# Shakespeare

THE GREENWOOD COMPANION TO

# Shakespeare

A COMPREHENSIVE GUIDE FOR STUDENTS

Volume IV

The Romances and Poetry

EDITED BY
JOSEPH ROSENBLUM

GREENWOOD PRESS
Westport, Connecticut • London

**Library of Congress Cataloging-in-Publication Data**

The Greenwood companion to Shakespeare : a comprehensive guide for students / edited by Joseph
Rosenblum.
     p.   cm.
    Includes bibliographical references and index.
    ISBN 0–313–32779–3 (set : alk. paper)—ISBN 0–313–32780–7 (v. 1 : alk. paper)—
ISBN 0–313–32781–5 (v. 2 : alk. paper)—ISBN 0–313–32782–3 (v. 3 : alk. paper)—
ISBN 0–313–32788–2 (v. 4 : alk. paper)   1. Shakespeare, William, 1564–1616—Criticism and
interpretation—Handbooks, manuals, etc.   2. Shakespeare, William, 1564–1616—Examinations—
Study guides.   I. Rosenblum, Joseph.
PR2976.G739   2005
822.3'3—dc22     2004028690

British Library Cataloguing in Publication Data is available.

Library of Congress Catalog Card Number: 2004028690
ISBN: 0–313–32779–3 (set)
     0–313–32780–7 (vol. I)
     0–313–32781–5 (vol. II)
     0–313–32782–3 (vol. III)
     0–313–32788–2 (vol. IV)

First published in 2005

Greenwood Press, 88 Post Road West, Westport, CT 06881
An imprint of Greenwood Publishing Group, Inc.
www.greenwood.com

Printed in the United States of America

The paper used in this book complies with the
Permanent Paper Standard issued by the National
Information Standards Organization (Z39.48–1984).

10 9 8 7 6 5 4 3 2 1

To Ida

Thou art the nonpareil

# Contents

## VOLUME I
## OVERVIEWS AND THE HISTORY PLAYS

### OVERVIEWS

### THE HISTORY PLAYS

## VOLUME II
## THE COMEDIES

# VOLUME III

## THE TRAGEDIES

# VOLUME IV

## THE ROMANCES AND POETRY

### THE ROMANCE PLAYS

### THE SONNETS

## THE LONG POEMS

# Alphabetical List of Plays and Poems

## The Plays

# A Preface for Users

O for a Muse of fire, that would ascend
The brightest heaven of invention!

(Henry V, Prologue, 1–2)

In the latter half of the seventeenth century, John Dryden revised William Shakespeare's *Troilus and Cressida*. Explaining why he tampered with the text of the man he had called "divine," Dryden wrote,

> It must be allowed to the present age, that the tongue in general is so much refined since Shakespeare's time, that many of his words, and more of his phrases, are scarce intelligible. And of those which are understood, some are ungrammatical, others coarse; and his whole style is so pestered with figurative expressions, that it is as affected as it is obscure.

The twenty-first-century student of Shakespeare will likely concur with Dryden's judgment. Shakespeare is hard. Even seasoned scholars differ on subjects ranging from the meaning of individual words to the implications of entire plays. No wonder, then, if high school students, undergraduates, and general readers are sometimes puzzled as they read one of Shakespeare's works or watch one of his plays. Literally thousands of studies of Shakespeare are published each year and recorded in the annual *World Shakespeare Bibliography*, which is updated annually and printed in the *Shakespeare Quarterly*, but this thicket of scholarship often renders Shakespeare more forbidding to students rather than less.

Throughout, *The Greenwood Companion to Shakespeare: A Comprehensive Guide for Students* aims to demystify Shakespeare so that students and general readers will be encouraged to appreciate the artistry of the writing and will come to a fuller appreciation of Shakespeare's genius. Students will find here what his works mean, how they came to be, how they make meaning, and how critics and directors have interpreted them over the centuries. No reference work can include all that is known or thought about Shakespeare, but the editor, contributors, and publisher have sought to make this *Companion* the best place to begin a study of this great writer. We hope that you will find the contents both useful and enjoyable.

## CONTENT AND ARRANGEMENT

The four-volume *Greenwood Companion to Shakespeare* includes seventy-seven essays offering a guide to the perplexed. All of these essays have been written expressly for this work by dedicated scholars commissioned because of their scholarship and teaching skills.

The first three volumes are devoted to the plays as follows:

- Volume I is divided into two sections: first, a series of essays about Shakespeare's age, his life, the theater of the time, the texts of his work, and the English language of his era—all of which will deepen the reader's understanding of the works; second, essays that focus on the history plays.

- Volume II explores the comedies.

- Volume III presents the tragedies.

- Volume IV begins with essays on the late plays called romances; the remainder of the volume discusses William Shakespeare's poetry, beginning with an overview of the sonnets. Thirty-one essays examine selected individual or paired sonnets, including full texts of each sonnet reviewed. Compared with the rest of Shakespeare's poetry, these sonnets are the most studied and reveal the widest range of subjects and attitudes. The other essays in this volume discuss the long narrative poems: *A Lover's Complaint*—that fascinating envoi to the sonnet cycle—immediately follows the sonnets, as it did when originally published with those poems; then, in chronological order, *Venus and Adonis*, *The Rape of Lucrece*, and *The Phoenix and Turtle*; *The Passionate Pilgrim* (in which two of Shakespeare's sonnets to the mysterious Dark Lady were first printed) has been placed last because most of the poems contained therein are not by Shakespeare.

The essays are arranged chronologically within genre. To further assist readers in finding essays on particular plays or poems, an alphabetical list of the works studied in this *Companion* follows immediately after the table of contents.

### Other Features

"A Shakespeare Chronology," preceding the overview essays in volume I, shows when William Shakespeare's works were written and published and provides basic facts about his life. An annotated bibliography accompanies each essay. At the end of volume IV, an appendix offers a selected, annotated list of Web sites about William Shakespeare and his work. Following that list is a selected bibliography. A subject index and an index of key passages concludes the work.

## THE ESSAYS

Forty scholars contributed essays to this *Companion*. Their writings add substantially to Shakespeare scholarship. These essays range in length from some 2,500 words for articles on particular sonnets to 26,000 words on *King Lear*. The articles dealing with the plays, subdivided into eleven sections for easy access, provide the following information to readers:

1. A scene-by-scene plot summary to help students understand what is happening on the stage/page.

2. A discussion of the play's publication history and, when relevant, its historical background context.

3. Sources for the play(s), including a discussion of controversies and recent findings.

4. A brief overview of how the play is put together in terms of structure and plotting.

5. The main characters, their actions, and their purposes within the play.

6. Devices and techniques (such as imagery) that Shakespeare used in the plays.

7. Themes and meanings of the play, citing opinions of various scholars.

8. A look at past and current critical discourse on the work to help students understand the issues that have engaged scholarly attention and to show that in many areas there is no single "correct" interpretation of these complex works. Students seeking topics to explore for their own papers may find this section especially helpful.

9. Production history, surveying the play's key theatrical and cinematic representation.

10. An explication of key passages, helping readers to understand sections of the play that are considered to be the most important.

11. An annotated bibliography for further study. This selection of sources will help students choose the most accessible works from the hundreds included in the *World Shakespeare Bibliography* or the dozens listed in bibliographical guides. The books and articles noted here include classic studies but concentrate on recent writing.

## The Essays on the Sonnets and Long Poems

The essays in volume IV discuss the poems. Compared with the essays on the plays they are briefer and contain fewer sections. For the sonnets, the essays provide the following key elements:

1. The sonnet itself, from *The Oxford Shakespeare*, edited by W. J. Craig and published in 1914 by Oxford University Press.

2. A prose paraphrase to explain the content of the work under discussion.

3. A discussion that situates the poem within the sonnet cycle.

4. An exploration of devices and techniques, and themes and meanings.

5. A description of the relationship of the sonnet to Shakespeare's other works, particularly the plays.

6. An annotated bibliography.

In the essays on the long poems the reader will also find discussions of publication history and sources (treated in the overview essay on the sonnets for those poems). All of the essays on the long poems conclude with annotated bibliographies.

## ISSUES IN THE SHAKESPEARE CANON

One poem that readers will not find in this volume is *A Funeral Elegy*. This 578-line poem was first printed by George Eld and published by Thomas Thorpe in 1612. Eld had printed and Thorpe had published Shakespeare's sonnets three years earlier. According to the title page, *A Funeral Elegy* was the work of "W. S." The identity of this W. S. has inspired some recent controversy. In 1989 Donald W. Foster published *Elegy by W. S.* (Newark: U of Delaware P), in which he discussed the question of attribution without reaching any conclusion. However, in the October 1996 issue of *PMLA* Foster argued that the poem was by Shakespeare. Because Foster had successfully identified the author of the "anonymous" novel *Primary Colors* (1996) as Joe Klein, Foster's view was credible enough for the editors of the revised Riverside edition of Shakespeare's works (Boston: Houghton Mifflin, 1997) to include the *Elegy*; they also included, however, something of a disclaimer by J.J.M. Tobin (pp. 1893–1895). In 2002 Foster recanted, arguing that the most likely author of the *Elegy* was John Ford.

This controversy reflects the unsettled state of the Shakespeare canon, which grows and shrinks. Brian Vickers's *Shakespeare, Co-Author* (Oxford: Oxford UP, 2002) assigns joint responsibility to five of Shakespeare's plays: *Titus Andronicus* (with George Peele), *Timon of Athens* (with Thomas Middleton), *Pericles* (with George Wilkins), and *Henry VIII* and *The Two Noble Kinsmen* (both with John Fletcher). Seeking to expand the canon, Eric Sams has argued that *Edward III* is an early work by Shakespeare (see *"Edward III": An Early Play Restored to the Canon* (New Haven: Yale UP, 1996).

On one point scholars agree: the William Shakespeare who wrote the plays and poems discussed in this companion was the son of John and Mary Shakespeare, was born in Stratford-upon-Avon in 1564, and died there fifty-two years later. Since the nineteenth century, various nonscholars have proposed dozens of alternative authors, including Francis Bacon, Queen Elizabeth, and Edward de Vere, seventeenth Earl of Oxford. Those readers curious about the authorship question may consult Samuel Schoenbaum's *Shakespeare's Lives*, new edition (Oxford: Clarendon P, 1991), section VI, which is aptly titled "Deviations." Arguments about the authorship of Shakespeare's works belong to the realm of abnormal psychology rather than literary criticism.

# A Shakespeare Chronology

*Note*: Titles in **bold** are discussed in this four-volume set. Dates for the plays (e.g., 1593 for ***Richard III*** and ***The Comedy of Errors***) indicate probable year of first performance.

| | |
|---|---|
| 1558 | Elizabeth I becomes queen of England. |
| 1564 | William Shakespeare born (ca. April 23). |
| 1576 | The Theatre (Shoreditch), built by James Burbage, opens. The Theatre is regarded as the first true London playhouse. |
| 1582 | Shakespeare marries Anne Hathaway (ca. December 1). |
| 1583 | Shakespeare's elder daughter, Susannah, born (ca. May 23). |
| 1585 | Shakespeare's fraternal twins, Judith and Hamnet/Hamlet, born (ca. January 31). |
| 1588 | Defeat of the Spanish Armada (July 31–August 8). |
| 1589 | Shakespeare probably in London, begins writing ***1 Henry VI*** (published in 1623). |
| 1590–1591 | ***2, 3 Henry VI*** written. The former first published as *The First Part of the Contention betwixt the Two Famous Houses of York and Lancaster* (1594), the latter as *The True Tragedy of Richard Duke of York* (1595). |
| 1592 | Robert Greene attacks Shakespeare in *A Groatsworth of Witte*. This is the first printed reference to Shakespeare as dramatist. |
| 1593 | ***Richard III*** (first published in 1597). |
| | ***Venus and Adonis*** published. |
| | ***The Comedy of Errors*** (first published in 1623). |
| | Shakespeare begins writing his **sonnets**. |
| 1594 | ***The Rape of Lucrece*** published. |
| | ***Titus Andronicus*** (first published in 1594). |
| | ***The Taming of the Shrew*** (first published in 1623). |
| | ***The Two Gentlemen of Verona*** (first published in 1623). |

*Love's Labor's Lost* (first published in 1598).

Lord Chamberlain's Men established.

1595    *King John* (first published in 1623).

*Richard II* (first published in 1597).

*Romeo and Juliet* (first published in 1597).

*A Midsummer Night's Dream* (first published in 1600).

1596    *The Merchant of Venice* (first published in 1600).

Hamnet/Hamlet Shakespeare dies, age 11 (ca. August 9).

1597    *1 Henry IV* (first published in 1598).

*The Merry Wives of Windsor* (first published in 1602).

Shakespeare purchases New Place, Stratford.

1598    *2 Henry IV* (first published in 1600).

*Much Ado about Nothing* (first published in 1600).

Francis Meres's *Palladis Tamia* lists a dozen plays by Shakespeare and praises him highly.

1599    The Globe Theater opens.

*Henry V* (first published in 1600).

*Julius Caesar* (first published in 1623).

*The Passionate Pilgrim* includes two of Shakespeare's sonnets (138, 144).

1600    *As You Like It* (first published in 1623).

*Hamlet* (first published in 1603).

1601    *Richard II* performed at the Globe (February 7) at urging of supporters of the Earl of Essex one day before his ill-fated rebellion.

*The Phoenix and Turtle* appears in Robert Chester's *Love's Martyr*.

John Shakespeare dies (ca. September 6).

1602    *Twelfth Night* (first published in 1623).

*Troilus and Cressida* (first published in 1609).

1603    Queen Elizabeth dies. James VI of Scotland becomes James I of England. James licenses the Lord Chamberlain's Men as the King's Men.

*All's Well That Ends Well* (first published in 1623).

1604    *Measure for Measure* (first published in 1623).

*Othello* (first published in 1622).

1605    *King Lear* (first published in 1608).

1606    *Macbeth* (first published in 1623).

1607    *Antony and Cleopatra* (first published in 1623).

Susannah Shakespeare marries John Hall (June 5).

Shakespeare's brother Edmund dies (ca. December 29).

1608    Elizabeth Hall, Shakespeare's only granddaughter, born (ca. February 18).

Shakespeare's mother dies (ca. September 7).

***Coriolanus*** (first published in 1623).

***Timon of Athens*** (first published in 1623).

***Pericles*** (first published in 1609).

1609    Shakespeare's ***Sonnets*** published, with ***A Lover's Complaint***.

***Cymbeline*** (first published in 1623).

The King's Men begin using the Blackfriars as an indoor theater.

1610    ***The Winter's Tale*** (first published in 1623).

1611    ***The Tempest*** (first published in 1623).

1612    ***Henry VIII*** (with John Fletcher; first published in 1623).

1613    Globe Theater burns down during production of ***Henry VIII***.

***Cardenio*** (with John Fletcher; lost).

***The Two Noble Kinsmen*** (with John Fletcher; first published in 1634).

1614    Second Globe opens on site of first Globe.

1616    Judith Shakespeare marries Thomas Quiney (February 10).

Shakespeare makes his will (March 25) and dies on April 23.

1619    Thomas Pavier attempts a collected (pirated) edition of Shakespeare. He publishes ten plays in quarto, some with false dates to conceal the piracy, before he is forced to abandon the project.

1623    The First Folio, the first collected edition of Shakespeare's plays, is published. It contains thirty-six plays, half of them printed for the first time.

# THE ROMANCE
# PLAYS

# *Pericles*

## Gary Waller

### PLOT SUMMARY

**1.Chorus.** The play opens with a Chorus in which the medieval poet Gower gives an account of the incestuous relationship of King Antiochus and his daughter. The king keeps her from marriage by giving all her suitors a seemingly impossible riddle; failure to answer it correctly means they will be put to death.

**1.1.** The play's hero, Pericles, Prince of Tyre, comes to Antioch as a suitor. He immediately guesses that the riddle tells of Antiochus's incestuous relationship with his daughter. Once Antiochus realizes that Pericles has succeeded in solving the riddle, he employs Thaliard, a lord of Antioch, to kill him.

**1.2.** Threatened by Antiochus's revenge, Pericles is melancholy and disturbed. He decides to flee Tyre and to hide in Tharsus, leaving the faithful Helicanus as his deputy in Tyre.

**1.3.** By the time Thaliard enters Tyre, Pericles has left.

**1.4.** Pericles heads for Tharsus, which is suffering a terrible famine. The governor, Cleon, learns that ships have been sighted. Cleon assumes he is being invaded, but it turns out that Pericles' ships are carrying corn with which Cleon can feed his people. There is much relief and joyful welcoming of the visitor.

**2.Chorus.** Gower tells us that when Pericles hears that Thaliard is in Tyre, he leaves Tharsus and sets forth on the Mediterranean. A storm destroys his ship, and only Pericles escapes death.

**2.1.** Pericles is washed up on the shore of Pentapolis. He discovers from fishermen that the country's king is the good Simonides, whose daughter, Thaisa, will be celebrating her birthday the following day. Suitors have been invited to joust for her hand in marriage. Pericles' armor has been rescued from the sea; though it is rusty, he decides to compete in the tournament.

**2.2.** The following day, Pericles is welcomed among the knights and wins the tournament.

**2.3.** Pericles, though poorly dressed, impresses both Simonides and Thaisa.

**2.4.** The play returns briefly to Tyre, where Helicanus reveals he has learned that the evil Antiochus and his daughter have been destroyed by the gods by a lightning bolt. In Pericles' absence, Helicanus is asked to become king. But he asks the Tyrean lords permission to take a year to try to find Pericles. If Pericles cannot be found, Helicanus will become king.

**2.5.** Back in Pentapolis, Simonides announces that Thaisa has vowed not to marry for a year, but she has decided she will indeed marry Pericles.

**3.Chorus.** In his opening chorus to this act, Gower informs us that Pericles and Thaisa, who is now pregnant, set out to return to Tyre.

**3.1.** However, while they are at sea, a fierce storm sends Thaisa into labor. The nurse Lychorida comes on deck with a newborn daughter but tells Pericles that his wife has died. The sailors insist that the body be thrown overboard in a chest, believing that the storm will not abate until the corpse has gone.

**3.2.** Washed ashore at Ephesus, the chest is taken to the house of a renowned physician named Lord Cerimon, who revives Thaisa, who was in fact not dead. Cerimon gives Thaisa a scroll he found in the chest which proclaims she is Pericles' wife.

**3.3.** Unaware that Thaisa is alive, Pericles at Tharsus prepares to return to Tyre. He asks Cleon and Dionyza to rear his daughter, who is named Marina, because she was born at sea.

**3.4.** Believing Pericles drowned, Thaisa becomes a priestess in the temple of Diana.

**4.Chorus.** Gower tells us that with Pericles back in Tyre, Dionyza becomes jealous of Marina, whose beauty, virtue, and talents, as she grows, exceed those of Dionyza's own daughter.

**4.1.** Leonine is hired by Dionyza to murder Marina, but just as she is about to be killed, she is kidnapped by pirates. The pirates carry her to Mytilene, another Greek port, and there they sell Marina to a brothel owner.

**4.2.** Pander, a nameless bawd, and Boult debate about how they may best sell Marina's virginity for the most profit.

**4.3.** Cleon discovers that Dionyza has arranged for Marina's murder and that she has had Leonine poisoned so that nobody will discover the cause of Marina's death.

**4.4.** Gower enters again and tells us that Pericles returns from Tyre to Tharsus to visit his daughter, only to be told of her decease. We see by dumb show how he sails off in despair.

**4.5.** Back in Mytilene, in the brothel, two clients encounter Marina, who has resisted all attempts to make her become a prostitute, and she converts them to virtue.

**4.6.** When Lysimachus, the governor of Mytilene, comes to the brothel, he too is overcome by Marina's virtue. In anger and despair at the threat to his trade, the brothel owner tells his servant to rape her, but she manages to convince him to stop and to find her alternative employment.

**5.Chorus.** Gower tells us that Marina is finally released from the brothel and that she finds work as a seamstress. He tells us that Pericles' ship has now arrived offshore near Mytilene, and that he is being greeted by Lysimachus.

**5.1.** Lysimachus learns of Pericles' grief for the death of Marina. Lysimachus states that there is a young girl famous throughout Mytilene for her healing virtue: perhaps she will be able to comfort Pericles. Marina comes onboard and starts to tell the distraught Pericles her life story. Gradually he realizes who she is. Father and daughter are reunited. The goddess Diana appears in a vision, telling Pericles he must go to her temple at Ephesus.

**5.2.** Gower says that Lysimachus wishes to wed Marina, but first Pericles and his entourage must sail to Ephesus. At Ephesus we see Thaisa and Cerimon ceremoniously awaiting Pericles.

**5.3.** Pericles and Marina tell their story to the priestess, who turns out to be none other than Thaisa. Husband, wife, and daughter are reunited. They depart for Pentapolis, where the marriage of Lysimachus and Marina will take place. Gower concludes the play with a summary and conveys good wishes to the audience.

## PUBLICATION HISTORY

The textual authenticity of *Pericles* has been much discussed. The play was not included in the First Folio; it appeared first in the Third Folio, of 1664. It had, however, already been published in 1609 in a quarto edition, which was reprinted the same year and then four more times by 1635 and was the basis of the 1664 text. The play must have been written before May 20, 1608, when it was recorded for publication in the Stationers' Register. The likely date of composition is therefore 1607–1608. Why it was not published in the First Folio is unclear. Perhaps the Folio editors were unsure about its authorship or believed the text of the quarto to be inauthentic (or at least partially so).

The textual history is complicated by the appearance, the year before the quarto was published, of George Wilkins's prose romance *The Painful Adventures of Pericles Prince of Tyre*. This work loosely follows the play's events, and many editors have suggested that Wilkins might well have been Shakespeare's collaborator in *Pericles*. Alternatively, and most likely, Wilkins's prose tale has been seen as based on Shakespeare's play, with Wilkins reconstructing, from memory, scenes and situations presented onstage. Although modern editors are unsure and often disagree significantly, a likely scenario is that Wilkins drafted the early scenes of the play; they were possibly worked over by Shakespeare, who then finished the rest of the play by himself; and Wilkins produced a prose tale based on the drama. Some modern editions (notably the Oxford edition) expand scenes in the play in the received text by drawing on Wilkins's tale, a practice also followed by many modern directors, especially the scene (4.6) in which Lysimachus visits the brothel and is converted from his predatory intents by Marina's virtues. Wilkins's prose version of the scene is longer and provides more motivation, so adding lines based on his story has often made the scene more convincing onstage. The text of the play is singularly obscure and confusing in this scene, with not only the contradiction between the vicious and the virtuous sides of Lysimachus but also lines that descend from forceful verse to stumbling prose—most likely caused by imperfect remembering of the play on the stage. Modern editors believe there may be up to 200 corrupt or misremembered readings or typesetting errors. At times, the reporter found remembering the lines too difficult as verse, and they come out as prose, a habit made worse by sloppy typesetting in the publication of the quarto. Not all of the quarto was reconstructed from memory, but there may have been enough gaps and mistakes to convince the editors of the First Folio that they should reject it from the collection.

## SOURCES FOR THE PLAY

Shakespeare's (and perhaps Wilkins's) primary source for *Pericles* was book 8 of *Confessio Amantis*—verse stories collected and related by the fourteenth-century poet John Gower, who appears onstage as a narrator in the play to link together the many episodes. The story of the wanderings (and moral lessons learned) by the main character, Appollonius of Tyre, was a traditional Greek and Roman tale that was popular in the Middle Ages. As *Pericles* took shape, details were likely added from Sir Philip Sidney's *Arcadia* (including Pericles' name) and possibly from Plutarch's *Lives of the Famous Greeks and Romans*, one of Shakespeare's favorite sources for plays about classical history. In addition, Lawrence Twine's translation (ca. 1576) of a French romance about Appollonius of Tyre, entitled *The Pattern of Painefull Adventures* (1594), was likely a further source for Wilkins's novel and probably for the play, especially the brothel scenes in act 4.

## STRUCTURE AND PLOTTING

For most readers, spectators, and critics, much of the first two acts of *Pericles* seems episodic and confusing. A large part of the text in the quarto edition was possibly either reconstructed by someone who saw the play performed or (more probably) printed from a script or scripts of parts in the play. Much of *Pericles* reads like a rough draft at different stages of composition and is crudely put together by comparison with the usual complex interweaving of plots of a Shakespearean play.

The episodic nature of the work, therefore, may have some relation to the textual corruption or to the possibility that Shakespeare did not adequately revise the script before it was acted and printed. The play's main structural continuity is provided by the figure of the medieval poet John Gower, coming onstage between scenes to recap previous episodes or to instigate dumb shows, wherein some action of the play is pantomimed. He also delivers the epilogue. It is possible that Shakespeare was experimenting with a combination of story-telling on the one hand and action with powerful language on the other hand in order to draw attention to the insights learned from fables, fairy tales, pageant, and music. *Pericles* has, for Shakespeare, an unusual balance between words and nonverbal communication.

The main narrative structure of the action that we are shown (as opposed to being told about) is built on a series of adventures. At the beginning of the play Pericles is in Antioch, from which he flees in order to avoid Antiochus's assassin, who has been instructed to pursue Pericles back to Tyre and kill him. Prone to melancholy, Pericles worries about Antiochus's trying to have him killed; to avoid this fate he sets off on more adventures and endures several shipwrecks. In many ways Pericles is a kind of classical hero figure, like Odysseus, always ready to enter a contest or competition, especially if the prize is a king's daughter. Pericles' subsequent journeys, moving from one place to another, may be seen as a fantasy of avoidance, with the original threat of the opening scene always returning in some form or other.

The external action, therefore, is meant to mirror an internal state. The quick change of scenes helps to portray a mind in turmoil, at least in concept if not easily manifest in the theater; onstage the play poses many problems of continuity and loose ends. Conceptually, however, it is clear that the successive scenes are "a pendulum swing of desire and dread" (Nevo, p. 72), with repeated immersions in and emergence from the sea, a series of images without seeming rational cause, as if a huge psychological disturbance is being acted out. The sea has been a recurring metaphor in human experience for the unpredictability and menacing aspects of human life; it is also a symbol of possibility and renewal, and (as will be explained in detail) it has often been especially associated with women. The author(s) of the first half of the play is/are clearly trying to draw on the richness of this complex metaphor to give some unity to the play. Even though it may not be totally successful, the structure of *Pericles*—with its quick, unexpected reversals, captures, and changing locales—is meant to emphasize what Ruth Nevo terms "the rhythm of vicissitude in human life, the rhythm of maturation: separation, dispossession, return" (74).

The other main device that tries to achieve some structural continuity is the birth, upbringing, and maturation of Pericles' daughter, Marina. After Thaisa's apparent death, Pericles leaves Marina in Tarsus with Cleon and Dionyza. Raised knowing she is a princess, yet without parents, Marina is melancholy and always aware of the losses she has sustained. But she is, we are told by Gower, both beautiful and determined. Faced with a murderer hired by Dionyza to kill her, she pleads eloquently for her life. Just as he is about to kill her anyway, she is kidnapped by pirates, who in turn sell her into prostitution in Mytilene. Her virtue prevails, however, and she convinces every man who wants to buy her that it would be a crime to take her virginity. The governor of Mytilene, Lysimachus, comes to the brothel and is impressed with her. Eventually she persuades the brothel keepers that she should be assigned to a more honorable and lucrative household task. When Pericles arrives in Mytilene she is summoned to help heal him—thus setting the stage for the discovery of their relationship and the eventual reconciliation of Pericles with his wife as well as his daughter.

## MAIN CHARACTERS

### Gower

The figure of the medieval poet John Gower plays the role of narrator for this play, providing continuity and a sense of the ancient and authoritative teller of tales. He is the stage narrator who both creates an atmosphere of antique medievalism: "To sing a song that old was sung, / From ashes ancient Gower is come" (1.Chorus, 1–2). Gower's story of Apollonius of Tyre, in *Confessio Amantis* (book 8), served as an important source for the play; while Gower is narrating, onstage, individual actors, with gesture and emphasis, may make the role more or less credible. Shakespeare uses comparable onstage narrators in *Henry V* (Chorus) and *The Winter's Tale* (Time). Gower's presence stresses that we are participating in a story, a fable, and are meant to learn from our experience. He reinforces the archaic nature of the story, and in an effective production he may become a significant commentator.

## Antiochus

Antiochus, King of Antioch, sets in motion the action of the play's first episode or adventure. Following his wife's death, he has entered into an incestuous relationship with his daughter. When young princes come calling to ask to marry her, he tests them by asking them to answer a riddle correctly or lose their lives. The action of the play starts when Pericles arrives in Antioch to undergo the test. Some critics see, conceptually at least, a connection between Antiochus's illegitimate father/daughter relationship and the potential for that of Pericles and Marina, but the parallel is not developed in the script. Antiochus and his daughter represent unbridled and illicit passion, inappropriate familial relations, and their actions lead to their deaths.

## Pericles

Pericles is the play's hero and the only adequately developed character. Many critics see his character as one-dimensional—not only passive, perfect yet continually victimized, but also without psychological depth. Yet to interpret Pericles as if he were Hamlet is to put too much strain on a role that, whatever a critic's overall interpretation, is not constructed to be a study of an individual. Even alongside the central figures of the other romances, such as Leontes or Hermione in *The Winter's Tale*, or Imogen in *Cymbeline*, Pericles remains sketchy. An excellent actor may lend depth to some of the scenes, but the part lacks complexity.

We can, however, see the pattern he exemplifies as a profound one. Throughout the play, Pericles moves from place to place, battered by misfortune. Pericles is shipwrecked in Pentapolis, where Simonides rules, and wins a jousting contest for the hand of Simonides' daughter, Thaisa. Simonides is impressed with Pericles and tries to jolt him out of his melancholy by offering to be his friend. Later, when he learns that his daughter wants to marry Pericles, Simonides tests Pericles by insulting his honor, and then allows the two to marry. In contrast to Antiochus, Simonides may be viewed as the good and careful father. Losses and disasters happen to Pericles, and he endures. As he goes through greater and greater misfortune, he becomes less active and finally ceases to speak altogether. Pericles is above all a good man and, despite his hardships, remains virtuous. He seeks a wife and finds that his choice is involved in incest; he is pursued by an assassin; he wins a bride in a tournament but loses her in childbirth; he is shipwrecked; his newly born daughter is rescued but then, when she reaches the age of fourteen, apparently dies. In short, he suffers misfortune to the point that he seems able only to suffer and endure. The play moves toward restoration and reconciliation: after fourteen years, at his nadir, he has both daughter and wife restored to him. The language and actions of the culminating scenes are designed to stress a sense of miracle, fantasy, and wish fulfillment. What has been most precious has been taken from him, and it is now restored. Finally he is revived by a young woman who turns out to be his supposedly dead daughter, Marina, and the two of them travel to Ephesus, where they discover Pericles' wife and Marina's mother, Thaisa.

One of Pericles' advisers in Tyre, Helicanus, cares for Pericles in his melancholy moods and recommends that he leave Tyre for a while after the events in Antioch. Helicanus takes over as temporary ruler of Tyre; when Pericles fails to return, the citizens want to crown Helicanus king. But Helicanus is loyal to Pericles, so he refuses. Helicanus is a genuinely good man, not touched by ambition, who believes that Pericles is the only true ruler of Tyre.

## Thaisa

Thaisa, the daughter of Simonides, expects to marry whoever wins the jousting contest in Pentapolis. She is very impressed with Pericles and writes to her father that she wants to marry him. Simonides sends away the other knights and challenges Thaisa, saying that Pericles is not a good match since they do not know his lineage. She insists she will have him, he agrees, and they are married. Later, at sea with Pericles on the way back to Tyre, Thaisa gives birth to Marina but seems to die during the birth. She shows great resolution and resourcefulness throughout the play, choosing her own husband and standing up to her father for him. Alone at Ephesus, she becomes a votary of the chaste goddess Diana.

## Marina

The daughter of Pericles and Thaisa, Marina was born at sea during a tempest. The late plays all contain a significantly developed younger woman as a central character. Marina is merely a sketch by comparison with Imogen in *Cymbeline*, Perdita in *The Winter's Tale*, or Miranda in *The Tempest*; in *Pericles*, the father-daughter relationship is explored briefly but profoundly. What we can see in Marina is Shakespeare feeling his way toward exploring a distinctive emphasis on strong, independent women who defy their apparently fixed roles in the fantasies of patriarchy. Most critics see Marina as a type of medieval saint, a victim who, through patience and virtue, is enabled by a providential force to overcome the most extreme circumstances. She has no mother, is brought up by hostile strangers, survives attempted murder and capture by pirates, is sold to a brothel, and wards off attempted rape. This melodramatic series of events is designed simultaneously to titillate and to appall an audience (and, to an extent, an audience likely to be male or at least taking patriarchy for granted). For such critics, she is an image of female patience, a romanticized saint.

However, as Deanne Williams argues, she can also be seen as one of Shakespeare's many articulate women, reflecting the emerging, new, educated ideal of early modern women, represented by Margaret Roper, Elizabeth I, Mary Sidney, and Lady Mary Wroth. Rather than stressing female silence and patience, Shakespeare writes Marina in the fifth act as a speaking woman. In this regard she is like the articulate, strong heroines of the comedies, such as Rosalind in *As You Like It* or Viola in *Twelfth Night*. What Marina brings to her father at the end of the play is the gift of speech. She tells a tale in which she has played a singular role; the result is, as Williams puts it, "father daughter incest, the subject of tragedy" transformed into a "reaffirmation of 'family values,' the matter of comedy" (598). By the end of *Pericles*, the play's male figure has been restored to his wife and has established a healthy relationship with his daughter, who has herself entered a new relationship with a lover/husband and has had her mother restored to her. Marina thus sets the pattern for later, more profound treatments of the redemptive roles women play in familial and wider social relationships—and within men's fantasies about them.

### Lysimachus

Lysimachus, the Governor of Mytilene, comes in disguise to the brothel where Marina works, either out of curiosity or as a potential client, but she convinces him to spare her. When Pericles comes into port, Lysimachus goes out to greet him and wants to help Pericles. When he discovers that Marina is Pericles' daughter, he has Marina brought to talk to Pericles. Later, he and Marina are engaged to be married. His main function in the play is to be redeemed, to show how virtue (perhaps, in particular, female virtue) can alter an individual. Significantly, his lust for Marina is translated into marriage; wild passion is civilized through a proper familial relationship. Again, this marriage contrasts with Antiochus's refusal to allow his daughter to marry because he, her father, has also become her husband.

## DEVICES AND TECHNIQUES

To many critics *Pericles* has seemed to mark the start of a new phase in Shakespeare's career. Its unsatisfactory textual quality may in part reflect experimentation or uncertainty. It seems likely that Shakespeare took over an imperfect script and found its material appealing. As he attempted to revise the text (recall that he was called on to serve as the script "doctor" to *The Booke of Sir Thomas Moore*), he brought to it many characteristic devices from earlier plays. As he worked, however, he started to anticipate theatrical techniques and thematic concerns he would use, more confidently, in the next plays he was to write: *Cymbeline*, *The Winter's Tale*, and *The Tempest*. These four plays are often referred to as the "late" or "last" plays, referring to their place in Shakespeare's chronology; or, more suggestively though not strictly accurately, as the "romances"—a category that does not occur in the Folio division of tragedy, comedy, and history but one that has gained popularity and near-unanimity since the nineteenth century. The Riverside edition (Boston: Houghton Mifflin, 1974; 2nd ed., 1997), one of the definitive modern collections, formally includes the "romances" as a separate major category. So does David Bevington's *The Complete Works of Shakespeare*, 5th ed. (New York: Pearson Longman, 2004).

The four romance plays are united by a common set of issues, concerns, motifs, and theatrical and narrative devices. These elements include lost children, father-daughter relationships, friendships and families broken and reconciled, coincidences, supernatural figures, storms and shipwrecks, magic, and characters that seem to stand for figures in our dreams or fantasies rather than reflecting plausible reality. Many explanations have been given for Shakespeare's returning incessantly to such motifs and dramatic techniques in this closely connected group of plays. These range from his alleged tiredness to his entering a period of new and almost effortless triumph; from his desire for experimentation to an obsessive reworking of personal or philosophical motifs. From a realistic viewpoint, these plays may appear naive, unmotivated, and superficial; but for many readers, critics, and spectators, they have been seen as among Shakespeare's most profound, prophetic works, with deep and perhaps even religious significance. Some critics have seen them as embodying Shakespeare's final insights into life, the measured wisdom of a philosophical mind looking deeply into what he has discovered. In that somewhat sentimental interpretation, Shakespeare becomes like his character Prospero in *The*

*Tempest*, a wise scientist-artist-magician who is trying, through the medium of theater, to articulate his understanding of life. Less sentimentally, critics have pointed to the radical theatrical experimentation in these plays. It is as if Shakespeare sets himself a series of difficult tasks to see whether he can overcome them, taking seemingly intractable material and trying to create dramatically convincing plays.

In particular, he is working with difficult sources from the tradition of prose and poetic romance. "Romance" may be best understood as a body of written and oral material that produces emotionally contradictory effects on its readers or spectators, mixing both "joy" and "terror," to use words from *The Winter's Tale* (4.1.1), culminating in an imaginative resolution of conflicts and vulnerabilities—an articulated wish fulfillment, like a dream or fantasy, that produces a utopian harmony. Its predominant form is a tale, or story, that amazes with its extremities, coincidences, and seemingly magical resolutions. Romance works less on an audience's rational response and more on its emotions. It attempts to entice us to bring our individual, collective, or historical vulnerabilities and fears into play, and it promises that we will find, after these feelings are intensified or deepened, a vision or scene where they are overcome. They may be conquered only momentarily, even only within the confines of art, but the aspiration of each of these plays is to indicate the possibility—whether permanent, universal, transcendent, or utopian—of some unprepared for or even undeserved achievement or happiness. As Joan Hartwig summarizes the pattern of the romances, "The main characters aspire towards some perfect relationship; that hope is shattered; and finally the original wish is fulfilled in a manner which leaves the characters amazed" (4–5).

"Romance," in short, is a serious art form, not the inherently trivial escapist entertainment earlier critics, from Ben Jonson (who sneered at *Pericles* as a "mouldy tale") to the early twentieth century, have denigrated. It aspires, in the view of many modern critics, to move theatrical experience close to a level of inspiration or at least comfort that traditional religions have offered. Many critics since the mid-nineteenth century, in fact, have seen these plays as either reinforcing Christian values but in a secular, mythologized context, or (more typically) providing, within a non-Christian context, an unimaginative equivalent to Christian insights. Many productions likewise choose religious or mythological settings to stress this level of vision or insight. Certainly the settings for *Pericles*—Ephesus, Tharsus, Antioch—recall the travels of Paul and the trials of the early Christian church.

In part because of its problematic textual status, with inconsistencies and loose ends in the text as we have it, an inclusive and coherent reading of the play may be difficult to achieve. Its outline, however, is simple. The basic structural device Shakespeare uses is an episodic succession of events—challenges, accidents, losses, and coincidences—suffered by the central character, Pericles. We are given a succession of scenes of loss and defeat, apparent triumph followed by even further losses. The play is not, however, intended to be a simple melodramatic story of fate endured and conquered. In terms of its devices, *Pericles* may be likened to the juxtapositions, quick transitions and cuts, backtracking and mixed reality of film as it works to achieve a vision of possibilities that go beyond the surface events. The desired effect of such a play, seen more clearly and richly in *Cymbeline* and *The Winter's Tale*, is to involve the audience less at the level of rational analysis and more at the level of emotional response. The audience has been presented with the story of a man suffering appalling losses and misfortunes; and now, finally, out of apparent

tragedy, restoration and reconciliation become possible. A new life can be anticipated.

Many critics have seen the story of the play as a "veiled version of the universal
narratives that humankind is fated to enact" (Ryan, p. 10). Shakespeare's major "device" in *Pericles*, as it is in the last plays generally, is to try to use theater to tap into
what modern psychoanalytical thinkers term the "unconscious," where individual,
family, and collective desires and fears exist and may determine or motivate our
conscious, waking actions. Earlier phases of our culture would have explained this
level of experience as "spiritual" or the "soul," and there are many critics or readers who still read the play in these terms. In the view of E.M.W. Tillyard, for
instance, Shakespeare is dramatizing a vision analogous to that of Dante, 300 years
before Shakespeare. At the culminating moment of the *Divine Comedy*, Beatrice appears to Dante who, like Pericles, has proceeded on a long journey of self-discovery;
she returns to him long after her death and instructs him to look at her and through
her to God. She has been lost to him, but now, after trials, challenges, and losses,
she is restored to him. The vision of *Pericles* is not as complex (or consistently powerful) as that of the other three late romance plays, let alone Dante's epic. But the
conceptual parallel is clear. Parallels with Dante are probably not intentional on
Shakespeare's part, but the play is certainly dramatizing experiences that are deeply
rooted in the Western religious tradition and in the tradition of romance story-
telling common to many cultures.

To speak of such near-universal narratives or of the play as a kind of fable is to
reach back far into how human societies have used stories to explain the nature and
purpose of human life. A fable is a story, usually episodic and simplified, that conveys a moral lesson or truths. With *Pericles*, it is the story of the stoical acceptance
of fate. Pericles is a man who receives blow after blow, loss after loss, and endures.
This series of episodes reflects the Greek origin of the tale: life is a series of misfortunes, and the most valuable lesson is to predict unpredictability and disaster
and especially to learn to survive despite them. Pericles compares himself to a ball
on a "vast tennis-court" (2.1.60), a plaything of forces he cannot control. This concept of fate is derived from the Greek version of tragedy, which Shakespeare had
explored in such works as *Hamlet* and *King Lear*. Tragedy stresses both human con-
tingency, the accidents and unpredictability of life, and the inevitability (often combined with a terrifying degree of unpredictability) of loss and death. But in *Pericles*
Shakespeare wants to invite us to imagine something beyond tragedy, a dimension
of human possibility that through pain and loss will lead to reconciliation and recovery. Or, to put it another way, romance offers that dimension to us as a tantalizing possibility, a fantasy of what we as humans hope for, might live for, and
should look to our own futures to find. This is to suggest that (as Freud put it) art
and love are those human creations that may (even though temporarily) defeat loss
and death.

## THEMES AND MEANINGS

The separation and individuation of child from mother; a child's discovery of
boundary conditions; the development of object relations; the delusions of omnipotence and fears of abandonment; and the search for a lost, pre-oedipal, poly-
morphous sexual fulfillment—all are concerns lying at the core of the thematic

richness of *Pericles*, even if they are worked out in detail only spasmodically. Many nineteenth-century critics read Shakespeare's preoccupations with family relations in the late plays as a reflection of autobiography. Whether there is some reflection of Shakespeare's personal and familial concerns cannot be determined, but *Pericles* certainly seems designed to draw out its audience's own preoccupations with belonging to, seeking, or losing precious family and generational ties. Family is a key concept in our cultural history, one that carries reverberations and contradictions far beyond its mere dictionary meaning. While the main narrative line concerns a single character, Pericles, the play emphasizes his family connections and the significance of his quest for and loss of them. *Pericles* is, in a phrase used famously by Freud, a "family romance," bringing to the surface a number of seemingly near-universal preoccupations with family ties: the search for and loss of love, childbirth, loss of children, abandonment, jealousy, and (most extremely) incest.

The incest motif is especially interesting. When we look at Shakespeare's sources, we find that incest lurks at the center of the original Apollonius story. Even if it is not fully worked out in the script as we have it, the play has similar concerns with the horror and fascination of incest. A common view of the play is that Pericles is seeking a wife, but she turns out to be involved in incest with her father; he is separated from his wife and daughter; and finally they are reunited in harmony and in a "proper" relation with both. However, some recent critics have taken a broader view of the theme of incest in the play, particularly from anthropological and psychological perspectives. Father-daughter incest is widely seen as the most violent and abusive expression of patriarchal male power. Psychologists have argued that it may incorporate both the father's urge to find a younger version of his aging wife and his nostalgic insecurity about lost youth. These elements are clearly featured in the initial scene: Antiochus is a tyrant, ostensibly bent on using his daughter's youth and beauty as a bargaining tool in dynastic marriage, though secretly enjoying her for himself. The daughter is silent and is never named: she is identified only as "Antiochus' Daughter." She is "spoken for," Williams notes, "in more ways than one" (602). That is, not only is she claimed but she does not even have a voice of her own. In the play she has only two lines.

But rather than simply providing an isolated incident at the opening of the play, incest remains an issue throughout. As Williams notes, "incest lurks in the dark corners of *Pericles*" (197). Even Pericles himself is portrayed as being not immune to the suggestions of incestuous attraction when he acknowledges that "all love the womb that their first being bred" (1.1.108). The daughter is compared to the Virgin Mary in language echoing the biblical vision of the woman "clothed with the son" (Revelation 12:1). Pericles himself sees her as a "Fair glass of light" (1.1.76) just as her father says, "Her face, like heaven, enticeth thee to view / Her countless glory" (ll. 30–31). Such metaphors continue throughout the play. Pericles hears of the great attractiveness of King Simonides' daughter, who is described in terms similar to those used for Antiochus's daughter. She is "beauty's child, whom nature gat / For men to see, and seeing wonder at" (2.2 6–7). It is the patriarchal language of seeing women as possessions valued for their visual attractiveness and prize-worthiness. Thaisa, like the unnamed daughter of Antiochus, is also protected by her father, offered as a prize, and is the object of paternal jealousy directed against her situation. Most critics read the episode with Thaisa as qualitatively different from the horrors of the opening scene, but Shakespeare's text keeps preoccupation with incest in the foreground. Williams even argues that Pericles leaves his daughter, following Thaisa's supposed death, to be brought up in Tarsus in part to avoid the temptation of incest. That may be pushing the argument, but there is no question that Pericles' relationship with his own daughter is the focus of the play's main actions. At the end, a balance is achieved. As Barker and Wheeler comment, "to find the mother in the daughter as Antiochus does in a fully sensual way, is what Pericles does in a sublime way . . . [he] achieves on a sublime level what he fled from on a degraded level" (313).

A second, closely related, major theme is Pericles' experiences not only with his daughter but also with women in general. Or, more accurately perhaps, with Woman; the reification of gender roles that have dominated Western patriarchal thought is a major focus of the play. Mother, daughter, sexual being, virgin, temptress, jealous harpy, goddess, religious figure: many of Western culture's fixations with the roles or images of women are played out here, as they are in all the late plays. This observation has been made by a variety of critics, mainly those writing in the psychoanalytical tradition derived from (though often radically different from) Freud, and by feminist critics who have drawn special attention to the play's treatment of issues of sexuality and gender. Long before Freud or modern developmental psychology, Shakespeare is providing insight into the anxieties of being gendered male in a society dominated by aggression, into some of the complexities of families, and into the roles of women in a patriarchal society.

The elevated praise of Antiochus's daughter, which we observe in the opening scene, for example, introduces a major characteristic of Western culture (and certain psychoanalysts and critics would speak of it as a universal): men tend to idealize women. Both Antiochus's daughter and Thaisa are described in idealized terms. Pericles says of the former: "See where she comes, appareled like the spring, / Graces her subjects, and her thoughts the king / Of every virtue gives renown to men!" (1.1.12–14). Simonides describes his daughter as "beauty's child," created to be seen and admired (2.2.6–7). Such idealization is a commonplace of Western discourse on love and women. Psychologically, it is built on what Freud termed "overvaluation": men in our history tend to "over-value" women, whether as mothers, lovers, wives, daughters, or some mysterious figure of insight or even a transcendent cosmic force. A woman, or a succession of women, are asked or needed by men to complete or compensate for internal weaknesses, inadequacies, or insecurities, to a degree that is often unattainable. At the same time, however, men may fear and frequently denigrate women, switching, as a modern psychotherapist expresses it, from "absolute idealization to complete denigration" (Estella Welldon, *Mother, Madonna, Whore: the Idealization and Denigration of Motherhood* [New York: Guilford P, 1988], 112). As Klaus Theweleit puts it, "what is really at work here . . . is a specific . . . form of the oppression of women. . . . It is oppression through exaltation" (*Male Fantasies*, trans. Stephen Conway et al. [Minneapolis: U of Minnesota P, 1987–1988], 1.284). Women are at once idealized and downtrodden, worshipped and devalued. In particular, because at least in part a woman is the source from where we all come, the bodies of women may at once be venerated and feared, worshipped and desecrated.

Shakespeare is not original or unusual in addressing this matter: the whole of Western culture has been haunted uneasily by women's alleged hold over men and the ways in which masculinity itself has been constructed by the predominant male perception of women. In that sense *Pericles* is a fantasy, a fable, written specifically by a man and in a sense offered as a confirming story to other men of what men supposedly know about women. Barber and Wheeler speak of the play's quest "to [recover] benign relationships to feminine presence" (11), but the overwhelming sense is of threat, potential evil, loss, or idealized purity. Woman is both goddess and whore, virgin and seductress, a contradictory collection of male fantasies that become explicit in the play's brothel scenes (4.2, 4.5–6).

Within the dominant ideology of Western culture, women are experienced by men (supposedly positively) as goddesses, mothers, or virgins, but also as seductresses and whores. Anthropologists explain that in "primitive" societies and (to a greater extent than we like to imagine) so-called "civilized" cultures, the contradictory pattern of goddess/whore operates within men's minds and within cultural assumptions, the dominant ideologies of gender and sexuality. Contemporary feminist critics point out that the supposed divinity of women and the desecration of them are traditionally brought together in the concept of the "sacred whore," a role that combines sexual vitality with a degree of often frightening (at least to patriarchal males) autonomy. Shakespeare's time sees the start of a major critique of such assumptions, a process that is still going on and from which, it may be argued, we might never escape. Western patriarchy has found it difficult to discard assumptions of the supremacy of male needs and continues to live out Western culture's fundamental dichotomy about women.

The succession of female characters in *Pericles*—daughters, wives, temptresses, betrayers, true and false nurturers—culminates in the deeply moving scenes at the end of the play. Having lost both wife and daughter, Pericles sails seemingly randomly and despairingly until he comes to Mytilene. The metaphor of the sea and its association with women is a crucial aspect of the play. Thaisa is lost at sea, and her body thrown overboard. Marina is named for her birth at sea, and eventually the sea brings Pericles back first to his daughter and then to his wife. The association of the sea with women, especially in the fantasies constructed historically by men about women, is in fact a recurring theme of Western literature, and far beyond. There is "a dread that lies in the hearts of all men, a dread of engulfment by the 'others' which is the mother, the sea or even the worst embrace of love," comments Theweleit, arguing that "in all of European literature (and literature influenced by it), desire, if it flows at all, flows in a certain sense *through women*. In some way or other, it always flows in relation to the image of women."

Pericles, then, sails the seemingly endless sea, a setting rich with symbolic meaning for the play's audiences, swearing "Never to wash his face, nor cut his hairs; / He puts on sackcloth, and to sea. He bears / A tempest, which his mortal vessel tears, / And yet he rides it out" (4.4.28–31). He is an image of self-obsessed depression, hardened into noncommunicative withdrawal. At the play's end, however, he is restored to himself, precisely by the return of the dual woman-figure on whose presence and power he has constructed his sense of being. The final scenes, in which both daughter and wife are miraculously restored to him, thus foreground the two roles for women that were presented in the play's opening scene: the virgin daughter and the wife/mother. The restoration of his daughter is hailed by Pericles in terms that echo Dante's prayer to Mary in *The Divine Comedy*, "Vergine madre, figlia del tua figlio" (Virgin Mother, daughter of your Son, *Paradiso*, 33.1):

> O, come hither,
> Thou that beget'st him that did thee beget;

> Thou that was born at sea, buried at Tharsus,
> And found at sea again. . . . This is Marina. (5.1.194–199)

In E.M.W. Tillyard's words, in *Pericles* Shakespeare was unwittingly creating a miniature version of Dante's *Commedia*. It needs to be emphasized that such a richly complex ending to the play is not fully realized, although on the stage a director can work toward a fuller embodiment of the concept of the play than the words of the text themselves have actually given. In part, the concept needs to be filled out in action rather than in words. The reunion between Pericles and Marina is then complemented, in a further intensification of the miraculous, by the restoration of Thaisa, and thus of the purified and matured family, which is completed by, in the final scene, Marina's betrothal to Lysimachus. However superficially—a sketching out, as it were, of more profound treatments in the next plays Shakespeare was to write—the multiple aspects of women that have haunted Pericles are now able to be seen harmoniously.

Criticism of the play, especially when it draws on our understanding of the psychology of the family and masculinity, may help us understand the way *Pericles* can produce in readers and spectators an uncanny mixture of what Time in *The Winter's Tale* calls "joy and terror" (4.1.1). Pericles is like so many of Shakespeare's male characters who seem engaged in continuous struggles within and beyond the family to form a secure gendered identity and to find (or reject) a place for women in that identity. The questions the play's ending raises include: Why has our culture produced such a recurring pattern of male loss and searching? Do we see the wish-fulfillment endings as complex projections of a male desire to project the all-forgiving and once always available mother upon their wives and lovers? Are men in our culture to be condemned, pitied, or accepted for such patterns? Are they built into the basic fantasy structure of being male, or are they characteristic of a particular phase of the history of the patriarchal family and the romances it has engendered?

These questions and the ideological framework in which they are put, however, are arguably gender-biased. Feminist readers would see them as distinctively male-centered. The desire for the daughter, the power of the mother, and the need to be revived or resurrected by youthful or mature female figures are recurring male fantasies. Shakespeare explores this male fixation with women as bearers of salvation or rescuers in both *Cymbeline* and *The Winter's Tale*. Here, in *Pericles*, it is sketched out, as if he were trying it out as dramatic material. The renewal of Thaisa, the beloved wife as well as mother, is presented as a religious ritual: heralded by Diana, accompanied by serenading virgins and marveling attendants, as if this male fantasy were a universal truth. A man has suffered unjustly, undergone terrible torments and losses, and now the central fantasy figures of his inner world—the virgin daughter/whore/mother/wise woman—appear to reassure him. *Pericles* enacts in these final scenes some of the great male wish fullfilments of our history.

## CRITICAL CONTROVERSIES

The ambiguous condition of the play's text has generated much debate; it is also the basis for other critical controversies. *Pericles* has generally been regarded as one of Shakespeare's least satisfactory plays, with undeveloped characters, much rough verse, episodic and confusing action. These problems have been attributed to the rough state of the text. Some early critics saw the play as an immature experiment. Victorian readers also took exception to the brothel scene and the concern with incest, characteristically attributing the more morally reprehensible parts to Shakespeare's collaborator or to a corrupt text. The character of Marina, however, was singled out for praise.

From the end of the nineteenth century until the 1930s critics tended to sentimentalize the play, while still regretting its imperfect textual state. It was often seen, as were all the romances, as signs of Shakespeare's tiredness, even boredom with the theater. However, parts of the play were admired: Marina for her delicacy and courage, Pericles for his fortitude, and (once a Victorian squeamishness about its subject matter was overcome) the brothel scenes for their realism. It was G. Wilson Knight in the 1920s and 1930s who first advocated regarding the underlying pattern (if not all the details) of the play as a whole and saw *Pericles* along with the other late romances as experimental and profound, and as evidence for Shakespeare's continuing vitality as a dramatist. Knight understood the play as embodying great symbolic opposites of destruction and reconciliation, and he played down the superficial characters and unreality of the story in order to look at the underlying themes. "In so doing," Skeele notes, "he overturned (or at least seriously challenged) centuries of critical opinion on *Pericles*" (7). Thus he set the tone of criticism of the play up to the present.

Knight's thematic approach was amplified by a series of others, mainly drawing on religious or psychoanalytic models to look at the play's overall pattern, including Ruth Nevo, Coppélia Kahn, C. L. Barber, and Richard Wheeler. Some critics (Barber, for instance) read the play as a Christian allegory of suffering, purgation, and reconciliation. These critics, in different ways, focused on the play's concern with family; with the masculine and feminine parts of the psyche; and the place of sexuality in human experience. They tended to focus on the pattern the play embodies rather than on whether this design is consistently carried out. In the 1980s and 1990s New Historicist critics tended to set it within Jacobean preoccupations such as the legitimacy of monarchy, changing patterns of family relationships, concerns about syphilis, and the education of women. Such approaches are useful for annotating special aspects of the play but go too far when they suggest that such matters account for the whole meaning of *Pericles*.

The most controversial aspect of *Pericles*, in part derived from its ambiguous textual status and how critics respond to that issue, is the degree of seriousness which the play actually achieves, as opposed to the seriousness of its underlying conception. Is what we have a rough draft? An experiment that does not quite work? A sketch for later, more profound plays? Or does the underlying design represent some profound vision of reality, an invitation to imagine a new future for humanity, "reaching forward . . . to social formations that still exceed the reach of our own" (Ryan, p. 130). Much depends on the weight given to Pericles' trials and especially the final scenes of discovery and recognition. The play is an attempt to go beyond the "happy ending" of most of the early comedies to comment on human hope or possibility. As Felperin puts it, *Pericles* aims to create "something which crystallizes the experience of a lifetime in to a moment . . . and which reaches out from the situation on stage to implicate our own situation and our own roles of father or husband, daughter or wife" (125). What do we learn? Is it that Pericles is like

Job, willing to bear continual burdens and losses, and like Job is finally rewarded? Or that a recurring and deep-seated human fantasy is for a universe where that should happen? Is Pericles' outburst on losing Thaisa, "O you gods! / Why do you make us love your godly gifts / And snatch them straight away?" (3.1.22–24), answered by receiving them back? Is that a reward for patience? A gift from the gods (or God)? Or chance? For Christian-oriented critics, it is as if, like Dante in the *Commedia*, Pericles has gone through hell, purgatory, and is now receiving a heavenly vision in earthly, familial terms. He gets not a vision of the divine—in Dante's poem Beatrice points beyond herself to God—but of the reunited human family and of appropriately differentiated roles and possibilities within that very human structure. At the play's end the hero is not shown heaven, but a very temporal space and set of relationships in which he must work out his human fulfillment.

While some critics do read the ending as a religious, specifically Christian, vision, most see it as the expression of a human fantasy. It can also be seen as sending the protagonist back into the world, to work out the future, much like the end of *The Tempest*. Prospero breaks his magic staff, drowns his book, and returns to the risky but real world of time, history, and unpredictability. Pericles likewise must now work on making his restored relationships function within human rather than mythical time.

## PRODUCTION HISTORY

The first quarto states that *Pericles* had been "divers and sundry times acted by his Maiesties Servants, at the Globe on the Banck-side." Along with the frequent reprinting in the early seventeenth century, that statement suggests this was probably one of Shakespeare's most popular plays, but in the eighteenth and nineteenth centuries it was rarely performed. Early twentieth-century productions remained relatively rare. Even as recently as 2001, Stephen Orgel could claim that Pericles "is a drama that editors and critics have, for most of the past century, found fascinating, but that the professional theater for three hundred and fifty years has either ignored or profoundly distrusted" (xlv). In part under the influence of changing critical fashion, it has gradually become a part of the repertoire in the great Shakespeare venues (Stratford-upon-Avon; The English National Theatre; Stratford, Ontario; Ashland, Oregon). In the 1990s and beyond, it has been frequently produced, and across America in 2003 it was shown on at least a dozen professional or college stages.

What characterizes most productions of *Pericles* (and may influence the choice to choose to stage it) is the freedom a director has, which, indeed, a director must take, to make the play a coherent experience for an audience. Its half-formed, or perhaps simply confused, textual state is a positive encouragement to see it as a script able to be shaped according to a director's tastes. Many directors feel free to rewrite parts of the first two acts, to use some of Wilkins's novel, smooth out the clumsiness of the verse, and reorder many of the speeches. The play also easily lends itself to spectacular settings. Toby Robertson's 1974 Prospect Theatre production, with Derek Jacobi as Pericles, was set in a male brothel, complete with cushions, transvestites, a "Bordello Band," acrobats, and whores, which dissolved as the seating dissolved for the reunion of Pericles and Marina. Terry Hands directed Ian Richardson at Stratford-upon-Avon in 1969 with the play being read as a Neoplatonic parable (under the influence of G. Wilson Knight) with a filmy, ethereal,

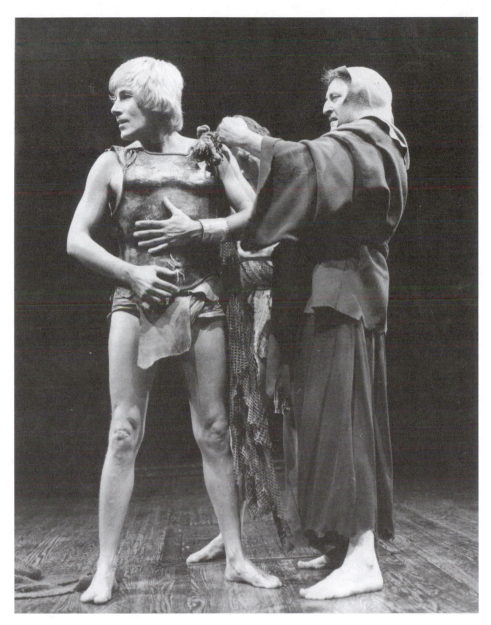

(Left to right) Nicholas Pennell as Pericles and Powys Thomas as 1st Fisherman in *Pericles*. Stratford Festival, Stratford, Ontario, Canada, 1974. Courtesy of Photofest.

quasi-religious atmosphere (and the doubling of the parts of Marina and Thaisa by Susan Fleetwood, suggesting the shared role of healer by the two women in Pericles' life); Ron Daniels, at Stratford's "Other Place" theater, produced it in 1979 on a bare stage, which became the setting for combat, a ship, and emblematic tableaux of episodic scenes. Like many other directors, he inserted new lines for Marina in the brothel scene (4.6) and for Thaisa as she wakes in Cerimon's presence (3.2). The BBC video (1983), directed by David Jones, used the television medium to overcome the rapidly changing scenes, and to provide visual background; again, it drew on Wilkins's prose text, especially in the brothel scene.

In short, *Pericles* offers a director both problems and possibilities of innovation to an unusual extent. Two productions in major venues illustrate this. The 2003 Stratford (Ontario) Festival production directed by Leon Rubin tackled the problem of the episodic first three acts by treating them as a spectacular travelogue, a tour of spectacularly costumed Asian cultures (thus moving the setting further east), introducing the peripatetic Pericles to a series of exotic peoples, settings, and customs. The laborious lines of much of the script could not easily be disguised, and the play relied on Gower as a linking device (superbly conceived as a scantily dressed ghost), urging the audience to follow and try to get through the halting action in the hope of arriving at something better. The second half, no less spectacularly draped, seemed as if a new playwright had taken over. There were witty, fast-moving brothel scenes, a superbly subtle meeting of father and daughter, a believably reformed Lysimachus, and a quiet but highly effective reunion of mother with father and daughter. As with most productions, Rubin's was successful despite the opening three acts. It served to underline what many editors and some critics assert, that we should consider the play as clearly divided into two parts (with the exception of a few lines here and there) and written by two authors.

The Bartlett Sher production, presented at Purchase and Brooklyn, New York, in 2004, also tackled the difficult textual situation head on. Sher's *Cymbeline* (2002) was the first American production to be mounted by the Royal Shakespeare Company under his direction, and his *Pericles* added to his distinction. Antiochus and the older Pericles were played by the same actor, and Antiochus's daughter and Marina by the same actress, thus stressing the incest associations, and he chose to handle the episodic first half of the play with a fast paced, unapologetic use of farce and pageantry. Such productions as Sher's and Rubin's reinforce the common critical and scholarly conclusion that Shakespeare took a poorly written episodic story, partly scripted out, and tried to do something with it, perhaps, in effect, lightly editing parts and heavily rewriting others. While not easily provable, such a division remains the most plausible explanation for the play's inconsistencies.

## EXPLICATION OF KEY PASSAGES

**4.2, 4.5–6.** In the eighteenth and nineteenth centuries, the brothel scenes occasioned general disapproval, either as being immoral or unseemly, or, at best, a distasteful arena where Marina with her heroic virtue could be displayed like a medieval saint surrounded by a sinful world. But the scenes certainly are not unusual in Shakespeare: they echo his earlier treatment of urban low life in *Measure for Measure* or *Henry IV*, and they have a remarkable energy. Nevo argues that the brothel family—the pandar, his wife, and their servant, Boult—is a parody of the family structure that will be restored at the end. More importantly, the brothel scenes embody in the contrast between Marina and her surroundings the virgin-whore contradiction, not in Marina, or even Lysimachus, but in the reader/spectator. Boult, also a pandar, advertises the arrival of a new virgin in the brothel, but she resists all attempts to prostitute her. Then Lysimachus, the governor, arrives at the brothel, disguised. This is clearly an important event in the play's development since, in the play's final scene, he is presented to Marina as her husband-to-be. Does he come as a customer and like the others is persuaded against having her by her virtue? Is he in disguise because he is investigating either the brothel or Marina? Would Jacobean audiences be horrified or amused?

Behind these scenes there lies a long tradition of medieval religious stories about the sufferings of virgin martyrs. Like St. Agnes (fourth century, Rome) and St. Lucia (283–304, Syracuse), Marina is presented to us as a pure, untouched, and highly talented upper-class Mediterranean virgin who possesses "a good face, speaks well, and has excellent good clothes," requiring only "[t]hese blushes of hers" to be "quench'd with some present practice" (4.2.47–48, 124–125). Medieval Christians saw the Virgin Martyrs of the early Church as embodying feminine virtue, beauty, and sexual purity, and successfully confronting "sadistic persecutors and potential rapists" in the person of prospective suitors, husbands, or clients (Karen Winstead, *Virgin Martyrs: Legends of Sainthood in Late Medieval England* [Ithaca: Cornell UP, 1997], 6). These largely mythological figures, notably Margaret, Cecilia, Agnes, Katherine, Agatha, Barbara, Lucia, and Ursula, served as Christian exempla, not only of perseverance in the face of persecution but also specifically of women taming their naturally rampant sexuality and therefore showing their fitness for heaven. At age twelve or thirteen Agnes was ordered to sacrifice to pagan gods and to lose her virginity by rape from an unwanted husband. She was taken to a brothel and tortured when she refused to turn against God, vowing she would keep her consecrated virginity intact, accept death, and see Christ. Such stories focus on young women's admirably denying the "natural" sinfulness of female sexuality, derived from the concupiscence of the Fall; many of the accounts linger over the sexual details of the threatened and tortured virgins. Like Marina, the typical virgin martyr is persecuted because she will not have sex. Often we are given graphic descriptions of violence against the women. Agnes is often depicted in medieval art forms carrying a tray on which her severed breasts are displayed; Cecilia, we are told, was mutilated and boiled alive. Intriguingly, in the many accounts of their tortures, they miraculously rarely feel what is being done to their bodies, just as medieval tradition insisted that the Virgin Mary suffered no birthing pains, a "male fantasy" in Theweleit's phrase, if ever there was one.

As we watch these scenes, the contradictory aspects of the patriarchal image of woman in Western history are on display. Just as Marina is both virgin and (potential) whore, Lysimachus is "a split character, indeterminately ravisher and protector" (Nevo, p. 83). Is that a consequence of an unfinished or contradictory text? Or is Shakespeare reaching to say something about the divided nature of male discourse about women? Directors (and some editors) add dialogue from Wilkins's prose tale to fill out the scene, but the questions remain unresolved in the script. Is Lysimachus reformed? Is he even likeable? Does he pretend to be a customer? Or is he really one? "I came with no ill intent" (4.6.109), he says after displaying what seems to be ill intent indeed.

**5.1, 5.3.** The first of the play's two final reunions, which shows Pericles reunited with his daughter (5.1), is among the finest scenes Shakespeare wrote. The second, with Thaisa (5.3), reads, however, like a sketch for the fuller culminating scenes he was to write in *Cymbeline* and *The Winter's Tale*. The overall pattern is clear, and the play's conclusion can be very moving, but the intense emotional impact of the scenes lacks the fullness of the statue scene in *The Winter's Tale* or the reconciliations and tableaux of *Cymbeline* or *The Tempest*.

Pericles arrives in Mytilene unable to speak, unshaven, withdrawn. He is greeted by Lysimachus, and it is suggested that the influence of a remarkable young woman in the town may help Pericles recover. Marina is ushered in and tells her story, sings, and Pericles does gradually respond; he then slowly recognizes her story and finally realizes that this person is his daughter. The poetry is superbly evocative, as if Shakespeare had realized where the script with which he had been tinkering was, finally, heading, and that he could link such scenes back to his own comedies and forward to plays that were as yet unwritten.

Act 5, scene 1 is succeeded by the ritual announcement by the goddess Diana that we will now experience a restoration of harmony. Gower's prophecies that all will be well will come true. The scene changes to a descent from heaven of the Goddess Diana, who instructs Pericles to go to her temple at Ephesus and tell his story. Gower tells us that Marina and Lysimachus will eventually marry and ushers in Pericles' arrival at Ephesus, where he relates his story, only to discover that one of the Vestals in the temple is Thaisa. They are reunited. Barber and Wheeler see Pericles' restoration, his "coming back to life" (139), as having such emotional resonance because it emphasizes the fundamental relationship between a child and the mother. It is an acting out of the desire to be encompassed in the womb and to see continuity in the next generation in the form of the daughter figure—once sought (at the start of the play) incestuously but now able to be accepted as an autonomous though loving being who (in the announced betrothal to Lysimachus) can be entrusted to another man. The family (at least in the patriarchal fantasy of the play's ending) is restored, purified, harmonious.

## Annotated Bibliography

Barber, C. L., and Richard Wheeler. *The Whole Journey: Shakespeare's Power of Development.* Berkeley: U of California P, 1986. Psychoanalytical approach, arguing that the play deals with subjects growing out of the psychology of the family.

Felperin, Howard. *Shakespearean Romance.* Princeton: Princeton UP, 1986. Focuses on the ambiguities of romance and its traditional story of developing virtue by trial.

Hartwig, Joan. *Shakespeare's Tragicomic Vision.* Baton Rouge: Louisiana State UP, 1972. Discusses the mixture of wonder and realism in the play, and the overall structure of the romance as working toward a revelation of wonder that fulfills an earlier fantasy in an unexpected way.

Kahn, Coppélia. *Man's Estate: Masculine Identity in Shakespeare.* Berkeley: U of California P, 1991. Study of Shakespeare's heroes and the underlying psychology of masculinity.

Knight, G. Wilson. *The Crown of Life.* London: Methuen, 1958. Classic study of the late plays, focusing on mythical themes and imagery.

Nevo, Ruth. "The Perils of Pericles." In *The Undiscover'd Country: New Essays on Psychoanalysis and Shakespeare.* Ed. B. J. Sokol. London: Free Association Books, 1993. 150–178. Close reading of underlying psychological dynamics.

Orgel, Stephen, ed. *Pericles, Prince of Tyre.* New York: Penguin, 2001. Excellent modern edition.

Ryan, Kiernan, ed. *Shakespeare: The Last Plays.* London: Longman, 1999. Useful collection of contemporary criticism.

Skeele, David, ed. *"Pericles": Critical Essays.* New York: Garland, 2000. Comprehensive collection of extracts of essays, reviews, historical documents, and theater history.

Tillyard, E.M.W. *Shakespeare's Last Plays.* London: Chatto and Windus, 1938. Sees the romances as developing out of the tragedies to produce re-creation from destruction.

Williams, Deanne. "Papa Don't Preach: The Power of Prolixity in *Pericles.*" *University of Toronto Quarterly* 71 (2002): 595–622. Highly provocative reading of the play's concern with incest.

# *Cymbeline*

### Gary Waller

## PLOT SUMMARY

**1.1.** We are in Roman Britain. Imogen, daughter of the King, Cymbeline, has alienated her father by marrying Posthumus, an orphan whom Cymbeline has raised in the court. We learn that Imogen's two brothers, Guiderius and Arviragus, children of Cymbeline's first marriage (as is Imogen), were abducted long ago when they were children and are presumed dead. Posthumus is exiled by Cymbeline. Before he departs to Rome, Imogen gives him a ring, and he gives her a bracelet.

**1.2.** Cymbeline's current queen has a boorish son, Cloten, who had been Cymbeline's preferred husband for Imogen. Cloten's servants make fun of him behind his back.

**1.3.** Pisanio, Posthumus's servant, who has stayed at the British court, gives an account to Imogen of his master's reluctant departure.

**1.4.** The scene shifts to Rome, where Posthumus is introduced to an Italian lord, Iachimo. They, along with other Romans, praise their mistresses. When Posthumus speaks of Imogen's virtue, Iachimo bets 10,000 ducats to the diamond ring, the present from Imogen, that he (Iachimo) can go to England and seduce this apparent paragon. Posthumus foolishly accepts the bet.

**1.5.** Back in Britain, the court doctor Cornelius is suspicious when the Queen collects poisonous plants. He decides to undercut any villainous plans she may have and tells the audience that what she thinks is a fatal poison is merely a sleeping potion. The Queen's plots take a further turn when she tries unsuccessfully to persuade Pisanio, servant to Posthumus who has remained in England, to join her against his master. She gives him what she believes to be a poison, telling him that it is a life-saving potion.

**1.6.** Iachimo arrives in Britain, and comes to the court. He brings Imogen a letter of introduction from Posthumus. Meeting her, he realizes he will lose the bet unless he can trick her in some way. He claims that Posthumus has himself been unfaithful and incites her to be revenged by sleeping with him. She is appalled by his suggestion and rejects him. He assures her he was merely testing her devotion to Posthumus and expresses his admiration for her steadfastness. He then requests that she keep a trunk full of valuables, partly owned by Posthumus, in her bedroom overnight for safekeeping, and he will leave in the morning.

**2.1.** That evening, Cloten is annoyed because he did not get to meet Iachimo.

**2.2.** We see Imogen asleep in her bedchamber, with Iachimo's trunk in the room. While she is asleep, Iachimo emerges from the trunk, and without waking her, takes notes on the details of her chamber and various marks on her body. He sees Posthumus's bracelet on her arm and, without waking her, removes it.

**2.3.** In the morning, Cloten tries to woo Imogen. She rejects him scornfully and, missing her bracelet, asks Pisanio to find it for her.

**2.4.** The scene returns to Italy, where Iachimo uses his knowledge of Imogen and her bedchamber and the evidence of her bracelet to convince Posthumus that he has seduced her. Posthumus is beside himself with grief and anger, and announces he will have revenge.

**3.1.** Back in Britain, Cymbeline refuses to pay tribute to Caesar, and as a consequence the Roman authorities declare war on him.

**3.2.** Pursuing his revenge against Imogen, Posthumus writes to Pisanio ordering him to kill her. Pisanio is appalled and will not believe she has been unfaithful. Posthumus further instructs Pisanio that in order to get her to leave the court so the execution can be carried out, he is to tell Imogen that Posthumus will meet her at Milford Haven.

**3.3.** We now meet a set of new characters—Belarius, who was long ago banished by Cymbeline and who, we discover, kidnapped Cymbeline's lost sons, Guiderius and Arviragus. They live together in a cave, near Milford Haven. The young men, not knowing they are princes, are becoming discontented by their rural life and yearn for the life of the court.

**3.4.** Imogen and Pisanio have traveled toward Milford Haven. Pisanio shows her Posthumus's letter in which he is ordered that she be killed. Pisanio refuses to kill her, though. He will tell Posthumus she is dead, but she should disguise herself as a boy and ask for employment with Lucius, one of the Roman nobles. As a gift, Pisanio gives Imogen the Queen's potion, which he believes to be a remedy for sickness, but we know to be a powerful sleeping potion.

**3.5.** Imogen is discovered to be missing from Cymbeline's court. The Queen wishes her to be dead or in exile so she may have more power over the succession to the aging Cymbeline. Thinking that Imogen is off to Rome with Lucius, Pisanio tells Cloten that she has gone to Milford Haven. Cloten decides to follow her, taking some of Posthumus's clothes as a disguise, vowing to kill Posthumus and rape Imogen.

**3.6.** Imogen, disguised as Fidele, finds Belarius's cave; she is exhausted and is welcomed by them with food and rest. The Romans in the meantime are planning the battle against Britain.

**4.1.** Cloten is drawing closer to Milford Haven, boasting of what he will do to Posthumus and Imogen.

**4.2.** In the cave, Imogen rests and takes the potion she received from Pisanio. Returning from hunting, Belarius sees Cloten and is afraid they have been discovered. Guiderius kills and beheads Cloten. The brothers return to the cave and find Imogen apparently dead. They lay her in a grave and pray and sing over her body. Imogen awakes. She sees Cloten's headless body dressed in Posthumus's clothes and assumes that Posthumus has been killed. She flies to join the Roman army where Lucius takes her under his protection.

**4.3.** Back in the court, Pisanio determines to fight against the Romans.

**4.4.** Fearing discovery, Belarius wants to flee, but the two boys want to remain to fight the Romans.

**5.1.** Posthumus has joined the invading Romans. He learns from Pisanio that Imogen has been killed as he ordered.

**5.2.** Posthumus abandons the Romans and dresses as a peasant to fight on the side of the Britons. Iachimo acknowledges having wrongly accused Imogen.

**5.3.** Posthumus describes how three unknown soldiers suddenly appeared and saved the Briton army. They turn out to be Belarius, Guiderius, and Arviragus.

**5.4.** Posthumus, now disguised as a Roman, is apprehended by the victorious Britons. He is imprisoned and takes it as his just desert. In prison, he receives a vision from the gods and awakes to discover a document containing a written prophecy that his fortune will improve, and that Britain itself will overcome its servitude.

**5.5.** Cymbeline presides over a victory celebration. He knights the mysterious soldiers, Belarius, Arviragus, and Guiderius, who have saved the day, but regrets he does not know the identity of one especially brave soldier (whom we know to be Posthumus). News comes that the Queen has died, at the end acknowledging her crimes and plots. Some Roman prisoners—Imogen, Posthumus, Lucius, and Iachimo—are brought before the King. Lucius successfully asks him for clemency for his page (whom we know to be Imogen). Then Fidele/Imogen asks that Iachimo provide an account of how he received the diamond ring he is wearing. Hearing Iachimo's confession, the griefstruck Posthumus leaps forward and pushes Fidele/Imogen away when she tries to explain. Pisanio steps forward to help her, and she turns on him, accusing him of poisoning her with the Queen's potion. The doctor who created the potion, Cornelius, in turn defends Pisanio. Belarius, Guiderius, and Arviragus, who are now bystanders to this new development, are amazed at Fidele's appearance. Guiderius admits he killed Cloten and is arrested by Cymbeline. Belarius then stands forth. He reveals who he is—and the identity of the King's two sons. Posthumus forgives Iachimo. Imogen and Posthumus embrace. "Pardon's the word to all" (5.5.422) pronounces Cymbeline, who announces that he will after all pay the traditional tribute to Rome, thus restoring peace between the Romans and Britain.

## PUBLICATION HISTORY

*Cymbeline* was likely written in 1609 or 1610: it was first performed in 1611, as witnessed and recorded that year by the diarist Simon Forman, who provides some account of the play's plot and characters but no other details. The play was first printed in the First Folio (1623). There was no earlier publication in quarto form. The text of 1623 is likely based on an authorial manuscript or perhaps a close copy of authorial material. Modern editors generally make minor emendations: the Oxford edition (1998) changes the traditional name Imogen to Innogen, and the name of the play's Italian villain Iachimo to its likely Italian original Giachimo. Forman calls the heroine "Innogen," but in the more authoritative Folio she is called "Imogen." Roger Warren, the Oxford editor, argues that "Innogen" has a special historical and symbolic appropriateness—it is the name of the legendary first queen of Britain. Also, it suggests innocence and so gives the heroine a name that matches Fidele, the name she uses when she becomes, in disguise, a Roman page. Most modern editions, however, including the Riverside Shakespeare, retain "Imogen," which has now long been a common name for girls. In the notes below, the Folio designation is maintained. Warren's argument, however, is worth considering from a theatrical perspective. He suggested that the revised name be tried out on an experimental basis in the rehearsals for the 1988 National Theatre production; and, he reported, that Posthumus's anguished repeating of the name of his supposedly murdered wife becomes a reminder of what he has done to her (58, 265).

## SOURCES FOR THE PLAY

The play is set mainly in early British history but has some actions set in what seems to be Renaissance Italy. These contradictions are a reflection of the play's sources. Shakespeare relied on Raphael Holinshed's *Chronicles* (1587) for the setting of the play and the name of the title character, Cymbeline, who, according to Holinshed, ruled Britain from 33 B.C. to A.D. 2. Boccaccio's Renaissance collection of stories, the *Decameron* (ninth novel, second day), which was written in 1353, provided the most prominent sources for the play's main story—the man who foolishly bets that his wife is the most faithful and would resist any attempt at seduction. Other medieval and renaissance sources record similar stories. Shakespeare certainly read the play *The Rare Triumphs of Love and Fortune* (1589), which provided him with the love story of Posthumus and Imogen, Posthumus's exile, and Cloten's desire to marry Imogen. No source has been found for the ending of the play, including the apparent death of Imogen (which echoes a plot device in *Romeo and Juliet*), the descent of Jupiter, or the story line regarding Belarius and the two kidnapped princes.

## STRUCTURE AND PLOTTING

"Nothing fits, everything goes in this wild play," says Harold Bloom; "the plot is a chaos, and Shakespeare never bothers to be probable." For Bloom, as for many critics, the plot, and especially its breathless conclusion, is "so contrived and so artificially resolved as to be ridiculous" (*Shakespeare: The Invention of the Human* [New York: Penguin, 1998], 615, 616). The play often appears to readers to be disorganized or disjointed, or at best, for those more charitably inclined, as some kind of bizarre experiment. While the moral force of the final act is clear—to show a fantasy of how we hope that although good people may be unjustly punished and persecuted in the short run, they may be rewarded in the end, either by desert or fortune—the goal is achieved through a remarkable series of seemingly impossible coincidences, revelations, and discoveries that may be emotionally powerful but are certainly unlikely. The extraordinary surprises of the ending of *Cymbeline* are not as radical as in the contemporary *The Winter's Tale*, where the statue of the seemingly dead Hermione comes to life; but their cumulative effect is (according to different perspectives) enormously moving or designed to strain (and even exceed) normal credibility. Anguish, loss, and threat are compensated by the final reunions and reconciliations of father and his (variously) lost sons and daughter, husband and wife, friends and acquaintances, so the overall effect is certainly 'comic' in a loose sense. But the happy ending expected in a comedy is preceded by a period when the audience knows a degree of great anxiety where any easy overall comic response is undermined; we must watch as characters with whom we have been asked to identify seem further and further from finding happiness. These are all typical devices of Shakespeare's late romances and are designed to work on an audience's emotional vulnerability to produce a mixture of anxiety and hope before the final scenes of reconciliation.

*Cymbeline*, then, posed for Shakespeare what (after writing *Pericles*) was becoming a major preoccupation for him: how to create a richly emotional mixture of potential tragedy, broad comedy, and the "miraculous" recovery typical of romance, and to make that mixture both acceptable on rational grounds and, more importantly, emotionally rich and persuasive.

While the overall pattern may be clear, the individual devices by which the play achieves its goal are often felt to be so extreme as to be ludicrous. But, as many critics have pointed out, none are especially original. All have been used by Shakespeare before—though not in the same play. It is as if Shakespeare assembles all the theatrical tricks he has used in the earlier comedies, some he used in the tragedies, and most immediately, some which a year earlier he had tried out in working over the initially unpromising material in *Pericles*—and then he decides to bring them all together. *Cymbeline* is made up of recycled stories and situations from earlier plays: these include the evil, plotting queen (*Macbeth*), the worn-out king who banishes his son-in-law and seemingly loses his daughter (*King Lear*), a villainous plotter (*Othello*), a heroine disguising herself as a boy (*Two Gentlemen of Verona*, *As You Like It*, *Twelfth Night*), and the discovery of once lost relations—sons, husband, wife, father (*Comedy of Errors*, *Twelfth Night*).

There are three interwoven plots. The primary plot strand of *Cymbeline* is the tale of Imogen and Posthumus, who marry against King Cymbeline's wishes and are parted by the king's sending Posthumus into exile. He travels to Italy and foolishly accepts the wager regarding Imogen's chastity. He is convinced that Iachimo has seduced her, orders her murdered, and believes her to be dead. This story occupies much of the first two acts and returns to dominate the last. The second story concerns the loss of Cymbeline's two sons, kidnapped as infants, who are eventually restored to him. This story is mentioned briefly in act 1, enters prominently in act 3, and joins up with the Imogen/Posthumus story in act 5. The third story is the confrontation of Rome and Britain, caused by Cymbeline's decision (heavily influenced by the queen and Cloten) to deny Rome its accustomed tax or tribute, a conflict that is finally resolved by Cymbeline's agreeing to pay tribute to Rome. This story is not developed until act 3, and joins the first two stories in act 5.

The scenes move rapidly among different places and settings (London, Rome, and Milford Haven); court, city, and country; peace and war; ancient Britain and (seemingly) Renaissance Italy. Shakespeare hurries the play's action along to reach the culminating scene in the Imogen/Posthumus story, in which Iachimo hides in a trunk left for safekeeping in Imogen's bedroom and emerges while she is sleeping to gather "evidence" of having slept with her. By the end of act 1, Posthumus has been exiled, gone to Rome, and foolishly made the bet with Iachimo; Iachimo has traveled to Britain and is presented to Imogen at court. He completes his mission by the end of the second act. Clearly, Shakespeare's goal was not verisimilitude. Rather, as in a film, he was providing snapshots of the significance of human actions, not a realistic portrait of the actions themselves. All of these multiple settings and the shifting combinations of tragedy, comedy, and even farce, culminate in the final resolution scene—the most remarkable in Shakespeare's plays—in which at least twenty-five (by some counts, thirty-two) plot complications are unraveled. Whether the play is felt structurally to be a success or failure, it is nonetheless a hugely ambitious undertaking and, to those who admire the play, a remarkable achievement. Like a juggler, Shakespeare keeps his characters (Imogen in particular) thinking they are in an unpredictably threatening and even tragic situation. By the play's middle scenes, signs of reassurance and hopeful possibility open up, but the level of threat to Imogen—from her father, from the exile of her husband, from Iachimo, from death by her own trusted servant instructed by Posthumus—creates a level of tension not present in most comedies. Imogen's level of entrapment adds a degree of anxiety to an audience's feelings, even if we know or look for hints of a happy ending. That tension is resolved in the final scene.

## MAIN CHARACTERS

### Cymbeline

Cymbeline is the king of ancient (and united) Britain. He is persuaded by his queen and her son Cloten to refuse to pay tribute to Rome, and after successfully battling the Roman army, has his lost children returned to him. He then agrees to return to a harmonious relationship with Rome and the wider European civilization it represents. Cymbeline represents kingship, fatherhood, and the authority of age and power in a patriarchal society. He is the father of the nation, father of his children, and also broadly embodies both the authority and the blindness of masculine power. In these roles, he finds his authority challenged and undermined and then at the play's end restored—though with far greater insight about his roles.

### The Queen

Cymbeline's queen (who has no name), the king's second wife, plots against Posthumus in order to gain Imogen for her son, Cloten. An expert in poisons, she gives Pisanio the (apparent) poison that seems to kill Imogen. One of the many revelations in the play's conclusion is that she confesses that she never loved Cymbeline. A stock figure of the evil stepmother, she embodies a common male fantasy of untrustworthiness and ruthlessness in a strong and manipulative woman.

### Imogen

Imogen (or Innogen), daughter of Cymbeline by a former queen, marries Posthumus against her father's will, escapes the court in disguise, encounters her lost brother, and then at the end finds her husband, who has believed her to be unfaithful and wanted her killed. Much critical controversy has focused on Imogen. Many of Shakespeare's plays contain heroines who fight back against male disregard and domination: Hero in *Much Ado about Nothing*, Mistress Ford in *The Merry Wives of Windsor*, Mariana in *Measure for Measure*, Helena in *All's Well That Ends Well*, and Hermione in *The Winter's Tale*. Imogen is likewise a substantial counterbalance to the dominant male world. In making the role of Imogen so central to the play, Shakespeare creates a rich and theatrically powerful character from what might have been merely a stereotype, whether as a heroine or a psychological savior for the male egos of the play, notably her husband and father. Imogen's underlying strengths emerge in the first three acts. We see her independence in her choice of a husband: she has chosen to marry a commoner, a fact marvelled at by the (male) courtiers. Yet we see immediately that such choice involves vulnerability. She becomes increasingly isolated. She is rejected by her father, her husband is exiled, her stepmother plots against her, Cloten pursues her. As one of the court lords exclaims: "Alas, poor Princess, / Thou divine Imogen, what thou endur'st, / Betwixt a father by thy step-dame govern'd, / A mother hourly coining plots, a wooer / More hateful than the foul expulsion is / Of thy dear husband" (2.1 56–61). Her strength in the face of isolation and persecution is seen especially in the scenes in which she rebuffs Iachimo's attempt to seduce her and Cloten's effort to woo her, and the terms by which women are described in such a world are displayed in the scene (2.6) in which he presents his "proof" on his return to Rome. In a misogynist society, such slandering and abuse of women as somehow inherently unfaithful (and as male possessions) is commonplace; the dominant assumptions of the age regarding women's infidelity and untrustworthiness are summarized in Iachimo's bravado and Posthumus's subsequent anger.

But matters get even worse. Pisanio takes her from the court under the pretence of meeting her husband; once they are in Wales, he reveals he has been ordered to kill her. She has to abandon her identity as princess, wife, and woman when she disguises herself as a boy trying to survive in the wilderness near the invading Roman army. Throughout, she remains committed to her marriage and admirable in her emotional solidity as she defies her father politely but firmly; she is dignified and disdainful to Cloten as she affirms her love for Posthumus: "His mean'st garment / That ever hath but clipt his body, is dearer / In my respect than all the hairs above thee" (2.3.133–135). She remains faithful to herself and to Posthumus, as her assumed name, Fidele, suggests. Until her apparent death in 4.2, *Cymbeline* might be read as the tragedy of Imogen—even if we know she is not really dead.

One of the recurring motifs in romance is the apparent death of a heroine and her miraculous restoration; this is common to three of Shakespeare's late plays. In *Cymbeline*, however, it is not merely part of the romance atmosphere but is also used to convey psychological insights and to raise questions about the nature of gender. A useful comparison is with the death of Hermione in *The Winter's Tale*, where there is an unmistakable sense that Shakespeare wants us to believe that the tragedy is complete, that on one level, Hermione is "really" dead. In *Cymbeline*, he was not so bold. The audience, moreover, knows that the poison is really a kind of sleeping draught and that she will eventually awaken.

Underlying the development of Imogen up to that point in the play are issues of men's treatment of women. These issues preoccupied Shakespeare in a number of plays and permeate the last romances. Like Hermione in *The Winter's Tale*, Imogen is idealized beyond merit, the degree of "over-valuation" a reflection of Posthumus's own obsessions and those of Western men before and subsequently who have too often tended to oppress women while seemingly adoring and idealizing them. This process of oppression through adoration is termed "over-valuation" in psychoanalysis. The tragedy of Imogen through act 4, then, is of broad cultural significance.

When Imogen disguises herself as a man, it is as if she is showing what kind of balance might exist in maleness. When s/he "dies" it is as if that ideal cannot survive in such a violent world. But the ending of the play gives us a vision of a possible understanding of humanity beyond the stereotypes of gender exploitation. We observe the coming together of father and daughter, brothers and sister, husband and wife. The ending of the play is, on one level, a male fantasy of forgiveness and redemption—that woman, at once worshipped and abused, will be ultimately there to reassure or, if needed, to rescue a man. But what Imogen poses to the play's readers and audience is a harder question: Can men learn a better way of living?

Imogen has been idealized not only within the play itself but also by male critics. For more than a century, what Richard Hosley has called "Imogenolaters" (*Cymbeline* [New York: Signet, 1963], xxxiv) have dominated criticism. In Imogen, A. C. Swinburne said in 1880, "we find half-glorified already the immortal godhead of womanhood" (Hosley, p. xv), and more recently Harold Bloom exclaims that Imogen's voice contains the notes of Shakespeare's "reinvention" of the human, the distinctive mark, Bloom believes, of Shakespeare's genius. Such terms retain the idealization that the play itself displays and then critiques, and it has taken twentieth-century feminist criticism to avoid such florid terms—to allow us to see Imogen as a study of a counterbalance to the destructive tendencies of the male world. As with Hermione in *The Winter's Tale*, we see a detailed and devastating critique of the dominant gender stereotypes; a view of women emerges not as objects of idealization (and denigration) but rather as equals, as partners.

### Cloten

Cloten, the loutish son of the current queen by a former husband, pursues Imogen when she leaves the court and is killed by one of Imogen's brothers. He is a crude representative of the masculine assumptions about women in the play. He believes his rank and riches, as son to the queen, will win him Imogen. Even Cymbeline himself speaks in this vein of his daughter to Cloten: "Some more time / Must wear the print of his [Posthumus's] remembrance on't, / And then she's yours" (2.3.42–44), he asserts. Cloten likewise assumes he can buy Imogen with riches: he woos her with paid musicians and boasts, "'Tis gold / Which buys admittance . . . / What can it not do, and undo" (2.3.67–68, 72–73). He views Imogen as a prize, and his reaction to her is a mixture of professed adoration and potential violence:

> I love and hate her; for she's fair and royal,
> And that she hath all courtly parts more exquisite
> Than lady, ladies, woman, from every one
> The best she hath, and she, of all compounded,
> Outsells them all. (3.5.70–74)

After dressing in Posthumus's clothes and determining to hunt down Imogen and rape her, Cloten is killed by Guiderius.

### Posthumus

Posthumus Leonatus, husband of Imogen, was brought up as an orphan in the British Court. Exiled to Rome, he too easily believes his wife to be unfaithful, orders her killed, repents, and helps defeat the Roman army before being reconciled to her. Leontes in *The Winter's Tale* is generally seen by critics as a persuasive portrait of jealousy fueled by insecurity and nostalgia for a lost childhood, but the character of Posthumus has never been seen as deserving such complex analysis. Harold Bloom, for instance, argues that not only does Posthumus join "that large company of Shakespearean husbands and lovers totally unworthy of their women" (619) but he also is plodding, boring, and marginal to the play's main actions. Other critics have seen a deeper significance to Posthumus. He is described at the play's start as "a poor but worthy gentleman" (1.1.7), and when his marriage to Imogen becomes known, we are told that all the courtiers support it: "[N]ot a courtier, / Although they wear their faces to the bent / Of the King's looks, hath a heart that is not / Glad at the thing they scowl at" (1.1.12–15). He is presented as a paragon of courtly, heroic virtue. As an orphan, adopted by Cymbeline and raised in the royal family, he has boldly challenged courtly prejudices against his status and won the princess's love on his own merits. Interestingly, even at the end, when many surprises are revealed, his relatively lowly status never changes: he is not found to be really a nobleman. Near the end, he has a dream vision of his parents; they are not, as might be expected in a romance, royal. His inherent worthiness, regardless of class origins, is an important detail. But regardless of his background he is still the quintessential hero—with all the strengths and weaknesses of what that means.

It is this degree of extreme idealization that proves to be Posthumus's weakness. We watch with bewilderment, indignation, and horror as he is all too easily manipulated by Iachimo. But the values we perceive among the courtiers in Rome are not only those of cynical Europeans. Posthumus's soliloquy after Iachimo has apparently proved Imogen's infidelity (2.5), with its echo of Othello's jealousy, violence, and self-destructiveness, is a frightening expose of the insecurities and dangers of male power, especially in its violent repudiation of the source in women—unknown yet deeply feared—of men's own insecurities. In his violence, he wants to destroy the "woman's part" in himself

> Could I find out
> The woman's part in me—for there's no motion
> That tends to vice in man, but I affirm
> It is the woman's part. (2.5.19–22)

This disintegration of Posthumus in the first two acts of the play has parallels in Shakespeare's other late plays. In *The Winter's Tale*, the central male character, Leontes, is overwhelmed by his jealousy and paranoia and, through increasingly destructive acts of tyranny, brings about the apparent death of his wife and two children. Anticipating Leontes (and with an echo of Othello's jealousy), Posthumus descends into an irrational rage, and, falling back on the now seemingly universal ethos of panicked masculinity, he orders Pisanio to kill his wife. It is as if the world of ego and competition has won him over—or he is revealed to be part of it after all. He will have to learn, as Barber and Wheeler put it, the "need men have to be validated by feminine presences" dramatized here, as in all the late romances, "as achieved in visionary revelations" (18).

### Belarius, Guiderius, and Arviragus

Belarius is a banished lord, living in the wilds of Wales under the name of Morgan. He kidnapped the two sons of Cymbeline when they were infants. Guiderius and Arviragus, the sons of Cymbeline and brothers to Imogen, are living with Belarius as his sons under the names of Polydore and Cadwal. They turn the battle against the Romans and discover their sister and father.

### Iachimo

Iachimo is a Roman gentleman, friend of Philario; he bets Posthumus he can seduce Imogen, then visits Britain and comes back to Rome with apparent proof of his success. Iachimo dominates the cynical tone of 1.4, where he and a group of European lords sit around gossiping about Posthumus as he comes to Rome. Iachimo offers an intriguing expose of the ethos of male authority and competitiveness that all the men of the play take for granted. When he meets Posthumus, he immediately attempts to victimize the exiled Britain; it is as if Iachimo and his highly sophisticated courtiers are looking for a chink in the newcomer's male armor, a weakness where Posthumus's masculinity can be probed, challenged, and overcome. Iachimo remarks cynically that Imogen's value rather than Posthumus's own worth commends him, as if such women were primarily useful only for building up a man's reputation among other men. Posthumus reacts angrily and naively, affirming his idealistic adoration of his princess and exposing himself to their victimization. That makes him Iachimo's victim.

Shakespeare reaches back to *Othello* for the situation he has thus set up between Posthumus and Iachimo—the naive, passionate outsider manipulated by the cunning, morally corrupt villain. Although less fathomless than Iago with his "motiveless malignancy," Iachimo is just as impressively developed, as Shakespeare links his flippant amorality with the values of the wider male society that he easily inhabits and with the peculiar vulnerabilities of his victim. Thus we see Iachimo's crude bravado in Rome; and then when he comes to the British court, we see his immediate recognition of Imogen's integrity. There is, unlike with Iago, no ambiguity about his motives: he is in competition with Posthumus, another man, a rival not in love but in ego. As G. Wilson Knight puts it, he is "a born exhibitionist, smug, suave, showy and bold as the occasion demands," who likes to be "put on his mettle, and follows any challenge as far as he can" (142). His verbal seduction of Imogen—just like his interactions with Posthumus—are calculatedly clever, looking for her weakness and finding it in her very truthfulness. By the end of the play, an abject Iachimo repents his deviousness and is forgiven as part of the general amnesty, but the damage he has done and what it represents about the male ego constitute a serious part of the play's concerns.

## DEVICES AND TECHNIQUES

In its history, from the First Folio (1623) on, *Cymbeline* has been variously listed among both the tragedies and the comedies—and it could almost be seen as a history play, since it derives from Holinshed's *Chronicles* and deals with supposedly factual events in early Britain. Most modern scholars classify it as one of the "romances," the closely linked group of plays Shakespeare wrote at the end of his career, which are accordingly grouped together in the Riverside edition (Boston: Houghton Mifflin, 1997). *Cymbeline* also has a number of important continuities with earlier comedies like *The Comedy of Errors* or *As You Like It*. But it contains situations more typical of the tragedies. Imogen's shock at apparently discovering Posthumus's beheaded body, her supposed death as "Fidele," and her moving funeral rituals performed by the three "wild men" (two of whom are, unbeknownst to her, actually her brothers) strike emotionally rich and tragic notes. Posthumus's naive and crass gullibility before the cunning of Iachimo is particularly anguished, especially because at that point we do not know how matters will work out. Posthumus's anger and violence threaten to turn into tragedy in the way that Leontes' jealousy and persecution of his wife Hermione do in *The Winter's Tale*. The play might best be described as a tragi-comedy, since it is a calculated combination of the effects of these two kinds of play.

But so extreme are the twists and turns of *Cymbeline* that, in fact, many critics see the play as chaotic, disorganized, full of contradictory emotions and very confusing to follow on a first reading or viewing. The play includes a vast array of moods. In the scene in which Imogen apparently dies, her brothers chant over her body what is often regarded as one of the most beautiful English lyric poems, "Fear no more the heat o' th' sun" (4.2.258–281). Then suddenly we experience a beheaded corpse! Such a radical juxtaposition of moods epitomizes the play's extreme theatricality. The play depends throughout on its audience's experiencing one extremity juxtaposed against another.

Adding to the theatrical effectiveness—and underlining the play's thematic continuities—are the multiple disguises and misprisions, both literal and metaphorical. These include the many living characters who are believed to be dead; and the characters who are believed to be truthful and are in fact false, like Iachimo and the queen, as well as those believed to be false but who are in fact true, like Imogen and Posthumus. The disguise/misprision motif is best represented by the changing role (over all five acts) of the sleeping potion that the queen concocts as a pupil of the court physician, Cornelius, who tells us that he is concerned about her dabbling in "devilish" arts (1.5.16) and so ensures that it is not a deadly poison but a sleeping potion that she concocts. But only in the final revelatory scene do we learn the truth about it from Cornelius himself.

Throughout the play, what seems to be can easily become perceived or revealed as something else: seeming truth as lies, good reputation as hollow, fidelity as faithlessness and vice versa. The king mistakes the nature of his scheming, self-confessedly murderous second wife, and is blind to the integrity and independence of his daughter; Posthumus is similarly naive, violent, and self-destructive in his reaction to Imogen's presumed unfaithfulness and in his reliance on a male ethos of narcissism and presumed superiority to women. The effect of this multiple technique is to create an atmosphere of anxiety and insecurity that helps to temper the overall optimistic movement of the play. "She is fool'd," says the doctor about the queen, "With a most false effect, and I the truer, / So to be false with her" (1.5.42–44). Cornelius here expresses a central motif in the play, being "the truer" by being false; and its reverse, pretending in order to reveal the truth, is a recurring device throughout the play—until all is revealed at the end, and the play in effect challenges its audience to adopt a new openness and to live the truth rather than simply take it for granted.

Many modern directors say that one of the greatest challenges in staging *Cymbeline* successfully is the rapid mixing of moods, the unpredictability of setting, and the seemingly deliberate anachronisms: Roman Britain, Renaissance Italy, ancient Wales. The shifting moods, settings, motives, and apparent truths are reflected not only in the characters' sense of the unexpected, but also in the members of the audience themselves, creating, at least in a successful production, the tragi-comic atmosphere of anxiety and wish fulfillment. By the end of the play an audience's hope for happy endings is indulged to an extent never attempted in any other Shakespearean play. Part of the play's effect is based on the degree of unpredictability and threat that has preceded the final scenes. Howard Felperin defines a romance as "a success story in which difficulties . . . are overcome . . . against impossible odds or by miraculous means" (10). While the audience anticipates a happy ending, the predominant effect aimed at is that of relief and surprise and what the late plays frequently refer to as "wonder." The mixing of tragedy and comedy and the multiple, even contradictory, feelings suggest a fruitful way of viewing the play as an experiment in achieving theatrical surprise. This intention certainly fits the play's thematic focus.

## THEMES AND MEANINGS

One of the shared themes of all of Shakespeare's late romances is forgiveness. In their different ways, they are all enacted parables or wish-fulfilment fantasies with a common pattern of loss and reconciliation, human mistakes and forgiveness. In *Cymbeline*, the key line is Cymbeline's own pronouncement, "Pardon's the word for all" (5.5.422) in the remarkable fifth act, after all the discoveries and reunions. Among the most prominent pardons, Cymbeline frees the Roman captives, Rome's rights to tribute are reaffirmed, and he forgives Belarius for kidnapping his sons. Posthumus forgives Iachimo for alienating him from Imogen; Imogen, in the play's central action, forgives Posthumus for doubting her fidelity and for wanting her murdered:

> *Imogen*: Why did you throw your wedded lady from you?
> Think that you are upon a rock, and now
> Throw me again.
>
> *Post*: Hang there like fruit, my soul,
> Till the tree die! (5.5.261–263)

Such a scene resembles Prospero's forgiveness of the conspirators in *The Tempest*, the reunion of Leontes and Hermione in *The Winter's Tale*, and of Pericles with Thaisa and Marina in *Pericles*. This theme is one Shakespeare wanted or needed to work over and over, as if in this last phase of his career, it was something he wished to dramatize and communicate theatrically, emotionally, and intellectually, to his audience.

This theme of forgiveness, with its dual phases of alienation and reconciliation, is seen most directly in the play's concern with the family. Besides being the father of his country, Cymbeline is embroiled in a complex family situation. He has three children by his first marriage, two of whom were kidnapped as infants; he has a daughter who has married against his wishes; and he has a second wife who is pushing the ambitions of her son from a first marriage. As in *Pericles* and *The Winter's Tale*, a suggestion of incest echoes in the play. Posthumus, the play's hero, has been taken into the royal family as an infant and brought up within it. His falling in love with Imogen is like deepening an existing brother-sister relationship. His rival, likewise, is part of the family: Cloten is her stepmother's son. Cloten refers to Imogen as his "sister" (2.3.86) as well as his wished-for wife. The emotional interactions of family life, negative and positive, provide a complex underpinning of the play's action.

The characters frequently yearn for different and less oppressive family situations. Freud termed the common human fantasy of wishing we were brought up in more advantageous family situations the "family romance" (*Standard Edition*, ed. and trans. James Strachey, 9 (1952), 237–241). The term refers to the common belief among children (though it has equivalents among adults as we grow older and look back on childhood) that one's "real" parents are more aristocratic, richer, wiser, more admirable in some way and that we ourselves were more advantaged. The playing out of the family romance in *Cymbeline* takes two main forms: the desire of Cymbeline's lost family members to discover their true natures, and Posthumus's orphan status, the complexity of his relationships with his lost "real" family and his consequent deep need for (and violent rejection of) Imogen. The psychology of male-female relationships, with Imogen's straightforwardness and Posthumus's tortuous internal conflicts, add a depth of insight to *Cymbeline* that belies any suggestion of the play's being merely escapist entertainment and that anticipates the even richer psychological vision of *The Winter's Tale*—with its focus on male paranoia and jealousy and the importance of the family in developing relationships based on mutuality rather than power or exploitation.

Even the political dimensions of *Cymbeline* connect with the familial theme. The play has some affinities with Shakespeare's Roman plays in that it is set in ancient Roman times and hints at some of the same political themes. Early twentieth-century critics like G. Wilson Knight saw the play as advancing the cause of British imperial power; more recently, the political dimension of the play has been singled out for its supposed tension between local autonomy of rule and international cooperation. "Britain's a world / By itself" (3.1.12–13) asserts Cloten belligerently, as Cymbeline debates whether to pay the Romans their traditional tribute. But by the end of the play a more harmonious acceptance of Britain's connection with the Roman Empire is affirmed. This is widely read by recent critics as Shakespeare's support for Britain's European connection—and is even linked by reputable scholars with Britain's twentieth-century preoccupation with joining the European Union! As Leah Marcus puts it, "The British and Roman ensigns wave 'Friendly Together', the fragmented kingdom of Britain is reunited, and the nation embarks on a new era and fertile era of peace" ("*Cymbeline* and the Unease of Topicality," in *Shakespeare: The Last Plays*, ed. Kiernan Ryan [London: Longmans, 1999], 142). Other recent critics see references to Jacobean politics: Posthumus as representing the Scottish outsiders wanting acceptance by James I's new English courtiers, or the

Roman scenes embodying what most early seventeenth-century audiences would widely accept as the corrupt and evil civilization of Catholic Italy, so that Posthumus was, at least in part, not to blame for his naïveté. The specifically Welsh setting has also been commented upon. While the play's actions pre-date the modern joining (or annexation) of England and Wales, it reflects something of early seventeenth-century Anglo-Welsh relations. Garrett A. Sullivan notes that there are in fact no Welsh in the play: "the political nation of pre-Roman Britain is figured only as English." Wales is a wilderness, "occupied by invaders or court figures in temporary exile and/or disguise." In particular Cymbeline's lost sons, dressed as rude mountain men who help beat the Romans "are as close as we come, but they, of course, are finally and fully reintegrated into the world of the court from which they came" ("Civilizing Wales: *Cymbeline*, Roads, and the Landscapes of Early Modern Britain," *Early Modern Literary Studies* 4.2/Special issue 3 [September 1998]: 14, 22).

While the dramatic tension Shakespeare builds up in the play's unfolding actions is rooted in an extremely complex familial network within the play's political concerns, much of the emotional power of the play rests on the recognition that an audience brings to these situations from their own real or potential family situations. By the play's end, all political and family complications have been overcome, and the audience is asked to rejoice and share the underlying wish fulfilment of togetherness and new starts. *Cymbeline* has his daughter and two sons returned to him. Imogen is reconciled with her father and is reunited with Posthumus, who has in turn been rid of his rival Cloten and his malicious stepmother. Cymbeline's two sons have found their rightful father and sister. Cymbeline now presides over a united family and a united kingdom, itself part of the wider European family of the Roman Empire. Whether in terms of family or nationalistic dynamics, the play's ending is a fantasy of universal reconciliation, forgiveness, and hope. In part this conclusion reflects Shakespeare's sources, but more importantly, it exemplifies his continuing experimentation with the tragicomedy form and the demands of dramatic romance to incorporate widely varied settings and emotions.

Perhaps the most important theme of all, one that unites both political and familial concerns, lies in the treatment of masculinity and, in particular, men's idealization of women. We are introduced to a key theme of the play when, in a revealing phrase, Posthumus describes himself as Imogen's "adorer, not her friend" (1.4.68–69). Men, to use a phrase of Freud's, frequently "overvalue" women: they idealize them and may just as extremely revile and denigrate them. As Klaus Theweleit observes, "It's as if two male compulsions were tearing at . . . women with equal strength. One is trying to push them away, to keep them at arm's length (defense); the other wants to penetrate them, to have them very near" (*Male Fantasies*, trans. Stephen Conway et al. vol. 1 [Minneapolis: U of Minnesota P, 1987–1988], 196). The idealization/denigration dichotomy, so starkly exemplified by Posthumus, is deeply rooted in European history and gender ideology. As Theweleit puts it, desire in the dominant discourses of Western civilization "flows in a certain sense through women. In some way or other, it always flows in relation to the image of women" (272). In such a context, women cannot live up to those cosmic expectations and suffer "oppression through exaltation" (284). "Every woman," he goes on, is "up against a set of expectations that were not from her, but that she was, nonetheless, supposed to fulfill" (381).

## CRITICAL CONTROVERSIES

The most controversial aspect of the play has been briefly touched upon under the discussion of characters and themes: Imogen's plight, her patience under extreme adversity, and her final forgiveness of Posthumus. The outline of the Imogen/Posthumus story is conventionally described by R. G. Hunter as a romantic comedy in which love is tested, and Posthumus proves worthy of forgiveness through sincere contrition, as well as by charitably refraining from killing Iachimo in battle. Hunter sees the play's themes as unambiguously Christian, with the Imogen/Posthumus story at the center (chapter 7). However, analyzing the play today, after fifty years of feminist criticism, instead of seeing forgiveness as an unambiguous affirmation of the play, critics now ask the more probing question that Cynthia Lewis reports from her students in the 1990s in their reactions to Imogen's faithfulness and forgiveness of her husband: "Why does she cling to a man who treats her so badly? [Why] does Shakespeare . . . sneak away from confronting her difficult marital situation by tacking onto 5.5 a vacuous, fairy-tale ending to her troubles?" (78). Such questions seem at once obvious and controversial. Yet how is it that previous generations of critics apparently overlooked this aspect of the play? Is it our projecting, from a feminist or post-feminist perspective, our own contemporary agendas? What is the play saying?

Long before modern developmental psychology, it is suggested, Shakespeare is providing insight not only into the anxieties of being gendered as male in a patriarchal society dominated by aggression and relationships based on power but also into some of the complexities of families and the roles of women in a patriarchal society. The Roman and English history plays, which focus strongly on the "public" world of dynastic struggle, war, politics, and heroic rivalries, all contain minor but important counterbalancing perspectives on male aggression, ego, violence, and war. Such critiques are often represented by minor female characters. In *Henry V* and *Julius Caesar*, the women largely stand for a set of values that critique the male violence of the main action. In *Cymbeline* that critique is especially strong: it focuses on both Cymbeline himself, as king and father, and on the romantic hero, Posthumus, who enacts a common pattern for the male characters of Shakespeare's tragedies, and the critique is focused on the major character of the play—a woman. All the men in the play, in fact, share at least one characteristic: a set of assumptions about the place and importance of women in their lives. *Cymbeline*, in short, dramatizes an especially powerful critique of the male-dominated world of war, ambition, bravado, rivalry, physical prowess, hunting, and nationalistic rivalries.

Given the history of *Cymbeline* criticism and production, such a reading remains controversial. Calling into question the nature of male heroism challenges a long, seemingly "natural" set of Western values. To call them "masculinist" as feminist criticism does, is to raise issues that go well beyond standard Shakespeare criticism and much of dominant Western culture. But that is what the play encourages us to do.

In a tragedy like *Romeo and Juliet* or *Othello*, the main male character starts the action apparently secure, undergoes misfortune or commits an error, and thereby sets in motion a chain of events ending in destruction or death. A similar pattern seems to be taking shape in the first half of *Cymbeline*. Posthumus starts the play praised by all the court (except for Cloten). Feminist criticism argues that Posthumus is no different from the other male characters. Posthumus's panicked anguish after Iachimo's apparent victory is in part understandable, a capitulation to the same masculinist world of ego, competition, and violence that implicates Iachimo, Cloten, and Cymbeline. In his reaction, he, too, shows that he sees women as suspect and even dangerous objects for which men must compete and over which they need control. In this way he is part of the masculine world. Why then, at the play's end, is he forgiven, to return to the students' question noted above? Either (as Bloom would have it) Shakespeare does not care, or the play is simply chaotic; or else something more profound is going on. Coppélia Kahn, for example, argues very suggestively that a prominent fantasy of men in our culture has been the male need to have women always, finally, to be available to accept, forgive, protect, and anchor them. To be forgiven for as destructive a reaction as Posthumus has to his wife is offered as an extreme male fantasy. Is it a revelation of a male desire to project the all-forgiving and once always available mother upon their wives and lovers? Are men in our culture to be condemned, pitied, or accepted for acting out such patterns? Are these patterns built into the basic fantasy structure of being male?

For the play's men, the problem is not them, but the women. "Who is't can read a woman?" asks Cymbeline (5.5.48–49). Clearly, the men of the play cannot "read" either women or themselves easily, or at least without women's help. It is a revealing remark given the play's ending when Cymbeline discovers his queen's treachery and Imogen is willing to forgive Posthumus. But it is a question that the play turns back to the male characters. Clearly, without women's help they cannot "read" much that matters. Men turn to women to compensate for what masculinity cannot, seemingly, provide. Further, is the man in this situation just Posthumus? Is it Shakespeare? Is it all Western males? The play apparently shows either that women have historically been given that compensatory role or, even more gloomily, that this is what the basic "wiring" of men is like. But the play seems more optimistic; it suggests that men need to move beyond that impasse. That is the play's hard lesson, one perhaps that men must learn over and over again. Put more positively, the play's ending shows the emergence of a vision of interactive relationships, whether in the family (Cymbeline, his sons, his daughter, and her husband) or in the most intimate of relationships, between husband and wife. For some readers and critics it is an unbelievable and unsatisfactory conclusion, with Imogen's forgiveness of her erring husband a capitulation to the worst of patriarchy, and as archaic as the subordination of Kate to Petruchio at the ending of *The Taming of the Shrew*.

What the play seems to be doing is opening questions for members of the audience to pose themselves. Approaching the play in that vein may help us understand the way it can produce in readers and spectators an uncanny mixture of what Shakespeare in *The Winter's Tale* calls "joy and terror" (4.1.1). The final scene in particular provides what psychologists refer to as a safe haven, almost literally a safe "play" space, for considering ourselves as gendered beings and as members of that once seemingly stable institution, the family. Especially from Freud onward there has been a marked preoccupation with the psychological dynamics of the family, with, for example, the separation and individuation of the child from the mother, a child's discovery of boundary conditions, and the development of object relations, delusions of omnipotence, and fears of abandonment.

## PRODUCTION HISTORY

*Cymbeline* long had a reputation for being rarely performed, but since the late twentieth century it, along with the other late romances, has been staged many times, and with startling success: notably by Sir Peter Hall at the National Theatre (1988), in an enriching and dynamic production directed by Bartlett Sher at The Theatre for a New Audience in New York (2002), and directed by David Latham at the Stratford (Ontario) Festival in 2004.

The earliest recorded performance was in 1611 at the Globe, as noted by Simon Forman; it was followed by a production at the indoor Blackfriars Theatre. Another early recorded staging was in 1634 at Whitehall Palace before King Charles I. The play requires some complex indoor scenes—Imogen's bedchamber, the cave near Milford Haven, the descent and ascent of Jupiter—and so lends itself to (or requires) some degree of elaborate stage effects, and that in itself may have inhibited additional performances in popular, outdoor venues.

The next recorded performance was not until 1682, when an adaptation, re-titled *The Injured Princess*, was performed at the Theatre Royal. Scenes and characters were cut out and modified into what Hosley terms "an unhappy piece of work— melodramatic ranting, sentimental, moralistic, overblown in style, cliché-ridden" (246). No record of the complete play being performed again occurs until 1744. Further adaptations occurred during the eighteenth century, including a popular version by David Garrick in the 1740s. In 1785, a more or less full version of the play, lavishly executed, was produced by John Philip Kemble. However, it excluded the vision of Jupiter scenes in act 4, which continued to be omitted in the occasional production that did occur during the nineteenth century. The most celebrated shortened version was by G. B. Shaw, who rewrote the fifth act as a "variation on Shakespeare's ending." It was produced in 1937 and published in 1946 as *Cymbeline Refinished*, written, according to Shaw, as if Shakespeare "had been post-Ibsen and post-Shaw instead of post-Marlowe" (George Bernard Shaw, *Geneva, Cymbeline Refinished, & Good King Charles* [New York: Dodd, Mead, 1947], 136). It is dull theatrically alongside the pyrotechnics of Shakespeare's ending.

With the advent of the Royal Shakespeare Company's (RSC) permanent home in Stratford-upon-Avon, a number of significant productions occurred from the late fifties on. Peter Hall's 1957 production featured Peggy Ashcroft as Imogen; as Hosley noted, it restored Posthumus's dream vision and the appearance of Jupiter, which occurred in an elaborate, masque-like atmosphere. John Barton's RSC production of 1974 featured Ian Richardson as Iachimo; Barton expanded the role of Cornelius, the doctor, to be something like that of the chorus-like Gower in *Pericles*, commenting and directing, using some of the stage directions. This technique was also used by Sher in his 2002 New York Theatre for a New Audience production when the lines of a number of minor figures were combined and given to two characters who provided links and continuity throughout the play. The Sher production featured Japanese Samurai costumes for the court party and Wild West dress for the "outlaws" in the wilds of Wales. These incongruities, like those of the text itself, surprisingly blended effectively, and with the minor characters providing a chorus the New Audience production was a theatrical tour de force and received outstanding reviews, even from critics who regarded the play as held together, as

(Left to right) Adam Greer as Guiderius, Andrew Garman as Arviragus, Stephanie Roth Haberle as Imogen, and Randall Duk Kim as Belarius in the Joseph Papp Public Theater/New York Shakespeare Festival production of *Cymbeline*, directed by Andrei Serban, 1998. Courtesy of Photofest.

one put it, by string and chewing gum. Another innovative production showing how the play has encouraged a variety of settings and approaches was Robin Phillips's provocative Stratford, Ontario, production of 1986, which had a World War I setting and featured a chorus singing "Lili Marlene" softly behind the final moments of the play by a seemingly never-ending procession of soldiers—to remind the audience of the violence and destruction that haunts the play and against which the emphasis of "pardon" in the final scene needs to be set. *Cymbeline* is now widely produced in Britain, the United States, and elsewhere, providing directors and audiences with an opportunity to see an extraordinary experimental work with some scenes and issues as momentous as any in the Shakespearean canon.

## EXPLICATION OF KEY PASSAGES

**2.2.11–51. "The crickets sing, . . . time, time!"** Though the scene where Iachimo emerges from his trunk (2.2) is improbable and foreshortened—three hours are covered in fifty lines—it is psychologically probing, theatrically powerful, and worth studying in detail. It opens with a clear echo of the culminating murder of Desdemona in *Othello*, with Imogen settling into bed, missing Posthumus, and accompanied by a woman servant. She reads and falls asleep. Then Iachimo, the play's Iago-figure, emerges from the trunk. As he looks at Imogen, he speaks in the play's characteristic mixture of idealization and dismissiveness, both in awe of Imogen's presence and businesslike in his task and his control of the situation. It is a scene that appeals to the guilty voyeur in men, evoking the male curiosity about invading female privacy; it stresses the vulnerability of a woman in such a society. Iachimo removes the bracelet that Posthumus gave his wife; again, however improbable this might be as a realistic action, the power of the poetry and the scene's concentrated focus creates a striking experience of violation, an impression reinforced by Iachimo's own observation of how his actions are like the subject of the book Imogen has been reading—the story of the rape of Philomella by Tereus from Shakespeare's favorite author, Ovid. It is not meant to be realistic or even wholly about Iachimo or the values he stands for; it is about us—the audience's fear of and attraction to secrecy, the fascination of being a voyeuristic invader, and about penetrating into some secret within not only Imogen but also the concept of masculinity and the male positioning of woman as desired object and object of conquest as proof of his masculinity. Her individuality, which by that point of the play has been stressed, is never considered by Iachimo; she is merely a challenge to his male competitiveness.

**2.5.1–35. "Is there no way . . . plague them better."** As 2.4 ends, Iachimo has convinced Posthumus that Imogen has been unfaithful. The brief 2.5 consists of Posthumus's soliloquy-diatribe against women. He begins by saying that everyone is illegitimate, including himself; he no longer believes that his own mother, regarded as "The Dian of that time" (2.5.7), was chaste. Then he reflects on Imogen's refusal to have sex with him before marriage, but Iachimo secured her consent "in an hour" (2.5.14).

From these reflections he concludes that all weaknesses of males derive from their feminine side: lying, flattering, "[l]ust and rank thoughts" (2.5.24), ambition, and others that he lists. He resolves to "write against" women (2.5.32) and to "curse them" (2.5.33), but then he concludes that he will pray "they have their will" (2.5.34)—a sly echo of Sonnet 135—because "The very devils cannot plague them better" (2.5.35).

Posthumus expresses the long-standing misogynist view of women here, one he shares with Othello, Leontes, and other misguided Shakespearean characters; he, too, will discover his mistake. However, even as he rails against women, he recognizes that he has a "woman's part" (2.5.20, 22). At this point in the play he would excise that portion of himself. But for Shakespeare the ideal is a fusion of maleness and femininity. The Fair Youth of the sonnets is the perfect "master mistress" (Sonnet 20.2). By the end of *Cymbeline* Posthumus will learn to combine bravery in battle with compassion, forgiveness, and love. It is noteworthy that at the end of the play, it is what Posthumus has identified as the "woman's part" that is triumphant, as *Cymbeline* proclaims, "Pardon's the word to all" (5.5.422).

**4.2.258–281. "Fear no more . . . by thy grave."** As 4.2 begins, Belarius tells Imogen, disguised as Fidele, to remain in the cave while he and his sons go hunting, since she is not feeling well. She takes some of the medicine that Cornelius has prepared, and when the men return they find her apparently dead. For the funeral rites the two brothers sing this lovely lyric, saying that Fidele now need fear nothing, not nature ("heat o' the sun," "winter's rages," 4.2.258, 259), not what humans can do ("the frown o' th' great," "the tyrant's stroke," 4.2.264–265), not malignant spirits ("exorciser," "witchcraft," "ghost," 4.2.276, 277, 278). Fidele has escaped, in short, all possible ills.

Even in this beautiful lyric Shakespeare cannot resist a pun: "Golden lads and girls all must, / As chimney-sweepers, come to dust" (4.2.262–263). On one level everyone, whether golden or covered with ashes, will return to dust. Shakespeare echoes the biblical passage of "dust to dust, ashes to ashes." But of course even when alive chimney-sweepers "come to dust"; that's their job. Samuel Johnson called the pun Shakespeare's Cleopatra, for which, like Marc Antony, he would willingly lose the world. But this bit of humor in the midst of solemnity is a fit emblem for *Cymbeline*, in which, finally, the only characters who really die (Cloten and the queen) are the ones we want dead, and the others end happily.

## Annotated Bibliography

Barber, C. L., and Richard Wheeler. *The Whole Journey: Shakespeare's Power of Development.* Berkeley: U of California P, 1986. Argues that the play addresses psychological needs arising from family interrelationships.

Felperin, Howard. *Shakespearean Romance.* Princeton: Princeton UP, 1972. A detailed study of all the late plays, stressing the mixture of realism and romance characteristics.

Hunt, Maurice. *Approaches to Teaching Shakespeare's "The Tempest" and Other Late Romances.* New York: MLA, 1992. Indispensable collection for teachers of all the late plays, with good interpretations as well as advice for instruction.

Hunter, R. G. *Shakespeare and the Comedy of Forgiveness.* New York: Columbia UP, 1965. Overview, stressing the presence of Christian themes.

Kahn, Coppélia. *Roman Shakespeare: Wounds, Warriors, and Women.* London: Routledge, 1997. Excellent on the ambiguous nature of masculinity and on connections with the Roman plays.

Knight, G. Wilson. *The Crown of Life.* London: Methuen, 1958. Classic critical study, stressing both the imperial politics and the poetic texture.

Lewis, Cynthia. "'With Simular Proof Enough': Modes of Misperception in *Cymbeline*." *Studies in English Literature* 31 (1991): 343–364. Insightful reading on the Imogen-Posthumus relationship.

Warren, Roger, ed. *Cymbeline.* Oxford: World's Classics, 1998. Focuses on theatricality, especially the interpretations of major modern directors. Extensive discussion of the "Imogen" versus "Innogen" controversy.

White, R. S. *Shakespeare and the Romance Ending.* Newcastle upon Tyne: School of English, the University, Newcastle upon Tyne, 1981. Close reading; psychological-historical approach; especially good on the ending.

# The Winter's Tale

## Gary Waller

### PLOT SUMMARY

**1.1.** Two lords—Archidamus, from Bohemia, and Camillo, from Sicilia—are discussing the friendship, started in boyhood and reinforced by a long visit to Sicilia, between their respective kings: Leontes of Sicilia and Polixenes of Bohemia.

**1.2.** Leontes urges his pregnant wife, Hermione, to try to persuade Polixenes to stay longer. She finally succeeds in getting him to remain a short while longer. But her attention to Polixenes makes Leontes jealous. He bitterly reveals that he is suspicious that Polixenes has in fact fathered the child with whom Hermione is pregnant. He tells his steward, Camillo, who is amazed at such suspicions. Undeterred, Leontes orders Camillo to poison Polixenes, but Camillo decides to inform Polixenes; and together they quickly leave Sicilia.

**2.1.** Hermione, late in her pregnancy, is playing with her son Mamillius and a number of her attendants. Leontes discovers that Polixenes has fled and so believes that is sure proof of guilt. He storms in and publicly accuses Hermione of being unfaithful. He orders her to be taken to prison. One of his lords, Antigonus, presents an indignant defense of Hermione. Leontes informs his court that he has sent to the oracle at Delphi to ask Apollo to reinforce his decision and reaffirm the guilt of Hermione.

**2.2.** Paulina, Antigonus's wife, coming to attend Hermione after her birthing, is refused access and then proposes bringing the new baby girl to Leontes, believing that seeing his daughter will overcome his jealousy and reconcile him to Hermione.

**2.3.** Leontes, still obsessed with his jealousy, asks after Mamillius, who is ill. Paulina does succeed in bringing the baby to Leontes. But not even her action helps him see his folly. He orders the child killed and then instructs Antigonus to take the child to some desert place and abandon it to die.

**3.1.** Cleomenes and Dion, the lords sent by Leontes to consult with the oracle at Delphi, return, hopeful that the oracle's message will convince Leontes of Hermione's innocence.

**3.2.** Hermione is put on trial. After the charges are read, she makes a powerful and dignified speech asserting her innocence. The oracle's statement is opened, and it affirms that Hermione is innocent, adding that Leontes' acts are tyrannical and that he will be condemned to live without an heir if what has been "lost be not found" (3.2.135–136). Leontes asserts that the oracle is false and orders the trial to proceed. Immediately, as if to punish him, comes the news that Mamillius has died. Leontes interprets his son's death as Apollo's punishment for his rejecting the oracle. Hermione faints and is carried out; Paulina enters to tell the king that the queen has died also. Leontes realizes his folly, too late, and recognizes that his future can only be grief and penitence for the destruction of his family, which he has brought upon himself.

**3.3.** Meanwhile, unaware of the king's belated repentance, Antigonus, who is carrying out his orders in regard to the newly born princess, lands on the coast of Bohemia. He names the condemned baby Perdita, signifying that she was lost, and puts her on the ground. Suddenly, a bear appears and chases him away. A Shepherd enters and finds Perdita. His son comes in and relates what he has seen—the storm, which has wrecked the Sicilian ship and its crew, and then the death of Antigonus, who was torn to pieces and eaten by the bear. The old man takes Perdita and finds gold and other things with her. It is as if the day has gone from disaster to happiness in an instant.

**4.1.** The figure of Time enters as a chorus and tells us that sixteen years have now passed. Polixenes' son Florizel, whom we have not yet met, has grown up, and Perdita, reared as a shepherd's daughter in Bohemia, is now sixteen.

**4.2.** The scene shifts to the royal palace of Bohemia. Camillo tells Polixenes that he wishes to visit his old home in Sicilia, and that the penitent Leontes wishes him to come back. Polixenes, however, is reluctant to let him go. He is also worried about Florizel, who has been reported to be secretly visiting a shepherd's daughter. Polixenes and Camillo decide to disguise themselves and spy on Florizel.

**4.3.** Near the Shepherd's home, we meet Autolycus, a traveling pedlar and con man, who convinces the Clown, the Shepherd's son, that he, Autolycus, has been robbed. Autolycus picks the Clown's pockets when the Clown tries to help the pedlar.

**4.4.** Florizel and Perdita enter, clearly in love. They are preparing for the sheepshearing feast, but Perdita is afraid that if the king finds out about their love, he will punish her. Polixenes and Camillo arrive, in disguise, and observe how remarkable she appears, seemingly "too noble" for her surroundings (4.4.159). Without knowing who they are, Perdita welcomes them graciously to the feast. Florizel informs them of his love for Perdita, but Polixenes and the Shepherd tell him he should have his father's permission before he can marry her. Florizel refuses. Polixenes then reveals his identity, announces that he will disinherit his son and that the Shepherd, for aiding Florizel and Perdita's rebellion, will be condemned to death. Florizel reasserts that he will be loyal to Perdita, choosing her over his father's favor and his inheritance as a prince. Camillo remains behind and suggests that they escape to Sicilia, and that Florizel present himself as on a visit with his princess, assuring them that Leontes will give them welcome. Autolycus is persuaded to change clothes with Florizel to aid in the disguise, and Perdita also disguises herself. Camillo decides, as a part of his plan, that he himself can return to Sicilia by telling Polixenes of the lovers' escape and going with Polixenes in pursuit of them. The Clown is persuaded to become part of the plan: if the old shepherd can prove that Perdita is not his daughter, he thinks, then he will also not be guilty. He tells his father to bring Polixenes the various things that Antigonus had left with Perdita when she was a baby. Autolycus goes as well, boasting that with his influence he can gain access to Leontes and save them from Polixenes' wrath.

**5.1.** Leontes has spent sixteen years in penitence for his wife's, his son's, and his daughter's deaths. Paulina, who has guided him in his repentance, makes him swear that he will not remarry, or will do so only with her approval. Florizel and Perdita arrive, saying they bring greetings from Polixenes. But almost immediately Polixenes' arrival is announced, and Florizel decides to confess the truth about his flight and the status of his supposed princess. Leontes, however, is not angry but forgiving, and, touched by their predicament, promises to take their part with his old friend, Polixenes.

**5.2.** The audience does not see the meetings and reconciliations that now occur: three court gentleman share their amazement at the emotional scenes that occur when Leontes learns Perdita's true identity. The Clown and Shepherd, who revel in their new status, promise Autolycus their support in making his way in the court.

**5.3.** As the culmination of the reconciliation of the two old friends and a father's reunion with his lost daughter, Paulina takes the two kings, their children, and their attendants to see a newly commissioned commemorative statue of the dead Hermione. Leontes is overwhelmed by its lifelike quality. Paulina says in fact the illusion of the artist is even more striking, for she can make the statue move. They prepare to watch this further achievement, and when it does indeed descend from its pedestal and embrace Leontes, all realize that it is not just a statue, but Hermione herself, who for sixteen years has been protected by Paulina until the prophecy of the oracle could be fulfilled. Hermione meets her lost daughter; Leontes urges Paulina and Camillo to marry and publicly asks forgiveness of his wife, Hermione, and his old friend, Polixenes.

## PUBLICATION HISTORY

*The Winter's Tale* first appeared in print in the First Folio (1623). It was placed at the end of the comedies. It appears that it may have been a late addition to the volume, probably set by the printer from a transcript of Shakespeare's foul papers. Most likely its divisions into acts and scenes were added by the Folio editors, not entirely happily, as the transition between the "tragic" and "comedic" phases of the play is not easily distinguished. Although there was no publication of *The Winter's Tale* before the Folio, we do have records of performances that help us date it to around the time Shakespeare was writing *Cymbeline* and *The Tempest*, plays that have close connections with it. The diarist (and self-styled magician) Simon Forman records seeing a performance at the Globe on May 15, 1611. A court performance on November 5, 1611, is also recorded, as is the play's presence in the repertory of works acted by the King's Men in honor of the marriage of James I's daughter Elizabeth in late 1612 or early in 1613. The play is therefore conventionally dated 1610–1611.

## SOURCES FOR THE PLAY

We can trace most of Shakespeare's play back to Robert Greene's romance, *Pandosto*, originally published in 1588, and reprinted three times before *The Winter's Tale* appeared. *Pandosto* is typical of the romantic prose tales popular with Elizabethans, telling of incredible adventures of noble characters in exotic places and full of recurring formulaic situations—lost lovers, abandoned children, hairbreadth escapes from pirates, invaders, or wild animals—and surprising, even incredible, endings occurring after remarkable coincidences and unexpected events, such as the return of apparently lost children, parents, or lovers. Shakespeare had drawn on such material throughout his theatrical career, but most intensely (and experimentally) in the other so-called "late" romances *Pericles* and *Cymbeline*, which immediately predate *The Winter's Tale*. He was also to draw on this material in *The Tempest*, which was likely written only a year or so later.

*Pandosto* gave Shakespeare many details for the play: the main plot, the setting, and most of the major characters. He changed Greene's characters' names, making them sound more Greek and therefore actually closer to the world of ancient romantic stories that Greene was imitating. However, Shakespeare made some far more significant changes that give us major clues as to his intentions and achievements. The most important change is having Hermione be "resurrected" (or returned, depending on the reader or director's interpretation). Greene's equivalent to Hermione, Bellaria, dies; King Pandosto is reunited with his lost daughter but, at first not recognizing her, falls in love with her before killing himself in horror at discovering his incestuous desires. By altering the melodramatic ending of Greene's story, Shakespeare thus brings the final tone of *The Winter's Tale* closer to that of *Pericles, Cymbeline*, and his earlier comedies, for example, *Much Ado about Nothing*. In *The Comedy of Errors* and *Pericles* we have long-lost family members reunited. A woman, seemingly dying, and returning to life, is a recurring plot trick in Shakespeare's comedies and romances, so it clearly had special significance for him.

The other major change from *Pandosto* is that Shakespeare compresses the abandonment and discovery of the newborn Perdita into two remarkable scenes, in which Antigonus's ship is wrecked, the baby abandoned, Antigonus eaten by a bear, and the baby found by the Shepherd. This brings about a sudden change of tone in the play, from tragedy to comedy, thus posing one of the major challenges to critics as well as directors—how to comprehend and stage such a dramatic shift in emphasis and apparent intention. Other minor changes include the transposition of the two settings, Sicilia and Bohemia, the creation of the key characters Paulina, who oversees Leontes' repentance, and the rogue Autolycus, who is especially useful in the creation of an atmosphere of jollity, anarchy, and self-indulgence in act 4. He also deepened the characters of Leontes and Hermione, on whose relationship most of play's first half is focused.

## STRUCTURE AND PLOTTING

The ingredients in the play's structure and plot came, as noted above, largely from Shakespeare's source: Greene's *Pandosto*. But many of the elements of *The Winter's Tale* are also found in Shakespeare's own plays. In the early comedies, he often used pastoral settings, young lovers struggling to establish their love against the wishes of their parents, and other "romance" motifs, such as lost children and reunited families, along with a touch of magic or the supernatural. In his tragedies, by contrast, he presented irrational and destructive male jealousy, the abuse of tyrannical power, and the suffering of women and children caught up in male conflict and violence. In the "tragi-comic" middle comedies like *Measure for Measure*, he combined a degree of both. *The Winter's Tale* is often, in fact, described as a "tragicomedy," a term used in the Renaissance to describe a widely recognized genre that mixed ingredients of comedy and tragedy. The movement of tragicomedy begins as if, like tragedy, it will produce catastrophe; but some chance or divine force intervenes, and a happy ending occurs. Aristotle, in his *Poetics*, had identified such plays as being associated especially with family relationships, a description that fits *The Winter's Tale*. Sir Philip Sidney spoke dismissively of "mongrel" tragicomedy, but it became a highly popular genre in the Renaissance—not always successfully, since it was a combination that could easily topple into melodrama that failed to provide emotional depth. In all his "late" plays—*Pericles*, *Cymbeline*, *The Winter's Tale*, and *The Tempest*—Shakespeare was evidently fascinated with the possibilities of the "mongrel" form, and in *The Winter's Tale* he arguably took on (and triumphed over) its most demanding challenges.

*The Winter's Tale* is, in fact, more than most of Shakespeare's plays, a highly experimental work. It is as if Shakespeare were deliberately setting himself a number of difficult compositional tasks: Can I get away with this or that? The challenges or even dares he takes on include how to combine deeply intense and destructive tragedy with light relaxed comedy, while—even more difficult—juxtaposing the climax of the tragic phase of the play with the beginning of the comic phase; "resurrecting" a major character; and ending the play with coincidences, reunions, and reconciliations to an extent only surpassed by the tour de force conclusion of *Cymbeline* with its multiple discoveries and reunions. For good measure, Shakespeare throws in a study of seemingly instantaneous, apparently unmotivated, jealousy; permits the survival of a baby seemingly abandoned as dead; gives land-bound Bohemia a sea coast; and in the central and most emotionally draining section of the play, brings in a bear, has the bear eat one of the characters (offstage), and then—a further surprise!—follows that scene with two comic rustics who discover an abandoned baby. Then a character introducing himself as "Time" enters and claims responsibility for the whole play! It is no wonder that critics ridiculed what seemed to be multiple absurdities. It is all the more curious that there has been a reversal in the play's critical reputation since 1900, such that many readers and spectators claim that *The Winter's Tale* is, as Wilbur Sanders puts it, "wonderful, moving, grand . . . a sublime diptych, a two-movement symphony whose music is only made richer by its overt structural diversity" (1). Few critics would now agree with Dryden's judgment in his essay at the end of the second part of *The Conquest of Grenada* (1672) that the play is a failure because it is "grounded on impossibilities." Other incidental criticism of coincidence and loose ends can be explained by the characteristics, acceptable in a theatrical performance in particular, of the romance genre in which Shakespeare is working.

The opening phase—acts 1, 2, and the first two or two and a half scenes of act 3—is a tight, closely worked out tragic action: a powerful king unjustly accuses his wife and oldest friend of adultery, arrests his innocent wife, and, tyrannically defying everyone else's opinion, including the explicit judgment of the gods, condemns her. He also condemns their newborn daughter to be left to die. By the end of the tragic phase of the play, the queen and their son are dead, the baby abandoned, and the king, realizing his errors too late and now devastated by the destruction his jealousy and tyranny have caused, is deeply repentant, vowing,

> Once a day I'll visit
> The chapel where they lie, and tears shed there
> Shall be my recreation. So long as nature
> Will bear up with this exercise, so long
> I daily vow to use it. Come, and lead me
> To these sorrows. (3.2.238–243)

As if to underline the relentlessly tragic mood, in 3.3 we see Antigonus laying down the final member of Leontes' family, his daughter, in the wilderness of Bohemia. He names her Perdita, meaning the lost one, because of instructions he tells us he received in a dream of the ghost of the dead Hermione, in the middle of the storm that will eventually destroy his ship. With the rising wind and the sound of a hunt getting louder, he tries to get back to his ship and is suddenly chased and eaten by a bear. With one of the most famous (or infamous) stage directions in his plays, Shakespeare suddenly wrenches us into a new world: "This is the chase; / I am gone forever!" (*Exit pursued by a bear*) (3.3.57–58). Depending on how a director has it played, the effect can range from farce to deeply threatening doom and everything in between. It is a deliberate and radical moment of discontinuity. Some productions take an intermission there, in the midst of act 3, scene 3. How should such a scene be played? With a real bear? A person in a bear suit? A dark shadow of a bear projected onto the wall? Directors have tried many alternatives.

And then, as if to underline the striking juxtaposition of tragedy, comedy, and something else yet to be defined, two characters we have never seen before amble onto the stage: an old shepherd and his son (the so-called "Clown"). They tell us about the wreck of the ship, the killing (and eating) of Antigonus by the bear, and then in yet another pivotal moment, the Shepherd shows his discovery of the child: "Heavy matters, heavy matters! But look thee here, boy. Now bless thyself: thou met'st with things dying, I with things new-born" (3.3.112–114). It is an extraordinary juxtaposition. As if to offer yet another challenge to directors, audiences, and critics, Shakespeare then brings onto the stage, much as he did in *Pericles* with Gower, a chorus figure, Time.

The second half of the play takes place sixteen years later. The baby who was lost has grown into a young girl, and the natural world, represented by the seemingly innocent seasonal cycle of sheep farming, festivals, personal maturation, and family unity create an atmosphere of harmony and relaxation. As R. S. White puts it, the play has given us first "a glimpse of childhood paradise" and then "a world of paradise lost, where even innocence itself is dubious," and it lets us enter a different version of paradise, the pastoral world (103), only to disrupt it again, this time by Polixenes' anger at his son's falling in love with a girl who is (apparently) a mere shepherd's daughter. The intervention of Polixenes and Camillo brings us sharply back to the play's beginning when Polixenes threatens Perdita:

> I'll have thy beauty scratch'd with briars and made
> More homely than thy state. . . .
>     if ever, henceforth, thou
> These rural latches to his entrance open,
> Or hoop his body more with thy embraces,
> I will devise a death as cruel for thee
> As thou art tender to't. (4.4.424–426, 437–441)

In its violence and crude misogyny, this speech returns us to the tyrannical insecurities of Leontes and links the two kings together in their inability to face aging, sexuality, and women, what Shakespeare in *Cymbeline* terms "the woman's part" in man and humankind generally (*Cymbeline*, 2.5.20, 22).

The final movement in this structural collage is the return, in the final act, to Sicilia, where we meet Leontes, sixteen years after he has lost his queen, son, daughter, and best friend. What Time brings forth is the reconciliation of father and daughter, father and son, and old friends. Finally in one of the greatest tours de force in Shakespeare's plays, we see the return of Hermione, initially as a statue and then in real life.

The structure of the play, then, is a remarkable combination of opposites. E.M.W. Tillyard in *Shakespeare's Last Plays* (London: Chatto and Windus, 1938) suggested that *The Winter's Tale* compressed the structure of Dante's *Commedia* into a single work. The hell that Leontes creates in the first three acts is succeeded by a Purgatory in which sixteen years are needed for repentance, penance, and learning. Then, finally, according to this reading of the play, Shakespeare's equivalent of Dante's *Paradiso* is celebrated by the miraculous reconciliations of the play's conclusion. That is something of a simplification and reflects Leontes' rather than the whole play's perspective. Such a scenario ignores the whole of act 4, the pastoral scenes, though they, too, might be fitted into such a scheme and seen as the needed healing—not so much the healing of Leontes as pointing to the time needed in general to heal, mature, develop, and reconcile. As Sanders puts it, "This is a play about interrupted continuities; about gaps that remain unfilled by natural growth and maturation; about matured developmental bonds; about sixteen years of fruitless penance and about equally frozen idealities which will tyrannize permanently over a budding nature, if 'dear life' does not redeem them" (11).

## MAIN CHARACTERS

### Leontes

At the play's start, Leontes looks back nostalgically to a mythical time of apparent innocence before he met his wife or experienced the complications of adult life. Nostalgia, the yearning to return to a lost paradise, whether a home, one's childhood or youth, a first love, early family togetherness, nature (or specific places, often in the countryside), is a near-universal feeling and one of the major ways by which we construct our identities, compensate for what is felt to be the inadequacies or frustrations in the present, and try to avoid our fears for the future. Adults often, and increasingly as they age or go through major transitions, look back to the loss of this world, and perhaps partly consciously but certainly on the level of the unconscious wish to return to its supposed security. Biographically inclined critics of this play, mainly in the nineteenth century, saw Shakespeare's own nostalgia, as a middle-aged man, reflected in these concerns. While it would clearly oversimplify the matter to see a direct biographical connection with details of the play, it is intriguing to speculate just how much of his own preoccupations he, consciously or unconsciously, works into it. Certainly the sheep-shearing celebration in act 4 recalls the Warwickshire of his youth.

Many recent critics have pointed to the uncanny psychological accuracy of Shakespeare's portrayal of Leontes. Specifically in the development of boys, espe-

cially within a social framework that emphasizes male power and responsibility embodied in political power, kingship and aggression, a nostalgia for childhood may
be overlaid with anxiety, and in particular with an ambivalence about the role of
women in the development of the male psyche. Long before Freud or modern developmental psychology, Shakespeare is providing insight into the anxieties of being
gendered male in a society dominated by aggression, into some of the complexities
of families, and the roles of women in a patriarchal society. Although by no means
unique among his plays for these concerns, *The Winter's Tale* is one of the most
powerful of Shakespeare's dramatizations of these matters.

Leontes' reaction is intensified by his position as King. His absolute monarchical power over everyone in Sicilia enhances his rage; as he becomes more out of
control internally, his "tyranny" (to use a phrase all who attempt to placate or advise him try to avoid, but which is obvious) becomes increasingly abusive. He orders Camillo to poison Polixenes, has his wife arrested and put on trial, orders his
baby daughter to be killed, rejects the oracle, and is directly responsible for the
deaths of his wife, daughter, son, and Antigonus, indeed, of the entire ship's crew
that sails to Bohemia with Perdita. When the truth is revealed, his repentance is as
extreme as his jealousy, a desperate craving for security and help, as he tries to undo
his past mistakes:

> I have too much believ'd mine own suspicion. . . .
>     Apollo, pardon
> My great profaneness 'gainst thine oracle!
> I'll reconcile me to Polixenes,
> New woo my queen, recall the good Camillo,
> Whom I proclaim a man of truth, of mercy. (3.2.151–157)

But it is too late. Confession and repentance may be necessary; however, the irreparable damage is done. His wife and son are dead, his daughter abandoned to
die. His suspicion, based on inner insecurities, immaturity, and violence have
brought about the tragic destruction of those closest to him. Leontes' victims are
exactly those in his adult life who could have compensated for his lost security—
his family and, in particular, his wife. Like Othello (and to an extent, Posthumus
in *Cymbeline*) before him, he has destroyed what he most relied upon.

### Hermione

The opening phase of the play centers on Leontes, but it can also be read as
Hermione's tragedy. Her plight is more singularly tragic in that she is unjustly accused, trapped in circumstances that destroy her integrity, relationships, and family.
She is a victim not only of her husband's tyranny but also of a whole masculine world
that all the men (and perforce, the women) in the play take for granted. Shakespeare
gives her some of the most dignified, emotionally controlled lines in all his plays to
show the enormous courage she demonstrates before the catastrophic events that
victimize her. She proves to Leontes what all the others see and are helpless to change,
that Leontes himself is dangerously childish. As Sanders says, Hermione discovers
"that it had been no kindness to cosset Leontes in his possessiveness, with continual assurances of love" (48). She defies him politely but firmly, and then when the

truth breathes through, she (along with her son and daughter) is the one who suffers what the audience believes is the tragic end. There is an unmistakable sense that by the end of the play's first phase, Shakespeare wants us to believe that the tragedy is complete, that Hermione is dead. Like Leontes, we hear Paulina's report of her death. We also hear him demand to see his wife's and son's bodies, his determination to have them buried together and his vow to visit their graves every day (3.2. 234–242). To this point in the play, we have witnessed a tragic end to the action. As Orgel comments, if, by the end of the play, "Leontes is being deceived by Paulina about the reality of death, so are we being deceived by Shakespeare" (36).

Hermione is one of Shakespeare's most admirable female characters, not merely in the dramatic development of the play, but in what she stands for in the play's moral scheme. Freud's insights into what he termed "over-valuation" are especially relevant here. In Western culture—and certain psychoanalysts and critics would say universally—men look to (and tend to idealize) women to compensate for the insecurities Leontes has so tragically displayed. In doing so they "over-value" women, whether as mothers, lovers, wives, daughters, or as some mysterious figure of insight or even a transcendent cosmic force. A woman, or succession of women, are asked for or needed by men to complete or compensate for internal weaknesses, inadequacies, or insecurities, to a degree that is often unattainable, or impossible.

## Perdita

The second half of the play highlights Perdita, who, abandoned as a child, has grown up, seemingly naturally, as if embodying the ideals of innocence to which Leontes and Polixenes looked back. In the play's emotional dynamic, she has "grown in grace" in Time's words (4.1.24), and we are shown what that grace consists of. Where Hermione has been "overvalued" by Leontes, simultaneously idealized and denigrated, Perdita insists that her lover be as honest and straightforward as she is. Whereas the kings recalled their lost innocence with nostalgia, regret, and anger, Perdita with her lover, Florizel is joyful, frank, and self-possessed—as if the tragedy of her birth and the destruction of what the audience knows is her original family is now far in the background. She expresses her frank concern about Florizel's deception of his father, is uneasy about the disguise Camillo and Florizel force upon her, and in her central speech, where she distributes flowers to all the participants at the annual sheep shearing, shows herself to be frank, open, and focused on the present moment.

The meeting of Perdita with her mother is quiet, understated, and subordinated to the reunion of Hermione with Leontes. One of the reasons some modern directors cast the same actress in both roles is to stress the continuity between mother and daughter, but an alternative is to stress newness, openness to the future, and new possibilities.

## Polixenes

Just as Leontes presides over the first half of *The Winter's Tale* (acts 1–3.2), set in Sicilia, so Polixenes reigns over much of the second half, which is set in his kingdom of Bohemia. As if to reinforce the ambiguities time will bring, even in the midst of celebratory idealization, comes Polixenes' intervention into the seemingly idyllic lovers' world, clearly echoing that of Leontes earlier in the play. He has his equivalent to Leontes' insecurities and cannot deal with his son's sexual maturity; it emphasizes his own aging, arouses his anxiety about women and sexuality that he had earlier articulated while visiting Leontes and rhapsodizing about their innocent boyhoods. Tragedy is once again threatening. But this time, the play wants to give us not another tragic sequence of events but the vision of other possibilities, and Polixenes' pursuit of the lovers leads to reunion and reconciliation.

### Paulina

Wife (and then widow) of Antigonus and supporter of Hermione, Paulina becomes Leontes' adviser after he has apparently caused his wife to die and regrets his actions. Emerging strongly in the later scenes of the play's first half, she is also Hermione's companion and defender, taking Leontes' abuse for her frank opposition to him and then, as his repentance sets in, stepping forward to act as his counselor. She, too, is fulfilling a male need, that of the "wise woman" who will step forward to pick up the pieces. The wise woman represents inherently a maturity that the men of the play find extraordinarily difficult to match, even if they can finally be led to acknowledge its importance. She acts as Hermione's surrogate to bring Leontes through the sixteen years needed for his real repentance and the growth of his daughter. At the end of the play, she reveals Hermione as living and marries Camillo.

### Autolycus

Autolycus is a captivating rogue who tricks innocents out of their money. Formerly a courtier, he has turned ballad-monger and thieving con man. "[L]itter'd under Mercury" (4.3.25), he is a "snapper-up of unconsider'd trifles" (4.3.26) who wanders through the fourth act fooling the honest, telling tales, singing and selling songs, and generally lightening the play's atmosphere. He represents carnival, relaxation, and theatrical self-indulgence; he provides comic relief between the emotional traumas of the play's first half and the renewed intensity of the play's conclusion.

## DEVICES AND TECHNIQUES

The title of *The Winter's Tale* is referred to in Mamillius's remark in 2.1 when, asked to tell a tale by his mother, he remarks, "A sad tale's best for winter" (2.1.25). So-called "winter's tales" were engrossing stories designed to help listeners relax and pass the time during the cold, dark days. But the meaning here is not so simple. The play is not relaxing, but rather gripping and full of incredible and often violent events. By the end, wonderment is what is stressed, and what occurs is "like an old tale, that the verity of it is in strong suspicion" (5.2.28–29), as one of the bystanders to the amazing events at the end says. The events are also described as being "[l]ike an old tale" (5.3.117). The play's story is also about "winter" in a metaphorical sense, about the darkness and destruction Leontes creates around him and the consequences of that dark phase of his (and his family's) life. It is not, however entitled "a" winter's tale; it is called "the" winter's tale, a dramatization of some of the basic, perhaps permanent, aspects of human nature.

Shakespeare faced a number of problems in constructing the play in addition to the radical mixing of genres discussed in "Structure and Plotting," above. As with both *Pericles* and *Cymbeline*, it is as if he set himself various especially difficult technical problems just to see whether he could solve them. These include adapting the multiple settings and actions of romance to the stage as well as combining the conflicting emotional demands of comedy and tragedy. Whether we think of *The Winter's Tale* as tragicomedy or romance or a hybrid genre of its own, it shares with *Pericles* and *Cymbeline* a set of devices and techniques that Shakespeare took from the romance tradition.

The play opens with an account of the two central male characters, King Polixenes and King Leontes, and we immediately discover that one of the techniques with which Shakespeare is experimenting is combining a remarkable degree of realism with the romance setting and story. As described by two of their lords, they have been friends from boyhood, and now that they are adults, the question is raised of how each looks back on his childhood—before the two men matured, married, and took on the responsibilities of the public world, especially kingship and the power that their public roles require. They were "twinn'd lambs that did frisk i' th' sun, / And bleat the one at th' other. What we chang'd [exchanged] / Was innocence for innocence" (1.2.67–69). Shakespeare uses these early scenes to probe the psychology of growing up and how memories and deeper unconscious experiences may determine adult behavior.

Another powerful device in the play is one that Shakespeare had used successfully in his early comedies, the pastoral. The pastoral's traditional trappings of shepherds, shepherdesses, song, lighthearted love, and an idealized simple life away from the complexities of court and city are familiar ingredients to earlier Shakespeare comedies, most notably *As You Like It*. Pastoral dramas were largely a Renaissance invention, since classical pastoral was primarily a poetic mode. Tasso's pastoral dramatic poem *Aminta* (1575) and *Il Pastor Fido* (1590), by Guarini, were European models for English courtly dramatists, but the more populist basis of London theater tended not to imitate the more staid, pure pastoral drama that was relatively static and emotionally detached. *As You Like It* is Shakespeare's fullest development of the genre, but there the pastoral is only one ingredient in a rich and complex dramatic whole, largely used to critique the corruption and complexity of court (and indeed country) life. The young lovers struggle to overcome barriers and misunderstandings, and at the end of the play there is a reunion of father and daughter, multiple weddings, and a celebratory conclusion. Likewise, *A Midsummer Night's Dream* has a pastoral setting and contains magic, coincidences, amazing conversions, changing identities, and reconciliations.

*The Winter's Tale* incorporates such typical pastoral elements into act 4, especially the long scene (4.4) centered on the sheep-shearing celebrations in which we see the now sixteen-year-old Perdita and her lover, Prince Florizel, who is disguised to all but Perdita as Doricles, a young shepherd. One of the functions of the pastoral scenes is to put Leontes' earlier actions out of our minds, to "lead us," as Sanders puts it "into forgetting just *how* ruinous Leontes' morbid preoccupations with good and evil have actually proved" (64). The celebration offers singing, dancing, and a culminating section where the two young lovers are about to announce their betrothal, when they are interrupted by Polixenes and Camillo, who have come in disguise to spy on the rumored affair between the young prince and his shepherdess. The buoyancy of the pastoral has lulled us into forgetting our anxieties and the losses we have seen accumulate in the play's first half. The violence of Polixenes' outburst ominously recalls Leontes' behavior in the first part of the play, and the pastoral atmosphere is suddenly upset by potential tragedy. We have been seduced into a lighthearted, seemingly natural world, when (just as in the play's opening phase) the actions of a jealous and possessive male clumsily and potentially destructively remind us that tragedy is always potentially present, even in the most immediate happiness. "*Et in arcadia ego*"; death lurks even in the most idyllic setting, as Nicholas Poussin's famous picture of that title (taken from Virgil's fifth eclogue) shows.

But this time there is an escape. The two young lovers, advised by Camillo, fly to Sicilia, and there unfolds the remarkable ending to the play. Act 5 has three scenes. The challenge Shakespeare faced, or set himself, was to build and maintain dramatic tension through a series of discoveries, climaxing in the unveiling of the statue of Hermione, sixteen years after she supposedly died. He handles this task by having the first discovery, the meeting of Leontes and Perdita, reported to us by three court lords (5.2). We do not see Perdita restored to her father or Camillo returning to his former employer. The unexpectedness and excitement of the scene is conveyed by the reports of the amazed bystanders: "They seem'd almost, with staring on one another, to tear the cases of their eyes. There was speech in their dumbness, language in their very gesture; they look'd as they had heard of a world ransom'd, or one destroy'd. A notable passion of wonder appear'd in them; but the wisest beholder, that knew no more but seeing, could not say if th' importance [meaning] were joy or sorrow" (5.2.13–19). "Joy or sorrow" echoes Time's terms as he had introduced the second phase of the play, referring to the mixture of experiences that Time brings to all humans (4.1.1).

The indirectness by which the joy is communicated through this scene prepares the audience for the following scene, one of the most remarkable (and difficult to stage) in Shakespeare's plays. The statue scene affirms not only the power of human compassion and forgiveness but also the power of art. In *The Tempest*, written shortly after *The Winter's Tale*, the artist is presented as a magician-visionary whose insights and perception are central to our understanding of the possibilities of human life. The statue of Hermione and its awakening into life anticipate that affirmation.

Although the culminating second revelation in 5.3 is clearly meant to operate primarily on a symbolic level, the boldness of what we see on stage cannot be underestimated. We behold the statue of Hermione, created by a master artist, as it is unveiled and admired; and then it turns out to be Hermione herself, sixteen years older. To achieve maximum emotional impact in this scene, Shakespeare put together many carefully constructed naturalistic devices designed to lower an audience's disbelief. The audience has not been taken into the secret: in fact the ending of the play's first phase gives a number of hints that Hermione has actually died. Paulina's affirmation—"I say she's dead; I'll swear't" (3.2.203)—and Antigonus's dream that she has died (3.3) are designed to convince first-time readers or spectators, and (on an emotional level) even those who know the ending, that she is actually dead.

By the time the final scene is reached, Shakespeare has been carefully adding in aspects of realism to what in some ways is going to be an "unrealistic" ending. The final scene is, as Orgel affirms, "an utterly implausible device that is nevertheless overwhelmingly moving" (62). Paulina shows the statue; Leontes is overwhelmed, and Shakespeare gives him the brief but moving, stammering lines: "Hermione was not so much wrinkled . . . as this seems" (5.3.28–29). Likewise, as the truth becomes known to him, his outburst is also simple but enormously moving: "O, she's warm!" (5.3.109). The scene's power is based on the perfect appropriateness of a statue, with its solidity, stone-like, inanimate nature, and artistic representation being the central focus. As Overton puts it, Leontes has "tried to condemn her, she has been dead to him. He has denied her very being, above all her femininity; she has become as stone" (83). Interestingly, as we read the play we must, more intensely than in many Shakespeare plays, envisage what is being enacted, not just what is said. Perdita says little. Shakespeare relies on actions, not words, to convey the significance of the meeting of mother and daughter, wife and husband. Even the words exchanged between Leontes and Hermione are sparse and simple, reinforcing what is occurring on the stage.

## THEMES AND MEANINGS

The power of *The Winter's Tale* is centered on its emotionally demanding and intellectually profound treatment of some of our basic human realities. These include our memories of childhood, family relationships, the insecurities of masculinity, and the multiple roles women play in relationships with men, each other, and their families, and the roles they are asked to play, especially by men, within the male-centered ideology of sex and gender that has dominated Western history. These points about the play have become increasingly made by a variety of critics, mainly those writing in the psychoanalytical tradition derived from (though often radically different from) Freud, and feminist critics, who have drawn attention to the play's focus on sexuality and gender. These critical approaches often incorporate the dominant critical tradition of the early and mid-twentieth century, where the emphasis was on the play's use of myth and the generic possibilities (and limitations) of romance.

The play's opening dramatizes a narcissistic idealization of childhood as a period when seemingly time did not pass; when together the two friends were "boy eternal" (1.2.65). Throughout the play, we are continually reminded of how childhood, and specifically boyhood, functions as a nostalgic reaction to the complexities of adulthood: "What we chang'd / Was innocence for innocence; we knew not / The doctrine of ill-doing, nor dream'd / That any did" (1.2.68–71). Both Leontes and Polixenes display nostalgia for their childhoods, along with an accompanying insecurity. Security and safety are identified with the pre-sexual and pre-marital. When Hermione suggests that the men have lost their boyhood innocence, Polixenes replies that when he and Leontes were youths, his own wife was but a girl, and Leontes had not yet seen Hermione. The suggestion is that sin has entered the men's world through their acquaintance with women.

In the present, it seems that only the existence of their sons can give them security, and even that is tinged with narcissism. They both look back on a seemingly uncomplicated time. It seems that nothing can return that sense of well-being, and any events between their idealized youth and the present have only increased their sense of threat and insecurity. In both Polixenes and Leontes, we are given sketches of male insecurity and immaturity. Polixenes' words, that they "were twinn'd lambs that did frisk i' th' sun, / And bleat the one at th' other" (1.2.67–68), speak for the special level of conflict around a man's separation from childhood, and his dependency on the unacknowledged mother figure. "Object love," the term psychologists use to define mature, intersubjective relationships, is achieved (if at all) only by growing beyond mere identificatory love, which is traditionally associated with the attachment, caretaking, and security of the mother, before complicating (and rival) affections develop.

The nature of masculinity is, in fact, a recurring preoccupation throughout Shakespeare's plays. The young lovers in comedies, the leaders and even national heroes (like Henry V) in the history plays, and the tragic heroes all show Shakespeare's fascination with the dangers and vulnerabilities of the masculine ego. The ambiguous desires and scanty self-knowledge of most of the male characters are often—whether lightly in the comedies or obsessively in some of the tragedies—accompanied by a reliance on or redemption by women. *The Winter's Tale* continues this preoccupation. As Carol Neely notes, Leontes' "conventionalized folly" resembles the tragic heroes' "pernicious swerve . . . from the idealization of women to their degradation" (172).

Modern developmental psychologists have shown the frightening accuracy of Shakespeare's portrayal of Leontes' descent into tragic destructiveness based on this dangerous combination of idealization and denigration. When, at Hermione's trial, he speaks of her as "too much belov'd" (3.2.4), he uses a phrase that points to his (and a broader gender-based) blindness about a "need" for Hermione to fulfill insatiable demands, and to a whole phenomenon widely explored in Shakespeare's plays. "Too much belov'd" turns all too rapidly into too much hated. The traditional polarities of woman as on the one hand corrupt, sexual, and seductive and on the other as goddess are not derived from women's own requirements or desires but rather from men's perceived needs. As Klaus Theweleit explains it, "What is really at work here . . . is a specific (and historically recent) form of the oppression of women . . . oppression through exaltation." As men continued "to measure every woman against an image of 'woman,' every woman ran up against a set of expectations that were not from her, but that she was, nonetheless, supposed to fulfill" (*Male Fantasies*, trans. Stephen Conway et al. [Minneapolis: U of Minnesota P, 1987–1988], 1.284, 381). It is as if Hermione is idealized into impossible and statuesque perfection as a counter to Leontes' insecurities. Hence, the figure of her as a statue is an appropriate metaphor for what Leontes' behavior has turned her into. But what *The Winter's Tale* shows is that this is not just Leontes' error or weakness. All the men in the play share this ethos. Sanders comments ironically that "from that fine and ancient . . . mess created by first deifying women as 'precious' / 'gracious' / 'sacred' and then treating them as property, the males flee in confusion. . . . They leave Hermione, as it were, holding the baby or—if we count Leontes—the babies" (33).

Familiarity in a relationship may overcome a man's primitive mystification of woman, but the implication is that awe and even dread of woman's power always remains alive. To abandon the fantasy of women as omnipotent (whether that is negative or positive) and to recognize women as independent subjects is therefore often difficult for men, who are conditioned to remain in an infantile status rather than accept the more disturbing but revolutionary appreciation of the other's independent subjectivity. Fantasies that are unrealized or unrealizable are projected upon women: the origins may not be immediate or concrete but instead be the fantasy of maternal omnipotence, combined with the inability to recognize women as other than oneself. Leontes reads his lost youth regressively and projects his losses upon Hermione. As Jessica Benjamin argues, it is a traditional Western paradigm that grants the woman too much responsibility and contains insufficient concern for her own subjectivity." Leontes cannot get a "glimmer that [a woman] is a person in her own right" (*The Bonds of Love* [New York: Pantheon, 1988], 89). In the early scenes, before Leontes' outburst, Hermione seems relaxed, vivacious, affectionate, acknowledging the different demands of love, motherhood, and friendship. She has a rich connection with her son, inviting Mamillius to tell her a tale, shooing him away when he is tiresome, and acting as what modern psychologists call a "good enough" mother. Shakespeare gives us, rarely for his plays, a glimpse of a rich and seemingly loving family environment. And then Leontes spoils it all.

When Perdita returns to Sicilia and meets her father, we get a striking reminder of both the opening scenes and Shakespeare's singular preoccupation in the other late romances, especially *Pericles*, of relations between fathers and daughters. Seeing his daughter, Leontes immediately thinks of Hermione. Shakespeare's source, *Pandosto*, makes much of incestuous desires: Pandosto propositions his daughter without knowing her identity but sensing a memory of his dead wife, and then, mirroring Oedipus, kills himself when he finds what he inadvertently tried to do. But now, as if he has learned from Hermione's warm but totally appropriate affection toward Polixenes at the play's start, Leontes' attraction to his daughter comes from a mature place in the psyche. What is now evident to him is a new, reformed sense of what his dead wife represented and perhaps what a new kind of relationship might be. The final scenes of the play are, indeed, about how he has come to terms with that relationship and its centrality in his experience. Neely argues that in the final scene "all of the characters need to recover Hermione" (182).

This breakthrough is represented in the statue scene, notoriously difficult to stage convincingly. Paulina, the second of the play's strong women, steps into the role of the healer-priestess. The play deliberately stages the "resurrection" of Hermione as a reminder to its audiences of the power of the "old" religion: Shakespeare's is a secular vision, but it draws heavily on the human yearning for miracle and ritual much as medieval plays on Christ's resurrection did. The statue itself is like a medieval Catholic image, to be venerated, even worshipped. Then it comes to life as Leontes evinces his grief and repentance, and he is rewarded by the return, in the flesh, of his wife. There is, as Overton puts it, an "unnerving aptness" (83) to the statue metaphor: Leontes has denied Hermione's otherness, her sexuality, and her humanity. He now asks, "does not the stone rebuke me / For being more stone than it?" (5.3.37–38). The statue is shown and admired; Hermione is lamented, and then the revelation occurs: "O, she's warm," exclaims Leontes (5.3.109), and it is the healing nature of human warmth, slowly, even clumsily and barely audibly, that comes through as a primary value. Sanders argues that "this is the single most important discovery of *The Winter's Tale*—the discovery of warmth" (118). As Theweleit puts it, we all (especially men) must learn to relate to a real not a fantasy woman, one "who is neither whiter-than-white virgin, nor statue, vision, nocturnal apparition, princess" (1. 49). The centrality of the play's exploration of families, marriage, parents and children, and women focuses on Hermione.

Hermione retakes her role as mother as well as wife, and, in a move that recalls many of the early comedies where minor characters are swept up into the happy ending, Camillo and Paulina are not left out, either.

Modern criticism of the play, represented at its most suggestive by Sanders, may help us understand the way the play can produce in readers and spectators an uncanny mixture of what Time calls "joy and terror" (4.1.1). It focuses especially on the family and the fragile relationships between men and women, and especially on the potentially tragic combination of power and violence in men as they face (or do not face) their vulnerability before women. Shakespeare's interest in this contradiction within masculine identity focuses on a male figure, Leontes, whose separation has been incomplete or problematic and for whom anxiety arises when he is called upon as an adult to be a friend, a husband, a father. As a husband, Leontes finds himself once again dependent upon a woman to confirm his identity, and he may easily reenact, either positively or negatively, in displaced or disguised forms, his early crises of masculine identity. Clearly, Leontes can be seen as projecting insecurities upon Hermione that go far beyond their apparent cause. For him, in his version of the family romance, bliss was in childhood, in his myth of an uncomplicated boyhood friendship with Polixenes, before the threat of otherness represented by falling in love, marriage, adulthood intervened. Hermione, marvelously serene in her "natural" motherhood as in her role as wife and friend, seemingly has all the self-completion that Leontes both yearns for and fears. The irrational rejection of Hermione in 1.2 and 2.1 can be read as enacting such contradictions, while Leontes' abjection when he believes Hermione to be dead is the extremity of the child who has destroyed the person whom he most loves and yet from whom he must assert his independence. In his suspicion and persecution of his wife, Leontes can be seen as projecting a nostalgic fantasy of a loss of an undifferentiated world upon her—attacking precisely what we in the audience are attracted by, her apparent serene oneness with her unborn child, her mature sexuality and easy friendship. Whether in idealization, identification, or envy, we too are likely to be disproportionately moved by the situation. Leontes repudiates her because he is threatened by her; and in his rage he adds to the arbitrariness of the political tyrant all the destructiveness of the patriarchally constructed male, along with the irrationality of the child who finds that he must cut himself adrift from his undifferentiated mother and yet resents having to do so.

The assumption here is that when we respond to and in a sense reproduce these plays within our own histories, we are led to draw on some of our most deeply encultured memories. The increased fascination of this play is the ways it draws out our most primitive experiences, whether we describe those as built into our basic biogrammar or (as some psychoanalysts argue) our fundamental psychological patterns, or as culturally determined, or as a mixture of all these. Indeed, if a combination of bio-psychological and cultural layering makes up the unconscious, then this play is among the works that draw most deeply on what that often contentious term stands for. That is why increasingly critics have seen *The Winter's Tale* as one of Shakespeare's great plays.

## CRITICAL CONTROVERSIES

The controversies in criticism of *The Winter's Tale* divide into two major categories. First—a view largely confined to pre-twentieth-century criticism—is that the action is unbelievable, unrealistic, and that therefore the play is a failure. For most pre-twentieth-century critics, *The Winter's Tale* was at best a strange and confused play. The main reason was its multiple settings and its apparently contradictory, even impossibly dislocated, emotional atmosphere. Comments between the late seventeenth and early twentieth century include "grounded on impossibilities" (Dryden), "beyond all dramatic credibility" (Hartley Coleridge), and "preposterous" (D. G. James). These comments, dating from 1672 to 1937, sum up the dominant viewpoint for 250 years (Orgel, p. 1). However, from the early nineteenth century, there also developed a gradual countermovement to the dominant view of the play, to the extent that many critics and readers now find *The Winter's Tale* to be among Shakespeare's most moving works.

More specific controversies focus on the character and motivation of Leontes and the implied message or vision of the play as a whole. One of the most controversial aspects of the play is the origin of Leontes' jealousy. While some critics see his outburst in 1.2 as unmotivated, most modern readers see a psychologically plausible, if briefly sketched out, motivation—not so much in his actions as in a state of mind that Leontes betrays (and which, as we see later in the play, Polixenes in part shares). Sexuality and marriage are areas especially subject to bringing out male insecurities. The two kings' idealizations of boyhood are the subject of fond teasing by Hermione as she listens to the two "twinn'd lambs" (1.2.67) identify their "[t]emptations" (1.2.77) with the onset of sexuality and their wives. Hermione jests that Polixenes turns his queen and her into "devils" (1.2.82) and laughs at the men. Hermione has, as Sanders puts it, "an elasticity and largeness, a free 'play' of spirit" (17) that shows no such dark insecurities, and when she persuades Polixenes to stay longer, she does so with generosity and without the least suspicion of any of the unconscious complexities that we see in her husband.

In Shakespeare's source, *Pandosto*, the jealousy of the king is seen as growing gradually and having plausible causes. Shakespeare's play gives us only half a scene for jealousy to arise, yet it becomes clear that the origins of Leontes' suspicions lie far back in childhood, beyond anything we see onstage. Like Othello, Leontes reads every little detail of speech or gesture as proof of his conviction that his wife is guilty, and in each case the audience sees increasingly that the errors lie deep within the husband's experience, not the wife's actions. Being forced to relinquish an irrational illusion can be traumatic, and Leontes' jealousy, which all those who come into contact with him attempt to point out, is based not on the real world but on his own insecurities and failure to grow up. When Hermione tries to cheer him up, to tease him, he digs himself deeper into self-delusion, seeing each detail as confirming his error; when at his request she tries to persuade Polixenes to stay longer, Leontes sees that action not as love for him but as proof of her deviousness. When she recalls their courting, his misgivings increase. She displays deep motherly fondness to their son; he creates fantasies that the boy, too, is a product of some earlier infidelity. When Camillo, his trusted servant, counsels against such fantasies, Leontes turns on him.

Much depends on how a director has the part played in a theater. Few critics argue that Leontes has real justification for his jealousy, but in some theatrical productions this has been suggested, an interpretation which then requires some major adjustment with the rest of the play if the work is not to seem incoherent.

Psychological criticism of Shakespeare has often been clumsy and reductive. But with this play it has proven highly instructive. Shakespeare's focus is clearly on the psychological roots of adult behavior, and he sees childhood experiences as crucial. Behind the acts and speeches of the two kings lie self-destructive insecurities that arise from separation from the mother, here (as elsewhere in the comedies and, not least, some of the tragedies like *Coriolanus* or *Hamlet)* represented by lost innocence, youth, nature. As a man looks back at his childhood, he recalls, often unconsciously, the perilous task of separation and individuation and transfers some of his ambitions and anxieties upon his adult experiences. Within the traditional patriarchal family, a boy's sense of becoming what his society defines as masculine is always endangered by that primary, profound (perhaps even primeval) oneness with the mother. Whether men "remember" that consciously or—what is certainly the case—try to revert to a core of imaginary oneness into which they simultaneously want to escape and to free themselves from, they may project these contradictory feelings, often violently, upon their adult lovers, wives, and children.

Also controversial is the question of how to summarize the play's overriding vision. Many, following Northrop Frye, understand it as an example of the healing powers of nature over civilization, with the pastoral scene as the soothing, renewing phase after the play's tragic opening. Other critics, notably S. L. Bethell, see the play as exemplifying a specifically Christian pattern of sin, forgiveness, and redemption. G. Wilson Knight places Hermione's "resurrection" and Leontes' repentance within the contrast of pagan myths of renewal; Bethel's point of view is more explicitly Christian. Sanders offers a persuasive correction to over-theologizing the play when he focuses on the term "grace," a key word in the play; he reads it not as specifically Christian but as the affirmation of a bodily based humanism centered on the warmth of human relationships. He points to the "radical humanism" of the play's ending and the "faith" that Paulina says is required as faith in human possibility. "We return," he affirms, "to the places of our defeat always with some strivings of inexcusable hope" (104). Sanders's is perhaps the best expression of this humanist reading of the play. He argues that the core of the play is focusing on "dramatizing the intolerable" and then, in the final scenes, and even "more profoundly, by awakening in the audience that exquisite aptitude for hope which lies at the heart of all experiences of loss" (106).

There is, however, an important critical alternative that surfaces in recent feminist studies. It is that the play's ending, stressing the triumph of human forgiveness and of love over loss and pain is itself based on a male fantasy. Such a view asks: The play dramatizes, but does it critique? The hope, built deeply into patriarchal psychology, is that a man will always be rescued by a woman, that the goddess will always be there to forgive and accept. Is Shakespeare aware of the gender-based fantasy his play's ending affirms? That there is something of a critique can be seen, perhaps, in the scene's explicit emphasis on Hermione's silence, which shows not just, as Sanders argues, her "warmth" but also her sternness. Shakespeare, comments Sanders, does not "minimize the scale of the repairs this relationship now must undergo" (116).

## PRODUCTION HISTORY

The perpetual challenge of *The Winter's Tale* for directors and actors is to combine the multiple elements of tragedy, comedy, and romance that lie at its core. Bartholomeusz' study of the stage history from 1611 to 1976 shows that the play's key moment, the statue scene, was rarely staged during the late seventeenth and eighteenth centuries, and most staging before the late nineteenth century located the play in an ancient Greek or classical venue. Shakespeare's notoriously mixed geography lends itself to multiple settings. Twentieth-century productions tended to focus on character and symbolism, with geographical location of secondary importance. Trevor Nunn's striking 1969 Stratford-upon-Avon production had the Sicilian scenes all in white (along with a huge white rocking horse that Leontes angrily struck, rocking it back and forth in his anger), and the Bohemian scenes in bright peasant costumes, with a rock band in tow. Some productions have tried to recreate the various "real" places and periods in which the play occurs. These have included the Renaissance (reflecting the sculptor Julio Romano, to whom the "statue" of Hermione is attributed), while a number of productions have attempted to reproduce the atmosphere and images of Renaissance painting. The 1997 Globe (London) production used tableaux in imitation of Brueghel or Carravagio, and the pastoral scene tried to reproduce scenes reminiscent of Botticelli's *Primavera*, with the shepherds dressed like Greek gods, including Bacchus, the Three Graces, and Pan.

Some productions have doubled the role of Hermione and Perdita, with a veiled substitute playing the silent daughter in the play's final scene. The classic instance of this is Judy Dench in the Nunn Stratford production of 1969. But whether or not a director chooses to do that, the statue scene remains the play's main challenge. Does an actress stand on display to the audience the whole time before she steps down? Does the production use curtains, or a revolving platform? The scene is open to many interpretations partly because Hermione never speaks directly to Leontes. The 1997 Globe production had the statue in the "discovery space," back and center, able to be closed by a curtain. Experiments during rehearsals led the director to push the scene farther forward (and actually the "statue" came to occupy the same space taken by a cage in which Hermione was imprisoned during the trial scene). A sense of remoteness and magic was conveyed by having the cast gather around, and by distancing the scene just far enough so the audience could not see the actress's breathing.

The remarkable theatrical popularity of all the late plays since the 1950s—in contrast with their relatively low reputation, except in the case of *The Tempest*, in earlier centuries—has been marked by many historians of the theater. It would seem that these plays have tapped into something central to the gender, sexual, and familial preoccupations of the post–World War II period. We are certainly as concerned within our own society with the family and its multiple romances as were the people in Shakespeare's audiences. Yet it should be stressed that the family is by no means idealized in these plays. Where many critics used to see the family as a symbol of stability in both the comedies and romances, it can also be seen as yet another site of instability, a place of confrontation between generations, where often one parent is missing, and where its harmonies are tentative, patched together, and founded on utopian wish rather than realistic expectation. Even here, the late plays, which, according to so many critics, serve to valorize reunited families, do so only through great strains and, as most poignantly in *The Winter's Tale*, without restoring all that was lost.

Consequently, *The Winter's Tale* is not an easy play to stage successfully. Moreover, the "exit pursued by a bear" (stage direction after 3.3.58), the rapidly chang-

Keith David as Leontes and Aunjanue Ellis as Hermione in the Joseph Papp Public The-
ater/New York Shakespeare Festival 2000 production of *The Winter's Tale*, directed by Brian
Kulick. Courtesy of Photofest.

ing emotions of the central scenes, and the statue scene are seriously challenging.
As one reviewer of the 1997 Shakespeare and Company (Lenox, Massachusetts) production put it, the play contains elements that work easily on film but are difficult
to simulate on stage. Productions should not rise or fall on one scene, but the centrality of the statue scene and its technical challenges do make it difficult to get
right. Conceptually, it works wonderfully well, but theatrically, the play poses difficulties to actors and directors.

## EXPLICATION OF KEY PASSAGES

**1.2.108–207. "Too hot, too hot! . . . How now, boy?"** Polixenes initially refuses to
extend his visit with his old friend, Leontes. Leontes then asks Hermione to plead
for a longer stay. Polixenes then complies, and Leontes' jealousy erupts. Much depends on the production as to how unmotivated this reaction appears onstage, but
it stands for more than one man's psychological problems. The scene is reminiscent of Cassio's with Desdemona in *Othello*, 2.1.167–177, where Cassio "takes [Des-
demona] by the palm" (2.1.167) and whispers in her ear. So here, judging from
Leontes' comments, Polixenes and Hermione are holding hands ("paddling palms
and pinching fingers," 1.2.115). Leontes begins to wonder whether his son, Mamillius, is really his. Hermione and other women have said that Mamillius is his son,
but "women say so, / That will say any thing" (1.2.130–131). Leontes' reaction also
recalls Posthumus's speech in *Cymbeline* 2.5. After Iachimo falsely claims to have
slept with Posthumus's wife, Posthumus doubts even his own legitimacy. So in persuading himself that Hermione is adulterous, Leontes projects his self-created in-

fection upon all others—his friend, his son, and turning to the audience at one point, upon all marriages:

> And many a man there is (even at this present,
> Now, while I speak this) holds his wife by th' arm,
> That little thinks she has been sluic'd in 's absence,
> And his pond fish'd by his next neighbor—by
> Sir Smile, his neighbor. (1.2.192–196)

Such paranoia finds evidence in every detail of life. Every ordinary event is evidence for the corruption and betrayal of all women, all relationships. The family, meant, in Leontes' eyes, to make him safe from his adult insecurities as he remembers his childhood, seems to betray him most. From its origin in Leontes' insecurities and in his very sense of being a man, dependent on women, the scene is set for a projection of this inner destructiveness onto a wider world.

**3.2.22–123. "Since what I am to say . . . Of pity, not revenge!"** Hermione's trial follows a relentless, seemingly unstoppable path. Hermione's richly dignified speech in response to the indictment is contrasted with the confusion and paranoia of her husband and his increasingly tyrannical imposition of his inner turmoil upon the rest of the world. In her opening address, Hermione declares that she defends herself only for honor, not because she values her life. She calls on Leontes to think of his feelings for her before Polixenes came to Sicily to visit and challenges him to point out any dishonorable act she committed during Polixenes' stay.

Like Othello, Leontes is deaf to reason, but Hermione resumes, noting that she behaved toward Polixenes "So, and no other, as yourself commanded" (3.2.66). To act otherwise than friendly would have been "disobedience and ingratitude" (3.2.68). Again Leontes ignores her argument and threatens her with death. "The bug which you would fright me with I seek," she replies (3.2.92). What has she left to live for, having lost the love of her husband, having been barred from her son, and having had her infant daughter taken away from her. Her existence is wrapped up in her husband and children. Without them she has no life. Still, she does care for her honor and appeals to Apollo for vindication. This she receives from the oracle, but Leontes at first refuses to heed even the god. Only when he learns that his wife and son are dead does he acknowledge, too late, that he was wrong.

**4.1.1–32. "I, that please some, . . . you never may."** The passage that opens act 4, Time's soliloquy, is a deliberate disruption of the flow of the action, giving the impression that the play's action or "tale" has a teller that has been in control right from the start: "I, that please some, try all, both joy and terror / Of good and bad, that makes and unfolds error, / Now take upon me, in the name of Time, / To use my wings" (4.1.1–4). Shakespeare's source, Greene's prose romance, had also focused on the importance of time, providing the moral, as the title page of *Pandosto* declares, that while "Truth may be concealed yet by Time in spight of fortune it is most manifestly revealed." But Shakespeare goes further, showing Time itself as a presenter—a confiding, friendly, homespun philosopher, who is concerned to comfort us and to hint at new possibilities that seemed to have been closed off. The speech looks forward to the statue scene when the central importance of Time and his reassuring prophecies becomes clear. As Time explains, it takes sixteen years not only for Perdita to grow up or Leontes to repent but also for Hermione to age and show that she is not a timeless symbol, somehow reflecting a lost, "fixed" ideal to be worshipped and denigrated. As Jessica Benjamin explains, Hermione becomes a person with "independent subjectivity with a shared reality" rather than part of an "omnipotent fantasy" (93). She can now become, through time, a genuine relational object. The dualism of unattainable transcendence and destructive rejection has been worked through. In developmental terms (and *The Winter's Tale* is profoundly concerned with human development), through time, "the other becomes the person who can give and withhold recognition in a relationship of mutuality" (Benjamin, p. 149).

The play here shifts from tragedy to pastoral, but it is Shakespearean pastoral. That is, the genre of pastoral traditionally rejects time. In the pastoral world the season is always spring; everyone is forever young. Certainly Perdita and Florizel fit the ideal pastoral couple, but Time itself introduces this world. Time, chance, and mutability exist even in this Arcadia, as events will prove.

**4.4.135–146. "What you do . . . are queens."** This passage, in which Florizel praises Perdita, looks both back and forward. Even in his idealization of his beloved, we see the beginnings of continuities between Florizel and the males of the earlier generation. Like all the other men in the play—and perhaps like all men—while Florizel wants to see Perdita grow, mature, and enter the future with him, he also wants her somehow to stay the same as she is in the present moment. In some of the play's most evocative lines, containing both homage and the makings of nostalgia, he sounds out a fundamental male dilemma when faced with a woman he adores. He wants her to be both fluid, flexible, changing, like "A wave o' th' sea" (4.4.141), for those are qualities he admires, and also still, in effect, a statue:

> When you dance, I wish you
> A wave o' th' sea, that you might ever do
> Nothing but that; move still, still so,
> And own no other function. (4.4.140–143)

The sea is one of humanity's most recurring metaphors for change, and here it is both an image of fixed beauty, a photo frame as it were, and an acknowledgment of the incessant changeableness of time. This is the poignant contradiction in human youth, beauty, and love. It lies at the core of the anxiety, panic, and violence we have seen at the play's beginning.

Like Leontes, he would freeze time, but only with death does time stop. Leontes spends sixteen years in a cemetery ("There was a man— . . . / Dwelt by a churchyard" [2.1.29–30], Mamillius begins the story he will never finish). At the end of the play Leontes will wish Hermione's statue unfrozen, and in the play's most moving words, he will exclaim, "O, she's warm!" (5.3.109). Redemption comes with the acceptance of flux, of time. So it is that Time itself inaugurates the new mood of the play, and Florizel will in his last speech appeal to Leontes for help by recalling time's passing: "Remember since you ow'd no more to time / Than I do now" (5.1.219–220).

### Annotated Bibliography

Barber, C. L. "'Thou that beget'st him that did thee beget': Transformation in *Pericles* and *The Winter's Tale*." *Shakespeare Survey* 22 (1969): 59–67. Provocative mythological and psychological approach.

Bartholomeusz, Dennis. *"The Winter's Tale" in Performance in England and America, 1611–1976.* Cambridge: Cambridge UP, 1982. Invaluable survey of theater history.

Bethell, S. L. *"The Winter's Tale": A Study.* London: Staples P, 1947. Christian reading of the play.

Frye, Northrop. *A Natural Perspective: The Development of Shakespearean Comedy and Romance.* New York: Columbia UP, 1965. Offers a theoretical approach to romance.

Hunt, Maurice, ed. *Teaching "The Tempest" and the Late Plays.* New York: MLA, 1996. Excellent for classroom use and teaching hints.

Knight, G. Wilson. *The Crown of Life: Essays in Interpretation of Shakespeare's Final Plays.* London: Methuen, 1947. Classic study of the mythology and imagery of the romances.

Neely, Carol Thomas. *Broken Nuptials in Shakespeare's Plays.* Urbana: U of Illinois P, 1993. Explores the treatment of marriage in the play.

Orgel, Stephen, ed. *The Winter's Tale.* Oxford World's Classics. Oxford: Oxford UP, 1996. Useful edition, especially for the Jacobean background.

Overton, Bill. *The Winter's Tale.* Atlantic Highlands, NJ: Humanities P, 1989. Close reading; especially good on critical approaches.

Sanders, Wilbur. *The Winter's Tale.* Brighton: Harvester P, 1987. The most thought-provoking modern close reading. A stimulating yet informal discussion of the play.

White, R. S. *Shakespeare and the Romance Ending.* Newcastle upon Tyne: School of English, the University, Newcastle upon Tyne, 1981. Close reading of the text; takes a psychological-historical approach; especially good on the ending.

# The Tempest

## Gina Macdonald

### PLOT SUMMARY

**1.1.** During a storm at sea, sailors struggle to keep their ship afloat as a royal party onboard (the King of Naples, Alonso; his brother, Sebastian; and the king's son, Ferdinand), returning home from celebrating the marriage of Alonso's daughter in Carthage, faces the grim and likely prospect of a watery grave. Accompanying the King of Naples and his family are Antonio, the current Duke of Milan; Gonzalo, an elderly honest and trusted adviser; and attendant lords Adrian and Francisco. The boatswain, out of patience with his high-ranking passengers getting underfoot, tells Antonio and Sebastian that they can either "keep below" (1.1.11) out of the way of the sailors doing their jobs or help the sailors. As the storm worsens, the panicked mariners seem to lose all hope; those onboard resort to prayer, fully expecting to go down with the ship. Gonzalo's final wish is for "barren ground" of any type (1.1.66), but the ship splits and all appear to be lost at sea.

**1.2.** The scene shifts to an island from which Prospero, the rightful Duke of Milan and a man well-versed in the arts of magic, and his daughter, Miranda, watch the ship sink. Observing the fury and violence of the storm and anxious for the lives of those onboard the ship, Miranda is comforted by her father, who explains to her that he has used his magical powers to orchestrate the storm: the tempest has been "So safely ordered" through his art that "no harm's done" (1.2.29, 15), no person injured, for all is working according to his plan. Taking off his "magic garment" (1.2.24), Prospero announces that the time has come for him to reveal to Miranda the hard truths of their past, truths from which he has long protected her. Twelve years before, when the now fifteen-year-old Miranda was a toddler and Prospero reigned as the Duke of Milan, he was much more interested in the joys of learning than in the affairs of state. To give himself more time to pursue his studies, the too-trusting and other-worldly Prospero assigned the management of his state to his Machiavellian brother, Antonio. Antonio liked the power, authority, and wealth of the office so much that he ultimately seized control and ordered Prospero and his three-year-old daughter cast adrift in a small boat unfit for sailing, fully expecting them to be lost at sea. Miranda has dim memories of attendant ladies but little else, and her attention seems to wander as Prospero speaks of events from their pre-island past, but she understands the tale of betrayal her father shares with her and remembers her terror. Prospero says that the sole reason Antonio did not simply have them killed was fear of public outrage, for Prospero had been popular with the people. The only kindness Prospero received before his banishment came from old Gonzalo, who secretly furnished them with provisions to help the castaways survive and with precious books from Prospero's library. Despite Antonio's plan, Prospero and Miranda arrived safely on the island. Before lulling Miranda to sleep, Prospero explains that since "most strange, bountiful Fortune" has brought his enemies to the island (1.2.178), he must, according to his astrological calculations, act quickly under the influence of "[a] most auspicious star" if he is to regain his rightful position and have revenge upon his enemies (1.2.182).

As soon as Miranda falls asleep, Prospero meets with Ariel, a spirit in service to Prospero, who reports that he has completed Prospero's orders: he has conjured the tempest, led the ship into a quiet harbor, put all the sailors to sleep, scattered the royal party, all unharmed, around the island, and dispersed the fleet, which now regrouped goes home in sorrow thinking their king's ship wrecked with no survivors. Ariel reminds Prospero of his promise to release him (Ariel) from bondage and asks for his freedom one year sooner than their previous agreement, but Prospero angrily reminds Ariel of the spirit's debt to his master. Years before Prospero arrived on the island, the island was ruled by a blue-eyed witch from Algeria named Sycorax and by her son, the devil-spawned Caliban. When Ariel refused to obey Sycorax, she cursed him by trapping him within a tree. Twelve years later, upon arriving on the island, Prospero released Ariel, who, in turn, agreed to serve him. Chastised for his impatience, Ariel apologizes and is promised freedom in two days—after Prospero has completed his plan.

After Ariel leaves, Prospero awakens Miranda, and the two meet with Caliban, who accuses Prospero of having taken the island from him, turned him into a wretched slave after Caliban had revealed all the virtues and secrets of the island, and prevented him from peopling the island with young Calibans as he had intended. Prospero retorts that Caliban had been treated generously and kindly by both Prospero and Miranda. Miranda had taken pains to teach Caliban language, but she found him too brutish to help: he learned to curse rather than to speak well. Since Caliban tried to rape Miranda, Prospero has controlled this "[a]bhorred" and "lying slave" (1.2.351, 344) through his magic, punishing his ingratitude and his threats with cramps and pinches, "each pinch more stinging / Than bees that made 'em" (1.2.329–330).

Rejoined by Ariel in the form of a water nymph, Prospero arranges for Miranda to see Ferdinand, who stumbles upon the scene, grieving for his drowned father and confused by the music he hears all around, music made possible by the invisible Ariel. One song is of the sea change that occurs in drowned men beneath the sea. Miranda, who has never seen another male besides her father and Caliban, is struck by Ferdinand's looks and bearing and falls in love with him, although at first she believes he must be a spirit. In turn, Ferdinand, upon sighting Miranda, is also dumbstruck by her and ready to make her his queen (thinking himself king of Naples since his father's supposed drowning). Prospero, secretly glad that his plan for their falling in love is working, treats Ferdinand harshly, calls him a traitor, and threatens him with torture and imprisonment, all so that Miranda will feel sorry for Ferdinand. He even tells Miranda that she cannot judge men, having seen only three, and that Ferdinand is a Caliban to the angelic men in the world she has not known, though she deems him good enough for her.

**2.1.** Alonso, Sebastian, Antonio, and Gonzalo find themselves miraculously alive and well on the seemingly uninhabited island, their clothes completely dry and fresh. Gonzalo, an eternal optimist, irritates Antonio and Sebastian with his moralizing on their good fortune. He is clearly trying to comfort Alonso, who believes his son Ferdinand to be dead, by pointing out the benevolence of Providence in rescuing them. Antonio and Sebastian mock his speeches, poking vicious fun at Gonzalo's attempts to make the best out of the situation, especially at Gonzalo's view of the island as a veritable utopia. Gonzalo, imagining himself manager of the island and speculating about what a perfect society would be like, asserts that he would abolish all titles and have a land of equality in which all would be free to be idle if they so chose, a Golden Age, though the others joke that despite this democratic ideal, he wants to be king. As Gonzalo fantasizes, Antonio and Sebastian carp at his naïveté, while Alonso, grieving for his presumed dead son and recognizing that his daughter Claribel, now married to a North African, is too far away to be of comfort, begs Gonzalo to be quiet. Their clothes have been made fresh by Ariel, who, invisible to all, plays a strange music that puts everyone except Antonio and Sebastian to sleep. Antonio then proposes that Sebastian join with him to kill Alonso, pointing out that now that Ferdinand is presumed dead, Sebastian could easily seize the throne with Antonio's backing. Just as they both draw swords to kill the sleeping lords, having agreed that Sebastian will follow Antonio's precedent, disposing of a brother to gain political power, Ariel awakens Gonzalo. Seeing Antonio and Sebastian with drawn swords, he raises an alarm and awakens everyone. Antonio and Sebastian then claim that they were reacting to strange and terrible noises that seemed to come from everywhere.

**2.2.** On another part of the island, Caliban, carrying wood for Prospero and cursing his master and his punishments, sees Trinculo, a servant (court jester) of Alonso, and, assuming that Trinculo is one of Prospero's spirits, falls to the ground, hiding under his own cloak. Trinculo, bothered by Caliban's fishy smell but terrified of some claps of thunder, hides under the cloak too. Stephano, another servant of Alonso, arrives. Quite drunk, when he sees the two sets of legs extended from the cloak Stephano believes that he sees a strange and rare monster. When Caliban screams for pity, Stephano gives him drink, but when he hears the voice of Trinculo cry out, he really thinks that he has encountered a four-legged monster with two voices, one of them English. Only when he pulls Trinculo out by his legs does he recognize his friend. Caliban, intoxicated by the "celestial liquor" (2.2.117)—he has never drunk spirits before—accepts as fact Stephano's joke that he is the Man in the Moon who has "dropp'd from heaven" (2.2.137) and believes him a god more deserving of his fealty than Prospero. Promising to show him "every fertile inch o' th' island" (2.2.148), to catch fish for him, pluck him berries, catch the island's edible creatures for him, and kiss his foot, Caliban leads them offstage, singing in wild abandon to his newfound master. At the same time, Stephano and Trinculo comment on what a credulous monster Caliban is and joke about being kings of the island, a lower-class parallel to the treacherous upper-class ambitions revealed in 2.1.

**3.1.** Ferdinand, now Prospero's servant, humbly carries and stacks quantities of logs, determined to prove to Prospero his love for Miranda, who is troubled by his strenuous labors and attempts to help him. As they express their self-sacrificing love for each other, Prospero watches at a distance, clearly pleased by the growth of "most rare affections" between the two (3.1.75). By the end of the scene, the two have agreed to marry, and Prospero is delighted.

**3.2.** Meanwhile, Stephano, Trinculo, and Caliban weave their way about drunkenly, plotting Prospero's murder so that Stephano can rule the island with Miranda as his queen, and Trinculo and Caliban his viceroys. Ariel, invisible to them, listens to their plans to sneak into Prospero's cell, kill Prospero as he naps, and make Miranda Stephano's queen. Imitating Trinculo's voice, Ariel interjects accusations of lies that produce dissension among the drunken plotters, as Caliban leads the way to Prospero's cell.

**3.3.** As Prospero looks on, invisible, Antonio and Sebastian continue to plot Alonso's murder, but they are interrupted by the appearance of strange spirits who bring in a banquet and invite the King and his party to eat. However, as soon as they attempt to do so, Ariel appears in the shape of a harpy, makes the banquet vanish, and accuses them of being "three men of sin . . . most unfit to live" (3.3.53, 58), who plotted against Prospero and now are suffering the consequences of their treachery, the death of Ferdinand being one of the punishments. Ariel then vanishes in thunder. Prospero is pleased with Ariel's performance and with having his enemies in his power. The grief-stricken Alonso goes offstage, followed by Antonio and Sebastian, leaving Gonzalo alone to worry about the effects of guilt for their actions.

**4.1.** Prospero says that Ferdinand has proven himself worthy of Miranda's hand. To celebrate their betrothal, Prospero presents a masque in which the goddesses Iris, Juno, and Ceres bless the couple. In the midst of the performance, Prospero suddenly remembers the "foul conspiracy / Of the beast Caliban and his confederates" (4.1.139–140) and, agitated, stops the revels. He asks Ferdinand and Miranda to retire to his cell. Using Prospero's description of the quickness with which the spirits vanish as the vehicle of the metaphor, Shakespeare makes a memorable statement about how quickly too the Globe Theatre and Shakespeare's "insubstantial pageant" (4.1.155) will fade away, even as will human beings, who are the stuff of dreams and sleep.

Ariel reports that he has led Caliban's party into a scum-filled pond right outside Prospero's cell, where they are dancing drunkenly. Prospero is dismayed that all his efforts to raise Caliban above his birth and nature have failed. Invisible, Prospero and Ariel then hang beautiful clothes upon a line to tempt the very wet Caliban, Trinculo, and Stephano. Although Caliban urges the entranced Trinculo and Stephano to forget the rich garments and to enter Prospero's cell, the two ignore his pleas. While they are preoccupied with dressing themselves (as if rich clothes will make them rich gentlemen), Prospero and Ariel have spirits in the shapes of dogs chase them offstage.

**5.1.** It is the sixth hour and all is going according to Prospero's plan; his charms are working, and his spirits are obeying him. Ariel reports that Alonso and his group are confined in a nearby grove. Describing their sad state, Ariel admits that if he were human, he would pity them, especially Lord Gonzalo. Ariel's admission moves Prospero to feel pity as well and to listen to his "nobler reason" and forgive rather than allow himself to follow his "fury" and continue to wreak vengeance upon those who have hurt him (5.1.26). Commanding Ariel to release them, Prospero is left alone onstage. With his staff he traces a magic circle around himself and, after wistfully acknowledging the great scope of his magical powers and his command of nature, decides to relinquish his magical arts, giving up "this rough magic" (5.1.50), promising to break his magical staff and bury it deep in the earth so it cannot be used again and to drown his book of spells.

Ariel arrives with Alonso, Gonzalo, Sebastian, Antonio, and the attendant lords Adrian and Francisco. Entering Prospero's circle, they stand in a trance. Prospero addresses each man, first praising the goodness and charity of Gonzalo, then identifying the crimes and weaknesses of Alonso, Sebastian, and Antonio, each in turn, and forgiving them despite the fact that their deeds have been against the laws of kinship and brotherhood. As the spell begins to lift, Prospero takes off his magic robes and appears as the Duke of Milan. As Prospero nostalgically thinks how much he will miss Ariel, the exuberant spirit, tasting the freedom shortly to come, does Prospero's final bidding, bringing together the shipwrecked men. Prospero embraces Gonzalo as a welcome friend and reveals himself to the penitent Alonso, and to the less penitent Antonio and Sebastian together. In an aside he warns the wicked Antonio and Sebastian that he could reveal their traitorous plots but will not at this time. His reservations about them are clear; clear, too, is his threat of future repercussions if they once again act on their ambitions. Alonso, in contrast to Antonio and Sebastian, is truly contrite. He immediately, by power of his kingship, restores the dukedom to Prospero and begs his pardon. He grieves for his son, and Prospero tells him that he himself has recently lost his daughter. Alonso wishes the two were alive and ruling in Naples. Prospero's greatest magic is then revealed, as the two fathers look in on a peaceful, loving scene, Ferdinand and Miranda, playing chess, and teasing each other lovingly. Alonso is overcome with joy and Miranda is so stunned to see so many human beings that she calls it a "brave new world / That has such people in it" (5.1.183–184). Her more cynical father simply notes that it is new to her. All remark on the wondrous quirks of fate that have led the daughter of an outcast duke to become the wife of a king.

The boatswain and his sailors arrive to report the amazing news that the ship is in perfect condition, and the still drunken Stephano and Trinculo repent for plotting to kill Prospero. Caliban rejects them, preferring to serve Prospero as his proper master. Prospero calls him a "thing of darkness" but acknowledges him as his own (5.1.275). All will spend the night on the island to hear more about Prospero's survival before journeying to Naples to attend the marriage of Ferdinand and Miranda. Prospero will then return to Milan, his rightful place. Ariel's final act of devotion to Prospero will be to assure a safe sea voyage home for all.

**Epilogue.** The play ends with an epilogue in which Prospero speaks directly to the audience, who hold an even greater power than that of the sorcerer/magician. As the character Prospero has been confined to the island, so the actor is confined to the stage until freed by the sound of applause, and Prospero asks the audience to release him.

## PUBLICATION HISTORY

Critics agree that there was a version of the play earlier than the 1623 Folio version, but they differ as to the earliest date. The date of *The Tempest*'s initial composition is usually linked to the publication and dissemination of pamphlets throughout London in the fall of 1610 describing the shipwreck of an English vessel in the Bermudas during the summer of 1609. Influenced by these narratives, Shakespeare might have written the play as early as November of 1610 but certainly some time before the first record of the play's performance: November 1, 1611. Some theorize that the play was a refurbished version of a longer earlier play, which Shakespeare condensed (hence the "fossil" rhymes, rhymes hidden in the midst of lines), though there seems to be more support for the theory that the play had a later date but was heavily revised, hence the occasional inconsistencies.

Traditionally, *The Tempest* has been regarded as Shakespeare's last play, a designation that has been quite influential in critical interpretations. Traditional readings have viewed it as Shakespeare's valediction to the theater and to his art, with Prospero serving as the artist-figure representing Shakespeare himself. In fact, Shakespeare did not stop writing after completing *The Tempest*. Shakespeare's *Henry VIII* was performed as a new play at the Globe in 1613, though it may have been written collaboratively. Shakespeare collaborated with Fletcher on two other plays, *The Two Noble Kinsmen* and *Cardenio*, after he wrote *The Tempest*. The imprecision of dating the final works suggests that *The Winter's Tale* could also have been written right after *The Tempest*, so all that can be said with certainty is that, as editor Stephen Orgel points out in his Introduction to the Oxford University Press edition of the play (1987), "Shakespeare was writing the play just after, or just before, or at the same time as *The Winter's Tale*" (64).

*The Tempest* was clearly influenced by the published narratives and public discourse about exploration and colonization. This was a period of discovery, adventure, and conquest, well documented in numerous accounts of travel; the Elizabethans were thinking in a global context and included North Africa, the Bermudas, the Caribbean, and the infant Jamestown colony as their fields of settlement and operation. Although England in 1611 was far behind other European powers in colonizing the New World, the political, social, and intellectual climate of the time focused on stretching old boundaries and testing new waters. Old World ways were being carried to new worlds that offered the Edenic promise of an unspoiled garden, new and startling peoples, and flora and fauna hitherto unknown to them. But there was also the possibility of untold wealth worth struggling for, material ambitions impossible in Europe. At the same time, freer travel meant a greater mingling of stories and literatures from different cultures, with the English being exposed to the mythologies of the Greeks and Romans in new, accessible translations, to the literature of the continent, poets and playwrights, philosophers, and scientists, to Magellan's as well as Drake's accounts of strange sights and wonders as they circumnavigated the globe.

*The Tempest*, the second-shortest play in Shakespeare's canon, was first published in the 1623 Folio of Heminge and Condell, appearing as the first play in the volume. That the last play—or one of the last plays—that Shakespeare wrote should appear as the first in the volume has led to much speculation as to the motivations of the publishers. Most arguments come down to two possibilities: (1) such a prominent placement of *The Tempest* indicates its importance as Shakespeare's most direct expression of his personal views on art and the theater; (2) pragmatically, publishers often opened volumes with works that might attract browsers. Frank Kermode in his introduction to his edition of the play (Cambridge, MA: Harvard UP, 1958) sums up some of the early speculation about the nature of this first edition: for example, that Shakespeare wrote the play in retirement at Stratford, hence the need

for detailed instructions about production issues in the stage directions and dialogue; that someone else inserted "literary equivalents" of the original theatrical directions; or that the editors provided details from productions they knew of but
made them present tense from habit (xi–xii).

Because *The Tempest* was a relatively new play that had not yet been printed and
because the Folio pages for this play are the cleanest of all, Sir Walter Greg (*The
Editorial Problem in Shakespeare* [Oxford: Clarendon P, 1942]) hypothesizes that it
was printed first as an editing model or guide; Trevor H. Howard-Hill, though not
in agreement with all of Greg's assumptions, concedes that the excellent appearance of the manuscript may have appealed to the printer and led to its choice as
the first play of the volume. (See his *Ralph Crane and Some Shakespeare First Folio
Comedies* [Charlottesville: UP of Virginia, 1972].) Clearly, the Folio's editors used a
transcription of the play by Ralph Crane, a legal scrivener, who prepared many of
Shakespeare's plays for publication in the Folio; his fondness for brackets, notes
Kermode, asserts itself through this play (xiii). According to John Jowett in "New
Created Creatures: Ralph Crane and the Stage Directions in *The Tempest*"
(*Shakespeare Survey* 36 [1983]: 107–120), Crane probably used Shakespeare's original manuscript or a fair copy of that original, perhaps one for a court performance
(107). He then edited the text to a certain extent, dividing the play into acts and
scenes, adding lists of characters in each scene accompanied by descriptions, and
probably inserting the anomalous, explicit, and most elaborate stage directions.
Greg and Jowett argue that the directions are written more for a reader than an
actor, in language a spectator would use to record staging.

In "Ariel and the Masque in *The Tempest*" (*Shakespeare Quarterly* 21 [1970]:
213–222), Irwin Smith claims "the masque [in 4.1] was inserted in the play as an afterthought" (214) and therefore advises cutting 113 lines from the play.

The 1623 text has few gaps or textual corruptions and is thus a very clear copy,
with, as noted above, more detailed stage directions than are usually found in
Shakespeare's plays. Some idiosyncratic spellings and formats occur (such as prose
lines written as if they were poetry and verse transcribed as prose). In addition to
the nature of the manuscript printed in the First Folio, another source of long-
standing editorial debate concerns Miranda's speech at 1.2.351 when she calls Caliban an "Abhorred slave." Although the Folio version ascribes the speech to
Miranda, many editors and scholars, beginning with John Dryden and Sir William
Davenant, have thought this speech was intended to be Prospero's, claiming the
speech which recounts the attempted rape by Caliban would have been inappropriate for a young girl to give. Furthermore, the verbal style of the speech is closer
to that of Prospero, and it is the only time when Prospero does not respond to Miranda's dialogue. In his introduction to his 1901 edition of *The Tempest* (London:
Methuen), Morton Luce has also argued that Miranda would not have been Caliban's tutor. However, since the mid-twentieth century, editors have gone back to
the Folio version of the speech, interpreting the shift in style as indicative of Miranda's understandable anger and outrage at Caliban's mockery of her. Miranda is
thus viewed as less passive and less sexually naive than in earlier interpretations. As
far as her serving as Caliban's tutor, Caliban himself in a later scene refers to her
teaching him about "the Man i' th' Moon" (2.2.138).

The Folio edition is carefully divided into acts and scenes, includes a dramatis
personae (cast list), and has excellent punctuation (see Percy Simpson, *Shakespearian
Punctuation* [Oxford: Clarendon P, 1911]).

## SOURCES FOR THE PLAY

*The Tempest* has produced plentiful studies of possible sources, yet no single source on which all critics can agree has been identified. Shakespeare clearly drew on a number of varied works around which to craft his play, a fact that led Robert Wiltenburg in his 1987 "The *Aeneid* in *The Tempest*," to conclude that this play, more than most others seems "a rich confluence of elements drawn from Shakespeare's diverse reading, conversation, and theatrical experience" (*Shakespeare Survey* 39: 159–168, 159). For his descriptions of the island, Shakespeare used narratives of a Virginia Company shipwreck in the Bermudas in July 1609, including those of Admiral George Somers, Sir Thomas Gates (the newly appointed governor of Virginia), William Strachey, Sylvester Jourdan, Richard Rich, and others. The most directly relevant of these are Richard Rich's ballad *News from Virginia* (October 1610), Sylvester Jourdan's *A Discovery of the Bermudas* (October 1610), William Strachey's *The True Reportory of the Wracke and Redemption of Sir Thomas Gates, Knight* (a manuscript report written in 1610 and published in 1625), and an official report, possibly by Sir Dudley Digges, entitled *The True Declaration of the Estate of the Colony of Virginia* (November 1610). Frank Kermode sums up the arguments of Lesley Hotson, C. M. Gayley, and A. W. Ward, among others, that Shakespeare was acquainted with members of the Virginia Company, particularly Southampton and Pembroke, men who had to consider the problems of the colonies; he knew the future governor of the colony (Lord De La Warr), and had personal connections that would have brought him into contact with both Sir Dudley Digges and William Strachey (xxvii–xxviii). F. E. Halliday in *A Shakespeare Companion* (Middlesex, Eng.: Penguin Books, 1964) focuses on Sir Dudley Digges as a direct aural source, for he visited Shakespeare's friend Thomas Russell at Alderminster, near Stratford, in September 1610 (486). Strachey's description of the horrendous storm and electrical display in *The True Declaration* clearly influenced Ariel's description in 1.2.196ff.

The long conversations in 2.1. and 3.3, among others, as well as the general concept of the island, also have their verbal parallels in Strachey's descriptions. He calls the Bermudas "The Devils Ilands" and describes them as "feared and avoyded of all sea travellers alive, above any other place in the world . . . there are no Rivers nor running Springs of fresh water to bee found" (Kermode, Appendix A, pp. 136–137). Although not published until 1625, Strachey's letter circulated among members of the Virginia Company, many of whom Shakespeare knew. However, Richard Hakluyt's *Voyages* (1598) also includes vivid descriptions of St. Elmo's fire lighting up the masts, and H. R. Coursen in *The Tempest: A Guide to the Play* finds a comparable biblical shipwreck tale in Act 27 about Paul's arrival on Malta. Sylvester Jourdan's *A Discovery of the Bermudas* could have also formed Shakespeare's vision of his island. According to Sylvester, the island's bad reputation was unwarranted: "yet did we finde there the ayre so temperate and the Country so aboundantly fruitful of all fit necessaries, for the sustenation and preservation of mans life" that they lived there comfortably for some time (Kermode, Appendix A, p. 141).

As to the plot of the play, German dramatist Jakob Ayrer, who borrowed from Elizabethan theater for his own works and who drew on some of the same sources as did Shakespeare, might have provided Shakespeare a plot source with his *Die Schöne Sidea*, though Kermode (xvi) and Halliday (47) find it more likely that he and Shakespeare drew on some unknown common source. *Die Schöne Sidea*, performed by English players in 1604, has a magician with a familiar spirit and a daughter, whom the son of the magician's enemy loves, but there is no magic island and no tempest (Halliday, pp. 434–435). Halliday finds it more likely that Shakespeare saw Italian actors who visited England perform "*Le Tre Satiri*," one of the commedia dell'arte scenarios that includes a shipwreck on an island ruled by a magician and inhabited by credulous islanders who think that the crew are gods (282). Quite possibly, says Halliday, Shakespeare drew on a fifteenth-century Italian source (391). In "The Sources of *The Tempest*" (*Modern Language Notes* 35 [June 1920]: 321–330), Henry David Gray finds the Caliban subplot derived directly from commedia dell'arte scenarios. G. C. Taylor finds Shakespeare's passage in which Gonzalo explains his plan for colonizing the island in 2.1 a recapitulation of Michel de Montaigne's essay "Of Cannibals," which describes an ideal community in America. In fact, Taylor notes in *Shakespeare's Debt to Montaigne* that the British Museum copy of Florio's Montaigne has in it the signature "Wllm Shakspere," which Capell noted in 1780 when he identified Montaigne's writings as a clear Shakespearean source (Halliday, p. 321). Montaigne speaks of Art in contrast to Nature, and of man's inability to reproduce nature even at its simplest level. The French essayist describes the virtues of cannibals as natural beings:

> The very words that import lying, falshood, treason, dissimulations, covetousnes, envie, detraction, and pardon, were never heard of amongst them . . . they live in a country of so exceeding pleasant and temperate situation, that as my testimonies have told me, it is verie rare to see a sicke body amongst them. (Kermode, Appendix C, pp. 146–147)

Gonzalo's description of his utopia in 2.2.144–163 echoes Montaigne's syntax and diction. Unlike Montaigne, however, Shakespeare goes on to contrast this ideal both with the limits of "natural man" and with the baseness of civilized corruption.

Whether Shakespeare used the original Latin or Arthur Golding's 1567 translation (edited by W.H.D. Rouse [New York: Norton, 1961]), he clearly drew on the description of Medea in Ovid's *Metamorphoses* for his depiction of Sycorax and adapts her incantations to the needs of Prospero. Kermode points out that lines 55–62 of Golding's prefatory statements are reminiscent of the "degradation of Stephano and Trinculo" (149). In fact, the standard travel literature of the Old World finds echoes in *The Tempest*, and 1.2.421ff, 4.1.102, and 3.3.52, 60 recall Virgil's *Aeneid* (See J.M. Nosworth, "The Narrative Sources of *The Tempest*," *Renaissance English Studies* 24 [1948]: 281–284). Indeed, in *Shakespeare and the Courtly Aesthetic* (Berkeley: U of California P, 1981), Gary Schmidgall explores the play as a compact version of the *Aeneid*, an "epic of a lost civilization rewon" (75), and Donna Hamilton in *Virgil and "The Tempest": The Politics of Imitation* (Columbus: Ohio State UP, 1990) agrees.

Critics have found analogues to Shakespeare's plays in much of the travel literature of the ancients and of the Renaissance (Greek, Hebrew, Spanish, Italian, German, even Bulgarian), though similar types of stories and concerns do not necessarily equal sources. They have also looked to real personages as models for Prospero, including King James I of England, Elizabeth I's beloved courtier Robert Dudley, and Shakespeare himself. The songs "Where the bee sucks" and "Full fadom five" have been attributed to composer Robert Johnson, who wrote songs for Ben

Jonson's masques. Overall, the inevitable conclusion of source studies for this play is that Shakespeare eclectically drew on and melded together many works to serve his dramatic purposes, but there is no scholarly consensus on the exact nature of any one influence. Whether one travelogue or another struck his imagination first is irrelevant to an understanding of his text. What is important is that a swirl of mythologies, stories, magic, and real events came together in his imagination to help him produce an innovative play in keeping with the spirit of his age.

## STRUCTURE AND PLOTTING

Described as a pastoral tragicomedy, *The Tempest* returns to the strengths of the five-act play that Shakespeare had used with such success in the past. Yet, its music, dance, elaborate sets, and motifs of wandering and disenchantment have made some critics, led by Enid Welsford (*The Court Masque* [Cambridge: Cambridge UP, 1927]), also see structural elements of the masque tradition. In this view, Prospero would be the masque presenter and act 1 scene 2 the masque induction. As presenter, Prospero manipulates the characters, and the narrative follows a pattern of uncertainty and confusion ended by choice, action, and transformation. Kermode and others are quick to recognize some elements that the play shares with masques, but they reject outright the idea that the masque dictates the play's structure (Kermode, pp. lxxi–lxxvi).

Instead of the loose form of a masque, in which the story line is the excuse for the beautiful sets and music, *The Tempest* is one of the most tightly and economically structured of Shakespeare's plays. Kermode asserts that Shakespeare presents "the redemptive achievement of Prospero as a single magical operation in five phases" and gives "maximum import, by the concentration of his method, to the interrelationship of event and character" (lxxvi). Mark Rose in *Shakespearean Design* (Cambridge, MA: Harvard UP, 1972) calls the play "one of the most disciplined, most severely controlled plays in the canon" (173). It conforms to the unities of time, place, and action, set on and around Prospero's island. The action unfolds in the course of a single afternoon, as Prospero instructs Ariel (1.2.240–241; 5.1.4–5), with all references to past history and other places recounted but not experienced by the playgoers, and is unified and directed by Prospero, who, throughout the play, is either in the scene or observing events, invisible or not, and intervening in the lives and minds of the other characters.

Structurally, this is an experimental play for Shakespeare, one breaking new ground, relying less on imagery and elaboration than before and more on a symmetry created by foils and contrasts. The arrival of Sycorax and her son, Caliban, parallels the arrival of Prospero and his daughter, Miranda. The deposition of Prospero from the dukedom of Milan before the play begins is set against two conspiracies within the play, both thwarted by Ariel's intervention, just as one pair of brothers (Alonso, King of Naples, and his brother, Sebastian) are played off against Prospero, the rightful Duke of Milan, and his brother, the usurping Duke of Milan. Alonso and his son, Ferdinand, parallel Prospero and Miranda. The trio Alonso, Antonio, and Sebastian find their distorted echoes in Stephano, Trinculo, and Caliban. The play opens with a shipwreck and ends with the same ship restored. The mysterious banquet served by strange shapes and gently swaying dancers in 3.3 disappears and Ariel as a harpy appears, just as the fantasy masque of betrothal, with its gentle spirits, suddenly disappears in 4.1 when the reality of Caliban and crew intrude. In a parallel scene the mysterious appearance of fine, rich clothing on a line (thanks to Ariel) diverts Stephano and Trinculo from their plot, and their appearance in stolen finery, say Virginia and Alden Vaughn in their introduction to the Arden edition of the play, is like an "antimasque" parody of the 4.1 betrothal spectacle (13). Echoing Harold Brook's comprehensive study of the play's repetitions ("*The Tempest*: What Sort of Play," *Proceedings of the British Academy* 64 [1978]: 27–54), David Lindley, in the New Cambridge Shakespeare edition of *The Tempest* (Cambridge: Cambridge UP, 2002) describes the play as resembling "a hall of mirrors," with reflection after reflection turning the play back on itself in a confining, even "claustrophobic" way (3).

Rose illustrates the tightness of the construction and contrast with a diagram of scenes, noting the progression from the natural tempest in 1.1 to the magical reconciliation in 5.1. Within this frame, the centerpiece, act 3 scene 1, concentrates on Ferdinand, the means by which the reconciliation will be played out, happily working to win Miranda's hand as Prospero observes from a distance (173). It is significant that the young couple concealed in Prospero's cell is playing chess in 5.1, because, while they exist apart from the world in a moment of time stopped for them, the world around them, the world at large, engages in the politics, war, ambition, plots, and conspiracies the chess game represents; and while Ferdinand and Miranda play without malice, their lines recall to listeners the darker conflicts played out before and after this innocent game, a very mild form of the traditional battle of the sexes. Chess here is iconographic, a visual metaphor for the political ambitions, struggle, and conspiracy outside the calm of their game. Yet their marriage will be the chess move Prospero hopes will capture a kingdom for his daughter.

Layered around this central tableau are double scenes, with the three main plot strands and the sets of characters of each in one certain order before the central tableau and in reverse order after it. Thus, 2.2 and 3.1 feature Caliban, Stephano, and Trinculo, and around them 2.1 and 3.2 feature Alonso, Sebastian, and Antonio, while around them 1.2 and 4.1 feature Prospero, Ferdinand, and Miranda. In 1.2 Ferdinand mourns a lost father; in 4.1 he gains a new father through marriage. The lack of interaction of characters outside their character sets is most unusual for Shakespeare, an extreme of plotting that necessitates a Prospero or an Ariel to link scenes otherwise connected only by way of contrast. Act 5 brings all the disparate and competing groups together with warnings and punishment, reconciliation and forgiveness. The marriage of Ferdinand and Miranda is a love match, but it is also a political marriage uniting the King of Naples with the Duke of Milan, thereby thwarting the schemes of Antonio and Sebastian, Stephano and Trinculo.

The play begins with heightened sounds of discord (tempest, screaming, frightened men), chaos, and darkness; it ends with harmony, music, sweet sounds, order, and the return of light. Each act concludes with powerful drama: Ferdinand subjugated (1.2), Caliban celebrating his freedom (2.2), Ariel as harpy castigating the frenzied lords (3.3), Caliban and his co-conspirators literally hounded away (4.1). Lindley argues that the custom at the Blackfriars Theatre was for a pause at each act-break to provide time to trim the candles, a pause Shakespeare turned to advantage in each of these dramatic scenes.

The separation of characters into distinctive and separate sets does not prevent Shakespeare from connecting them thematically. For example, Shakespeare explores various degrees of evil, guilt, and self-centeredness in his characters. Ferdinand and Miranda, despite their naïveté and innocence, share the human potential for error (hence Prospero's cautions of restraint, 4.1.14–23). Prospero himself neglected the proper ends of government and his duties to the state; however, he repents, rectifies the situation, and returns to humanity and worldly responsibilities. Alonso was partially responsible for Prospero's banishment, but he repents his past acts, mourns his son, accepts his responsibility, and purges his guilt through remorse and recognition of family responsibilities. Sebastian is ambitious; gulled into a plot to kill Alonso, he denies his natural bonds and remains selfish. Antonio through envy and ambition usurped power and damned his brother, Prospero, to exile, disregarding that natural bond. Trinculo and Stephano are tainted with lower-class vices: drunkenness, greediness, vulgarity, and anarchy. Their reason is degraded. Finally, Caliban, the offspring of a witch, is pathetic yet bestial, driven by animal instincts and characterized by a total absence of reason; contact with the outside world simply leads him to greater wrong.

Another structure that lies behind the play is the unifying concept of the Great Chain of Being, whereby the universe is ordered in a hierarchy of degree that would have been apparent to Renaissance playgoers:

Providence

Higher level of spirits (like Ariel)

Fairy World of elves and other lesser spirits

Mature, intelligent, reasonable humans (like Prospero)

Decent humans guided by intuition: Ferdinand, Miranda, Gonzalo

Upper-Class Schemers, capable of reason: Alonso, Antonio, Sebastian

Lower-Class Humans, driven by passions: Trinculo, Stephano

Bestial: Caliban (cannot be tamed by reason)

There is also a thematic organization as disorder and discord threaten order and harmony but are then overcome, as noise is replaced by music, and as earth-bound creatures yield to airy ones (Caliban versus Ariel). Imagery also relates to structure, with images of the sea and sea voyages running throughout the play. In terms of chronology, the events begin with Prospero and Miranda thrust upon the sea and voyaging, unawares, to the island they make their home; the play too begins with a sea voyage, as Alonso travels to Tunis for his daughter's wedding, then is cast ashore by a violent sea. Ariel sings of the "sea-change" drowning brings (1.2.401) and later describes the "three men of sin" (Alonso, Sebastian, Antonio) as belched up by "the never-surfeited sea" (3.3.53, 55). In between, Alonso suffers much sorrow as he thinks of the sea cruelly swallowing his son, and has little hope it will quickly cast him forth. At the end of the play, the sea proves as merciful as does Prospero, for Ferdinand lives, and calm waters carry the sojourners home safely.

Throughout the play Prospero is a unifying force, calling on spirits to do his bidding, stage managing the action, listening in, moving events along according to plan, with Ariel as almost an extension of himself, sent out to bring his plans to fruition, just as he himself seems an extension of Shakespeare, raising questions of justice and retribution, of forgiveness and reconciliation, of nature and art.

Despite the tightness of the structure and the compactness of events, the play leaves many loose ends, including Antonio's son, mentioned only in 1.2.439, Alonso's daughter, Claribel, in Tunis, the unexplained absence of Prospero's wife, Sycorax's history, and Caliban's future. The play exists in a final limbo, complete but incomplete, the plot lines brought together, but danger still potentially there, and the actor waiting for the final applause that will free him to go home, as Prospero wishes to do.

## MAIN CHARACTERS

### Prospero

Prospero, whose kingdom and title were usurped by his brother, Antonio, is the rightful Duke of Milan, the magician who holds sway on his island, and the choreographer who plans a play of his own making to bring about justice and reconciliation. His name suggests that he will prosper, as he eventually does. He has survived a plot on his life and shipwreck, has gained control of the spirits of the island, and now directs them to acts of magic as Oberon did in *A Midsummer Night's Dream*. Prospero justly rules his land, though ironically he has usurped the island from its former heir, Caliban, who had himself usurped the land from some unknown others. Having once foolishly yielded his rights and responsibilities to his brother with dire consequences, Prospero now engages in various machinations to redeem the future for his daughter. He makes sure that Alonso's ship wrecks on the island, so he can get his revenge on his brother and his brother's associates for their wrongdoing. Prospero's narrative in 1.2 demonstrates his contradictory feelings as he reassures Miranda of the safety of the shipwrecked men; but he is angry and vengeful when he recalls past treachery against him and his daughter by his perfidious brother.

His art requires discipline, temperance, learning, and control. He demonstrates in his deeds that control over self and nature leads to restoration of human and political harmony, that art can control nature and make the world a better place. Prospero is a Renaissance scholar who has dabbled in the black arts and in the end rejects them. He chose the world of mind over the world of political involvement and suffered the consequences. At the end of the play, he is older and wiser and far more cynical than he once was, but he takes responsibility for his past, corrects his present, and ensures a good future for his daughter. In the final act of the play, he notes, "Though with their high wrongs I am stroock [struck] to th' quick, / Yet, with my nobler reason, 'gainst my fury / Do I take part" (5.1.25–27).

Prospero stands for civility, for reason over passion, for control of appetites and fancies. Fortune has placed his enemies at his mercy, but instead of killing them, he forgives them and seeks to guide them to repentance. He at times seems a harsh taskmaster, but his harshness to Ferdinand tests the power of the young man's love and makes him better appreciate the worth of his prize; it also ties Miranda more fiercely and protectively to Ferdinand with a depth of emotion normally impossible in so short a time. Prospero commands Ariel but frees him at the end. He has taken the island from Caliban, but Caliban was not original to the island and did not develop its wealth; hence, in Elizabethan terms, he is not worthy of owning it. Prospero certainly torments Caliban when the monster engages in wrongdoing, but

Prospero has tried to teach him language and civilize him. Prospero is no Gonzalo with hopes of a utopian existence; he views the nature of human beings cynically, as his experiences have taught him to do. He expects the very worst and hence is sometimes pleasantly surprised.

## Ariel

Described by Prospero as "quaint," "delicate," "dainty," and "tricksy" (1.2.317; 4.1.49; 5.1.95, 226), Ariel is an intelligent and powerful spirit of the island, whom Prospero has saved from Sycorax and freed from imprisonment in a pine tree. Out of gratitude, Ariel is indentured to Prospero for a limited time, a time that runs out at the end of the play. Despite such servitude, Ariel possesses high powers and is committed to Prospero only out of a sense of responsibility and duty. His conflict with Sycorax resulted from his absolute refusal to carry out commands he considered abhorrent. He rebels momentarily against Prospero in 1.2, but Prospero's promise of only two more days of duties contents him. He is the agent of Prospero's magical powers, and the stage manager of his plot, causing the tempest of the title and much of the magic, and bringing together many of the conspirators in the play. Though working for Prospero somewhat against his will, Ariel is intelligent and capable, and at the play's end rejoices to be free. The name Ariel possibly comes from a Hebrew name in Isaiah chapter 29 meaning the "lion of god," but it may just as likely come from the traditions of magic and magicians, where it frequently occurs. Ariel is associated with the element of air and fire (flying about and causing St. Elmo's fire onboard Alonso's ship; causing lightning to set the sky ablaze) but is at ease in all elements. Ariel, like Puck in *A Midsummer Night's Dream*, torments many of the earthlings in the story, at Prospero's bequest.

## Caliban

Caliban, in contrast, is clearly a lesser being, associated with earth and rock, yet his importance to the play is undeniable, as is his importance to critics. The Vaughans, quoting Martin Spevack, point out that he has 30 percent of the lines in the play, second only to Prospero (24). Caliban and his mother ruled the island before Prospero arrived and took control. He becomes Prospero's subject, performing manual labor, yet he continues his past existence to some degree, hiding in subterranean caves and living off the land (its berries, fish, and so forth). We know little of his appearance, relying on hints from such imprecations as "freckled whelp," "filth," and "Hag-seed" (1.2.283, 346, 365), "beast" (4.1.140), "misshapen knave" (5.1.268), and "savage" (1.2.355). Trinculo reacts to Caliban's fishy smell, demeaning him as a "deboshed fish" and "half a fish and half a monster" (3.2.26, 29). Prospero refers to him as "this thing of darkness" (5.1.275), which could be metaphorical rather than literal. Other references have to do with his paternity, his unkempt appearance, his growing uglier with age, and his oddness: Alonso calls him "a strange thing as e'er I look'd on" (5.1.290). Yet producers have expended such energy creating varied creatures that the Vaughans have devoted a whole book to his stage metamorphoses (see "Annotated Bibliography," below).

Caliban tried to rape Miranda, and he is therefore shunned by both Miranda and Prospero. All who encounter Caliban regard him as sub-human, or reprehensible, because of his different looks and strange ways. However, Caliban has a capacity for poetry and for appreciating beauty, as shown by his speech at 3.2.135–143, which is one of the most poetic, beautiful, and descriptive of the play. Gonzalo is the only one within the play who even tries to evaluate Caliban and his kind fairly; the others, blinded by prejudice, mistreat him to various extents. E. K. Chambers argues that the name derives from *cauliban*, a Romany word for "blackness" (*William Shakespeare: A Study of Facts and Problems* [Oxford: Clarendon P, 1930], 1.494). Various critics have found his name an anagram for "cannibal," or associated it with "Carib," a Renaissance term for savage New World Indian islanders. The byproduct of a wicked witch and an incubus, Caliban is frequently denounced as "devil-born" and hence deformed. He is associated with uncontrolled appetites.

Although he is frequently seen as an icon for enslaved Native Americans or Africans, his mother was an Old World witch, and he is an intruder on the island, not a native, despite his claims of ownership. Moreover, he is an intruder anxious to rape the inhabitants and to people the island with his offspring, while glutting himself on the rich variety of foods available. He becomes as drunken as Stephano and Trinculo, and is clearly in their sorry league to some degree, though in some ways he is smarter than they (recognizing a trap when they do not) and more experienced with the consequences of wrongdoing (fearing the resulting pinches and cramps).

### Ferdinand and Miranda

The two characters most central to both Shakespeare and Prospero's plot are Ferdinand, Alonso's only son, and Miranda, Prospero's only daughter, whose name means "wondrous" or "to be astonished at" in Italian. She has little memory of anywhere but the island, whereas Ferdinand is heir to the kingdom of Naples. Young (barely fifteen) and innocent, she is also intelligent (having learned much from her father), and headstrong. In accord with her father's plan, she falls in love with Ferdinand at first sight and would willingly undergo trials and tribulations for his sake, as he does for her. Bound to her by mutual infatuation, Ferdinand is Prospero's means to regain for his daughter what he lost through inattention to duty. When Miranda and Ferdinand decide to marry, though they have been pawns in Prospero's plan to reclaim his dukedom, their affection for each other is genuine, and Ferdinand gladly endures much for Miranda's sake. Presumed dead by his father because they were separated during the shipwreck, Ferdinand is overjoyed when Prospero brings father and son together. Having already won Prospero's approval of his engagement, he is heartened by his own father's response. Together Ferdinand and Miranda will rule Naples when Alonso retires.

### Alonso, Sebastian, and Antonio

The three characters at whom Prospero aims his plot are Alonso, King of Naples; Sebastian, Alonso's brother; and Antonio, Prospero's brother, now Duke of Milan. Alonso assisted Antonio in his plot to overthrow Prospero. A flawed politician, Alonso is not an evil man. He has just married off his daughter, Claribel, and is returning home with his son and heir, Ferdinand, when the shipwreck occurs. When he finally confronts Prospero, he is so undone by the loss of his son and so guilt-ridden at what he had done that he quickly and truly repents and is quite earnest when he wishes his returned son might marry Prospero's daughter and seal their friendship and political commitment. He drops Antonio without hesitation and restores the dukedom to Prospero.

In contrast, Alonso's brother, Sebastian, and Prospero's brother, Antonio, seem unredeemable. They are flawed personalities, driven by political ambition and just plain meanness. Antonio feels no remorse for his brother's supposed death or for plotting with Sebastian to seize his brother's crown. Both are punished by the magic of the spirit Ariel, and Prospero warns both to beware his vengeance if they force him to act. Instead of being grateful that his brother trusted him with his dukedom, Antonio lusted so much after power that he usurped the dukedom of Milan while Prospero was absorbed in study; he also had Prospero and his daughter dumped at sea. Antonio urges Sebastian to murder Alonso and seize the throne of Naples, though Ariel's magical powers prevent these traitorous acts. He is sarcastic and unrepentant. In fact, throughout the play the mocking wit of Antonio and Sebastian marks them as separate from their party, as do their bitingly negative responses to Gonzalo's benign remarks. When Gonzalo describes the beauty of the green grass, they assert that "the ground indeed is tawny" (2.1.55). When Gonzalo notes that despite being wet through by the sea their clothes are "rather new dy'd than stain'd with salt water" (2.1.64–65), they say that he "lies" (2.1.67). Heedless of others, Sebastian and Antonio are arrogant and quick to argue. They constantly bicker, insult, and backstab until Prospero provides their eventual comeuppance.

## Gonzalo

Gonzalo stands in direct contrast to these three, an honest, kind-hearted man, disgusted with politics and political corruption. A counselor to the king, he is an optimist, always looking on the bright side. He helped Prospero and Miranda survive Antonio's plot to murder them. Gonzalo is unquestionably good, with no dark side and no dark secrets. He dreams of a utopian society in which rank is abolished and man and nature live in harmony. His utopian vision may be naive, especially given the mean streaks in Antonio and Sebastian that are at odds with Gonzalo's picture of natural man, but his speech in 2.1.144–165 represents the Renaissance spirit of political idealism and the interest of the Jacobean Age in new worlds and new possibilities.

## Trinculo and Stephano

Trinculo, a drunken jester and servant to Alonso, and Stephano, a drunken butler and friend of Trinculo, are always onstage together, often with Caliban. Trinculo's name probably comes from the Italian verb *trincare*, meaning to drink greedily. As he reels about, alternately fearful and insulting, he provides a slapstick type of comic relief. Caliban takes an instant dislike to him, egged on by Ariel's taunts uttered in Trinculo's voice. Trinculo joins in Caliban's plan to murder Prospero and take over the island but is too ineffectual and out of control to have much success at anything. Stephano likewise is inebriated throughout much of the play, but he is jollier than Trinculo; somehow Caliban sees virtue in him, taking his drunken braggadocchio as truth and accepting him as the man in the moon and his new master. Caliban thinks that Stephano has magical powers. Stephano agrees to Caliban's plot to make him ruler of the island and to make Miranda his queen. Nonetheless, like Trinculo, he is completely incapable of bringing the plan to fruition.

## DEVICES AND TECHNIQUES

Shakespeare pulls out all the stops to give his audience what they want. He appeases the groundlings' taste for entertainment in a variety of forms, providing fairies, masques, strange sights and sounds, a harpy, and idyllic love. The play offers magic, a shipwreck, assassination plots, drunken sailors with bawdy songs reeling on stage, and a grotesque, misshapen beast such as the common people would have paid a penny to see in some traveling sideshow. For that same price they get an entire play. At the same time, Shakespeare is at his most esoteric: His play obeys the classical unities of time, place, and action. That is, the play on stage takes approximately the same time to perform as the number of hours from shipwreck to reconciliation. The action takes place in only one location, on and around the island. The scenes are tightly controlled. There are nine short scenes; the fifth scene is the center of the play and is surrounded by a triple frame composed of groups of distinct characters.

Music is very important to this play, perhaps even more than in *Twelfth Night*. The enchanted island is full of sounds, with its shrieking winds, croaking frogs, hissing adders, or Ariel's playing of the tabor and pipe. Directions for music emphasize "Solemn and strange" (s.d. after 3.3.17) or "soft" (s.d. after 3.3.82); these contrast with the cacophony of sounds produced by the singing of drunken sailors and Caliban's chant of freedom. Music wakens characters and puts them to sleep. Ferdinand and Caliban remark on the magic of the sounds in the air or earth.

Magic, too, dominates this play, with the music a direct result of Prospero's powers at work, commanding elves and spirits, sending Ariel to perform such tasks as cleaning and freshening the attire of the shipwrecked company, putting characters to sleep or awakening them at significant moments, thwarting plots, and punishing offenders. Prospero is indeed the magus, with book, staff, and robe, and the play is his final magical performance. Through the alchemy of his magic, he hopes to transform or at least reform his human subjects. He succeeds with those who are redeemable and fails only with those tainted by evil. The masque embedded in 4.1 is a product of this magic, one meant to evoke awe and wonder in the young couple and to impart lessons and warnings about love and marriage. This Jacobean court form is more than a musical interlude, for it has a stage set and spirit-actors who speak and dance at Prospero's command in their guise of Roman goddesses. It provides an iconographic rendering of the four elements—earth, air, fire, and water—coming together harmoniously as a royal marriage and universal order go hand in hand.

Allusions to classical stories like those involving the Roman goddesses occur throughout the play. References to *The Aeneid*, in particular, are common. For example, Claribel's African wedding leads Antonio and Sebastian to debate about the "widow Dido" and whether Carthage and Tunis are the same place (2.1.75–86). *The*

*Tempest* is roughly set in the same geographic region as Virgil's work, with Alonso's ship probably taking the same route that Aeneas took from Carthage to Naples before the shipwreck, a fact that brings to the work the political realities explored by Virgil rather than those of New World colonies. Another obvious parallel to *The Aeneid* appears in the scene with Ariel as a harpy with a dire prophecy (3.3.52). In book 3 of *The Aeneid* the harpy Celaeno predicts famine for the Trojans.

As throughout his canon, Shakespeare engages in many forms of wordplay. Antonio and Sebastian, for example, use puns to mock others. When the somewhat long-winded Gonzalo begins to entreat the king, Sebastian teases that he is "winding up the watch of his wit, by and by it will strike" (2.1.12–13). Then, when Gonzalo opens his mouth again, Sebastian shouts out, "One," as if Gonzalo, clocklike, has struck the hour (2.1.15). Gonzalo goes on to speak of grief that is "entertained" or received (2.1.16); Sebastian plays on the word "entertaining" to mean "being paid to amuse others," hence his reference to "A dollar." Gonzalo immediately responds, playing on the closeness in sound between the words "dollar" and "dolor" to suggest that sufferers indeed entertain "dolor" (2.1.18, 19). The nasty edge to their wordplay, especially against so honest and open a character, reveals their unsavory character. Likewise in 3.2.16–19 Trinculo and Stephano pun on the word "standard" in the meaning of a standard-bearer or ensign as they joke about how drunk (and hence unable to stand) Caliban is. For more on Shakespeare's language, see Barbara Mowat and Paul Werstine's introductory discussion in the New Folger Library Shakespeare edition, *The Tempest* (New York: Washington Square Press, 1994).

Like wordplay, imagery is an ever-present Shakespearean device. Earlier in this chapter I discussed the variations on sea and sea changes, but there are many running images of change and transformation as well as images of disease, sores, cankers, plague, and the poisonous effects of guilt. The opening storm image, a visual and auditory experience, is a conventional Renaissance metaphor for a storm-tossed mind and brings with it comments on the vicissitudes of human life, helplessness before fortune, and loss of reason and self-control. But the turbulent action, complete with technical naval commands and wet sailors, extends the image to suggest disordered elements that parallel the inversion of the social hierarchy onboard ship. The boatswain questions the authority of the king and of Gonzalo's courtly counsel and thus prefigures questions of power and control raised throughout the rest of the play.

## THEMES AND MEANINGS

*The Tempest* contains many of the themes and techniques Shakespeare had used earlier in his career, but here they appear in a new, mellow mood, more tolerant of humanity's faults than in the darkest plays, yet less confident of virtue's invulnerability than in the light comedies. Among the issues the play addresses are nature's abundance, the appeal of the natural life, the reclamation of nature, the Golden Age, justice and mercy, man fallen and redeemed, questions of decorum of language and action, the nature of government, the obligations of leaders, the effects of travel, the joys and dangers of new territories, and the brave new possibilities opening up for humankind. In his "Introduction to *The Tempest*" (*The Norton Shakespeare* [New York: W. W. Norton], 1997), Stephen Greenblatt calls the play an "echo chamber of Shakespearean motifs," resonating with "issues that haunted

Shakespeare's imagination throughout his career" (3047). However, in "'A Quaint Device': *The Tempest* at Blackfriars," in Alden and Virginia Vaughan's 1998 collection *Critical Essays on Shakespeare's "The Tempest"* (New York: G. K. Hall), Keith Sturgess goes a step further and calls the play "both a summation of Shakespeare's writing career and a radically experimental new departure" (107). Indeed, it looks both back and forward in its strategies and themes.

Whether or not this play was his farewell to the stage, Shakespeare here pulls together techniques and images from his canon and recreates them for new purposes. These devices include the drunken slapstick of early comedies, the fairies and spirits of *A Midsummer Night's Dream*, and the dream imagery of both *A Midsummer Night's Dream* and *The Taming of the Shrew*. The pratfalls, ditties, and drunken absurdities of Stephano and Trinculo echo similar scenes in Shakespeare's early comedies, while the masques throughout the play suggest the romantic escapism of *A Midsummer Night's Dream*. The uniting of old enemies through the marriage of Ferdinand and Miranda is a counter-ending to *Romeo and Juliet*, one appropriate to a more sanguine view of the world. Gonzalo even suggests that the heavens are responsible for the happy ending (5.1.201–204), in contrast to the malevolent influence of the stars in *Romeo and Juliet*. In spite of the low comedy, romance, and happy ending, however, the triumph over evil is not easily won; for the island, a hotbed of intrigue, is a displaced microcosm of Milan and Naples rather than the utopias of Athens (*A Midsummer Night's Dream*) and Illyria (*Twelfth Night*). *The Tempest* reflects Shakespeare's concern with art and play-acting and with the theme of appearance versus reality as in *Hamlet* and *A Midsummer Night's Dream*, but this play is more modest about art's powers. The theme of illusion runs throughout *The Tempest*, beginning with the storm that seems to illustrate human helplessness against nature's wrath, when in fact it is the work of an illusionist who causes and choreographs the storm and shipwreck. Furthermore, as in *King Lear*, *Julius Caesar*, and *Othello*, an external tempest reflects an internal storm. The play offers political intrigue and usurpation as in *Hamlet* and in *Richard III*, and Miranda is a naive and innocent heroine like Desdemona or Lady Anne. Shakespeare's final romances (*Pericles*, *Cymbeline*, *The Winter's Tale*, *The Tempest*) reveal an interest in intimate human bonds (unity of family), time, and passion as necessary to heal divisions of estrangement. Fathers lose children through passion-driven folly (at the beginning). Suffering and remorse follow estrangement (central action); the plays conclude with magical transformations and with lost children restored. As in *Measure for Measure* a duke has abstained from his duties and deputized a replacement through whom he learns the negative effects of power, the limits of human goodness, and the hypocrisy with which all rulers must contend.

However, the connections between Shakespeare's other works and *The Tempest* are not merely superficial. They help readers see the progression of Shakespeare's interests and concerns, his working out of themes, and his life-long interest in the nature of human beings. In the earliest plays, the malevolence of which some men are capable seems controllable through the intercession of good men. Nonetheless, good men may fail, as does Friar Lawrence. The history plays show how kings and great men are still weak humans tempted by power; evil is eventually driven out in *Richard III* and *Henry IV Part I*, but only after its time has passed and many lives have been lost. While the great tragedies encompass general philosophical and psychological themes, they focus on the specific faults that destroy great men: Othello's blind jealousy, which makes him easily susceptible to Iago's evil; Hamlet's hesitation and over-intellectualizing; Lear's foolishness and selfishness; Coriolanus's arrogance and intolerance. Even though evil is a constant threat in *The Tempest*, the play, nonetheless, returns to some of Shakespeare's earlier optimism, which allows goodness to prevail. The outcome of *The Tempest* is tempered by a mature awareness of the limits of human goodness, but it is not as grim as those of the great tragedies.

Caliban is, of course, the best symbol of nature unchecked, an earthy creature dominated by desire and ambition. In Renaissance terms he is passion, the most basic force, analogous to the id, and Prospero himself may represent reason: the intellectual part of man that ascertains the good and works to achieve it. Frank Kermode calls Caliban a central element, "the natural man against whom the cultivated man is measured" (xxiv), nature unnurtured and unrefined by civilization, his function one of contrast: to set off the world of "art, nurture, civility" (xxv). Like the Duke in *Measure for Measure*, whose behavior he parallels, Prospero works quietly behind the scenes, keeping order in his state. He has learned the danger of withdrawal into higher pursuits, and his deposition is a constant reminder that the good ruler must practice an active life, exercising an almost tyrannical, though ultimately benevolent, control. (Notice Prospero's tight rein on Ariel, a higher spirit whom he must continually bribe with the promise of freedom in order to assure precise obedience.) Shakespeare critic Hardin Craig is right in complaining about the overemphasis placed by modern interpretations on Prospero's magic; true, he "has everything his own way" (*The Complete Works of Shakespeare* [Chicago: Scott, Foresman, 1951], 1249), but the issue is in some doubt until the end, and the happy result is a tribute to his skill rather than to a determined, prearranged triumph over evil. Miranda would have represented intuition for the Renaissance. Like Desdemona, her innocence causes her naturally to seek the good without recourse to reason, but unlike the comic heroines of the early plays, she is a rather flat character, one managed by Prospero rather than one who determines her own life. Shakespeare's mature judgment is that innocence and good intentions may point the way but need the guidance and wisdom of reason to get there.

Shakespeare's hero is Prospero, a skeptical, careful, mature person who is nevertheless determined to struggle for order and decency, while practicing the benevolence others have often denied him. Through Prospero, *The Tempest* strikes a balance between the naive optimism of the first comedies and the often all-pervading gloom of the major tragedies. It recognizes man's limitations but provides a solution for overcoming them and for establishing justice and decency.

Part of the lesson of *Coriolanus* was the need for self-discipline and self-control. Coriolanus is an honorable man, but he yields to anger and passion when confronted with the cowardice, dishonesty, and duplicity of man; anger at the citizens' guilt leads to his personal loss of self-control and hence his fall. Shakespeare, in *The Tempest*, deals with the necessity of discipline, hard labor, and restraint in order to attain freedom and honorable goals. First of all, Shakespeare is disciplining himself, forcing himself to control the structure and form of his play (adhering to the three unities) in order to produce a masterpiece that holds the mirror up to the audience and shows them their basic nature: their weaknesses and their strengths. Thus, one of the lessons he teaches is the need to control creative impulses in order to produce the desired final result. Likewise, Prospero, another creator, must discipline himself. He lost his freedom and his kingdom through self-indulgence and rejection of restraint and responsibility/duty, and he can regain what he has lost only when he learns to discipline himself and to govern both his own impulses and those of the citizens of his new commonwealth, restraining Caliban and employing Ariel usefully. He must use art and magic to mend the nature of his enemies by showing them their guilt and by helping them recognize their personal responsibilities instead of seeking cruel revenge. Ariel, too, earns freedom through hard work and loyalty. Ferdinand must undertake physical labor and practice self-discipline to earn Miranda's hand, and Miranda must discipline herself and pay attention to her father's strictures and advice to learn who she is and to earn the right to Ferdinand's love and respect. Both young people must also learn sexual restraint.

In contrast, Caliban proves incapable of learning because of his bestial nature. He has no self-discipline. Likewise, neither Trinculo nor Stephano can be taught because drink and license steal their reason. They fit neatly with Elizabethan images of masterless men up to no good, plotting treason and subversion of the state. The songs they sing of freedom and the chaotic lack of restraint confirm their inability to learn and to change for the better.

Thus, this play revisits themes and concerns, strategies and approaches of earlier works, contrasts the pragmatic political realist and the philosophical idealist, sees the world changing and power shifting, captures the enduring force of nature and its fecundity summed up in the sea, postulates chess as a metaphor for political ambitions, and depicts time past redeemed to assure the future and transform the present. Prospero proves he is no longer the egocentric man he was in his youth, and he looks to the next generation with hope—not for himself but for a better world for his grandchildren.

## CRITICAL CONTROVERSIES

In the 1968 New Pelican Shakespeare edition of *The Tempest* (Harmondsworth, Eng.: Penguin), editor Anne Barton observes that the play is "an extraordinarily obliging work of art" for it will "lend itself to almost any interpretation, any set of meanings imposed upon it" (22). David Lindley, in the New Cambridge Shakespeare edition of *The Tempest*, adds a list of the most common critical readings of the play: "as a romance of reconciliation, a Christian allegory of forgiveness, a meditation on the powers of the imagination and the limits of art, a psychological drama of fatherhood, a play about Jacobean politics, and a dramatisation of colonialist or patriarchal ideology" (1).

H. R. Coursen in *"The Tempest": A Guide to the Play* contrasts the various critical approaches to the work and finds in and between each category areas of controversy and contention: New Critical (a close examination of text, seeking clues to Shakespeare's themes and intent), Feminist (a consideration of the gender roles and Miranda's submissiveness), Generic (debate about the type of play and the implications of such classifications), Linguistic (what the linguistic patterns reveal about the themes and concerns of the play; the significance of names and image clusters), Psychological (exploration of family dynamics; Prospero as authoritarian father-figure; the divided self; Freudian interpretations of relationships and acts; Jungian shadows of inner selves), Historicist (the influence of social, political, philosophical attitudes and events of the time; the play as a historically determined literary artifact, subordinated to history), Colonialist (politically edged attack on British cultural materialism as propagated in the play), Religious (allegorical significance; Christian icons; questions of guilt and redemption), and Postmodernist Criticism (the indeterminacy of interpretation; the play as signifying different things to different audiences, regardless of authorial intent). The historicist critic can accept no interpretation that fails to consider the history and culture of the time, while the New Critics examine the text closely, largely to the exclusion of biographical or historical background. The range of disagreement, then, is quite broad, with, for example, New Critic J. Dover Wilson in "The Enchanted Island" from *The Essential Shakespeare* (Cambridge: Cambridge UP, 1932, 131–145) calling the play "the most consummate of all Shakespeare's masterpieces" (132). But feminist Gayle Greene in "Margaret Laurence's *Diviners* and Shakespeare's *Tempest*," finds the play Shakespeare's "most sexist" and "most racist" creation (in *Women's Re-Visions of Shakespeare*, ed. Marianne Novy [Urbana: U of Illinois P, 1990], 165–182), and historicist Donna Hamilton regards the play as a mirror for magistrates, a set of instructions to kingship for James I ("Shakespeare's Romances and Jacobean Political Discourse," in *Approaches to Teaching "The Tempest" and Other Late Romances*, ed. Maurice Hunt [New York: MLA, 1992], 64–71). Clearly, Stephen Orgel is on target in his 1987 "Introduction" to his Oxford edition of the play: "*The Tempest* is a text that looks different in different contexts, and it has been used to support radically differing claims about Shakespeare's allegiances" (11). Orgel goes on to summarize the very different images of Prospero as "a noble ruler and mage, a tyrant and megalomaniac, a necromancer, a Neoplatonic scientist, a colonial imperialist, a civilizer" and of Caliban as "an uneducable brute, a sensitive savage, a European wild man, a New-World native, ugly, attractive, tragic, pathetic, comic, frightening, the rightful owner of the island, a natural slave" (11).

The colonialist/historicist approaches to the play have provoked the greatest controversy to date. In "'This Thing of Darkness I Acknowledge Mine': *The Tempest* and the Discourse of Colonialism" (in *Political Shakespeare: New Essays in Cultural Materialism*, ed. Jonathan Dollimore and Alan Sinfield [Ithaca: Cornell UP, 1985], 48–71), Paul Brown argues that the play reveals contradictions in colonialist discourse about both the New World and Ireland as it plays euphemisation, or the effacement of power, against Prospero's enslavement of Caliban. In "Prospero in Africa: *The Tempest* as Colonialist Text and Pretext" (in *Shakespeare Reproduced: The Text in History and Ideology*, ed. Jean Howard and Marion O'Connor [London: Methuen, 1987], 99–115), Thomas Cartelli cites the use of the play in Kenyan and West Indian writing to support his belief that it expresses western power and ideals in the catch-phrases of "predatory" colonialism. The following list of essays reflects only a brief selection of critical takes on *The Tempest* as colonialist literature: Philip Brockbank, "*The Tempest*: Conventions of Art and Empire" (in *Later Shakespeare*, ed. John Brown and Bernard Harris [London: St. Martin's P, 1966], 183–202); Trevor Griffiths, "'This Island's Mine': Caliban and Colonialism" (*Yearbook of English Studies* 13 [1983]: 159–180); Octavio Mannoni, *Prospero and Caliban: The Psychology of Colonization*, trans. Pamela Powesland (Ann Arbor: U of Michigan P, 1990); and Rob Nixon, "Caribbean and African Appropriations of *The Tempest*" (*Critical Inquiry* 13.3 [Spring 1987]: 557–578). In "Discourse and the Individual: The Case of Colonialism in *The Tempest*" (*Shakespeare Quarterly* 40 [Spring 1989]: 42–69), Meredith Anne Skura sums up the contrast between past critical interpretations of the play and the new historicist readings, the debate over whether they are indeed ahistorical and project onto the past modern concerns of no real interest to Shakespeare and Elizabethans, whether they see subsurface readings that reflect the sociological biases of the time that were and remain inherent in celebrations of colonialism, or whether they make dominant "the Europeans' exploitative and self-justifying treatment of the New World and its inhabitants" when, in fact, it is but a minor concern in the larger text. Basically, she finds the revisionist impulse "salutary" in correcting New Critical "'blindness' to history and ideology" but finds it in danger of "fostering blindness of its own" (46). She asks how we know that *The Tempest* "'enacts' colonialism" rather than simply alluding to the New World or that Caliban is indeed "part of the 'discourse' of colonialism" (47). She wisely concludes that, whatever our critical persuasion, conflicting readings of text confirm the individuality or uniqueness of the play and enrich our understanding of text and context.

The nature of Caliban has been in such dispute that the controversy and the transformations of the vision of him from age to age and critic to critic have led to Alden and Virginia Vaughan's *Shakespeare's Caliban: A Cultural History* (see "Annotated Bibliography"), with its exploration of the multifaceted debate, particularly questions of Caliban's genesis and allegorical or emblematic nature. Is he a deformed monster? A noble savage? A cannibal? An American Indian? An aquatic monster? A Darwinian missing link? Natural man? An orphaned African slave? A symbol for the victimization of Third World peoples? The ultimate answer to these questions affects the debate over his physical embodiment on the stage, where he has been portrayed variously as the Id, a black militant, and a punk rocker.

## PRODUCTION HISTORY

The earliest surviving record of the play's performances during Shakespeare's lifetime indicates that it was presented by Shakespeare's acting company, the King's Men, on "Hallomas nyght," November 1, 1611, at the Banqueting House at Whitehall before King James I (*Revels Account*, noted in F. E. Halliday's *A Shakespeare Companion*, p. 486). Tradition suggests that the play was performed at the Globe, the Cockpit (a royal preserve off Whitehall), and Blackfriars Theatre (see Kermode, p. 151). Andrew Gurr in "*The Tempest*'s Tempest at Blackfriars" (*Shakespeare Survey* 41 [1989]: 91–102) contends that this was the first Shakespearean play designed for a Blackfriars performance. According to the *Chamber Account*, in 1613, *The Tempest* was one of fourteen performances at court as part of the celebration of the February marriage of Princess Elizabeth, James I's daughter, to the Elector Palatine, leading to the speculation that, given the presence of the Jacobean-style wedding masque in act 4, the 1611 version of the play was revised to make it more suitable to the occasion of a wedding. The addition of the masque (as well as the elaborate stage directions with their emphasis on spectacle) has led some scholars to argue that *The Tempest* was specifically written or revised for a court audience (Kermode, p. xxii). However, many have also argued that such an argument overemphasizes the importance of *The Tempest* at the wedding festivities, especially since it was only one of fourteen plays performed, many of which were not particularly tied to the theme of marriage. Some have also argued that the masque can be read as an integral part of the play's structure and theme, despite its necessarily distinct style, and that the non-court venues, such as the Blackfriars Theatre and the Globe, had elaborate stage machinery for special effects. In any case, the existence of the two court records does not contradict the likelihood that the play was first performed at the Blackfriars Theatre. Few contemporary allusions to the play remain, though Ben Jonson's reference to it in his satiric play *Bartholomew Fair* suggests that it was clearly popular. Samuel Pepys, reports George C. D. Odell in *Shakespeare from Betterton to Irving* (New York: Scribner, 1920), saw the play eight times (1.22), though not all these performances were of Shakespeare's version. Pepys also saw John Dryden and William Davenant's 1667 lighthearted comedic adaptation, which began with much lightning and thunder, an agitated sea, darting spirits, a sinking ship, and a shower of fire. This adaptation was very popular well into the nineteenth century, despite its major changes to the original, including providing Miranda with a sister, Dorinda, and a male parallel, Hippolito, and giving Caliban a sister named Sycorax. Thomas Shadwell's 1674 Dorset Gardens production also featured an agitated sea and Ariel flying from top to bottom of the stage (Coursen, p. 145). David Garrick's eighteenth-century version cut 442 lines and added only fourteen, but not until 1838 was Shakespeare's original production again performed in its entirety, without the musical comedy additions of characters and spectacle, thanks to Charles Macready's restoration of Shakespeare's text (Coursen, p. 146).

Charles Kean's version, presented at the Princess Theatre (London) in 1857, featured elaborate machinery, necessitating 140 stagehands to produce the effects (Coursen, p. 146). Eighteenth- and nineteenth-century productions cut the words of the opening scene, substituting music and storm sounds. F. R. Benson's first performance of the play at Stratford-upon-Avon, in 1891, substituted Haydn's *Der Sturm* for dialogue and had Prospero waving his wand at a painted backdrop of a shipwreck and airborne spirits. Ariel was played as a female, despite Shakespearean pronouns to the contrary. There were few early twentieth-century performances, but a 1945 New York City production with the black actor Canada Lee as Caliban opened the gateway to modern revivals of the play.

Lindley describes the striking effects of the 1951 Mermaid Theatre (London) production, with its claps of thunder, rigging falling from above, mariners clambering up through a trap-door, courtiers reeling in through side entrances, the illusion of hurricane-force seas, and no word of the text lost (9). In America, experiments with theaters in the round in the 1960s and 1970s led to interesting productions that brought audiences into the midst of the action, with spirits running up and down the aisles, sailors falling into the sea of viewers, and Ferdinand and Miranda playing chess only a few arm's lengths away from the audience. The intimacy of such performances (like the Dallas 1966 theater-in-the-round production) brought to life for modern playgoers the intimacy of the Elizabethan stage.

A 1970 Jonathan Miller production at the Mermaid Theatre, London, cast two black actors to depict Caliban as an uneducated field hand and Ariel as a clever house slave so that Prospero's role was defined and limited in colonialist terms (Coursen, p. 154). Aimé Césaire's *A Tempest* (1969), a rewriting of Shakespeare's play, prescribed the use of masks to signify racial identity, with Caliban black, Ariel mulatto (both Prospero's slaves), with a Yoruba trickster god, and with the action a struggle between a colonizing European master and the colonized indigenous slaves (see "Addicted to Race: Performativity, Agency, and Cesaire's *A Tempest*," *College Literature* 25 [Spring 1998]: 17–30).

(Left to right) Frank Langella as Prospero, B. D. Wong as Ariel, and Jill Larson as Miranda in the Roundabout Theatre Company's 1989–1990 production of *The Tempest*. Courtesy of Photofest.

Peter Hall's 1974 minimalist production purposely downplayed and silenced the external storm with only a few sounds to punctuate the dialogue in order to make the internal storm of the second scene more noisy (Roger Warren, *Staging Shakespeare's Late Plays* [Oxford: Clarendon P, 1990], 160–161). Hall's production featured John Gielgud as one of the most striking of modern Prosperos, a performer who communicated a sense of balance and control, with reason controlling passion and bringing civilization amid savagery, lonely and detached.

The physically powerful tempest in Giorgio Strehler's Italian production (Milan,

1978) lasted five minutes, with the billowing sea reproduced by a billowing silken cloth and with Prospero at scene's end revealing the sixteen stagehands who produced the effect. In this production, Prospero's magic is that of the theater. He has such powers as a director would possess, no more and no less. Ariel flies, but the audience can see the wire and harness that allow that movement. When Prospero breaks his staff at the end of the play, the set collapses. Ariel is again played by a woman; Prospero frees her by releasing her from her cable. (See Dennis Kennedy, *Looking at Shakespeare: A Visual History of Twentieth-Century Performance* [Cambridge: Cambridge UP, 1993], 305.)

*Prospero's Books* (London: Chatto and Windus, 1991), Peter Greenaway's formidable adaptation of Shakespeare's *The Tempest*, works at three separate levels: (1) as a homage to Sir John Gielgud, who plays Prospero; (2) as a showcase for the next wave of film and video technology; and (3) as the latest phase of Greenaway's exploration of the potential of cinema as an art form. Greenaway uses the latest video technology to layer his haunting images and to create three overlapping or superimposed images. For Greenaway, the entire play unfolds in Prospero's mind. This version is visually lush and sensuous.

British filmmaker Derek Jarman's 1979 screen adaptation of *The Tempest* anticipated many of the distinctive strategies of Peter Greenaway's piece, argue Diana Harris and Macdonald Jackson in "Stormy Weather: Derek Jarman's *The Tempest*" (*Literature Film Quarterly* 25 [1997]: 90–98). Jarman eliminated a great deal of Shakespeare's dialogue and rearranged what he kept, transforming Prospero (played by Heathcote Williams) from a wise ruler and stand-in for Shakespeare into a deeply disturbed protagonist, tyrannical, repressive, and insecure, a representative "of British empire-building which robs the indigenous peoples of their native inheritance in the name of civilization" (90). They find Jarman's "anti-establishment style" challenging or mocking "the designs of empire," as well as "gender stereotyping, and other forms of ideological policing" (98).

## EXPLICATION OF KEY PASSAGES

**2.1.148–168. "I' th' commonwealth . . . the golden age."** In an attempt to distract Alonso from grieving for his son, Ferdinand, who is apparently drowned, Gonzalo offers a utopian vision of government. So enchanted is he by the island, its fresh air, lush grace, and abundant food that Gonzalo begins to fantasize about the commonwealth he would like to establish here. His rule would differ from any other. There would be no commerce or business, no magistrates or judges, no legal documents (maybe no schools or places of required learning), no rich, no poor, no servants, no contracts, no legal matters of any sort, not even private property or even tilled land. His idea is a return to nature and natural ways, before writing and laws that limited and restricted behavior and action. Nor would anyone need coined money or gold or other traditional means of trade or usury. There would be no need to have a profession or work; everyone could be "idle" (2.1.155), enjoying the fruits of nature rather than working hard for sustenance; all would be innocent and pure. Most importantly, there would be no kings or rulers or class system of any kind. All would be equal, and all would live as they pleased. There would be no treason or felony, no torture, no weapons of any kind. Instead, everything would be in harmony with nature and all would benefit from the abundance of nature, which would produce to perfection (much as Caliban says the island does with its berries and clams and readily available food of every sort). His populace would be nature's children, innocent (Sebastian and Antonio joke about the citizens all being "whores and knaves," 2.1.167, if there were no marriages and no work). This vision draws from the biblical Eden, Thomas More's *Utopia* (1516), Montaigne's essay "Of Cannibals," and narratives about Bermuda (see "Sources for the Play"). This speech reveals Gonzalo's good nature and offers one vision of government.

In response to such idealism, the cynical and disparaging Antonio and Sebastian mock Gonzalo, arguing that in such a free and equal paradise, Gonzalo would still wish to be king, so that his final statement of no king or sovereign contradicts his beginning. While Gonzalo's vision is mocked in the text, it is disparaged by the most villainous of characters in the entire play. By implication then, Gonzalo is voicing a positive image of a "brave new world" (5.1.183) peopled by free men and women. Some critics have taken this to be Shakespeare's image of the potentials of the American colonies, if the impulse for trade and exploitation of native peoples could be overcome. Others have seen it to some degree reflected in the island lives of Prospero and Miranda, while still others have noted its direct contrast to the model provided by Prospero of a benevolent master, supervising and controlling as magistrates did.

**4.1.57–138. "Now come, my Ariel . . . In country footing."** Prospero calls on Ariel to produce an entertainment for the newly betrothed Ferdinand and Miranda, a masque of a type popular in the early seventeenth century for weddings of state and court functions. Masques like this one were ritualistic and highly stylized. Iris, the messenger of the gods and goddess of the rainbow, calls on Ceres to come forth and join in the celebration of a true love contract. Ceres, credited with teaching humans agriculture and civilized ways, presides over the masque as a symbol of order and plenty. Ceres is fearful of encountering Venus, who helped Pluto kidnap Ceres' daughter, Proserpine, in a nature myth not only explaining the reason for the seasons but also thematically relevant to the events that follow: the dark and light of life, good times and bad, evil mixed with good. Her lesson is one the innocent Miranda has yet to learn. Juno, Ceres, and Iris together bless the engaged couple and wish them prosperity and honor, a long life together, many children, and great joy. Their message reinforces Prospero's injunction against sex before marriage (4.1.96–97). The poetry celebrates the fecundity of nature and growing things.

However, just as Iris is calling on the nymphs and reapers to join in a celebratory dance, the magic and high dignity of the masque are interrupted by the drunken sounds of Caliban and crew. Prospero ended up on the island because he had been so absorbed in his art that he ignored the real danger of his brother's ambition; here he is again absorbed but is able to shake himself from his reverie, and he becomes conscious of events he must act on. Prospero admits he has been so entranced by the product of his own magic (a lesson to the young couple in the palatable guise of an entertainment) that he forgot to keep track of what was going on in the real world (of Shakespeare's play): a plot on his life. He is humanized here, transported by his truly enchanting magic but aware of his mortality, his forgetfulness, and the limits of that magic.

**4.1.148–163. "Our revels . . . with a sleep."** When Ferdinand and Miranda remark on Prospero's disturbed and angry passion, these lines are Prospero's reply. He calls an end to the revels, and the masque disappears instantaneously. He notes that the actors, all spirits, because of their nature, were bound to melt into thin air. In fact, all the world's a stage, with its backdrop scenery of palaces and temples, of high towers; and all of these, indeed, "the great globe itself" (4.1.153) as both world and Globe Theatre, and all its inhabitants, are ephemeral, an "insubstantial pageant" (4.1.155) that will fade away and leave no trace behind. His works of magic are all in vain, made of "baseless fabric" (4.1.151) that will not last. From the insubstantiality of the masque, Prospero broadens his statement to include the insubstantiality of our lives, which are "little," are the stuff of dreams rather than reality (4.1.156–157), and which end in a "sleep" or death (4.1.158).

This is a somber moment in the play, as Prospero seems to realize his human frailty, his human limitations. Prospero apologizes to Ferdinand for his inattention, uses the excuse of the weakness of age and a troubled brain, and encourages the young man to rest a bit in Prospero's cave while Prospero takes a short walk to calm his agitated mind. This admission of his "weakness" (4.1.159) and "infirmity" (4.1.160) explains the events that follow, as he renounces his magic and, as he says at the play's end, makes every third thought a contemplation of the waiting grave. His musings here on the emptiness of life echo those of Hamlet as he contemplates the skull of the court jester.

**5.1.33–57. "Ye elves of hills . . . my book."** These lines are Prospero's farewell to his magic powers. He calls on fairies and elves, "demi-puppets" (5.1.36), who nightly flit by moonlight throughout nature (on land and water, along the sea shore, in the air), leaving no footprints as they perform odd tasks like making the sour-grass rings around toadstools (sometimes called fairy rings) and growing mushrooms overnight. They "rejoice / To hear the solemn curfew" (5.1.39–40) because afterward they can walk abroad and get up to mischief. These masters of their own domain have helped Prospero eclipse the noonday sun, make winds blow, cause turbulent storms at sea, create roaring thunder, and cause lightning to strike at his command (even against Jove's sacred oak tree). With their help, Prospero has made strong mountains shake, pulled up pine trees and cedars by the roots, and even opened graves and made dead men walk. This "potent art," this "rough magic" (5.1.50), which enables him to turn the violent powers of nature against his enemies, he here renounces.

He uses this art one last time to conjure "heavenly music" (5.1.52) of the sort the audience can hear even as he speaks, music that works upon the senses with soothing, healing power. Then he will break his magic staff and bury it deep in the earth, where no one can find it to use its powers again. His final source of magic, his book of spells, he will send deeper into the sea than any human devices for measurement can go.

This is an important speech, for Prospero is willingly and purposefully rejecting the supernatural powers that have helped him survive, protect his daughter, and safely confront his enemies. Now he will stand alone as one human being before another, bereft of special effects, armed only with his reason and his heart. Shakespeare's description derives from Ovid, particularly Medea's speeches in the *Metamorphoses* wherein she recounts her power over elves and spirits to call forth fire and dim the heavens. However, unlike the sorceress in Shakespeare's source, and Sycorax, the witch whose evil acts Prospero disparages, Prospero is a mature man who is rejecting magical powers, whether black or white magic, and who is prepared to face the harshness of reality and the corruption of human nature without props. When Prospero was young, his fascination with the study of magic lost him his dukedom. He paid no attention to his brother's steady acquisition of power. Now his arts have served his purposes well, helping him right the wrongs of the past, with no harm to any involved. He is far more cynical than he was when he set out unwilling on the journey that brought him to the island, but he is also more of a man of the world than he was in his youth. He sees hope for the future in the reconciliation of enemies, in the marriage that makes allies of two households. At the same time, he is firmly aware of the dangers still latent in his brother Antonio and Sebastian, and of the chaos that the lower orders (Stephano, Trinculo, Caliban) could unleash.

Yet when he chooses to give up his magic, he has won a battle within himself. He accepts responsibility for Caliban, Sycorax's offspring, and the dark qualities that Caliban represents to him: "this thing of darkness I / Acknowledge mine" (5.1.275–276). He uses his one remaining source of magic, the spirit Ariel, who will be set free once he has completed this final act, to protect the young couple on their journey to Naples, to speed their ships with gentle breezes, and to ensure the safe arrival of friends and former enemies alike.

Interestingly, Prospero's relinquishing of his magic is followed shortly by descriptions of its power. In 5.1.229–239, the stunned boatswain describes the strange fate of the ship, including the noises ("roaring, shrieking, howling, jingling chains" and other diverse and horrible sounds, 5.1.233). When Alonso asks about such matters, Prospero modestly promises to reveal his devices later on, revelations put off until there is more leisure, perhaps before they sail, perhaps never.

**Epilogue. "Now my charms . . . set me free."** The final twenty lines of the play in a nutshell are a request that the audience by applauding to show their appreciation for a job well done thereby free the actors to go home. The passage parallels Puck's similar request in *A Midsummer Night's Dream*. Yet here, these rhymed couplets are responsible in large part for critical controversy about this play being Shakespeare's farewell to the stage. In act 5 Prospero had abjured his magic; in act 4 he suggested the insubstantiality of life and of the great globe of the world, a reference unquestionably tied to Shakespeare's own Globe Theatre. The play has demonstrated his powers to create fantasies, to manipulate characters, to perform magic. Now at the play's close, the magic is over. The charming play is done, and the charmer's task complete. Worn out from his exertions, almost faint from his heavy tasks, he himself is trapped in a magic spell of enchantment—one produced by the audience. His dukedom restored, Prospero is ready to return to the ordinary life he left behind when he landed on the magic island that has been his home for so many years. Now the island is bare; the magic gone.

However, just as Ariel was bound to the island and to Prospero until released, so Prospero (and the actor who plays him) is bound on the little island of the stage until released by the applause of the audience. If they clap their approval of this play, a reward for his performance, he will be content to sail away to Naples, to other duties and other projects. His aim has been to please, but if they will not clap their approval of his efforts, he will remain bound to the stage. In other words, the actor who played Prospero has stepped out of the illusion of the play to join the real world, a character from fiction no longer in his fictional role. The final couplet sums up the play, crimes pardoned, the enchanted and enchanter freed. Now it is the audience that has the power of Prospero to forgive error and to restore reality, and the actor/character/author who is the guilty party seeking pardon. If the spectators wish to be pardoned in the future for their offences, say the final lines, then they should be generous, as Prospero was generous, and free the actor to go about his private business. This is a most unusual ending for a Shakespearean play. The audience holds the power and determines what will happen next, whether the character Prospero will go on to Naples or not, whether the actor playing his role will go home satisfied or not, whether the author will complete his play or not. All remains unfinished and unresolved until the audience claps. Then the spell will truly be broken, and reality restored.

If this is indeed Shakespeare's valedictory speech, then he is by analogy asking for validation of his career and permission to quit it. If this is not Shakespeare's last work and final farewell, and the ending is simply Prospero's leave-taking, the close is still startling in its modernity. Like an early twentieth-century modernist playwright, Shakespeare violates theatrical illusion, highlighting the artificiality of the artistic process. It is a bravura ending, whether of a play or a career.

## Annotated Bibliography

Breight, Curt. "'Treason Doth Never Prosper': *The Tempest* and the Discourse of Treason." *Shakespeare Quarterly* 41 (1990): 1–28. Prospero's stage managing a series of fictional conspiracies suggests subversively the possibility that so-called treasonous plots might have been stage managed by monarchs to display their power.

Cefalu, Paul A. "Rethinking the Discourse of Colonialism in Economic Terms: Shakespeare's *The Tempest*, Captain John Smith's Virginia Narratives, and the English Response to Vagrancy." *Shakespeare Studies* 28 (2000): 85–119. Cefalu explores the play in the larger context of colonialism, providing background historical information on the Virginia narratives of author John Smith and on the decline of feudalism and rise of capitalism in England.

Coursen, H. R. *"The Tempest": A Guide to the Play*. Westport, CT: Greenwood P, 2000. This valuable work provides a thorough approach to the play, with sections on textual history, contexts and sources, dramatic structure, themes, critical approaches, and the play in performance.

Fox-Good, Jacob. "Other Voices: The Sweet, Dangerous Air(s) of Shakespeare's *Tempest*." *Shakespeare Studies* 24 (1996): 241–274. Fox-Good critiques the music in the play, discussing the centrality of sound, despite assumptions about music that have made critics slight its significance, and providing background on Shakespeare's music.

Hamlin, William. "Men of Inde: Renaissance Ethnography and *The Tempest*." *Shakespeare Studies* 22 (1994): 15–45. Hamlin contextualizes the play (English colonialism in the late sixteenth and early seventeenth centuries), analyzes the dramatic allusions, samples the interchanges and dramatic incidents, explores the reciprocity of the relationship between Prospero and Caliban, and comments on what other critics have argued about Shakespeare's style of discourse.

Murphy, Patrick M., ed. *"The Tempest": Critical Essays*. London: Routledge, 2001. Part of the *Shakespeare Criticism* series, this book provides a history of interpretations of the play, followed by essays from the early critics like John Dryden, Samuel Taylor Coleridge, and William Hazlitt as well as later definitive pieces by critics like Arthur Kinney, Stephen Orgel, and Richard Wheeler; a section on performances of the plays; and then a final section on twenty-first-century essays on the playwright's voice, print history, political allegory, and modernist versions of the play. This work defines the critical issues of the play.

Schneider, Ben Ross. "Are We Being Historical Yet?: Colonialist Interpretations of Shakespeare's *Tempest*." *Shakespeare Studies* 23 (1995): 120–145. Schneider challenges historicists who marginalize the play as a paradigm of early modern colonialism and a justification of colonial oppression by British imperialists. He explores the storm as representation of social disorder, Prospero's self-contradictory and contradicted prologue, the idea that Shakespeare is the universal man, and images of anger and freedom in the play.

Simonds, Peggy Muñoz, and Clifford Davidson. "'Sweet Power of Music': The Political Magic of the 'Miraculous Harp' in Shakespeare's *The Tempest*." *Comparative Drama* 29 (1995): 61–90. The article studies the mythological use of Orpheus in the play: the symbolization of Orpheus in the iconography of Renaissance emblem books and civic pageants, the relationship between the cosmic aspects of Orphic music and human politics, and the meaning of the Renaissance vision of marriage.

Slights, Jessica. "Rape and the Romanticization of Shakespeare's Miranda." *Studies in English Literature* (John Hopkins) 41 (Spring 2001): 357–377. Slights provides a feminist reading, with Miranda embodying alternative models of selfhood, moral agency, and community life.

Vaughan, Alden T., and Virginia Mason Vaughan. *Shakespeare's Caliban: A Cultural History*. Cambridge: Cambridge UP, 1991. This text explores Caliban as a durable cultural signifier, his flexible image appropriated and reshaped from generation to generation to fit the concerns and assumptions of the time. This interesting study begins with Caliban's debut on the Elizabethan stage, explores the historical and literary contexts that spawned him, and then tackles the varied receptions reflected in literary criticism in England and America. Discusses colonial metaphors, stage and screen history, as well as artists' renditions and modern poetic invocations. It concludes with an overview of Caliban through all his transformations in literary and artistic criticism, his odyssey toward our modern vision of him and an unknown future transformation that will fit other philosophic, psychological, historical, and sociological needs.

# The Two Noble Kinsmen

## Yashdip S. Bains

### PLOT SUMMARY

**Prologue.** The prologue likens new plays to maidenheads: "Much follow'd both, for both much money gi'n, / If they stand sound and well" (ll. 2–3). In addition to the bawdy humor intended to amuse, this speech introduces the play's themes of virginity and marriage. The speech goes on to acknowledge the play's debt to Chaucer; hence the play should please everyone.

**1.1.** A boy sings a wedding song, or epithalamium, "Roses, their sharp spines being gone" (1.1.1–24). Theseus, duke of Athens, and Hippolyta (queen of the Amazons and recently captured by Theseus), in the company of the Athenian general Pirithous and Hippolyta's sister, Emilia, enter for their wedding. They see three mourning queens, whose husbands have died in battle against Creon of Thebes and have been refused burial. Kneeling before Theseus, they plead that he should delay his marriage until he has subdued Creon. After being urged by Hippolyta and Emilia, Theseus grants their request.

**1.2.** Palamon and Arcite, two cousins in Thebes, criticize the cruel nature of Creon's rule, but they still get ready to fight for Creon against Theseus.

**1.3.** Pirithous says farewell to Hippolyta and Emilia, who are considering the contrary possibilities of same-sex friendship and love. Emilia reminisces about her dead friend, Flavina.

**1.4.** Theseus defeats Creon. Theseus notices the wounded Palamon and Arcite, who had fought nobly. He orders that the two should be attended to but kept in prison.

**1.5.** The three queens prepare for the funerals of their husbands to the dirge, "Urns and odors bring away" (1.5.1–10) and depart after solemn farewells.

**2.1.** The Wooer discusses with the Jailer his upcoming marriage with the Jailer's Daughter, who feels sorry for and admires Palamon and Arcite, her father's prisoners.

**2.2.** Palamon and Arcite lament their loss of liberty and take vows of eternal friendship. Emilia is strolling in her garden when Palamon and then Arcite see her from their prison window. Both of them fall instantly in love with her and become jealous rivals. Theseus pardons Arcite but insists that Arcite live permanently in Thebes, so the Jailer releases him. Palamon finds himself confined to a windowless cell.

**2.3.** Arcite puts on a disguise to stay near Emilia. When some countrymen tell him that Theseus is sponsoring wrestling matches and races, Arcite welcomes the opportunity to show his strength—and to see Emilia.

**2.4.** The Jailer's Daughter indulges her fantasies over Palamon and plans his escape so that he will love her in gratitude.

**2.5.** Arcite wins the wrestling contest, and Pirithous appoints him servant to Emilia.

**2.6.** The Jailer's Daughter has let Palamon escape to the woods. She prepares to leave her father's house and to join him with food and files to cut off his shackles.

**3.1.** Theseus, Emilia, and their party go into the woods for their May morning hunt, and Arcite goes there, too. Arcite savors his proximity to Emilia and imagines that Palamon would be jealous over his good fortune. Just then Palamon appears out of the bush and challenges Arcite. Arcite consents to bring meat, wine, and files for his cousin, and the two agree to fight a duel after Palamon recovers his health.

**3.2.** The Jailer's Daughter has been searching in vain for Palamon in the woods. She worries that wolves may have devoured him. She notes that her father has been sentenced to death because he is suspected of helping Palamon escape. Thinking Palamon dead, she wishes she were, too.

**3.3.** While eating and drinking, Palamon and Arcite exchange memories of their loves in the past.

**3.4.** The Jailer's Daughter has lost her mind and begins to hallucinate.

**3.5.** Gerrold, a schoolmaster, is rehearsing five countrymen (one dressed as a "bavian," that is, a baboon), Nell and four other country wenches, and a taborer for a morris dance in Theseus's presence. They discover they need a sixth woman and take the Jailer's Daughter in. The schoolmaster welcomes Theseus and his party with his rhyming oration, and the dancers entertain the group.

**3.6.** Getting ready for a duel, Arcite meets Palamon, whom he supplies with a sword and armor. They help each other to arm themselves, but their plans are frustrated with the unexpected appearance of Theseus, Hippolyta, Emilia and Pirithous. Theseus finds out who they are and why they are engaged in a clash. He condemns the two to death. Emilia and Hippolyta beg for their pardon. Arcite and Palamon reject Emilia's proposal that they go into exile. They do not wish to abandon their dispute over Emilia, and she refuses to choose one or the other. Theseus decides to let them fight a duel in a month when each will appear with three knights. The winner will wed Emilia, and the loser and his companions will be executed.

**4.1.** The Second Friend relieves the Jailer's anxiety by telling him that, according to Palamon, his Daughter had helped him escape from prison. Theseus therefore has pardoned the Jailer. The Wooer informs the Jailer that his daughter has gone mad. The Wooer has seen her wandering in the woods and singing mad tales of Palamon's strength. The Jailer's Daughter comes in and fantasizes taking a boat in search of Palamon. The Jailer and others go along with her fancies to keep her calm.

**4.2.** Emilia scrutinizes the pictures of Arcite and Palamon and still cannot choose between them. Theseus praises the companions Arcite and Palamon have enlisted for their duel.

**4.3.** The Jailer and the Wooer consult a doctor, who speaks to the Jailer's Daughter and recommends that the Wooer should feed her fantasy and pretend to be Palamon.

**5.1.** Palamon and Arcite bid farewell to Theseus and his party. Arcite kneels before the altar of Mars, and the god blesses him with clanging of armor and thunder. Palamon kneels before the altar of Venus, who shows her approval through her music and fluttering doves. Praying to Diana, Emilia agrees to marry the winner of the duel if she cannot stay a maid. Diana sends her away with a sudden twang of musical instruments, and a rose falls from the tree, indicating that Emilia will be married.

**5.2.** The Wooer, dressed like Palamon, is following the doctor's advice. As the scene ends, the Wooer and the Jailer's Daughter go off to bed.

**5.3.** Emilia is too nervous to attend the fight, but she follows it from offstage shouts and a servant's report. Theseus introduces Arcite, who has won the combat. Arcite speaks emotionally of the vanquished Palamon's nobility and bravery.

**5.4.** Palamon gives his purse to the Jailer for his Daughter's marriage and places his head on the block for execution. Pirithous enters in haste and reports that Arcite has suffered injuries when his horse trampled him during his entry into Athens. Theseus and others bring Arcite in on a chair. Arcite offers Emilia to Palamon and dies with a kiss from her. The conquered man has triumphed, and the victor has lost.

**Epilogue.** Asking the audience if they liked the play, the Epilogue hopes that they will have many chances "to prolong / Your old loves to us" (ll. 16–17).

## PUBLICATION HISTORY

Not included in the First Folio (1623), *The Two Noble Kinsmen* was entered in the Stationers' Register (the list of books licensed to be printed) on April 8, 1634, and published in a quarto the same year by Thomas Cotes for John Waterson. According to the title page, it was "Written by the memorable Worthies of their time; Mr. John Fletcher, and Mr. William Shakespeare, Gent." After analyzing the variant spelling and distinctive features of style, meter, and diction, most editors divide the play into two mismatched halves allotted to Shakespeare and Fletcher (1579–1625) in the following way:

| | |
|---|---|
| 1.1–2.1. | Shakespeare (but 1.4 and 1.5 uncertain) |
| 2.2–2.6. | Fletcher |
| 3.1. | Shakespeare |
| 3.2–5.1.33. | Fletcher (but 4.3 uncertain) |
| 5.1.34–173. | Shakespeare |
| 5.2. | Fletcher |
| 5.3–5.4. | Shakespeare |

The prologue and epilogue as well as the play's opening song are also assigned to Fletcher. Brian Vickers divides the play slightly differently, giving Shakespeare 1.1–1.4, 2.1, 3.1, 4.3, 5.1.34–173, and 5.3–5.4 and the rest to Fletcher.

In other words, Shakespeare essentially wrote the scenes with Theseus and the opening and end of the Palamon-Arcite plot. Fletcher wrote the scenes of rivalry between Arcite and Palamon and the Jailer's Daughter's scenes. It appears that Fletcher may have collaborated with Shakespeare in the writing of at least one other late play, *Cardenio* (a lost play) and perhaps *Henry VIII*. Nobody knows anything about the method of collaboration between the two playwrights. Hence the dual authorship makes it difficult to assign portions of the text to Fletcher or Shakespeare with any certainty.

A substantially altered version of the play, entitled *The Rivals*, usually attributed to Sir William Davenant, appeared anonymously in 1668. The second Beaumont and Fletcher Folio of 1679 included *The Two Noble Kinsmen*, and until the end of the twentieth century it was treated as part of the Fletcher canon.

The play was most probably written in 1613 and performed at the Blackfriars Theatre. Ben Jonson's *Bartholomew Fair*, dated "the one and thirtieth day of October, 1614," refers to Palamon. The schoolmaster's entertainment in 3.5 of *The Two Nobe Kinsmen* is borrowed from Francis Beaumont's *Inner Temple and Gray's Inn Mask*, performed at Whitehall on February 20, 1613. Beaumont and Fletcher were frequent collaborators. Perhaps the same troupe of dancers appeared in *The Two Noble Kinsmen* and in Beaumont's masque.

## SOURCES FOR THE PLAY

Shakespeare acknowledged his primary source in the Prologue (ll. 13–14): "Chaucer (of all admir'd) the story gives; / There constant to eternity it lives." The play stages Chaucer's "The Knight's Tale," the first of *The Canterbury Tales*. Shakespeare and Fletcher might have been familiar with Chaucer's source, Boccaccio's *Teseida*, in which Arcite's horse crushes him by falling backward on him instead of throwing him off headlong as in Chaucer. The two collaborators modified Chaucer's tale considerably by altering the scenes of the three queens interrupting the progress of Theseus's marriage and seeking his help in defeating Creon. In Chaucer, for example, the queens are called "A compaignye of ladyes, tweye and tweye, / Ech after oother" (I. 898–899). Only one of them, "whilom wyf to kyng Cappaneus" (I. 932), speaks to Theseus. Shakespeare and Fletcher changed Chaucer also by adding the condition that the loser of the duel between Arcite and Palamon must die.

Shakespeare and Fletcher invented the scenes with the Jailer's Daughter who helps Palamon in escaping from prison and who goes mad on account of her unrequited love for Palamon. The Jailer's Daughter appears in nine complete scenes and in the morris dance as the sixth wench. The playwrights created elaborate scenes in which the countrymen discuss May games and tell Arcite about them (2.3) and the morris dance in 3.5.

## STRUCTURE AND PLOTTING

This play contains many of the structural features of romances like *The Winter's Tale* and *The Tempest*, and it can be best examined as a tragicomedy that culminates in a funeral and a wedding. It has an elaborate, sensational, and episodic sequence of events that the playwrights inherited from Chaucer, and they made it more complicated and melodramatic by adding the Jailer's Daughter plot and a few other details. The characters are developed to the extent that they serve the plot, and the emphasis is on the narrative drive. Arcite and Palamon undertake dangerous and heroic challenges and walk a hazardous path for Emilia's hand. Their fortunes are constantly affected and altered by improbable and unlikely events. Emilia, a disciple of Diana, finds herself having to make a choice between the two kinsmen, something she had not contemplated, and she cannot bring herself to choose one or the other. In the subplot, the Jailer's Daughter is on a quest of her own, in search of Palamon and the quenching of her sexual desire.

The play opens with an elaborate wedding procession for Theseus's marriage with the Amazonian queen, Hippolyta. Three Queens interrupt the proceedings and urge Theseus to help them bury their husbands properly by defeating Creon, who has denied them this right. The first act introduces the main characters in the primary plot and provides the medieval context of chivalry and romance for a story set in classical Athens and Thebes. It underlines the ideals of nobility and friendship. Two grand spectacles of the wedding procession and the "funeral solemnity" for the burial of the kings (stage direction before 1.5.1) open and close the act. Before they leave, the Three Queens strike a somber note, saying that "death's the market-place," where diverging streets meet (1.5.16).

The first act employs a technique that is used throughout the play: interruption. Theseus must interrupt his marriage ceremony to launch a military campaign against Creon; Arcite and Palamon, unhappy at the state of Thebes under Creon, plan to leave but stay to fight in Creon's army. Emilia's friendship was cut short by Flavina's death. Palamon and Arcite, closest of friend, become rivals in love after catching a glimpse of Emilia. The Jailer's Daughter, who had helped Palamon to escape from prison, begins to have mad fantasies when Palamon ignores her. Thus, her union with the Wooer is delayed. The kinsmen, fighting in the woods, are interrupted by the unexpected appearance of Theseus. Theseus issues a decree for their death, but changes his order after the pleas of Hippolyta, Emilia, and Pirithous. Emilia's determination to stay a virgin is softened when she realizes that the two cousins have fallen in love with her; she pities them and feels attracted to them. Arcite wins the duel but is destroyed by a fatal accident. Palamon's execution is stopped, and he gets Emilia's hand. The play ends with a funeral to be followed by Palamon's wedding.

The interrupted action and sudden turns in the plot reinforce the feeling that the course of life does not run smoothly for anybody. Gods, fortune, and unexpected events produce an ominous atmosphere of incompletion. Hence Paula Berggren characterizes the play as "an interrupted poem, with a beginning that sets out a group of problems that never truly resolve themselves and an ending that is glorious, terrifying, and finally mute in the face of the universe it conjures up" ("'For what we lack / We laugh': Incompletion and *The Two Noble Kinsmen*," *Modern Language Studies* 14 [1984]: 14–15).

From the opening of act 2, the play unfolds in a pattern of scenes of the main plot alternating with those of the subplot and focusing on developments in the lives of the four principal characters. The six scenes of the second act depict the initial stages of the Jailer's Daughter's love for Palamon and the two cousins' love for Emilia. The Jailer's Daughter has been observing the prisoners: "It is a holiday to look on them" (2.1.53). In 2.2 Palamon and Arcite turn into rivals instead of friends after a glimpse of Emilia. Thus the playwrights establish a link between the three who catch the sickness of love. The Schoolmaster and the Countrymen break this order of alternating scenes with their rehearsals for Theseus and Hippolyta's marriage. Suddenly in their midst they find the Jailer's Daughter, "a dainty mad woman" (3.5.72) who suits their needs perfectly. Theseus, Pirithous, Hippolyta, Emilia,

Arcite, and train enter without any warning. The entertainers "are all made" (3.5.158) when Theseus sees them "all rewarded" (3.5.152).

The main plot of Palamon and Arcite complements and modifies that of the Jailer's Daughter, who stands as a counterpart to Emilia. Both Emilia and the Jailer's Daughter are faced with a conflict—one's lack of desire for a man and the other's intense yearning for one. Neither can have what she wants. The Jailer's Daughter cannot marry Palamon, and Emilia cannot remain a virgin. Both are pathetic figures who have difficulty maintaining their balance. Shakespeare and Fletcher create a tragicomedy by interweaving the noble kinsmen's pursuit of a worshipper of Diana and the Jailer's Daughter's loss of her mind in search of Palamon.

## MAIN CHARACTERS

### Theseus

Theseus presides over the play not as the embodiment of ideal human behavior, but as someone who develops these traits in response to external pressures. When the Three Queens interrupt his wedding and request his help in burying their husbands by defeating Creon, Theseus is not inclined to grant their petition. His first impulse is to say: "Forward to th' temple. Leave not out a jot / O' th' sacred ceremony" (1.1.130–131). The Three Queens have to plead again, and Hippolyta and Emilia kneel before him to beg that he "do these poor queens service" (1.1.199). In the course of these pleas, Theseus begins to realize that in denying the Queens' appeal he is succumbing to his sensual desires instead of living up to his chivalric principles. Once he has agreed to their request, the three pay him a sincere tribute. They praise him for making "good / The tongue o' th' world" (1.1.226–227), that is, living up to what everyone says of him, and place him "Equal with Mars" (1.1.228). In spite of being a mortal, the Third Queen remarks, he "makes affections [passions] bend / To godlike honors" (1.1.229–230). Theseus, in other words, puts aside his desire to wed and bed Hippolyta to undertake honorable deeds worthy of the gods. Touched by the drift of their tribute, Theseus modifies his perception of himself and suggests that by "being sensually subdu'd," he would have lost his "human title" (1.1.232–233). Thus he regains his humane traits under pressure.

Theseus had encountered numerous situations when he was under pressure and did things he would not have done otherwise. He empathizes with Arcite and Palamon:

> Since I have known frights, fury, friends' behests,
> Love's provocations, zeal, a mistress' task,
> Desire of liberty, a fever, madness,
> Hath set a mark which nature could not reach to
> Without some imposition, sickness in will
> O'er-wrastling strength in reason. (1.4.40–45)

Under these varied circumstances, Theseus has made decisions that reflect his capacity to act beyond the limits of pure will.

Still, Theseus tends to act arbitrarily. He keeps Palamon in prison and releases and banishes Arcite for no apparent reason; later he orders that, since they are traitors, they "shall sleep forever" (3.6.184), that is, die. He cannot be trusted in taking the right action without some help from others. Hippolyta and Emilia intercede immediately in behalf of the two cousins. The two sisters allude to their tie of marriage, Theseus's spotless honor, his faith, his "virtues infinite" (3.6.199), and his valor, and Pirithous supports them on the basis of his friendship with Theseus and their participation in wars together. Theseus, still planning to execute the men, introduces a new element by linking Emilia with the love the two profess for her; he addresses his sister-in-law directly:

> Every day
> They'ld fight about you; hourly bring your honor
> In public question with their swords. Be wise then
> And here forget 'em; it concerns your credit
> And my oath equally. (3.6.220–224)

Emilia does not want the two cousins executed on account of their love for her. Theseus should not act in a rash and angry manner, she suggests. Finally, Arcite and Palamon agree to fight a duel for Emilia's hand.

Theseus earned fame and renown by fighting Creon to make possible the burial of the three husbands and by commuting his death penalty into a duel between Arcite and Palamon. He also provides an interpretation of the meaning of the events at the end of the play. He is a chivalric idealist who is willing to accept the outcome of strange and unpredictable events he has witnessed and participated in. In the end he observes,

> O you heavenly charmers,
> What things you make of us! For what we lack
> We laugh, for what we have are sorry, still
> Are children in some kind. Let us be thankful
> For that which is, and with you leave dispute
> That are above our question. Let's go off,
> And bear us like the time. (5.4.131–137)

Theseus has been so puzzled and mystified by events that he still feels like a child who cannot understand why things happen. The gods keep their secrets and are still a mystery to him. Human wisdom lies in not entering into disputes with gods.

## Hippolyta

One of Theseus's notable achievements is his conquest of Hippolyta, who has had a martial past. For the Second Queen, Hippolyta is a model (1.1.90). The Amazonian Queen has been a warrior and experienced the worst horrors of bloodshed. This has made her so tough that she cannot act weak and sentimental about atrocities committed on the battlefield or even cannibalism (1.3.18–22). Now that Theseus is her lord, Hippolyta can cultivate the virtues that would make her a civilized wife. Once subjugated by Theseus, she becomes a loyal and obedient spouse who is still bold enough to disagree with him at significant moments like helping the Three Queens and saving Arcite and Palamon from Theseus's sentence of execution.

## Arcite and Palamon

Shakespeare and Fletcher place Arcite and Palamon in the context of Creon's cruel wars and the deplorable conditions to which Creon has reduced Thebes. They are acutely conscious of the anger they feel at what Creon has wrought and would like to move away from him (1.2.1–12). But when they are needed in Thebes' war with Theseus, their sense of honor and kinship with Creon, their uncle, compels them to fight for their country, as Palamon explains (1.2.107–113). Arcite and Palamon have gone through similar experiences in love and war. Palamon proposes a toast "to the wenches / We have known in our days!" (3.3.28–29). Despite their bonds of blood and a shared past, one glimpse of Emilia from their prison window severs their friendship and sets them apart. Theseus adds a twist of his own by setting Arcite free and sending him into exile while keeping Palamon behind bars.

Emilia shares with the audience her feelings based on knowing the two youths. If nature were a woman she "would run mad" for Arcite: "What an eye, / Of what a fiery sparkle and quick sweetness, / Has this young prince!" (4.2.12–14). Palamon, in contrast, is "a mere dull shadow; / He's swart and meagre, of an eye as heavy / As if he had lost his mother; a still temper, / No stirring in him, no alacrity, / Of all this sprightly sharpness not a smile" (4.2.26–30). But she quickly changes her mind and perceives Arcite as "a mere gypsy" and Palamon "the noble body" (4.2.45, 44). In other words, there is little reason to prefer one to the other. Both men are paragons.

However, the playwrights (following their source) distinguish the two on the basis of their devotion to Mars and Venus. Arcite, a devotee of Mars, resolves to stay near Emilia by putting on a disguise. He tells Theseus he possesses

> A little of all noble qualities:
> I could have kept a hawk, and well have hollow'd
> To a deep cry of dogs; I dare not praise
> My feat in horsemanship, yet they that knew me
> Would say it was my best piece; last, and greatest,
> I would be thought a soldier. (2.5.10–15)

Pirithous and Theseus dub him a "perfect" and "a proper man" (2.5.15, 16). Emilia concurs with this assessment and speculates that "his mother was a wondrous handsome woman" (2.5.20). Hippolyta agrees that she has "not seen so young a man so noble" (2.5.18).

Arcite and Palamon may have the same chivalric ideals and an intense love for Emilia. They may appear to be identical, but in act 5 they show that they differ, and their final destiny places them apart. Arcite's imagination is filled with "the hearts of lions / And breath of tigers" (5.1.39–40). His "prize / Must be dragg'd out of blood" (5.1.42–43). Arcite prays to a Mars "that makes the camp a cestron [cistern] / Brimm'd with the blood of men" (5.1.46–47). As a follower of Mars's drum, he hopes to win with military skill in his battle with Palamon. Arcite believes that war provides a solution for degenerate societies (5.1.34–68). Bleeding was a treatment for diseases of excess. Blood is on Arcite's mind, and by shedding blood he thinks he can win his love.

Unlike Arcite, Palamon prays to Venus. His "argument is love" (5.1.70). For him the goddess of love possesses the "power / To call the fiercest tyrant from his rage" (5.1.77–78). Palamon has never violated her laws. He has not seduced anybody's wife and has not read the slanderous distortions of love and attacks on women by licentious wits. He has never betrayed a woman by talking about her in public. He has condemned those who boast of their sexual triumphs and demean women. Palamon's idea of love for Emilia includes sex and procreation but also a profound respect for women. The two cousins who have appeared to be so similar up to this point reveal themselves to be quite the opposite of each other, as Mars is the opposite of Venus. Arcite is from Mars, Palamon is from Venus. Mars loses; Venus gives Emilia to Palamon.

## Emilia

Emilia is a strong woman; she is, after all, sister to the former Queen of the Amazons, Hipployta. She participates actively in decision making and asserts her opinions about various matters. She acts immediately in response to the Third Queen's request for help: "What woman I may stead that is distress'd / Does bind me to her" (1.1.36–37). She is full of sympathy for the suffering Queens and shares their grief. She also claims to shun marriage, a position that Hippolyta questions, even while acknowledging that at the moment Emilia believes what she says. Emilia argues that "true love 'tween maid and maid" can be as real and as strong as that between persons of different sex (1.3.81).

As so often happens in Shakespeare's plays and sonnets, though, love proves too powerful. When she meets the disguised Arcite she tells him, "If you serve faithfully, I dare assure you / You'll find a loving mistress" (2.5.56–57). She pays close attention to the noble and heroic qualities of Arcite and Palamon when she is studying their pictures (4.2.1–54). Finally she acknowledges her erotic desire to herself: "I am sotted, / Utterly lost. My virgin's faith has fled me" (4.2.45–46). She recognizes that she now longs for both men equally.

Hence, when Emilia prays to Diana in 5.1, her speech differs from that of her namesake in *The Knight's Tale*. Chaucer's Emelye prays that Diana will let her remain a virgin and will make both Palamon and Arcite stop loving her. Only if that request cannot be granted does she ask to marry the man who loves her more. Chaucer's Emelye concludes, "Syn thou art mayde and kepere of us alle, / My maydenhede thou kepe and wel conserve, / And whil I lyve, a mayde I wol thee serve" (I.2328–2330). In the play, Emilia confesses to Diana that she loves both men so much that she cannot choose between them. Hence, she prays for the man who loves her more. As an afterthought she adds, "or else grant / The file and quality I hold I may / Continue in thy band" (5.1.160–162). At the end of the play Emilia prepares to marry Palamon and so completes her journey from innocence to experience.

## The Jailer's Daughter

The Jailer's Daughter makes a strong contrast with Emilia in her search for love and sexual fulfillment. She has a Wooer, who is negotiating his dowry with her father and getting ready for her marriage (2.1.1–14). But she also relishes observing the two prisoners. She falls in love with Palamon and so interrupts her wedding plans. She is aware of her low social status and realizes that she has little chance of a union with a nobleman. Still, she cannot help herself. Palamon kissed her once, and she says that she "lov'd my lips the better ten days after" (2.4.26). She therefore decides to help him escape.

Once she releases Palamon, the Jailer's Daughter reveals her propensity to fantasize and the possibility of losing her mind when she imagines that she would be a martyr for love if she loses her life for her crime. Palamon has not even thanked her for her brave deed, but her hope is that "this love of mine / Will take more root within him" (2.6.27–28). She imagines running off with him somewhere, and by his side, "like a shadow," she will "ever dwell" (2.6.34–35). As she wanders the woods looking for her lost lover, her mind starts to wander:

> Good night, good night, y' are gone. I am very hungry;
> Would I could find a fine frog! he would tell me
> News from all parts o' th' world. Then would I make
> A carreck of a cockleshell, and sail
> By east and north-east to the King of Pigmies,
> For he tells fortunes rarely. (3.4.11–16)

Later, believing that her father is the master of a ship, she directs him to head north to the forest "where Palamon / Lies longing for me" (4.1.144–145). She narrowly escapes the fate of the mad Ophelia when the Wooer rescues her beside a lake.

### The Jailer

The Jailer expresses much sympathy for his daughter's condition. He has observed her closely and gives a heartbreaking account of her state:

> She is continually in a harmless distemper, sleeps little, altogether without appetite, save often drinking, dreaming of another world and a better; and what broken piece of matter of soe'er she's about, the name Palamon lards it, that she farces [stuffs] ev'ry business withal, fits it to every question. (4.3.3–8)

He seeks medical help for his daughter. The Doctor gives his diagnosis: " 'Tis not an engraff'd madness, but a most thick and profound melancholy" (4.3.48–50). He prescribes that her delusion should be combated with falsehood and the Wooer should pretend to be Palamon. He also recommends that The Wooer should have sex with her. Apparently the Wooer and the Jailer's Daughter leave at the end of 5.2 to follow the doctor's advice, and apparently it works. The Jailer later tells Palamon, "Sir, she's well restor'd, / And to be married shortly" (5.4.27–28). Desire drives her mad, but it also leads to her cure.

## DEVICES AND TECHNIQUES

Ceremonies and spectacles are among the chief devices Shakespeare and Fletcher use in this tragicomedy. They present a sequence of grand and stately scenes beginning with the wedding in the opening act. Each spectacle unfolds at a slow pace toward the completion of a ceremony until an intruder or a person's decision interrupts the action and diverts it in another direction. The Three Queens send Theseus into a war with Creon. This leads to the capture of Arcite and Palamon and their imprisonment. The two kinsmen fall in love with Emilia, and this love leads finally to their duel for Emilia's hand. One interruption after another lies at the basis of new directions, movement, and action in the play. The Jailer's Daughter would have continued to be with her Wooer if Palamon had not been her father's prisoner. Her encounter with Palamon leads to her madness, which resolves itself in her marriage with the Wooer.

Shakespeare and Fletcher also draw upon the court masque form, which was popular in the early seventeenth century. Although there is no solid proof, most editors agree that the morris dance in 3.5 was based on a similar scene in the *Masque of the Inner Temple and Gray's Inn*, by Francis Beaumont, staged at Whitehall on February 20, 1613. The wedding procession in 1.1, Theseus's intervention in the duel between Palamon and Arcite in 3.6, and the prayers of Arcite, Palamon, and Emilia in 5.1 are examples of the masque.

Shakespeare and Fletcher use horses significantly in relation to Emilia and Arcite. Remembering their past knightly amusements, Palamon regrets that the two of them will never exercise their arms again and "feel our fiery horses / Like proud seas under us" (2.2.19–20). Central to their lives as knights, the horse also represents controlled or uncontrolled passion. Neptune was the god of the sea and horses. Arcite is associated especially with the horse when he tells Palamon, "When I spur / My horse, I chide him not; content and anger / In me have but one face" (3.1.106–108). Emilia is keenly interested in and owns horses. When Arcite does not have a horse, Emilia promises to get him one (2.5.53–57). Arcite thanks the Lady Fortune that Emilia has presented him with

> A brace of horses; two such steeds might well
> Be by a pair of kings back'd, in a field
> That their crowns' titles tried. (3.1.20–22)

She finally gives him a black horse in recognition of his victory over Palamon for her hand:

> a black one, owing
> Not a hair-worth of white, which some will say
> Weakens his price, and many will not buy
> His goodness with this note. (5.4.50–54)

While Arcite tries to control it, the "hot horse, hot as fire" (5.4.65) causes his death, and Emilia must grieve over the unfortunate gift she had given him.

## THEMES AND MEANINGS

*The Two Noble Kinsmen* deals with the nature of friendship between the same sexes. It takes up the conventions of chivalry and a knight's oath to serve the community and protect it from danger. Theseus, Arcite, Palamon, and Emilia try hard to live and act nobly and often put duty ahead of personal preference. Courtesy, politeness, and liberality are part of the chivalric code, as are compassion and pity for the weak. In 1.1.205–215, Theseus, for example, agrees to the request of the Three Queens for help in burying their husbands. When Theseus and his party come upon Arcite and Palamon in the forest preparing to engage in a duel, Theseus orders that both be executed, Arcite for returning from exile, Palamon for escaping from prison (3.6.184). Emilia, Hippolyta, and Pirithous appeal to his honor, faith, friendship, and valor and beg him to show mercy to the two cousins. Theseus changes his mind and orders them to return to their country and come back with three knights each to fight a duel for Emilia's hand (3.6.288–299). Although Arcite and Palamon agree that their uncle Creon is "a most unbounded tyrant," they still resolve to fight in his army because "to be neutral to him were dishonor" (1.2.63, 100). When given the opportunity to choose between Arcite and Palamon, Emilia is unable to do so because to choose one would be wrong to the other. All these decisions are rooted in the code of chivalry to which the four of them subscribe. In a display of liberality and compassion, Palamon inquires of the Jailer about his Daughter's health; Palamon and his companion knights give a purse to the father to supplement her dowry (5.4.22–35). Theseus, Arcite, Palamon, and Emilia thus pursue the high ideals of chivalry through their noble values.

Shakespeare and Fletcher take up the theme of love, rivalry, and jealousy by contrasting the sexually starved Jailer's Daughter with the Diana's devotee Emilia and by delineating the consequences of Palamon and Arcite's falling in love at first sight. Emilia is so absolute in her defense of chastity that for some time she cannot consider a life of marriage and sex. The Jailer's Daughter, in love with Palamon, is so deranged by her passion that she cannot live without sex and marriage. Emilia strives to preserve her innocence, while the Jailer's Daughter is seeking experience through sex. Theseus and Hippolyta represent the middle ground of married love in 1.1, and by the end of the play Palamon and Emilia, the Jailer's Daughter and the Wooer, will also arrive there by their different routes.

In Thebes, Palamon and Arcite were aware of "temptings" (1.2.4) and determined "to / Be masters of our manners" (1.2.43–44). In Theseus's prison, they lament that they will live "unmarried" and never enjoy "[t]he sweet embraces of a loving wife" (2.2.29–30). Catching a glimpse of Emilia in her garden, the cousins fall in love at first sight in accordance with their rules of chivalry. Love undermines their vows of loyalty, and they are no longer willing to "tell the world 'tis but a gaudy shadow" (2.2.103). They undergo a series of hardships and tests to maintain their loyalty to their love and make an arduous journey from innocence to experience.

Friendship between males with males and females with females gets tested in different ways. Pirithous and Theseus have been friends for years. As Emilia perceives it, their relationship "has more ground, is maturely season'd, / More buckled with strong judgment" (1.3.56–57). They are attached to each other in loyalty and brotherhood. Emilia and the now-dead Flavina became friends in their early girlhood and spoke of "things innocent" (1.3.60). Flavina's death left Emilia in mourning and convinced her "That the true love 'tween maid and maid may be / More than in sex dividual" (1.3.81–82). She is certain that she will never love "any that's call'd man" (1.3.85). Her ideal of chastity erodes over time, and she accepts Palamon as an unavoidable choice.

Love also undermines the friendship between Arcite and Palamon. Arcite imagines himself spending his life in prison with Palamon and notes some of the advantages of their brotherly bond:

We are an endless mine to one another;
We are one another's wife, ever begetting
New births of love; we are father, friends, acquaintance;
We are, in one another, families:
I am your heir, and you are mine; this place
Is our inheritance. (2.2.79–84)

Palamon returns this sentiment with strong conviction: "Is there record of any two that lov'd / Better than we do, Arcite?" (2.2.112–113). Everything changes drastically once they begin arguing contentiously about Emilia. Arcite employs a few wily arguments to justify his rivalry: "Am not I liable to those affections, / Those joys, griefs, angers, fears, my friend shall suffer?" (2.2.187–188). He accuses his cousin of uncourtly behavior, as if it were natural that they should fall in love and become rivals:

Why then would you deal so cunningly,
So strangely, so unlike a noble kinsman,
To love alone? Speak truly: do you think me
Unworthy of her sight? (2.2.189–192)

Then Arcite changes his premise and talks about an enemy in a battle:

Because another
First sees the enemy, shall I stand still,
And let mine honor down, and never charge? (2.2.193–195)

Rivalry has destroyed their friendship, and the two are willing to fight to the death. When Theseus is considering their deaths, Palamon even wishes that Arcite would die first "That I may tell my soul he shall not have her" (3.6.179). The happiness of one is contingent upon the other's demise. With Arcite's death, Theseus declares that Palamon's "day is length'ned, and / The blissful dew of heaven does arrouse [sprinkle] you" (5.4.103–104).

   The power of fortune and the inscrutable workings of the gods form a significant theme of the play. Responding to the appeals of the three Queens for revenge against Creon, Theseus alludes to "the fortunes" of their husbands with much "lamenting" (1.1.56–58). At the end, he acknowledges the impact of unfathomable fortune on the lives of Arcite, Palamon, Emilia, and others:

Never fortune
Did play a subtler game. The conquer'd triumphs,
The victor has the loss; yet in the passage
The gods have been most equal. (5.4.112–115)

He also recognizes that human beings are like children because they never understand the operation of the mysterious forces on individual lives:

O you heavenly charmers,
What things you make of us! For what we lack
We laugh, for what we have are sorry, still
Are children in some kind. (5.4.131–134)

The fortunes of Arcite and Palamon change so arbitrarily from their life in Thebes to their end in Theseus's Athens that they cannot possibly comprehend the twists and turns in their fates. God and gods that control the destiny of Arcite and others are mentioned thirty-six times. To the dying Arcite, Palamon cannot help saying in grief, "The gods are mighty" (5.4.87). "The impartial gods," Theseus had said early in the play, "behold who err, / And in their time chastise" (1.4.4–6). Despite all the vicissitudes of life, *The Two Noble Kinsmen* illustrates that, in Hamlet's words, "There's a divinity that shapes our ends, / Rough-hew them how we will" (*Hamlet*, 5.2.10–11).

## CRITICAL CONTROVERSIES

All the controversies about the play are the result of the authorship debate, as Potter has stressed: "The dominance of the authorship question in the nineteenth century, though it led to some close analysis of the writing, had otherwise a dire effect on criticism: whether the play had any interest outside its own historical context was seen as depending only on Shakespeare's presence in it" (96). Since the play was not entirely Shakespearean, no editor would include it in that playwright's works until Charles Knight did in 1839–1841. Even Knight omitted "without hesitation" the passages that he believed Shakespeare did not write. For example, he excluded 2.3.32–36 from the text on the ground that they were Fletcher's "grossnesses," which "are the result of impure thoughts, not the accidental reflection of loose manners. They are meant to be corrupting" (*The Works of Shakespeare*, Imperial Edition, 4 vols. [New York: Patterson and Neilson, 1873–1876?], 4.589). Similarly, W. W. Skeat, W. J. Rolfe, and W. R. Thayer edited out what they deemed the non-Shakespearean matter from their editions.

Among later critics unhappy with *The Two Noble Kinsmen* can be mentioned Theodore Spencer, who has objected that "the story of Palamon and Arcite, whether told by Boccaccio, Chaucer or Shakespeare and Fletcher, is intrinsically feeble, superficial, and undramatic" ("*The Two Noble Kinsmen*," *Modern Philology* 36 [1938–1939]: 256). Ann Thompson considers it a failure on account of its "many tensions and inconsistencies" (*Shakespeare's Chaucer: A Study in Literary Origins* [Liverpool: Liverpool UP, 1978], 166). E. Talbot Donaldson rejects it outright as "that most distressing of plays." He also dislikes it because "it is a very unpleasant one in which the dark side that Shakespeare saw in *The Knight's Tale* when he was writing *A Midsummer Night's Dream* is fulsomely re-expressed" (*The Swan at the Well: Shakespeare Reading Chaucer* [New Haven: Yale UP, 1985], 50).

The most detailed defense of the play comes from Paul Bertram, who examines its action "as falling into three movements—the war against Creon (Act I), the May Day contests (Acts II and III), and the final tournament (Act IV and V)" (265). He "refute[s] the common assumption that the play lacks any controlling organization or consistent development—that some scenes are 'easily detachable' from the rest." He argues that Palamon and Arcite "are quite effectively distinguished in the play, and the distinction is one that anyone beholding the stage would apprehend immediately, whether he were capable of articulating it in words or not. . . . Despite the careful and necessary balance in sympathy," Bertram proposes that "there is no question but that we are made to take greater interest in Palamon" (268).

The very defects for which the play had been condemned have found favor with scholars: "its remote and artificial story, its highly charged sexuality, and the difficult language of the non-Fletcherian scenes" (Potter, p. 96). Richard Hillman adopts a favorable approach on the ground that it is "possible, especially in a postmodern critical climate, to take the play's internal jars, what ever their origin . . . as integral to the text." The playwrights "expose as disingenuous and destructive, not merely the ideals of all the characters—notably including Emilia—but, more provocatively, idealism itself ("Shakespeare's Romantic Innocents and the Misappropriation of the Romance Past: The Case of *The Two Noble Kinsmen*," *Shakespeare Survey* 43 [1991]: 70–71). Alan Stewart argues that "rather than being a failed attempt at a play about idealised male friendship," it "is rather a play about a failed attempt at idealised male friendship." He suggests that "this failure derives from the juxtaposition of both classical-humanist and chivalric modes of male friendship with the realities of social relations, and a particular form of kinship, in Jacobean England" ("'Near Akin': The Trials of Friendship in *The Two Noble Kinsmen*," *Shakespeare's Last Plays: New Readings*, ed. Jennifer Richards and James Knowles [Edinburgh: Edinburgh UP, 1999], 58). Fletcher and Shakespeare, Stewart concludes, "indulge their audience in the comfortable humanist myth of *amicitia* [friendship], and the reliable codes of chivalric courtship, only to force the audience to accept the fact that ultimately these are no more than myths and codes, and that they cannot thrive together" (71).

Considering the play in terms of its treatment of "human division and separation," Julia Briggs underlines Shakespeare's "sense of the limitations set upon happiness when nothing can be gained without a corresponding loss." She stresses Shakespeare's anticipation of the themes found in modern playwrights like Samuel Beckett:

> *The Two Noble Kinsmen* comes as close as its moment allowed to questioning the existence of a benevolent providence, and in the process generated for itself a dramatic structure that enacts and even reinforces that doubt. In this respect, it anticipates, albeit at an enormous distance, the dramatic structures of Samuel Beckett, as it registers the brave new direction taken in this, the last of the late plays. ("Tears at the Wedding: Shakespeare's Last Phase," in *Shakespeare's Last Plays: New Readings*, ed. Jennifer Richards and James Knowles [Edinburgh: Edinburgh UP, 1999], 226, 227.)

## PRODUCTION HISTORY

*The Two Noble Kinsmen* had been "Presented at the Blackfriers by the Kings Maiesties servants, with great applause," according to 1634 quarto's title page. James Burbage acquired Blackfriars, an abandoned monastery in the Blackfriars section of London, in 1596, and the King's Men used it as a private theater in the winters from 1609 to 1642. This roofed house held about 700 seats, which cost more than at the public theaters. The King's Men appear to have kept the play in their repertory in the 1620s.

It seems that after the closing of the theaters in 1642, the play did not get produced again until 1928, having been absent from the stage for some three hundred years, unless one includes William Davenant's version of 1664, entitled *The Rivals*, at Lincoln's Inn Fields. The Old Vic presented *The Two Noble Kinsmen* in 1928 for six performances. Reviewers welcomed the play's medieval setting as "an experiment in prettiness" or "a fragrant, wholly unreal romance of chivalry" (Potter, p. 78). Ernest Milton played Palamon "as a comic character in a red wig" and, in the words of Rupert Hart-Davis, "gently burlesqued it for the rest of the evening, stealing the show and most of the notices" (Waith, p. 34). Reviewers like A. G. Macdonell felt embarrassed by " 'the nobility of character and sentiment' in the conversations between the kinsmen, but he was impressed by Jean Forbes-Robertson's outstanding performance, and commented that the Jailer's Daughter goes mad 'in the most beautiful, touching, Ophelian way' " (34).

The Royal Shakespeare Company first produced *The Two Noble Kinsmen* in 1986 at the Swan Theatre in Stratford-upon-Avon. Barry Kyle, its director, "attempted to recreate the sense of a warrior society (largely Japanese in imagery) with elaborate rituals of love and war, according to Potter (81). Nancy Maguire describes the beginning:

> The opening scene was like an overly ornate Kabuki drama: actors frozen in constrained poses and holding shiny gold masques to their faces formed a backdrop, and characters in red and black oriental robes flitted about the lengthy promontory stage. With startlingly surreal effect, roses fell out of Hippolyta's bosom when Theseus, after pursuing and shooting her with bow and arrows, pulled out the arrow. (*Shakespeare Bulletin* 4.4 [1986]: 8–9)

Not everyone liked the Japanese conventions. For Waith (39), they "were mainly a distraction—a needless complication added to a seventeenth-century version of a medieval elaboration of Greek legend."

Kyle received praise for "matching the difficult Shakespearean speeches with highly stylized costumes and delivery, while doing justice to the more naturalistic subplot and the less stylized parts of the main plot" (Potter, p. 82):

> These two plots were strongly linked through imagery that made the most of the sexual ritual of the morris and the references to horses: in 3.5, the Jailer's Daughter rode in upon a phallic maypole that spewed out long, white silk ribbons (referred to in rehearsal as the "ejaculation" [RSC, "Promptbook"]) and was later seen in a bridle which served as her straitjacket. (82)

"In her mad scenes," as Waith has stressed, Imogen Stubbs "made her uninhibited sexuality both amusing and touching" (40).

Shakespeare's Globe Theatre produced the play in the summer of 2000, directed by Tim Carroll. It "opens stunningly with a blizzard of confetti and the wedding procession of Theseus and Hippolyta carving its amorous, exhibitionist way at knife-point through the crowd" (Paul Taylor, London *Independent*, 7 August 2000). Carroll "opted for extreme simplicity," according to Potter ("This Distracted Globe: Summer 2000," *Shakespeare Quarterly* 52 [Spring 2001]: 126). "The one scenic device," according to Potter, "was a structure suggesting a crude siege tower or catapult, topped with the giant skull of a horse and a tail":

> As something primitive and incomprehensible, like Peter Shaffer's *Equus*, it represented the three gods who are addressed in the temple scene. In the final scene it became both Palamon's scaffold and, by a turn as sudden as that of the story, the place where Arcite lay dying. (127)

(Left to right) Brian Sgambati as Arcite and Graham Hamilton as Palamon in the Old Globe's 2004 Shakespeare Festival production of *The Two Noble Kinsmen*. Photo by Craig Schwartz © 2004.

The "simple and unspectacular" signs given by the gods in the temple scene (5.1) were "a brief flare-up of flame for Arcite, smoke for Palamon, and, for Emilia, a rose whose petals crumble in her hand" (126). Jasper Britton as Palamon and Will Keen as Arcite "manage to come across as both dangerous obsessives and endearing chumps, awkwardly trapped in extremist postures that it's an almost comic strain for them to sustain." Keen's "clean-shaven, gaunt Arcite is stoical" while "Britton's unkempt, chubbier Palamon flies into tantrums" (Kate Bassett, London

*Daily Telegraph*, 7 August 2000). In the Jailer's Daughter's "notoriously show-stealing role, which includes three consecutive soliloquies, Kate Fleetwood played to the whole house effectively but was admirably disciplined in avoiding the temptation to exploit her relationship with the audience" (Potter, p. 127).

Directed by Darko Tresnjak at the Martinson Hall in the Joseph Papp Theatre, New York City, "this strange, tonally ambiguous amalgam of comic plot and tragic lamentation is enthralling," stated Bruce Weber (*New York Times*, 21 October 2003, B1+). There was "too much emphasis on the sinister and not enough on the flip, in its other meaning: lighthearted." Mr. Tresnjak "begins the play with a forceful dramatic thrum, which makes the onset of the play's comic elements, in the jail cell scene between Palamon and Arcite, abrupt and wrenching." Emilia, played by Doan Ly, "seems to have been encouraged to overemote." Graham Hamilton, in the role of Palamon, "has identified the character's shifting passions, and plays them with physical robustness, but his delivery of the language is without any subtlety or idiosyncrasy at all." David Harbour as Arcite was "physically fastidious—there's a lovely bit in which he sets a perfect table in the middle of the forest—and his line readings give you the idea that he's seeking an identifiable personality for his portrayal." Jennifer Ikeda, as the Jailer's Daughter, "is both skillful with the language and pentameter and traces a beautiful arc from hopeful, innocent maid to bride whose happiness is twisted by delusion. Indeed, at the end of the play, she is seen in a harshly ironic image of joy, the very emblem of the final sentiment of the play," concluded Weber.

## EXPLICATION OF KEY PASSAGES

**1.3.54–82. "Yes. / You talk . . . in sex dividual."** Emilia is reminiscing about her love for Flavina, when both of them were eleven. Emilia speaks admiringly of the love between Pirithous and Theseus. Their love has a firm basis; it has lasted for many years, and it is supported with strong judgment. In their military roles, one has watered the "intertangled roots of love" for the other (1.3.60). Flavina and Emilia were innocent and inexperienced, loved simply because they did, and were like the four elements of earth, air, fire, and water, the basic parts of all material objects, that produce, without knowing what or why, wonderful results by their operation. Similarly, their souls produced the wonderful result of love. Without any further discussion or examination, Emilia approved of whatever Flavina liked and condemned what she disliked. Whenever Emilia plucked a flower and put it between her breasts, Flavina would long for it until she had found a similar one and placed it in her breast, where, like the phoenix, the flower died and was reborn as a perfume. Emilia could not wear any trifling ornament if it did not match Flavina's. She admired and imitated even the most casual choices of Flavina's dress. If Emilia happened to have come upon a new melody or hummed a new tune or musical improvisation by chance, it became a melody Flavina would also memorize and dwell on and sing it in her sleep. This account of their love, Emilia says, proves that two maids may develop a love relationship even stronger than one between two persons of different sexes.

Such same-sex bonds are common in Shakespeare's plays. One thinks of Helena and Hermia in *A Midsummer Night's Dream*, for example. Helena recalls how she and Hermia, "like two artificial gods, / Have with our needles created both one flower, / Both on one sampler, sitting on one cushion, / Both warbling one song, both in one key, / As if our hands, our sides, voices, and minds / Had been incorporate" (3.2.203–208). Rosalind and Celia in *As You Like It* are similarly inseparable. On the male side there are Valentine and Proteus in *The Two Gentlemen of Verona*, and in *Love's Labor's Lost* a group of men foreswear women's company to create an all-male academy.

Invariably love disrupts these same-sex relationships, which are treated by Shakespeare and others as a form of narcissism because it rejects otherness. This same-sex love is a stage on the way to maturity, which is represented by married love. Tragedy results when characters fail to move beyond same-sex friendship to love. Romeo chooses to avenge his friend Mercutio rather than to spare the kinsman of Juliet. Othello trusts Iago rather than Desdemona. Emilia will learn to accept a husband, just as Hippolyta predicts.

**2.4.1–33. "Why should I . . . shall love me."** The Jailer's Daughter is assessing her relationship with Palamon and the possibility of his love for her. In this soliloquy, she is trying to decide what she should do to get close to Palamon. She begins by saying that he will never love her because she is low-born and socially inferior to him. Her father is just a lowly keeper of this prison, and Palamon is a prince. She can never hope to marry him, and it would be stupid to have sex with him without marriage and become a whore. She is disgusted with the idea and with her situation, but girls are driven to extreme measures once they turn fifteen and past the age of puberty.

The Jailer's Daughter traces the evolution of her love. First she saw Palamon and was impressed by his physical beauty. Next, the Daughter felt sorry for him. Any young woman of her age and her conscience would do the same. Then, she loved him, loved him extremely, loved him infinitely. He also had a cousin who was fair like him, but in her heart the Daughter has only Palamon, who keeps her heart in turmoil. It is heaven to hear him sing in the morning, even though he sings only sad and sorrowful tunes. No gentleman speaks more nobly than he does.

When the Jailer's Daughter brings him water in the morning, he first bows to her, and then he greets her thus: "Fair gentle maid, good morrow. May thy goodness / Get thee a happy husband" (2.4.24–25). Once he kissed her; she did not wipe her lips for ten days afterwards. She wishes he would kiss her every day! He grieves too much, and seeing his misery makes her sad. What should she do to let him know she loves him, for surely she would be eager to have and enjoy sexual relations with him? Suppose she ventured to free him? How would the authorities react to her action? The Daughter resolves to set Palamon free, and in a day or two, this night or tomorrow, he will surely love her.

This speech shows how love progresses from a superficial physical attraction to deep emotion. It also reveals how the Jailer's Daughter can delude herself. At the beginning of her speech she acknowledges the great social gulf between herself and Palamon, and she recognizes that he will not marry her. She also understands that becoming his mistress is foolish. Yet within thirty lines she has persuaded herself that Palamon can love her, will love her, and she is apparently willing to give herself to him even without benefit of clergy.

**4.2.1–54. "Yet I may . . . cry for both!"** Because Emilia will not choose one of the two noble kinsmen, Palamon and Arcite, to marry, Theseus has decided that Palamon and Arcite will fight a duel for Emilia's hand; the winner will marry her and the loser and his knights will be executed. Emilia must accept this decision; otherwise both of them will perish. Emilia, alone with the pictures of Palamon and Arcite, is debating with herself whether she can stop the fight by choosing one or the other. She does not want such young and handsome men to die on her account.

Looking at Arcite's picture, she observes that he has a sweet face. If Nature, with all her wisdom, endowed with all the beauty she gives, and possessed of "The coy denials of young maids" (4.2.11), were to be transformed into a young woman, she (Nature) "would run mad for" Arcite (4.2.12). This young prince has beautiful eyes, full of "fiery sparkle and quick [lively] sweetness" (4.2.13). In his face, Cupid "himself sits smiling" (4.2.14). Arcite is like Ganymede, a beautiful youth whom Jove, in the form of an eagle, carried off to be his cupbearer. Eventually Ganymede formed a bright constellation, Aquarius. Arcite's forehead is like Juno's, only more pleasant, and smoother than Pelops's shoulder, which was made of ivory. (Tantalus killed his son Pelops and presented him as food to the gods; they restored him to life. Since Demeter had already eaten a part of his shoulder, they replaced it with ivory.) Emilia believes that fame and honor should take up residence on Arcite's forehead, and from there sing of the epic battles and great loves of gods and heroes.

Turning to Palamon's picture, she observes that he is nothing but Arcite's "foil" (4.2.26), who sets him off by contrast, just a pale shadow of him. Palamon is dark (in an age that valued pallor) and thin. He looks as if he has just lost his mother, and he has a lethargic temperament, without any of Arcite's animation. But then Emilia begins to change her mind. Maybe, she considers, these supposed blemishes suit Palamon. Narcissus was a serious boy but also beautiful.

Calling herself a fool, Emilia changes her mind. Kneeling to Palamon's picture, Emilia begs his pardon. She considers him uniquely beautiful. His eyes "command / And threaten love" (4.2.39–40), and no young maid would dare oppose them. Palamon's brown manly face possesses "a bold gravity" and is yet also inviting (4.2.41). This dark complexion is the only one that she prefers now. She sets Arcite's picture aside, calling her former favorite "a changeling . . . , a mere gipsy" compared with his cousin (4.2.44).

But in the end she cannot choose. She no longer wants to remain a virgin, but if Theseus had asked her which of the two she loved, she would have run for Arcite; if Hippolyta put the same question, she would be more inclined to Palamon. If Theseus and Hippolyta stand together and ask her which man she prefers, she will look in vain for an answer. One's affection is like a child that, presented with two equally pretty and equally sweet objects, is unable to choose between them "but must cry for both!" (4.2.54).

Emilia's speech resembles that of the Jailer's Daughter in 2.4. Both begin with an attempt to be rational. The Jailer's Daughter knows that she can never have Palamon; Emilia knows that she should choose one of the cousins and so prevent them from killing each other. But in the course of the speech passion triumphs, and neither woman can act on what she knows is right. The Jailer's Daughter wants Palamon. Emilia is so in love with both men that she cannot choose and so prevent a duel. Emilia has, however, abandoned the view that she maintained in 1.3, where she rejected heterosexual love.

**5.1.34–173. "Knights, kinsmen, lovers, . . . signs were gracious."** Arcite and Palamon have agreed to fight a duel, and the victor will marry Emilia. Before the fight, Arcite, Palamon, and Emilia pray to their respective patron deities. At the altar of

Mars Arcite addresses his supporters. He exhorts them to be brave and to banish fear. He tells his fellow knights to pray to Mars for the courage of lions and for the endurance, ferocity, and speed of tigers. Arcite urges them to remember that Emilia cannot be won without bloodshed. They must act with force and perform warlike deeds so that he can wear the garland, the victor's wreath, and also Emilia, the prize. Arcite and his knights now pray to Mars.

Arcite addresses Mars as the deity who has turned the green sea red with blood. Comets warn of Mars's approach; fields full of skulls bear witness to his mayhem; his hot winds can destroy the harvests of fertile Ceres, the goddess of fruit and grain; with his mightily armed hand appearing from warlike clouds he can destroy the turrets that had been built by masons for war and for protection against enemies. Mars should instruct Arcite, his youngest pupil, so that Arcite can triumph. Then he asks Mars for a sign.

At this point Arcite and his companions fall on their faces; they all rise and bow to the altar once they have heard the clanging of armor, with a short burst of thunder, like the sound of battle. Arcite then resumes his prayer. He speaks of Mars as the "great corrector" of corrupt times (5.1.62), the shaker of corrupt countries; he is the grand arbiter of old claims, who can heal the earth with blood when it is sick and cures the world of human excess. He assures Mars that he is taking his signs as favorable and will march forth boldly in his name. Then Arcite tells his knights to leave the stage.

Palamon and his knights observe the same rituals that Arcite and his knights have performed, but Palamon seeks to win Venus's favor for their cause. He acknowledges that this day will bring success or death. Since the subject of their quarrel is love, if Venus grants love she will give them victory. Palamon asks Venus for her favor.

At this point the members of Palamon's party advance to the altar of Venus and fall on their faces; then they kneel. They invoke the goddess as queen of secrecy in love, who can make the fiercest tyrant weep like a girl. With a single look Venus can quell conflict. She can cure a cripple faster than Apollo, the god of medicine. Venus can force a king to become a subordinate of his slave and can inspire an elderly man to dance. The goddess can make an old bachelor of seventy, who avoided passion in his youth, sing love songs.

What an immense godlike power does Venus exercise over other gods! She has scorched the sun. All wet and chaste, Diana, the goddess of chastity, threw away her hunting bow and began to sigh for Endymion under Venus's influence. Palamon prays that Venus will take him under her protection. Palamon has never spoken carelessly against Venus's code of love, never revealed a lover's secret because he did not know any, but he would not have done so even if he had known them all. He never seduced anyone else's wife, and he has never read the slanderous misrepresentations of love by licentious writers. At great feasts, he has never disclosed the private affairs of ladies but has felt embarrassed for those who did. He has been harsh to the men who grossly boast of many sexual conquests, angrily reminding them that they had mothers who are women, and in their malice they are wronging women.

Venus has breathed life into the dusty bones of a half-dead old man who, at the age of eighty, married a girl of fourteen. He was disease-ridden, and yet the young and beautiful mate of this skeleton of a man gave birth to a healthy son. The girl swore the child was his, and Palamon believed her, as who would not?

In short, Palamon is no companion of a rake who has done what he boasts of. He challenges and defies those who injure women's reputations for no reason. He rejoices with those who tried but were not successful in love. He has no regard and love for anyone who discloses the secret affairs of others in foul detail and openly discusses things that should be kept hidden. Palamon asserts that there has never been a truer lover than he. Therefore he asks for victory and for a sign of Venus's favor.

Music is heard at this moment; doves, sacred to Venus, appear. Palamon and his knights fall again upon their faces, then on their knees. Palamon addresses Venus: You who reign supreme in the lives of human beings from the age of eleven to ninety, whose hunting ground is this world and for whom people are the figurative herd of animals you shoot with love's arrows, thank you for this sign of your favor. He urges his followers to rise, bow before Venus, and depart.

Finally, Emilia enters, dressed in white, with a wreath made of wheat (symbol of fertility, like the rice commonly thrown at weddings). She approaches the altar of Diana. Addressing the chaste goddess, she tells of her plight. She is dressed as a bride but still has the heart of a virgin. She has been assigned a husband but does not know who he is. She knows she should choose either Palamon or Arcite, but she cannot because she loves them both. Therefore she asks Diana to give her the man who loves her more, or else let her remain a virgin.

Emilia had placed a silver deer (symbol of Diana as huntress) filled with incense on Diana's altar. The deer vanishes and is replaced by a rose tree bearing one rose. At first Emilia thinks that this sign means that she, like the rose, will remain "un-pluck'd" (5.1.168). But then the rose falls from the tree, and Emilia understands that she will be married. She leaves the scene uncertain of Diana's will, but she hopes that Diana will be pleased.

Shakespeare (who is credited with this portion of the play) uses this scene to reveal character. Arcite is warlike. As a worshipper of Mars, he deserves to win the battle, but Palamon as the true lover, the follower of Venus, deserves to get Emilia. Emilia herself still cannot choose between the men, but when she sees the rose fall from the tree she understands that Diana "here dischargest me" (5.1.170). These words can mean simply that Diana is telling her to go, but it can also mean that Diana is freeing her devotee from her vow of chastity, which Emilia apparently is eager to abandon. All three worshippers will have their prayers answered.

**5.4.112–137. "Never fortune . . . like the time."** Arcite, who had won the duel for Emilia's hand, has been trampled to death by his black horse, and Palamon will marry her. This change of fortune has shocked everyone. As Arcite's body is being carried out, Theseus delivers his final words on the uncertainty of luck in human affairs.

Theseus notes that Fortune has never played a more subtle game. The conquered one has triumphed, and the victor has lost. Yet, in the combat between Arcite and Palamon, the gods have been most impartial and given the same to each. Even Arcite had admitted that Palamon had the first right to the lady since he had seen her first and had been the first to proclaim his love for Emilia. Hence Arcite has restored Emilia to Palamon and wished that Palamon would send him to the other world with words of forgiveness. The gods have taken away Theseus's right to deliver justice and have become the executioners themselves. (Theseus had intended to execute the losers in this duel.) Theseus tells Palamon to take his lady and call the knights who had accompanied him to the duel away from the scaffold where they are still waiting. Theseus will now befriend them. Theseus and others will mourn Arcite's death sadly for a short while and graciously prepare for his funeral. At its conclusion, everyone will put on the cheerful look of the bride and bridegroom and smile with Palamon. For an hour Theseus had been sorry for Palamon and glad for Arcite; now he is glad for Palamon and sorry for Arcite. Addressing the gods who work through charms or supernatural powers, Theseus wonders what they have made of human beings! We laugh for what we do not have; we are sorry for what we have. Instead, we should be thankful for what we have, and we should desist from arguing about matters we do not understand.

Although Theseus begins his speech by addressing fortune, in fact he is positing a providential world. Palamon really deserved Emilia because he had seen and loved her first. Arcite had acted like a thief, and his fate is deserved. Theseus also recognizes the validity of tragic-comedy, which mirrors life. The victor one moment may become the vanquished the next. Because life is so unpredictable, people should accept the will of the gods and be thankful for whatever happens.

## Annotated Bibliography

Bertram, Paul. *Shakespeare and "The Two Noble Kinsmen."* New Brunswick: Rutgers UP, 1965. Examining the "elements of design in the language and structure of the play," Bertram's purpose is "to demonstrate its integrity" and "to prove the case for Shakespeare" as the sole author (244).

Bruster, Douglas. "The Jailer's Daughter and the Politics of Madwomen's Language." *Shakespeare Quarterly* 46 (1995): 277–300. The play highlights the relations of power and comments on Jacobean culture and social change.

Edwards, Philip. "On the Design of *The Two Noble Kinsmen.*" *Review of English Literature* 5 (1964): 89–105. Regards the play as masterfully crafted. Shakespeare presents the progress from innocence to experience.

Frey, Charles H., ed. *Shakespeare, Fletcher, and "The Two Noble Kinsmen."* Columbia: U of Missouri P, 1989. Ten scholars discuss the text and questions of authorship, the tradition of ideas behind the play, its social and economic settings, and the history of stage performances. Includes a selective bibliographical guide.

Metz, G. Harold, ed., with introduction. *Four Plays Ascribed to Shakespeare.* Columbia: U of Missouri P, 1989. Metz's introduction includes sections on publication, date, authorship, sources, and stage history. Reprints Chaucer's *The Knyghtes Tale*, and excerpts from Beaumont's *The Masque of the Inner Temple and Grayes Inne*, the fourth book of Sir Philip Sidney's *The Countess of Pembroke's Arcadia*, Dryden's translation of Plutarch's *The Lives of the Noble Grecians and Romans: The Life of Theseus*, and Sir Philip Sidney's *The Lady of May.*

Potter, Lois, ed. *The Two Noble Kinsmen.* The Arden Shakespeare. New York: Routledge, 1997. Discusses problems of date and collaboration; historical, cultural, and performance contexts; survey of critical approaches; detailed notes and commentary on the text.

Shannon, Laurie J. "Emilia's Argument: Friendship and 'Human Title' in *The Two Noble Kinsmen.*" *ELH* 64 (1997): 657–682. Emilia's characterization "revises the definitional prejudices of the male model regarding both gender and sexuality" (676). She "offers a rebuttal to Renaissance commonplaces about female friendship's impossibility" (675). By showing Emilia's innocent love for Flavina, the play places homoerotics within the scope of female friendship.

Vickers, Brian. "*The Two Noble Kinsmen.*" In *Shakespeare, Co-Author: A Historical Study of Five Collaborative Plays.* Oxford: Oxford UP, 2002. 402–432. Vickers identifies the separate shares of Shakespeare and Fletcher by analyzing their language and style. Vickers examines various arguments for assigning sections to Shakespeare.

Waith, Eugene M. *The Two Noble Kinsmen.* The Oxford Shakespeare. Oxford: Oxford UP, 1989. Discusses early publication and performances, text and collaboration, sources, stage history, and critical approaches.

# THE SONNETS

# Overview of the Sonnets

## James B. Gutsell

Shakespeare's *Sonnets* was published in 1609 under mysterious circumstances. It is known from a work by Francis Meres, *Palladis Tamia* (1598), that in the 1590s some of the sonnets circulated in manuscript, as was fashionable with such poems. Meres speaks of Shakespeare's "sugared Sonnets among his private friends." The next year sonnets 138 and 144—two of the more shocking and unusual sonnets—together with three lyrics taken from *Love's Labor's Lost* were printed in *The Passionate Pilgrim*, a book of twenty poems, of which fifteen were falsely attributed to Shakespeare. Clearly the public knew of the sonnets and wanted to buy them.

The *Sonnets* was printed with another piece by Shakespeare called *A Lover's Complaint*. Joining these two works as a kind of bridge were two sonnets, printed as the last two of the sonnet sequence but not belonging to it. There is no satisfying explanation of who collected this material in reasonably good condition and planned the book. Shakespeare, it is generally thought, was not responsible for the publication, but he was the person most likely to have possessed the manuscripts. The common but not necessarily true belief that the sonnets were printed in wild disorder supports the opinion that Shakespeare was not involved with their printing. The intimacy of the sonnets also seems to rule him out as the source of their publication, but the temptation of financial compensation might have come at a weak moment, or Shakespeare might have known that the sonnets already had circulated widely, so he simply decided to let them be printed. Alternatively, he might have regarded them (correctly) as unique and important to his life's work.

If Shakespeare was involved in publishing the sonnets, some explanation is needed for the role of the actual publisher, and for his mysterious dedication of the work:

TO. THE. ONLIE. BEGETTER. OF. / THESE. INSVING. SONNETS. / MR. W. H. ALL. HAPPINESSE. / AND. THAT. ETERNITIE. / PROMISED. / BY. / OVR. EVER-LIVING. POET. / WISHETH. / THE. WELL-WISHING. / ADVENTVRER. IN. / SETTING. / FORTH. / T.T.

The initials "T.T." are known to stand for Thomas Thorpe, for he officially entered "a Book called Shakespeares sonnettes" in the Stationers' Register on May 20, 1609. He was the publisher, and the volume was printed on contract by John Eld.

Since "onlie begetter" seems an obvious reference to the Youth who inspired the bulk of the poems, much effort has gone into fitting known and lesser-known young men to the initials "W.H." or "H.W." The initials of Henry Wriothesley, third Earl of Southhampton, were H.W., and in many ways he seems a likely candidate; as a result, much argument has been made for him as the Youth, with blame for this deception going to Thomas Thorpe. Shakespeare himself might have been capable of a little deception in this matter, a point not usually conceded. He might have decided to publish the sonnets, involved Thomas Thorpe to see them through the press, and written a carefully laid trail to mislead the general reader as to the Youth's identity. Although "private friends" would have known who the young man was, the dedication effectively disguised him, and no information or speculation from that day has come down.

The sonnets abound with mysteries. Who is the fair Youth to whom most of the poems are addressed? Who is the Dark Lady? Who is Mr. W.H., to whom the 1609 edition is dedicated? What is the correct order of the sonnets? When were they written? Who provided the sonnets to the publisher? What was Shakespeare's sexual orientation? Research into the mysteries of the people involved—particularly the "Mr. W.H." of the dedication, the Youth, and the Dark Lady—has occupied the careers of many scholars. It would be interesting to know the identities of these people and equally interesting to know how the sonnets were obtained and who arranged them. But none of that really matters, for the poems are what they are, and the relationships stated and implied will never be better understood by means of certain identification of the unknown people. That is information for biographers, not for sonnet readers.

These mysteries, whether delightful or maddening, have deflected attention from the sonnets as literary works and as unusual and fascinating personal expressions by Shakespeare. If we take the sonnets for what they claim to be, they can, in a fashion, render the author to our loving (though distant) embraces. William Shakespeare's sonnets are rich, difficult, and tantalizing for the glimpses they offer into the author's life and mind. The situations presented are unusually personal, often obscurely private, and frequently embarrassingly intimate.

The scholarly community in recent times has given attention to the poetry as poetry, a great improvement in focus of attention, but such criticism can err by treating the poems as discrete entities and focusing exclusively on the discovery of complex internal literary patterns and strategies within individual poems. In the case of a sonnet sequence, where the poems exist in a community of related works that carry on a kind of dialogue and fall into groups, the intense critical analysis of sonnets in isolation from each other loses track of the larger dialogue, of the more immediate grouping, and of the purposes of the sequence as a whole. There are obvious practical reasons for examining individual sonnets without complicated references to the whole, but when doing so the larger body tends to be lost from sight and individual works lose important contextual meanings.

The primary purpose of the sonnets was not to exercise poetic craft, although they certainly do that deliberately and self-consciously. The sonnets were, primarily, focused acts of communication between Shakespeare and two other people.

Clearly, he expected these people, the Youth and the Dark Lady, to be able to read these poems without unusual technical skills of interpretation, and he expected them to respond to what he had written as a consequence of their sharing his feelings and understanding his thoughts. At the same time, the sonnets are also deliberately innovative exercises in this newly popular genre of poetry.

This overview will be based on two assumptions. First, the sonnets were, in their primary purpose, just what they present themselves as being: verse epistles written mainly to a young man or a young woman regarding their private affairs. Second, the sonnets were also serious, innovative exercises in a newly popular genre through which Shakespeare apparently intended to improve his standing as a serious poet, an effort he was also making with his verse narratives (*Venus and Adonis*, 1593; *The Rape of Lucrece*, 1594). In conjunction with this purpose, Shakespeare clearly identified the Youth as a patron as well as a friend, a situation further complicating matters. Shakespeare's desire for a new and different social reputation presumes the existence of a significant audience beyond that of the two people to whom the sonnets are addressed. Since the poems, or the events behind them, are often private, we can only guess that the larger, secondary audience consisted of friends of the Youth. They would have known something of the personalities and circumstances involved and would have appreciated the sonnets as bringing something original to the literary scene. It is difficult to imagine Shakespeare distributing the sonnets to any other circle of acquaintances. The daring aspect of the sonnets lies in their very commitment to the claim that sonnets always made of reporting on the private longing of lover-poets. Shakespeare brought his sonnets out of the study and in doing so exposed himself and others to a degree of scrutiny that almost certainly caused problems.

Attention is given here to Shakespeare's uses and departures from the sonnet tradition; for without some awareness of this literary context a reader can appreciate neither the poems' daring originality nor their traditional literary clothing. An approach that allows the sonnets to be both personal and public works of art permits us to view Shakespeare as something other than the unreliable speaker that modern critical assumptions propose for all first-person poetry. To understand the sonnets well and to see the parallels between Shakespeare's evolution in thought and craft as a writer of sonnets and of plays would do much to reveal the rich personality he displayed so openly from the beginning of his career. No complete understanding of Shakespeare or his sonnets is possible, but better understandings can be achieved by allowing the sonnets the unheard-of openness that they offer.

An introduction such as this, covering the whole scope of the sonnets, does not permit detailed commentaries; the intention here is to offer a way of reading the sonnets as a coherent sequence presenting common human experiences of love, disappointment, weakness, and perseverance. More attention is given to the early sonnets in order to establish the necessary setting for reading the later ones, which are among the best. The sonnets are radically innovative, uneven, and complex, but collectively they are a great achievement, enormously interesting, and completely unparalleled.

In the summer of 1592 Shakespeare was twenty-eight years old and had been residing and working in London as an actor since about 1588. He had written at least three successful plays concerning the reign of Henry VI and had probably finished *Richard III*, a play that set new standards for dramatic writing in London. With his dramatic career assured, Shakespeare would soon begin his efforts to become a more literary kind of poet. During the summer of 1592 a severe and prolonged outbreak of plague led to a nearly two-year closing of the theaters. Threatened with economic destruction, the acting companies left London and toured the countryside to earn a living. Shakespeare, however, stayed in London and wrote in quick succession two narrative poems: *Venus and Adonis* and *The Rape of Lucrece.* He probably also began his sonnets during this period. Sonnet 104 indicates that he continued writing sonnets for at least three years. That being said, however, it is important to remember that almost every position taken on the history of the sonnets and their relationship to Shakespeare's life has been questioned. Given the paucity of certain information, arguments for this or that conclusion about the sonnets depend on complex perspectives that cannot be proven. The best one can do is to struggle with the internal logic of the material within the slight framework of available fact.

The position taken here is fairly conventional as to dates of composition; the sonnets were probably written over a period of at least three or four years, possibly longer, beginning between 1592 and 1594. To put this span of time into the context of Shakespeare's plays, in 1593–1594 he wrote *A Comedy of Errors* and *The Taming of the Shrew*; in 1595–1596, *Romeo and Juliet* and *A Midsummer Night's Dream*; and about 1600–1601, *Hamlet.* As for content, the sonnets show every indication of being genuinely and painfully autobiographical, and for that reason and others they were innovative. In relation to Shakespeare's larger career, the sonnets were being written at the time of his major breakthrough as a dramatist, which is particularly noticeable in *Romeo and Juliet* and *A Midsummer Night's Dream*, when he discovered the inner lives of his characters and the language to make them convincing and fully alive. The great emotional breadth of his own experiences and his discovery of language to give life to those events undoubtedly became a perpetual spring of inspiration for his plays. As one reads through the sonnets and the plays, the latter seem crowded with the types of emotions described in the former, such as naive adoration, idealistic commitment, jealousy, self-deprecation, and rage. These plays, epitomized by *Hamlet*, are essentially modern in their psychological realism, more modern than any drama in the next three centuries.

This modernity is also true of the sonnets. Despite the obvious social and literary conventions of the day that Shakespeare employs in his phrasing and ideas, he defies the fundamental convention of looking at existing models for content and shows himself determined to learn his own truths. Finding these became a complex act of personal and literary investigation into unexplored territory, and part of what Shakespeare discovered was the extent to which uncertainty underlies even our firmest convictions. Allied with uncertainty are strange relativities of perspective often requiring opaque and abstract language, where images of nature play no role, as in the opening obscure quatrain of Sonnet 121:

> 'Tis better to be vile than vile esteemed,
> When not to be receives reproach of being.
> And the just pleasure lost, which is so deemed
> Not by our feeling, but by others' seeing.

These explorations led Shakespeare to new perspectives about love and produced a personal breed of surprising metaphors to describe it, such as could be found in accounting and moneylending.

Shakespeare's dramatic characters become freed, in the later 1590s, from the conventional stage language and mannerisms of the day, in which emotions are named and motives stated rather than revealed naturally as aspects of behavior and thought. In *Richard III*, which precedes the sonnets, Shakespeare's concepts of psychology and morality are at best simple and obvious. Richard, the Duke of Gloucester and future king, announces in his opening soliloquy that he is so physically deformed "That dogs bark at me as I halt by them" (1.1.23). From this defect follows his whole being and plan:

> And therefore, since I cannot prove a lover
> To entertain these fair well-spoken days,
> I am determined to prove a villain
> And hate the idle pleasures of these days. (1.1.28–31)

This is a play with a dynamic villain and dramatic gusto but little subtlety and no mysteries of personality or motivation. In subsequent plays, Shakespeare did not abandon evil people, but he probed the complexities of thought and behavior that contribute to the realization of evil. In comedy, even at its broadest moment, he found his humor not in slapstick but in the willingness of people to deceive themselves and indulge in folly.

*Romeo and Juliet*, a breakthrough work, gushes with more complexity and subtleties than most directors and actors can realize in a production. The main characters defy easy summary. Romeo is likable, genuine, and well meaning, but he is also in the grip of youthful hormones, blindly impulsive, and violent. His love is genuine but also, as one might expect of a teenager, a bundle of romantic clichés in its expression. His plans are poorly conceived and badly managed. He kills the innocent Paris, then himself, and finally causes Juliet's death. His good friend Mercutio is loyal, witty, poetic, obscene, manic, and violent. His irresponsible fight with Tybalt triggers the worst disasters of the play. Yet we like him. In the end, assigning blame for the tragedy has a very modern aspect, for there is no simple cause; instead, we must credit the disaster to some mix of fate, feuding parents, society, the cult of romantic love, and youthful excess. Hamlet, much like Romeo, is attractive and sympathetic. Although a victim with whom we sympathize, he becomes cruel and destructive. With his world and his own perspectives unhinged, it is easy to imagine Hamlet muttering, " 'Tis better to be vile than vile esteemed." It is hard to imagine Hamlet's existence without the sonnets.

An enormous synergy existed between Shakespeare's activities as playwright, actor, and sonnet writer, with each of these interests contributing to his success in the others. The playwright and actor, for instance, reveals himself in a number of the sonnets where the speaker is a man thinking out loud as in a dramatic soliloquy or monologue, with thoughts taking shape and shifting direction as they come. In *Romeo and Juliet* the sonnet writer even provides the lovers with sonnets for dialogue (1.5.93–106). However the interaction of interests and practices worked out, it can hardly be doubted that Shakespeare's sonnet writing played a major role in his subsequent development as a playwright.

It is a common assumption in contemporary Western cultures that love poetry is inherently personal in some way, but in fact love is the most conventionalized emotion in literature and has been since romantic love was invented in the eleventh century by the knightly troubadours of Provence, a semi-autonomous region in southeastern France. Medieval romantic love, often called courtly love, usually involved an illicit relationship between a worshipping knight and an idealized lady, often the wife of the knight's overlord. Such relationships proposed adultery as their natural destination and were often considered a kind of madness. The tragic and destructive triangle of King Arthur, his best friend (Lancelot), and his wife (Guinevere) illustrates this situation. Although these conventions of adoring lovers and ideal women have changed with time, they have not vanished. We have little trouble understanding Romeo, Shakespeare's purest example of the romantic lover. Even if Juliet was not quite married to Paris, she was not available and had to be courted in secret. As in the best tradition of courtly love, Paris, Romeo, and Juliet die.

Sixteenth-century writers of the English love sonnet inherited a particular set of courtly love conventions from the fourteenth-century Italian writer Francesco Petrarch (1304–1374). Petrarch, a great scholar and poet, spent many years addressing sonnets and songs to a woman he seldom saw and who died of the great plague that swept Europe while he was halfway through his project. His version of courtly love had become particularly idealized and intellectualized. It had also become the literature of a middle-class scholar.

Since the woman to whom he addressed his sonnets, a married lady he called Laura, was not available, his adoration of her could be a perpetual round of longing, celebration, hope, and struggle within himself between reason and passion. The great popularity of his sonnets lies partly in the craft of individual pieces and partly in the sense they give of a prolonged psychological study of love in its emotional states as conventionally understood. Petrarch, at once a medievalist and a classical scholar, provided drama for his imaginary love affair through myth and allegory. He warred with Cupid and sailed the stormy seas of passion.

Petrarch made his strongest impact in England through translation and imitation. Sir Thomas Wyatt (1503–1542) and Henry Howard, Earl of Surrey (1517?–1547), worked through the problems of basic English metrics, and in doing so both translated Petrarch and composed their own individual and unconnected sonnets. Wyatt's translation of Petrarch's *Rime 140* offers a good example of Petrarch's poetic method and a marker by which to judge Shakespeare's evolution:

> My galley charged with forgetfulnesse,
> Through sharpe seas, in winter nightes doth passe,
> 'Twene rocke, and rocke: and eke my fo (alas)
> That is my lord, stereth with cruelnesse:
> And euery houre, a thought in readinesse,
> As though that death were light, in such a case.
> An endlesse wynd doth teare the sayle apace
> Of forced sighes, a trusty fearfulnesse.
> A rayne of teares, a clowde of darke disdayne
> Haue done the weried coardes great hinderance,

Wrethed with errour, and wyth ignorance.
The starres be hidde, that leade me to this payne.
Drownde is reason that should be my comfort:
And I remayne, dispearyng of the port.

The pleasure of this work occurs largely in working out its allegorical devices. The ship lost at sea is Petrarch lost in the dangerous irrationality of desire. The cruel lord who drives on the ship is his passion, or Cupid. The lost stars that should guide him would be his ideals of rational and moral behavior. Although an old theme, this tale of reason subjected by passion is made vivid and engaging. It offers some generalized truth, in that we have all found ourselves in uncontrolled, emotional situations. The appeal of Petrarchan sonnets lies partly in their generalized depictions of love, but modern readers may miss the voice of a particular person engaged with actual problems.

Neither Wyatt nor Surrey undertook a sonnet sequence. It was not until Sir Philip Sidney (1554–1586) wrote his *Astrophil and Stella* that an English sequence appeared, and that circulated in manuscript until after Sidney's death, when an unauthorized edition was published in 1591. These sonnets appealed to a community of writers prepared to jump on an agreeable literary bandwagon, and soon many took to sonnet sequences, including Shakespeare. Another particularly notable sonneteer during that poetic scramble was Edmund Spenser (1552–1599). Spenser's sonnet sequence, *Amoretti* (1595), celebrated his courtship with his wife. His literary affinities were much more with Petrarch's age than with the kind of modernism initiated by Shakespeare. Even a brief examination of sonnets by Sidney and Spenser can do much to suggest where Shakespeare's work stood in relation to sonnet conventions.

In his first sonnet Sidney addresses the issues of persuasion and stylistic originality. He examines the writing of others for methods and inspirations, and then in the last line he concludes to himself, "Fool, . . . , look in thy heart and write." Having opted for actual experience and personal feelings, he begins the narrative in the second sonnet by describing how he fell in love:

Not at first sight, nor with a dribbed [random, ineffectual] shot,
Love gave the wound, which while I breathe will bleed:
But known worth did in mine of time proceed,
Till by degrees it had full conquest got.

The imitation of Petrarch is obvious. The originality and personal truth the speaker claims to seek may lie in the slowness of the process by which Love conquers him, but the sonnet ends with the basic Petrarchan submission of the rational self to the Lord of Love: "I call it praise to suffer tyranny" (2.11). The sonnet succeeds; it is lively, graceful, and complex, but also very Petrarchan. Sidney was neither seeking radical new truths nor abandoning old devices. His most interesting innovations, found in other sonnets, were to draw occasionally on some apparently personal experiences and to find fresh imagery for standard emotions. He could not have imagined what Shakespeare was to do by seriously exploring his own experiences. Sidney, a born Petrarchan sonneteer, easily found a light, artful grace with sonnets—a grace that was entirely unnatural to Shakespeare's very different talents and his effort to dig out the deeper moral and psychological dimensions of experience.

Spenser, in his Sonnet 67, also remains conventional as he adopts the medieval allegorical mode to describe his courtship and his wife's consent to marriage; he is the hunter and she the doe he chases with his hounds. Spenser's poem, although about a stressful decision and a struggle of wills, conveys no sense of conflict. The events are all idealized and then hazed over with deliberately Chaucerian language, as if life were no more than an old painting or tapestry. His Sonnet 33 directly adapts Petrarch's *Rime 140*:

> Lyke as a ship that through the Ocean wyde,
> by conduct of some star doth make her way,
> whenas a storme hath dimd her trusty guyde,
> out of her course doth wander far astray. (ll. 1–4)

Unlike his predecessors and contemporaries, Shakespeare decided to practice what Sidney advocated; he looked into his heart for both subject and method, and he quickly found himself in unexplored territory. Although Sidney wrote about an actual relationship he had with a woman and Spenser wrote about courting his wife, neither spoke in his own voice or allowed the problems abounding in real relationships to find their way into the grander matter of high love and noble poetry. Shakespeare, for his part, chases no does, sails no ships in stormy seas, dispenses with ruby lips and golden tresses, and entertains Cupid only briefly. He writes, instead, about his devotion to a young man and about a sexual relationship with a married woman. He idealizes the Youth, but the Youth and the Dark Lady become lovers. Shakespeare's sonnets are about idealism and reason and passion and hope and disappointment, but he addresses those matters as they are encountered in the course of life—where failures are regular and guaranteed, and success becomes a matter of survival while holding onto bits of integrity for oneself and keeping shreds of faith in and with others.

Before tracing our way through the sonnets, it would be useful to consider the form Shakespeare chose for his work. Known now as the Shakespearean, or English, sonnet, it consists of three groups of four lines, called quatrains, and a couplet. The quatrains have alternating internal rhymes that usually do not interconnect with the rhymes of other quatrains. The Shakespearean sonnet, then, has four parts with the following rhyme scheme: *abab cdcd efef gg*. This division in rhyme establishes a sense of distinct units and directs the English sonnet toward a division of content corresponding to the four separate rhyming sections. The writer of English sonnets tends to develop an idea through three distinct stages, one for each quatrain, as parallel illustrations that collectively unify into a single larger point in the couplet.

The couplet that follows the three quatrains becomes the critical element of the whole structure. An effective couplet can summarize the sonnet in some way, or it can twist the whole content with a moment of clever wit. A sonnet with an unsuccessful couplet feels weak no matter how adequate the rest of the poem may be. Shakespeare's couplets could become the tail that wagged the dog; or when the energy of the poem had run its course in twelve lines, the couplet could feel redundant. One solution to the couplet problem was to treat the whole poem, despite the rhyme scheme, as a two-part Petrarchan structure; this took the pressure off the couplet by allowing a six line conclusion.

The Petrarchan form consists of two parts, an octave of eight lines and a sestet of six lines. Both units can have varied rhyme schemes. The usual octave is either *abbaabba* or *abababab*. The sestet can be more varied in its rhymes, but it is most commonly *cdcdcc*, or *cdecde*, or *cdcdee*. Sidney often employed a combination of rhymes that look somewhat Shakespearean if divided into quatrains: *abab abab cdcd ee*. The repeated rhymes are very different, however, and, unlike Shakespeare, Sidney did not treat the octave as two quatrains and seldom used the ending couplet as an independent, concluding unit. The Petrarchan form usually produced multiple couplets, as in *abbaabba cddcee*, which has five. To look at another sonnet option, Spenser elected three quatrains, but he connected the quatrains with overlapping rhymes: *abab bcbc cdcd ee*. This form actually produces three couplets, one between each quatrain, and the last two lines of the poem.

Shakespeare had two obvious reasons for choosing a four-part form. The first lies in the advantages of development in three parts. The second lies in minimizing rhyme. Sidney's and Spenser's sonnets are heavily musical. The very word sonnet in Italian and Provençal means "little song." In Italian, rhymes are easily created because of the frequency of feminine endings. In English, however, much ingenuity and artifice in phrasing and vocabulary are required for repeated rhymes. The Shakespearean form abandons the music of rhyme in favor of more natural expression and flexibility of thought.

The content of the sonnets suggests that Shakespeare's life at the time he wrote the sonnets was in a state of emotional flux. The sonnets tell us that he was both idealistic and passionate. His reading and his playwriting had made him an explorer of emotional experience through the lives of others. It is unlikely that someone with his personality would remain in an emotional vacuum and live on imagined experience. In the sonnets his expressed worries about age make clear his concern that he was getting too old for romantic attachments. He probably was feeling a need to explore love while he could expect to succeed. In launching a new career as a nondramatic poet, he had turned his attention to the erotic affairs of Venus and Adonis as narrated by his favorite Roman author, Ovid (43 B.C.–A.D. 17), and to Sidney's newly published sonnets. With a dramatic synchronicity between his personal life and his literary interests, Shakespeare apparently became involved with a passionate woman and fell in love with a beautiful young man. These two affairs allowed Shakespeare to investigate the polar opposites of the field of love with marvelous efficiency. Love for the Youth started him down the path of Plato and Petrarch in devoting himself to idealized beauty, and through his involvement with the Dark Lady he was able to explore the erotic world of passion found in Ovid.

There is no evidence within the sonnets to determine which loved one came into Shakespeare's life first. The sonnets to the Youth certainly begin the sequence. Yet when the Mistress appears in the sonnets to the Youth, she does so in a way that suggests she had been a part of Shakespeare's life before the Youth. Since the sonnets to the Mistress may not be in their order of composition, it is impossible to trace the evolution of the relationship, but it appears that the earliest sonnets to her are those that celebrate her special qualities. This sense of joy in the relationship is soon largely displaced by complaints about her infidelity. She had an affair with the

Youth, but whether this begins Shakespeare's complaints or is only one more reason for them cannot be determined. The Mistress was married, and probably much younger than Shakespeare, who was then twenty-eight or so. The Youth would have been in his teens, independent in his affairs, wealthy enough to be a patron of poets, and probably aristocratic. Their polar roles in Shakespeare's life are not only evident from the sonnets in general but are also suggested by Sonnet 144, in which the Youth is depicted as an angel and the Mistress as a devil.

The initial set of seventeen poems (excluding Sonnet 15) is formally dedicated to the idea of persuading the Youth to marry, beget children, and so preserve his great beauty through progeny. Shakespeare's motives for devoting this much attention to arguments for marriage addressed to a young man out of his social circle has been treated as a great puzzle, one suggestion being that he was under contract to a worried parent whose wayward son was resisting the usual expectations of an arranged marriage. The hired-pen theory, however, does nothing to explain Shakespeare's deep admiration for the Youth's beauty from the first sonnet. By Sonnet 10 this admiration is being expressed as love ("Make thee another self for love of me," 10.13). Sonnet 13 calls the young man "dear my love" (13.13). By Sonnet 14 the Youth has become the embodiment of both "truth and beauty" (14.11). Sonnet 15 concludes with "for love of you, / . . . I ingraft you new" (15.13–14); that is, Shakespeare will give the fair youth new life through poetry as time takes its toll. By this point the argument for marriage and children had lost its energy in favor of a new relationship; in return for love, the poet will provide a superior kind of immortality through his sonnets. Sonnets 16 and 17 return to the theme of begetting children to ensure immortality. Then the much admired Sonnet 18 makes a full confession of love, although without any actual statement to that effect. With this sonnet Shakespeare gives the world a new voice in verse and love poetry through his special talent in evoking nature's beauties: "Shall I compare thee to a summer's day? / Thou art more lovely and more temperate" (18.1–2).

With his devotion fully declared in Sonnet 18, Shakespeare's immediate problem, therefore, was to define this love, particularly in respect to its sexuality. A popular explanation of Shakespeare's relationship with the Youth makes it no different from ordinary close friendships between males during the Elizabethan Age when men could speak of loving each other. Devoted friendships between men who shared much in their public and military lives have been greatly celebrated through the ages, from Plato in the fourth century B.C. to Shakespeare's contemporary Sir Francis Bacon (1561–1626). But Shakespeare quickly makes it clear that his feelings are distinctly romantic and speaks to this issue with frank and comic directness in Sonnet 20. In the poem's second line Shakespeare declares the Youth to be "the master mistress of my passion." The "master mistress" paradox captures the ambiguity of his feelings and sets the tone of much of what follows in the sonnets. Shakespeare carefully notes that his sense of the Youth's sexual ambiguity is not unique; all men and women are similarly struck by the Youth's attractions. The third quatrain tells a little tale, in the manner of the Roman poet Ovid in his *Metamorphoses*, about how the Youth was supposed to have been a woman but became a man instead because Nature fell in love with the image she was making and changed the female to a male "By adding one thing to my purpose nothing. / But since she prick'd thee out for women's pleasure, / Mine be thy love, and thy love's use their treasure" (20.12–14).

The pun on "prick'd" is typically Shakespearean in carrying a multitude of simultaneous meanings. It strikes us first for its most obvious ribald meaning; the Youth was given a "prick" to please women. But then the image grows comically, for to "prick out" was to indicate the outline of a pattern by making pinpricks in the material prior to cutting it out. So Dame Nature, busy with her sewing, made a pattern of the form-to-be of the Youth as a woman, then she changed her plan; thus the "prick" was "prick'd out."

In Sonnet 20 Shakespeare says that he expects no sexual activity but admits to the romantic and nearly sexual nature of his feelings. Later sonnets refer to scandal that might have resulted from distribution of the sonnets, so Shakespeare is fully aware of the quasi-sexual character of his emotions. It is a basic aspect of the sonnets and perhaps a deliberate source of emotional tension. Shakespeare is not coy in his confessions, and so, without proof to the contrary, readers have little reason to doubt that his love for the Youth involved boundaries. His instincts seem basically divided between, on the one hand, his worship of the beautiful male, who is usually a little distant both emotionally and socially, and on the other his sexual attraction to the sexually predatory female (the Dark Lady), who is intimate but unfaithful.

Sonnet 20, among other things, celebrates a bond that had been developing since the beginning of the sequence. Shakespeare's willingness to raise the sexual issue and his freedom to treat his aristocratic friend's "prick" as a joke indicates not only some pressing need to clarify a delicate matter but also a quality of frankness reaching almost to social equality. That desired equality now becomes the greater impediment to an enduring friendship. Sonnet 20 has some of the character of a wedding or an engagement in which understandings are announced in a state of heightened joy. But such events only herald the real work to come. In Sonnet 1 and still in Sonnet 20 Shakespeare knew this Youth to be self-centered and deceptive. The young man is the prince of charm, who with the seeming largess of his affections excites all his acquaintances in both sexes. Shakespeare dances attendance in that crowd. As a rising playwright and promising poet, he is allowed to run with the manored set and amuse it for a time, but he will never be of it. As the suitor, the patron-seeking poet, and the social climber, he would be foolish to hope for an extended commitment from the Youth, but he also apparently had received a degree of commitment, some encouragement, hope, and hope's illusions.

The sonnets following Sonnet 20 provide continued glimpses into the affection, hope, and insecurity that Shakespeare endured following this profession of love, though the poems contain more uncertainty and wishing than satisfaction. For a time Shakespeare shows a disturbing eagerness to forgive serious violations of friendship and dignity in the name of a love that endures all and forgives all (sonnets 35, 41–42). But he is not always patient. His position could feel galling, as is evident in sonnets 57 and 58, in which he repeatedly calls himself the Youth's "slave" (57.1, 57.11, 58.1). This sarcasm finds voice in other sonnets where the Youth's character rather than Shakespeare's dependency is the issue, and Shakespeare can express outright anger, such as in Sonnet 40 ("Take all my loves, my love, yea take them all," l. 1), where he can address the Youth with the extraordinary, bone-cutting paradox of "[l]ascivious grace" (l. 13). Before long, separation becomes the more common situation, and the subservience of the earlier sonnets tends to disappear in the face of mutual failure and self-confidence in his own dignity that allows Shakespeare to speak out in his own defense.

The first twenty sonnets to the Youth exhibit a coherence lacking in the remainder of the sequence. (The sonnets to the Mistress, 127 through 152, form a group by subject but are not otherwise unified, nor do they appear to be sequential.) Sonnets 21 through 126 to the Youth are composed of many small groups that explore situations or variations on a theme, often the same activity. The only other extended group involves agitation over a rival poet. These begin with Sonnet 76 and extend to at least Sonnet 86. The problems Shakespeare comments on here go beyond simple poetic rivalry to a serious cooling in friendship. We understand from Shakespeare's complaints that the rival poet has flattered his way into the Youth's good graces. Exactly where this sequence ends is unclear, for the next dozen or so sonnets focus on Shakespeare's complaints and criticisms of the Youth for his lack of constancy in friendship and may be continuous with the rival poet series.

The other sonnets to the Youth tend to fall into groups of two to five poems. The existence of groups has been thought the signal of an editor at work arranging the manuscript for the printer by putting together sonnets that have a common subject. There can be no certainties on this matter; someone probably made editorial decisions, such as keeping the opening poems together and placing those to the Mistress at the end. Possibly some groups elsewhere were formed by an editor, but many groups were quite clearly composed together to explore a problem or to expand a poetic theme. Small groups of two or three poems might have been written at one sitting, or at least in fairly quick succession, as new reflections or new methods of development occurred to the poet. A short poem requires a commitment to the opening impulse and method, but in the process other methods or ideas can occur, suggesting other poems. Likewise, one response to a personal problem may lead to other, more considered responses. Or a sequence could evolve quite consciously as a step-by-step approach to explaining an issue. Shakespeare, the memory-trained actor, might have composed in his head, while walking to morning rehearsals or quaffing an ale with friends in the evening to unwind after a performance. He apparently wrote at least one poem of a pair while on horseback (Sonnet 50, "How heavy do I journey on the way").

A quick composer, he may have had more than one sonnet in his head by the end of a day. Knowing so well the importance of one's angle of perception in discovering truths, he seems to have enjoyed the exercise of exploring different angles and finding the truths to which they pointed. For Shakespeare to have written only one sonnet on a situation would have been less likely than his writing several. Groups were his natural method for giving substance to an idea. If he had felt a strong need to make a point, fourteen lines would hardly succeed in exploring a complex problem or imposing its significance on the busy and possibly inattentive Youth. The differing versions of his plays indicate that Shakespeare was an inveterate reviser, and the sonnets show a similar penchant for revisiting and reframing a topic.

The first twenty sonnets mix criticism of the Youth with praise, but the criticism is directed at a rather special being whose failure to marry and start a family has no threatening effect on Shakespeare: quite the opposite. It is not until Shakespeare makes his declarations of love that the Youth's character becomes an issue, along with Shakespeare's age and his inferior social position. Clearly Shakespeare wrote

Sonnet 20 feeling an assurance that his devotion was returned. He had been seek-ing and earning that friendship with his splendid sonnets, but immediately after his celebration of mutual friendship in Sonnet 20, he begins worrying. In the sonnets following 20, Shakespeare carefully explores the new ground of this relationship. Although desiring mutuality, he clearly remains the cautious suitor and the poet making his sonnet offerings.

In Sonnet 21 Shakespeare makes a major promise; he will write of the Youth truthfully, and by this promise he will depart from the exaggerations of common Petrarchan lovers and sonneteers. He does not promise to show the warts and all here, for he is not focusing on deeper problems, but he does mean to base his af-fection on the wonderful things that he knows rather than on impossible perfec-tions to be imagined. It follows that he expected to be a poet of real experience.

In Sonnet 22 Shakespeare addresses a problem he often returns to, his age. He may be only ten or eleven years older than the Youth, but he remains uneasy. He fears that the Youth will find him incompatible as a heart's companion. He felt a generation older than the Youth, as he did with the Mistress. In Sonnet 22 Shake-speare's proposed solution to the difference in ages is to abolish it through the union of true hearts, an idea based on the traditional wedding service in which two people metaphorically become one flesh. If two people share a single heart or exchange hearts, they are as one and thus of the same age in their sense of each other. As Shakespeare works through this idea in Sonnet 22, he promises, in the third quat-rain, to protect the Youth's heart as a "tender nurse her babe" (22.12). This is the most touching moment in the sonnet. In contrast to this peaceful and caring prom-ise, the couplet strikes a new and jarring note that tells us more than is revealed in the first twelve lines. Shakespeare fears that his own heart will not be protected, and he reveals how shaky the proposed union feels: "Presume not on thy heart when mine is slain, / Thou gav'st me thine not to give back again" (22.13–14). Here the poem travels a remarkable circle from certainty in friendship to anticipation of fail-ure, and in so doing captures the basic emotional unease that informs a large per-centage of the remaining sonnets to the Youth.

Sonnet 23 makes an important request. Shakespeare has realized that his poems need to acquire a new degree of seriousness, and he wants the Youth to attend to them carefully. Although sonnets played a significant role in the development of the friendship, they now become even more critical to maintaining it, for they will be Shakespeare's only effective means for complicated communications. Shakespeare, like a tongue-tied actor, writes that he cannot express the love he feels in direct, personal address. This problem is entirely understandable. How much can one say without causing embarrassment, particularly if meetings tend to have a social set-ting? He anticipates that the sonnets will become important in bridging the awk-ward limits of conversation. It was one thing to be an older man writing flattering and scolding poems about marriage; it is another entirely to use verse as a serious means of maintaining an intimate, somewhat one-sided friendship. Hence, the son-nets, as Shakespeare's best voice, "plead for love, and look for recompense" (23.11).

Sonnet 24 revisits the uncertainty of Sonnet 22 by again addressing the Youth's character in terms of the union of hearts. Shakespeare remarks in the final couplet, which makes a neat reversal of the first twelve lines and so alters the whole poem, that his knowledge has one important limitation; he does not know the nature of the Youth's heart. Two problems are implied here: the Youth's hidden heart may not be as beautiful as his visible exterior, and Shakespeare's reciprocal portrait may not be painted there. Sonnet 25 forms a pair with Sonnet 24 and celebrates some assurance received between the poems of his permanent place in the Youth's love. The sonnets apparently are working as effective letters in managing the relationship, and we can infer that some conversation has occurred as a result of the poems.

In the evolution of Shakespeare's friendship with the Youth, Sonnet 26 is critical, for it addresses a major crisis that contrasts the relationship for many sonnets to come. On the face of things, the poem begins openly with the language of a courtly lover addressing the loved one: "Lord of my love, to whom in vassalage / Thy merit hath my duty strongly knit" (ll. 1–2). It is the Youth's "merit," not his social position, Shakespeare carefully notes, that has caused this "vassalage." Shakespeare, full of humble obedience, conceded this sonnet to be a poor thing, lacking "wit" (26.5). Shakespeare hopes that the Youth will supply what is missing. The sonnet shows that the Youth and poet are physically separated, since the sonnet is being sent, not presented in person. Is this separation the result of the poet's banishment from the Youth?

The particular problem alluded to in Sonnet 26 reappears in the opening lines of Sonnet 36:

> Let me confess that we two must be twain,
> Although our undivided loves are one:
> So shall those blots that do with me remain,
> Without thy help, by me be borne alone.

The sonnet suggests that this separation may be permanent because of their disparity in social status:

> I may not evermore acknowledge thee,
> Lest my bewailed guilt should do thee shame,
> Nor thou with public kindness honor me,
> Unless thou take that honor from thy name. (36.9–12)

Traditionally, the male author/speaker of sonnets in the courtly love tradition claimed to be of lower rank than the female addressed (often the wife of the speaker's lord). Shakespeare employs that convention here, though if the Youth was the third Earl of Southampton or the Earl of Pembroke, the conventional fiction would, in fact, have been a reflection of the truth.

Another cause of separation, apart from one of status, seems to be the guilt or failing on the part of the speaker. The specifics of the situation cannot be inferred and may not matter, although Shakespeare's reputation during his lifetime is obviously of interest. While there is little point in speculation, rumors of a sexual relationship could easily have developed. If the sonnets were in circulation among the Youth's friends, and possibly among friends of friends, some of these readers naturally would have assumed that Shakespeare's romantic attachment had an overtly sexual character. That interpretation would sully both reputations, but particularly Shakespeare's for writing the sonnets.

Concerns regarding his reputation continue to show up in Shakespeare's poetry. In sonnets 110 and 111 he writes bitterly of the disgrace that his life in the theater has imposed on him, as though it had actually corrupted his nature. In Sonnet 112 the problem seems personal, but the "vulgar scandal" (112.2) mentioned could mean simply a disreputable condition caused by social position or profession. Since "vulgar" means "common," Shakespeare may merely be lamenting the fact that he becomes a spectacle on the stage as an entertainer of the public several afternoons a week. His many roles in plays now long forgotten could have made him a well-known figure of little dignity as he walked the streets. The masses would have recognized the actor rather than the playwright of growing eminence.

The problem of reputation becomes strikingly personal in Sonnet 121, where Shakespeare writes, " 'Tis better to be vile than vile esteemed" (l. 1). Yet the vileness accredited to him here seems to refer to specific deeds, not a general condition such as being an actor. He accepts a reputation for being "sportive" (l. 6), a word that suggests sexual activity, but he denies other criticisms he encounters in the accusing eyes he meets. He also rejects criticism for acts that he personally thinks "good" (l. 8). He says that the criticism comes from hypocrites who are morally weaker than he. In other sonnets he bewails the guilt and dishonor thrust on him by his profession, but here his sense of self-worth and outrage bursts out with defiant self-identification. Paraphrasing God speaking to Moses, he writes enigmatically of himself: "I am that I am" (l. 9). It is some time before he arrives at that point of indignation. In the meantime, he suffers more as one defeated.

In sonnets 27 and 28 Shakespeare goes on a journey, creating physical separation from the young man and requiring that his epistles be posted back to the city. He seems deeply troubled, but it is difficult to determine exactly why. Lying in the dark, he imagines the Youth's face, "Which like a jewel hung in ghastly night, / Makes black night beauteous, and her old face new" (27.11–12). This imagery is designed to be unsettling. A jewel can be a beautiful thing, but it is cold and reflects light produced elsewhere, such as by one who wishes to admire it. Perhaps it is because the imagined face is so cold that this mental "pilgrimage" (27.6) back to the worshipped Youth offers Shakespeare no relief, as the couplet states: "Lo thus by day my limbs, by night my mind, / For thee, and for myself, no quiet find" (27.13–14).

The force of the concluding "quiet" clearly provides the problem with more substance than mere loneliness. The fatigue of travel and loneliness of separation are facts of the poem, but the poem combines these conditions into a metaphor for a disturbed emotional situation. The poem radiates simultaneous feelings of alienation and attraction; beyond that the situation and emotions remain elusive. Sonnet 28 again depicts the speaker's unhappiness in being separated from the youth.

Sonnets 29, 30, and 31, which describe the speaker's experience of being depressed and then finding a cure in thoughts of the Youth, form a natural continuation of the two preceding poems about separation. They make an excellent set of variations on a theme. Sonnet 29 abandons the three-part form of development with a summarizing couplet in order to organize the material as an octave and sestet. The octave sets out the condition of misery and depressed spirits, and the sestet allows six lines of reversal to build up a grand sense of rising spirits, like the meadow larks that fly up at dawn to hover almost out of sight above their nests in damp meadow grass, singing joyfully (ll. 11–12). The other two sonnets in this group conclude with similar but briefer reversals, employing only the couplet for this purpose. These allow more space to the development of the melancholic condition and necessarily have less developed but more dramatic reversals of idea and mood.

Sonnet 32 returns to two established topics: (1) the difference in age between the Youth and the speaker and (2) the quality of the poems ("These poor rude lines," 32.4). Shakespeare, indulging in obvious pathos of self-pity and playing the old man card, imagines himself dying and the Youth continuing to read his sonnets, not for their style but for their love. Shakespeare's artistic insecurity may have been genuine, or it may have been an expression of modesty, or it may have been a ploy in begging for attention and compliments, or all of those, but it is difficult to sympathize with artistic insecurity when the work is so excellent.

Sonnets 33, 34, and 35 concern an unnamed event identified in Sonnet 35 as "sensual" (35.9). In sonnets 40, 41, and 42 an affair between the Youth and the Mistress is clearly named. These six sonnets certainly pertain to an extended event that may have gone through some progression. We are forced at this point to take into account the Mistress. Sonnet 144, which is part of the group addressed to the Dark Lady but treated as a soliloquy that might be included in either group, speculates on whether the Youth and Dark Lady have yet had sexual relations; sonnets 133 and 134, which seem to follow Sonnet 144 chronologically, lament the Mistress's possession of the Youth as her lover. It appears that the Youth and the Mistress became lovers in the period of Shakespeare's absence from the Youth. This betrayal would have realized all of Shakespeare's darkest forebodings about the Youth's more casual interest in friendship with the speaker, as well as Shakespeare's jealous knowledge of the Mistress's inclinations to roam freely in her sexual conquests. Shakespeare, having been banished to safeguard the Youth's reputation, has been doubly betrayed by a conspiracy of the two people he loves.

Sonnets 33, 34, and 35 offer a particularly striking situation for considering Shakespeare's use of groups, or clusters, of poems. The three have a progressive development of analysis and reaction to a difficult situation that required either a dramatic rupture of relations with the Youth or a cautious and diplomatic response involving much humiliation. The rupture would have canceled a relationship in which Shakespeare had invested great emotion and poetic effort. He was not ready for that step. Shakespeare's relationship with the Mistress was equally complicated, and to her he was also enthralled by dependency and desire.

These three sonnets, in which Shakespeare first confronts the relationship between the Youth and the Dark Lady, display either a changing perspective or a carefully considered response that appears to evolve. Sonnet 33 opens grandly with a metamorphosis of the Youth into a sun deity whose emotional warmth had shown his sunny beams on Shakespeare as the heavenly body blesses the earth with its presence:

> Full many a glorious morning have I seen
> Flatter the mountain tops with sovereign eye,
> Kissing with golden face the meadows green,
> Gilding pale streams with heavenly alcumy. (33.1–4)

This magnification of the Youth has several possible implications, but Shakespeare employs it, at the overt level of the poem, to excuse the Youth, as any reader of classical myth would do, since the gods can be neither controlled nor judged by mere mortals—a point underscored by the final line: "Suns of the world may stain, when heaven's sun staineth" (that is, lose their brightness, 33.14). Forgiveness that comes so easily feels weak in this serious situation, as if Shakespeare as both person and poet had failed to confront the situation realistically. The end, however, suggests another intention opposite to the apparent point. Shakespeare almost certainly aims to induce guilt by admitting to such elevation of the Youth in his life. A good deal is expected of the deity you worship. By forgiving the betrayal in the terms presented, he actually magnifies the deception while seeming to excuse it.

Sonnet 34 reaps the benefits of the guilt that was successfully induced by Sonnet 33. The Youth's acknowledgment of the betrayal allows a more serious tone to be put forward, so the speaker begins with the same basic image of a sun that permits a storm to overtake him. In both sonnets Shakespeare avoids direct accusations by treating the sun as passive in allowing the battering storm, though in fact the Youth is the cause. In Sonnet 34 Shakespeare comes closer to an accusation of betrayal in the opening line. The sun, here a little less the deity, had made a promise but then had broken it, leaving Shakespeare exposed and defenseless. Next we learn that the Youth has apologized and wept, literally or figuratively. Thus, Sonnet 33 did its work. But Shakespeare delays accepting the apology and begins a lecture that assumes greater personal dignity than he has previously displayed. He becomes the adult lecturing the inexperienced young man, explaining that apologies and repentance do not abolish pain, particularly the pain of betrayal by a friend. Apologies also do not cure the "disgrace" incurred (34.8). The poem here reverses the Youth's earlier concern about the disgrace that might come to him through association with Shakespeare. The affair between the Youth and the Mistress has become known, and Shakespeare has been humiliated.

Shakespeare's use of the "cross" in 34.12 to depict his suffering suggests the innocence of Jesus, who suffered for the sins of others. This parallel to the deity who pardons repenting sinners is carried on in the couplet as Shakespeare forgives the Youth after seeing tears of true contrition. These tears suggest the biblical "pearls of great price," alluded to in 34.13, that must be valued. A reversal of roles has occurred. The Youth, as a nature deity, has been superseded by the poet as a crucified deity of forgiveness, and in this process the Youth loses his elevated status and becomes human and immature. This is the first moment in the sonnets that Shakespeare asserts his own worth and dignity as factors in the relationship. It marks the beginning of a movement away from the role of suitor and toward that of equal.

Sonnet 35 takes its point of departure directly from the conclusion of the preceding sonnet, where Shakespeare identified himself as a painfully crucified martyr of love who is offering forgiveness. Now Shakespeare makes a remarkable leap of focus and understanding by turning his accusing eye on himself and identifying the basic problems as his own complicitous behavior and exaggeration of his martyrdom. Cured, for the moment, of his tendency to apologize, Shakespeare launches the sonnet with a quatrain full of sarcasm aimed jointly at the Youth and himself: at the Youth for being less than he seems and at himself for being all too eager to offer an excessive bounty of forgiveness. Referring back to the closed rose of the first sonnet and the clouded sun of the two immediately preceding sonnets (33 and 34), Shakespeare adds a third yet more powerful image: the dirty fountain. Here the discrepancy between the seeming brilliance of the beautiful and expensive piece of garden art—which might dispense refreshing water—when seen from a distance and the actual filth of the basin when viewed from nearby carries particular weight. Shakespeare adopts a tone of weary recognition in offering these well-known facts and their relevance to the Youth, but he applies his criticism mainly to himself for "[a]uthorizing thy trespass" and thereby "[m]yself corrupting" (35.6, 7). He has, he writes, also exaggerated the Youth's "sins" (35.8) in order to gain merit from forgiving them, thus further corrupting himself. The sestet reveals the speaker's state of fundamental emotional contradiction, in which he notes the "civil war" that is being waged within himself (35.12).

The critical insight brought to this final poem of the first trio on betrayal offers an entirely revised understanding of the dynamics of the relationship. Now Shakespeare clearly articulates what he had previously hinted: that he himself is deeply divided. However, while the perspectives are different, the situation has not changed; the Youth remains the worm-eaten bud and an expensive dirty fountain, and Shakespeare remains entangled with the graceful beauty of appearances. Still, the insights of the poem act like a watershed moment when the emotional flow has imperceptibly changed directions.

The next four sonnets—36 through 39—act as a group collectively dedicated to praising the Youth and reassuring him of Shakespeare's unreserved devotion. These sonnets have the odd effect of serving as a buffer between the three sonnets that explore Shakespeare's complicated response to the Youth's "sensual" betrayal (sonnets 33, 34, and 35) and the next group—sonnets 40, 41, and 42—which record and respond to the affair between the Mistress and the Youth. Sonnets 36 through 39 offer a brief respite between blows to the relationship, a respite in which Shakespeare rededicates himself to the Youth, as if to demonstrate that his love is undamaged by betrayal and banishment. Having cheerfully pardoned the Youth's offense, the speaker then suffers another attack on his honor, self-esteem, and love. The purpose of this group of poems seems to be to dispel the anger of the preceding three sonnets and to bring the relationship back to a more innocent condition in which the Youth deserves all the praise and Shakespeare is again the subservient suitor and praising poet. However, things have happened that need to be dealt with, such as Shakespeare's banishment, so Shakespeare takes these up in a very positive manner. Images of spoiled rose buds disappear in the light of good cheer. While these poems are dedicated to dismissing problems, we sense a degree of excessively positive praise that testifies to their continued though underlying presence, and in Sonnet 38 the praise is clearly undercut with irritation. Sonnet 39 seems designed to recover the cheerful tone that leaked away in Sonnet 38.

In sonnets 40, 41, and 42 Shakespeare faces the major betrayal of the sequence. First the Youth betrayed him; now he and the Mistress jointly do so. Although the Mistress is not mentioned, the events of sonnets 33, 34, and 35 may have involved some prelude to this event. Shakespeare's hopeful attempts to put the earlier betrayal behind him with a set of four praising sonnets did not succeed, for the problems inherent in his relationship with the Youth could not be wished away. Shakespeare probably entertained no illusions about the loyalty of the Mistress, since the sonnets to her suggest that she was perpetually and openly busy with men. By Sonnet 40 the picture of dual betrayal may already have been clear, so that Shakespeare responded less with shock than with tired recognition of and resignation to the inevitable. Sonnets 41 and 42 lumber through half-hearted rationalizations for undeserved forgiveness, delivering small stabs of annoyance along the way. Shakespeare explained in Sonnet 35 that in his divided self he excused too easily and thereby contributed to the offense, but he continues all too easily, it seems, on this road.

Sonnets 43 through 47 form a cluster centering on the difference between bodies and thought, seeing and imagining, and the elements of air, earth, fire, and water as they play their roles in perception and mood and contribute to loving. Continued separation of Shakespeare from his two loves is not only implied but even stated. Sonnet 48 laments the loss of the Youth, who has now been stolen by some "vulgar thief" (48.9). This reference could be to the Mistress, but may involve someone else.

In Sonnet 49 Shakespeare writes in powerful and ironic anticipation of a formal break in his friendship with the Youth. It is also one of his better poems of double meaning. The overt gist of the poem lies in Shakespeare's offer to take the Youth's side and to support this break, for he can think of no reason why the Youth should love him. The language used to describe the Youth's imagined behavior, however, conveys a different message; it makes the Youth into a banker who keeps books and does audits to check his profit and loss, who converts currency and adopts a manner of grave formality in his business proceedings. It is to this calculating manner of conducting friendship that Shakespeare has nothing to offer, for real love is not a matter of audits and currency exchanges. Shakespeare's apparent humility, his confession of not deserving so rich a friend, only slightly disguises the scorn carried in his characterization of the Youth as a banker or accountant of emotions. The images of this poem once again draw attention to the social and economic distance between Shakespeare and the Youth and (as elsewhere) suggest that wealth has a corrupting effect on its privileged possessors.

Sonnets 50 and 51 both treat Shakespeare's journeying away from the Youth, and both focus with mild comedy on the horse carrying him. If these sonnets retain their original order, it has to be assumed that some reconciliation took place and the banishment was lifted, for these poems make no mention of forced separation and yet they assume the disruption of a social relationship.

Traditionally, sonnet sequences can be graphed as sine waves, with oscillations in the relationship before the lovers ultimately part. Only Spenser's *Amoretti* ends in marriage. In Sidney's *Astrophil and Stella*, after a series of sonnets lamenting his mistress's indifference, Astrophil rejoices in Sonnet 69, "Gone is the winter of my misery, / My spring appears; O see what doth here grow! / For Stella hath, with words where faith doth shine, / Of her high heart giv'n me the monarchy" (ll. 7–10). After another group of poems rejoicing in Stella's love, Sidney's Sonnet 86 begins, "Alas, whence came this change of looks?" Similarly Shakespeare's Sonnet 50 implies that the speaker and Youth are enjoying one of the peaks in their love/friendship.

The remaining sonnets addressed to the Youth present an unnerving seesaw of attitudes and tones. The rival poet group tends to be sarcastic, but not uniformly. The most famous of love sonnets come from this group, but so do the largest number of openly angry poems. This shift to open irritation largely displaces the poetry of repressed anger, as in the veiled accusations of emotional accounting of Sonnet 49.

Sonnets 55, 60, 64, and 65 introduce a new emotional tone that is entirely impersonal. In these, Shakespeare's efforts lie entirely in the art of the sonnet, not at all in exploring intense personal emotions. For all of its fame, Sonnet 65 is emotionally empty compared with sonnets 21 and 23. The lack of real intimacy and the impersonal focus on craft go far to make good the promise first declared in Sonnet 15 that Shakespeare would write poems to immortalize the Youth, to "ingraft" him with timeless verse (15.14).

Shakespeare's new openness in anger is signaled by Sonnets 57 and 58 ("That god forbid that made me first your slave," 58.1). In this pair open sarcasm dominates. Previously buried ironies come to light for what they are. As with Sonnet 35, however, Shakespeare is not interested in breaking off the friendship. Unlike the problem in Sonnet 35, the situation here is of a general nature—having to wait for promised attention and being disregarded in the busy life of a great man—and for that reason no anguished decision is required. However, the patience expressed at the end of Sonnet 57 seems exhausted by the conclusion of the next poem: "I am to wait, though waiting so be hell, / Not blame your pleasure, be it ill or well" (58.13–14). The last line suggests that the Youth engages in unattractive activities while he keeps Shakespeare waiting.

Sonnets 93 through 96 again take up the basic discrepancy Shakespeare notes between the Youth's appearance and his behavior, and sets this out with special and personal clarity in Sonnet 93:

> So shall I live, supposing thou art true,
> Like a deceived husband, so love's face
> May still seem love to me, though alter'd new. (93.1–3)

Shakespeare's mixture of deep commitment and anxiety is captured more effectively in the opening lines of this sonnet than anywhere else. His confession to having the feelings and fears of a husband signals the existence of much friendly intimacy, at least from time to time. The Youth has been charming and accepting. The speaker, by announcing that he is like a deceived husband who remains innocent of his spouse's true feelings and behavior, is quite obviously saying just the opposite; he is calling attention to his suspicion and frustrated inability to detect the truth. But the perpetually loving looks on the Youth's perfectly innocent face almost succeed in abolishing suspicion.

Shakespeare begins to push toward the probability that he really is like the cuckolded husband and brings up the Garden of Eden story and God's curious responsibility for the bewitching beauty of the apple and the sin it inspired. "[H]eaven" (93.9) has made the Youth seem beautiful and innocent, like the beautiful apple, and perhaps like the beautiful Eve. But the apple turned out to be evil. Thus, the evil apple, created by God, and the beautiful woman, also created by God, brought evil into the world. In the Renaissance view it is Eve's temptation of Adam that plays the critical role in the downfall of mankind, not Adam's weakness. In Sonnet 93, the beautiful apple with its load of evil is Heaven's work, and the Youth with his beautiful unreadable face is as well. At this point the Youth appears to be associated with the apple as a temptation a wise man might avoid. Sonnet 92 ends on a similar note: "But what's so blessed-fair that fears no blot? / Thou mayst be false, and yet I know it not" (92.13–14).

These two poems and a number of others coming toward the end of the sonnets to the Youth share the curiosity of existing in a sort of timeless loop, in which new poems do not refer back to earlier situations from which Shakespeare would have obtained certain knowledge, or as if Shakespeare lived in a kind of perpetual state of optimism that erased the past and allowed the relationship to recommence uncontaminated by experience. Elaborate rearrangements of the order of the sonnets might solve some of these discrepancies between ignorance and certain knowledge, but in general the later poems are more open, as this one is, in stating the problems addressed.

Certain themes reappear throughout the sequence and over several years. The fame that these sonnets will bring; the wearing effects of time; the perfect, eternal, and inspiring form of the Youth's beauty; Shakespeare's committed devotion in the face of all discouragements; his suffering unjustly: all of these themes bob up with perfect regularity, as if chosen topics of sonnet meditation.

Shakespeare's confessions of his own failings offer a new theme for the later sonnets to the Youth. He can be very open in depicting his own deficiencies of various sorts—particularly his shortcomings as a true friend. This confession makes an agreeable reversal in loyalties. Shakespeare's self-criticism suggests an increase in self-confidence, an assertion of equality, and a relief from his previous frequent complaints of martyrdom. In Sonnet 102, Shakespeare admits to a lessening of his initial fervor of enthusiasm in an unusually lyrical moment. With its reference to Philomel it is a sonnet that John Keats (1795–1821) must have admired greatly, for the third quatrain rings through his *Ode to a Nightingale* some two centuries later.

In Sonnet 109 Shakespeare confesses to having "rang'd" (l. 5) to find other affections, but never so far as to lose his unity with the Youth. In the end he can return from his voyages in affection to wipe off the stains that his behavior has created, for the Youth in the "wide universe" is his "rose" (ll. 13, 14).

Likewise, in Sonnet 110 Shakespeare admits to much wandering. The first quatrain provides perhaps the most interesting comment we have of Shakespeare on himself:

> Alas, 'tis true, I have gone here and there,
> And made myself a motley to the view,
> Gor'd [wounded] my own thoughts, sold cheap what is most dear,
> Made old offenses of affections new. (ll. 1–4)

Here is an obvious comment on his stage profession. He has been like a court jester in his costumes. He may also be referring to foolish social behavior in his associations with the rich and powerful whose favor he craved; he certainly must have felt the fool at times in the company the Youth kept. Then he goes on to more obscure and deeper criticisms of his basic character, perhaps as a writer, but more likely in his personal life. The particulars remain obscure, but the passage has the tone of a deeply felt confession.

Sonnet 116 famously paraphrases 1 Corinthians 13.4–8 in a kind of marriage ceremony. Yet immediately following this poem about love's constancy, Shakespeare in sonnets 117–119 admits, "I have hoisted sail to all the winds / Which should transport me farthest from your sight" (117.7–8). In the earlier sonnets the speaker had been banished by the Youth. Now the speaker anticipates Coriolanus's claim that "There is a world elsewhere" (*Coriolanus*, 3.3.135) and says in effect, "I banish you!" (3.3.123).

Sonnet 118 digs into the darker reaches of the psychology of friendship and the physiology of appetite and constipation. The opening quatrain runs through a double simile of considerable distaste about eating sour things to improve the appetite and taking laxatives to ease constipation and prevent disease. Thus Shakespeare, who feared he was growing sick of his friend, administered emotional purges to himself by means of new friends. In Sonnet 119 the speaker again states that he has strayed from the Youth, but in the concluding couplet the poet returns "to my content" (l. 13). In an ironic twist, then, these sonnets depicting the speaker's inconstancy end up confirming Sonnet 116's assertion of love's permanence, since in the end the speaker returns to the Youth.

Sonnet 120 is particularly interesting for the assertion that his role with the Youth has reversed. He suggests no satisfaction here in obtaining revenge through the actions described in sonnets 117 through 119, but his willingness to call in emotional debts suggests confidence in the relationship and in himself. The poem speaks with particular frankness in reviewing reciprocal pain: "For if you were by my unkindness shaken / As I by yours, y' have pass'd a hell of time" (120.5–6).

There is no final, easy summation to be made about Shakespeare's relations with the Youth or about the sonnets that followed that friendship. There seems to have been deep affection and deep ambiguity to the very end, as though Shakespeare had made a commitment that he would see through, as with a marriage in which the relationship was initially uneven but in time achieved some balance. The last poem addressed to the Youth, Sonnet 126, is a twelve-line lyric with paired rhymes. In one of the richest and most complicated poems of the series, Shakespeare returns to the theme of time's effects on the Youth. Shakespeare reverts to his mythological framework to depict the Youth as a kind of plaything of Nature (recalling Sonnet 20), who is using him in her contest with Time to see which is more powerful. She has succeeded in keeping Time's effects away from the Youth, but she cannot do so forever:

> She may detain, but not still keep, her treasure!
> Her audit (though delay'd) answer'd must be,
> And her quietus is to render thee. (126.10–12)

The final image uses one of the bookkeeping metaphors Shakespeare employed for various purposes. The image is cold, as in Sonnet 49. Nature has favored her special boy, but Time cannot be defeated. The Youth will be handed over in a delayed payment. The poem moves from a rich set of merged images involving Time's sickle, the hourglass, and the crescent moon in the opening to this simple unemotional ending. The tone of the work is that of someone with wisdom purchased through Time speaking to someone inexperienced in time's meanings. "Lovely boy" (126.1) feels both tender and condescending. There is little sense of the Youth's facing a tragic destiny, only a warning: "[I]f it be not now, yet it will come" (*Hamlet*, 5.2.221–222).

The sonnets to the Mistress constitute a second history, so to speak, and thus quite sensibly were printed as a separate group. Whoever possessed the sonnets and delivered them to the printer may well have acquired the two groups as separate collections. The sonnets to the Mistress begin with two complimentary love poems; because they are uncomplicated by jealousy and betrayal it seems as if they might have been the first sonnets written to her. No further efforts to establish a sequence are evident until the last two sonnets, which were not originally connected to any of the others in the collection but were placed at the end of it as a bridge to *A Lover's Complaint*—the other work printed in the original 1609 quarto edition. It is particularly noticeable that the three poems having to do with the Youth are not sequential, for the one that obviously comes first (Sonnet 144) is printed last.

Taken together, the sonnets addressed to the Dark Lady involve fewer inhibitions and less self-deprecation than those to the Youth. With the Mistress, Shakespeare is not fighting for a relationship to which he must be admitted by another's social grace and patronage. As in the sonnets to the Youth, situations in this group remain unspecified, but their general character is less varied and easier to understand. Most of the problems Shakespeare explores here involve the Dark Lady's infidelity and Shakespeare's attempts to cope with his feelings of attraction and jealousy. He speaks forthrightly in naming the faults and weaknesses on both sides. Although many of these sonnets involve limited success in love and much pain, Shakespeare is generally able to respond without tortured justifications for either party and at times can see the whole relationship as fundamentally comic.

Shakespeare reveals very little about the Mistress. Sonnets 142 and 152 tell us that she, like him, is married; that she, like him, has had other adulterous affairs; and that at the moment she is impatient with his desire to hold her to him, for she is in active pursuit of others. In Sonnet 128, her skill with a keyboard instrument suggests that she came from a family with advantages in both money and culture. She is young by Shakespeare's standards, he being twenty-eight to thirty. Since he makes much of the difference in their ages, she can hardly be more than twenty and may be even younger.

In Sonnet 133 we discover that the Mistress and the Youth are friends who see each other when Shakespeare is not with them, so we can infer that she moves in circles to which the Youth belongs—with arranged marriages and much freedom for adulterous relationships as long as reasonable discretion was maintained. We know that she has dark hair, dark eyes, and "dun" colored breasts (130.3)—in contrast to the more conventional object of love poems, with blonde hair, blue eyes, and milky skin. Most likely, her coloring gives her the title of "Dark Lady," a designation that perhaps conveys more mystery than was intended.

From the content of the sonnets we can infer that she was intelligent, appreciated wit, and had much independence of spirit—indeed, too much for Shakespeare, since the qualities that made her attractive and available also made her impossible to hold. Because the Mistress was the primary reader of the sonnets that were addressed to her, it can reasonably be assumed that her ability to respond was a factor in Shakespeare's treatment of the material. With the Mistress, Shakespeare was wittier, more outspoken, earthy, and certainly less humble than with the Youth. He doted on her but did not view her in anything remotely like Petrarchan or courtly love terms. Sharing a bed with her apparently produced in Shakespeare a particular quality of frankness.

The "Dark Lady" sonnets thus reverse Petrarchan conventions in a variety of ways. Whereas in every other sonnet sequence the beloved is of a higher social station than the speaker, the Dark Lady does not appear to be aristocratic. She defies Petrarchan ideals of beauty. Traditionally, the speaker of sonnet sequences laments because his lady is physically inaccessible. The Dark Lady, on the contrary, is all too accessible, not just to the speaker but to others as well, including the Youth.

It would be reasonable to assume that the Mistress, in addition to being a friend of the Youth, would have read the sonnets that Shakespeare wrote for the Youth. Her interest in men being unquenchable, she might well have regarded the Youth not only as a handsome, wealthy, popular, and available young man, but also as a rival. In his sonnets to the Youth, Shakespeare leaves little noticeable room for any other deeply felt love, a slight that the Mistress might have found distressing. She might have read Sonnet 20. Not long after that poem was written and during Shakespeare's banishment, she seduced the Youth, or so Shakespeare asserts in both Sonnet 41 and Sonnet 144. Although only speculation this reasoning is not out of keeping with the complexities of the situation—one in which two men with close but strained ties share the favors of a young married woman.

To Shakespeare, the Mistress was beautiful, interesting, erotic, and elusive, but she was also weak, treacherous, and maddening. She was a serious challenge in herself and posed a challenge to his friendship with the Youth. The main challenge she offered Shakespeare was less that of keeping her attention than that of maintaining his reason and balance in the face of the temptations and annoyances she continuously threw in his path. A number of sonnets to the Mistress may reference her affair with the Youth, but only three sonnets are certain to do so: 133, 134, and 144. Of these, Sonnet 144 appears to be the earliest, for it speculates with a certain savagery on whether the relationship between the Mistress and the Youth has yet become sexual, and suspects it has. Sonnet 144 may be associated with sonnets 33, 34, and 35, involving the "sensual" betrayal.

Sonnet 144 is not addressed to the Mistress. It is a soliloquy that begins with the imagery of a traditional morality play, with a good angel and a bad angel fighting each other for Shakespeare's soul, although the only real issue is whether the good angel, the Youth, can survive the temptations offered by the bad angel, the Mistress. Just as a large portion of the heavenly host followed Satan into Hell, so the Youth seems doomed to a similar fate of a sexual nature:

> And whether that my angel be turn'd fiend,
> Suspect I may, yet not directly tell,
> But being both from me, both to each other friend,
> I guess one angel in another's hell. (144.9–12)

The dark "hell" of the Mistress refers to her vagina.

The sonnet ends on a note of ambiguous comedy, as several of them do, with speculation on how Shakespeare can learn the truth: "Yet this shall I ne'er know, but live in doubt, / Till my bad angel fire my good one out" (144.13–14). The image here is entirely sexual and has several possibilities, probably all intended. One is that she will discharge him from her sexual embraces, as one fires an object from a cannon, or otherwise drive him out of her or away from her. Or she may burn out his passion through excessive indulgence. Or since fire could mean a wasting affliction, she might give him a venereal disease. In any case, Shakespeare does not expect immediate or definitive information. The situation is a continuing one. The cutting allusion to venereal disease may only be a counterthrust designed to cause trouble where it is deserved.

Sonnet 133 again deploys the much-worked theme of the unity of lovers, this time with Shakespeare bonded to both parties. This union of hearts among three produces a "torment thrice threefold" (133.8) and Shakespeare's total imprisonment in the bosom of the Mistress. Sonnet 134 is a continuation of 133 but switches the basic metaphor from imprisonment to mortgage and debt. The speaker here asks that the Dark Lady restore the Youth to him but knows she will not. She will keep both the friend, who has paid Shakespeare's debt (by having sex with the Dark Lady), and the speaker, who is "not free" (134.14) to leave because he still loves her. In the financial world, if someone pays another's debt, the debtor is no longer tied to the creditor. Love works differently.

Sonnet 151 breaks new poetic ground in English poetry by introducing frank sexual arousal as central to love and then treating it with amusement. In the sonnet tradition, certainly, no poet had previously so completely stripped away from love the romantic fabric of idealized passion. Although graphically sexual and startling, the poem is comic and affectionate rather than obscene—and very Shakespearean in that it depends on a complex argument to explore the basic psychological and moral character of sexual attraction. The key word of the poem, "conscience" (ll. 1, 2, 13), was little distinguished at that period in history from "conscious." Both words mean self-awareness. "Conscience," however, can also mean the moral sensibility and may refer simultaneously both to general self-awareness and to moral self-awareness.

The poem opens by introducing the youthful Cupid, god of unthinking love, in order to establish the basic paradox surrounding passion: erotic love is so direct, primitive, and pre-rational that its basic impulses are thoughtless and innocent. At the same time, however, the acting out of sexual impulses, innocent in itself, requires suppression of the moral self-awareness with which all adult sinners are burdened. Cupid—the offspring of Love (Venus) and War (Mars) and armed with his erotic arrow, or irrationality—is a complex figure. The observation about love's producing both moral awareness and greater self-awareness invokes the Christian understanding of the Old Testament myth of the Garden of Eden, where Adam, who should have obeyed God's commandment not to eat the fruit, allowed his erotic attraction to Eve to lead him astray. His sin produced guilt and punishment, giving him a conscience, previously unneeded, and a new form of humanizing self-awareness.

Love, then, carries a whole set of basic human attributes and contradictions: on the one hand, it is infantile, willful, mindless, and even innocent, but on the other hand, it is awakening, creative, humanizing, conscience-producing, and guilt-ridden. The poem quickly moves from paradox to a jesting argument. Shakespeare is sexually aroused by the Mistress. She calls attention to the sin of his adultery, to which he responds by claiming her attractions have led him astray and caused him to repress his adult conscience. Now his "flesh" takes over and "rising at thy name doth point out thee / As his triumphant prize" (ll. 8–10). His uninhibited, unreflective male organ rises to full attention at the mere thought of her name. This condition briefly transforms Shakespeare into the image of a prize-winning knight who has fought for his lady, and with lance erect claims victory in the tournament. The image of this triumphant erection is brief, however, for the victorious knight soon becomes the conquered vassal who "is contented thy poor drudge to be, / To stand in thy affairs, fall by thy side" (ll. 11–12). He is put to a great deal of work, but happily. The final couplet combines a sweetness of affection with the comedy of unhampered desire and, referring back to the opening lines where thought is abandoned, Shakespeare enjoys a childishly simple and sensual erotic moment completely lacking either conscience or consciousness: "No want of conscience hold it that I call / Her 'love' for whose dear love I rise and fall." Use of the present tense effectively contributes to the transitory quality of such uninhibited pleasure. This sonnet has no rivals in the English tradition for its confessional sexual comedy.

Indulgence in thoughtless sensuality was not, however, Shakespeare's primary mode. Sonnet 129 is the most intense and self-lacerating of the sonnets. Although offered as an exclamation about the irrationality and violence of sexual desire generally, it leaves no doubt about its source in personal experience. The object of Shakespeare's anger is not the Mistress or the Youth involved with her, although they would be contained by the general indictment. He rails against his own passionate, uncontrollable self. This mad irrationality has its primary cause in its limitless desire, but it then produces equally irrational self-loathing, like a poison put down for rats that drives them mad before killing them. Lust begets a world without moderation where virtue itself becomes a vice. If Sonnet 151 is the "yin," or thesis, of sensual poems, Sonnet 129 is the "yang," or antithesis. All innocence of flesh has vanished in this diatribe against the betrayal of "the nobler part" (151.6), the consciousness so happily abandoned in Sonnet 151.

Three kinds of sonnets within the "Dark Lady" group give Shakespeare his best works: those appreciative of the Mistress, those particularly frank in their presentation of the sexuality of the relationship, and those with the most perceptive demonstrations of self-analysis. The least successful may employ the same themes but fall back on metaphor that promotes ingenuity over fresh thought, such as those relying on the bonding of hearts.

Sonnets 127, 128, and 130 are among Shakespeare's lightest and best. Sonnets 127 and 130 may be the two best anti-Petrarchan sonnets written, for here Shakespeare directly denies the clichés of female attractiveness. Sonnet 127 attacks Petrarchan conventions indirectly by attesting to the downfall of modern standards of beauty, which now allow black to be beautiful, but this observation becomes a compliment, for Shakespeare lived in an age of cosmetics. In this world of artifice, only this Mistress possesses uncontaminated beauty. Sonnet 130 takes up the same theme and was probably paired with 127 in composition. In the opening quatrain, Shakespeare simply denies all the standard clichés about female beauty:

> My mistress' eyes are nothing like the sun;
> Coral is far more red than her lips' red;
> If snow be white, why then her breasts are dun;
> If hairs be wires, black wires grow on her head.

As with Sonnet 127, Shakespeare loves her for the genuine thing she is and not for the fictitious attributes commonly imposed by poets on the women they love: "And yet, by heaven, I think my love as rare / As any she belied with false compare" (130.13–14).

Sonnet 138 may be the most psychologically analytical and profound work of the entire sequence. Here Shakespeare explores, in a completely modern manner, the neurosis of mutual dependency yet without loss of poetic richness, as in the paradox of the second line: "I do believe her though I know she lies." It is in poems of this sort, where direct insight combines with strong emotion, that Shakespeare does some of his best work. In his most productive manner, he concludes by allowing multiple meanings and an ambiguous tone to hover over the final insight, particularly with the pun on "lie" and the many overlapping meanings of "flattered": "Therefore I lie with her, and she with me, / And in our faults by lies we flattered be" (138.13–14).

The love they share is here defined as the consequence of transparent but successful attempts at mutual deceptions. These dishonesties bring them to a sexual act that is only a pretense of love. They tell lies in order to lie in bed together having sex; and that act is a lie about love. They lie in all these meanings of the word in order to be "flattered," which can mean delighted, or pleased by obsequious behavior, or insincerely praised, or gratified through vanity, or tricked, or inspired with false hope, and probably all of that. They have needs, and their needs are being met, each by cooperative exploitation of the other. She, the adulterous wife and unfaithful mistress, and he the adulterous and aging man, want to recapture what they have lost, and they do so with behavior that seems to gloss over the losses but actually only confirms them. But that is their game. The couplet concludes with a final twist of unflinching analysis but also with an odd shrug of acceptance, a little laugh at them both.

Sonnet 143 is a good work on which to draw this discussion to a close. Although neglected, it stands as one of Shakespeare's most amusing, self-deprecating, original, and successful sonnets. It is based on the kind of self-awareness shown in Sonnet 138 but goes much further with the comedy of Shakespeare's infatuation with the Mistress and her insatiable appetite for men. It is a poem without name-calling or spasms of anger. Shakespeare turns to his occasional narrative gift, as in Sonnet 20, and spins a domestic tale in which the Mistress becomes a housewife who must cope with a flock of chickens and a clinging toddler. Shakespeare is the toddler. The rooster who runs away is a young gallant (possibly the Youth) whom the distracted mother chases as he tries to escape her flock.

Shakespeare's recognition of himself, who is older than the Mistress, as a weepy and stumbling baby is as insightful as is his perception of himself as a liar in Sonnet 138, and much funnier. Presenting his Mistress as a rustic keeper of chickens who wants to maintain control of her flock and will neglect her baby, the speaker makes tolerable her need to control as many men as possible. In several sonnets to the Mistress and in a few of the later sonnets to the Youth, Shakespeare puns on his name, usually as here with a double meaning of "sexual desire" and Will Shakespeare. So Will offers her both himself and her pleasure with others, hoping she might soon return to her proper chores and comfort him after her busy chase. Everyone is reduced to a barnyard farce that might easily have sprung out of *The Nun's Priest's Tale* from Chaucer's *Canterbury Tales*. It is good to see Shakespeare, the great master of the ludicrousness in the lives of others, turn his humor on himself, for it must have been a strong antidote to much melancholy and irritation.

Sonnet 145 seems slightly anomalous. Written in iambic tetrameter rather than the pentameter of the other sonnets, it employs rather simpler diction than is characteristic of the sequence. The sense of the poem could fit with the other Dark Lady Sonnets, but line 13 offers a tantalizing possible pun: " 'I hate' from hate away she threw." Shakespeare was of course married to Anne Hathaway, whose last name in the late sixteenth century would have been pronounced "Hate-away." Might this have been a poem originally addressed to Anne? Could Shakespeare have recycled it (as other poets have) for a new love? Or did someone—Shakespeare or another—slip it into the sequence?

Sonnets 153 and 154, discussed elsewhere in this volume, both are and are not part of the Dark Lady sequence. They are not addressed to her, and they present an Ovidian myth-making tale that serves as a bridge to *A Lover's Complaint*. But the speaker who flees to Bath to be cured of his love discovers that no remedy is possible; he can be happy only with his beloved, who is presumably the Dark Lady.

The Dark Lady sequence, like that to the Youth, ends inconclusively. Perhaps *A Lover's Complaint* offers the only resolution. In that poem a woman complains that she was betrayed by her lover. Yet even after all the pain she has suffered, after the discovery of how false her lover was, she says that she might do it all "again for such a sake" (*A Lover's Complaint*, 321). Shakespeare put the matter more bluntly in Sonnet 129.13–14, "yet none knows well / To shun the heaven that leads men to this hell." This is how love is, the poems say, and how it will always be. There is no resolution. As constable Elbow admonishes the suspected malefactor Pompey, "Thou art to continue now, thou varlet, thou art to continue" (*Measure for Measure*, 2.1.191–192).

In these sonnets Shakespeare the man stands revealed. He is a little naive in an agreeably hopeful sense. We can judge him to be in many ways a rationalist and a skeptic, but he stands also as an idealist. But he is much more. He wants love and suffers at not being accepted for who he is and what he has to offer. He wants passion but gets only part of what he desires. He confesses to many failures. He compromises to keep a friendship that a modern reader might consider to be of little value, or perhaps he is merely determined in his commitments—an idealist forced to accept imperfection. He feels himself to be some sort of social outcast and is aware of public censure. Most important, his sonnets display an openness to working with actual experience that was unique at the time, and it is this openness to experience that fed his plays so wonderfully.

**Annotated Bibliography**

Bloom, Harold, ed. *Shakespeare's Sonnets and Poems*. Broomall, PA: Chelsea House, 1999. Brief anthology of short selections from major essays on seven sonnets and other major poems. Designed for school libraries.

Booth, Stephen, ed. *An Essay on Shakespeare's Sonnets*. New Haven: Yale UP, 1969. An intense response to reading the sonnets considering a number of methods by which they were organized. Of special interest to advanced students.

———. *Shakespeare's Sonnets*. New Haven: Yale UP, 1977. Photocopies of the original 1609 edition with facing text in modern spelling and punctuation, followed by extensive line-by-line notes on each sonnet. Indispensable for any reader truly interested in Shakespeare's work.

Hubler, Edward. *The Sense of Shakespeare's Sonnets*. New York: Hill and Wang, 1962. Useful series of studies on the sonnets and their connections to Shakespeare's other work. Appropriate for undergraduate and advanced students.

Leishman, J. B. *Themes and Variations in Shakespeare's Sonnets*. New York: Harper and Row, 1963. An interesting scholarly study on major themes and their sources. A scholar's essays for scholars.

Smith, Hallett. *The Tension of the Lyre: Poetry in Shakespeare's Sonnets*. San Marino, CA: Huntington Library, 1981. Considers the sonnets in the context of Shakespeare's total body of work. Mainly for advanced students.

Vendler, Helen. *The Art of Shakespeare's Sonnets*. Cambridge, MA: Harvard UP, 1997. Vendler examines each sonnet individually, focusing on the linguistic artistry of the poems. Not dwelling on the narrative pattern, she points out how Shakespeare uses language in startling and innovative ways.

Willen, Gerald, and Victor B. Reed. *A Casebook on Shakespeare's Sonnets*. New York: Thomas Y. Crowell, 1964. A photocopy of the 1609 edition with extensive notes and a useful anthology of essays. For students at all levels.

# Sonnet 3

## Michelle M. Sauer

Look in thy glass and tell the face thou viewest
Now is the time that face should form another,
Whose fresh repair if now thou not renewest,
Thou dost beguile the world, unbless some mother.
For where is she so fair whose unear'd womb
Disdains the tillage of thy husbandry?
Or who is he so fond will be the tomb
Of his self-love, to stop posterity?
Thou art thy mother's glass and she in thee
Calls back the lovely April of her prime;
So thou through windows of thine age shalt see,
Despite of wrinkles this thy golden time.
   But if thou live, remember'd not to be,
    Die single, and thine image dies with thee.

### PROSE PARAPHRASE

Look into your mirror and tell the face that you see there that it should dupli-cate itself right now by procreating. If it is not copied now, you will cheat the world and deprive some woman of the blessing of motherhood. Where can you find a woman with an "unear'd [unplowed] womb" (3.5), that is, a virgin, no matter how beautiful, who will reject your advances? And what man is so foolish and so nar-cissistic that he will end his lineage in his grave?

You are your mother's mirror image, and she is reflected in you as she looked in the prime of her youth. So you, despite your wrinkles caused by age, will see your youth represented by your children. But if you intend not to be remembered, do not marry; and your image will die with you.

## THE PLACE OF THE SONNET IN THE CYCLE

Sonnet 3 is part of the "procreation" series, which is comprised of the first 17 sonnets, and are addressed to the fair youth. Heather Dubrow argues that these sonnets, even more than the later ones, establish the counter-Petrarchan tradition. These sonnets urge carnal desire, love as the fulfillment of social obligations, and procreative sexuality. Still other critics explore the nonprocreative sexualities in this sonnet set. Much recent critical attention has been given to the explorations of homosocial desire between Shakespeare (or at least the sonnet persona) and the lovely boy. Within the first 20 sonnets, there is a progressive development of sexual feelings that were initially repressed. By Sonnet 18, the persona claims his desire and suggests that his words will become the young man's descendants, especially since they reflect his beauty. Sonnet 3 emphasizes this idea of preservation, and it marks the entry of the word "love" into the sequence, although it is introduced as "self-love."

A great deal of critical attention has also been devoted to finding the "true story" behind the sonnets. Who was the lovely boy? Who was the beautiful mother? What was Shakespeare's relationship to them? Sonnet 3 is not an exception to this narrative hunt. It has been suggested that the young man in question was William Herbert, the future third Earl of Pembroke, who was one of the dedicatees of the First Folio (1623). However, there is no evidence of a connection between him and Shakespeare during the time the sonnets were composed. Another candidate for the young man is Henry Wriothesley, third Earl of Southampton. If Wriothesley were indeed the lovely boy, then the mother of lines 9–10 would have been Mary, Countess of Southampton. In 1594, the year her son was to enter his inheritance, she would have been a widow for thirteen years.

Despite this drive to find the "real story," nothing has been proven conclusively. Still other scholars have looked into other stories to be told by the sonnets. Robert Crosman suggests that "there is a discernible story in Shakespeare's sonnets," a view he supports through a reading of sonnets 1–17 (470). Crosman believes that the procreation sonnets are the "preamble" to the later love poetry that the sonnets become. In this way, Shakespeare used them to ingratiate himself with the upper class by offering artificial advice meant to placate powerful patrons. However, in doing so, Shakespeare ultimately undermines his own position—for having spent time with the young man, he falls wildly in love, and then is unable to recapture his beloved's trust.

Even without an apparent change of heart, Sonnet 3 occupies an interesting position in the procreation set. As the main point of these sonnets is to urge the lovely boy to have children, most rely heavily on images of life rather than death, although age is a common image, too. Helen Vendler suggests that Sonnet 3 encapsulates a series of "alternatives," both death-dealing and life-giving (58–60). The images of death include the unblessed mother (l. 4), the disdained husbandry (l. 5), and stopped posterity (l. 8). Corresponding images of life include replication (l. 2), the accepting woman (ll. 5–6), and the man who is not foolish (ll. 7–8). Overall, the poem urges life; ultimately, it concludes with a "death-curse" couplet. This series of complications is connected to the notion of *dédoublement* (aesthetic self-reflection), which is an integral part of the sonnets.

Despite the focus of Sonnet 3—and indeed of the entire procreation subset—on the male reproductive role, the concept of motherhood, albeit as a womb-incubator, is introduced immediately. Sonnet 3 focuses on mother-as-womb in suggesting that no woman would refuse her womb to the young man. Much has been made, for example, of the lines comparing the young man to his mother instead of to his father. Some scholars have suggested that the father is dead. Others believe the maternal comparison is deliberate. Sonnet 20 claims that the fair youth has "[a] woman's face" (20.1) and "[a] woman's gentle heart" (20.3). By likening the youth to his mother, Sonnet 3 already introduces the element of androgyny that pervades the entire fair youth sequence (sonnets 1–126).

Naomi J. Miller examines the procreation subset in connection with the burgeoning new literary genre: the maternal advice book. Specifically, she focuses on the phrase "unbless some mother" (l. 4) as being directly connected to the "resonance of the 'mother's blessing' texts," which had begun appearing contemporaneously with the sonnets. In light of these texts, "the narcissistic discourse of physical vanity that marks [S]onnet 3 . . . may be read against an incipient counterdiscourse of maternal love and responsibility" (353). These advice books suggested that mothers contributed more to their children's existence than simply incubation and nurturing. Instead, such works emphasized the need for maternal participation in instruction and development, from birth through adulthood. Moreover, motherhood was considered the ultimate ambition and defining role for Early Modern English women. The real sin, then, is less the deprivation of the world, and more the refusal to fulfill the anonymous woman's destiny.

## DEVICES AND TECHNIQUES

Structurally, Sonnet 3 fits into Shakespeare's overall scheme for the sonnet sequence. It is written in iambic pentameter, has three cross-rhymed quatrains, and ends with a couplet. Of the 154 sonnets, most have seven rhymes; however, twenty-one have fewer. Of these, Sonnet 3 is the only one to have five rhymes: *abab cdcd* followed by *dede dd*. While the resultant 8-6 structure is similar in nature to the Petrarchan (Italian) form, the content does not reflect Petrarchan ideals. For instance, Sonnet 3 does present a "summary" in the third quatrain, but the new idea of the young man's reflecting his mother's beauty is also introduced, with the possibility of the nubile young wife ignored. Thus, despite its failure to reflect a pure 4-4-4-2 form, Sonnet 3 holds more to the English (Elizabethan) sonnet structure than to the Italian.

There are also internal rhymes (couplet ties) in this sonnet. In particular, the repetition of the *re* sound both connects the poem internally and recalls the "theme" of regeneration and renewal. The *re*- words include: f**re**sh, **re**pair, **re**newest, whe**re**, unear'[e]d, **re**membe**re**'[e]d. Another internal, connecting rhyme is -*age*: till**age**, **age**, im**age**.

The ultimate goal of the sonnet is to persuade the youth of the advantages of producing a child. The first two lines of the poem form a synecdoche, wherein "face" stands in for the entire lovely boy whom the persona will address. Initially, direct exposition outweighs persuasion, as the sonnet opens in the imperative mood, with the persona instructing the youth. This tone quickly gives way to persuasion through flattery, which is followed by two rhetorical questions. As a persuasive device, these questions free the persona from continuing to make obvious statements and instead let the youth reach obvious conclusions without further directive. Line 9 contains a metrical surge, smoothly and effectively making the transition from questions to declarative statement.

Grammatically, lines 9–14 are one sentence. This device lends a sense of unity to the close despite the break in rhyme. It also distinctly separates the physical/sexual reproductive images from the reflections of the youth's beauty. The ethical responsibility to reproduce his beauty for the world is detached from the act itself.

Sonnet 3 contains a clear reference to the story of Narcissus from Ovid's *Metamorphoses*. Like that lovely boy, the fair youth apparently asks: "Why woo at all? What I desire, I have; the very abundance of my riches beggars me" (book 3). Further allusions to the *Metamorphoses*, particularly book 15, as well as Ovid's other works, such as *Medicamina Faciei* and *Ars Amatoria*, are implied in the latter half of the sonnet. These works contain the fairly standard Ovidian connection between age and wrinkles, which are created through plowing. For instance, in *Ars Amatoria*, Ovid writes: "Soon to you too, lovely boy, will come white hairs, soon will come wrinkles to plough your body" (2.117–118). Although the plowing metaphors in Ovid are not sexualized, they are ravaging.

## THEMES AND MEANINGS

There is no single controlling image found within Sonnet 3; however, there are consistent ideas. The governing objective is, of course, procreation, and this goal is represented through extended agricultural metaphors. Like the fertile field waiting to be plowed, all attractive, virginal women are waiting to be approached by the lovely young man.

Besides agricultural metaphors, the sonnet depends on a number of references to *glass*. The word *glass* connects the octet and sestet both in form and content. *Glass* often referred to a mirror, although in the sonnets, it frequently refers to an hourglass as well. Though mirror is the intended definition, the hourglass concept is not without reverberations. *Glass* is used in the first line, and the second contains the word *time*. The glass referred to in lines 9–10 is a living mirror—children. Combining *glass* with *calls back* further extends the hourglass implication. In function, hourglasses are used to tell time, and they accomplish this by being reversed, in essence by running time backwards. Another more oblique reference to *glass* is presented in line 11, which makes reference to windows. Metaphorically, "windows" refers to the young man's eyes. Beyond that, however, windows are *glass* barriers, meant to keep out the elements while allowing the inhabitant contact with the outside world. If there is an imperfection in the window-*glass*, the view will be warped. Similarly, mirrors both capture and distort the real world. In Sonnet 3, the youth's image is replicated in the mirror, as it would be in his children—an idea confirmed by his mother's use of him as a "glass" of her youth. Thus the idea of reproduction is dually formed. People can be replicated by looking in a mirror and by procreating. Moreover, the persona seems just as interested in the reflection as he is in the actual replication, for both fulfill his craving for beauty. As the sonnet cycle continues, the emphasis on physical reproduction will be replaced by an appreciation for memories of beauty. Thus, in the final line, *image* has three senses: fame in this world, reflection in the mirror, and children in your life (Booth, p. 139).

The notion of children being living images of parents is one that Shakespeare utilized elsewhere as well. Intriguingly, Shakespeare often connects offspring with the parent of the opposite sex. Sonnet 3, for instance, compares the lovely youth to his mother. In *The Rape of Lucrece*, it is the father who claims that his image had been found within his daughter (ll. 1751–1764). Using the same language as found in the sonnets, Lucretius bemoans the loss of his "glass" (l. 1768) that is the mirror image of himself, but he also mourns the loss of his image within the world. Not only will the world be deprived of Lucrece's beauty, but it will also feel the loss of Lucretius's physical appeal, too. This speech echoes a position Shakespeare takes in *Venus and Adonis*. For instance, in her attempt to persuade Adonis into a sexual relationship, Venus emphasizes that the pleasure of bearing his child would not be for her sake alone, but for the sake of the world, that his beauty might live on: "By law of nature thou art bound to breed, / That thine may live when thou thyself art dead" (ll. 171–172). Thus lack of reproduction—or destruction of the product of that reproduction—is a selfish and foolish ("fond") act.

This selfishness is expressed in the double use of the word "glass" noted above. The glass as mirror reflects back the image of the person looking into it and has long been a symbol of vanity. The glass as window allows the gazer to see not himself but others and thus represents sharing. It can even serve as a means of entering the world, or letting the world in. The sonnet urges the fair youth not to imitate Narcissus (who drowns in his mirror) but rather to look beyond himself.

## THE RELATIONSHIP OF THE SONNET TO SHAKESPEARE'S OTHER WORKS

The procreative theme is emphasized in line 3 with the juxtaposition of *fresh repair* with *renewest*. Both of these phrases indicate refurbishment of something that probably does not yet need it. As Stephen Booth points out, this combination also suggests a double meaning behind repair. Not only does it imply restoration, but it could also be taken as a punning compound of the Latin prefix *re-* and the French noun *père* (father), altering its meaning to "fathering again" (139). *Repair* is used twice more in the sonnets, both times as a verb, and in both cases, the suggested pun seems likely: "Seeking that beauteous roof to ruinate / Which to *repair* should be thy chief desire" (10.7–8); "So should the lines of life that life *repair*" (16.9). The dual nature of *repair*, connecting restoration and fatherhood, is also found within the plays, as illustrated in this passage from *King Lear*: [Cordelia] "O my dear father, restoration hang / Thy medicine on my lips, and let this kiss / Repair those violent harms that my two sisters / Have in thy reverence made" (4.7.25–28). The connection between *repair* and fatherhood is also found in *All's Well That Ends Well* when the King says, "It much repairs me / To talk of your good father" (1.2.30–31).

Agricultural images of sexuality and reproduction recur throughout Shakespeare's works. In lines 5–6, the words "unear'd," "tillage," and "husbandry" sustain this extended imagery. "Unear'd" implies two meanings simultaneously. The first refers to ripeness. A stalk of corn or wheat that is "uneared," without ears of fruit, is not yet ready for harvest. Similarly, a woman with an "unear'd" womb is one that has not yet borne fruit (given birth). The other meaning, though closely related, is derived from the etymology of *uneared*. In Early Modern English, "to ear" meant to till or to plow. This verb was derived from the Old English verb "erian," which means "to plow." Thus, an "unear'd" womb can also mean an un-tilled womb—one that has not been part of sexual intercourse. In tilling a field, the farmer's plow enters the soil, he then sows it with seeds, which in turn lead to the growth of crops. The soil must be fertile in order to produce a crop, but it is the seed that generates the produce. Similarly, in sexual intercourse, a man penetrates a woman, and implants his "seed" (semen) within her fertile soil, which may re-sult in pregnancy.

It is precisely this type of plowing that Agrippa refers to in *Antony and Cleopa-tra*: "She [Cleopatra] made great Caesar lay his sword to bed; / He ploughed her, and she cropp'd" (2.2.227–228). After her affair with Caesar, Cleopatra gave birth to Caesarion. Earlier in that play, the verb *ear* is also used to denote plowing: "Menecrates and Menas, famous pirates, / Makes the sea serve them, which they ear and wound / With keels of every kind" (1.4.48–50).

The connection between tillage and impregnation is further strengthened by the pun on the word *husbandry* in line 6. Again, this is a reoccurring image in Shake-speare's plays. In *Measure for Measure*, Lucio tells Isabel,

> Your brother and his lover have embrac'd.
> As those that feed grow full, as blossoming time
> That from the seedness the bare fallow brings
> To teeming foison, even so her plenteous womb
> Expresseth his full tilth and husbandry. (1.4.40–44)

Claudio and Juliet embody the result of good tillage; unfortunately, they are not yet married. In this case, husbandry is somewhat ironic, as Claudio is not yet able to completely fulfill the role.

Elsewhere, "husbandry" upholds a series of bawdy puns by itself. For instance, in *2 Henry IV*, Falstaff and Mouldy take great delight is their rowdy exchange:

> [*Falstaff.*] Prick him. [That is, draft him for the army.]
>
> [*Mouldy.*] I was prick'd well enough before, and you could have let me alone. My old dame will be undone now for one to do her husbandry and her drudgery. You need not to have prick'd me, there are other men fitter to go out than I. (3.2.110–115)

The lewd banter contains a large number of double entendres, with "husbandry" and "prick'd" providing keys to the sexual undercurrent. The metaphorical exten-sion can also be found in *Henry V*: "Alas, she [Peace] hath from France too long been chas'd, / And all her husbandry doth lie on heaps, / Corrupting in its own fer-tility" (5.2.38–40). In this case, without proper husbandry—tillage—fertility is run-ning rampant and is therefore producing tainted offspring, in this case noxious weeds and poisonous plants. The "husbandry" here also refers to all the husbands slain in the wars between the English and the French, again linking agricultural and matrimonial metaphors.

James Winny believes that the idea of self-love as an impediment to procreation is a theme that is touched on in several of Shakespeare's works as well as expressed within the sonnets. These include *Venus and Adonis*, *Twelfth Night*, *Measure for Measure*, and *King Lear* among others. Adonis, of course, considers himself too good for anyone, including the goddess of love herself, because of his physical perfection, and as pointed out earlier, is gently rebuked by Venus for his attitude. Similarly, in *Twelfth Night*, Viola reproaches Olivia for hoarding her beauty. Though Olivia does not fall in love with her mirror image, she does become infatuated with Viola in disguise; thus, she displaces her love onto a mirror of herself in the sense of gender, and at the same time, through her choice, denies procreation. (Winny, *The Master-Mistress*, pp. 146–152). This same form of self-love in the guise of loving another woman rather than a man underlies Emilia's reluctance to marry in *The Two Noble Kinsmen*.

Interestingly, in *A Lover's Complaint*, the female speaker suggests that self-love would have saved her from her tragic fate: "I might as yet have been a spreading flower, / Fresh to myself, if I had self-applied / Love to myself, and to no love beside" (ll. 75–77). This passage contains echoes of the scene from *Twelfth Night*, in that self-love prevents procreation. However, in Olivia's case, she should have been seeking constructive sexuality, whereas the speaker in *A Lover's Complaint* says she should have been avoiding it.

### Annotated Bibliography

Crosman, Robert. "Making Love Out of Nothing at All: The Issue of Story in Shakespeare's Procreation Sonnets." *Shakespeare Quarterly* 41.4 (1990): 470–488. Suggests that Shakespeare began the sonnets as a way to curry favor with the aristocracy, but ends up writing about a true passion that he developed. Claims that except for the sonnets, Shakespeare's homosexual leanings are practically indiscernable.

Dubrow, Heather. *Echoes of Desire: English Petrarchism and Its Counterdiscourses.* Ithaca: Cornell UP, 1995. Discusses Shakespeare's sonnets in light of the popular sonnet movement, particularly against the Petrarchan ideals.

Miller, Naomi J. "'Playing the 'Mother's Part': Shakespeare's Sonnets and Early Modern Codes of Maternity." In *Shakespeare's Sonnets: Critical Essays.* Ed. James Schiffer. New York: Garland, 1999. New Historical examination of the concept of motherhood in the sonnets as a whole, with a special emphasis on the procreation sonnets. Makes careful and exceptional use of contemporaneous texts about maternity, "huswifery," and the like.

Vendler, Helen. *The Art of Shakespeare's Sonnets.* Cambridge, MA: Harvard UP, 1997. Each sonnet is prefaced by both the 1609 quarto version and a modern rendition, and is subsequently examined in greater detail on an individual basis. Includes careful examination of language and sounds.

Winny, James. *The Master-Mistress: A Study of Shakespeare's Sonnets.* New York: Barnes & Noble, 1968. Debunks the scholarly trend to find biographical explanations for the sonnets, and focuses on the "inner life" of the poetry itself. Emphasis on apparent contradictions and juxtapositions.

# Sonnet 12

## Charles R. Forker

When I do count the clock that tells the time,
And see the brave day sunk in hideous night;
When I behold the violet past prime,
And sable curls, all silvered o'er with white;
When lofty trees I see barren of leaves,
Which erst from heat did canopy the herd,
And summer's green all girded up in sheaves,
Borne on the bier with white and bristly beard,
Then of thy beauty do I question make,
That thou among the wastes of time must go,
Since sweets and beauties do themselves forsake
And die as fast as they see others grow;
    And nothing 'gainst Time's scythe can make defence
    Save breed, to brave him when he takes thee hence.

### PROSE PARAPHRASE

When I reckon up the ticks and strikes of the clock and see the bright day submerged by night's darkness, when I observe the violet decline from its peak of perfection in the spring and dark hair turned to gray, when I see tall trees stripped of their leaves, which formerly shaded the cattle from heat, and the green unripened barley or wheat of summer all trussed up in bundles and carried on the handbarrow (or wagon) with their bleached and beardlike bristles—then I speculate about your beauty, considering that you too must be destroyed by time, since all sweet and lovely things change from what they once were and die as quickly as they see others grow to replace them. Nothing can be a defense against Time's scythe except offspring procreated in defiance of the day when Time takes you away.

## THE PLACE OF THE SONNET IN THE CYCLE

This sonnet belongs to the so-called marriage group—the opening sequence of seventeen sonnets that urge the "lovely boy" (126.1) to conquer time by marrying and begetting children who will become the youth's copy. The marriage sonnets, somewhat more formal in tone than the increasingly more passionate and personal poems to follow, may have been commissioned by the family of the young man addressed, who, according to some scholars, was probably William Herbert, the future third Earl of Pembroke. In the mid-1590s Herbert was a teenager and is known to have resisted pressure to marry for the sake of extending his aristocratic bloodline. As the Victorian critic Edward Dowden noticed, the poem gathers up and reconfigures ideas, images, and vocabulary already used in sonnets 5, 6 and 7 (Evans, p. 125). Shakespeare, for instance, repeats the notion of hours passing (5.1–4), of seasonal change (5.5–8, 6.1–2), of flowers withering (5.13), of light fading (7.1–10), and of posterity as the enemy of death (6.11–12); he also echoes earlier words such as "hideous" (5.6), "leaves" (5.7), "summer" (5.5, 5.9, 6.2), "beauty" (5.11, 6.4, 7.7), "sweet" (5.14. 6.3), and "breed" (6.7). Line 12 ("And die as fast as they see others grow") echoes language from the preceding sonnet ("As fast as thou shalt wane, so fast thou grow'st," 11.1), altering the emphasis from a child's growth to the disintegration of everything.

Sonnet 12 is one of the numerous poems in the large group addressed to the fair youth (1–126) that plays variations on the theme of mutability or the ravages of time, a favorite Elizabethan motif (as in Spenser's *Ruines of Time* and "Mutabilitie Cantos" from *The Faerie Queene*). In sonnets 15, 17, 18, 19, 55, and 60, for instance, the poet affirms or hopes that he may defeat time by enshrining the lad's perfection in the enduring art of his verse; then in sonnets 64 and 65 he loses faith in the possibility of any remedy against oblivion unless some "miracle" should reverse the universal law of decay and allow his love to "shine bright" forever "in black ink" (65.13–14). Sonnet 115 toys with the paradox that even the poet's love, once claimed as absolute, is itself subject to alteration since what seemed in the past like perfect love continues to increase rather than diminish. Then several of the last sonnets to the handsome boy (116, 123, 124, 125) redefine love in metaphysical terms as transcending temporality and all material evidences of transience. Sonnet 126, a quasi-sonnet in six couplets and therefore symbolically incomplete, concludes the poems addressed to the beautiful boy by asserting the tenuous power over time granted him by nature, while warning that, since he is finally mortal, nature must ultimately render "her treasure" (l. 10) up to death. The sonnets that come after 126 (127–154) center for the most part on a dark woman demeaned as lustful and destructive (despite her sexual magnetism) whom the poet contrasts with his male beloved (idealized despite his faults); this is the "woman color'd ill" whom the poet, borrowing an image from the morality plays, casts in the role of diabolical temptress or "worser spirit" trying to "win" him from his "better angel"—the "man right fair"—and so from "comfort" to "despair" (144.1–6).

As Helen Vendler notices (97), Sonnet 12 is the first poem in the set in which the pronoun "I" is allowed to dominate, giving us a sense for the first time of the speaker as a meditating presence; the previous sonnets had made the addressee (the "you" of the relationship) the focus of syntactic attention so that even in the one instance where "I" does appear (10.9), it occurs only in a subordinate clause. Sonnet 12, then, marks the beginning of the poet's ascendancy in the love drama to be unfolded in the sonnets that follow.

## DEVICES AND TECHNIQUES

Although this sonnet illustrates the standard Shakespearean form of three quatrains and a couplet (rhymed abab cdcd efef gg), its syntax suggests the Petrarchan or Italian arrangement of octave and sestet. The poem consists of a single long sentence, a series of three subordinate clauses that begin with "When" (ll. 1, 3, 5) taking up the first eight lines, and the main clause, which begins with "Then" (l. 9), filling the remaining six. The three "When" clauses contain two main verbs ("count" and "see," 12.1–2) or a single main verb ("behold," 12.3; "see," 12.5) with double object ("violet" and "curls," 12.3, 4; "trees" and "summer's green," 12.5, 7), so that the octave builds up a sense of the universality and inevitability of change through its rich *copia* or accumulation of examples (the striking clock, the faded day, the withering violet, the gray hair, the trees without their leaves, the cattle deprived of shade, the grain of summer cut and harvested, the corpse carried to the grave). The octave also conveys the idea of time affecting both the realms of nature (day, night, flowers, trees, cattle, grain) and of human life (clocks, hair, corpses, beards). One of Shakespeare's most effective devices is his fusing of imagery from both categories so that a single word-picture elicits a double level of reference—vegetative and human. The sheaves of wheat or barley with their bleached and beard-like awn (the bushy ends) being carried on a wagon or barrow to the barn for threshing simultaneously evoke a dead body with its grizzled beard or white stubble (which may continue to grow after death) being borne on a hearse or bier to its grave. Shakespeare may also have meant to evoke the image of a harvest-home procession—a country ceremony in which "the last load of grain is brought in with flowers and images" (Kerrigan, pp. 188–189)—which would merge suggestively with the idea of a funeral cortege. The final two lines of the octave where this conflation occurs gather up and unite the evocations of plant and human life presented separately at earlier points.

Having drawn disparate images from nature and humanity into a conceptual oneness centered on the theme of ineluctable change, the poet now applies the idea to a unique individual—the boy whose beauty will be subject to the same process of decay that destroys everything and everyone else. He too must go "among the wastes of time" (l. 10), a phrase that in its ambiguity suggests not only that he is one of the desirable things that Time must inevitably waste away and obliterate but also that he himself may have wasted time, failing to make full use of the brief opportunities thus far afforded him in life. Additionally, there may be some suggestion of the boy's being on the point of journeying into the wastes (or desiccating deserts) of time as though he were already about to forfeit the perishable bloom of his youth by becoming an adult. From the speaker's perspective, the boy embodies both "sweets and beauties"—virtues or moral strengths as well as physical allure, inward as well as outward attractions (Vendler, p. 98); the "I" or persona of the poem thus celebrates not only the youth's aesthetic appeal but also traits such as his sweet nature or instinctive kindness of the sort already anticipated by the detail of trees offering shade to cattle. "Sweet" also suggests odor, thus glancing backward at the violet (l. 3), notable for its delicate scent. The concluding couplet employs the conventional emblem-image of Time personified as the grim reaper, invoking the familiar figure of Death with his scythe, who cuts down all humankind as the farmer harvests his crop (cf. 60.12, 100.13–14, 116.9–10). This image again embraces both vegetable and human categories, linking up effectively with the dual meanings of bier as farm wagon (or barrow) and funeral hearse.

Finally we should notice the poet's striking use of sound effects. The opening line is a splendid example of onomatopoeia, its succession of monosyllabic words ("When I do count the clock that tells the time") beautifully reproducing the monotonous ticking away of the minutes and striking of the hours; alliteration, the use of repeated initial consonants ("count the clock," "tell the time") reinforces the effect of uninterrupted sameness. A reiteration of "s" sounds in subsequent lines— "sable curls all silver'd" (l. 4), "trees . . . leaves" (l. 5), "summer's green . . . sheaves" (l. 7), "sweets and beauties do themselves forsake" (l. 11), "fast . . . others" (l. 12), "time's scythe . . . defense" (l. 13), "takes thee hence" (l. 14)—subtly conveys the sense of beauty irresistibly slipping from the poet's control, while alliterations such as "past prime" (l. 3), "Borne on the bier with . . . bristly beard"(l. 8), and "breed, to brave him" (l. 14) create an undertow of resistance to the flow of time. Thus Shakespeare renders musically the psychic counterpoint between the speaker's melancholy acquiescence to inevitable flux and his urge to challenge or combat it.

One especially telling effect is the use of the word "brave" in two syntactically and denotatively contrasting ways: in line 2 it is an adjective meaning resplendent, gorgeous, or showy and, as the modifier of "day," sets up the opposition to "hideous night"; then the speaker uses the word again in line 14, now as a verb meaning to confront boldly or defy the ceaseless advance of time that has erased the splendor evoked in line 2. The verbal repetition ties the beginning and end of the sonnet together, at the same time marking a transition in the speaker's psyche from passive observation of time's annihilating effects to an effort to excite strenuous resistance in the lad addressed. The word "breed," which alliterates assertively with "brave" in the final line, is usually glossed as a noun meaning offspring; but it is possible also to construe it as a verb (= breeding, to breed), a more active sense that effectively conveys the sexual energy involved in the act of procreation. Duncan-Jones observes, however, that the final effect of the progression "is almost self-canceling, for the poetic evocation of time's all-inclusive operation is so persuasive as to leave the remedy in doubt" (134). Shakespeare helps to suggest the insistent onslaught of time by introducing the word in line 1 and then repeating it in lines 10 and 13.

## THEMES AND MEANINGS

Numerology seems to play a role in the significance of certain sonnets. Thus the twelfth in sequence neatly suits the opening image of the clock with its twelve numerals or hours struck, just as Sonnet 52 with its allusions to annual "feasts" (l. 5) and "the long year set" (l. 6) reinforces the idea of the fifty-two-week calendar, and as Sonnet 71 with its anticipation of the speaker's death (l. 1) glances backward to the familiar biblical notion of man's life span as seventy years, or three score and ten (Duncan-Jones, p. 100). Flower symbolism also signifies, for the violet, briefest and most perishable of all spring blossoms, was traditionally associated with faithfulness as well as with the fragility of youth. Thus the speaker hints sadly that the fidelity of the boy's relationship to his admirer may be as mutable as his physical charms. A contrast between fertility and infertility also enters the poem in the opposition between the lush greenness of the growing season and the bleakness of autumn; the trees that were once thick with leaves are now "barren" (l. 5), a word that in the context of a plea to beget an heir also connotes the inability to bear children and may subtly adumbrate the imbedded pun on "nothing" in the penultimate line; the word "nothing" (a form of "no thing") was sometimes used with indecent innuendo (as in *Hamlet*, 3.2.117–118) to refer to the vulva—the nought or cipher that "lie[s] between maids' legs." As Vendler suggests (99), Sonnet 12 discriminates "three models of dying—vanishing, being scythed down, and freely choosing to breed and being willing to die," each of them, however, "melt[ing] insensibly from one to the next . . . without harsh juxtaposition or acknowledged conflict." What Vendler (97) refers to as an "intransitive" model of death in which things gradually disappear or innocently waste away yields to a more "transitive" one in which Time violently murders his victims.

An important influence on this sonnet (as also on sonnets 55, 60, 63, 64, 65, and 73), was Ovid's *Metamorphoses*, known to most Elizabethans in Arthur Golding's popular translation of 1567. The theme of Ovid's entire poem is the propensity of everything in creation to undergo change; but the passage that seems to have suggested much of this sonnet's imagery is part of a discourse by Pythagoras from book 15 (lines 199–216; Golding, 221–237), in which the progress from youth to age is likened to seasonal changes and in which details such as green plants and flowers flourishing in summer and then losing their vitality at harvest time, or human hair turning grey or white in wintry old age, are prominent. Significantly, an account of changes in the heavens from day to night (lines 186–198; Golding, 206–220; cf. "the brave day sunk in hideous night," l. 2) comes just before the passage comparing the youth-age sequence to its seasonal counterpart. A passage in another of Ovid's poems, the *Ars Amatoria* (2.113–120), which illustrates the transitoriness of youthful beauty by references to the fading violet and to white hairs, may also have been influential. Shakespeare's probable use of Ovid shows the strain of classical humanism and literary sophistication in his work. But the freshness and realism of the sonnet's pastoral details undoubtedly owe as much to the poet's personal experience of English rural landscapes as to books.

## THE RELATIONSHIP OF THE SONNET TO SHAKESPEARE'S OTHER WORKS

Parallels to the themes and imagery of this sonnet proliferate throughout Shakespeare but are especially notable in the Elizabethan rather than the Jacobean phase of his output. The pastoral image of herds canopied by shady trees (ll. 5–6) reappears, for instance, in *3 Henry VI*, where the King, having retired from battle, idealizes the shepherd's life:

> Gives not the hawthorn bush a sweeter shade
> To shepherds looking on their silly sheep
> Than doth a rich embroider'd canopy
> To kings that fear their subjects' treachery? (2.5.42–45)

The collocation of "summer's green" with "bristly beard" after the corn has been cut and bundled (ll. 7–8) relates strikingly to Titania's reference in *A Midsummer Night's Dream* to "green corn" that has rotted before the youthful farmer has "attain'd a beard" (2.1.94–95); and the suggestion of a funeral procession as the grain, whitened like the beard of an old man, is "Borne on the bier" (l. 8) to its receiving barn reminds us of Ophelia's deranged song about her suddenly murdered father: "They bore him barefac'd on the bier" (*Hamlet*, 4.5.165). Another image of hair color as a mark of aging—"sable curls all silver'd o'er with white" (l. 4)—resurfaces in Horatio's description of the "grisl'd" beard of Hamlet'd ghost: "A sable silver'd" (*Hamlet*, 1.2.239–241).

Violets, of course, occur frequently in Shakespeare, but "the violet past prime" (l. 3), an image of youth fading and possibly also of unstable fidelity, recalls Laertes' cynical advice to his sister to regard Hamlet's "trifling . . . favor" as "A violet in the youth of primy nature, / Forward, not permanent, sweet, not lasting" (*Hamlet*, 1.3.5–8). Later, Ophelia, dispensing wildflowers, refers to "violets" that "wither'd all when my father died" (*Hamlet*, 4.5.184–185). The flower's impermanence takes on a political meaning in *Richard II* when the Duchess of York inquires of Aumerle after Bullingbrook's usurpation, "Who are the violets now / That strew the green lap of the new-come spring?" (5.2.46–47). In Shakespeare's erotic epyllion, the goddess of love, trying to seduce the beautiful boy Adonis, invokes a carpe diem argument that reminds us of Sonnet 12's content and vocabulary:

> Make use of time, let not advantage slip,
> Beauty within itself should not be wasted.
>> Fair flowers that are not gath'red in their prime
>> Rot, and consume themselves in little time. (*Venus and Adonis*, 129–132)

This passage, probably composed during the same period as the earliest sonnets, uses four key words of Sonnet 12 in close conjunction ("time," "beauty," "prime," "waste") in addition to the related concepts of flowers withering and of "sweets and beauties" forsaking or consuming themselves. Shakespeare's loaded phrase, "the wastes of time" (l. 10), receives a fresh configuration and context in Richard II's long meditation on his sad career in relation to transience: "I wasted time, and now doth time waste me" (*Richard II*, 5.5.49). Not surprisingly, the King's soliloquy invokes in the very next line the image of a "numb'ring clock" (cf. "When I do count the clock," l. 1) and relates the idea of "still-breeding thoughts" (5.5.8; cf. "Save breed, to brave him when he takes thee hence," l. 12) to the concept of "minutes, times, and hours" (5.5.58) slipping away and to a man's eventually "being nothing" (5.5.41).

### Annotated Bibliography

Booth, Stephen. *An Essay on Shakespeare's Sonnets*. New Haven: Yale UP, 1969. A sophisticated analysis of the entire sequence as well as of the individual sonnets. Emphasizes the "multitude of different coexistent and conflicting patterns—formal, logical, ideological, syntactic, rhythmic, and phonetic" (ix).

———, ed. *Shakespeare's Sonnets*. New Haven: Yale UP, 1977. Presents a conservatively modernized text of the 1609 quarto. Booth attempts to recreate what "a Renaissance reader would have thought as he moved from line to line and sonnet to sonnet" (ix). Also offers detailed commentary with valuable paraphrases and illustrates the richness of the poems' many-faceted meanings.

Duncan-Jones, Katherine, ed. *Shakespeare's Sonnets*. The Arden Shakespeare. London: Thomas Nelson and Sons, 1997. A modernized edition of the sonnets with a full and illuminating commentary that absorbs much of the earlier scholarship and contains an important introduction making a compelling case for William Herbert, Earl of Pembroke, as the fair youth addressed in sonnets 1–126. Contextualizes the sonnets historically and argues that the sequence underwent several phases of revision before being released for publication in 1609.

Evans, G. Blakemore, ed. *The Sonnets*. The New Cambridge Shakespeare. Cambridge: Cambridge UP, 1996. Contains a valuable textual apparatus and commentary with an introductory note by poet Anthony Hecht summarizing "what we actually know, and, equally important, how much we do not know about the genesis of the Sonnets and about Shakespeare's relationship to them" (110).

Kerrigan, John, ed. *Shakespeare: "The Sonnets" and "A Lover's Complaint."* Harmondsworth, Eng.: Penguin, 1986. An influential edition with an introduction and notes that focuses on the inadequacy of strictly biographical or formalist approaches and suggests that when Shakespeare was writing *A Lover's Complaint* (which Kerrigan dates 1602–1605) he was "consciously shaping [his] collection" of sonnets (12). Kerrigan sees the 1609 sequence as patterned after those published in the 1590s, such as Samuel Daniel's *Delia* (1592) and Thomas Lodge's *Phillis* (1593). Argues that *A Lover's Complaint* serves as a conventional conclusion to the sonnets and so is an integral part of the sequence.

Rollins, Hyder Edward, ed. *The Sonnets*. New Variorum Edition. 2 vols. Philadelphia: J. B. Lippincott, 1944. Historically indispensable. Provides an exhaustive record of what was written about the sonnets from 1609 until the early 1940s.

Vendler, Helen. *The Art of Shakespeare's Sonnets*. Cambridge, MA: Harvard UP, 1997. Contains a sensitive and detailed interpretation of each sonnet as a self-contained poetic artifact.

Wilson, John Dover, ed. *The Sonnets*. Cambridge: Cambridge UP, 1966. An older-style edition still valuable for its comprehensive notes, historical learning, and eloquent, wide-ranging introduction. Wilson's account of the relationship between the poet and the fair youth seems somewhat old-fashioned and naive.

# Sonnet 15

Patrick Perkins

When I consider every thing that grows
Holds in perfection but a little moment,
That this huge stage presenteth nought but shows
Whereon the stars in secret influence comment;
When I perceive that men as plants increase,
Cheered and checked e'en by the self-same sky,
Vaunt in their youthful sap, at height decrease,
And wear their brave state out of memory;
Then the conceit of this inconstant stay
Sets you most rich in youth before my sight,
Where wasteful Time debateth with decay
To change your day of youth to sullied night,
　And all in war with Time for love of you,
　As he takes from you, I engraft you new.

## PROSE PARAPHRASE

When I reflect upon the fact that all things that grow maintain their most perfect state for but the briefest period of time, that this transitory, ephemeral world, which is shaped by mysterious planetary forces, yields nothing either substantial or constant, when I see that humans are no different from plants, for both are subject to the changing whims of the sky, both make a show of their vigor while young, begin to decline the instant they reach their peak, and then disappear and are no longer remembered—then the thought of the struggle with mutability brings to my mind you in all your glory, surrounded by time and decay, which fight to disparage your beauty. In a desperate attempt to save you from the ravages of time, for I love you, as time detracts from your beauty, I restore it through my poetry.

## THE PLACE OF THE SONNET IN THE CYCLE

Sonnet 15 is part of a seventeen sonnet sequence in which the poet encourages a young friend to extend his life through procreation. In many of these poems the youth is warned that he will age, that his "proud livery" will become "a tattered weed, of small worth held" (2.3–4), unless he preserve himself through his progeny. In these sonnets Shakespeare repeatedly figures the young man as a spring or summer flower about to fall victim to seasonal change (cf. 2.1–4, 3.9–12, 5.5–14, 12.3–14). The final couplet of Sonnet 5, where the speaker claims that "flowers distill'd, though they with winter meet, / Leese [lose] but their show; their substance still lives sweet," anticipates the last two lines of Sonnet 15, as in both poems Shakespeare responds to the ravages of time without breaking from the botanical metaphor.

Sonnet 15 also initiates a five sonnet series where the poet considers eternalizing his love in and through his verse. These five poems, like the previous fourteen, and like many other poems in the cycle, are reflections on temporality. Sonnet 16 reverses the poet's claim in the couplet of the previous poem, declaring that verse alone cannot make the young man live again, and that there are "many maiden gardens, yet unset" that would bear the young man "living flowers" more like him than an artist's "painted counterfeit" portrait of him (16.6–8). Sonnet 17 worries that the poet's high praise of the man will not be believed unless the young man's descendants stand as living proof of the poet's verse. Sonnets 18 and 19, like Sonnet 15, complete the five poem series, once again confidently asserting the life-giving force of the poet's pen. "But thy eternal summer shall not fade," claims Shakespeare in Sonnet 18, "Nor lose possession of that fair thou ow'st, / Nor shall Death brag thou wand'rest in his shade, / When in eternal lines to time thou grow'st" (18.9–12). The word "lines" has a dual meaning here, referring both to lines of verse and lines of descent, though the final line of the poem—"So long lives this, and this gives life to thee"—amplifies the former reading (Duncan-Jones, p. 146). This quatrain reminds us that poems, like children, can be numbered among the things that grow. In Sonnet 18 growth is not the threat it is in Sonnet 15, nor is time, for the poet's metrical verse allows his love to grow "to time." A variation of this play on phrases containing the word "time" can be found in Sonnet 60, where the poet first claims that "Time doth transfix the flourish set on youth, / And delves the parallels in beauty's brow" (60.9–10), but then asserts "And yet to times in hope my verse shall stand, / Praising thy worth, despite his cruel hand" (60.13–14).

Structurally, Sonnet 15 is similar to sonnets 2, 12, 30, and 64, reflections on mutability that all open with the subordinator "when." Sonnet 15 is almost a mirror image of Sonnet 12, which also has two "when" quatrains followed by a "then" quatrain (Vendler, p. 109). In sonnets 55, 60, 63, 65, and 74 Shakespeare also advances the idea that his verse will withstand the forces of time. In Sonnet 55 the poet claims his verse will "outlive" the "gilded monuments / Of princes" (55.1–2) and tells his love " 'Gainst death and all-oblivious enmity / Shall you pace forth" (55.9–10), for "You live in this, and dwell in lovers' eyes" (55.14). In Sonnet 65 the poet asks, "Or what strong hand can hold his [Time's] swift foot back, / Or who his spoil of beauty can forbid?" and concludes, "O none, unless this miracle have might, / That in black ink my love may still shine bright" (65.11–14).

## DEVICES AND TECHNIQUES

Sonnet 15 is a single fourteen line sentence comprised of two subordinated "when" clauses, which form the first two quatrains, followed by a "then" clause, which forms the third quatrain and couplet. As Vendler notes, the poem moves from the general to the specific, from a consideration that nothing in this world is permanent to a realization that the poet's beloved will also be laid waste by time (Vendler, p. 108). The poet is not only asserting that everything is subject to change; first and foremost he describes a mental event or exercise and its effects: he contemplates the impermanence of all and is moved to take action. Sonnet 15 shares this quality with Sonnet 29, where the speaker's honest, unsparing account of his own condition leads him to depression, at which point he remembers his friend and is uplifted. The descent, it would seem, makes the ascent possible, as it provokes what Duke Vincentio from *Measure for Measure* would call "heavenly comforts of despair" (4.3.110).

That which threatens permanence or stability is growth, for all growing things are subject to change. Though we may first think of sentient beings when we read "everything that grows," we might also note that lines, sentences, poems, and sonnet cycles can be numbered among those things that grow. Sonnet 15 points back to the opening line of the cycle—"From fairest creatures we desire increase" (1.1)—and challenges its claim, suggesting that growth or increase makes things vulnerable to the forces of change. The main verb in the relative clause that begins with "everything that grows" is either "holds" or "holds in"; either everything maintains a perfect state for but a brief period of time, or is able to "hold in" its perfection only temporarily (Booth, *Shakespeare's Sonnets*, 155). The feminine rhymes at the end of the eleven syllable lines two and four provide audible evidence that the state of perfection can be retained but momentarily, as the perfect iambic line is lost as the additional syllable augments the line. As Booth points out, the scope of Shakespeare's topic shrinks as the poem itself grows. The poet's first words are "When I consider everything," and with the addition of "that grows," the topic diminishes considerably. It is further narrowed when Shakespeare adds, "holds in perfection but a little moment," for it then becomes clear that "everything that grows" is part of a relative clause, and that the poet is not considering everything, or everything that grows, but rather that everything that grows is subject to decay (ibid., pp. 155–156).

Critics have found the perspective of the speaker to be of interest. As Booth notes, "The act of imagining *this huge stage* presupposes the vantage point of the stars" (*An Essay*, 183). The speaker's is an astral vision, as he looks down on earth from above, surveying all and finally lighting on his particular love. Like the stars in the sky that comment on the lives of the earthlings, so the poet, who seems both of the earth and beyond it, reflects on his beloved. Vendler finds two distinct perspectives in the poem, claiming the poet looks down as one above but feels as one below. "Much of the pathos of this and other sonnets," says Vendler, "derives from the capacity of the philosophical mind to rise to impersonal grandeur or cold self-inspection while the sensual mind remains below, in thrall to passion" (Vendler, p. 108).

Shakespeare mobilizes three primary fields of discourse, or what Booth calls "ideological frames of reference" (Booth, *An Essay*, 182), as he works through his conceit, borrowing terminology from horticulture, theater, and astrology. Once one of these fields is mobilized, it remains in the air, and many lines refer to two or more of these fields simultaneously (Booth, *An Essay*, 183–184). The central metaphor of the poem is that which compares people to plants, which the poet states explicitly at the start of the second quatrain, but which is operative from the opening lines: "When I consider everything that grows / Holds in perfection but a little moment." As the poem develops, humans and plants become virtually indistinguishable, with lines six through eight describing the fate of both simultaneously. Line three introduces theater terminology as the speaker considers that "this huge stage presenteth nought but shows." All earthly things, people and all of their enterprises included, have no more permanence, no more staying power, than a plant or a production at Shakespeare's theater (Duncan-Jones, p. 140). Line four, "Whereon the stars in secret influence comment," uses astrological terms to suggest that the stars mysteriously control the destiny of all below.

Astrological references reappear in lines six, eleven, and twelve. "Cheered and checked ev'n by the self-same sky" (15.6) suggests that the sky is either duplicitous or fickle, and opens up the possibility that the sky itself is not beyond mutability. If we look back to lines three and four, "That this huge stage presenteth nought but shows / Whereon the stars in secret influence comment," we may notice that "whereon" can modify "stage" as well as "shows," and we wonder whether the stars and their comments are part of the brief show—and therefore subject to mutability—rather than apart from it. These lines, as Booth points out, simultaneously configure the stars as an audience that encourages and discourages the players on stage (*An Essay*, 183). In lines eleven and twelve, "Where wasteful Time debateth with Decay / To change your day of youth to sullied night," the poet figures time and decay as abstract cosmic forces determined to destroy his love's youthful beauty.

The theatrical discourse, initiated by the word "stage" in line three, resurfaces in lines six through eight as we are told that people are "cheered and check'd" by the sky, "[v]aunt in their youthful sap" and "wear their brave state out of memory." While this last phrase suggests that the "brave state" of plants and humans eventually wears out and is forgotten, it also implies that all living things hopelessly attempt to maintain this state out of habit or memory, feigning youth and bravery in ridiculous denial that their "youthful sap" is lost. The word "vaunt" in line seven suggests that even the initial "brave state" itself is no more than a show, the braggart's swagger or the mistaken confidence or conceit of the short-sighted, for time will not allow such a state to be maintained.

The phrase "even by" in line six argues that the sky does not play favorites, that the sky that cheers and checks plants cheers and checks humans as well. The verb "sets" in line ten extends the metaphor, figuring the poet's love as a flower arranged between time and decay. The final couplet of the poem neatly exploits the horticultural metaphor as the poet claims he renews his plant-like love by grafting the youth as one would a scion to a stock. Though a person's plant-like nature feels like a liability in the opening twelve lines of the poem, it suddenly becomes an unforeseen blessing in the final couplet. If an individual is like a flower, then he can be grafted. "And all in war with Time for love of you," writes Shakespeare in lines 13–14, "As he takes from you, I ingraft you new." The function word "as," which refers to both time and manner in line 14, revises "When I perceive that men as plants increase" (15.5), where "as" refers exclusively to manner. The poet, at war "with Time"—"with" meaning both "against" and "accompanied by"—begins to write in a timely fashion.

Since the word "ingraft" in the final line of the poem has no stated indirect object, it is not clear to whom or what the poet grafts his love. As Booth points out, since the poet has yet to offer versifying as a way to preserve his love's beauty, the reader may first understand the word as a reference to the poet's endeavor to join the young man to a woman (*Shakespeare's Sonnets*, 158). The opening lines of Sonnet 16, however, which read like a continuation of Sonnet 15, suggest that "ingraft" refers to the poet's attempt to preserve his love in verse. Here the poet says to the young man, "And fortify yourself in your decay / With means more blessed than my barren rhyme" (16.3–4), making it clear that the closing couplet of Sonnet 15, punning on the etymology of *graft* (from the Greek word *graphein* meaning *to write*), imagines grafting as a metaphor for immortalizing a loved one through verse. Katherine Duncan-Jones points out that the "youth" is made "new" in a very literal manner: Time takes the "th" from "youth" in line ten, leaving him a bare "you" in line 11, and the poet then transforms the blighted "you" to "new" with his final rhyme.

## THEMES AND MEANINGS

Until its final line, Sonnet 15 has a melancholy tone, asserting that since death and decay are inevitable, all things are meaningless and illusory. All earthly things are no more real than a play, and those who "[v]aunt in their youthful sap, at height decrease, / And wear their brave state out of memory" (15.7–8) are all base actors, not far removed from the swaggering Pistol in *Henry V*, who, as Gower says, is an imitation soldier, one who memorizes his part, who "now and then goes to the wars, to grace himself at his return into London under the form of a soldier" (3.6.67–69). Even truly brave figures, such as Hotspur in *1 Henry IV*, are forced to concede that "thoughts, the slaves of life, and life, time's fool, / And time, that takes survey of all the world, / Must have a stop" (5.4.81–83).

This meditation on impermanence in Sonnet 15, though, paradoxically yields a solution, for it is the realization that the human condition is no different from that of a plant that generates the final metaphor. Eternal life, the poem suggests, is made possible by temporality. The grafting metaphor, while it suggests versifying, also alludes to chapter 11 of St. Paul's Epistle to the Romans, where Paul distinguishes between faith and works by using grafting as a figure for the former (Freinkel, pp. 244–246). The gentiles, Paul claims, though of a "wild olive tree," are "graft in . . . and made partaker of the root and fatness of the olive tree" through faith in Christ. "I would not that this secret should be hid from you my brethren (lest ye should be wise in your own conceits)," Paul forewarns the gentiles, "that partly blindness is happened in Israel, until the fullness of the gentiles be come in: and so all Israel shall be saved." This secret teaches that branches are hewn off so as to be grafted on at a later date. "As ye in time past have not believed God," says Paul to the gentiles, "yet have obtained mercy through their unbelief: even so now have they not believed the mercy which is happened unto you, that they also may obtain mercy. God hath wrapped all nations in unbelief, that he might have mercy on all."

Though Shakespeare's poem reads as a secular reflection on mutability, one that imagines salvation through poetry rather than faith, it echoes and parallels Pauline theology. Like Paul's "secret," which teaches that works fail so that we may be grafted to God through faith, the poet's rumination on our "inconstant stay" (15.9), on the fact that "perfection" is unsustainable, leads him to "ingraft" his love in eternal verse. The poet, one could claim, like the stars above, has a "secret influence" upon his love, one that he holds in reserve until the final line of the poem, forcing readers to despair over their fragility and impotence only to rescue them in the end.

There may be a trace of sexual innuendo present in the sonnet as well. The poet's concern that "everything that grows / Holds in perfection but a little moment" (15.1–2), that men "Vaunt in their youthful sap" and "at height decrease" (15.7), sounds like an oblique reference to male performance anxiety and recalls Troilus's words to Cressida: "This is the monstruosity of love, lady, that the will is infinite and the execution confin'd, that the desire is boundless and the act a slave to limit" (*Troilus and Cressida* 3.2.81–83).

## THE RELATIONSHIP OF THE SONNET TO SHAKESPEARE'S OTHER WORKS

Meditations on man's transitory state are ubiquitous in Shakespeare's work. The opening quatrain of Sonnet 15 echoes the speech of the melancholic Jaques in *As You Like It*. "All the world's a stage, / And all the men and women merely players; / They have their exits and their entrances, / And one man in his time plays many parts, / His acts being seven stages" (2.7.139–143). In his comparison, Jaques suggests that all of these stages are ridiculous, and that everyone plays his or her final role "[s]ans teeth, sans eyes, sans taste, sans every thing" (2.7.166). Upon the report of his wife's death, Macbeth sums up the meaninglessness of life by resorting to the same metaphor: "Life's but a walking shadow, a poor player, / That struts and frets his hour upon the stage, / And then is heard no more. It is a tale / Told by an idiot, full of sound and fury, / Signifying nothing" (5.5.24–28).

The grafting metaphor found in the couplet of Sonnet 15 reminds one of the conversation between Perdita and Polixenes in *The Winter's Tale*. Perdita claims that she will neither grow nor collect "carnations and streaked gillyvors," or gillyflowers, for they are "Nature's bastards." She worries that "There is an art which their piedness shares, / With great creating Nature" (4.4.82–83, 87–88). Polixenes, however, defends such art:

> Yet Nature is made better by no mean
> But Nature makes that mean; so over that art
> Which you say adds to Nature, is an art
> That Nature makes. You see, sweet maid, we marry
> A gentler scion to the wildest stock,
> And make conceive a bark of baser kind
> By bud of nobler race. This is an art
> Which does mend Nature—change it, rather; but
> The art itself is Nature. (4.4.89–97)

Polixenes' defense of grafting, which contradicts his apparently misguided opposition to the match between his son and Perdita, also anticipates Paulina's presentation of Hermione in the final scene of the play. Like the poet in Sonnet 15,

Paulina renews or preserves a loved one through holy artifice. Sounding much like Paul in Romans, Paulina prefaces her display of Hermione by telling the inconstant Leontes that "It is requir'd / You do awake your faith" (5.3.94–95).

### Annotated Bibliography

Booth, Stephen. *An Essay on Shakespeare's Sonnets*. New Haven: Yale UP, 1969. Booth concludes his work with an insightful close reading of Sonnet 15, arguing that the sonnet form allows Shakespeare to utilize an "unusually high number of systems of organization" (174).

———, ed. *Shakespeare's Sonnets*. New Haven: Yale UP, 1977. Presents the 1609 edition of the sonnets side by side with a modernized text. Provides careful and comprehensive line-by-line analysis of each sonnet, teasing out variant readings.

Duncan-Jones, Katherine, ed. *Shakespeare's Sonnets*. The Arden Shakespeare. London: Thomas Nelson and Sons, 1997. Modernized edition. Provides clear and creative glosses on the sonnets and comprehensive introduction to the sonnets and to biographical controversy surrounding them.

Freinkel, Lisa. "The Name of the Rose: Christian Figurality and Shakespeare's Sonnets." In *Shakespeare's Sonnets: Critical Essays*. Ed. James Schiffer. New York: Garland, 2000. 240–261. Traces influence of Luther and reformation theology on the sonnets.

Kaula, David. "'In War With Time': Temporal Perspectives in Shakespeare's Sonnets." *Studies in English Literature, 1500–1900* 3 (1963): 45–57. Study of poems in which Shakespeare makes use of the figure of time.

Vendler, Helen. *The Art of Shakespeare's Sonnets*. Cambridge, MA: Harvard UP, 1997. Presents both 1609 edition and modernized text alongside exceptionally keen readings of each sonnet. Focuses particularly on Shakespeare's language.

Waddington, Raymond B. "Shakespeare's Sonnet 15 and the Art of Memory." In *The Rhetoric of Renaissance Poetry*. Ed. Thomas O. Sloan and Raymond B. Waddington. Berkeley: U of California P, 1974. 96–122. Claims that Sonnet 15 makes use of artificial memory systems in order to defeat time. "To defeat Time, to protect the young man from his ravages, the poet translates him from the public, temporal genre of theatre to the private, non-temporal dimension of the immortalizing sonnets. As line 13 intimates, Time's love for the young man is natural; and, as the grafting connotations suggest, in a sense the poet's love is unnatural. He wants to take the young man out of nature or, to follow the implications of the memory theatre more precisely, *above* nature" (117).

# Sonnet 18

## Roze Hentschell

Shall I compare thee to a summer's day?
Thou art more lovely and more temperate:
Rough winds do shake the darling buds of May,
And summer's lease hath all too short a date:
Sometime too hot the eye of heaven shines,
And often is his gold complexion dimmed,
And every fair from fair sometime declines,
By chance, or nature's changing course untrimmed:
But thy eternal summer shall not fade,
Nor lose possession of that fair thou ow'st,
Nor shall death brag thou wander'st in his shade,
When in eternal lines to time thou grow'st,
    So long as men can breathe, or eyes can see,
    So long lives this, and this gives life to thee.

### PROSE PARAPHRASE

Should I equate you to a day in summer, when days are loveliest? You are more beautiful and even-tempered. Blustering winds disturb the lovely new May flowers, and summer's allotted time expires much too soon. At times in the summer the sun shines too intensely, and often it is clouded over. Beauty eventually fades from every beautiful thing, stripped of its loveliness by accident or natural decay. But your ageless beauty will not decline. You will not lose the beauty you own, nor will Death proclaim that you walk in his shadows, when you become a living part of time in immortal verses. As long as humans exist or eyes gaze, this poem will endure, endowing you with life.

## THE PLACE OF THE SONNET IN THE CYCLE

Sonnet 18 is one of the many (1–126) addressed to or dealing with a fair young man whom the speaker intensely admires. While some of the poems in this cycle arguably suggest the speaker's homoerotic attraction to the youth, the sonnets in this grouping are largely concerned with a platonic yet intense friendship between the speaker and the highly idealized youth. Sonnet 18 follows the poems on the theme of procreation, the so-called "breeding" or "marriage" sonnets (1–17), in which the speaker urges the youth to defeat the ravages of time and preserve his youth by begetting children. Just as those poems are concerned with the destructive nature of time, so, too, is Sonnet 18. As Charles Forker shows in his essay in this volume on Sonnet 12, there are numerous sonnets in the cycle that take up the trope of time's degenerative qualities, which was, as Forker notes, "a favorite Elizabethan motif." However, in Sonnet 18 the speaker addresses the problem posed by time not by suggesting that the youth procreate or indicating what ill fate awaits him if he does not (as in sonnets 1–14, 16–17), but rather by emphasizing the power of poetry to grant immortality. Thus it ties in most explicitly with sonnets 15 and 17 before it and 19, 55, and 60 after it. While Sonnet 17 doubts that the youth's physical perfection will be believed in future generations solely through the power of the speaker's "rhyme" (l. 14), and thus the youth is encouraged to breed to leave behind evidence of his beauty, Sonnet 18 emphasizes how an affirmation of the youth's qualities can be found in poetry rather than progeny (Duncan-Jones, p. 146).

While some critics often group Sonnet 18 with the procreation sonnets, others deny any relation to these sonnets because sonnets 18 and 19 "flatly contradict the overriding procreation theme of 1–17" (Evans, p. 131). Unlike children, poetry is immune to the ravages of time, a theme developed in Ovid's *Amores* and Horace's *Odes*. By immortalizing the youth in verse, the speaker goes procreative practices one better. While breeding children can guarantee one generation further, poetry has the power to live eternally. It is impervious to the "thousand natural shocks / That flesh is heir to" (*Hamlet*, 3.1.61–62). In this sense, Sonnet 18 is most closely aligned with Sonnet 55, which asserts the power of poetry to "praise" (55.10) the youth for "all posterity" (55.11), not just for one generation. Verse will persevere until "the ending doom" (55.12); it laughs in the face of "sluttish time" (55.4).

The speaker, however, emphasizes in Sonnet 18 and elsewhere that the poetry so capable of "giv[ing] life" (18.14) is his verse (18.14; 19.14), thus indicating the speaker's own involvement in immortalizing the youth. While the youth will be grafted to "time" through the "lines" of the poem (18.12), the poem still belongs to the author. In this sense, Sonnet 18 ties in more closely with the procreation sonnets than initially suggested. Here, then, the speaker is intimately involved in this new type of breeding. By writing, or giving birth to, a poem on the subject of the youth (a theme seen in Philip Sidney's sonnet cycle, *Astrophil and Stella*, when the speaker asserts he is "great with child to speak" [1.12]), he is able to contribute significantly to the defeat of time and "death." The speaker thus becomes a sort of parent himself, able to produce and generate.

While many of the first 126 sonnets idealize the young man's beauty, a few compare him specifically to the sun. In Sonnet 7 he is likened to the sun, whose setting in the west is an image of the youth's decline should he not procreate. And in Sonnet 33 the youth is regarded as "my sun" (33.9), who left the speaker one morning like a sun that has been dimmed by clouds. In Sonnet 76 the speaker compares the repetitive themes of his own verse to the sun, which "is daily new and old" (76.13). In Sonnet 18 the comparison between the youth and the glorious sun falls short, not necessarily because the sun is less stunning than the youth, but because the sun is inconstant. This theme of the youth's constancy and temperance appears particularly in Sonnet 53, where the youth is praised for his "constant heart" (l. 14), and in Sonnet 117, where the speaker "strive[s] to prove / The constancy and virtue" of the youth's "love" (ll. 13–14).

## DEVICES AND TECHNIQUES

Sonnet 18 follows the format of the "English" or "Elizabethan" sonnet, the three quatrains and couplet pattern introduced by Henry Howard, Earl of Surrey and popularized by Shakespeare, which has a rhyme scheme of *abab, cdcd, efef, gg*. The rhetorical logic of the poem, however, follows a formula aligned with the Petrarchan pattern of an octave and sestet. The first eight lines of this poem present the speaker's dilemma: should he compare the young man with summer? On the surface this seems like a good plan. Summertime was proverbially the best of all things to be compared to. But the rest of the octave goes on to describe how such a comparison is ultimately inadequate. Summertime, especially in England, can be windy and thus "shake" the new "buds" of "May" (18.3); the English Julian calendar in the 1590s lagged about two weeks behind our Gregorian calendar, and so May was considered early summer. The sun, "the eye of heaven," is sometimes too intense or obscured by clouds, "his gold complexion dimm'd" (18.6). Additionally, summer has to come to an end, thus being as susceptible as anything else to the ravages of time. Like summer, each thing of beauty must "decline" (18.7) either by unforeseen events or by natural degenerative processes. Comparing the youth to a summer's day, it seems, is not such a grand idea after all.

The sonnet's sestet, which is introduced by the "But" of line 9, indicates a shift in argument. As Stephen Booth indicates, this is the same technique Shakespeare uses in sonnets 7, 14, 41, 44, 54, 63, 138, 141, 151, and 153 (*An Essay*, 3). Unlike summer and presumably all that is living, the beauty of the young man will never fade or depart. One of the most striking elements of the sestet is that it unfolds like a mystery. If all things must eventually be time's victim, how is it possible that the youth can defy it to possess his beauty "eternal[ly]" (18.9, 12)? How can he perform the seemingly impossible to be immune to death itself? The answer, of course, lies not in anything the youth does, but in the possibility that poetry praising the youth is that which can defy time and even death. As Evans suggests, "the phrase 'eternal summer' is syntactically difficult, since the youth's summer is not 'eternal' in itself but only in so far as it is caught and preserved in the verses" (131).

While beginning the sonnet with a question is not unique among the other poems in the sequence, it is unusual. The questions that begin fifteen other sonnets are usually asked over two or more lines and are directed at the youth ("Who will believe my verse in time to come / If it were fill'd with your most high deserts?"[17.1–2]) or to a general audience ("Why is my verse so barren of new pride? / So far from variation or quick change?" [76.1–2]). Sonnets 8 and 18 are the only ones in the sequence that begin and end the first line with a question. It is a question, however, that in its very asking is about the nature of poetry and the Petrarchan tradition. "Should I do what traditional sonneteers do and compare you to that which is proverbially the best?" In other words, "How should I write this poem?" The question that opens the sonnet invites a world of possibility. But positive answers to this question are undermined by the fact that it is a question rather than an assertion. What follows gives us a tentative answer to the initial question: "No. A comparison between you and summer fails since summer falls short of your beauty and constancy." But in the very catalog, we nonetheless receive a comparison. "Here are a few of the many ways in which you are not like summer but far exceed it." Then the logic becomes this: "I will compare you to a summer's day, but it is a faulty comparison." The failure of the comparison is what gives the poem its depth and moves us away from a simple Petrarchan conceit. As in Sonnet 130, where the speaker turns traditional and trite poetic comparisons on their head by asserting that his "mistress' eyes are nothing like the sun" (l. 1), here he also upends common metaphors by enumerating the inadequacy of comparing the youth to a summer's day (Kerrigan, p. 30).

We then move from the expected—the figurative comparison of an object of affection to something beautiful—to the surprising—a statement on the permanence of verse. As Vendler has suggested, the poem progresses from the "light, innocuous, dulcet" first line to eternal art: "It is only with the *short date* . . . on summer's lease that a somber quality enters, and we realize that from the lovely day we have come far, to the end of the season" (120). The highly alliterative "chance or nature's changing course" (18.8) indicates the harshness that comes with the passing of time. Through the poem's progressing diction we find a "widening of scope and deepening of gravity," which is seen nowhere more clearly than in the series of alliterative "D" words: we move from "day" (l. 1) and "darling" (l. 3) to "dimm'd" (l. 6), "declines" (l. 7), and, finally, "Death" in line 11 (Vendler, pp. 120, 121). But this poem does contain promise, and the possibility that the youth will live forever, that he will grow "in eternal lines to time" (18.12), is indicated in the attenuated internal rhyme. The final couplet, however, as in many of the sonnets, is ambiguous. The initial sense is that the lines of the poem will live eternally, will exist until doomsday. The youth will be triumphantly immortalized. The monosyllabic words emphasize this finality and permanence, while the use of anaphora, or the repetition of words at the beginning of successive phrases, reiterates the promise of immortality. But this can be only "so long as men can breathe or eyes can see" (18.13). In the couplet the speaker "concede[s] that art has human perpetuity rather than transcendent eternity" (Vendler, p. 121). This idea is echoed in Sonnet 60, which states "to times in hope my verse shall stand" (60.13), indicating a hoped-for future, but one that is ultimately unknowable.

## THEMES AND MEANINGS

A prevalent theme in Sonnet 18 is that of legal possession and ownership. Summer is said to have a "lease" (18.4), an allotted time that it can remain. Like any other temporary ownership, this lease must expire. The youth is represented as possessing or owning his beauty forever, unlike the summer that merely can "lease" its. Despite the strong legal connotations, as Burrow suggests, "these terms are not synonymous in law. *Possession* (especially when applied to land or property) means occupancy . . . but it does not necessarily imply ownership; hence to enjoy something fully one must have both ownership and permanent possession over it," as the youth has over his beauty (416). Although "fair thou ow'st" (18.10) is usually glossed as "beauty you own," it also connotes debt, "the beauty you're supposed to repay" (Kerrigan, p. 196). How the youth is meant to repay his beauty is unclear. Is it through procreation (thus linking it to the "breeding" sonnets), or through being immortalized as the subject of the speaker's poem?

The boy will keep ownership and possession of this beauty when he grows to time, or becomes a living part of time (18.12). This wording introduces the grafting metaphor that is seen more prominently in Sonnet 15: "As [time] takes from you, I ingraft you new" (15.14). The image here is of splicing a plant and combining it with the root-stock of another. "Eternal lines" (18.12), then, indicates cords or ropes, that which would have been used to bind a graft to the stock of another plant. The young man's growth onto time, bound with "eternal lines," will ensure his growth with time, rather than as a victim of it. Of course, the "eternal lines" that the youth will "grow" to are usually regarded as a reference to the actual written lines of verse. They may also carry the connotation of blood lines, or "lines of life" (16.9) that would align this poem with those on the topic of breeding. The "lines of life" were also the threads that would have been spun by the Fates in mythology: "the fates decided the length of each human life and cut each man's thread accordingly. *Eternal lines* would be threads never cut" (Booth, *Sonnets*, 162).

Part of the gravity of Sonnet 18 comes from its allusions to the youth's triumph over the darkness of death, which on one level implies a sort of religious experience. When the youth is immortalized by verse, "Death" cannot "brag" that the young man "[wanders] in his shade" (18.11). This image suggests the "shades" of the underworld and the shadows, or the inhabitants, of Hades (Booth, *Sonnets*, 162). It also echoes Psalm 23.3: "Yea though I walk through the valley of the shadow of death I will fear no evil." It is through one's faith in God that one can overcome the fear of death and can defeat the "brag[art]" Death, as we see in 1 Corinthians, "O death, where is thy sting?" (15.55) and John's Donne's "Holy Sonnet X," "Death be not proud" (1). That which can defeat death in Sonnet 18, the immortality found in verse, is akin to the power of faith to save one's soul.

## THE RELATIONSHIP OF THE SONNET TO SHAKESPEARE'S OTHER WORKS

The imagery in Sonnet 18 is developed in other of Shakespeare's works in more figurative terms. In Sonnet 18 the speaker asserts that "rough winds do shake the darling buds of May" (18.3) simply to suggest that the wind in summertime can often be blustery and somewhat disruptive to fresh young flowers. In *The Taming of the Shrew*, Kate uses this image in her controversial final monologue as a simile for a wife's shrewishness to her husband:

> dart not scornful glances from those eyes,
> To wound thy lord, thy king, thy governor.
> It blots thy beauty, as frosts do bite the meads,
> Confounds thy fame, as whirlwinds shake fair buds. (5.2.137–140)

Looking disdainfully at one's husband, Kate argues, ruins one's reputation ("confounds thy fame"), just as the wind destroys the new-formed flowers. A wife's reputation, she suggests, is fragile and in need of protection, especially from herself. In a much later play, *Cymbeline*, Imogen compares her father's interruption of her farewell to Posthumus to the "tyrannous breathing of the north / [that] Shakes all our buds from growing" (1.3.36–37). In all cases, the wind is seen as a destructive force, and the "buds" as having the potential to be ruined.

The "eye of heaven" in Sonnet 18 is a straightforward reference to the sun that is sometimes "too hot" in summer. In *Richard II*, rather than referring to the sun as that which gives off heat, it is represented, like God, as that which is all-seeing and can reveal evil deeds. The king, who has just landed in Wales after fighting in Ireland, draws the comparison between himself and the "eye of heaven." Like the sun that is "hid / Behind the globe" at night and cannot perceive "thieves and robbers" who work in darkness, while Richard was away from England he could not keep his eye on "this thief, this traitor Bullingbrook" (3.2.37–38, 39, 47). Similarly, in *The Rape of Lucrece*, the sun is seen as a protector of the virtuous. The would-be rapist, Tarquin, is glad that "The eye of heaven is out, and misty night / Covers the shame that follows sweet delight (ll. 356–357). Here the image is of the sun that has been extinguished ("out") and is therefore incapable of shedding light on the "shame" that will come from the rape of Lucrece.

In a larger sense, Shakespeare repeatedly explores the validity of the language being used. Richard II believes himself to be the sun, a standard image for a king, but he soon discovers that he is human:

> For you have but mistook me all this while.
> I live with bread like you, feel want,
> Taste grief, need friends. (*Richard II*, 3.2.174–176)

Juliet teaches Romeo to avoid the traditional oaths that lovers swear. When he asks, "What shall I swear by?" she replies, "Do not swear at all; / Or if thou wilt, swear by thy gracious self" (*Romeo and Juliet*, 2.2.112–114). To cite but one more example, Brutus famously argues that "There is a tide in the affairs of men, / Which taken at the flood, leads on to fortune" (*Julius Caesar*, 4.3.218–219). Here, as throughout the play, Brutus creates and then falls prey to his lovely language; his argument leads him to Philippi and death.

**Annotated Bibliography**

Booth, Stephen. *An Essay on Shakespeare's Sonnets*. New Haven: Yale UP, 1969. Booth explores various patterns in the sonnets, such as patterns of sound and vocabulary. Includes close readings of some of the poems.

———, ed. *Shakespeare's Sonnets*. New Haven: Yale UP, 1977. Booth provides a facsimile of the 1609 first printing of the sonnets together with a modern edited edition. Following the text are copious notes that illuminate the poems.

Burrow, Colin, ed. *The Complete Sonnets and Poems*. Oxford: Oxford UP, 2002. A carefully annotated edition of Shakespeare's complete poems, which synthesizes prior work and contributes valuable additional commentary.

Duncan-Jones, Katherine, ed. *Shakespeare's Sonnets*. The Arden Shakespeare. London: Thomas Nelson and Sons, 1997. In addition to useful notes to all the sonnets, Duncan-Jones provides an excellent introduction. Includes a survey of the debate over the biographical nature of the sonnets.

Evans, G. Blakemore. *The Sonnets*. Cambridge: Cambridge UP, 1996. Evans offers a good intro-
    duction, followed by detailed analysis of each sonnet. Discusses the text of the 1609 edi-
    tion.

Fineman, Joel. *Shakespeare's Perjured Eye: The Invention of Poetic Subjectivity in the Sonnets*. Berke-
    ley: U of California P, 1986. Argues that the sonnets disrupt the conventional nature of a
    poetic persona and create a new kind of poetic subjectivity. The poems are part of a tra-
    dition that reveals the ironies of praise.

Innes, Paul. *Shakespeare and the English Renaissance Sonnet: Verses of Feigning Love*. New York:
    St. Martin's P, 1997. Sees Sonnet 18 as a bridge between the first seventeen, which urge the
    fair youth to marry, and the rest of the sonnets. In Sonnet 18 the speaker appropriates the
    ideals of beauty for the youth, so that the youth becomes the owner of those qualities.

Kerrigan, John, ed. *Shakespeare: "The Sonnets" and "A Lover's Complaint."* Harmondsworth, Eng.:
    Penguin, 1986. This useful edition includes a lengthy introduction that looks at the se-
    quence in an historical context. Kerrigan annotates each sonnet and includes a section on
    "Variants and Further Sonnets."

Vendler, Helen. *The Art of Shakespeare's Sonnets*. Cambridge, MA: Harvard UP, 1997. Vendler pays
    particular attention in her notes to the language of the poems and how Shakespeare uses
    that language to make meaning.

# Sonnet 19

## Priscilla Glanville

Devouring Time, blunt thou the lion's paws,
And make the earth devour her own sweet brood;
Pluck the keen teeth from the fierce tiger's jaws,
And burn the long-liv'd phoenix, in her blood;
Make glad and sorry seasons as thou fleetst,
And do whate'er thou wilt, swift-footed Time,
To the wide world and all her fading sweets;
But I forbid thee one most heinous crime:
O! carve not with thy hours my love's fair brow,
Nor draw no lines there with thine antique pen;
Him in thy course untainted do allow
For beauty's pattern to succeeding men.
   Yet, do thy worst old Time: despite thy wrong,
   My love shall in my verse ever live young.

## PROSE PARAPHRASE

All-consuming Time, you may blunt the fierce claws of the lion, and destroy Nature's generative forces with the cycle of the seasons, diminish the power of even the tiger and destroy the long-lived Phoenix. I give you permission to spread joy and sorrow through the seasons, and do whatever you choose, swiftly passing Time, to the world's delights, which are under your influence. But I will not let you commit one most horrid crime: Oh, do not wrinkle my love's brow, or draw lines there; as you continue on your destructive march, leave him untouched so he remains a model of ideal beauty for future generations. Yet if you do commit this most horrid of crimes, despite your unjust actions, my love will remain eternally young in my poetry.

## .THE PLACE OF THE SONNET IN THE CYCLE

One of the 126 sonnets addressed to a lovely young male friend, Sonnet 19 presents the speaker's desire to save his young muse from the ravages of time. As in other sonnets addressed to the fair youth, the speaker is here primarily concerned with the physical effects of time. While, in its entirety, the first sonnet group explores the central themes of procreation and art as means of escaping the snares of time and the particular necessity of perpetuating beauty through such means, Sonnet 19 is often described as a turning point in the sequence. It is often suggested that Sonnet 19 is the last of the mild and somewhat distanced calls for marriage and procreation as means of countering time's ravaging of beauty, a theme expressed on a more personal and impassioned level in the sonnets that follow Sonnet 19. In the early sonnets, the youth is championed as one of the "fairest" from whom future generations require "increase" (1.1), or children, as "beauty's legacy" (4.2), rather than as a love interest of the speaker himself. The speaker's attitude, in these first sonnets, alternates between praise of the young man's beauty, mourning of "beauty's waste" (9.11) by one who "murd'rous shame commits" in refusing to marry (9.14), and subsequent promises to "ingraft" (15.14) and immortalize the youth and his beauty through verse.

The sequence begins with an initial lauding of immortality rendered through marriage and procreation and moves into an expression of frustration at the youth's seemingly selfish rejection of the two states. After Sonnet 14's apocalyptic foretelling of "truth's and beauty's doom and date" (14), Sonnet 15 marks the point at which the second alternative to mortality—immortality through art—is first proposed. In sonnets 16 and 17, the speaker qualifies this proposition by affirming that procreation is a more exact means of self-perpetuation than inspiring representation in verse. In Sonnet 18, the speaker vacillates again, praising the ability of "eternal lines" (18.12) to thwart the ravages of Time. In Sonnet 19, this ability surfaces as the theme of the closing couplet, a position often reserved for a sonnet's summation or final insight: "Yet, do thy worst, old Time: despite thy wrong, / My love shall in my verse ever live young" (19.13–14). Here the speaker seems both to face the inevitability of Time's consuming power and to accept the necessity of answering that power himself. The lines that the poet inscribes on paper will counteract the lines that Time inscribes on the fair youth. One might also say that with the close of Sonnet 19 the focus shifts from perpetuating the youth's idealized Platonic beauty for the edification of future generations to the speaker's increasing obsession with the young man as an object of personal and artistic desire.

The distanced champion of Platonic beauty gives way to an impassioned speaker whose increasing eroticisation of his subject has long been a focal point of critical debate among Shakespeare scholars. Such is the voice that surfaces in Sonnet 20 to bemoan the fact that Nature "painted" the beauty of the young man—now described as the "master mistress" of his "passion"—to defeat him (20.1–2). Poignantly, the weapon Nature uses to ensure his defeat is a deeper love than that which may be aroused by fickle "women's pleasure" (20.13). Interestingly, Sonnet 20 is upheld as both an example of the homosexual undertones of the sonnets and as evidence that the speaker's interest in the young man is purely Platonic. Regardless of its sexual undertones, this "fair" love (21.10) bonds artist and muse in both heart and soul in Sonnet 22 and matures into an alternately "fierce" (23.3), "silent" (23.13), and "tottering" (26.11) obsession in the following sonnets.

## DEVICES AND TECHNIQUES

Following the pattern that distinguishes the Shakespearean sonnet from other sonnet forms, Sonnet 19 is divided into four parts: three four line quatrains (with an *abab cdcd efef* rhyme scheme) followed by a rhymed couplet (*gg*) that provides a concluding summation or insight. The sonnet contains two sentences. The first is a twelve-line denunciation of the abuses of Time, and the second is a response to the first.

Each quatrain is built around a unifying metaphor: Time's voracious appetite (ll. 1–4), bittersweet effects (5–7), and artistic affinity for transforming material reality (9–12). The sonnet moves from a piling up of jarring imagery (quatrain one), to a central paradox (quatrain two), and to an extended metaphor (quatrain three) that is carried, like a refrain, through the closing couplet.

In this sonnet, the speaker personifies and directly addresses Time, which places the young muse in the role of silent auditor. One may thus see the poem as a dramatic monologue. Set within fluid five-foot lines, a piling up of irregularly stressed commands, "blunt . . . make . . . pluck . . . burn . . . make" and "do" (19.1–6) opens the poem and well reveals the horror Time's corrosive power inspires in the speaker. In the second quatrain, a harried tone is conveyed through the increased use of alliteration, such as repeated "s," "l," and "w" sounds: "Make glad and sorry seasons as thou fleet'st / And do what e're thou wilt, swift-footed Time, / To the wide world and all her fading sweets" (19.5–7). By the third quatrain, expressions of horror and frustration give way to personal outrage as Time directs its power toward the idealized beauty of the young man. Such outrage reaches its pinnacle and technical climax in the sonnet's defiant final couplet. By the poem's conclusion, we see that the speaker no longer intends to engage in civil discourse with Time, a force clearly represented as immune to reason or appeal. Instead, the speaker will vindicate his friend's beauty and preserve it in verse, rendering Time irrelevant.

One should note the poignant use Sonnet 19 makes of Eastern mythology, Neoplatonism, and parable. For instance, the "long-liv'd Phoenix" (l. 4) of the poem is the famed red-plumed bird of Egyptian mythology. According to legend, this Arabian eagle-like bird lived for a 500-year cycle. At the close of this cycle, it would build a nest, ignite its new home and itself, and give way to a new bird born from its ashes. Thus, it was associated with the rising and setting sun and worshiped as a manifestation of the Egyptian gods Ra and Osiris. In like fashion, the young man's beauty, however ravaged by the abuses of Time, will emerge refreshed and untouched in the poet's verse. As the Phoenix is immortal but not entirely immune to the passing of Time, the young man's material glories may fade, but he will nevertheless remain an untouched and pristine delight for the poet's admiring audience.

As the mutability of the phoenix reflects the influence of Eastern mythology, it also reflects the mystical philosophy of Neoplatonism. The idea that the young man's beauty must remain an unmarred icon for the edification of future generations reflects the Neoplatonic ideal of metaphysical perfection represented in material form: a material appropriation of the perfection that exists beyond the limits of human comprehension. In an age in which a rigid hierarchy, known as the Great

Chain of Being, is still largely thought of as ordering all existence, from the realm of pure spirit (God) to that of inanimate objects, the young man's beauty offers a re-connection to the state of perfect spirit from which human beings are distanced at birth. Likewise, critics often note that the muse's call to marriage and procreation champions the message of Matthew 25 and its parable of the talents, which exhorts those who are gifted or blessed to make the most of their bounty—indeed, to multiply it—rather than squander or hoard it. In the sonnet sequence, the gift being squandered is the supreme beauty of the young man, a gift best and more widely served through procreation. As Time is guilty of warring against such beauty, the youth himself is guilty of failing to perpetuate it through alternate means.

## THEMES AND MEANINGS

Clearly, the central theme of Sonnet 19, a theme nearly ubiquitous in Shakespeare's sonnet sequence as a whole, is the corrosive effect of Time. This is a pervasive message not only in Shakespeare's sonnets but also in Renaissance artistry in general. While the Great Chain of Being came under increasing scientific scrutiny, the dissolution of the monasteries under Henry VIII led to large parcels of land being divided and sold to speculators. This redistribution of large amounts of property helped to deflate the supremacy of the landed gentry, while a surge in urban development engendered the prosperity of a rising mercantile class. At the same time, continuing hostility between Protestants and Catholics inundated the political landscape with intrigue, espionage, blackmail, and dynastic instability. Taken as a whole, such profound changes led to an overall sense that life was spinning out of control—that religious, political, and social norms were fleeting while Time and death alone remained constant. Thus, it is not surprising that the cultural products of the Renaissance reflect a sense of urgency coupled with an ambiguous attitude toward change. In Sonnet 19, such ambiguity gives way to a climate of horror and rejection. For this speaker at least, the march of Time is the most egregious scourge of stability and beauty. As his age must come to terms with shifting astronomical and social constructs, the speaker must come to terms with the precarious love of beauty at the heart of Renaissance spiritual, secular, and artistic constructs. Time is the ravager of all.

As is typical with Shakespearean sonnets, the central theme of Time and its abuses is organized into quatrains and a concluding couplet. In this instance, the first quatrain of Sonnet 19 is distinguished by a building up of images that present the cyclical journey from birth to death through jarring jungle imagery. As Time insures that the bounty of spring and the raptures of summer give way to the closing icy breath of fall, the earth will be forced to "devour her own sweet brood" (l. 2). Predators soon become prey, as voracious Time stops the "fierce tiger's jaws" (l. 3). In a phantasmagoric instant, the ancient Phoenix is boiled in her own blood (l. 4).

The second quatrain of Sonnet 19 introduces one of the central paradoxes for which the Romantics so admired Shakespeare: the idealization of beauty that must die. In this quatrain, the seasons are both "glad" and "sorry" (l. 5), for spring's bounty and summer's ripeness are overshadowed by the foreknowledge of fall's speed and winter's icy breath. Life is more poignant and beautiful—the "fading sweets" of "the wide world" are sweeter (l. 7)—because they are not immune to the ravages of "swift-footed Time" (l. 6). The third quatrain then develops the central metaphor of Time as an artist, in particular an artist whose "antique pen" (l. 10) has ever been the scourge of civilization and must not be permitted to mar the Platonic beauty of the young muse. Thus, Time becomes a metaphor for the unsettling scientific, political, and social fluctuations with which the age had to contend. If Platonic beauty provides a sole point of connection to the realm of pure spirit, the loss of that beauty reflects the loss of humanity's last stabilizing effect. Even the very artistry that is upheld as a link to immortality is an ambiguous tool. In the hands of the poet, creativity wields eternal life, but Time, too, is an artist, and Time best celebrates beauty by rendering it tragic.

## THE RELATIONSHIP OF THE SONNET TO SHAKESPEARE'S OTHER WORKS

In Sonnet 19, Shakespeare uses violent images of consumption to describe the ravaging of Nature, beauty, and, as an aftereffect, humanity's connection to the realm of the spirit. Such is not an uncommon theme in Shakespeare's work, nor is the jarring jungle imagery through which it is delivered. Many of Shakespeare's dramatic pieces likewise feature terrifying and bestial appetites that gnaw away the heart of a stabilized social and cultural fabric. For instance, in *Hamlet* and *King Lear* jarring and poignant jungle imagery, images of consumption in particular, are used to reflect the instability of the age and its institutions. As Prince Hamlet suggests, in a world in which political and social hierarchies give way to chaos and instability, the worm is an "emperor" in its diet, for "we fat all creatures else to fat us, and we fat ourselves for maggots," making a "fat king" and a "lean beggar" but "variable service, two dishes, but to one table" (4.3.21–24). Likewise, such courtiers as Rosencrantz and Guildenstern are kept like "an apple" in their King's jaw: "first mouth'd, to be last swallow'd" (4.2.18–19). Because the world is "an unweeded garden" possessed by "things rank and gross in nature" (1.2.135–136), our futile existence of competition and strife provides but one constant, and that constant is our march toward death. *King Lear* is another work that features animal appetites gone amuck. For example, Lear's covetous and bloodthirsty daughter Goneril is "serpent-like" (2.4.161) in her poisonous speech, a "vulture" in her "sharp-tooth'd unkindness" (2.4.135), and a tiger (4.2.40) in her ruthlessness. As Albany suggests, the world of King Lear is a destabilized realm in which humanity, no longer cradled by a solid political and social hierarchy, will "perforce prey on itself, / Like monsters of the deep (4.2.49–50). Indeed, life is so chaotic, so perversely futile, that Gloucester concludes, "As flies to wanton boys are we to the gods, / They kill us for their sport" (4.1.36–37). Like the world of Sonnet 19, that depicted in *Hamlet* and *King Lear* is a far cry from a pastoral Eden. It appears rather a hell in which gross appetites wield power over unstable social, political, and spiritual norms. In such a world, the only absolute is the speed with which Time summons us to the grave, for, as Ulysses notes in *Troilus and Cressida*,

> . . . beauty, wit,
> High birth, vigor of bone, desert in service,
> Love, friendship, charity, are subjects all
> To envious and calumniating Time. (3.3.171–174)

Another theme that Sonnet 19 shares with Shakespeare's other works is that of beauty rendered immortal through procreation. This theme is well dramatized in *Twelfth Night* when the cross-dressing Viola chides Olivia for not marrying and perpetuating her beauty through issue. As the speaker of the sonnet sequence chides the young muse for not marrying and having children, Viola describes Olivia as "the cruell'st she alive" in her decision to "lead these graces to the grave, / And leave the world no copy" (1.5.241–243). Because Viola is in love with Orsino, on whose behalf she woos Olivia, her frustration may be due in part to her sense that Orsino, too, has a responsibility to perpetuate his idealized beauty. Here, as in Sonnet 19, it is not perpetuation of the body that is ultimately at stake but preservation of the soul. If beauty is perpetuated through issue, the dissolution of the Great Chain of Being need not signify a chaotic and alienated existence. Platonic beauty may be marred by Time—as are Nature, political and social institutions, and love itself—but it can thus arise, Phoenix-like and pure, from the cradle of its own ashes. Thus, beauty remains a link to the unseen creator—a sole point of connection and stability in a world of flux and confusion. The longing for eternal beauty—as represented in Sonnet 19, in Shakespeare's sonnet sequence as a whole, and in multitudinous products of Renaissance artistry—is ultimately proved to be a longing for the self. Thus, in Sonnet 19, as in many of his works, Shakespeare transcends the boundaries of text and genre to define the universal search for identity at the heart of the human condition.

## Annotated Bibliography

Bloom, Harold, ed. *Shakespeare's Sonnets: Modern Critical Interpretations*. New York: Chelsea House, 1987. Part of the quite helpful Modern Critical Interpretations series, this work provides six general but highly informative articles by established Shakespeare scholars. As a whole, the collection analyzes the sonnets' form and major themes from varied and engaging critical perspectives. Novice readers of Shakespeare's work, as well as novice readers of poetry in general, will find this text particularly helpful.

Hedley, Jane. "'Since First Your Eye I Eyed': Shakespeare's Sonnets and the Poetics of Narcissism." *Style* 28.1 (Spring 1994): 1–30. Hedley examines the diction and syntax of Shakespeare's sonnets, arriving at the conclusion that their language, structure, and contradictions reveal the psychic makeup of a speaker suffering from narcissism. Thus, Hedley proposes, as the speaker reveals the narcissism of the young man, he does so in conscious awareness that he is simultaneously working through his own psychic difficulties.

Hubler, Edward. *The Sense of Shakespeare's Sonnets*. Princeton: Princeton UP, 1952. In this formalist and reader-friendly overview of Shakespeare's sonnets, Hubler provides an introduction to the form and meter of the sonnets, an analysis of the speaker's characterization of the young muse and dark lady, and chapter length discussions of such central themes as mutability, immortality, and repudiation of goodness. Readers who are interested in the nature and Neoplatonic imagery of the work will find chapters three and four particularly helpful.

Jungman, Robert. "Untainted Crime in Shakespeare's Sonnet 19." *American Notes & Queries* 16.2 (Spring 2003): 19–21. Jungman examines the specific diction of the poem, treating its adoption of jousting, hunting, and legalistic metaphors. In doing so, he arrives at a central paradox often overlooked in critical discussion of the poem: the fact that Time and the speaker ultimately present the same threat to the young man's idealized beauty.

Pequigney, Joseph. *Such Is My Love: A Study of Shakespeare's Sonnets*. Chicago: U of Chicago P, 1985. In this well-received study, Pequigney examines the homoerotic undertones of the themes, language, and structure of the sonnet sequence.

Swisher, Clarice et al. *Readings on the Sonnets*. San Diego, CA: Greenhaven Press, 1997. This resource is an excellent starting place for novice readers of Shakespeare and his sonnets.

Opening with an interesting biography, the collection proceeds through speculations concerning the identity of the young muse and Dark Lady to an overview of themes and poetic techniques featured in the sonnet sequence as a whole and analysis of the more prominent poems among the sonnets. It closes with a helpful historical timeline, a glossary of literary terms, and suggestions for further reading.

# Sonnet 20

## Roze Hentschell

A woman's face with nature's own hand painted,
Hast thou, the master mistress of my passion;
A woman's gentle heart, but not acquainted
With shifting change, as is false women's fashion:
An eye more bright than theirs, less false in rolling,
Gilding the object whereupon it gazeth;
A man in hue all hues in his controlling,
Which steals men's eyes and women's souls amazeth.
And for a woman wert thou first created;
Till Nature, as she wrought thee, fell a-doting,
And by addition me of thee defeated,
By adding one thing to my purpose nothing.
   But since she prick'd thee out for women's pleasure,
   Mine be thy love, and thy love's use their treasure.

### PROSE PARAPHRASE

You, who are both the master and mistress of my heart, have the naturally beautiful face of a woman. You also have the kindness of a woman, but lack the fickleness that is so typical of females. Your eyes—more brilliant than a woman's—are not as likely to be attracted by one person after another (or to feign interest and excitement). Rather, you add luster to that which you look upon. Masculine in physical form, you surpass everyone, male and female, in beauty. You are admired by men and captivating to women. You were initially conceived of as a woman, until Nature, when she formed you, became infatuated with you and therefore endowed you with an additional object (a penis). This additional thing is of no use ("nothing," that is, no thing) to me (l. 12). But since Nature selected you to delight women, let me have your love and let your physical enjoyment be women's valuable possession (or let "their treasure," that is, their vaginas, be for your physical pleasure).

## THE PLACE OF THE SONNET IN THE CYCLE

Sonnet 20 is a part of the first sequence of poems addressed to or dealing with a young, physically attractive, and virtuous man. Unlike the poems that precede it, this poem does not urge the youth to procreate (sonnets 1–14, 16–17), nor does it fixate on the speaker's desire to immortalize the youth in his verse (15, 18–19). Some critics have seen a departure in Sonnet 20, both in introducing a more intimate tone as well as more sexually charged language into the sequence. The poem therefore provokes much speculation regarding the addressee and the nature of the speaker's relation to him. First, Sonnet 20 has been seen to demonstrate possible evidence of the identity of the young man in the sonnets. In his essay on Sonnet 12 in this volume, Charles Forker describes the possible candidates for the youth, focusing on the initials W.H. as the "onlie begetter" of the sonnets, identified in Thomas Thorpe's title page to the 1609 quarto first edition of these poems. There has been no end of heated investigation into the initials and for whom they might stand, and Sonnet 20 has only helped to fan the flames.

In Sonnet 20, the speaker asserts that the object of his affection is "a man in hue" (7). In the 1609 quarto (known as "Q"), "hue" was capitalized, italicized, and spelled thus: "*Hews.*" This word has prompted generations of speculation, beginning with Edmond Malone in the eighteenth century, that "Hews" could refer to a W. Hughes, or William Hughes, the W. H. of the title page. Hyder Edward Rollins playfully laments that Malone "created a spook harder to drive away than the ghost of Hamlet's father (Hyder Edward Rollins, ed., *The Sonnets*, New Variorum Edition, 2 vols. [Philadelphia: J. B. Lippincott, 1944], 1.181).

In the late nineteenth century, Oscar Wilde wove the intriguing (but entirely specious) yarn that one Willie Hughes was a boy actor in Shakespeare's company who left the Lord Chamberlain's Men for a rival troupe and thus drove Shakespeare to write a sonnet sequence to him. *HEWS* has also been construed as an anagram for Henry Wriothesley, third Earl of Southhampton, the most popular candidate for the youth. However, the reader cannot lend too much weight to arguments based on the fact that the word was italicized and capitalized—all italicized words in Q were capitalized, and italicization seems to be arbitrary. Further, there is no evidence that Shakespeare had any ties to any of the William Hugheses that were "dragged from deserved obscurity" (G. Blakemore Evans, ed., *The Sonnets* [Cambridge: Cambridge UP, 1996], 133).

Like most of Shakespeare's other sonnets, Sonnet 20 has provided fodder for an autobiographical reading. Those critics who have read the sonnets in this manner have tended to use Sonnet 20 as a touchstone, either to prove that Shakespeare had homoerotic feelings for a young man (because the sonnet refers to a hoped-for physical relationship) or to refute such a claim (because the sonnet ultimately does not allow for this relationship). While each argument has its potential merits, to claim that the sonnet denies Shakespeare's homoerotic love or provides evidence of Shakespeare's homosexuality is ultimately futile. The voice in the sonnets is that of a speaker, a persona, no less constructed of language than the addressee. As Stephen Booth has stated, "The sexual undercurrents of the sonnets are of the sonnets; they probably reflect a lot that is true about their author, but I do not know what that is" (*Shakespeare's Sonnets* [New Haven: Yale UP, 1977], 549). As much as we would like to solve the mystery of the youth's identity (if it is indeed one person he is addressing) and Shakespeare's relationship to him (if it is indeed "Shakespeare" and not a fictionalized persona-speaker), these are quixotic enterprises. The sonnets as a whole do not tell us Shakespeare's sexual orientation, nor do they fully indicate the nature of the relationship between the speaker and the addressee.

Just as wrongheaded is to suggest that Sonnet 20 is radically different from the other sonnets in the sequence. Sonnet 20 reinforces the theme of the youth's physical beauty made clear in the earlier (and later) sonnets. Outward beauty, which had been lauded for generations in love sonnets written by men to women, is redirected onto the young man, thus presenting a fresh object of affection. In line 2 the traditional mistress of sonnet sequences is made a "master mistress"—a man who excels women in all areas. Throughout the poems addressed to the youth, his physical perfection is brought up several times: In Sonnet 1, the youth is counted among the "fairest creatures" (l. 1); he is urged to give his "sweet semblance" to another (13.4); the speaker acknowledges his verse is inadequate in showing "your most high deserts" and "the beauty of your eyes" (17.2, 5). The young man's beauty, "with Nature's own hand painted" (20.1), is alluded to again when the speaker asserts that "I never saw that you did painting need" (83. 1).

Neither is the ardent tone of "master mistress of my passion" (20.2) or the declaration of the speaker's love much of a departure from the way in which other sonnets in the sequence refer to the youth. Elsewhere the speaker addresses the youth as "dear my love" (13.13), proclaims the addressee "Lord of my love" (26.1), and refers to him as "my love" three times in Sonnet 40 (ll. 1, 3, 5). Sonnet 20 develops the theme of the youth's dominant position in relation to the speaker as well as other people. While the youth has "all hues in his controlling" in line 7 of Sonnet 20, in Sonnet 53 he has "millions of strange shadows" that "tend" upon him (l. 2). In Sonnet 20 the youth is the "master mistress" of the speaker's "passion," thus introducing a theme of dominance over the speaker, which is extended in sonnets 57 and 58 when the speaker refers to himself as a "slave" to the youth (57.1, 11; 58.1). Finally, the androgynous appearance of the youth (he has "[a] woman's face," l. 1) that readers find so provocative in Sonnet 20 is referred to again in Sonnet 53, when the speaker asserts that images both of Adonis and Helen are "painted new" in the youth's beauty (l. 8).

## DEVICES AND TECHNIQUES

While Sonnet 20 follows the typical Shakespearean rhyming pattern of three quatrains and a couplet, the logic of the sonnet is much more aligned with the octave-sestet of the Italian sonnet. In the octave, the speaker compares the youth to women, asserting the young man's natural beauty, kindness, and constancy. Despite his likeness to women, the young man is described as superior to them and is able to "amaze" them (l. 8). The sestet offers a creation myth, wherein the young man's origin and the fate of the speaker are described: Nature, who first molded the youth as a woman, fell in love with her own creation, gave her creation an "addition" (a penis), and so deprived the speaker of physically enjoying the youth. The youth, thus "prick'd . . . out" (l. 13), must give his physical body to women but still can give his love to the speaker. As Joseph Pequigney has argued, "the two sections have parallel movements; each begins by remarking the youth's feminine aspects and closes by distinguishing male from female reaction to his person" (32). In both sections of the sonnet, females benefit from the young man. They are enchanted by his physical beauty in the octave, and the lucky recipients of his "love's use" in the sestet (l. 14).

This sonnet on gender confusion is the only one in the sequence that uses the feminine rhyme throughout. Also called a double-rhyme, the end rhyme is on the last two syllables of each line, and there is an additional unstressed syllable. This pattern has the effect of attenuating each line, perhaps placing greater emphasis on the rhymes themselves. Thus we have "painted" (l. 1) explicitly being tied to "acquainted" (l. 3). The falsehood of women found in their use of cosmetics might be tied to their quaint, a Middle English word for female genitalia. Similarly, "Nature . . . fell a-doting" (l. 10), thus allowing the speaker to have "nothing," pronounced "noting" in Shakespeare's day (l. 12). It is Nature's infatuation and her subsequent "addition" that deprives the speaker of the "thing" he desires. According to Colin Burrow, feminine rhymes in poetry are commonly used in the sonnets of romance languages and often surface at sexually charged moments (Colin Burrow, ed., *The Complete Sonnets and Poems* [Oxford: Oxford UP, 2002]). Feminine rhymes are of course appropriate for a sonnet describing a man who is almost a woman.

## THEMES AND MEANINGS

The poem has fascinated and frustrated critics over the years primarily because, in the Quarto, the youth is referred to as "the master mistress of my passion," thus introducing the theme of androgyny. The phrase "master mistress" appears to be unprecedented (Burrow, p. 420) and is most readily glossed as "sovereign mistress." Initially, then, it appears that the addressee may be a woman. This reading, however, seems implausible after we discover that the addressee is being compared to women, but is not one. After we get to line seven we conclusively realize the speaker is addressing a man ("a man in hue"). Many editors have hyphenated "master-mistress" to suggest the sense of "man-mistress," or "one loved like a woman but of the male sex," or one who appears to possess the qualities of both man and woman. "Passion" (20.2) in these readings, then, suggests "desire," specifically "sexual desire." Martin Friedman points out that that "Master" and "Mistress" are interchangeable terms for "something which is an object of passionate interest or a center of attention" and are terms from lawn bowling. They are names for the small bowl "thrown out at the beginning of a game as a mark for the players to aim at" (189). Friedman cites several other instances in Shakespeare's work in which he uses such bowling terms and follows the game's imagery through the sonnet ("rolling" in line five, the friend as object of a contest between the speaker and nature, and the notion of one who must be defeated). Despite this fascinating suggestion, the reading has not managed to overtake the more conventional and suggestive sense of the line as a declaration of love for a womanish-man.

The last line of the sonnet suggests the limits of the relationship between the speaker and the addressee in economic terms, introducing the theme of usury, the practice of lending money with interest taken on return. The speaker asserts that the youth should give his "love" to the speaker while giving "thy love's use" to women. "Use" here can mean "usefulness," but also "interest" as opposed to capital. Thus, "thy love's use" would translate either as "the actual physical act of your love" or "the interest left over from your love." The speaker, in this sense, would receive the capital ("thy love"), while women would only receive the interest ("thy love's use"). Although usury was almost universally derided in Shakespeare's time as immoral, was proscribed in Deuteronomy 23:20, and especially vilified in Shakespeare's play *The Merchant of Venice*, it was also legal. Crucial to the operation of mercantile culture in a time when there were no banks, usury (that is, interest) was regarded as a necessary evil. Francis Bacon saw it as "a thing allowed because of the hardness of men's hearts." The sense that "use" is necessary, however unpleasant, is reinforced in Sonnet 20. The speaker admits that the youth's "use" must be given to women, no matter how distasteful he finds such a notion. Shakespeare employs the economic meaning of "use" throughout the sonnets, most explicitly in Sonnet 4, where the addressee is called a "Profitless usurer," who, in his refusal to have children, is not collecting any interest on his beauty (l. 7). This phrase suggests that the "use" given to women is that which would allow for sexual procreation, that is, semen, thus linking Sonnet 20 with the procreation sonnets. If this is the case, the "treasure" that the women would gain would be the children. We see this sense in Sonnet 6 when the speaker tells the addressee to

> treasure thou some place
> With beauty's treasure ere it be self-kill'd.
> That use is not forbidden usury,
> Which happies those that pay the willing loan. (ll. 3–6)

Here, "use" of this sort is encouraged by the speaker. It is "not forbidden," but rather will bring joy to the recipient. In Sonnet 20, however, the speaker is resigned to the "use" that the speaker must give to women instead of him. However, this tone of "defeat" is tempered. As Peter Herman has suggested, "use" is linked with sexuality and "subordinated to the homoerotic relationship" (277). Procreation is marginalized and the means of procreation, sex with women, is subordinated to the more lofty "love" which the speaker will share with the addressee.

Sonnet 20 also introduces a favorite theme of Renaissance writing, that of a woman's artificiality and fickleness. Women are accused in the sonnet of artifice in their use of cosmetics, of possessing the "fashion" of "shifting change" (l. 4) indicated in both desire for modish apparel and their changes of heart, and of having a "rolling" eye (l. 5). According to the theory of the four humors that dates back at least to Aristotle, women were supposed to have a phlegmatic temperament, which was governed by the moon, thus leading to fickleness and changeability (Evans, p. 133). The use of cosmetics was an outward indication of women's changing nature. Hamlet repeats this charge in his tirade to Ophelia: "I have heard of your paintings, well enough. God hath given you one face, and you make yourselves another" (3.1.142–144). The notion that women go against their God-given nature in painting their faces is underscored by their lack of steadfastness and loyalty. The youth in Sonnet 20, impervious to "shifting change" (l. 4), is pitted against "woman's love," which is "brief" (*Hamlet*, 3.2.154, 153).

## THE RELATIONSHIP OF THE SONNET TO
## SHAKESPEARE'S OTHER WORKS

Intense friendship between men is a hallmark of Shakespeare's work. Although the homosocial relationship is regarded as superior to love between a man and a woman, heterosexual relationships more often than not are privileged dramatically, especially in comedy. In Sonnet 20, the speaker admits his "passion" for the youth, but ultimately must concede "defeat" (l. 11) as the youth gives his "love's use" to women. In *The Merchant of Venice*, Antonio's fierce devotion to Bassanio allows him to assure Bassanio that "My purse, my person, my extremest means, / Lie all unlock'd to your occasions" (1.1.138–139). Yet, at play's end, when Antonio believes he must die for Bassanio, he acknowledges the primacy of Bassanio's relationship to his new wife, even as he reiterates the importance of their homosocial love:

> Commend me to your honorable wife, . . .
> Say how I lov'd you, speak me fair in death;
> And when the tale is told, bid her be judge
> Whether Bassanio had not once a love. (4.1.273–277)

In the closing scene, Antonio is relegated to being merely a guest in the marriage festivities and in the home of Bassanio's new wife, Portia. Another Antonio, the sea-captain of *Twelfth Night*, similarly expresses his ardor for another man, Sebastian. After they have landed in Illyria, Antonio pleads to follow Sebastian, begs to be his "servant," and proclaims, "I do adore thee so" (2.1.36, 47). Later, sounding much like the speaker in the sonnets, Antonio suggestively expresses that his "desire, / (More sharp than filed steel)," along with his "willing love" urged him to follow Sebastian (3.3.4–5, 11). Despite Antonio's declarations of love and loyalty, Sebastian happily marries Olivia, a woman whom he hardly knows and who has mistaken Sebastian for his twin sister. The multiple homoerotic plots are subordinated to the tidy marriages at play's end; and Antonio, dumbfounded at seeing the twins, Viola and Sebastian, reunited can only utter what are his melancholic last words: "Which is Sebastian?" (5.1.224).

### Annotated Bibliography

Casey, Charles. "Was Shakespeare Gay? Sonnet 20 and the Politics of Pedagogy." *College Literature* 25.3 (1998): 35–52. Casey discusses the questions surrounding Shakespeare's sexual identity brought up by the sonnets and Sonnet 20 in particular. He demonstrates how pedagogical methodology is intrinsic in the way students come to the issue of Shakespeare's sexuality.

Cousins, A. D. *Shakespeare's Sonnets and Narrative Poems.* Harlow, Eng.: Longman, 2000. In his commentary on the sonnets, Cousins discusses the homoerotic element of the poems to the youth, and especially Sonnet 20, in the context of classical and Renaissance discourses on male-male friendship. He highlights the idealization of such relationships as well as the implicit misogyny in them.

Friedman, Martin B. " 'Master Mistris': Image and Tone in Sonnet 20." *Shakespeare Quarterly* 22.2 (1971): 189–191. Friedman claims that Sonnet 20 has received perhaps more attention than it merits because of line 2, where the speaker calls the youth the "master mistress of my passion." He claims that critics who see the sonnet as highly erotic have "falsified" the tone. Rather, he reads "master" and "mistress" as terms from bowling, thus seeing the tone as "sportive."

Herman, Peter C. "What's the Use? Or, The Problematic of Economy in Shakespeare's Procreation Sonnets." In *Shakespeare's Sonnets: Critical Essays*. Ed. James Schiffer. New York:
Garland, 1999. 263–283. This essay discusses the first twenty sonnets in economic terms.
Herman argues that the inclusion of economic imagery in these sonnets "arise[s] from
and intervene[s] in the economic developments of the early 1600s" whereby humans are
reduced to commodities (264). He discusses the word "use" in Sonnet 20 as economic interest. "Use" is explicitly tied to heterosexual pleasure, which is subordinated to the homoerotic relationship developed in the sonnet.

Melchiori, Giorgio. "Love's Use and Man's Hues in Shakespeare's Sonnet 20." *English Miscellany:
A Symposium of History, Literature and the Arts* 23 (1972): 21–38. The author discusses how
Sonnet 20 emphasizes women (as a whole) as inferior to men. Women are associated most
particularly with false appearances and with bald sexuality. By contrast, the youth in the
poem is genuine, true, and constant.

Pequigney, Jospeh. *Such Is My Love: A Study of Shakespeare's Sonnets*. Chicago: U of Chicago P,
1985. As a whole, the author reads Shakespeare's sonnets as homoerotic amorous verse
rather than an expression of platonic male friendship. In discussing Sonnet 20, he argues
that it is the youth's seeming unattainability that may be the primary cause of the arousal
of intimacy between the friends.

# Sonnet 29

## Robert G. Blake

When in disgrace with fortune and men's eyes
I all alone beweep my outcast state,
And trouble deaf heaven with my bootless cries,
And look upon myself, and curse my fate,
Wishing me like to one more rich in hope,
Featured like him, like him with friends possessed,
Desiring this man's art, and that man's scope,
With what I most enjoy contented least;
Yet in these thoughts my self almost despising,
Haply I think on thee,—and then my state,
Like to the lark at break of day arising
From sullen earth, sings hymns at heaven's gate;
    For thy sweet love remember'd such wealth brings
    That then I scorn to change my state with kings.

## PROSE PARAPHRASE

When I am suffering from miserable luck and loss of reputation I weep to find myself a pariah, isolated, and ignored by others. My prayers to heaven for help go unanswered, and I feel lost and curse my life and my condition. In these periods of near total despair I look about me in envy of others. I wish that I could be like someone else who is in a state of hope, or who is handsome, or who has friends. I envy those whose artistic achievements are superior to my own and those whose learning is greater than mine. I even derive no pleasure from that which I enjoyed the most. In this state of destructive thought I come close to despising myself utterly; but then if by accident I think on you, my friend, I am miraculously changed into such a happy person that I would not exchange my condition with anyone, not even with a king.

## THE PLACE OF THE SONNET IN THE CYCLE

This sonnet is part of the cycle addressed to the poet-speaker's friend about whom nothing is definitely known, even whether he is just one person. The cycle comprises 126 sonnets of the total number of 154 in the generally accepted order of Thomas Thorpe, who published the first printed edition of the sonnets in 1609. In the first 17 sonnets the poet adjures the friend to propagate children, thereby ensuring his beauty for posterity. That this method of immortalizing oneself is hardly foolproof, as Shakespeare may sadly have found in his personal life, need not concern us here. By Sonnet 29 in the cycle the poet resorts to a variety of other issues in the relationship, including complexity of the poet's feelings for his friend (Sonnet 75), the inadequacy of the poet's writing to do justice to the friend's worth (Sonnet 103), the effect of the friend on the poet's perception of the external world (Sonnet 113), the changes in the poet's feelings for his friend over time (Sonnet 115), the friend's stealing the poet's mistress (sonnets 40–42, 133), and the power of the very memory of his friend to affect the poet's emotional state as in this sonnet.

Sonnet 29 conveys a complex of feelings addressed in other sonnets as well. These emotions include but are not limited to melancholy (Sonnet 30), victimization by Fortune (Sonnet 37), envy of other writers (Sonnet 76), loss of reputation (Sonnet 88), and dependence on the friend for emotional health (Sonnet 112). This cycle dedicated to the friend does not present a straightforward narrative of the poet-friend's relationship but rather disparate themes based on that relationship. In fact, the narrative component of the sonnets regarding the poet, his friend, the rival poet, and the Dark Lady is so opaque that it could have profited for clarity's sake from the practice of Dante and Petrarch to give prose links to explain the relations among sonnets in their sequences. In his edition of Shakespeare's works, David Bevington points out that "the typical Elizabethan sonnet sequence offers a thematically connected series of lyrical meditations, chiefly on love but also on poetic theory, the adversities of fortune, death, or what have you" (*The Complete Works of Shakespeare* [New York: HarperCollins, 1992], 1614).

## DEVICES AND TECHNIQUES

Edward Hubler in *The Sense of Shakespeare's Sonnets* acutely observes that "No sonnet beginning with 'When' is an undistinguished poem" because the adverb "introduces a subordinate clause which must, perhaps after more subordinate matter, lead to a main clause, thus creating an arrangement of logically ordered elements in an emphatic sequence" (25). Hubler's observation is well illustrated in this sonnet. The first four lines convey a grammatically complete thought, expressing the poet's depression, self-abasement, and isolation, while the next four employ a periodic construction based on participles and dependent on the final six lines for its completion of meaning. The sibilance and dark vowels of the first two lines create a doleful, melancholy tone that is sustained through line nine. This tone is broken by the simile in the last lines comparing the speaker's change of mood to a lark flying heavenward at "break of day," which refers not only to the time of the bird's flight but also to the poet's emergence from the dark night of the soul to the very entrance to heaven. The simile is remarkable for its soaring rhythm as well as content which together prepare for the concluding couplet, here typically giving point to the whole.

Helen Vendler in *The Art of Shakespeare's Sonnets* makes the point that more than three quatrains and a couplet are necessary for a poem to qualify as a Shakespearean sonnet. The poem must be beautiful and "the theme must be freshly imagined, the genre must be renewed, and the words must surprise and satisfy from the point of view of proportion, musicality, and lexical vivacity" (4). Moreover, even if the theme is preserved without what George Santayana calls "our literary baggage" the resulting poem, in Vendler's view, is not a true Shakespearean sonnet. She uses Santayana's modern English transcription of Sonnet 29 to illustrate her point, stating that "In spite of its resemblance to the original in theme, sentiments, and rhyme, this [modern rendition] is not a Shakespearean sonnet" (8).

The first two quatrains of Sonnet 29 display a depth of melancholy characteristic of what would now be called clinical depression and, coupled with the last six lines, could be deemed bipolar disorder. The extreme shift of mood from black depression to ecstatic rapture is primarily used for the poetic purpose of complimenting the friend, but if taken biographically it could suggest a serious psychological instability, albeit an occasional one. The word "trouble" in line three accentuates the poet's ego-erosion as if not even heaven would be bothered by him. "Featured" in line six indicates the poet's feelings of inferiority about his physical appearance. The lines "Desiring this man's art, and that man's scope, / With what I most enjoy contented least" (ll. 7–8) are particularly interesting considering they come from the pen of the greatest writer of Western literature. Could it be that Shakespeare might have envied the genius of Thomas Kyd or Christopher Marlowe and the scope or learning of Ben Jonson or Francis Bacon in moods of near despair, even questioning his own worth as a dramatist? Is such envy even more likely early in the Bard's career when many scholars believe most of the sonnets were written?

## THEMES AND MEANINGS

Technically, the theme of Sonnet 29 is the power of friendship, but only the concluding couplet explicitly expresses that idea, while most of the sonnet concentrates on the poet-speaker's miserable condition, as does Sonnet 30. Of the sonnet form William Wordsworth wrote, "with this key / Shakespeare unlocked his heart" (*Selected Poetry of William Wordsworth*, ed. Mark Van Doren [New York: Modern Library, 2001], 641). Certainly many of the sonnets that express personal feelings rather than philosophical reflections or general observations possess such a high degree of emotional power and apparent authenticity that it is difficult to take issue with Wordsworth's assertion despite Robert Browning's objection in "House":

> " '*With this same key*
> *Shakespeare unlocked his heart,*' once more!"
> Did Shakespeare? If so, the less Shakespeare he!

Sonnet 29 feels as if it is written from the heart and if so, one can only conjecture about what plunged Shakespeare into such despair.

Although the identity of the poet-speaker as Shakespeare in all of the sonnets is far from certain, it is clear that sonnets 135 and 136 are indubitably autobiographical because of the play on *Will*; and the emotional intensity of the later sonnets about the Dark Lady, particularly Sonnet 147, is of similar quality to that of Sonnet 29. Depression often accompanies creation, which can serve as a sublimating process, as Hubler points out in his discussion of this sonnet. Taking a biographical approach, Hubler writes that "the sonnets certify that [Shakespeare] was not always discouraged and that the intensity of the discouragement, when it existed, was not constant" (121). He goes on to say that the poet's friendship compensated "for the ills which the poet endured" (121) and that the best example of such compensation is this sonnet.

Hubler makes the interesting suggestion that the melancholy tone of Sonnet 29 reflects Shakespeare's ambiguous attitude about his profession. Not only was he deeply aware of the lack of respectability of the theater and the Puritan opposition to it (on economic as well as religious grounds), he also "was aware of an indecency inherent in the practice of literature" (120). All evidence points to Shakespeare's overriding interest in money and that he saw playwriting as a means of making it. It is highly doubtful that he respected *belles-lettres* or saw himself except in trying moments as a *litterateur*. Hubler quotes Sonnet 72, "I am sham'd by that which I bring forth" (l. 13), and he could have quoted Hotspur in *1 Henry IV*: "that would set my teeth nothing an edge, / Nothing so much as mincing poetry. / 'Tis like the forc'd gait of a shuffling nag" (3.1.131–133). If Hubler's view is correct (and line 8 of Sonnet 29 would seem to support it), it may be that Shakespeare occasionally used the subjective form of the sonnet as a way to sublimate more effectively his moments of shame in being a writer than he could do in drama.

If the sonnets were not written *en bloc*, but over an indeterminate period of time (as seems likely), it is not improbable that Sonnet 29 reflects the poet's general depression over his relationship with the Dark Lady, a depression that would permeate his whole outlook on life. Line 8 could just as easily support this view as Hubler's. Moreover, in sonnets 40, 41, and 42 his friend has taken his mistress, and the tone of the last of these, although not as dark as that of Sonnet 29, is bleak, as evidenced by "grief" (40.11) and "this cross" (42.12). The concluding couplet of Sonnet 29 is ingenuous but does not ring true as a palliative for the poet's hurt.

Whether one accepts Hubler's theory that the depression of Sonnet 29 is attributable to Shakespeare's feelings about his profession or the idea that the sonnet reflects the torment occasioned by the Dark Lady, one cannot help but observe that the sequence is filled with numerous expressions of self-abasement, which suggest a biographical basis. Many of these expressions refer to the poet's vocation as a writer. For example, Sonnet 76 confesses a sameness of style and form because the subject matter is always the same, that is, the friend. Sonnet 85 refers to "My tongue-tied Muse" (l. 1) that can add nothing to the words of the rival poet in praise of his friend, and in the next sonnet the poet enviously attributes the rival poet's inspired writing to supernatural inspiration. Sonnet 103 avers that the friend's beauty "overgoes my blunt invention quite, / Dulling my lines, and doing me disgrace" (ll. 7–8). His pathetic efforts to do justice to his friend in words is even said to be "sinful" (l. 9). Expressions of low self esteem in a number of the sonnets have no clear or discernible cause, making them more mysterious. Examples of these would be sonnets 71, 72, 88, 89, and 90. Sonnet 71 is the best known of these, and it expresses bitterness more than sadness. It appears to have a curious connection to the first two lines of Sonnet 90: "Then hate me when thou wilt, if ever, now, / Now, while the world is bent my deeds to cross" (ll. 1–2). In all probability, we will never know for certain which sonnets reflect the Bard's personal feelings and under what circumstances, but speculating about this issue will undoubtedly remain grist for the critical mill.

## THE RELATIONSHIP OF THE SONNET TO SHAKESPEARE'S OTHER WORKS

G. Wilson Knight in *The Mutual Flame* makes a cogent argument that the corpus of Shakespeare's sonnets encapsulates the major themes of the plays. He writes that "All melancholia is in [S]onnet 29" (110). This may be something of an exaggeration, but the psychological torment of this sonnet is exceeded, if at all among the sonnets, only by the desperate obsession of Sonnet 147. The tone of this sonnet, not the content per se, is repeated in the tragedies by various of Shakespeare's characters who express a near suicidal despair when they reflect on life. Hamlet's "To be or not to be" soliloquy (3.1.55–87) may come first to mind in this connection, only his religious conviction and fear of the unknown (and of course the necessity of continuing the play) preventing him from taking his life. Macbeth's "To-morrow, to-morrow, and to-morrow" speech (5.5.19–28) is one of utter darkness and asserts the absurd meaninglessness of life. Even in the comedies, reflections on the human condition are generally dark. One has only to remember Ulysses' remarks to Achilles in *Troilus and Cressida* that "Love, friendship, charity, are subjects all / To envious and calumniating time" (3.3.173–174) or in *As You Like It* Jaques' "from hour to hour we rot and rot" (2.7.27) or his "Seven Ages of Man" speech (2.7.139–166).

Neither the character nor the complexity of the friendship theme of the sonnets is to be found in the plays because in the sequence Shakespeare enjoyed the luxury of relating multifarious aspects of the poet-narrator's relations with his friend in considerable autonomy without having to provide narrative or any other kind of continuity or any explanation of divergent or contradictory views. Such freedom is patently not possible in drama, which is the servant of continuing action, motivation, and verisimilitude.

This is in no way to suggest that friendship does not play an important role in many of the plays, but rather that it is presented dramatically in particular contexts rather than analytically as in the sonnets. If we consider well-known friendships in a variety of plays—comedies, tragedies, and histories—we can arrive at certain generalizations. In the sonnet sequence the poet is younger and of lower social status than the aristocratic friend. The approximate parallels to these conditions in the plays would be Hamlet–Horatio, Julius Caesar–Antony, and Lear–Kent. All of these are ended with the death of the principal. Horatio wants to die with Hamlet, but he is persuaded to live and tell his friend's story. Antony sets his mind and heart to avenge his friend's death. Kent does all that he can to protect his friend against the savagery of the world and to assuage his suffering. On a level of social equals Bassanio would give his life to save Antonio's, and Romeo in trying to aid Mercutio causes him to be fatally wounded. These are examples of positive and enduring friendships in Shakespeare's plays. They resemble the friendship of the sonnets only in the love that the speaker has for the noble youth. Other friendships are not so happy. When Prince Hal becomes King Henry V he rejects Falstaff, banishing him on pain of death "Not to come near our person by ten mile" (*2 Henry IV*, 5.5.65). Macbeth has his friend Banquo slain as a potential progenitor of future kings, and Richard III dismisses Buckingham after the king has finished using him. The only overtly sexual friendship is that of Achilles and Patroclus, whom Thersites refers to as Achilles' "masculine whore" (*Troilus and Cressida*, 5.1.17).

Much has been written about the sexual nature of the friendship of the sonnets. Many commentators refer to it as "Platonic" friendship, implying that it is strictly spiritual without sexual content. Of course, this is an incomplete understanding of Socratic/Platonic friendship, which emphasized pederasty as a means of bringing beautiful young boys into a higher order of spirituality. In Sonnet 20 Shakespeare clearly disavows any sexual interest on the part of the poet for his friend. All the language that would suggest otherwise is pure Renaissance embellishment.

Shakespeare's sonnet sequence stands alone in its emphasis on a male as the major recipient of the narrator's love, although that emphasis is somewhat tempered by the twenty-five sonnets concerning the Dark Lady. The sonnets, like most of Shakespeare's other works, attest to his fiercely original genius.

## Annotated Bibliography

Hubler, Edward. *The Sense of Shakespeare's Sonnets*. Princeton: Princeton UP, 1952. After more than fifty years Hubler's remains a useful study. Economically written, it explores various facets of the sonnets with insight. This study is particularly provocative in regard to the sonnets concerning the Dark Lady.

Knight, G. Wilson. *The Mutual Flame*. London: Methuen, 1955. Knight is one of the classical Shakespeare scholars, and his insights and learning remain undiminished by time and changing critical approaches. He is adept at relating specific sonnets to Shakespeare's plays.

Vendler, Helen. *The Art of Shakespeare's Sonnets*. Cambridge, MA: Harvard UP, 1997. This is an ambitious study that seeks to identify the components that comprise a Shakespearean sonnet, and it provides a separate analysis of each of the 154 sonnets. Offers close readings of the poems, emphasizing their language.

# Sonnet 30

### Barry B. Adams

When to the sessions of sweet silent thought
I summon up remembrance of things past,
I sigh the lack of many a thing I sought,
And with old woes new wail my dear time's waste:
Then can I drown an eye, unused to flow,
For precious friends hid in death's dateless night,
And weep afresh love's long since cancell'd woe,
And moan the expense of many a vanish'd sight:
Then can I grieve at grievances foregone,
And heavily from woe to woe tell o'er
The sad account of fore-bemoaned moan,
Which I new pay as if not paid before.
    But if the while I think on thee, dear friend,
    All losses are restor'd and sorrows end.

## PROSE PARAPHRASE

Whenever I am in a ruminative, reflective, or nostalgic frame of mind, I find my-self recalling sad or sorrowful experiences, such as the death of friends, an unhappy love affair, and more generally my failure to achieve as much as I had hoped to achieve. In fact, such recollections, by in effect repeating the experiences themselves, actually intensify my sadness. However, as soon as I think of you, my friend, I am no longer sad.

## THE PLACE OF THE SONNET IN THE CYCLE

This sonnet is securely linked to those immediately preceding and following. Al-though the link is secure, it is not as tight as that which binds some of the poems in the collection into pairs, as when a sonnet begins with such words as "But" or "Thus" (as in sonnets 16, 51, and 74), thereby creating a grammatical and semantic dependence on the sonnet that comes before. Each of the three sonnets in the short sub-sequence that runs from Sonnet 29 to Sonnet 31 can stand alone as a coherent linguistic unit. All three also convey basically the same theme though with different emphases and through different poetic techniques. In each case the speaker contrasts his general mood (which is sad, melancholy, or despondent) with the mood that comes upon him whenever he thinks of the man to whom he is addressing these three sonnets. In Sonnet 30, the contrast comes suddenly, in the concluding couplet. In Sonnet 29, it comes closer to the midpoint of the poem, at the onset of the third quatrain (which in an Italian or Petrarchan sonnet marks the beginning of the sestet, the second of two major structural units), while in Sonnet 31 it comes at the very beginning: the speaker has achieved that more positive, hopeful outlook even before he begins to speak. To that extent, Sonnet 31 is dependent upon or presupposes its immediate predecessor in the development of what may be called, loosely, the psychological narrative of the cycle. By contrast, Sonnet 30 does not presuppose Sonnet 29 but rather reiterates it with a different emphasis.

The identity of the "dear friend" to whom the poem is addressed remains an intriguing mystery. This is the first of several occurrences of the phrase or its variant "fair friend" in the sequence. It is natural to suppose that it refers to the same person each time, and that this person is the one addressed as "thou" or "you" (and in Sonnet 13.1 as "love"; see also "my love" [401]) and the person referred to as "he" or "him" in most of the first 126 sonnets. From internal evidence it is clear that the speaker's attitude toward that person changes with the circumstances of their relationship. But there is and will probably never be a consensus about the particulars of that relationship or the identity of that person. Some have argued that he is the "Mr. W. H." who is characterized by the printer of the 1609 edition of the *Sonnets* (the first edition, and the only authoritative one) as their "onlie begetter," and that this person is Henry Wriothesley, Earl of Southampton, to whom Shakespeare dedicated two of his narrative poems, *The Rape of Lucrece* and *Venus and Adonis*. Others have argued that he is William Herbert, third Earl of Pembroke, whose initials match more closely those of the putative begetter. Still others have speculated that he is someone named William or Willie Hughes, whose name may be introduced punningly in Sonnet 20. In the absence of more compelling evidence, it is best to concentrate on the internal structures of the poems and on meanings that are not dependent on knowing the circumstances of their composition.

## DEVICES AND TECHNIQUES

The opening lines of Sonnet 30 make figurative use of legal language ("sessions," "summon up"), but this imagery is not sustained or developed. Instead the poem shifts to a more literal plane of discourse to introduce the subject of memory, which becomes its major theme. The phrase "remembrance of things past" in line 2 has been immortalized as the title of the best known English translation of Marcel Proust's *A la recherche du temps perdu*. It also appears in several English translations of the Bible. The apocryphal Book of Wisdom (also known as The Wisdom of Solomon), printed between the Old and New Testaments in Protestant Bibles of the sixteenth and seventeenth centuries, speaks of a "double grief" felt by the enemies of the Israelites, double because these enemies witnessed the Israelites being favored by a God who was at the same time punishing them, the Israelites' enemies, along with a "mourning, and the remembrance of things past." This is the translation found in the Geneva Bible, first published in 1560—the English version with which Shakespeare was most familiar. The more famous King James version, also knows as the Authorized Version, which was not published until 1611, two years after the publication of the *Sonnets*, also employs the phrase "remembrance of things past."

Shakespeare's development of the remembrance theme moves in tandem with the idea of doubleness, though not the kind of doubleness referred to in the biblical verse. Shakespeare's doubleness is not a simultaneous balancing of one entity against another but the repetition of the same experience in the course of time. The pertinent phrases in Sonnet 30 are "old woes new wail" (l. 4), the unity of the phrase reinforced by the phonetic repetition of alliteration, which is extended to "waste" at line's end; "weep afresh" (l. 7), with a glancing allusion to the renewing effect of water; "grieve at grievances foregone" (l. 9), the repetition of the lexical root mimicking the fact of repetition and perhaps recalling the word "grief" from the biblical passage cited above; and "from woe to woe" (l. 10), a more direct functional repetition, this time of a whole word rather than a lexical root. This series of repetitions concludes with another repetition based on a lexical root in "new pay as if not paid before" (l. 12) immediately preceding the abrupt reversal of the speaker's melancholy train of thought.

That reversal is announced simply but emphatically with the conjunction "But" that introduces the concluding and resolving couplet. The rhetorical strategy of the sudden reversal reinforces the idea that the mere thought of his dear friend, mentioned for the first time only at the very end of the poem, outweighs all the thoughts and emotions mentioned, inventoried, and reiterated in various direct and indirect ways over the course of the poem's twelve-line body.

The argumentative movement of Sonnet 30 is more clearly telegraphed than in most other sonnets in the collection. The verbal markers come at the beginning of the four main structural units—the three quatrains and the couplet, which are introduced by the colorless but structurally significant function words "When," "Then," "Then," and "But." The two middle markers are not only the same word, they form part of a single repeated phrase: "Then can I," "Then can I." The thematically linked sonnets that precede and follow this one avoid this manner of marking structural units. Sonnet 29 runs the thought and the syntax from one quatrain to the next, and even from the third quatrain over into the couplet. Sonnet 31, with its easily discernible breaks between the three quatrains and between the last quatrain and the couplet, comes closer to the pattern of Sonnet 30; but even though each of its structural units consists of a complete sentence, it does not mark those units as overtly as does Sonnet 30.

As is generally the case with Shakespeare's sonnets, the most obvious patterning of Sonnet 30 is supplied by the rhyme. The first quatrain consists of four lines arranged in alternating rhymes, the first line rhyming with the third and the second with the fourth in a scheme conventionally represented as *abab*. The second and third quatrains adopt the same pattern with different rhymes, producing the scheme *cdcd efef*, which is followed by the rhyming couplet *gg*. For modern readers of Sonnet 30, two sets of rhymes are phonetically irregular: the vowel sounds of "past" and "waste" in lines 2 and 4, respectively, are different enough to create something other than a "true" rhyme, and the same is true of the vowels in "foregone" and "moan" in lines 9 and 11. But the sounds of spoken English are not the same today as they were in the sixteenth and seventeenth centuries, and there is good reason to believe that the "a" sound in "waste" was much closer to if not indistinguishable from our typical pronunciation of the "a" in "past." Similarly, in Shakespeare's pronunciation the second "o" in "foregone" may well have been indistinguishable from that in "moan." With only one exception, the word "moan" whenever it appears in the *Sonnets* falls in a rhyming position, and in every one of these instances the rhyme is less than exact or true by current standards. In Sonnet 44 and again in Sonnet 71, it rhymes with "gone," and in Sonnet 149 with "upon."

Other particulars of Sonnet 30 that may cause a modern reader to stumble, at least on a first reading, include the meaning of the word "foregone" (l. 9), which is "former" or "gone before" rather than "abstained from" or "allowed to pass." (Nowadays the word is spelled without the medial "e" and conveys the latter meanings. In the edition of 1609, it appears with the medial "e" as well as a hyphen but without a final "e": "fore-gon.") The primary meaning of "expense" (l. 8) is "loss," but it frequently carries a secondary sense closely related to the modern sense in contexts that deal with financial matters. The verb "tell" (l. 10) is also related to financial matters (a relation that survives in the job title of those bank employees known as "tellers"), although its more basic meaning has to do with the arithmetical action of counting. The financial references in these words along with "account" (l. 11; obviously related to the verb "count"), "pay," and "paid" (ll. 11 and 12) contribute to a unifying theme for the final quatrain, one that is glanced at in the word "losses" in the last line of the poem. The verb "summon" in line 2 is related most immediately to the legal references already noted (and which survive today in one of the specialized meanings of the noun "summons"), but on re-reading it is possible to detect anticipatory wordplay based on the phonetic similarity of this word to the counting and financial term "sum." The word "date" in Early Modern English carries specifically legal and financial connotations, referring in appropriate contexts to the moment when a legal or financial obligation falls due. Thus the "dateless night" of line 6 would be one that never expires, a characterization that is obviously appropriate as a metaphor for death. Shakespeare makes use of the same metaphor in *Romeo and Juliet* when Romeo on the verge of suicide speaks of his "dateless bargain to engrossing death" (5.3.115).

The conspicuously poetic features of Sonnet 30 are for the most part matters of sound rather than sense. Even though Shakespeare makes use of legal and commercial discourse to achieve conceptual or thematic unity, he is no less interested in the comparatively superficial rhetorical figure of alliteration. The first line introduces this figure with the three-fold repetition of an initial "s" sound in "sessions," "sweet," and "silent." The word "summon" in the next line extends the figure somewhat less emphatically until it is reintroduced with "sigh" near the beginning of the third line and "sought" at the end of that line. The fourth line features another triple alliteration in "woes," "wail," and "waste." It is even possible to add the preposition "with" to make this a quadruple alliteration. Although prepositions and other such insignificant words do not ordinarily contribute much if anything to phonetic texture, this one carries a perceptible stress by virtue of its position as the second member of an iambic foot. The initial sound of "drown" in line 5 anticipates the alliterative phrase "death's dateless" in the following line, and each of the next six lines contains an example of the same phonetic figure: "weep" and "woe" (as well as the phrase "love's long"), "moan" and "many," "grieve" and "grievances" (and perhaps the second syllable of the compound "foregone," which would receive stress even in a prose passage), "woe" and "woe," "fore-bemoaned moan" (granting the second element of the compound "bemoaned" the status of a word), "pay" and "paid." The final couplet avoids this figure, at least in its more prominent and easily detectable form. In doing so it projects an air of sincerity consistent with the governing purpose of the sonnet, which is to assert the overriding power of the dear friend, or more precisely, the irresistible power of the speaker's simple remembrance or calling to mind of his friend. At the same time, it is possible to detect a quasi-alliterative repetition of the s sound in "losses," "restored," and "sorrows," a repetition that recalls the more conspicuous and emphatic alliteration of the poem's opening line.

## THEMES AND MEANINGS

Although it touches on such common human experiences as sorrow, loss, death, and the power of memory, Sonnet 30 lacks the universalizing or cosmic suggestiveness of some of Shakespeare's sonnets. On the other hand, the broad sweep and lofty sentiment of some of these better known sonnets can be deceptive. Thus Sonnet 55, which begins "Not marble nor the gilded monuments / Of princes shall outlive this pow'rful rhyme," after a number of profound observations on death and the "ending doom," comes to rest finally on the praise of his friend as he is represented in the speaker's own poetry: "You live in this [that is, this verse of mine], and dwell in lovers' eyes." Similarly Sonnet 60, after devoting twelve lines of memorable poetic description to the effects of time and the aging process, concludes with a consoling comment about the friend and the poet's verse: "And yet to times in hope my verse shall stand, / Praising thy worth, despite his cruel hand." Sonnet 30, by contrast, avoids altogether the exalted, philosophical sentiment that Shakespeare uses to launch these other sonnets. It is from the outset much more private, as suggested by the phrase "sweet silent thought" of line 1, and also much more personal, as reflected in the frequently reiterated first-person pronoun from line 2 on ("I summon up," "I sigh," "I sought," and so forth). Sonnet 55 has no first-person pronouns and Sonnet 60 only one.

## THE RELATIONSHIP OF THE SONNET TO SHAKESPEARE'S OTHER WORKS

The ability to recall is one of the most important and distinctive human powers. It allows us not simply to satisfy a nostalgic yearning for events from the past but to guide our actions in the present and the future. Even more fundamentally, it is a prerequisite for any knowledge other than the momentary flash of insight. It is therefore all but inevitable that a serious literary artist, especially a dramatist, would introduce the topic of memory into his works, in passing if not as an explicit theme. Shakespeare does so in a number of places, but perhaps most notably in Hamlet's first encounter with his father's ghost. Here the issue is not abstract or philosophical but highly personal, as it is in Sonnet 30. The Ghost's parting words, "Adieu, adieu, adieu! remember me" (Hamlet, 1.5.91), provoke Hamlet to a barely controllable paroxysm of references to memory and remembering:

> Remember thee!
> Ay, thou poor ghost, whiles memory holds a seat
> In this distracted globe. Remember thee!
> Yea, from the table of my memory
> I'll wipe away all trivial fond records,
> All saws of books, all forms, all pressures past
> That youth and observation copied there,
> And thy commandment all alone shall live
> Within the book and volume of my brain,
> Unmix'd with baser matter. (*Hamlet*, 1.5.95–104)

The remembering that Hamlet harps on is obviously different from the remembrance of things past invoked by the speaker of Sonnet 30, yet they both testify to the importance of this ability and to Shakespeare's interest in it. The focus of Hamlet's memory is verbal—not just a person or an event but the words spoken by a person at a given moment in time. What the speaker of Sonnet 30 recalls, by contrast, is mostly vague and unspecified: "things past" (l. 2) "precious friends" (l. 6), "many a vanish'd sight" (l. 8). The one exception is the "dear friend," who is, like the ghost of Hamlet's father, an individual person rather than a concept or an event. Moreover, the mental activity involved in this exceptional case is not clearly one of remembering or recalling but the more inclusive act of thinking ("I think on thee," l. 13), which leaves unanswered the question of whether the friend exists within or outside of the speaker's set of memories. This unanswered question should be viewed not as a failure but an artful ambiguity, one that serves further to exalt the dear friend by inviting us to see him as a force existing both in the past and in the present.

A concern for friendship, the subject of the sonnet, runs throughout Shakespeare's plays, from *The Two Gentlemen of Verona* to *The Two Noble Kinsmen*. According to Renaissance theory that derives from Plato's *Symposium* and Cicero's *De amicitia*, same-sex friendship is more enduring than heterosexual love. Shakespeare's plays invariably demonstrate that in reality love is, and indeed should be, more powerful. When characters choose same sex friendship over male-female love, tragedy ensues. The comedies show same-sex friendship yielding to love. Even in the sonnets the fair youth apparently betrays the male speaker by sleeping with that speaker's mistress. However, the sonnets still privilege friendship over love, and Sonnet 30 celebrates the power of that friendship to redeem all losses.

**Annotated Bibliography**

Kerrigan, John, ed. *Shakespeare: "The Sonnets" and "A Lover's Complaint."* Harmondsworth, Eng.: Penguin, 1986. Includes a useful general introduction to the *Sonnets* as well as sensible comments on Sonnet 30.

Leishman, J. B. *Themes and Variations in Shakespeare's Sonnets*. London: Hutchinson, 1961. Provocative comments on the quasi-idolatrous character of Sonnet 30 and other of Shakespeare's "more 'hyperbolical' sonnets."

Mahood, M. M. *Shakespeare's Wordplay*. London: Methuen, 1957. The chapter on the Sonnets includes a subtle analysis of Sonnet 30 and the way in which neutral diction is turned to emotive ends.

# Sonnet 35

Jeremy Lopez

No more be griev'd at that which thou hast done:
Roses have thorns, and silver fountains mud:
Clouds and eclipses stain both moon and sun,
And loathsome canker lives in sweetest bud.
All men make faults, and even I in this,
Authorizing thy trespass with compare,
Myself corrupting, salving thy amiss,
Excusing thy sins more than thy sins are;
For to thy sensual fault I bring in sense,
Thy adverse party is thy advocate,—
And 'gainst myself a lawful plea commence:
Such civil war is in my love and hate,
   That I an accessary needs must be,
   To that sweet thief which sourly robs from me.

## PROSE PARAPHRASE

Do not be upset any longer about what you have done. All beautiful things have their faults: "Roses have thorns," and sediment collects in "silver fountains" (l. 2). Even the brightness of the moon and sun can be dulled by clouds and eclipses, and flowers are destroyed by disease. All men make mistakes. Even I have made a mistake: I have justified your error by arguing from analogies. I thereby corrupt myself even as I smooth over what you have done wrong. In doing so, I have sinned even worse than you: for I have made your reckless and unthinking mistake seem reasonable. I, who should condemn you, have pleaded your case, and pleaded against myself. I am so torn between my love and hate for you that I have made myself your accessory—helped you, whom I love, take everything that you can from me.

## THE PLACE OF THE SONNET IN THE CYCLE

This is one of the 126 sonnets addressed to the fair youth. By itself, Sonnet 35 could refer equally plausibly to a woman or a man. It is a conventional lover's complaint, in which the lover invokes conventional ways of understanding the wrongs his beloved has done him (the trite metaphors of lines 1–4), only to discard this understanding in favor of vexed self-abasement. The gender specificity of "All men" in line 5 could be understood as the speaker's identifying himself with a group of men his female lover has duped ("I am like all men who have succumbed to your wiles"); or it could be understood as part of the speaker's tendency to make excuses for his male lover ("Your mistakes are understandable because all men make mistakes.")

In context, Sonnet 35 is one of a brief series of sonnets that turn rather suddenly sullen and complaining (sonnets 33–36) between two series of sonnets that either glow with excited praise for the beloved (sonnets 25–32), or seem to attempt to forgive and supplicate to the beloved (sonnets 37–41). It is in this context, in the specific echoes of the sonnets around it, that we most clearly understand that the lover's complaint of Sonnet 35 is addressed particularly to a man. Sonnet 33 laments a moment of falling out of the beloved's favor—"alack, he was but one hour mine" (l. 11)—and does so by means of a cloud and sun metaphor: "The region cloud hath mask'd him from me now. / Yet him for this my love no whit disdaineth: / Suns of the world may stain, when heaven's sun staineth" (ll. 12–14). The puns on sun/son and the image of staining are echoed in line 3 of Sonnet 35. The thief metaphor of Sonnet 35 (l. 14) is repeated in Sonnet 40 (l. 9), just two sonnets before Sonnet 42, in which the speaker becomes relatively explicit about a situation that has driven himself and his beloved asunder: "That thou hast her, it is not all my grief, / And yet it may be said I lov'd her dearly" (ll. 1–2). Rather surprisingly, these lines in Sonnet 42 introduce a love triangle as a reason that the relationship between the speaker and his male beloved has soured, which was described in Sonnet 41 (l. 8).

## DEVICES AND TECHNIQUES

The first eight lines of the sonnet (its octave) evenly divide two different parts of the speaker's argument between the two four-line groups (quatrains). The first quatrain claims that the beloved should not be upset over his mistake and gives some examples of beautiful things that sometimes turn out to be less than beautiful. In the second quatrain the speaker claims that the beloved's fault is merely an example of a universal tendency, and goes on to heap blame upon himself for being similarly faulted in his desire to forgive the beloved.

At the beginning of Sonnet 35's last six lines (its sestet) is a conventional word, "For" (l. 9), to mark a shift or turn in the argument. In the structure of a Petrarchan (or Italian) sonnet, an argument is developed over the course of the octave and taken in a new direction with the sestet. Turn-words are usually conjunctions like "for," "but," or "yet"; or logical connectors like "therefore" or "thus." What is noteworthy about this sonnet's turn is that it does not really turn the sonnet. The word "For" in line 9 merely continues the thought begun in line 5; the sestet continues to list the ways in which the speaker is foolish, even sinful, for agreeing to forgive his beloved. Indeed, "For" continues not only the idea but in fact the sentence begun in line 5. Whereas the poem's first sentence consisted of four orderly, straightforward lines that listed parallels between the beloved and beautiful things in nature, the second sentence stretches itself over seven lines, beginning with a reference to the beloved ("All men make faults") and quickly turning its attention to, and keeping that attention fixed on, the speaker. The extension of the poem's second sentence and the use of the turn-word "For" to signal, but not deliver, a change in the nature of the argument are among the most important physical devices the poem relies on to express the character of its speaker's voice: the speaker is droning on rather strenuously, introducing the subject of his beloved and what his beloved has done only so that he can talk about himself and what he has done.

The poem's dominant metaphors are legal in nature: they have to do with courtrooms and crime. The speaker claims that he has authorized his beloved's "trespass" (l. 6) and that he now acts as a lawyer ("advocate" [l. 10]) for the beloved in a case in which the speaker himself is a plaintiff. In the final line, the beloved is thought of as a "thief." Alongside this metaphorical pattern is a slightly less prominent one having to do with disease and decay: "corrupting" and "salving" in line 7 are words that suggest a bodily disease (or wound) and its healing. These words echo the "canker" that destroys the flower in line 4. The flower in line 4 is part of a cluster of related metaphors that do not attain the prominence the poem suggests they will. The first four lines suggest that the poem will be concerned with pastoral imagery or the imagery of nature. These lines suggest that the extended conceit of the poem might argue that the beloved is similar to beautiful things in nature not only in his ability to be "stained" or "corrupted," but also in his ability to regenerate and return to his natural beauty. The expectation these lines create about the poem's metaphors is similar to the expectation they create about the poem's focus: just as the speaker brings up the beloved only to stop talking about him, so he invokes conventional images of natural beauty only to suggest that he is not really interested in talking about them at all.

## THEMES AND MEANINGS

Like virtually all of Shakespeare's sonnets, Sonnet 35 is very specific in its tone and implications, but very vague about what it is actually talking about. The insistently legal language of the poem ("trespass" [l. 6], "fault" [ll. 5, 9], "adverse party" [l. 10], "advocate" [l. 10], "lawful plea" [l. 11], "accessary" [l. 13]) keeps the reader, and the speaker, at considerable distance from the actual substance of the conflict. One gets the sense that the speaker is trying to explain as calmly and rationally as possible a situation that makes him intensely emotional; he thus resorts to language that is as far away as possible from the language that would actually represent the situation. Thus, insofar as words like "sensual" (l. 9), "love" (l. 12), and "sweet" (l. 14) suggest that the poem is about a problem of romantic love, the poem is characteristic of the way in which the sonnets are simultaneously eager to talk about sex and guilty talking about it.

"Sensual fault" in line 9 has definite implications that the beloved has wronged the speaker in a sexual way, or by means of sexual attentions toward someone else. This oblique reference to lust is as explicit as the poem gets. But its language is demonstrably preoccupied with the subject: "stain" (l. 3) and "corrupt" (l. 7) are words frequently used by Shakespeare and his contemporaries to describe sexual defilement. "Robs" in the poem's final line has suggestions of the sexual possibilities inherent in the word "take." The thorny roses in line 2 hint at the "prick" (a sexual pun that was centuries old even in Shakespeare's time) that the poem goes on to suggest has done the speaker wrong. All of these images are similar in that they suggest that the sexually charged interaction between the speaker and his beloved is painful, troubled, and to some extent coercive.

The "civil war . . . in my love and hate" (l. 12), an image of the self divided, is persistent in the sonnets. The speaker in these poems is frequently ambivalent about his feelings toward someone else, divided in his affections (see, for example, Sonnet 144), divided in his behavior toward others (see, for example, Sonnet 138), or physically divided from his beloved (see, for example, Sonnet 113). The theme of division is echoed formally, and constantly, in the paradoxes and antitheses that are so frequent in these poems. Examples of antithesis in this poem include "Myself corrupting, salving thy amiss" (l. 6) and "that sweet thief which sourly robs from me" (l. 14). Thematic antitheses involve the conflict between reason ("sense") and emotions, or the body ("sensual fault," l. 9); or between forgiveness ("Authorizing") and self-abasement ("myself corrupting") in lines 6–7. These oppositions are echoed in other sonnets such as "All days are nights to see till I see thee, / And night's bright days when dreams do show thee me" (43.13–14), and "All the world well knows, yet none knows well / To shun the heaven that leads men to this hell" (129.13–14). The vivid representation of the divided mind, wrestling with irreconcilable opposites, wanting the thing it claims not to want, is perhaps the most enduring and characteristic achievement of Shakespeare's sonnets.

## THE RELATIONSHIP OF THE SONNET TO SHAKESPEARE'S OTHER WORKS

The conflict between reason and emotion or/and the conflict between reason and the body is a persistent theme in Shakespeare's plays. Othello has no reason to believe his wife is unfaithful to him, but he is overcome by his own passionate jealousy once Iago has planted only the smallest seeds of it. Coriolanus knows that the ritual of humility he must endure before becoming consul is merely a ritual, but he cannot overcome his passionate pride and thus brings about his own banishment from Rome. King Lear knows his youngest daughter loves him more than either of her sisters but opts for the destruction of himself and his kingdom when Cordelia will not utter the words he wants to hear. Shakespeare's great dramatic characters are frequently, if not always, massively selfish, insisting to the uttermost on the thing they desire even as they are aware of the way in which that thing is irrational and destructive. The speaking voice of the sonnets is frequently the same way.

In Sonnet 35 this voice begins with only the tritest pastoral metaphors (perfunctory references to flowers, fountains, sun, and moon) in order to give only the most cursory attention to the person it claims to be addressing. The speaker then launches into a tedious and self-serving list of the wrongs done him and the sacrifices made by him, making use of formal devices—the breaks between quatrains, the *turn*—only to make them useless. Then, only two sonnets later, the speaker is once more in virtual awe of his beloved, now abasing himself in a different way: "As a decrepit father takes delight / To see his active child do deeds of youth, / So I, made lame by Fortune's dearest spite, / Take all my comfort of thy worth and truth" (37.1–4). The rapid changes in mood and tone, the desire to express with great rhetorical power a sense of self-satisfaction, is a characteristic the sonnet speaker shares with Hamlet, King Lear, Othello, and any number of other great Shakespearean characters.

In its simultaneously explicit and submerged homoeroticism—the attraction the speaker conveys for his lover even as he disavows it with the hidden "prick" pun in "Roses have thorns"—Sonnet 35, and many other of the sonnets addressed to the "young man," are similar to some of the more famously ambiguous moments in Shakespeare's plays. Roman Coriolanus and Volscian Aufidius spend much of *Coriolanus* trying to kill each other, but when Coriolanus is banished from Rome and throws himself on the mercy of the Volscians to get revenge, Aufidius tells him, "I lov'd the maid I married; never man / Sigh'd truer breath; but that I see thee here, / Thou noble thing, more dances my rapt heart / Than when I first my wedded mistress saw / Bestride my threshold" (4.5.114–118). In *Othello*, Iago claims at different times to pursue revenge because he loves Desdemona, and because he suspects Othello of having slept with Emilia, Iago's wife. Iago is terrifying in his quest to provide Othello with proof of Cassio's way with women. But when called upon in 3.3 to produce some such proof, he comes up with a story about sleeping in the same bed as Cassio and being the subject of Cassio's erotic dream: "In sleep I heard him say, 'Sweet Desdemona, / Let us be wary, let us hide our loves'; / And then, sir, would he gripe and wring my hand; / Cry, 'O sweet creature!' then kiss me hard" (3.3.418–422). There is an interesting (though probably unintentional) echo of Sonnet 35's botanical metaphors in Iago's description of this scene, where he goes on to say that Cassio kissed him as if Cassio "pluck'd up kisses by the roots / That grew upon my lips" (3.3.423–424).

## Annotated Bibliography

Booth, Stephen. *An Essay on Shakespeare's Sonnets*. New Haven: Yale UP, 1969. A detailed critical examination of the sonnets, both as a sequence and as individual poems. Booth argues that the sonnets always provide a reader with the "comfort and security of a frame of reference, but the frames of reference are not constant, and their number seems limitless" (187).

———, ed. *Shakespeare's Sonnets*. New Haven: Yale UP, 1977. A useful edition with parallel modern and early modern (1609) texts and with excellent commentary on each sonnet. These annotations range from explanatory glosses to full-length critical essays.

Evans, G. Blackmore, ed. *The Sonnets*. The New Cambridge Shakespeare. Cambridge: Cambridge UP, 1996. This edition provides commentary devoted largely to explicating difficult phrases. Discusses textual variants and historical context.

Fineman, Joel. *Shakespeare's Perjured Eye: The Invention of Poetic Subjectivity in the Sonnets*. Berkeley: U of California P, 1986. A compelling and provocative study. Argues that the sonnets shift between poetry that idealizes and praises a beloved and poetry that focuses attention on the writer's problematic desire, revealing fissures and paradox within the narrative voice and, effectively, a different and more complex sense of self.

Vendler, Helen. *The Art of Shakespeare's Sonnets*. Cambridge, MA: Harvard UP, 1997. A thoughtful and accessible series of close readings of each sonnet, focusing primarily on the poem's aesthetic features but also addressing its ideas and psychological mood.

# Sonnet 55

### Gayle Gaskill

Not marble, nor the gilded monuments
Of princes, shall outlive this powerful rime;
But you shall shine more bright in these contents
Than unswept stone, besmear'd with sluttish time.
When wasteful war shall statues overturn,
And broils root out the work of masonry,
Nor Mars his sword, nor war's quick fire shall burn
The living record of your memory.
'Gainst death, and all-oblivious enmity
Shall you pace forth; your praise shall still find room
Even in the eyes of all posterity
That wear this world out to the ending doom.
   So, till the judgment that yourself arise,
   You live in this, and dwell in lovers' eyes.

## PROSE PARAPHRASE

In this poetry, you have a more enduring memorial than the stone that is carved and ornamented for a monarch, for in these lines your life will still glow while time, like a lazy housekeeper, lets cold royal grave-markers grow obscure with the dust of neglect. Wars will come with sword and fire to topple monuments and lay waste the sturdiest fortifications, but even Mars himself cannot destroy this eternal tribute to you. You will triumph over both death and forgetfulness as generation after generation honors you until the end of the world. So until Judgment Day, when your body rises incorruptible from the dead to be united with your immortal soul, this poetry assures that you will be admired and loved forever.

## THE PLACE OF THE SONNET IN THE CYCLE

Shakespeare proclaims the enduring power of poetry in this and several other sonnets to the young man, notably Sonnet 18, where "eternal lines" last "so long as men can breathe or eyes can see" (ll. 12, 13), and Sonnet 65, which braves the inexorable destruction of the passing years as it proclaims that "in black ink my love may still shine bright" (l. 14). Sonnet 55 also caps a trio of contiguous sonnets on "artistic description," as Booth points out (227). All three address the young man from a respectful rhetorical distance as "you"; none slips into the intimate familiarity of "thou" and "I." Sonnet 53 portrays the poem's subject as a reincarnation of the legendary Adonis and Helen, as the metaphorical embodiment of springtime and harvest, and yet as superior to all these "for constant heart" (l. 14). Sonnet 54 continues the theme of constancy in art as it compares rank "canker-blooms," which fade, to the "[s]weet roses" from which a perfumer extracts and retains the essence of summer (ll. 5, 11). That sonnet's concluding couplet applies the metaphor to the poet's art: "And so of you, beauteous and lovely youth, / When that shall vade [pass away], by verse distills your truth." Finally, in Sonnet 55 the heroic language of warfare supersedes the delicate perfume simile as the creator of a memorial scorns an "unswept" gravestone (l. 4) in favor of a "living record" from which the beloved shall "pace forth" for "all posterity" (ll. 8, 9, 10).

Of the three sonnets, only Sonnet 55's triumphant conclusion extends the promise of immortality beyond the power of art into the Christian commitment to what the Burial Office in the Anglican Book of Common Prayer calls a "sure and certain hope of resurrection to eternal life, through our Lord Jesus Christ, who shall change our vile body that it may be like to his glorious body." Compared to the classical pledge of immortal fame through poetry, which Shakespeare regularly reiterates, this specific allusion to church doctrine is rare in the sonnets; it recurs only in Sonnet 146. By that late point in the sequence, though, the speaker focuses solely on his own religious hope for immortal life, when "Death once dead, there's no more dying then" (l. 14). In Sonnet 55 the doctrinal allusion elevates the tribute to the beloved by surrendering the highest claims for poetry to the promises of religion.

## DEVICES AND TECHNIQUES

Like almost all of Shakespeare's sonnets, Sonnet 55 comprises three discrete iambic pentameter quatrains and a concluding couplet. These are linked, as Vendler notes (268–269), by the key word "live," which the poem repeats once in each of its four units as "outlive" (l. 2), "living record" (l. 8), "all-oblivious enmity" (l. 9), and "you live in this" (l. 14). Moreover, the pronoun "you" and the auxiliary verb of command or promise, "shall," are each repeated five times as the poem outlines a mythic contest between time and the beloved young man. Thus the initial quatrain boasts that "not marble . . . nor monuments / . . . shall outlive" the poetry that praises the beloved (ll. 1–2), but "you shall shine" through "this pow'rful rhyme" (ll. 2–3). Lest the youth's victory seem easy, the second quatrain foretells that "wasteful war shall" (l. 5) destroy statues and masonry. By the third quatrain, however, the speaker promises his beloved the victory: in defiance of death "shall you pace forth" (l. 10). Finally, "your praise shall still find room / . . . in lovers' eyes" (ll. 10, 14), with the word "still" meaning always. This concluding prophecy recalls John Donne's contemporary poem "The Canonization," where lovers "build in sonnets pretty rooms" and invite all posterity to invoke their devotion as an ideal pattern for intimate affection. The two other repetitions of "you" similarly offer the beloved unending life: "The living record of your memory" (l. 8) and "you live in this" (l. 14).

Alliteration further links the sonnet's three quatrains and couplet, notably the alliterated "m" of "marble" and "monuments" (l. 1), "masonry" (l. 6), and "memory" (l. 8); the "w" of "wasteful war" (l. 5) and "wear this world out" (l. 12), and the "p" of "princes" and "pow'rful" (l. 2), "pace forth" and "praise" (l. 10), and "posterity" (l. 11). Finally, the alliterated "l" enhances the concluding emphasis on "live" and "lovers' eyes" (l. 14). Internal rhyme yokes "nor Mars his sword" with "nor war's quick fire" (l. 7) to create a zeugma that stresses the chaos of battle in language that is illustrative rather than grammatically precise: G. Blackmore Evans, among others, points out that "a sword cannot be said to burn anything" (*The Sonnets* [Cambridge: Cambridge UP, 1996], 163). In contrast to war's wasteful confusion, it is the beloved's serene destiny to "pace forth" (l. 10), which Duncan-Jones observes is "a surprisingly gentle word" that suggests peace and rhymes internally with "praise" (220). Linguistically, the sonnet opposes wars and princes to the beloved, monuments and masonry to poetry, and it is through poetry that the beloved triumphs.

## THEMES AND MEANINGS

The enduring potency of poetry is a classical theme that was widely familiar to the Sonnets' first readers. Ovid concludes his *Metamorphoses* by boasting that poetry will assure him everlasting fame (15.871–79). Ovid borrows the theme from Horace (Odes 3.30), as Booth points out while citing the Loeb translation from the Latin: "I have finished a monument more lasting than bronze. . . . I shall not altogether die, but . . . on and on shall I grow, ever fresh with the glory of after time" (Booth, pp. 227–228). Many of Shakespeare's Renaissance contemporaries, including Samuel Daniel and George Chapman, repeat that classical theme.

Yet Sonnet 55 diverges from the well-worn claim to immortality through verse in two original ways. First, as John Kerrigan points out, the poet does not require eternal fame for himself but offers it to the beloved ("*The Sonnets*" and "*A Lover's Complaint*," rev. ed. [New York: Penguin, 1995], 241). Ovid proposes to extend his own afterlife through the reputation of his literary achievement, but Shakespeare's self-effacing speaker disappears into the poem while he asserts that the "you" he addresses five times in this sonnet will live till the end of time. Moreover, the beloved lives not in the book of fame through a poetic catalogue of his public achievements but in the private universe of "lovers' eyes" as an icon of whatever loveliness readers may imagine, value, and desire.

Second, the poem resigns its own authority to extend a mortal life to the larger Christian doctrine of the resurrection of the body and the life everlasting. Vendler reads the sonnet as "the gradual transformation of a memorializing and commemorative impulse into a resurrective one" (268). The speaker begins where Ovid ends, with congratulations for his own skill to extend the memory of a man long beyond his lifetime, but he concludes with the faithful hope to recover the beloved himself rather than to rest satisfied with the fictive image of the beloved that lies in his poetry.

## THE RELATIONSHIP OF THE SONNET TO SHAKESPEARE'S OTHER WORKS

Shakespeare frequently portrays both injurious time and the living memorials that endeavor to defeat it. The combined subjects recur throughout the sonnets to the young man, right through the last one, Sonnet 126. Notably among the non-dramatic poems, the title character in *The Rape of Lucrece* apostrophizes time as well as "thy servant Opportunity" for eleven stanzas as she curses Tarquin, who has ravished her and escaped into the night (ll. 925–1001). Like the speaker of Sonnet 55, Lucrece defines time as mutability with its power

> To ruinate proud buildings with thy hours,
> And smear with dust their glitt'ring golden tow'rs. (ll. 944–945)

Far from defying time, Lucrece comforts herself with the hope that one day Tarquin will "have time to wail th' abusing of his time" (l. 994). The drama of her discourse builds with incremental repetition of the word "time."

When the poetic contest between memory and oblivion occurs in his English history plays, Shakespeare turns the playhouse into a living record of national recollection. For example, *Henry V* is both a gilded monument of princes and a powerful rhyme, as Duncan-Jones hints in a gloss on Sonnet 55 when she says the initial pair of lines "suggests gilded tombs of monarchs in marble chambers, such as that of Henry V in Westminster Abbey" (220). The play's Chorus echoes line 7 of Sonnet 55 when he claims that had he "princes to act, / . . . the warlike Harry . . . [should] Assume the port of Mars, and at his heels / . . . famine, sword, and fire" (Pro. 3–7). The military undermining of Harfleur with gunpowder (*Henry V*, 3.1) dramatizes the "broils [that] root out the work of masonry" in Sonnet 55 (l. 6). Moreover, King Henry's valiant battle speech on St. Crispin's Day depicts a future veteran as his own memorial for all posterity:

> Old men forget; yet all shall be forgot,
> But he'll remember with advantages
> What feats he did that day.
>
>       \*    \*    \*
>
> This story shall the good man teach his son;
> And Crispin Crispian shall ne'er go by,
> From this day to the ending of the world,
> But we in it shall be remembered. (4.3.49–51; 56–59)

In the final account, however, the theater can only extend an imperfect memory; it cannot restore the hero's life or recover his conquests. The play's sonnet-epilogue bemoans both the author's "rough and all-unable pen" (Epi. 1) and the "small time" (Epi. 5) of his royal subject's influence.

In the tragedies, Shakespeare portrays memorial verse, stone, and ceremony with dramatic irony as a sorry substitute for the lost beloved. As *Romeo and Juliet* plays out its melancholy last scene outside the Capulets' monument, Montague makes a promise to Juliet's father that paraphrases Ovid's expectation of fame as enduring as Rome:

> For I will [raise] her statue in pure gold,
> That whiles Verona by that name is known,
> There shall no figure at such rate be set
> As that of true and faithful Juliet.

In the spirit of capitulation or competition, Capulet makes the like fruitless offer of a matched statue that wasteful war shall quite possibly overturn:

> As rich shall Romeo's by his lady's lie,
> Poor sacrifices of our enmity! (5.3.298–304)

The "glooming peace" that concludes this tragedy of young lovers who act out the Petrarchan hyperbole of love and despair finds small consolation in a public offer that their "praise shall still find room, / Even in the eyes of all posterity" (55.10–11).

   *Hamlet* treats the memorial as a wry and bitter joke. "Remember me," commands the father's departing ghost, and Hamlet instantly and powerfully revises the living record of his memory:

> Remember thee!
> Ay, thou poor ghost, whiles memory holds a seat
> In this distracted globe. Remember thee!
> Yea, from the table of my memory
> I'll wipe away all trivial fond records. (1.5.91; 95–99)

Hamlet's resolved memory denotes his enmity to his father's murderer, whom he immediately records as a "smiling, damned villain" (1.5.106), but leads only to self-loathing, not to action. Before he redeems that memory Hamlet jokes with the gravediggers. Only the gravedigger can make the house that "lasts till doomsday" (5.1.59), not sonneteers who promise to "find room [for your praise] / . . . to the ending doom" (ll. 10–12). The summary displacement of Yorick's body by Ophelia's illustrates the absurdity of trusting memory to monuments, though Ophelia's histrionically grieving brother demands, "What ceremony else?" (5.1.225) and leaps into the grave to prolong her futile obsequies. Hamlet sneers at him, "Dost thou come here to whine? / . . . Nay, and thou'lt mouth, / I'll rant as well as thou" (5.1.277; 283–284). At last, however, even Hamlet's skepticism cannot compel him to relinquish his own hope—not for "gilded monuments"—but for a living record of his memory. Dying, Hamlet asks his friend Horatio to "draw thy breath in pain / To tell my story" (5.2.348–349). Even then, he cannot die as a private man, hoping to "dwell in lovers' eyes" (14) but as a prince, struggling to clarify his political succession.

   The plots of several of Shakespeare's comedies and romances reward grieving family members by reuniting them with those who have faithfully kept the living record of their memories. As in Sonnet 55, a metaphorical allusion to the religious mystery of the resurrection intensifies the action and makes it dramatically credible. In *Twelfth Night*, for example, fraternal but indistinguishable twins who are separated by shipwreck gradually recognize each other as the sister "whom the blind waves and surges have devour'd" and the brother who went "to his watery tomb" (5.1.229, 234). Each twin, convinced that the other had died, perceives the miraculous meeting, as expressed in Sonnet 55 (l. 13), as a kind of "judgment that yourself arise." Each breathlessly sets aside a living record of memory for the living beloved he or she gazes on.

A more detailed dramatization of Sonnet 55 appears in the fortunes of the callow bridegroom Claudio in *Much Ado about Nothing*. Convinced that his ignorant treachery has killed Hero, his bride, Claudio ceremoniously hangs an epitaph on her monument. The dry little verse does not invite Hero to "dwell in lovers' eyes," but offers her fame, the reward of princes:

> Death in guerdon of her wrongs,
> Gives her fame which never dies.
> So the life that died with shame
> Lives in death with glorious fame. (5.3.5–8)

After Claudio pledges his yearly renewal of the memorial ceremony, Hero's father restores his living daughter to the amazed young penitent, who is instructed to interpret the occasion in terms of a rising from death. Hero explains, "One Hero died defil'd, but I do live, / And surely as I live, I am a maid." Don Pedro interjects, "The former Hero! Hero that is dead!" and Hero's father assures him, "She died, my lord, but whiles her slander liv'd" (5.4.63–66). Fame, the monument of princes, ultimately yields not to poetry or memory but to the expectation of new life.

In the romances the resurrection motif replaces memorials more magically and triumphantly than in the comedies. Finding his daughter's monument "in glitt'ring golden characters" (4.4.44), the eponymous Pericles sinks into impenetrable grief, but with his discovery that "she is not dead . . . as she should have been" (5.1.215) he hears "the music of the spheres" (5.1.229) and receives a divine vision that leads him to his lost wife. He only asks her rescuer, "Will you deliver / How this dead queen relives?" (5.3.63–64). He does not ask to have old false reports corrected but to have his faith in the resurrection renewed. In *The Winter's Tale* Leontes similarly discovers a lost daughter, and that event yields to a breathtaking miracle as a memorial statue of his dead wife becomes the woman herself. The steadfast courtier Paulina directs him, "It is requir'd / You do awake your faith" (5.3.94–95). Next, to the sound of music she commands the seemingly dead wife to "bequeath to death your numbness; for from him / Dear life redeems you" (5.3.103–104), and his beloved literally paces forth to dwell in lovers' eyes in her own person. In miniature, Sonnet 55 summarizes the themes of several plays as it rejects public princely monuments for the intimate living record of a beloved who is commanded at the ending doom to rise from the grave. Ultimately it points artfully beyond art toward a religious hope.

### Annotated Bibliography

Booth, Stephen, ed. *Shakespeare's Sonnets*. New Haven: Yale UP, 1977. Offers comprehensive annotations for each sonnet.

Burrow, Colin, ed. *The Complete Sonnets and Poems*. Oxford World's Classics. New York: Oxford UP, 2002. Provides extensive and helpful annotations.

Burto, William, ed. *The Sonnets*. Rev. ed. Signet Classic Shakespeare. New York: Signet, 1999. Includes an introduction by W. H. Auden, an updated bibliography, and critical essays by William Empson, Hallett Smith, Winifred M. T. Nowottny, and Helen Vendler.

Duncan-Jones, Katherine, ed. *Shakespeare's Sonnets*. The Arden Shakespeare. London: Thomas Nelson and Sons, 1997. A thorough and helpful annotated edition, with an introduction that historically contextualizes the sonnets and persuasively nominates William Herbert, the future third Earl of Pembroke, as the fair young man.

Rollins, Hyder Edward, ed. *The Sonnets*. New Variorum Edition. 2 vols. Philadelphia: J. B. Lippincott, 1944. The most comprehensive critical survey of commentary on each sonnet from 1609 until 1944.

Vendler, Helen. *The Art of Shakespeare's Sonnets*. Cambridge, MA: Harvard UP, 1997. Original close readings of the sonnets that focus on a schematic of key words and couplet links.

# Sonnet 60

## Robert G. Blake

Like as the waves make towards the pebbled shore,
So do our minutes hasten to their end;
Each changing place with that which goes before,
In sequent toil all forwards do contend.
Nativity, once in the main of light,
Crawls to maturity, wherewith being crowned,
Crooked eclipses 'gainst his glory fight,
And Time that gave doth now his gift confound.
Time doth transfix the flourish set on youth
And delves the parallels in beauty's brow,
Feeds on the rarities of nature's truth,
And nothing stands but for his scythe to mow:
    And yet to times in hope, my verse shall stand
    Praising thy worth, despite his cruel hand.

## PROSE PARAPHRASE

Just as the ocean waves move one after the other toward the rocky shore, our minutes swiftly devour each other in an ongoing procession. As we mature from infancy and childhood and approach our prime we are paradoxically closer to dissolution and death, time being the fickle enemy of us all. Time gives us youth and beauty only to take them away in a great betrayal. Everything is the victim of Time's sharp sickle. Nevertheless, my writing in your praise will prevail over the effects of time, namely aging and death.

## THE PLACE OF THE SONNET IN THE CYCLE

According to Thomas Thorpe's original arrangement of Shakespeare's sonnets, Sonnet 60 is almost in the middle of the long sequence that is largely devoted to the unknown friend. The first seventeen of these try to persuade the friend to propagate children to ensure his continuance into the future. But several of these seventeen speak of the poet's art as another, albeit inferior, way to perpetuate the friend's memory, and in Sonnet 18 the focus shifts from procreation to the characteristic Renaissance view of art as a means of immortalizing the friend. Almost twenty sonnets in the whole sequence explicitly affirm the power of poetry to keep the friend's memory green for future generations, most of these making the affirmation in the concluding couplet. C. L. Barber makes the point that usually more than the last two lines are necessary to give weight to the promise of art to ensure immortality and cites Sonnet 55 as a more convincing argument (19). Although Sonnet 55 is among the greatest of the sonnets, Barber could with equal justice have cited Sonnet 63, which also is devoted entirely to the power of rhyme to defeat time and ensure the friend's memory for perpetuity. Edward Hubler selects Sonnet 60 along with several others as having a less than auspicious conclusion (27). And G. Wilson Knight writes of the concluding couplet of Sonnet 60, "This is at once slack poetry and cold comfort" (81).

## DEVICES AND TECHNIQUES

The fundamental character of Shakespeare's thought is analogical. Probably better than any other poet in western literature he is able to see similarities in dissimilarities and to use sensory images to concretize the abstract. The first two lines of Sonnet 60 illustrate this ability as well as anything that Shakespeare wrote. Anyone who has seen the ocean can visualize the first line and connect the movement of the waves to the sense of the ongoing succession of time. The opening lines introduce the subject of the poem, which is the general nature of the journey of life. Line four makes the transition from the ongoing process of the ocean waves and the minutes of time to life's successive stages, all change being seen as arduous and painful. The fifth line is one of the most fascinating in Shakespeare. According to the *Oxford English Dictionary*, "nativity" in Shakespeare's time as in ours means birth, not infant or newborn, as numerous editors have maintained. Why, then, do we not have "Infants, once in the main of light"? By using a word that refers to birth in general, Shakespeare seems to refer to the human condition, not mere individuals. And "the main of light" may refer to the world of endless possibilities of experience and relationships awaiting all newborns. If this interpretation is sound, the line could anticipate by hundreds of years David Darling's recent theory of secular reincarnation, buttressed by neuroscience, which holds that any infant is potentially capable of becoming anyone because our "early environment and interpersonal relationships determine the precise neural circuitry of our brains, and this circuitry in turn determines who we are" (*Zen Physics: The Science of Death, the Logic of Reincarnation* [New York: HarperCollins, 1996], 21).

Once one reaches maturity, which is the prime or apex of life, "Crooked eclipses 'gainst his glory fight" (60.7); and time, now personified, attacks the individual in deadly ways, through aging and all the infirmities that go with it. Time that gave youth now robs one of it and therefore is a treacherous and deceitful giver of bounty. It would be difficult to imagine a more evil image than "crooked eclipses." Eclipses in Shakespeare's day were portents that foretold disaster in the state or cosmos, and "crooked" is generally interpreted to mean vicious or evil, so that the two words together are deeply disturbing, especially as a general verdict on the human condition. So concentrated is Shakespeare's language in the sonnets generally and in this one especially that here lines five through eight state essentially what Jaques takes twenty-eight lines to say in *As You Like It* in the well-known "Seven Ages of Man" speech (2.7.139–166).

In the final quatrain of Sonnet 60 Shakespeare moves from time's destruction of physical beauty—"delves the parallels in beauty's brow" (l. 10)—to a more insidious and inclusive damage to all that is most precious in nature. In fact, so bleak is the outlook of this sonnet that Shakespeare states that "nothing stands but for his [Time's] scythe to mow." The concluding couplet seeks to affirm the power of this particular poem to survive time's destruction, but any comfort intended by the line is lost in the dismal outlook of the previous twelve.

Helen Vendler offers an interesting verbal analysis of Sonnet 60, taking as her starting point the word "stand" and applying it to each of the quatrains. *Stand* is the single thing that the subjects of the quatrains are unable to do: waves move inexorably; maturity, the crown of life, does not last and neither does the vegetation of the earth; everything is mowed down. Vendler sees the concluding couplet as failing to achieve the intended "optimistic reversal" because of the syntactical placement of "cruel hand" (l. 14), "with *cruel* being the last echo of the destructive *cr-* words (*crooked*, and so forth) of the tragic paradigm" (285). Vendler notes that in the first two quatrains time's destructive action follows the dissolution of its objects, while in the third quatrain the destroying verbs "transfix," "delves," and "feeds" come before the subjects of time's effects. This reversal is important, according to Vendler, because it shows that "Shakespeare gives us his own analytic and philosophical model in place of the victim's chronological one" (286). We perceive our lives chronologically, but the philosopher objectively regards them analytically, "perceiving the undeflectable end even in the flourishing beginning. The ensuing philosophical despair . . . is consequently believably motivated, and the suggestion of malign destiny . . . is made plausible" (286).

## THEMES AND MEANINGS

The titular theme of Shakespeare's sonnets is Neoplatonic friendship. Approximately 80 percent of the corpus is devoted to it, but almost as high a percentage is devoted to the subject of time and its deleterious effects. Numerous students of Shakespeare have written about time in the sonnets, none more expansively and provocatively than G. Wilson Knight, who devotes an entire chapter of his book-length study of the sonnets to it. Although Knight sees the sonnets as "a poetic war with Time" (74), he eventually arrives at the conclusion that for Shakespeare poetry in its deepest sense represents a metaphysical triumph over time, that "poetry enjoys an authority, or exists from a dimension, to which all temporal fabrications and engagements are as nothing" (101). This Socratic idea is heartening, but, like religion, not everyone subscribes to it.

In the sonnets Shakespeare demonizes and personifies time, usually capitalizing the word and ascribing to it various epithets and characteristics, e.g., "never-resting time" (5.5), "Time's scythe" (12.13), "wasteful Time" (15.11), "Devouring Time" (19.1), "swift-footed Time" (19.6), "sluttish Time" (55.4), "Time's injurious hand" (63.2), "Time's fell hand" (64.1), and "Time's tyranny" (115.9). Not once in the sonnets does Shakespeare portray time in a positive light, much less as benevolent, and seldom is a complete sonnet devoted to it. Which of the various couplets achieve an "optimistic reversal," to use Helen Vendler's term, must be left to the reader's discretion, but it clearly is not those of sonnets 60 or 65: "And yet to times in hope my verse shall stand / Praising thy worth, despite his cruel hand" (60.13–14) and "O none, unless this miracle have might, / That in black ink my love may still shine bright" (65.13–14). Both of these are far too tentative to inspire confidence in the reader. At the other extreme of the scale of assurance stands Sonnet 55, C. L. Barber's example. In that sonnet Shakespeare faces and stares down time: "Not marble nor the gilded monuments / Of princes shall outlive this pow'rful rhyme." Shakespeare's lesser known Sonnet 107 also convincingly maintains that not only the friend but also the poet will "live in this poor rhyme" (107.11).

## THE RELATIONSHIP OF THE SONNET TO SHAKESPEARE'S OTHER WORKS

One must not expect to find many direct echoes of the sonnets in the plays since we are dealing with entirely different genres. Nevertheless, one exception must be noted. Sonnet 66 in enumerating "the whips and scorns of time" and viewing death as a blessed release from them has affinities with Hamlet's "To be or not to be" soliloquy (3.3.55–87), the "golden lads" song from *Cymbeline* (4.2.258–281), and the Duke's speech on death to Claudio in *Measure for Measure* (3.1.5–41). Shakespeare's vision of the human condition is essentially tragic. Time, in his view, is the root cause of aging and death, those inescapable stations on the human journey.

In *The Tempest*, written near the end of Shakespeare's career, Prospero speaks of "the dark backward and abysm of time" (1.2.50) and avers that "our little life / Is rounded with a sleep" (4.1.157–158). In *Romeo and Juliet* time is precious because it is fleeting. Hamlet is obsessed with the short length of time between his father's death and his mother's remarriage, and in *Troilus and Cressida* time is personified as the thief of accomplishments, "a great-siz'd monster of ingratitudes" (3.3.147). In none of the plays is time given the prominence that it enjoys in the sonnets, and the reference just cited in *Troilus and Cressida* is the closest that Shakespeare makes time out to be a villain in the plays.

It is not possible from the references to death in the plays to infer exactly how Shakespeare regarded it. Isabella in *Measure for Measure* says that "The sense of death is most in apprehension" (3.1.77), but her brother Claudio does not agree. He expresses more powerfully than in any other of Shakespeare's writings the human fear of death as he seeks to persuade Isabella to sacrifice her virginity to save his life:

> The weariest and most loathed worldly life
> That age, ache, penury, and imprisonment
> Can lay on nature is a paradise
> To what we fear of death. (3.1.128–131)

Hamlet would commit suicide except "that the dread of something after death, / The undiscover'd country, from whose bourn / No traveller returns, puzzles the will" (3.1.77–79). Romeo and Juliet, on the other hand, eagerly seek death rather than live without the other, as do Antony—("I come, my queen" 4.14.50)—and Cleopatra—"I have / Immortal longings in me. . . . Methinks I hear / Antony call" (5.2.280–284). Othello takes his life to escape the anguish of having killed Desdemona. Caesar proclaims that "Cowards die many times before their deaths, / The valiant never taste of death but once" (2.2.32–33), and after Caesar's assassination Casca says, "[H]e that cuts off twenty years of life / Cuts off so many years of fearing death" (3.1.101–102). Death comes as a boon to King Lear after his horrific suffering. Kent is compelled to exclaim "Vex not his ghost. O, let him pass, he hates him / That would upon the rack of this tough world / Stretch him out longer" (5.3.314–316). Just as we will never know Shakespeare's religious beliefs, it is not possible to know what he thought about death. Except for Horatio's exclamation when Hamlet dies, "Good night, sweet prince, / And flights of angels sing thee to thy rest!" (5.2.359–360) there is nothing Christian about the Bard's view of death.

Aging and old age itself are consistently portrayed in the plays as worse than death. Virtually the only positive view of old age is paradoxically spoken by Macbeth: "that which should accompany old age, / As honor, love, obedience, troops of friends, / I must not look to have" (5.3.23–25). Macbeth's "Tomorrow" soliloquy (5.5.19–28) is often interpreted as Shakespeare's most dismal commentary on the human condition, but it can be argued that for an even darker vision we must go to the comedies, namely, Jaques' "Seven Ages of Man" soliloquy in *As You Like It*. The tragic truth of the sixth and seventh stages of life is witnessed by patients in nursing homes or in a work of literature like *King Lear*. Adam in that play claims, "Though I look old, yet I am strong and lusty" (2.3.47). In the forest of Arden his strength gives out, though. Orlando must carry him to Duke Senior's encampment, and in his last line in the play he states, "I scarce can speak to thank you for myself" (2.7.170). Sadly, old age and death in the plays are unredeemed by the hope of immortality by biological reproduction or poetry as in the sonnets.

### Annotated Bibliography

Barber, C. L. "An Essay on Shakespeare's Sonnets." In *Shakespeare's Sonnets*. Ed. Harold Bloom. New York: Chelsea House, 1987. 5–27. Barber's is a sophisticated essay divided into six sections: for example, "The Sonnet as an Action" and "Eros: Tyrannos." About the friend's affair with the Dark Lady Barber writes, "Most men would bury the event in silence, or else turn injury into anger. Shakespeare turns injury into poetry" (23).

Hubler, Edward. *The Sense of Shakespeare's Sonnets*. Princeton: Princeton UP, 1951. Especially valuable for an extended appendix effectively debunking the misguided idea that someone other than Shakespeare wrote the works attributed to him and the naïve notion that the sonnets are an account of a homosexual episode in his life.

Knight, G. Wilson. *The Mutual Flame*. London: Methuen, 1955. Erudite discussion of various aspects of Shakespeare's sonnets drawing on a wide range of literature to support his insights. His chapter on "Time and Eternity" is especially incisive.

Vendler, Helen. *The Art of Shakespeare's Sonnets*. Cambridge, MA: Harvard UP, 1997. Ambitious work with a helpful introduction and perceptive close readings of all 154 sonnets.

# Sonnet 65

### Barry B. Adams

Since brass, nor stone, nor earth, nor boundless sea,
But sad mortality o'ersways their power,
How with this rage shall beauty hold a plea,
Whose action is no stronger than a flower?
O! how shall summer's honey breath hold out,
Against the wrackful siege of battering days,
When rocks impregnable are not so stout,
Nor gates of steel so strong but Time decays?
O fearful meditation! where, alack,
Shall Time's best jewel from Time's chest lie hid?
Or what strong hand can hold his swift foot back?
Or who his spoil of beauty can forbid?
   O! none, unless this miracle have might,
   That in black ink my love may still shine bright.

### PROSE PARAPHRASE

How can something as fragile as beauty survive in a world in which everything is subject to the inexorable force of Time—a force that is responsible for human mortality but also for the degeneration or destruction of even the hardest physical objects, such as brass or stone, as well as the most far-reaching and all-pervasive physical elements imaginable (the earth, the sea)? After posing this question in various forms, the speaker concludes, tentatively, that the celebration of his love's beauty in verse will prove a miraculous exception to this universal law of nature.

### THE PLACE OF THE SONNET IN THE CYCLE

Sonnet 65 picks up language and themes from the two preceding sonnets as well as from Sonnet 60. Each of these four poems dwells on the wasting or destructive effect of time and relates this effect specifically to the object of the speaker's affection, presumably the "dear friend" who is the topic of most of the first 126 sonnets of the collection. Sonnet 64 stands out in this small, broken cluster by failing to deliver a consoling counter-statement to balance or qualify the speaker's melancholy reflection on the ravages of time. Its concluding couplet in fact offers a powerfully pessimistic summary of his rumination: "This thought is as a death, which cannot choose / But weep to have that which it fears to lose." In sonnets 60, 63, and 65, by contrast, the speaker reaches a more optimistic conclusion with more or less emphatic and confident claims about his own verse. Sonnet 2, which is also very much concerned with the effects of time on human existence, offers a similarly optimistic resolution, but a significantly different one. Like a number of closely related sonnets from the first set of seventeen poems in the collection, it urges a young man (again presumably the same "dear friend") to beget children. The parallel between children and poems, both of which are in some sense products of human acts of creation, is exploited most fully in sonnets 15, 16, and 17. The first of these concludes with the speaker's promise to perpetuate the memory of his friend by means of his verse: "And all in war with Time for love of you, / As he takes from you, I ingraft you new" (15.13–14). The opening of the next sonnet, however, robs this promise of some of its force: "But wherefore do not you a mightier way / Make war upon this bloody tyrant Time?" That "mightier way," as the speaker goes on explain, involves his friend's own biological creativity. The third in this short series of poems recommends a combination of means, one neatly expressed in the summarizing couplet: "But were some child of yours alive that time, / You should live twice, in it and in my rhyme" (17.13–14). Sonnet 65 offers a simpler consolation: the miracle of verse will preserve the young man's beauty.

## DEVICES AND TECHNIQUES

In Sonnet 65, the controlling thematic idea is first developed in a series of rhetorical questions that in effect repeat the indisputable fact that time destroys everything until that fact is called into question, or at least significantly qualified, by the concluding couplet. Line 9 announces a shift from the rhetorical question pattern of the first two quatrains, specifically a summary reflection ("O fearful meditation"), but the third quatrain actually presents two other rhetorical questions, and the meditation's answer is postponed to the concluding couplet. The quatrain structure is emphasized by the placement of repeated exclamatory "O"s at the beginning of lines 5 and 9, but then modified by the appearance of a third "O" introducing the concluding couplet. The effect of this last verbal repetition is to modify (if not to nullify) the normal 4+4+4+2 structure of the English or Shakespearean sonnet by blurring the distinction between couplet and quatrain. Yet the argumentative structure of the poem insists on that distinction, since the concluding couplet is designed precisely to qualify or even contradict the observations in the three quatrains.

As noted above, this argumentative movement, in particular the sudden change of direction at the end, is markedly different from the movement of Sonnet 64, where the speaker offers nothing but sorrow and tears in response to his melancholy ruminations on time. For cases more like that of Sonnet 65, in which the concluding couplet embodies a change in direction, we may turn to sonnets 60 and 63, both of which put forward the notion that poetry, or more specifically poetry about the speaker's friend, offers an effective remedy to time's depredations. Sonnet 60 does so with considerable force: "And yet to times in hope my verse shall stand, / Praising thy worth, despite his cruel hand" (60.13–14).

The change of direction is signalled overtly by "And yet" and reinforced by the unexpected introduction of an addressee in the final line. The first twelve lines of the sonnet are of the most general sort, consisting of philosophical reflections addressed to no one in particular but instead put forth as indisputable observations about time and its effects. Only with the reference to "my verse" in line 13, followed by "thy worth" in the next line, are these observations tied to anything immediate, concrete, or circumstantial. Sonnet 63 concludes with a similarly confident assertion by the speaker about the power of his verses, though here the subject of those verses (who is, we may again presume, the "dear friend") is referred to in the third person: "His beauty shall in these black lines be seen, / And they shall live, and he in them still green" (63.13–14).

The connection with Sonnet 65 extends to the verbal level in the phrase "black lines," which reappears in slightly modified form as "black ink." In both cases the color reference is explained by the fact that early printing was predominantly monochromatic, making little or no use of colored inks. The inky blackness of Sonnet 63 is set in opposition to greenness, a common symbol of life. In Sonnet 65, that blackness is set in opposition to brightness, which here and elsewhere suggests beauty. Both poems also place considerable thematic weight on the deceptively simple word "still," which in Elizabethan English could mean what it means today, "up to now" or "even after a specified time," but could also mean "always" or "forever." In the contexts of sonnets 60 and 65, the stronger Elizabethan sense of the word, now obsolete, is dominant.

Time so considered invites treatment by means of the rhetorical and poetical figure of personification, in which abstract attributes are expressed through human forms or actions. Some basic personifications have been so thoroughly assimilated into common speech that we tend to overlook their figurative nature. Father Time, for example, is typically portrayed as old and decrepit to illustrate the effects of extreme age on the human body. In modern renderings he frequently appears holding an hourglass, thereby reinforcing the putative cause of his condition, namely the passage of time rather than disease or some other abnormality. He may also carry a scythe (as in Shakespeare's Sonnet 123) or a sickle (as in his Sonnet 116), suggesting the end of growth, which is by extension identified with death. This iconic detail, which calls attention to agency rather than effect, does not harmonize logically with the underlying personification, which is designed to embody effect rather than agency. Alternatively, it is possible to focus on the fact that time is fleeting and generate a personification like that glanced at in Shakespeare's Sonnet 19, which is addressed to a figure called "Devouring Time" in line 1 and "old Time" in line 13, as well as "swift-footed Time" in line 6. The several attributes of time captured in these expressions all have an obvious rightness, and the fact that they do not come together naturally to form a single unified picture is, poetically speaking, of little consequence. Sonnet 126 contains a more complex poetic personification in which Time is first opposed to Nature (another personification) and then effectually aligned with her when Nature is characterized as "sovereign mistress over wrack": that is, both Time and Nature are working to the same end, which includes the destruction of the dear friend's beauty, later if not sooner. The speaker's movement from one view of Time to the other represents the development of a more insightful philosophical outlook.

## THEMES AND MEANINGS

The ravaging effect of time, particularly on human life, was a familiar theme both in classical literature and in the Hebrew scriptures. For Shakespeare and his more literate contemporaries, the Roman poet Ovid's phrase "tempus edax rerum" (time consumes all things), with its partially suppressed image of time as a gluttonous beast, would have been an expression so commonplace as to have become stale. The "Devouring Time" of Shakespeare's Sonnet 19, in fact, has the ring of a cliché. The "all-eating shame" of Sonnet 2, on the other hand, is an imaginative play on the commonplace idea and expression, one that obliquely applies some of the relevant attributes of Ovid's Time to an ad-hoc personification of the psychological condition shame. Shakespeare and his contemporaries, including less literate ones, would have been even more familiar with passages from the Old Testament that harped on the shortness of human life. According to the prophet Isaiah, for example, "All flesh is grass, and all the glory thereof is but as the flower of the field: when the flower of the grass is withered, the flower falleth away, when the wind of the Lord bloweth upon it. The people surely is grass, the which drieth up, and the flower fadeth away" (40.6–8). The prophet Job employs similar imagery to deliver much the same message: "Man that is born of woman, living but a short time, is full of manifold miseries. He springeth up like a flower, and fadeth again, vanishing away as it were a shadow, and never continueth in one state" (14.1–2).

The views expressed in these quotations sound like what moderns have been taught to associate with patristic and medieval Christianity. But such sentiments survived into post-Reformation England, as is evident from the fact that these biblical verses are here quoted from the First Book of Homilies, a collection of sermons officially sanctioned by the government of Queen Elizabeth, which required them to be delivered each Sunday from the pulpit of every church in the realm. The passages from Isaiah and Job are among the dozen or so biblical passages of the same tenor scattered throughout this sermon, which is entitled "Of the Misery of All Mankind and of his Condemnation to Death Everlasting by his Own Sin." Such ideas crop up from time to time in the *Sonnets*, sometimes in small clusters but more often in individual poems. And although they are fairly pervasive, such ideas seldom dominate the sonnets in which they appear. One noteworthy exception, Sonnet 64 with its concluding reference to death, tears, and fears, has already been cited to highlight the significantly different conclusion of Sonnet 65. Another is Sonnet 146, in which the speaker addresses his own soul and recommends a more explicitly religious response to the painful realization of the brevity of human life by urging his soul to "Buy terms divine" by renouncing material pleasure (146.11). More commonly these ideas reside in the background, ready to serve as a foil or defining contrast, or even as a springboard from which to execute a surprising poetic turn.

The countervailing theme, according to which the devastating effects of time may be defeated or overcome by means of poetry, is rooted in classical culture. In a well-known passage from the end of his third book of Odes, Horace reflects on his achievement:

> I have finished a monument more lasting than bronze and loftier than the Pyramids' royal pile, one that no wasting rain, no furious north wind can destroy, or the countless chain of years and the ages' flight. I shall not altogether die, but a mighty part of me shall escape the death-goddess. On and on shall I grow, ever fresh with the glory of after time. (Quoted in Booth, pp. 227–228; other translations give "brass" for "bronze" in the first sentence.)

Unlike Ovid's "devouring Time," Horace's claim for poetry is not reinforced by the Judeo-Christian tradition. The Hebrew scripture contains rich poetry (for example, the Psalms and Song of Solomon), all of it in some sense religious, but the idea that poetry or any other form of art can render eternal something that is natural and hence mutable goes against fundamental Jewish beliefs about the nature of the Deity. Similar constraints along with others associated with doctrines of the afterlife obtain in the realm of Christian theology as well, but Christian poets, especially post-medieval Christian poets touched by the revival of classical learning, had no difficulty incorporating the Horatian topos into metaphorical expressions designed to exalt their creative activity.

## THE RELATIONSHIP OF THE SONNET TO SHAKESPEARE'S OTHER WORKS

In Shakespeare's plays, the effects of time are most apparent in his portrayals of characters conspicuous for their old age. Such characters tend to be portrayed sympathetically, either on account of the wisdom that comes from experience (John of Gaunt in *Richard II*) or on account of the vulnerability that comes from infirmity (Adam in *As You Like It*, Belarius in *Cymbeline*). More memorable and interesting are those that break the mold, such as King Lear and Falstaff. Both of these characters lack wisdom (though Lear acquires something like it in the course of his tragic suffering). Falstaff displays the physical debility that usually comes with age, especially in *2 Henry IV*, but this condition is presented in a semi-satirical fashion, not as something that elicits unqualified sympathy. The contrast with Lear is particularly noteworthy: at the beginning of the play the king is physically very active despite his advanced years, and his extraordinary energy extends close to the end of the play, when we are told that he killed the soldier who was hanging his daughter Cordelia (5.3.275). Yet at the very end, what dominates is his pathetic helplessness.

Time is not always portrayed negatively in the plays. Viola in *Twelfth Night*, for example, calls on time to "untangle" the knot of complications and confusions that confront her (2.2.40). That is indeed what happens in the course of this romantic comedy, the implied message of which is that if one waits long enough, things will turn out happily or fortunately. With this topic as with so many others, Shakespeare has no single thematic program to promote but operates as a dramatic artist rather than a philosopher.

**Annotated Bibliography**

Booth, Stephen. *Shakespeare's Sonnets*. New Haven: Yale UP, 1977. Presents a photocopy of the 1609 edition with facing modernized texts of each sonnet as well as a reliable digest of the many theories about their composition (543–549), but its chief value lies in the analytic commentary, notable for its close attention to linguistic detail.

Duncan-Jones, Katherine, ed. *Shakespeare's Sonnets*. The Arden Shakespeare. London: Thomas Nelson and Sons, 1977. Valuable summary of scholarly and critical issues surrounding the sequence as well as acute observations on individual sonnets.

Leishman, J. B. *Themes and Variations in Shakespeare's Sonnets*. London: Hutchinson, 1961. Contains a useful sketch of the "devouring time" topos from classical Greece to the English Renaissance.

# Sonnet 71

## Robert Appelbaum

No longer mourn for me when I am dead
Than you shall hear the surly sullen bell
Give warning to the world that I am fled
From this vile world with vilest worms to dwell:
Nay, if you read this line, remember not
The hand that writ it, for I love you so,
That I in your sweet thoughts would be forgot,
If thinking on me then should make you woe.
O! if, I say, you look upon this verse,
When I perhaps compounded am with clay,
Do not so much as my poor name rehearse;
But let your love even with my life decay;
    Lest the wise world should look into your moan,
    And mock you with me after I am gone.

### PROSE PARAPHRASE

After my death do not mourn for me very long. Do not mourn for me past the time when you hear the gloomy, solemn town bell toll to note my death. No, if you read this verse do not even remember the hand that wrote it. I love you so much that if thinking about me after my death should cause you pain, I would rather you forgot about me.

Listen. If you read this verse after my death, when I have perhaps turned into clay, do not even speak or think my name. Let your love decay as I have myself decayed. Otherwise people—the "wise world" (71.13)—will examine your suffering, and mock you along with me (or because of me) after I have died.

## THE PLACE OF THE SONNET IN THE CYCLE

Sonnet 71 is the first of four sonnets in a sequence where the speaker thinks about his death and what it will mean for the young man (assuming that it is to the young man that the speaker is addressing himself). In these poems the speaker assumes that he will die before the young man, sooner rather than later, and that both of them know this will happen. Where the young man seems to have little to worry about on his own account, at least so far, the poet is a living symbol of impending old age and death: he has gone grey; he is going bald. As Sonnet 73 also suggests, the poet is losing his natural heat—the heat of youth, as we would still say today, although the reference is to an obsolete scientific notion. He is already going cold.

Previously, the poet has been mainly concerned, in spite of the young man's vigor, with the youth's mortality. Ever adopting the stance of an older man to a younger—though Shakespeare himself was not anywhere near as old as the speaker of the poems seems to feel himself to be—he has worried that the young man is incapable of seeing beyond present, youthful glory and so is not preparing for the future. He has advised the young man to marry and have children. He has praised the young man's temporarily flourishing beauty while insisting that the possessor of such beauty needs either children to carry on after his beauty fades or else a great poet—the speaker of the poems—to immortalize him in verse. The speaker has worried about the inconstancy of love, and examined ways in which the love he and his young man share may never change, or die, or be forgotten. He has had to worry about this bond in the face of the young man's own fickleness in matters of love, in the face of an affair the young man is having with a woman the poet has also been involved with. In later poems the speaker will worry about his own fragility as a human being, and praise the young man as someone whose love, or image, or virtues, can give him the strength to go on, or at the very least to write more memorializing poems. To the end of the young man sequence as a whole (that is, sonnets 1–126) the poet will see the young man and the poet's relationship with him as reminders of the impermanence of human affairs, and will look for resources in many places for overcoming the devastating impact, the "thievish progress" (77.8) of Time.

In sonnets 71–74, however, the poet looks squarely at the image of his own death: when he mentions the "surly sullen bell" in Sonnet 71 under discussion (l. 2), he is imagining what the world will be like without him. And in all four poems he is worrying about how the relationship between himself and the young man may be affected by the specter of death. He worries about how their relationship will appear to the world after his death, if anyone should learn about it. He worries about how the language with which he and the young man communicate with one another, especially the language of the sonnets themselves, will forestall or undermine the meaning of his mortality and the timeless, wordless love between them.

In this sonnet and sonnets 72 and 74 the speaker sometimes plays a game of false modesty, suggesting that the words of praise that the world will expect of the young man on the occasion of the speaker's death will be more than the speaker has ever deserved. He also suggests that language, which he and the young man and all the world so much count on, is inherently imperfect. Only love is true, he suggests. The person loved and the language used to describe the person loved are of a lesser order than love itself. So it is better to be silent; it is better not to memorialize; it is better not to remember.

The poet does not, perhaps, really mean all this. It has been suggested (by Stephen Booth among others) that the poet means the opposite of what he is saying. He wants the young man to remember him, to memorialize him, to speak on his behalf, to feel the pain of his passing away and let people know about that pain. After all, as Sonnet 73 argues, the mortality of the poet should make the young man love the former all the more strongly. Sonnet 71, the deepest in feeling of the four poems of the sequence, also uses the trick of saying the opposite of what is meant. But the poet uses this trick in order to transcend the limits of the language of love and death.

## DEVICES AND TECHNIQUES

The "trick"—which is, in fact, key to the poem's meaning—unfolds in the opening words: "No longer mourn for me when I am dead." The thought is completed only in the next lines, but it seems as if the thought is already finished when we come to the word "dead." The chief sense is: do not mourn for me any longer than you have to. Therefore, do not mourn for me longer than the official commemoration of my death by the town bell requires you to mourn. But the opening line seems to communicate two other meanings as well. One is, do not mourn for me anymore just now. The second, even more important meaning, which we also hear even if what we hear is not the right meaning, is, "mourn for me": "mourn for me when I am dead," even, "No, longer mourn for me when I am dead." There may not be a term for what Shakespeare is doing here, but the effect of what he is doing is like the effect of a pun: it is to say one thing literally and other things figuratively, by suggestion. Sound patterns and syntax evoke this effect, but what creates it above all is the fact that what Shakespeare is literally saying is so unexpected, so extreme, violating our sense of what a dying lover or potentially dying lover ought to be saying to his beloved. He should not be saying, "Do not mourn for me." He should not be saying "when I am dead." One ought to be less direct than this. One should not be thinking these thoughts. And so we hear, "No, longer mourn for me when I am dead."

The violence of the idea is underscored by other turns of language. If the first quatrain begins with the word "no," a word that we do not want to hear in its literal meaning, the second quatrain begins with "Nay," the third with "O"—exclamations betokening nervousness, and echoing the "No" with which Sonnet 71 begins. The nervousness is additionally betokened by the parenthetical comments "(I say)" and "(perhaps)" (ll. 9, 10), which signify hesitancy on the part of the speaker, a recognition that what he is saying does not go without saying, and may encounter resistance. As for the suggested, non-literal contrariness of what the poet is saying, it is continued in such statements as "if you read this line, remember not / The hand that writ it" (ll. 5–6). Now, as the person to whom the poem is addressed reads these lines, it is illogical to suggest what to do "if you read" it, since he is already reading it. And it is a familiar, deliberately self-defeating paradox to say, "remember not" such-and-such, since the effect on a reader told not to remember something is for the reader to remember what he or she is not supposed to remember. Indeed, the way the language is constructed, while the addressee is told, literally, not to do certain things in the future (mourn, remember, think, rehearse), in being told not to do them the addressee is already doing them. Moreover, if the reader reads this poem in the future, that is re-reads it, he will necessarily read the poem as a remembrance of the person who wrote it. In any case, the rhetorical force of the poem, over and above its literal meaning, is to cause the addressee to think in advance about the speaker's death, to imagine a world without the speaker. Hence, it has the effect of causing the reader to mourn in advance the death of the poet, and actually thus to "longer mourn."

The fundamental structure of the poem is typical of the *Sonnets*. A first quatrain expresses an idea, a second and then a third quatrain develop the idea by amplification, though perhaps in unexpected ways. The concluding couplet wraps up the argument of the poem by amplifying the meaning of the last quatrain and at the same time introducing a fresh paradox. Versification and rhyme follow the usual pattern of *abab, cdcd, efef, gg*. And as is often the case, though it is especially appropriate here, the lines end with strong end-stopped sounds, fixed upon a strong ending beat: for example, "dead," "bell," "fled," "dwell." There may be two exceptions in this sonnet. Line 6 ends with an accented syllable and includes both a long vowel and longish, aspirated consonant: "so." But the way we are likely to hear it both emphasizes the meaning and rushes us into the next line. The "gone" at the very end of the poem, in the original (1609) printed text spelled "gon," may seem to be a near-rhyme rather than an exact rhyme with "moan" (in the original text spelled "mone"), ending the poem on what is perhaps an appropriate note of incomplete resolution, and perhaps accentuating the connection between this poem and the one that follows it. The next sonnet begins with an "O" into which a "gon" may nicely slide. Yet "gon" is rhymed with "mone" elsewhere in the sonnets, as are, for example, "none" and "stone." Perhaps it both is and is not a near rhyme.

Sonnet 71 frequently employs alliteration: "mourn for me when I am" (l. 1); "shall hear the surly sullen bell" (l. 2); "warning to the world" (l. 3); "vile world with vilest worms" (l. 4). The effect is somewhat dirge-like. Perhaps in the rhythms that the alliteration accentuates we hear the tolling of the very bell the poem discusses.

## THEMES AND MEANINGS

The bell we are caused to think about is an object betokening a world we have lost—a world where the church steeple dominated the urban landscape, and communities were compact enough, and cohesive enough, to mourn collectively the passing of one of its members by way of a single clanging piece of metal. As the bell tolls in a church steeple it reminds us that in the communities of Shakespeare's life and imagination most people were practicing Christians. But the vision of death the poem articulates seems to have dropped one of the standard components of the Christian system of belief, the eternal soul. It would be orthodox enough of Shakespeare to emphasize that after death the body flees from the vileness of the world to cohabit in a grave with vile worms, or for his body after death to be compounded with clay. But that is not what he says in Sonnet 71. He says, "I am fled" (l. 3) and "I . . . compounded am with clay" (l. 10), tempering the last remark, to be sure, with a "perhaps." In this poem (and others) the poet is either unsure or dismissive of what he has been told about the afterlife. It is not just his body, but his self that decays and mixes with the earth. In that situation, blasphemously, the existence of the soul or the self after death depends upon others' living memory, or on the language that a living memory is empowered to "rehearse" (l. 11). The mortal individual is dependent on those who survive him, and of course especially on those who loved him. Everything comes down here then to the intimate relationship between two men, a lover and a beloved.

And yet, two contrary claims are being made as a consequence of "I love you." The first is, I love you so much that I do not want you ever to suffer. Therefore, do not suffer when I am dead and gone: do not mourn for me; do not even think or talk about me. I do not want the occasion of my death to interrupt your peace of mind. After all, I am not even worthy of such an interruption. The second claim is, from the point of view of the poet communicating the message, I am thinking about my death; I am thinking about you when I think about my death; I am thinking about the fact that I will be annihilated, "food for worms," when I die (1 Henry IV, 5.4.87). When I think about my death I think about the death of my love for you, the death of what little I can do for you while we are together, the death of our so-called eternal love, the inevitable death of your love for me, the death of everything we have meant to one another apart from the words that will remain behind me, your words above all, your hesitant, inadequate words. I am thinking all these things, and I am putting a good face on it: I am converting my fear of death to a courageous gesture on your behalf, putting your interests above mine. But deep down, when I think about the town bell tolling to mark my death, I am myself overwhelmed with grief.

## THE RELATIONSHIP OF THE SONNET TO SHAKESPEARE'S OTHER WORKS

Some of the images of the poem appear in the Henriad: Prince Hal says that Percy is "food for worms" (1 Henry IV, 5.4.87); the idea appears in other plays as well. A "sullen bell" is noted in advance of the news of Hotspur's death in 2 Henry IV, 1.1.102. That said, one must also think about how this poem about death and memory plays a part in the overall mediation on the subject that pervades the Shakespearean oeuvre. One can place this poem side by side with some of the comments in Hamlet: the ghost crying out to the young Hamlet, "Remember me" (1.5.91); Hamlet himself, as he lays dying, telling Horatio to "report me and my cause aright" (5.2.339). One may also think about the entombing of dead heroes not in the earth, where worms can get at the corpse, but in monuments of stone, as at the end of Romeo and Juliet and Antony and Cleopatra. The lovers and heroes in Shakespeare's tragedies are not usually allowed to pass away without being mourned and remembered.

While the sonnet in its paradoxical way laments the speaker's death, it also recognizes death's inevitability. This theme, too, recurs in Shakespeare's plays. Juliet contemplates her death even on her wedding day (3.2.21). Hamlet refuses to put off his fatal fencing match with Laertes despite misgivings because "If it be now, 'tis not to come; if it be not to come, it will be now; if it be not now, yet it will come— the readiness is all" (5.2.220–222). Cranmer at the end of Henry VIII recognizes that however great Elizabeth will be, "she must die" (5.4.59).

Sonnet 71 may be regarded as yet another attempt to find a stay against this mortality. In the procreation sonnets (1–17) that stay is children. Elsewhere, as in sonnet 18 or 55, art offers permanence. Despite its ostensible request for oblivion, Sonnet 71 in fact belongs with these latter poems, since the beloved will read the speaker's lines after the speaker himself has died. Life is short, but art endures.

**Annotated Bibliography**

Booth, Stephen. *An Essay on Shakespeare's Sonnets.* New Haven: Yale UP, 1969. The book that changed the way we read the sonnets, emphasizing complexities and unresolvable tensions and contradictions in the experience of reading the poems.

———, ed. *Shakespeare's Sonnets.* New Haven: Yale UP, 1977. An indispensable edition that includes a reproduction of the 1609 quarto, amply and ingeniously annotated.

Fineman, Joel. *Shakespeare's Perjured Eye: The Invention of Poetic Subjectivity in the Sonnets.* Berkeley: U of California P, 1986. The most influential book on the sonnets since Booth's *Essay.* Often difficult to read, it studies the sonnets by way of the theme of Shakespeare's poetics of praise, adopting the language and critical tools of poststructuralism and Lacanian psychoanalysis.

Kerrigan, John, ed. *Shakespeare: "The Sonnets" and "A Lover's Complaint."* Harmondsworth, Eng.: Penguin, 1986. A fine edition with useful commentary.

Pequigney, Joseph. "Sonnets 71–74: Texts and Contexts." In *Shakespeare's Sonnets: Critical Essays.* Ed. James Schiffer. New York: Garland, 1999. 285–304. A sound reading of Sonnet 71 and the subsequence to which it belongs. Concludes, however, with a tendentious argument about autobiographical resonances in the sequence.

Schiffer, James, ed. *Shakespeare's Sonnets: Critical Essays.* New York: Garland, 1999. A cornucopia of important readings, including Joseph Pequigney's essay cited above.

# Sonnets 73 and 74

## Nicholas Birns

### Sonnet 73

That time of year thou mayst in me behold
When yellow leaves, or none, or few, do hang
Upon those boughs which shake against the cold,
Bare ruin'd choirs, where late the sweet birds sang.
In me thou see'st the twilight of such day
As after sunset fadeth in the west;
Which by and by black night doth take away,
Death's second self, that seals up all in rest.
In me thou see'st the glowing of such fire,
That on the ashes of his youth doth lie,
As the death-bed whereon it must expire,
Consum'd with that which it was nourish'd by.
   This thou perceiv'st, which makes thy love more strong,
   To love that well which thou must leave ere long.

### PROSE PARAPHRASE

You see that I have grown old, like the year in autumn when the trees are losing their leaves, when the boughs are abandoned by the birds that used to sing upon them but do so no longer. You see that I am at the stage of life where day is ending and passing into twilight and then night. The darkness of night anticipates that of death, which is ultimate night for everybody, eventually taking up and confining all of life. You see that what remains of my life is like glowing fire-coals sitting on top of ashes. These coals will soon burn up and become ash themselves. The ashes smother the fire that, when the ashes were wood, was sustained by them. This same process that has given me life will one day take it. Because you know that I am near death, you love me even more. Because you know that you will lose me, your love for me is even stronger now than it was before.

###  ❈  Sonnet 74

But be contented when that fell arrest
Without all bail shall carry me away,
My life hath in this line some interest,
Which for memorial still with thee shall stay.
When thou reviewest this, thou dost review
The very part was consecrate to thee:
The earth can have but earth, which is his due;
My spirit is thine, the better part of me:
So then thou hast but lost the dregs of life,
The prey of worms, my body being dead;
The coward conquest of a wretch's knife,
Too base of thee to be remembered.
   The worth of that is that which it contains,
   And that is this, and this with thee remains.

## PROSE PARAPHRASE

I will be carried away to death for good, being no longer able to stave it off as a prisoner who posts bail prevents himself from being put in jail. But there will be some consolation for you. When you read this poem, you will read the very aspect of life that I dedicated to your name. My memory will live in your mind, and you will savor my memory especially because I loved you so much. My earthly tomb will only have my body, which is nothing but matter. But you will have my soul, which is my poetry, and that is really the important part of me. All you have given up is a body which, like every other part of matter, ends up decaying and being subject to ignoble degradation. The body is but a container for the soul. Through my poetry the memory of my soul will remain with you after I die.

## THE PLACE OF THE SONNETS IN THE CYCLE

These poems participate in the great theme of the cycle: love and how love endures, if it indeed does. But they have a special slant on this theme. They talk not about the death of the beloved, but that of speaker of the poems, and how the loss of the poet's voice will affect the object of that voice's praise.

The speaker, for once, is not devaluing himself. He is letting his beloved know that there will one day be a time when the speaker no longer exists physically, and that he may well be missed. The tone is both one of warning, of preparatory advice, and of consolation. There is here a kind of immediate tactical purpose—of letting the beloved know that his admirer will not be there forever and, therefore, that this admirer should be appreciated more while he lives. This near-at-hand rhetorical goal coexists with an idealistic sense of the immortality of the soul, assured, among other things, by the material survival of the poetry the soul has produced. By extension, this belief in immortality suggests a belief that love can survive the external limitations earthly life imposes upon it by surviving within what Joseph Pequigney calls a "private vicarious existence" (192). This is a very different kind of immortality than that he suggests to the beloved in the first set of sonnets (1–17). Here, the beloved is advised to seek immortality by siring children and thus perpetuating himself. The implicit sense of self-worth that the speaker exhibits in these two sonnets makes the tone in sonnets such as 87 and 88, when he returns once again to a self-devaluing mode, seem almost exaggerated and/or desperate.

The last two lines of 74 recall the conclusion of Sonnet 18: "So long lives this, and this gives life to thee." Sonnet 18 is preoccupied with the beloved's perpetuating himself through the lover's poetry. Sonnet 74, on the other hand, refers to the poet's perpetuating himself through his own poetry. In both cases, the poetry written by the speaker is the active immediate agent of this perpetuation. This is what Joseph Pequigney (192) calls the poet's "memorializing himself." Both the internal and external aspects of memorial come into play here. In the earlier sonnets, there is a sense of the poet's legacy comparable to the "gilded monuments / Of princes" (55.1–2). But Sonnet 74 offers a more emotional and improvisational sense of memory. This is a sense of how the poet's image will be conjured, after his death, in his friend's heart. If sonnets 1–126 are, on the immediate level, about various maneuvers the lover uses to impress his beloved, those of sonnets 73–74 are atypical. Instead of invoking the poet's constancy and power, these poems forecast his passing and reveal his human weaknesses. We continue here the dynamic described by A. L. Rowse: "the constant contrast between the modest view of himself as a man and the confidence in himself as a poet" (151). In the immediate vicinity of the two sonnets, we see Sonnet 71, in which the poet, as person, cannot evade the fate of dwelling with "vilest worms" (l. 4). Only as poet/lover can he achieve permanence. As Rowse implies, this attitude reverses the terms on which most of sonnets 1–126 are premised.

The bail imagery used in Sonnet 74 is also found in Sonnet 133: "But then my friend's heart let my poor heart bail" (l. 10). The distinction in its employment in the two sonnets is indicative of how particular the quality of the 73/74 diptych is within the cycle. In Sonnet 133 both the poet and his friend are caught by the erotic undertow of the same woman. When the friend is emotionally imprisoned, the speaker offers his own heart as bail to secure his friend's release. In Sonnet 74, on the other hand, bail is missing. Here, though, bail, along with its kindred image of interest, actually stands for continued life. It represents something substantial, an achievable immortality.

Whereas in Sonnet 94 the beloved is likened to those who "have the power to hurt and will do none" (l. 1), here the speaker has the power to hurt—through dying. The specter of his death is one of the few ways the speaker is confident of breaching the emotional imperviousness of his beloved.

Most scholars suppose that Sonnet 75, which begins with the conjunctive "So," continues on from 74. Its guiding metaphor of appetite and consumption, though, does not, on a literal level, depend on the previous two sonnets' images of mourning and memory.

## DEVICES AND TECHNIQUES

Though sonnets 73 and 74 share the same theme, the way they operate rhetorically could not be more different. This is virtually a textbook case of how a common meaning can be expressed though completely different kinds of language. This linguistic difference, in turn, alters the effect if perhaps not the underlying meaning of the two sonnets.

Both poems concern what we lose and gain as we age, concede life, move toward death—both are by a speaker addressing a younger person, informing him about what is happening and what is to come. Sonnet 74 is far less popular than Sonnet 73 because it is less lyrical, and because its register of images is different. The functional diction ("interest," "review") reads more like the financial pages than high poetry, and is plain and down-to-earth. But Shakespeare's triumph in Sonnet 74 lies in conjuring emotion out of this very functionality. What is explicit in Sonnet 73—paradoxically, through gilded metaphor: leaves, sunset, fire—is implicit in the latter, paradoxically, through everyday speech. Shakespeare's mixing of high and low, plain and fancy styles gives his language an extraordinary fluidity even when he is, as here, writing in a fixed lyric form.

The sequence of metaphors in Sonnet 73—autumn, then twilight, then fading coals—are cognate, but not identical, with each other. They express the same sense of beauty's evanescence, and of the way things are somehow most beautiful at the moment at which they are about to fade. But each image becomes more tangible, closer to our own direct experience. The autumnal leaves appeal to us visually, whereas with ashes, even though we see them, their gross palpability easily lends the association with the reality of death that literary language has recognized from time immemorial. The falling of leaves can be seen as something external to us. Besides, we know the leaves will come back the next year. The passing of day bears a more direct resemblance, in miniature, to the diminution of our time alive with every passing year. But there will be a new day tomorrow. With the fading coals, we know that the coals, as such, will never come back. There is no way they will be reconstituted, and so their final orange glow is truly final. It will never be there again. The sense of the reality of death reaches here a physical crescendo that disturbs any sense of insulating detachment the reader may have. Similarly, the time-span of the analogy contracts, from the season of the year to the twilight of the day to the instant of the glow of the fading coal. The effect of the images, in other words, is not just serial. It is cumulative. The three are placed one after another in order to escalate to maximum impact.

The way the rhyme-words are arranged matters to the verbal meaning as well as the metrical structure of the poem. "Hang" and "sang," "fire" and "expire" are particularly effective in that they juxtapose fire and failure, vigor and the lapse of vigor. In both poems "away" is coupled with a word that denotes constancy or presence, "day" in Sonnet 73, "stay" in Sonnet 74. The words rhyme, but they denote diametrically opposite states, thus creating a semantic tension that enriches the poem's language and stance.

The image of trees in autumn is used as a metaphor for human aging and death. But the trees are evoked through figurative language, conjured elliptically rather than with bare directness. The image of the bare ruined choirs not only describes the trees, but is itself an example of a kind of spare beauty amid, and betokening, desolation. The trees, in lacking the full plenitude of summer's warmth, possess the compensation of what the twentieth-century poet Wallace Stevens, in his poem "The Motive for Metaphor," was to call "the half colors of quarter-things" (Wallace Stevens, *The Palm At the End of the Mind* [New York: Vintage, 1972], 240). Because of this doubled image of bittersweet fading, rather than simply see the trees, we feel what it is to be among their forlorn beauty. The evocation of the absent birds, whose singing was once heard, heightens the multi-sensory effect of the early lines. This image also recalls the once gorgeous abbeys and churches that have gone to ruin since the English Reformation.

The images in Sonnet 74 are much less elevated. Their common motif is the economic idea of borrowing and return, of investing money or assets, actions involving a momentary separation of property from oneself that is followed by a several-fold return on what was originally possessed. The theme of the poet's soul being preserved through his own poetry is also expressed in rather functional language: "When thou reviewest this" (74.5), for instance, as compared with "you shall shine more bright in these contents" (55.3). In addition, the immortality of the poetry is ascribed less to the intent of the author, more to its active preservation by the reader—the beloved.

The scansion of the poems is, for the most part, regular. Sometimes, as in Sonnet 74, line 2, "Without all bail shall carry me away," a certain syllable, in this case the latter one of the fourth iamb, does not carry the emphasis that a stressed syllable usually does, although "me" in this strategic position does call attention to the selfhood of the speaker. A similar example appears in the following line, where if the sixth word, "line," were to be given a maximum stress, the result would sound mechanical. (Of course, the very presence of the word "line" within the line of poetry is a self-conscious gesture on the part of the poet.) Also, in this line, "interest" is three syllables, whereas at other points in the sonnets (for example, 31.7) the same word is read as having only two syllables. So sometimes words that are, in theory, stressed are elided by the spoken voice, creating de facto pyrrhic feet (that is, feet in which both syllables are unstressed) between the end and beginning of a given pair of putative iambs. Sometimes stress can affect meaning. "This" and "that" always occupy the stressed half of an iamb to indicate that these ordinary helping words, generally bypassed for stronger nouns or verbs, are here key.

## THEMES AND MEANINGS

The image of "bare ruined choirs" in Sonnet 73 has often been interpreted as a reference to the dissolution of the abbeys by Henry VIII in the 1530s. This measure was part of the expropriation of monastic properties that accompanied the switch from Roman Catholicism, an international Christianity under the supervision of the Pope in Rome, to Anglicanism, a national Christianity under the temporal suzerainty of the English monarch. This interpretation seems convincing. Many commentators have gone further and seen the reference to what A. L. Rowse calls "the roofless shells" of monasteries as indicating that Shakespeare was a closet Roman Catholic, lamenting this change and surreptitiously expressing his Catholic tendencies. This reading is far less persuasive, and is a product more of critical wishful thinking than of actual response to the words on the page. In all his writing, and especially in the sonnets, Shakespeare uses, as examples, images from a variety of registers. The reference to dissolved abbeys means no more that he had a personal stake in them than the reference to bail in the next sonnet means that Shakespeare had been jailed and subsequently been released by posting bond.

The "bare ruined choirs" line, though, does express a spirituality, a tender searching for something beyond the constraining givens of life, that suffuses Sonnet 73. The bare tree is beautiful. It expresses the melancholy of fading, a beauty about to be lost and thus that we love all the more. It also expresses the idea of the trees in leaf. Even though the leaves have fallen and the birds have left, their absence in a way instances their presence more vividly than their presence, in its fullness, would ever have. This sense of a kind of cleansing nothingness extends to the poem's depiction of death itself. The phrase in line 10 of Sonnet 73, "the ashes of his youth," signifies a consciousness of death, not of being at death's door itself, but on the verge of reflective middle age—not unlike Dante's sense of being in the middle of the journey at the beginning of his poetic pilgrimage through the afterlife. There is a sense of spiritual awareness. The poet feels the chill of death's proximity. But he also feels the compensating exhilaration of what survives death: poetry, memory, the soul. Helen Vendler speaks of his "gradual withdrawal from the idealization of his own youth" (Vendler, p. 335). He is cajoling his beloved to regard him with more value. The speaker is trying to console the beloved for the impending loss of his presence. And he is in a way trying to spread the good news of what survives death. Within the frame of the poem's melancholic melody and images of autumnal afterglow, there is a genuine optimism. We glimpse a joy in finding that adversity can make "love more strong" (73.13).

Sonnet 74 uses more worldly metaphors. One can hardly find a more humbling circumstance than being jailed. When the speaker says that he lacks the bail money to extricate himself from death, the prison-metaphor he uses implies that the imprisonment is not for some sort of noble resistance against a flawed order but for an ordinary if not banal crime. When the poet reassures the beloved that "My life hath in this line some interest" (74.3) he is using not only a financial register but a kind of half-joking, bantering tone, as if he is saying, playfully, that he, the poet, should not be counted out, that he has a few trump cards in his pocket which can still be played. One of these cards is the poetry that has been generated by his love and that will preserve and honor that love after the poet himself has died. Stephen Booth also sees this line as suggesting that the beloved will, in legal terms, be the literal heir of the speaker (Booth, p. 261). When the beloved, whether literally or metaphorically, looks over the terms of the speaker's will, he will find his inheritance is greater than he imagined—though this inheritance does not have to do with money, but with memory.

Even when spiritual words such as "consecrate" (74.6) appear, they are used with a kind of mock-epic hyperbole. The consecration has nothing to do with a collective sacredness. It pertains to the private affection of the relationship. Of note here is the intensity with which the body is dismissed. Even though the point is to assert the superiority of the soul, and the poetry the soul produces, to the body, the body's materiality is asserted in so gross and unpalatable a way that the image lingers in the reader's mind despite the poem's manifest dismissal of the embodied. One has only to compare the equally dark but much less gritty address to a personified Death by Juliet's father in *Romeo and Juliet* (4.5.35–40) to see how this sonnet emphasizes the ugly and disturbing side of the physical cessation of human life.

The body is penetrated both by animal scavengers and human weapons; it is not only mutable but vulnerable. The body, because of its tendency to decay, cannot last. But, equally, because of its lack of beauty and its minimal barriers against contagion by the unlovely, it should not last. Sonnet 74 is in several ways less romantic in presentation than its predecessor. But the underlying point is equally romantic in both—that love, as a principle, will survive the corporeal existence of the person who first enunciated that love.

Sonnet 74 powerfully argues for the immortality of the soul and the negligible status of what is embodied—the dismissal of earth is reminiscent of Jesus's words in the Gospel, "Render unto Caesar what is Caesar's, render unto God what is God's," with the implication that what is not God's really does not matter. Also, there is an echo of the Anglican burial service, where the body is conveyed in the final stage of its course from "earth to earth, ashes to ashes, dust to dust." Although more elevated and stately in Sonnet 73, this assertion of how a human being is both mortal and immortal is in a way more abstract in Sonnet 74 precisely, and paradoxically, because of the very common words "this" and "that." These words, both colloquial and indirect, guide the reader's attention away from visible absolutes to invisible pointers that evoke referents that are not directly there.

The poems are addressed by the speaker to his beloved. But they are also about the speaker himself. Though true of all the sonnets, this is especially the case with these two because in these the speaker puts himself into play. His continued existence is not assured; he may and will one day vanish; his presence is not a constant. In talking about his death, he is not only cajoling or admonishing the person whom he is addressing. He is also conceding some of his own authority as a speaker. He is not in control of everything. He will one day die. In fact, in the very eloquence of his own words he tells us of his own certain death—and how his love will survive it. This endurance is confirmed by the fact that the vast majority of those who have read these poems have done so after the death of the man who wrote them. Notwithstanding death, Shakespeare's voice speaks more resonantly to us then ever. This is the point of the poems—that beauty, and our love for it, can outlast death.

## THE RELATIONSHIP OF THE SONNETS TO SHAKESPEARE'S OTHER WORKS

The immediate resonance the reader will notice with respect to Sonnet 73 is Macbeth's speech, "My way of life has fallen into the sere, the yellow leaf" (5.3.23), spoken when the Scottish usurper knows his downfall is imminent. The life situations and characters of the two speakers are different. The sonnet writer is a peaceable, lovelorn poet. Macbeth is a hardened, murderous politician. In an indirect way, this difference illustrates the universality of the golden fading, the beautiful perishing of life the lines evoke. The eighteenth-century critic Samuel Johnson thought the Macbeth metaphor imprecise. Johnson argued that one can hardly picture a "way of life" turning yellow as a concrete image. This imprecision, in what most critics after Johnson have considered a positive fashion, informs the general mood of melancholy that informs both the *Macbeth* and Sonnet 73 lines.

Less literally, Sonnet 73 also, in tone, recalls the endings of two of Shakespeare's great tragedies. In *Hamlet*, the dying Prince urges Horatio to "Absent thee from felicity awhile" (5.2.347) to tell his, Hamlet's, story, to those who remain. The beloved in the sonnet is cast as Horatio to the poet's Hamlet—the one who will recollect him, explain him to posterity. (This stance presents quite a reverse from most of the sequence, where it is the poet immortalizing his beloved.)

The bail imagery of Sonnet 74 is also used in *The Comedy of Errors* (4.1.80), when the Ephesian Antipholus says, "I do obey thee, till I give thee bail," and then, at line 107 of the same scene requests that Adriana be told of his plight and instructed to bring a purse of ducats as that "shall bail me." Adriana then says (5.1.382), "I sent you money, sir, to be your bail." It is found in *Measure for Measure*, where Pompey says, "I hope, sir, your good worship will be my bail" (3.2.73), and Pompey uses the word again ten lines later; in 5.1.352 the Duke says, "Let me bail these gentle three." And in *All's Well That Ends Well* Diana says to the old widow, "Good mother, fetch my bail" (5.3.285).

Bail in these references is used as a literal plot device, one that often offers either the promise or reality of new hope, new developments in characters who had been thought or had thought themselves foredoomed. But it also signifies the idea of keeping afloat, prolonging life, prolonging the drama. These plays were written at different times. They possess very different tones. But they are all dramas about impersonations, mistakes, bungled opportunities. Similarly, Sonnet 74 begins with the vista of a tragic situation, whose futility verges on the absurd and the farcical. There is no way out. But what remains, though it looks paltry and ordinary—like the dregs of interest one gets on an unexciting bank account—can percolate and, correctly tended, bring renewed life. Memory, even the kind of memory not so melodramatic that it is more treasured than simply reviewed, can mean everything. It can mean renewal of the spirit. It can evoke the absent dead. It can transcend death itself. From the poem's understated beginnings comes a more unguardedly affirmative sentiment than anything in the more grandiloquent Sonnet 73.

The image of the body, after death, being eaten by worms is one used again and again by Shakespeare. It is used three other times in the Sonnets ("make worms thine heir," 6.14; "with vilest worms to dwell," 71.3; "worms, inheritors of this excess," 146.7) and in *The Merchant of Venice*, a play concerned, among other things, with hoarding and possession (2.7.69, "Gilded tombs do worms infold"). It is also to be found in history plays such as *Richard III*, 4.4.384–386, where the widowed Queen Elizabeth says to Richard, "And both the Princes . . . / Thy broken faith hath made the prey for worms"; *Richard II* ("Let's talk of graves and worms and epitaphs," 3.2.145); and *1 Henry IV* ("For worms, brave Percy," 5.4.87). In these history plays, there is a particular emphasis on the idea that even those who wield supreme worldly power will end up in the humiliating position of being consumed by worms. This truism is expressed most eloquently in the graveyard scene of *Hamlet* ("This might be my Lord Such-a-one, . . . now my Lady Worm's, chopless, and knocked about the mazzard with a sexton's spade," 5.1.84, 88–90).

The thrust of all these references is multiple. The universality of death is heightened, brought home by the visceral imagery. But there is also a certain satisfaction in seeing arrogant humanity get its comeuppance. The poet, strikingly, extends this satisfaction to himself. The part of him that is selfish, that is merely material, will be ground down with the rest. Yet the part of him that has gained immortality through loving someone and recording that love in poetry will remain, and should remain, alive in the heart of the beloved.

Sonnet 74's forthright stance towards the inevitability of death is notable. The violent and graphic imagery of the knife in line 11 of Sonnet 74 has led some crit-ics to allege that the speaker is contemplating suicide. This is most likely an overly florid reading. It is also an overly literal one. The image could make good sense just as a token of the unwelcome nature of most varieties of death. The speaker's own disgust is not merely at his own impending death. It is occasioned by the body's propensity to suffer such processes. The body is open to its own disintegration.

## Annotated Bibliography

Booth, Stephen. *Shakespeare's Sonnets*. New Haven: Yale UP, 1977. Popular, enduring, meticulous commentary. Sees sonnets 73 and 74 as alluding to the Latin poet Ovid, the biblical book of Job, and the Anglican prayer service.

Duncan-Jones, Katherine, ed. *Shakespeare's Sonnets*. The Arden Shakespeare. London: Thomas Nelson and Sons, 1997. Annotated edition. Independence of judgment is instanced by the opinion that the bareness of the autumnal trees in Sonnet 73 is an allusion to Shakespeare's own baldness!

Fineman, Joel. *Shakespeare's Perjured Eye: The Invention of Poetic Subjectivity in the Sonnets*. Berke-ley: U of California P, 1986. Theoretically dense but rewarding in its demonstration of how mutable and vulnerable the speaker's persona is, how indicative of the splintered self-consciousness of the modern individual. Given the "change of position" of the speaker in sonnets 73 and 74 when compared with most of the rest of the cycle, Fineman's observa-tions very much inform a close reading of the poems.

Giroux, Robert. *The Book Known As Q*. New York: Scribner, 1982. Speculative study of the identity of the addressee of sonnets 1–126 by a famous publisher of modern poetry. At times Giroux neglects the poetry in the midst of historical defective work, but the book generates valu-able insights into the psychology of the two poetic personalities involved.

Hieatt, A. Kent. "The Genesis of Shakespeare's Sonnets: Spenser's *Ruines of Rome*: by Bellay." *PMLA* 98 (October 1983): 800–814. Seminal article that illuminates the connection be-tween the poet's claims in the sonnets for personal and poetic immortality and the his-torical arguments for the endurance of the memory of the Roman Empire as outlined by earlier poets such as Edmund Spenser. Shakespeare transmutes Spenser's claims for Rome into "an image of the exemplary but physically and morally vulnerable beloved, a pattern of antiquity, who inspires the *Sonnets* and thus gains eternity" (802). Hieatt manages to anchor the sonnets' sometimes lofty claims to immortality within a historical and cultural matrix.

Pequigney, Joseph. *Such Is My Love: A Study of Shakespeare's Sonnets*. Chicago: U of Chicago P, 1985. The first thorough look at the homoerotic nature of sonnets 1–126; valuable for the study of sonnets 73 and 74 because of its understanding of the passion of the personal re-lationship represented in the poem.

Rowse, A. L. *Shakespeare's Sonnets*. London: Prometheus, 1984. Short annotations of the sonnets; links them to their hypothesized time of production, such as the time of year in which Shakespeare may have written them.

Vendler, Helen H. *The Art of Shakespeare's Sonnets*. Cambridge, MA: Harvard UP, 1997. Formalistic annotation of all the sonnets; deeply attentive to their linguistic energy. Sees Sonnet 73 as verbally self-conscious and calling attention to "the material and mediating function of verse." Vendler notes the sonnet's resort to "the appeal of mental decline" (335).

Waller, Gary. *English Poetry in the Sixteenth Century*. Essex: Longman, 1986. Places the lyric of the period in a social context. Helpful in understanding the financial images of Sonnet 74. Waller also discusses how the poems participate in the Renaissance desire to "escape the burden of temporality" (234), a dynamic very much visible in Sonnet 73.

# Sonnet 76

### Yashdip S. Bains

Why is my verse so barren of new pride,
So far from variation or quick change?
Why with the time do I not glance aside
To new-found methods and to compounds strange?
Why write I still all one, ever the same,
And keep invention in a noted weed,
That every word doth almost tell my name,
Showing their birth, and where they did proceed?
O! know sweet love, I always write of you,
And you and love are still my argument;
So all my best is dressing old words new,
Spending again what is already spent:
    For as the sun is daily new and old,
    So is my love still telling what is told.

## PROSE PARAPHRASE

In the opening eight lines, or octave, the speaker is asking himself questions about his style. Why is his poetry so conspicuously lacking or deficient in new images? Why can he not write in an ostentatious style or use gaudy and ornamental language? Why can he not make his diction varied and lively? Why is he unable to respond to changes of style quickly and search for newly discovered devices or modes of procedure for writing and look for unusual methods of composition? Why must he always compose in the same monotonous manner without any variation and keep his inventive skills or literary creation under restraint, using only familiar, old-fashioned expressions for his thoughts so that every word betrays and reveals him as the author?

The speaker provides an answer in the sestet. He says to his beloved that he, the author, is always writing about his "sweet love" (76.9), that is, the Fair Youth, and about love. Hence all his best efforts consist in arranging old words in new ways.

He uses his words like old coins that can change hands in repeated transactions. His affection and his expressions of that sentiment are like the sun that appears every day and is both an emblem of monotonous repetition and a harbinger of the new.

## THE PLACE OF THE SONNET IN THE CYCLE

Sonnet 76 is one of the first 126, which deal with the tensions and complexities of a friendship between a young man and an older person. The youth may be imagined as complaining about the monotony of style and a repetition of old-fashioned words and images in the older man's verses. Instead of apologizing for his style as offensive or a failure, Shakespeare defends it by answering that the young man's objections are untenable.

One of the poet's anxieties centers on the difficulty of saying something new in a language that is fashionable and current. Shakespeare had addressed this question famously in Sonnet 18, where he rejects the conventional image of the beloved as a "summer's day" (l. 1). Still, the young man apparently believes that many of Shakespeare's lines are monotonous and dull and will not give eternal life to the subject.

Shakespeare broods over the problem of style and content in many of the sonnets. In Sonnet 38 the poet declares that he cannot lack invention so long as his friend "dost breathe" and provide his "own sweet argument" (ll. 2, 4). Shakespeare comments constantly on his search for suitable images. If there is nothing new to say, can he find something in what has already been written? He cannot find anything worthwhile in old writings because "the wits of former days / To subjects worse have given admiring praise" (59.13–14). The poet's muse has invoked his friend often for assistance because the poet himself is ignorant, and this subject has made his work far better than that of other learned ones who surround the young man (78.13–14): "But thou art all my art, and dost advance / As high as learning my rude ignorance." Rewriting the idea of Sonnet 78, Shakespeare laments the decayed state of his own craftsmanship (79.1–4):

> Whilst I alone did call upon thy aid,
> My verse alone had all thy gentle grace,
> But now my gracious numbers are decay'd,
> And my sick Muse doth give another place.

But this is no reason to praise the rival poet because "what he owes thee, thou thyself dost pay" (79.14).

Shakespeare complains about his Muse repeatedly. Sometimes she is just forgetful (100.1–2). At other times she is truant, neglectful, and silent (101.1–9). The Muse is impoverished and misses the chance "to show her pride" (103.1–4):

> Alack, what poverty my Muse brings forth,
> That having such a scope to show her pride,
> The argument all bare is of more worth
> Than when it hath my added praise beside.

Shakespeare asks in Sonnet 108: "What's new to speak, what now to register, / That may express my love, or thy dear merit?" (ll. 3–4). This awareness of problems of invention and the fear of monotony and dullness appears frequently in the sonnets; Shakespeare overcomes it again and again by assuring his friend that, as he concludes in Sonnet 76, he is always expressing his love for the Fair Youth.

Sonnet 76 also belongs to a group dealing with the rival poet. Sonnets 76, 78, 79, 80, and 82–86 are generally assigned to the group. It is difficult to identify this rival with any certainty. Among the candidates are Christopher Marlowe, George Chapman, and Ben Jonson, important contemporaries of Shakespeare. Shakespeare wonders whether his competitor is seeking "the prize of all-too-precious you," that is, the Fair Youth (86.2). Nobody can say whether Shakespeare was too conscious of his own limitations as a poet on account of his limited schooling when he writes or whether he is losing in the competition because the other poet is "of tall building and of goodly pride" (80.12).

## DEVICES AND TECHNIQUES

Sonnet 76 is written in the standard Shakespearean form of three quatrains and a couplet (rhymed abab cdcd efef gg). But it follows the Petrarchan or Italian arrangement of octave and sestet in its presentation of its argument. In the octave, Shakespeare summarizes the questions the young man has raised about his monotonous and dull style that is "so barren of new pride" (76.1). The octave consists of three questions of self-scrutiny, beginning with "Why"? Through the repetition of why, the speaker is questioning his own inadequacies. He is challenging himself to account for his failure to match the stylistic expectations of his young friend. The "I" here is self-effacing, skeptical, and timid about his capabilities. The repetition of "Why" serves as confirmation of the poet's inability to express himself in new ways.

There is a distinct transition at line 9 from the octave to the sestet. The sestet offers a defense of the poet's craftsmanship. In line 9, Shakespeare changes his tone with the opening "O know, sweet love," from questioning to an assertion regarding his style. He reveals a logical link between the daily appearance of the sun and his use of words. The sun is "daily new and old" (76.13). Similarly, Shakespeare's "love" is "still telling what is told" (76.14). Shakespeare's style is always new and always old; what is told is old, but his telling is new. His style is "monotonous," because it reflects the "monotony" of his faithfulness and devotion to his young friend.

Through his repetition of certain words, Shakespeare stresses the basis of his self-defense. The word "new" appears in lines 1, 4, 11, 13; "old" in 11, 13; "tell," "telling," and "told" in 7, 14; "love" in 9, 10, 14; "still" in 5, 10, 14; and "so" in 1, 2, 11, 14. Instead of being unvaried and monotonous, Shakespeare is redefining "new" and "old" in each context so that by the end of the sonnet the young friend's "new" loses its force and new and old become examples of "new pride" instead of being barren. The same old words keep taking on new significance. Variation and quick change become superfluous because to vary and change would signify infidelity. Hence it is crucial that every word should announce the author of the lines about "you and love" (76.10).

Shakespeare employs the imagery of dress, parent-child relations, spending, and the rising and setting sun to underline the gravity of his intent. He reflects ironically on the relationship of content to form by pointing to his inability to produce a fashionable piece of clothing for his vain friend. His comparison exposes the limitations of his range as a poet, but it also enables him to belittle his friend's demands. What could be more mundane than asking for something ostentatious and gaudy? Shakespeare also presents himself as a parent who has been unable to give birth to a worthy child. This classical image appealed especially to Renaissance poets, who use it frequently. Shakespeare is hardly happy about his issue, but he turns things around and blames the problem on his friend. The idea of words as money and spending and counting the same treasure again and again turns also into a sexual pun. To spend is to have sexual intercourse, which can be enjoyed repeatedly like the spending of money. Sex does not lose its vigor, just as words and coins do not lose their value in transactions. The sun renews itself afresh as a promise of the new and sets daily to signify the old. As Booth explains in his edition of *Shakespeare's Sonnets* (1977), the sun simile "is also a potential emblem of glorious and eternally Phoenix-like rejuvenation" (265–266). The poet's love possesses a similar contradictory quality in that it is always new and always old. Through these images Shakespeare transforms the old into new and renders redundant the distinction between the old and the new.

## THEMES AND MEANINGS

Shakespeare explores the nature of style and the limitations and constraints of language through his preoccupation with his young friend's supposed criticism and his reply in self-defense. Can language be detached from the poet's argument? The words in the language are old but cannot be dismissed as stale and worn-out. Helen Vendler sums up Shakespeare's theme: "The extreme simplicity of Shakespeare's defense of *style* as the *true* measure of novelty marks his refusal to concede to the young man's standard of ever-changing fashionable elaboration as the *stylistic* test of literary value (he has already refused the young man's standard of variety of subject as the *thematic* test of value)" (*The Art of Shakespeare's Sonnets* [Cambridge, MA: Harvard UP, 1997], 345). Vocabulary in a language is "still all one, ever the same" (76.5). The young man's fondness for "new-found methods" and "compounds strange" (76.4) reveals his shallow and superficial values in matters of linguistic skills. He does not comprehend the nature of language.

Shakespeare establishes a clear link between "still my argument" (76.10) and "dressing old words new" (76.11). His style would change only if his topic were to change. Hence style and subject matter are inseparable for the poet. Style cannot be isolated as an ornament that can be added to a subject to make it attractive to others. The demand for "new pride" is shallow and misleading. It does not show a real grasp of the problems of writing. Sonnets cannot be constantly revised and updated to conform to the young friend's desire for the fashionable. Constancy in style speaks for the poet's constancy in love.

Shakespeare is alerting his young friend to the fact that the latter's taste is so superficial that it cannot become the basis of a rich and complex expression of genuine sentiment and feeling in poetry. The Fair Youth is rejecting the stale conventions and old rhetorical devices. Shakespeare is mocking his Elizabethan and continental predecessors like Petrarch and Sydney, who dressed their sonnets in a distinctive and recognizable style or "noted weed" (76.6). But his own writing excels because it is part of a dialogue with a friend and is conditioned by the terms of an exchange between lovers.

The poet is also exploring whether or not it is better to seek change because constancy in love is incompatible with the stylistic practice of seeking "variation or quick change" (76.2) and ostentatious images. He loves "not less, though less the show appear" (102.2). His poetry is "to constancy confin'd" (105.7). Shakespeare's verse constitutes his signature. His genuine style will develop out of his loyalty to his love. He rejects the expectation that his work should alter with fashion and offer praise in a constantly varying manner. While this sonnet is largely about style, it also confirms the consistency of the poet's love. It thereby serves as a critique of the fair youth's affections, which, as the "rival poet" sonnets demonstrate, is less steadfast.

## THE RELATIONSHIP OF THE SONNET TO SHAKESPEARE'S OTHER WORKS

The young friend's challenge to Shakespeare was to produce something that would appeal to shallow and superficial minds. Shakespeare ridiculed this kind of writing constantly in the plays. Orlando's compositions for Rosalind in *As You Like It* and Hamlet's for Ophelia provide examples of such fashionable (and silly) compositions. In one of Shakespeare's early plays, *The Two Gentlemen of Verona*, Proteus gives this advice to Thurio, who is wooing Silvia in vain and is desperately looking for help:

> You must lay lime to tangle her desires
> By wailful sonnets, whose composed rhymes
> Should be full-fraught with serviceable vows. (3.2.68–70)

Shakespeare is describing what many lovers in his comedies do and get ridiculed for their feeble attempts at writing. The lovers in *Love's Labor's Lost* and *Much Ado about Nothing* compose sonnets when they are falling in love. To some, it is a sign of weakness to possess and read books of sonnets. Master Slender in *The Merry Wives of Windsor* would trust a collection of sonnets for success in love: "I had rather than forty shillings I had my Book of Songs and Sonnets here" (1.1.197–198). Shakespeare is mocking the sonnet vogue the same way he could mock theatricals in plays like *A Midsummer Night's Dream*. That is, he is making fun of bad sonnets and bad plays.

### Annotated Bibliography

Booth, Stephen. *An Essay on Shakespeare's Sonnets.* New Haven: Yale UP, 1969. A reading of the entire sequence and individual sonnets, with stress on the "multitude of different coexistent and conflicting patterns—formal, logical, ideological, syntactic, rhythmic, and phonetic" (ix).

———, ed. *Shakespeare's Sonnets.* New Haven: Yale UP, 1977. In his conservatively modernized text of the 1609 edition, Booth seeks to provide what "a Renaissance reader would have thought as he moved from line to line and sonnet to sonnet" (ix). Full commentary on the richness of language and shades of meaning.

Burrow, Colin, ed. *The Complete Sonnets and Poems.* The Oxford Shakespeare. Oxford: Oxford UP, 2002. Discusses date of composition, order of the sonnets, and structural influences.

Argues that the sonnets present various themes and thoughts rather than a systematic sequence about specific relationships.

Dubrow, Heather. "'Conceit Deceitful': The Sonnets." In *Captive Victors: Shakespeare's Narrative Poems and Sonnets.* Ithaca: Cornell UP, 1987. 169–275. Shakespeare's sonnets are more subtle in their use of narrative and dramatic techniques than those of other Renaissance poets.

Duncan-Jones, Katherine, ed. *Shakespeare's Sonnets.* The Arden Shakespeare. London: Thomas Nelson and Sons, 1997. A modernized text of the sonnets, with detailed notes and commentary; a full introduction to historical, intellectual, and cultural contexts of the sonnets, with a review of critical approaches.

# Sonnet 87

## Barry B. Adams

Farewell! thou art too dear for my possessing,
And like enough thou know'st thy estimate,
The charter of thy worth gives thee releasing;
My bonds in thee are all determinate.
For how do I hold thee but by thy granting?
And for that riches where is my deserving?
The cause of this fair gift in me is wanting,
And so my patent back again is swerving.
Thy self thou gav'st, thy own worth then not knowing,
Or me to whom thou gav'st it else mistaking;
So thy great gift, upon misprision growing,
Comes home again, on better judgement making.
   Thus have I had thee, as a dream doth flatter,
   In sleep a king, but waking no such matter.

### PROSE PARAPHRASE

Sonnet 87 is addressed to the speaker's friend, who has apparently announced his intention to end their relationship. In bidding this friend "farewell," the speaker professes to be resigned to his new state of affairs and proceeds to analyze why the separation, though regrettable, is at least understandable. The explanation he offers is that the friend was (and still is) in some undefined way superior to the speaker and had entered into their relationship without fully realizing the speaker's un-worthiness. The speaker now ruefully reflects that the happy period during which their relationship flourished was fundamentally unreal, like a dream.

### THE PLACE OF THE SONNET IN THE CYCLE

Sonnet 87 marks a significant turning point in the story of a personal relation-ship. To use this sonnet to interpret the one immediately preceding adds an intriguing element but not enough light to clarify the relationship between the speaker, the addressee, and the "rival poet" who is the principal subject of Sonnet 86 and who is referred to more or less explicitly in the eight preceding sonnets. That poet, who has never been satisfactorily identified, is not simply a professional rival but one who is competing for the affections of the "dear friend" being addressed in both of these sonnets as well as the person addressed elsewhere in the cycle as "dear friend" or "fair friend." Reading forward in the cycle from Sonnet 87, it is possible to trace a narrative thread up through Sonnet 95. All of these sonnets involve direct address to the same person mixed with criticism of this person for leaving the speaker. The basic situation is the same even though the speaker's outlook or attitude changes. Construed somewhat more broadly, as an account of the separation of two friends rather than an abandonment or rejection of one by the other, the narrative may be seen to extend to Sonnet 99. Even Sonnet 94, which unlike all the others in this sequence is not cast in the form of direct address, contributes to the theme. Readers seeking ordinary narrative satisfaction, however, will be disappointed, for there is no clear or definite conclusion to the story of rejection or separation. The cycle continues to Sonnet 126 with additional poems to or about the friend in which artistic unity or coherence is achieved by means of thematic rather than narrative means.

## DEVICES AND TECHNIQUES

As is usual in Shakespeare's sonnets, the rhyme scheme of Sonnet 87 divides the poem into three quatrains and a couplet. What is unusual in this sonnet is the prevalence of what are known as "feminine" rhymes, in which the repeated vowel sound that is an essential feature of all rhyme occurs in the next-to-last syllable of the line, with this syllable rather than the final one carrying metrical stress. A feminine rhyme may be triple (for example, *comparison* : *garrison*), the rhyming vowel being followed by two unstressed syllables instead of just one. Whereas a triple feminine rhyme usually has a comic effect, double rhymes typically project a sense of poetic skill and virtuosity without being humorous. Both artificiality and virtuosity are intensified when the double rhyming is multiplied, as it is in Sonnet 20 (the only other sonnet by Shakespeare to make extensive use of this device) and in Sonnet 87. Sonnet 20 displays a bawdy humor entirely absent from Sonnet 87. In his edition of the *Sonnets* (New York: Harper & Row, 1964), A. L. Rowse says that feminine rhymes by their very nature contribute a sense of melancholy to a poem. This is by no means a widely accepted belief, though it agrees well with Helen Vendler's contention that the feminine rhymes of Sonnet 87 express the speaker's reluctance to let his friend go: the line lingers an extra syllable before it ends.

In Sonnet 87, the final syllable in all but two of the rhyming pairs is the same: the enclitic *-ing*. The first four rhyming *-ing* words are gerunds and the remaining six are participles. In addition to these rhyming *-ing* words there is the participle "waking" in the middle of line 14, which may deliberately echo the words "a king" earlier in the same line.

Aside from its unusual reliance on feminine rhymes, the external form of Sonnet 87 is the conventional Shakespearean one of three clearly marked quatrains followed by a couplet. This is the form first introduced into English by the Earl of Surrey in the early years of the sixteenth century and commonly designated the English or Shakespearean sonnet form as opposed to the Italian or Petrarchan, which follows a two-part design of octave and sestet. Yet like many of Shakespeare's sonnets, Sonnet 87 contains vestigial traces of the Italian form. For example, the second quatrain, introduced by the function word "For," is closely tied to the first by supplying its logical support and thereby creating what amounts to a unified octave. The third quatrain, beginning "Thyself thou gav'st," represents a fresh start as the speaker speculates on the possible reasons for the friend's behavior. For someone familiar with the Italian sonnet form, this fresh start would signal the beginning of the sestet. But the poem's conclusion, the summarizing couplet introduced by the narrative and logical pointer "Thus," frustrates this expectation and brings the poem closer to the norm for the English sonnet.

Although Sonnet 87 is part of what may easily pass as a brief narrative sequence about the speaker's separation from his friend, considered in itself it is more like a playlet than a short story. The poem creates the impression of a speech delivered to a single person in a specific situation. In this it differs from the other poems in the sequence that begins with Sonnet 86. Although all but one of these, Sonnet 94, have an explicit addressee (the second-person pronoun "thou" or "you"), which by itself creates a sense of the dramatic, only Sonnet 87 gives the impression of the speaker actually addressing that person at a definite time and in a particular place. This effect is achieved in part by the consistent use through the first two quatrains of present-tense verbs tied to a sense of time rather than to an atemporal universality, as in the proverbial present of the last line of Sonnet 94, "Lilies that fester smell far worse than weeds." Such general sentiment is designed to promote acceptance of or reflection on an abstract truth, not to construct in imagination a situation in which individuals are engaged in an exchange of words.

The poem's diction draws heavily on language that straddles legal and more general registers of discourse. Words like "charter," "bonds," "patent," and "misprision" have an obvious legal flavor, which colors more neutral words like "possessing," "releasing," "granting," and even "judgment," playing on their latent legalistic senses. The underlying idea of commercial exchange backed by the force of law is implicitly set over against the notion of something offered freely and without legal obligation, a notion echoed in the poem's surprising number of *give* words: "gives" in line 3, "gift" in lines 7 and 11, and "gav'st" in lines 9 and 10. The tension between free gift and legal obligation constitutes the poem's thematic axis.

While such word choice is certainly skillful and thematically effective, it is not notable for its poetic or rhetorical embellishment. The words are not colorful, nor (with the possible exception of the concluding couplet) do they provoke strong or memorable mental images. Most of them are either commonplace words with no discernible poetic status or else hard-edged abstract terms that seem almost antipoetic. The last line of the second quatrain actually links these two sorts of words in an illuminating way. The legalistic "patent" (that is, the speaker's legal right to retain possession of his friend's affections) is said to be "swerving"—or more precisely, swerving "back again" (87.8), which is to say that it has been rescinded or retracted by the agent, that is, the friend, who initially granted that right. The conjunction of abstract words like "patent" with concrete words like "swerving" is common throughout these sonnets. Such conjunction tempts a reader to construct more or less vivid mental pictures, as when the speaker of this sonnet says that his "great gift . . . / Comes home again," but the intervening phrase "upon misprision

growing" as well as the appended one "on better judgment making" will be difficult if not impossible to incorporate into whatever picture he or she may begin to
conjure up (87.11–12).

Still, the general sense of the passage is reasonably clear. It is in essence a reiteration of the statement about the swerving patent or the rescinded right. The second element of the phrase "Comes home" suggests an animate being, perhaps a
farm animal, returning to its usual abode after feeding on "misprision." It is this
last word, abstract and legalistic, that first defeats any attempt at imaging. The concluding phrase, "on better judgment making," partly because its syntactical ties to
the rest of the sentence are so loose, adds to that sense of defeat. An extended paraphrase would run as follows: So is it that your gift of yourself to me, which was
based on and for a time nourished by your misunderstanding of who or what I was,
returns as if of its own accord (a natural enough expression if the friend is thought
of not just as the gift but also as the one who granted the gift), after you, the gift-
giver, have given more thought to the gift and especially the recipient.

## THEMES AND MEANINGS

The thematic center of gravity of Sonnet 87 is the speaker's sense of his own un-
worthiness, the grounds of which are never stated but only taken for granted. It is
not clear if this unworthiness is a matter of social standing or something more innate, such as intelligence or taste. Such self-criticism reappears in Sonnet 88, but
there it is subjected to a witty examination leading to the ingenious conclusion that
the speaker's failings are in reality proof of his friend's worthiness as well as his own.
This ingenuity may lead us to question the sincerity of the basic feelings being expressed. Sonnet 72 projects a less clever and hence more sincere sense of unworthiness. It is also more focused. The speaker there is distressed by the quality of his
own verses. As he puts it in the concluding couplet, "For I am sham'd by that which
I bring forth, / And so should you, to love things nothing worth." Since the subject
of the verses is the one addressed ("you," presumably the "dear friend" or "fair
friend"), such criticism amounts to indirect praise of the addressee as well as appreciation of him for valuing the speaker's poetic efforts as little as he does.

## THE RELATIONSHIP OF THE SONNET TO
## SHAKESPEARE'S OTHER WORKS

In his exchange with Ophelia that follows directly on his "To be or not to be"
soliloquy, Hamlet claims to be "very proud, revengeful, ambitious, with more offenses at my beck than I have thoughts to put them in, imagination to give them
shape, or time to act them in" (*Hamlet*, 3.1.123–126). Like Malcolm's confession to
Macduff (*Macbeth*, 4.3.50–100), this claim should not be taken uncritically as the
speaker's sincere and literal statement of fact, but it does express, admittedly in an
extreme fashion, a sense of unexplained and unjustified unworthiness akin to that
of the speaker of Sonnet 87. Hamlet's earlier soliloquy in which he accuses himself
of being "a rogue and peasant slave" (2.2.550ff) is more realistically motivated and
less extravagant than this one, being grounded as it is on his inability to act upon
the obligation imposed by the ghost of his father, but even his milder self-criticism
is much more intense than that of the speaker of Sonnet 87. In fact, that speaker

may be said to express a sense of personal inadequacy rather than anything more serious. A comparable sense of inadequacy is noticeable in Viola, the heroine of Shakespeare's *Twelfth Night*. Unlike such Shakespearean heroines as Portia from *The Merchant of Venice* or Rosalind from *As You Like It*, Viola is essentially passive, allowing herself to be used by Count Orsino and even at one point humiliated by Sir Toby Belch. The issues are treated for the most part lightheartedly, but the resigned quality of Viola's behavior throughout is not unlike what we detect in the voice of the speaker of Sonnet 87.

The speaker's sense of his own inadequacy excludes resentment at his friend's behavior. This has led one critic to characterize his feelings as a "possessionless love" comparable to that ordinarily associated with religious commitment (Leishman, p. 229). That inadequacy is also devoid of self-pity, another sentiment that would arise naturally from the situation as described in this sonnet. By way of contrast, we may consider the title character of Shakespeare's *Richard II* as he contemplates his defeat at the hands of his rival Bullingbrook and his followers. In some of his most lyrical poetry, Shakespeare has the defeated king explicitly reject the consolation offered by his friends:

> of comfort no man speak:
> Let's talk of graves, of worms, and epitaphs,
> Make dust our paper, and with rainy eyes
> Write sorrow on the bosom of the earth. (3.2.144–147)

Richard's extended aria continues uninterrupted for another thirty lines. The same attitude emerges in the last two acts of the play, when Richard is brought before his supplanter (4.1.161ff) and later when in prison (5.5.1ff). Shakespeare's presentation of competing emotions in these scenes is complex, but they all include a large dose of self-indulgence entirely foreign to the speaker of Sonnet 87.

**Annotated Bibliography**

Hecht, Anthony. Introduction. In *William Shakespeare, The Sonnets*. Ed. G. Blakemore Evans. The New Cambridge Shakespeare. Cambridge: Cambridge UP, 1996. Contains an extended interpretation of Sonnet 87 along with a sensitive appreciation of the entire cycle with particular attention to poetic meter.

Leishman, J. B. *Themes and Variations in Shakespeare's Sonnets*. London: Hutchinson, 1961. Includes a useful treatment of the theme of "compensation" as it applies to the "dear friend."

Mahood, M. M. *Shakespeare's Wordplay*. London: Methuen, 1957. Chapter on the sonnets analyzes Sonnet 87 to show an irony that aligns it closely with Sonnet 88.

Vendler, Helen. *The Art of Shakespeare's Sonnets*. Cambridge, MA: Harvard UP, 1997. A stimulating, microscopic analysis of each of the sonnets, attending to poetic technique more than thematic significance.

# Sonnet 91

Jeremy Lopez

Some glory in their birth, some in their skill,
Some in their wealth, some in their body's force,
Some in their garments though new-fangled ill;
Some in their hawks and hounds, some in their horse;
And every humour hath his adjunct pleasure,
Wherein it finds a joy above the rest:
But these particulars are not my measure,
All these I better in one general best.
Thy love is better than high birth to me,
Richer than wealth, prouder than garments' cost,
Of more delight than hawks and horses be;
And having thee, of all men's pride I boast:
 Wretched in this alone, that thou mayst take
 All this away, and me most wretched make.

## PROSE PARAPHRASE

Some are proud of having been born noble, some are proud of their own cleverness; some are proud of their wealth, some are proud of their strength; some are proud of their clothes, even though those clothes, however fashionable they may be, are ugly; some are proud of their hunting animals, some are proud of their horses; and each individual temperament has a corresponding pleasure, in which it finds more joy than in any other. But pride in such particular things is not the standard by which I judge happiness; I have something that makes me more happy, and in fact encompasses the happiness provided by all these other things. Your love is better than noble birth to me, makes me feel richer than money can, and more attractive than the nicest clothes; your love is of more delight to me than any hunting animals and, in that I have you, I can boast that I have something equivalent to everything else that makes all other men proud. I am miserable in only one way: I know that you have the power to take all this away, to leave me, and make me miserable.

## THE PLACE OF THE SONNET IN THE CYCLE

By position, Sonnet 91 seems to belong to the group that addresses the young man (sonnets 1–126). It is, however, strangely detached from the tone and subject matter of those poems immediately on either side of it. Sonnets 87–90 and 92–93 are very concerned with the potential that the beloved might leave the speaker—a concern that is expressed only in the final couplet of this sonnet. Sonnet 91 begins by discussing something very general (the kinds of things that different kinds of men like) in order to draw a comparison between the speaker and everyone else in the world (the speaker is much happier). The speaker does not directly address the beloved until line 9 ("Thy love . . ."), and the focus of the poem has been so general up to this point that the expression of love seems very general as well. That is, this seems like a love poem that any poet could write to any person—a conventional poem that expresses the insignificance of all other things in comparison to love itself. By contrast, sonnets 87–90 and 92–93 all begin by addressing the beloved directly, and all seem to represent one half of a conversation already in progress: "Then hate me when thou wilt, if ever, now" (90.1); "But do thy worst to steal thyself away" (92.1). Whereas sonnets 87–90 and 92–93 represent a very particular vexed relationship apparently in the midst of a crisis, Sonnet 91 is cheerfully conventional about the glories of the beloved, and might be thought to bring up the potential misery of love in its final couplet only to suggest that this potential is not very real.

## DEVICES AND TECHNIQUES

The poem is symmetrical, and this is a large part of why it seems cheerful and conventional in spite of its final couplet. The first four lines, or quatrain, of the poem list "birth," "skill," "wealth," "garments," "hawks," and "horses" as things one might be proud of; the last quatrain before the couplet (lines 9–12) reintroduces each of these things only to point out that they are not as good as the love the speaker is shown by his beloved. In the first quatrain's list, the use of anaphora (repetition of the first word of consecutive lines, here "Some") allows the speaker to achieve a comprehensive tone: he sounds as though he is talking about all the different kinds of people one might be able to think of. He also sounds as though he is talking about all the different kinds of pride or happiness one might have. This comprehensive feeling makes the poem's turn—the point at which the argument goes in a new direction—particularly emphatic: line 7, "But these particulars are not my measure," announces that we have not really considered all the things that might make one happy.

Sonnets can typically be divided into two parts: the first eight lines constitute the octave and the final six lines constitute the sestet. Typically, the direction of the sonnet changes after the octave: the ninth line is usually referred to as the turn. The position of the turn in Sonnet 91 is interesting because it is early: it comes in line 7 ("But these particulars") rather than in line 9. The somewhat irregular position of the turn has two possible effects. One is to increase the poem's symmetrical feeling: line 7 is the 14-line poem's midpoint, and after the contrasting idea it intro-duces the poem will go on to repeat the terms of its first half. The second effect of the early turn is possibly to suggest the speaker's eagerness to expostulate on the joys of his beloved: having run through as many different types of people and hap-piness as he can think of, he hurtles forward into his counter-examples.

Sonnet 91 is structured around two particularly important puns. The first is a pun on the word "better." In line 8 the speaker uses this word as a verb meaning "to get the better of" or "to outdo." The reason the speaker is able to "better" the happiness of all other men is that his love is better than everything that makes other men happy. The speaker uses "better" in this latter sense, as an adjective, in line 9. The second pun is less explicit and has to do with the words "Some" and "all." On the most obvious level, these words are contrasted by the speaker throughout the poem: while some men experience some pleasures, the speaker has something bet-ter than all the pleasures of all men. More subtly, "some" puns with the word "sum," and "all" and "some" pun with the common phrase "all and sum," mean-ing totality. We can paraphrase line 12, "And having thee, of all men's pride I boast" to understand more clearly the work of the pun: this line can be said to mean "And having thee, I can boast of having something greater than the sum of all men's pride."

## THEMES AND MEANINGS

Sonnet 91 makes a conventional statement about the value of love to the exclu-sion of all other things, and in particular, material things. Most of the items that give men pride listed in the first four lines of this poem suggest wealth and status. While the explicit, general meaning of this poem is "I am happier with your love than I could be with anything else," a more specific, underlying meaning seems to be, "Even though I am not rich and powerful, I am happy because I have your love." In the second half of the poem, the speaker repeats only the most material of the items he listed in the first half. He leaves out "skill" (line 1) and "body's force" (line 2). In these omissions we might see a certain preoccupation with material things on the speaker's part. That is, we might think of the poem's symmetry as repeti-tive—as an expression of the way the speaker is trying to convince himself that, as long as he has love, he does not need anything else.

The poem's apparent cheerfulness is potentially undercut again in its final cou-plet. On one hand this couplet is also quite conventional: it is typical of a love poem in which the speaker acknowledges the power of his beloved, and hopes aloud that the beloved will not desert him. To this extent, it does not make the poem seem much less joyous than it is. On the other hand, the suddenness with which the cou-plet's contrasting voice erupts makes that contrasting voice rather emphatic. "Wretched," a word whose first syllable is stressed (that is, a trochee), breaks abruptly into the regular iambic rhythm (alternating unstressed syllables followed by stressed syllables) of the previous two lines. "Wretched" echoes, in sound as well as meter, the word "Richer" in line 10, and the echo suggests an explicit contrast between two very different states of mind. The word "wretched" was (and is) fre-quently used as a synonym for impoverished, and in the way the final two lines sep-arate themselves from the rest of this sonnet, the speaker suggests that everything he has said up to this point is a mere fantasy. The visions of wealth and status his beloved allows him to entertain are revealed to be nothing more than visions, and the poem ends with a statement of self-abasement rather than confident love.

The insecurities of the speaker in Sonnet 91 are not really at the surface level: they are revealed only upon an interrogation of the poem's insistent, conventional cheerfulness. Insofar as the poem represents an insecure speaker trying to convince himself not only that he is truly rich, but also that he is truly beloved, it is similar to the anxious, self-contradictory, and self-abasing voice of many of the other sonnets. In Sonnet 91 the speaker suggests first that he has nothing, and second that everything he does have can be taken away from him by his beloved. These suggestions are made under a veneer of joy, where the speaker claims himself to be the luckiest man alive. An even less pleasant version of this occurs only two poems previously, in Sonnet 89, where the speaker insists that his beloved cannot "disgrace me half so ill, / . . . / As I'll myself disgrace, knowing thy will" (89.5–7). As in Sonnet 35, where the speaker finds himself an "advocate" against himself, justifying his beloved's bad behavior, so in Sonnet 89 he promises to "vow debate" (89.13) against himself, loving himself only if his beloved does not hate him. This literal self-contradiction is expressed in the form of Sonnet 91, where the couplet contradicts everything said in the first twelve lines. And we see another version of this double vision, now addressed to the Dark Lady, in Sonnet 147, where the speaker regrets that he has "sworn thee fair, and thought thee bright, / Who art as black as hell, as dark as night" (147.13–14).

## THE RELATIONSHIP OF THE SONNET TO SHAKESPEARE'S OTHER WORKS

The simultaneously confident and insecure voice of the lover in this poem is reminiscent of Othello who, even in his most vehement statements of affection for Desdemona, sows the seeds of his own jealousy. "Excellent wretch!" he says of her after she has tried to convince him to take Cassio back into his favor. "Perdition catch my soul / But I do love thee! and when I love thee not, / Chaos is come again" (3.3. 90–92). Not even 200 lines later, chaos has come again, and Othello is virtually convinced of his wife's infidelity. At this point, Othello lists a variety of reasons that Desdemona might leave him, denies that these reasons are plausible, and, finally, accepts their plausibility: "Haply, for I am black, / And have not those soft parts of conversation / That chamberers [those who spend their time in ladies' chambers; gallants] have, or for I am declin'd / Into the vale of years (yet that's not much), / She's gone" (3.3. 263–267). The vacillation between uncertainty and conviction, as well as the fear of the beloved's power that it implies, is very similar to the structure of Sonnet 91.

Othello, like the speaker in Sonnet 91, also frequently imagines himself as someone who has nothing—he is not eloquent, not a scholar, not officially part of Venetian society, not the type (or color) of man Venetian girls would normally marry—but also as someone who has everything because he has love. Othello, like the speaker in Sonnet 91, deludes himself in two ways: sometimes he imagines that he is happier than he is, and sometimes he imagines that he is less happy than he is.

The self-tormented state of mind that comes about from having the thing one wants, and feeling that one does not deserve or cannot hold onto it is a recurrent subject of Shakespeare's plays. As soon as Hamlet has confirmation of the thing he

most desires to know, that his father was killed by Claudius, the necessity for action drives him to self-doubt and delay, premised in part upon the possibility that
"The spirit [of old Hamlet] that I have seen / May be a dev'l, and the dev'l . . . /
Abuses me to damn me" (*Hamlet*, 2.2. 598–603). In *The Winter's Tale*, Leontes fab-
ricates a belief in his wife's infidelity out of thin air and works with terrifying single-
mindedness to destroy his happy marriage, only to recognize and regret, too late,
that he has erred.

Leontes is fortunate: the sixteen years that pass between the third and fourth acts
of *The Winter's Tale* give him the chance to be forgiven by and reunited with the
woman whom he knows he should have trusted all along. Shakespeare is usually
less optimistic in his view of the processes, internal and external, that take away
from us the things we actually want. The four lovers in *A Midsummer Night's Dream*
treat each other terribly and with hyperbolic affection by turns, subject to the forces
of a magical flower that they know nothing about. There is no convincing way to
argue that at the end of this play any one lover gets what he or she really wants.
The plot of *Romeo and Juliet* is an extended version of the conventional statement
Sonnet 91 makes about the triumph of love over everything; and as with the plot
of *Romeo and Juliet*, Sonnet 91 ends considerably less happily than we might hope
it will.

**Annotated Bibliography**

Booth, Stephen. *An Essay on Shakespeare's Sonnets*. New Haven: Yale UP, 1969. A detailed critical
        examination of the sonnets, both as a sequence and as individual poems. Booth argues
        that the sonnets always provide a reader with the "comfort and security of a frame of ref-
        erence, but the frames of reference are not constant, and their number seems limitless"
        (187).
———, ed. *Shakespeare's Sonnets*. New Haven: Yale UP, 1977. A useful edition with parallel mod-
        ern and early modern (1609) texts and with excellent commentary on each sonnet. These
        annotations range from explanatory glosses to full-length critical essays.
Fineman, Joel. *Shakespeare's Perjured Eye: The Invention of Poetic Subjectivity in the Sonnets*. Berke-
        ley: U of California P, 1986. A compelling and provocative study. Argues that the sonnets
        shift between poetry that idealizes and praises a beloved and poetry that focuses atten-
        tion on the writer's problematic desire, revealing fissures and paradox within the narra-
        tive voice and, effectively, a different and more complex sense of selfs.
Spiller, Michael R. G. *The Development of the Sonnet*. London: Routledge, 1992. A clear discussion
        of the history of the sonnet from its thirteenth-century origins in Italy through the son-
        nets of Milton in the seventeenth century. The focus is largely on the changing nature of
        the speaking voice and on notions of subjectivity. Includes a chapter on Shakespeare's
        sonnets.
Vendler, Helen. *The Art of Shakespeare's Sonnets*. Cambridge, MA: Harvard UP, 1997. A thought-
        ful and accessible series of close readings of each sonnet, focusing primarily on the poem's
        aesthetic features but also addressing its ideas and psychological mood.

# Sonnet 94

## Robert Appelbaum

They that have power to hurt, and will do none,
That do not do the thing they most do show,
Who, moving others, are themselves as stone,
Unmoved, cold, and to temptation slow;
They rightly do inherit heaven's graces,
And husband nature's riches from expense;
They are the lords and owners of their faces,
Others, but stewards of their excellence.
The summer's flower is to the summer sweet,
Though to itself, it only live and die,
But if that flower with base infection meet,
The basest weed outbraves his dignity:
    For sweetest things turn sourest by their deeds;
    Lilies that fester smell far worse than weeds.

## PROSE PARAPHRASE

They who are able to hurt other people's feelings and will not do so, who do not do what they seem most likely to do, who attract other people but are themselves unmoved by anyone, who do not respond to other people's attractions and resist temptation—they make proper use of (or deserve) the good fortune they receive. They preserve the riches of nature, keeping them from being expended. They are the masters of their faces. Others are mere caretakers of the excellent qualities with which they have been endowed.

The summer flower is sweet to the summer, even if that flower lives and dies alone. But if the flower is infected with a disease, the lowliest of plants is more beautiful and dignified. For those things that are sweetest by their actions may turn into the sourest of objects. For example, lilies that rot "smell far worse than weeds" (94.14).

## THE PLACE OF THE SONNET IN THE CYCLE

Sonnet 94 is one of a group of poems (91–96) that worry about the young man's attractiveness to other people. Unlike most other poems apparently addressed to the young man, these sonnets entertain the idea that the young man may be imperfect, lacking the virtues that someone in his position ought to possess. Sometimes the poems not only worry about the young man's character, but even caution him against misbehaving. "How like Eve's apple doth thy beauty grow," the poet warns the young man in Sonnet 93, "If thy sweet virtue answer not thy show!" (ll. 13–14). The poet is concerned that the object of his intentions may seem to feel or behave one way and actually feel or behave another. What he is worried about most of all is that the young man will be unfaithful to him—though it is not clear if unfaithfulness in this case involves sexual conduct or some other kind of behavior. "[T]hou mayst take / All this away," the poet frets in Sonnet 91, referring at once to all the young man's love and all the benefits his love confers upon the poet—and hence "me most wretched make" (ll. 13–14). In the last two poems of the sequence, 95 and 96, the recriminations go even further, as when the poet writes in Sonnet 95, "O, in what sweets dost thou thy sins enclose!" (l. 4).

Sonnet 94 is usually regarded as the climax of this particular sequence, the poem that brings the sequence's concerns to a culminating set of sentiments and observations. However, it is also considered to be an especially enigmatic poem, difficult if not impossible to decipher. It is the sonnet that has been the most written about and argued over during the last one hundred years. In *An Essay on Shakespeare's Sonnets* Stephen Booth has claimed that the problem lies not in the poem but in strategies of reading that attempt to impose a single, unambiguous meaning on a text that is inherently resistant to such strategies. Critics will argue about the poem because they think that there must be one specific interpretation of it, and if two critics interpret it differently, one of the interpretations must be wrong. But the sonnets, according to Booth, work by engaging in language that is inherently equivocal, registering unresolved and ambivalent feelings. Sonnet 94 only takes this engagement with ambivalence a bit farther than most other poems in the sequence. More recently, in *Bodies and Selves in Early Modern England* Michael C. Schoenfeldt has argued that critics have found the poem enigmatic partly because they have brought to the poem a set of ideas about psychology and morality that the poem simply will not accommodate. According to Schoenfeldt, the poem's mixture of psychology and morality stems from a conventional, pre-modern understanding of the body and the mind and their relation to psychic "interiority." It seems to correspond to modern expectations concerning statements about virtue, physical attraction, and erotic behavior but in fact corresponds to the conventions of Galenic medicine and early modern moral thought, where stoicism and temperance are often keys to happiness. But the essay that began the modern debate about the poem, William Empson's "They that have the power," in *Some Versions of Pastoral*, sees the poem as part of the long sequence of poems to the young man that respond ambiguously and even uncertainly to him because the poet is uneasy about his own feelings and because one of his chief defenses against his uneasiness is irony.

Sonnet 94 reminds us of many of the earlier sonnets addressed to the young man, especially the procreation or marriage sonnets (1–17). The image in the procreation sonnets of the young man as a flower, usually a rose, is recalled in Sonnet 94 by the images of the summer flower and the lily. The theme of the procreation sonnets is recalled so far as the later sonnet poses the problem of what one should do about or with one's beauty. The extended meditation featured in the procreation sonnets on saving, expending, and husbandry is recalled in Sonnet 94 as well. The young man in both the procreation sonnets and Sonnet 94 is cautioned about what he should do with his natural talents, and in all cases is admonished not to waste them. The early sonnets, however, advise the young man to save his vital spirits for marriage and procreation: the emphasis is on producing offspring and siring replicas of his beauty. Sonnet 94, by contrast, seems to advise the young man not to do anything at all, lest his behavior sully his beauty. And in putting this advice in terms of acting "as stone" (94.3), on the one hand, and of preserving himself as a summer flower, on the other, it seems to recommend a kind of selfishness. However, we may also be reminded of Sonnet 20, "A woman's face with Nature's own hand painted" (20.1), which speaks about a face that complicates the young man's gender identity as well as the poet's relation to the young man, not to mention the question of the how the young man's beauty may be exploited.

## DEVICES AND TECHNIQUES

Although the sonnet follows the usual Shakespearean procedure, being composed out of four quatrains and a concluding couplet in the usual rhyme scheme (*abab*, *cdcd*, *efef*, *gg*), the development of meaning in the sonnet follows Italian convention, and is constructed by way of an opening octave and a complementary sestet. The octave (*abab*, *cdcd*) states an argument. The sestet (*efef*, *gg*) states a different, though related argument, providing an elaboration and conclusion. However, as is sometimes the case in Italian verse as well, the first and second parts of the poem are actually very different from one another, and perhaps do not fit together quite as well as the structure of the poem as a whole suggests they should. The two parts differ from one another in tone, imagery, diction, and thought; and it is difficult to see how the concluding sestet, if it "concludes" anything at all, really resolves the issues raised by the opening octave.

As has often been noted, this is an impersonal poem: it contains neither "I" nor "you," and we can only associate its language with an imagined "I" and "you" by virtue of the poem's position in a sequence where we know that one person (the poet) is writing to another (the young man), worrying about their relationship. As an impersonal poem, the sonnet opens with a proposition with apparently universal implications: Those who have the power do harm but do not use that power are using their gifts properly. Yet as we read this poem in the context of the sequence, we assume that the poet is talking about his young man and telling him something he needs to learn. The poem makes a general argument but expresses it for the benefit of a single person under a single set of circumstances. So the opening octave talks about a "they," implying that the never-directly-addressed young man is (or could be or should be) one of those who have the power to hurt but do not, who are themselves as stone, and so forth. The concluding sestet, equally impersonal, goes on to talk about a "summer flower" and, in the plural, "lilies," again implying that the young man is or could be like this summer flower or those lilies. Although we read the poem as a personal communication between two intimate friends, and apply what the speaker says in general to what we think the speaker is saying to his friend in particular, the impersonal nature of the rhetoric of the poem has a distancing effect. The distancing is only exacerbated by what may be called the sententious character of both parts of the poem. A "sentence" in Shakespeare's age is a high-minded and pithy saying, the tradition for which was inherited from ancient Roman writers as well as from the popular folklore of proverbial expressions. Both parts of the poem are "sententious" in the sense that they briefly communicate high-minded moral observations that might be made by a Roman moralist or the proverb tradition, and which therefore brook no rebuttal.

The language of the octave is generally abstract: key words include "power," "hurt," "thing," "show," "temptation," "inherit," "nature," and "faces." The images are sparing: in the first place, an unmoved and cold "stone"; in the second place, a "husbanding" of nature, suggesting agricultural pursuits, though this image is not taken very far, and indeed is undermined by its application. A "husband" in the sense of someone who pursues the profession of "husbandry" is a male head of a household who tills the ground and manages a farm, usually his own farm; by extension, to "husband" resources is to manage them well, prudently and economically, laying some resources aside for the future. But here "nature's riches"—not the resources that result from shrewd cultivation, but natural products, natural "riches"—are husbanded, and they are husbanded, simply, from expense. They are kept from being used. The implied promise of continued fertility and of what the procreation sonnets call "use" is curtailed: we are reminded of the unmoved stone mentioned before, and made to think about the "faces" that such unmoved creatures are "lords and owners" of as cold and static (94.7). One may speak of the face of a cliff or the faces of a diamond as well as of the face of a human being. "Faces" in the context of a sentence about being "as stone" (94.3) is not only unlike what we think of as "selves," rational beings with an inward sense of their identity, but also unlike what we think of as "persons," fully human selves, with insides as well as outsides, with vulnerabilities as well as strengths, with openings as well as closed surfaces.

The concluding sestet, obviously, shifts away from much of this kind of language. The "they" of the octave has been dropped for something more definite. The images are lively: a "summer's flower," a "basest weed," "lilies that fester." The verbal units used to express the speaker's ideas are emphatic: "live and die," "infection meet," "outbraves," "turn sourest," "fester," "smell." However, even if the language of the sestet is lively and colorful, the ideas in it still communicate something incompletely active. The summer flower not only lives but also dies. The danger the sestet harps upon is the danger of going rotten, of contracting a disease and putrefying. The opening octave argues that by being unmoved, "as stone," one inherits riches (and/or "graces") and saves them from use. The concluding sestet adds that in the case of flowers, death and decay are inevitable. Yet somehow one wishes to avoid too much decay, to prevent oneself from going sour, or to protect oneself from festering. Lilies, lush-smelling flowers that traditionally symbolize purity and remind us of the innocent biblical "lilies of the field," in fact stink worse than other flowers when they rot.

## THEMES AND MEANINGS

The poem challenges us to agree to an argument, or perhaps several arguments, to which we many not always find it easy to assent. We may like the idea that people who can hurt others may avoid doing so. We may not be so sure that we like acting "as stone." We may like the idea of inheriting "heaven's graces" or of husband-ing "nature's riches." We may not be so sure that one "rightly" does so (either "by rights" or "in the right way") simply by acting as stone. We may like the idea of people being lords and owners of themselves, but that is not what the poem says: it says that people who act "as stone" are the lords and owners of "their faces." Al-though the other poems of the sub-sequence worry about virtue and convention-ally contrast outward show with inward conviction (or inward depravity), this poem seems to suggest that appearance is in fact what counts: keeping up a good appearance by not giving in to temptation, by not allowing oneself to be moved or compromised by contact with others, is what makes one the lord and owner of one's identity. And this is desirable, so desirable that it may be equated with inheriting heaven's graces (that is, either inheriting such beautifying attributes as we associ-ate with heavenly creatures or inheriting, in fact, "grace," which is to say salvation). The sestet, though it changes the terms of the poem, may even be said to accentu-ate this challenging argument. For what it worries about is the deterioration of the look, the taste, and the smell of the natural objects, a deterioration that results from contact with infectious agents.

There may be, as William Empson suggested, something "Machiavellian" about the argument. For we can see in the praise of those "That do not do the thing they most do show" (94.2), who inspire others to act but themselves are impassive, the very model of the ruler whom Machiavelli cynically extols in his famous 1516 trea-tise named *The Prince*. Machiavelli's Prince may cause his followers to believe and feel all kinds of things that he is himself indifferent to, the better to keep his sub-jects in their place, in awe of his power and ready to serve him. And so the poet ad-vises the young man both to restrain his feelings and to keep them to himself for the sake of personal advantage. The connection between the poet's advice and Machiavelli is further underscored by the subtle allusion to an "unmoved mover." It was as an "unmoved mover" that Aristotle characterized God, and it is in such terms that Machiavelli sometimes imagines his manipulative absolute monarch, the Prince.

It is perhaps in keeping with the idea of a Machiavellian unmoved mover that the young man is asked to think of those who "rightly do inherit heaven's graces" (94.5). If we imagine that there is a wrong way to inherit heaven's graces, as well as a way of inheriting them wrongfully, then to rightly inherit heaven's graces is in part to do well with that by which one has been divinely endowed; it is to take what God gives one in the right way, by the path of virtue. Yet if "rightly" to inherit heaven's graces is also to do so "by rights," the poem also asks us to think about the "right" by which a monarch claims authority, or an aristocrat claims his aris-tocratic privileges. Whether in the cynical context of Machiavellian thought or in the more idealistic context of English humanism of the sixteenth century, this is to claim authority at least in part by divine right. However, whether the primary sense is to inherit heaven's graces in the right way or else by rights, by virtue or by divine dispensation, the individual who inherits heaven's graces in this way is involved in something peculiar: to inherit heaven's grace is to "husband" one's riches and to be the "lord and owner" of one's face. (In the original, that is, 1609, spelling, "lord" is capitalized, and the word thus suggests both the idea of mastery and the idea of aristocratic privilege.) It is to sustain the outward show of one's identity, and to do so, again, both in the right way and by rights. Others are mere "stewards," that is hired hands, administrators; they are the merely salaried managers. They are the managers either of their own excellences (that is, their own "graces," which they seem to have inherited wrongly) or else, even worse, the excellence of others, which is to say the excellence of those who know how to act as stone, and (rightly) husband their natural riches. One way or the other, the implication is that they do not manage what they do either in the right way or by rights. They lack privilege.

Acting in this way, staying in possession of one's "face" by remaining unmoved by the causes of excitement to which one is exposed, as Michael Schoenfeldt argues, may also be to exemplify the values of stoicism that were commonly praised in the early modern period. To remain "as stone" is not to repress one's emotions; it is not to stay bottled up, in denial; it is rather to remain imperturbable in the face of temptations and excitations. It is to exercise moderation by exercising a productive mastery of one's impulses.

Yet both the Machiavellian and the stoic lines of thought in the poem are challenged by the argument of the sestet. The "summer's flow'r" is said "to live and die . . . [only] to itself" (94.9–10). But what is both attractive and bothersome is not what the flower is in itself, to itself, but what it is to the summer, or to those who look upon it in the summer. Alone, to the air and to its observers, the summer flower is sweet, brave, dignified. But if it should be exposed to a contaminating agent, it will rot. And whatever it is, again, to itself, to others it will be sour, ugly, undignified, and smelly. The advice thus seems to be that one should keep oneself free from contamination—not to remain impassive, but to remain untouched, in order not to be infected by disease. But what kind of advice of this? The summer flower that only lives and dies is a far cry from the "rose" that in the early sonnets is encouraged to procreate and reproduce itself, and whose sweetness entails an inward as well as an outward quality. It is a far cry, for that matter, from the unmoved mover of the octave. The lily is a far cry from a stone, and its fragility and perishability are qualities that make it an unlikely analogue for a stoic.

To come to terms with this poem it may well be necessary to see it as deeply ironic—as not meaning what it says, as actually condemning where it seems to be praising, as recommending contact, liveliness, motion where it seems to be praising isolation, deathliness, and unmoved stoic calculation. It may also be necessary to attribute a dramatic character to the poem, to locate it within the context of an ongoing drama between a lover and a beloved where the lover's admiration, his genuine appreciation of his beloved's beauty and talent for self-possession, is mixed with anger and contempt. It may be the case that within the context of this moment in the drama of the speaker's emotions, there is no satisfactory way out. Poems that follow will have to change the terms of the problem. But for now, the speaker seems both to treasure and detest the attractive, at once stone-like and flower-like beauty of his beloved.

## THE RELATIONSHIP OF THE SONNET TO SHAKESPEARE'S OTHER WORKS

The "lily" appears often in Shakespeare's works as a symbol of purity, innocence, and feminine beauty. The whiteness of the lily, to be sure, was already a cliché in the sixteenth century, particularly in the context of the "lily hand" of a beautiful woman of leisure—an image that opens Spenser's sonnet sequence, *The Amoretti*. Shakespeare commonly uses the idea in this borrowed, hackneyed sense. But in *Henry VIII* we encounter Queen Katherine saying in despair that "[l]ike the lily, /

That once was mistress of the field, and flourish'd, / I'll hang my head and perish" (3.1.151–153). And in *Venus and Adonis*, though Venus is earlier said to have "lily fingers" (228), when she takes Adonis by the hand, it is Adonis who is associated with the lily: "Full gently now she takes him by the hand, / A lily prison'd in a jail of snow" (361–362).

Images of stones and stoniness recur throughout Shakespeare's works, with a large range of applications. To have a "stony" heart is sometimes a good thing, as when one needs to act with resolution. In *2 Henry VI*, the young Clifford, at the sight of his slain father, readying himself to exact revenge, remarks that "Even at this sight / My heart is turn'd to stone: and while 'tis mine, / It shall be stony" (5.2.49–51). However, to be like a stone may also mean to be cold-hearted, lacking a capacity of pity, as when in *The Two Gentlemen of Verona* the clown Launce comically remarks about his dog, "yet did not this cruel-hearted cur shed one tear. He is a stone, a very pibble [pebble] stone, and has no more pity in him than a dog" (2.3.9–11). The climax of *The Winter's Tale* comes when the marble statue of Hermione is transformed into a human being, Paulina having invoked the statue to "be stone no more" (5.3.99), and Hermione's husband having lamented, "[D]oes not the stone rebuke me / For being more stone than it?" (5.3.37–38). Othello, in fact, when first resolved to punish his wife for her supposed infidelity, exclaims, "Ay, let her rot, and perish, and be damn'd to-night, for she shall not live. No, my heart is turned to stone" (4.1.181–183).

The emotions registered in Sonnet 94 are perhaps most similarly evoked in *Venus and Adonis*. Venus complains of Adonis,

> Fie, liveless picture, cold and senseless stone,
> Well-painted idol, image dull and dead,
> Statue contenting but the eye alone,
> Thing like a man, but of no woman bred! (211–214)

But Shakespeare's most extended meditation on the issues raised in Sonnet 94 and the images they evoke come in *Measure for Measure*. There we find Angelo, an administrator, a steward of the state, who struggles between extremes. At first he seems too hard-hearted, too "precise," a man who "scarce confesses / That his blood flows, or that his appetite / Is more to bread than stone" (1.3.50–53). But later he is clearly too quickly moved to temptation, and, being moved, to hurt others—and not just their feelings. Meanwhile the pure and innocent Isabella struggles between her vow of chastity and the need to use her body to save her brother from execution, and the libertine Lucio finds himself first delighted and then condemned to stay in contact with an underworld of brothels, pimps, and prostitutes, a world that the play consistently associates with contagious and ignoble diseases, with "base infection." It may well be that *Measure for Measure* is no more successful at resolving the conflicts its themes and imagery raise than Sonnet 94; but to read the sonnet in the context of the play, or the play in the context of the sonnet, is an instructive exercise. What it may encourage us to do—though the critical literature so far has yet to take this step—is to read the uneasy, perhaps conflicting themes of the poem as a reflection not so much on the young man as on the speaker, the poet, who in a certain situation could advise the young man to live unmoved, as stone or as uninfected lilies.

**Annotated Bibliography**

Booth, Stephen. *An Essay on Shakespeare's Sonnets.* New Haven: Yale UP, 1969. The book that
   changed the way we read the sonnets, emphasizing complexities and unresolvable tensions and contradictions in the experience of reading the poems. The section on Sonnet
   94, pages 152–168, gives a provocative account of criticism of the poem through 1969.
———, ed. *Shakespeare's Sonnets.* New Haven: Yale UP, 1977. An indispensable edition that includes a reproduction of the 1609 quarto, amply and ingeniously annotated. The original
   spelling text included may be especially helpful in the reading of Sonnet 94.
Empson, William. *Some Versions of Pastoral.* London: Chatto and Windus, 1968. 89–118. A land-
   mark study, in the case of Sonnet 94 opening the twin problems of ambiguity and ambivalence for analysis.
Kerrigan, John, ed. *Shakespeare: "The Sonnets" and "A Lover's Complaint."* Harmondsworth, Eng.:
   Penguin, 1986. A fine edition, with useful remarks on Sonnet 94.
Schoenfeldt, Michael. *Bodies and Selves in Early Modern England.* Cambridge: Cambridge UP,
   1999. 74–95. A provocative attempt to locate the themes of the sonnet historically and culturally.

# Sonnets 97 and 98

Jeremy Lopez

## Sonnet 97

How like a winter hath my absence been
From thee, the pleasure of the fleeting year!
What freezings have I felt, what dark days seen!
What old December's bareness every where!
And yet this time remov'd was summer's time;
The teeming autumn, big with rich increase,
Bearing the wanton burden of the prime,
Like widow'd wombs after their lords' decease:
Yet this abundant issue seem'd to me
But hope of orphans, and unfather'd fruit;
For summer and his pleasures wait on thee,
And, thou away, the very birds are mute:
   Or, if they sing, 'tis with so dull a cheer,
   That leaves look pale, dreading the winter's near.

### PROSE PARAPHRASE

My separation from you, who give me my only happiness in this world, has been like a winter! What sadness I felt, what dark days I have seen! The world has seemed as bleak as the earth in December. And yet, we were separated during the summer and then the autumn, which arrives bearing summer's fruits, like a widow giving birth after her husband has died. But the bountiful harvest was no more satisfying to me than the blighted hopes of orphans: the delights of summer mean nothing without you. Without you, birds do not even wish to sing. Or, if they do sing, they sing so sadly that the leaves look pale, as if they are afraid that winter is near.

## ❖ Sonnet 98

From you have I been absent in the spring
When proud-pied April, dress'd in all his trim,
Hath put a spirit of youth in every thing,
That heavy Saturn laugh'd and leap'd with him.
Yet nor the lays of birds, nor the sweet smell
Of different flowers in odour and in hue,
Could make me any summer's story tell,
Or from their proud lap pluck them where they grew:
Nor did I wonder at the lily's white,
Nor praise the deep vermilion in the rose;
They were but sweet, but figures of delight,
Drawn after you, you pattern of all those.
    Yet seem'd it winter still, and you away,
    As with your shadow I with these did play.

### PROSE PARAPHRASE

I have been separated from you in the spring-time, when colorful April makes everything, and everyone, no matter how gloomy and sluggish, seem youthful and vibrant. But neither the songs of birds nor the sweet smells of all the many different flowers could make me speak of pleasant things, or pick flowers happily. I was not impressed with the whiteness of the lily or the deep red of the rose. These things are little more than the superficial signs of happiness; they were made in your image. You are the pattern of all things that are delightful. So in your absence it seemed always to be winter; and, while you were away, I played with the flowers and felt that I was playing with your shadow because they are pale reflections of your loveliness.

### THE PLACE OF THE SONNETS IN THE CYCLE

In these poems the speaker does not talk so much about his beloved as about his own state of mind when he and his beloved are separated. The same basic sentiment is conveyed in each sonnet, and in each Sonnet it is done only slightly differently: Sonnet 97 says that the joys of summer mean nothing when the beloved is not nearby; Sonnet 98 says that the joys of spring mean nothing when the beloved is not nearby. The use of the seasons to express an emotional state is conventional to virtually all love poetry.

These poems occur amidst a sequence of sonnets, beginning with Sonnet 94, that rely fairly heavily on natural imagery. The "summer's flow'r" that meets with "base infection" in Sonnet 94 (ll. 9–11) is echoed in the "canker in the fragrant rose" of Sonnet 95 (l. 2); these images find their complements in the image of "summer and his pleasures" at 97.11 and the list of flowers in Sonnet 98. The images of "youth," "gentle sport," and even "lambs" in Sonnet 96 resurface in the spring imagery of Sonnet 98. And the flowers that steal beauty and sweetness from the beloved in Sonnet 99 recall the flowers that are but his shadows in Sonnet 98.

Sonnets 87–93 deal, to varying degrees, with a separation of the speaker from his beloved that seems indeterminate in length and not of the speaker's choice. That is, in those sonnets, the speaker seems to be trying to resign himself to the fact that his beloved has left him. Sonnets 100–103 lament the loss of the beloved in terms particularly pertinent to poetry: the speaker says that, without his beloved, he has lost his "Muse." The voice in all of these sonnets speaks in the present tense. By contrast, the voice of sonnets 97 and 98 speaks in the past tense, suggesting that he is no longer separated from the beloved. The seasonal metaphors suggest, in important contrast to the other sonnets, that the separation has only been temporary—only a matter of time.

## DEVICES AND TECHNIQUES

Both sonnets rely heavily on the word "yet." Sonnet 97 uses this word to mark the beginning of each new group of four lines or quatrain. The "And yet" of line 5 reveals that the physical qualities of winter invoked in the first quatrain were meant only to represent states of mind, not the actual weather. Lines 5–8 describe the beauties of summer; the "Yet" of line 9 renders them unimportant. The first quatrain of Sonnet 98 works in a way that is similar to the second quatrain of Sonnet 97. That is, the speaker describes the beauties of spring in lines 1–4 and then uses a "Yet" in line 5 to negate them.

The various instances of "yet" discussed above are moments where the argument of each poem turns in a similar way—toward the negation of some pleasure that has just been described. But the two poems do not always turn in the same way. Lines 1–12 of Sonnet 97 conclude with a claim about the sadness of summer in the absence of the beloved: "And thou away, the very birds are mute" (l. 12). The couplet then opens up the possibility for some more positive image of summer with the word "Or." Immediately, however, the possibility of a positive image is negated—"Or if they sing, 'tis with so dull a cheer . . ."—and we are back where we began, "dreading the winter's near" (ll. 13–14). The "Or" of the poem's thirteenth line ends up working just like the word "yet" in line 5 and line 9. In Sonnet 98 "or" and its cousin "nor" are used in lines 8–10 to extend the idea created by the "Yet" of line 5. "Or" and "nor" help the speaker create a dreary list of ways in which he could not enjoy the spring without his beloved. The dreary list continues until line 12. In line 13, the speaker introduces the word "Yet," again suggesting the possibility of something different from the dreariness that has preceded the couplet. But the couplet goes on to say very much the same thing that the rest of the poem has said: it seems like winter, and flowers provide no joy, when the speaker is without the beloved. Each sonnet works to shut down every possibility for perceiving or experiencing something pleasurable.

To a certain extent these poems seem to suggest that the separation of the speaker from his beloved was something temporary—something that, like the seasons, has passed. At the same time, however, there is some temporal confusion that might work to make the separation feel more indefinite, more permanent than the speaker attempts to suggest. Line 5 of Sonnet 97 says that the time of separation "was summer's time"; line 8 then begins with a different time, the "teeming autumn." Given the birth metaphors that follow, it is possible that Shakespeare intended "summer's time" to mean "the end of the summer's term of pregnancy," that is, the time when fruits are harvested. But given line 11, "For summer and his pleasures wait on thee," and given the speaker's use of "winter" to describe his emotional state, it is likely that a reader assumes the poem is talking about summer. The potential confusion between summer and autumn suggests that the months are collapsing together as the speaker tries in vain to think that the separation will soon be over. A similar confusion occurs in Sonnet 98, where the subject is spring but the speaker says that he is not inspired to tell "any summer's story" (l. 7).

## THEMES AND MEANINGS

In their assertion that nature's beauty and bounty are meaningless without the beloved, these sonnets recall the opening lines of one of Shakespeare's most famous sonnets: "Shall I compare thee to a summer's day? / Thou art more lovely and more temperate" (18.1–2). In all three poems, nature seems to exist entirely for the purpose of providing the speaker with ways to praise his beloved, or providing the speaker with ways to express his own state of mind. The exact season the speaker is referring to in Sonnet 97 is not as important as are the connotations of "winter" as a metaphor for the speaker's state of mind. Sonnet 98 constructs a long catalogue of the pleasures of spring (birdsong, the smell and colors of flowers) only to say that the speaker had no interest in looking at these things.

In these poems, as so frequently is the case in the sonnets, the nature of one's experience of external things is entirely dependent on what one feels internally. In both poems the speaker employs considerable hyperbole, or exaggeration: "the very birds are mute" (97.12) and "They were but sweet, but figures of delight / Drawn after you" (98.11–12) are just two examples. But even while it is clear that the speaker is using nature to make exaggerated metaphorical claims, it is also clear that he does not hear the birds with any pleasure, and does not find any sweetness in the flowers. He is aware of the possibility of pleasure in such things without experiencing it at all. An even more extreme version of this relationship between internal feelings and external experience can be seen in Sonnet 113, where the speaker claims that, while separated from his beloved, every thing he sees, "bird, . . . flow'r, . . . shape" (113.6), is made by his mind to look like the person he loves.

These poems explicitly equate, or contrast, the speaker's emotions with the weather. Somewhat less explicitly, they demonstrate a concern with youth and youthfulness: they suggest not only that the speaker feels more youthful when the beloved is around, but also that the speaker is worried that his relationship with the beloved has grown old. "December's bareness" in 97.4 presents an image of a frozen landscape; the word "bareness" also suggests the *barrenness*, or inability to produce offspring, that becomes the dominant concern of lines 6–11. The first quatrain of Sonnet 98 says that April "Hath put a spirit of youth in every thing" (98.3), but the implication of the next 10 lines is that the speaker is one important exception. The implicit anxieties about age and the passage of time in these two poems are later brought more closely to the surface in sonnets 100 and 102. In the former, the speaker asks for the beloved, his "Muse," to return and inspire him to write poems that will counter the effects of time by memorializing their love—poems that will "make Time's spoils despised every where" (100.12). In the latter, the speaker notes sadly that while once "Our love was new, and then but in the spring" (102.5), things have changed: "the summer is less pleasant now" (102.9).

## THE RELATIONSHIP OF THE SONNETS TO
## SHAKESPEARE'S OTHER WORKS

Shakespeare's plays are replete with moments where a character's internal state is connected to external experience—and especially to natural phenomena such as the weather or the seasons. Because actors in Shakespeare's plays performed on a stage without sets or movable scenery, it is frequently difficult to tell how, as a spectator, one is supposed to understand external experience beyond the way in which it relates to characters' internal states of mind. The third scene of act 2 in *Titus Andronicus* provides an excellent example. At the beginning of this scene the evil Tamora, queen of the Goths, gleefully plots revenge against Titus Andronicus with her lover Aaron. They are in the woods, and Tamora refers to the "melody" of birds, the "sweet shade" of the trees, and the "babbling echo" of a brook (2.3.11–17). Only a few lines later, after Tamora has become involved in a confrontation with Lavinia and Bassianus, and seeks the aid of her sons, she refers to the woods as a "barren detested vale," with trees "forlorn and lean, / . . . / Here never shines the sun, here nothing breeds" (2.3.93–96). Like the speaker of sonnets 97–98, Tamora observes nature only in order to make it reflect her emotional state from one moment to the next.

Perhaps the most famous example in Shakespeare of a connection between external phenomena and internal states of mind is *King Lear*. After King Lear has been stripped of his power by his daughters and shut out of their homes, he wanders outside in a terrible storm and "Strives in his little world of man to outscorn / The to-and-fro-conflicting wind and rain" (3.1.10–11). Though everyone in the play confirms that a storm actually is occurring, the spectators in Shakespeare's Globe would have had to rely mainly on Lear's emotional storming to fill in whatever stage technology and special effects could not. When Lear screams, "Blow, winds, and crack your cheeks! rage, blow!" (3.2.1), he is screaming equally out of rage at his daughters and his degraded state (the storm that comes from within) and at the weather (the storm that comes from without).

The use of seasons to represent both the decaying and the healing potential of time is also common in Shakespeare's plays, and one of the best examples is *The Winter's Tale*. The play's title alludes to a kind of ghost story typically told at festive winter gatherings. The climax of the play's action occurs in the third act when the jealousy of King Leontes is declared to be unfounded—an oracle proclaims that his wife has not cheated on him. Leontes defies the oracle and his wife is, apparently, immediately struck dead. The infant child she had by him is left on a distant coast. This act ends with a terrible storm, the infant being rescued at the last minute by a passing shepherd. The play's fourth act begins with a narrator figure announcing that we are to imagine sixteen years have passed. The first scene of this act shows us springtime among shepherds, and from here the action works toward a wonderful and improbable resolution: Leontes and his wife and their child are united. Somewhat more optimistically than sonnets 97–98, or those around them, the passage of the seasons in *The Winter's Tale* allows "December's bareness" to give way to "summer and his pleasures" once more (97.4, 11).

### Annotated Bibliography

Booth, Stephen. *An Essay on Shakespeare's Sonnets*. New Haven: Yale UP, 1969. A detailed critical examination of the sonnets, both as a sequence and as individual poems. Booth argues that the sonnets always provide a reader with the "comfort and security of a frame of reference, but the frames of reference are not constant, and their number seems limitless" (187).

———, ed. *Shakespeare's Sonnets*. New Haven: Yale UP, 1977. A useful edition with parallel modern and early modern (1609) texts and with excellent commentary on each sonnet. These annotations range from explanatory glosses to full-length critical essays.

Evans, G. Blackmore, ed. *The Sonnets*. The New Cambridge Shakespeare. Cambridge: Cambridge UP, 1996. This edition provides commentary devoted largely to explicating difficult phrases. Discusses textual variants and historical context.

Fineman, Joel. *Shakespeare's Perjured Eye: The Invention of Poetic Subjectivity in the Sonnets*. Berkeley: U of California P, 1986. A compelling and provocative study. Argues that the sonnets shift between poetry that idealizes and praises a beloved and poetry that focuses attention on the writer's problematic desire, revealing fissures and paradox within the narrative voice and, effectively, a different and more complex sense of self.

Vendler, Helen. *The Art of Shakespeare's Sonnets*. Cambridge, MA: Harvard UP, 1997. A thoughtful and accessible series of close readings of each sonnet, focusing primarily on the poem's aesthetic features but also addressing its ideas and psychological mood.

# Sonnet 106

## Kirk Bazler Melnikoff

When in the chronicle of wasted time
I see descriptions of the fairest wights,
And beauty making beautiful old rime
In praise of ladies dead and lovely knights,
Then, in the blazon of sweet beauty's best,
Of hand, of foot, of lip, of eye, of brow,
I see their antique pen would have express'd
Even such a beauty as you master now.
So all their praises are but prophecies
Of this our time, all you prefiguring;
And, for they look'd but with divining eyes,
They had not skill enough your worth to sing:
    For we, which now behold these present days,
    Have eyes to wonder, but lack tongues to praise.

## PROSE PARAPHRASE

Sonnet 106 begins with the speaker's describing his response to reading past poetic praise of beautiful "ladies" and "knights" (l. 4). Such descriptions, which catalog the particular perfections of men and women of yore, make him believe that these poets would have wanted to represent the young man's beauty. The speaker decides that these past poetic descriptions in fact prefigure the young man and that had these poets actually had the opportunity to see the young man, they would have been able to express his beauty effectively. The speaker concludes that this situation in the past (of having the poetic ability but not the perfect object) inversely corresponds to his own present where poets have the perfect object (i.e., the young man) but not the poetic ability to do him justice through representation.

## THE PLACE OF THE SONNET IN THE CYCLE

Sonnet 106 is one of 126 sonnets addressed to the unidentified young man. It has further been categorized as one of sixteen sonnets (starting with Sonnet 102) that in one way or another treat of love's power to defy time. Among these sonnets, some suggest that love can defeat time; still others argue that love can stop time. In the former category are sonnets 102, 107, and 115. Just as the speaker in Sonnet 102 reassures the young man that "My love is strength'ned, though more weak in seeming" (l. 1), so in Sonnet 115, the speaker asks, "Alas, why, fearing of Time's tyranny, / Might I not then say, 'Now I love you best'[?]" (ll. 9–10). Similarly, in Sonnet 107, the speaker contends that nothing "Can yet the lease of my true love control" (l. 3). Falling generally into the latter category are sonnets 104 and 116. In Sonnet 104, the speaker promises that "To me, fair friend, you never can be old" (l. 1). And in the well-known Sonnet 116, which begins, "Let me not to the marriage of true minds / Admit impediments" (a favorite reading in many a marriage ceremony), the third quatrain argues that "Love's not Time's fool," and that "Love alters not with his brief hours and weeks" (ll. 9, 11).

More narrowly, Sonnet 106 is closely related in "verbal echo" and theme to the following three sonnets (107–109). The word "time" is used at least once in each of these four sonnets (106.1; 107.9, 11; 108.14; 109.7), and forms of the time-related terms, "antique" (106.7 and 108.12) and "prophecy" (106.9 and 107.1), are repeated in this group. Indeed, it is the ravaging power of time that becomes a common theme at this point in the cycle. To Sonnet 106's beginning "wasted time," Sonnet 107 adds the ending image of a future time "When tyrants' crests and tombs of brass are spent" (l. 14). Sonnet 109's assurance that the speaker will be able to return from an absence "not with the time exchang'd" (l. 7) responds to Sonnet 108's recognition of "the dust and injury of age" (l. 10). This group of sonnets suggests that poetry has the ability to transcend the ravages of devouring time. Just as Sonnet 106 suggests the transcendent power of "beautiful old rhyme" (106.3), sonnets 107 and 108 present poetic writing as a powerful albeit enigmatic mode of expression. In Sonnet 107, the speaker promises that despite death "I'll live in this poor rhyme" (l. 11), and Sonnet 108 begins by asking, "What's in the brain that ink may character / Which hath not figur'd to thee my true spirit ?" (ll. 1–2).

Like the majority of Shakespeare's sonnets, Sonnet 106 was first published in the 1609 quarto. It does, however, also exist in two seventeenth-century commonplace books: one preserved at the Rosenbach Museum and Library (Philadelphia) and the other at the Pierpont Morgan Library (New York City) and called "the Holgate Commonplace Book." Both of these manuscript versions of Sonnet 106 essentially bear the title "On his Mistris Beauty." According to G. Blakemore Evans, both of these books appear to have been derived from a manuscript source that may have contained legitimate authorial variants (286). The more significant of these approximately twenty-one variants occur in the final four lines. In line 11, the Rosenbach's commonplace book has "deceiving" where both the quarto and the Holgate commonplace book have "divining"; in line 12, both commonplace books have "skill" where the quarto has "still"; and in line 13 the Rosenbach's commonplace book has "pleasant" where both the quarto and the Holgate Commonplace Book have "present." It is the quarto's "still" in line 12 that has been subject to the most emendations.

## DEVICES AND TECHNIQUES

Sonnet 106 employs iambic pentameter and the conventional English sonnet rhyme form of three quatrains followed by an ending rhymed couplet (*abab cdcd efef gg*). Syntactically, however, the sonnet also belongs to the older Italian tradition which organized a 14-line sonnet into an octave and a sestet. As such, the first and second quatrains together comprise one sentence (separated by a comma) with the first quatrain being a clause of causation (indicated by its beginning "When") and the second quatrain being a clause of effect (indicated by its beginning "Then"). The ninth line opens the sonnet's third quatrain with the inductive "So," and this more generalized conclusion that "all their praises are but prophecies" yet "[t]hey had not still enough your worth to sing" (106.9, 12) also functions as a consequence of the fact that "we which now behold these present days, / Have eyes to wonder, but lack tongues to praise" (106.13–14). In effect, the structure of Sonnet 106 suggests a typological scenario where essentially causes and effects are chronologically reversed. Just as the poem begins with a causational clause, it also ends with one.

Like other sonnets and dramatic verse by Shakespeare, Sonnet 106 contains disruptions of its regular iambic meter that serve to stress significant words and phrases. In the octave, disruptions occur in linked pairs, and they subtly underscore the poem's thematic concern with time. The sonnet's first irregularly stressed word "When," for example, which suggests both a happening in the past and in the future, is echoed by the fifth line's irregularly stressed "Then," a word that both introduces the consequence of "I see" (l. 7) and repeats the historical connotations of "When." The octave's rhythmic linkings are continued when the fifth line's ending "of sweet beauty's best" (a phrase with three stresses in its final four syllables) is coupled with the eighth line's ending "as you master now," the later phrase echoing and superseding the former. The octave ends with the stressed "now," and this word also recalls the sonnet's beginning "When." Sonnet 106's ending sestet continues these purposeful disruptions. It, however, stresses difference over continuity. In lines 9–12, the sestet regularly departs from its regular iambic meter in referring to poets from the past ("their" [106.9], "they" [106.11, 12]) as distinguished from the present and the young man ("our" [106.10] and "your" [106.12]). The ending irregular rhythm of the sonnet's final couplet also underscores this discontinuity. Ending with the pessimistic idea that present poets are not able to express praise effectively, the couplet disrupts its beginning smooth flow of language—set up by the essentially regular line "For we which now behold these present days"—with the ending phrase "but lack tongues to praise" which has four stressed word in its final five syllables.

Sonnet 106 contains a wealth of wordplay. As has been pointed out, the word "praise" reverberates throughout the poem. Introduced in line 4, "praise" can be sensed in the following words "of Ladies," in the seventh line's "expressed" and then again (after "praises") in the ninth line's "prophecies" and the tenth line's "prefiguring." Such reverberations come to a provocative climax in the final couplet when the thirteenth line's "present days" is compacted in the sonnet's final rhymed word "praise." These reverberations serve to link the poem's focus upon poetry and upon prophecy. Moreover, the final quatrain, by having its first rhyming construction ("prophecies" / "eyes") vaguely echo the rhyme of the couplet, constructs in miniature a situation where the future can be sensed in the past.

## THEMES AND MEANINGS

Perhaps the most consistently noted theme in Sonnet 106 is that of typology. Just as Christ was thought to have been prefigured by many of the stories of the Old Testament, the speaker of this sonnet imagines that the young man is prefigured in the past "descriptions of the fairest wights" (l. 2). Shakespeare, however, adds his own spin to Christian typology in that it is the young man and his great beauty, not Christ and the promise of redemption, being prefigured by "antique pen" (l. 7). According to Helen Vendler, Shakespeare's secularizing of Biblical prophecy is clearly blasphemous, and this blasphemy would have been immediately apparent to any early-modern reader.

Vendler has also pointed out how the sonnet falls into the ample lyric tradition of poems about the impossibility of writing poetry. Examples from Shakespeare's lifetime include the first sonnet in Sir Philip Sidney's *Astrophil and Stella*, which records Astrophil's frustration at wanting "in verse [his] love to show" but being "helpless in [his] throes," and the third sonnet from Spenser's *Amoretti*, which describes how the speaker "would write [his beloved] titles true" but "ravisht is with fancy's wonderment." Shakespeare's sonnet not only openly laments the fact that the speaker and other contemporary poets "lack tongues to praise," but it also enacts such an inability in the poem's movement. Whereas descriptive words such as "fairest" (l. 2), "beauty" (l. 3) "sweet," and "lovely" (l. 4) fill out the sonnet's first octave, such words disappear in the final sestet. In effect, the ample yet vague praise of the past is coupled with an essentially silent "wonder" in the present.

## THE RELATIONSHIP OF THE SONNET TO SHAKESPEARE'S OTHER WORKS

In making "prophecies" and "prefiguring" focal points of its meaning, Sonnet 106 is reminiscent of Shakespeare's thematic concern with the interconnections between divine providence and the political world in the first tetralogy dealing with the reigns of Henry VI, Edward IV, and Richard III. It is in the concluding play of this tetralogy, *Richard III*, that Shakespeare most consistently deploys the various forms of the word "prophesy." Not only are many of the characters in the play plagued by disturbing "prophecies and dreams" (1.1.54), but the play even turns Queen Margaret into a "prophetess" (5.1.27). Shakespeare's dramatic ode to the Tudor line of kings culminates in *Richard III* and puts a divine spin on the function of prophecy that does not so clearly exist in Sonnet 106. Whereas the shady realm of dreams in *Richard III* functions to imply a divine intent behind Richard's purgation of the English court in order to make way for Henry VII, the prophetic in Sonnet 106 is imagined only to prefigure "Even such beauty as you master now" (l. 8).

Like a number of sonnets that are self-conscious about the difficulty of "making beautiful . . . rhyme" (106.3), Sonnet 106 can also be linked to many plays from the first half of Shakespeare's career. In *Love's Labor's Lost*, for example, the immaturity of the lords of Navarre is clearly figured by their weak poetry, or, as the French Princess describes the King's poetry, "as much love in rhyme / As would be cramm'd up in a sheet of paper" (5.2.6–7). Similarly, in *As You Like It*, the tension between Orlando's personal passion and his conventional expression is well bespoke by the poetry that he affixes to the trees in the Forest of Arden, poems that Touchstone calls Orlando's "very false gallop of verses" (3.2.113). Indeed, in a passage reminiscent of Sonnet 106, Rosalind says of Orlando's poems of praise that "I was never so berhym'd since Pythagoras' time, that I was an Irish rat, which I can hardly remember" (3.2 176–178). In these comedies, such poetic failings are remedied either through marriage or the promise of marriage in the end. In plays like *Romeo and Juliet* and *Titus Andronicus*, however, such poetic failings lead to tragic consequences. In the former play, Romeo's empty Petrarchan language at the beginning suggests an immaturity that will prove destructive both to himself and to Juliet. In the latter play, Lavinia's rape and disfigurement symbolize not simply her lack of agency within hyper-masculine Rome but also the objectification of the female body by romantic discourses full of Petrarchan clichés. Such troubling objectification is perhaps most apparent in Marcus's long poetic response to the sight of the ravished Lavinia the end of act 2. In effect, neither Rome nor Verona is shown to be capable of envisioning a man's love for a woman outside of the objectifying idealism of Petrarchan poetic expression—what Sonnet 106 calls "the blazon of sweet beauty's best, / Of hand, of foot, of lip, of eye, of brow" (106.5–6).

Sonnet 106 can be associated with works by other contemporary writers as well. There is an obvious connection to be made between Sonnet 106 and the first quatrain of a sonnet written by Henry Constable that is preserved in manuscript: "Miracle of the world! I never will deny / That former poets praise the beauty of their days; / But all of those beauties were but figure of thy praise, / And all those poets did of thee but prophesy" (quoted in Kerrigan, 312). Because we do not know the date of composition of this poem (or of Sonnet 106, for that matter), however, the line of influence can only remain conjectural. Sonnet 106 has also been argued to be reminiscent of the forty-sixth sonnet in Samuel Daniel's *Delia*, published in 1592. In a manner somewhat akin to Shakespeare's sonnet, Daniel's begins with a rumination upon poets (in this case contemporary poets) who have sung of "Knights and Palladines." Just as Shakespeare's speaker suggests that antique poets were limited in their ability to capture beauty because they were not able to see the young man, Daniel's speaker implies that poets who have not chosen Delia as their poetic object have ensured the inferiority of their poems. Daniel's speaker, however, lacks the pessimistic attitude towards his own poetic abilities that so defines the speaker of Sonnet 106. Whereas Daniel's speaker—in the vein of Ovid in his epilogue at the end of his *Metamorphoses*—confidently asserts his ability to create "Arkes and Tropheis [ . . . ] / That fortifie thy name against old age," Shakespeare's speaker ends by admitting that he and other poets "lack tongues to praise" (106.14).

**Annotated Bibliography**

Evans, G. Blakemore, ed. *The Sonnets*. Cambridge: Cambridge UP, 1996. An edition of Shakespeare's sonnets that includes a basic introduction, a detailed commentary on each sonnet, and a short textual analysis of the 1609 quarto.

Kerrigan, John, ed. *Shakespeare: "The Sonnets" and "A Lover's Complaint."* Harmondsworth, Eng.: Penguin, 1986. A frequently cited edition of Shakespeare's sonnets that argues for the importance of "A Lover's Complaint" as the concluding element of the sequence. It includes a relatively long introduction that articulates Kerrigan's historicist approach, detailed commentary on each sonnet, and a useful section on "Variants and further Sonnets."

Vendler, Helen. *The Art of Shakespeare's Sonnets*. Cambridge, MA: Harvard University Press, 1997. An often compelling work that considers each sonnet as its own poetic entity. It includes an accessible introduction and an admirably detailed analysis of each sonnet.

# Sonnet 116

### Annalisa Castaldo

Let me not to the marriage of true minds
Admit impediments. Love is not love
Which alters when it alteration finds,
Or bends with the remover to remove:
O no! it is an ever-fixed mark
That looks on tempests and is never shaken;
It is the star to every wandering bark,
Whose worth's unknown, although his height be taken.
Love's not Time's fool, though rosy lips and cheeks
Within his bending sickle's compass come:
Love alters not with his brief hours and weeks,
But bears it out even to the edge of doom.
   If this be error and upon me prov'd,
   I never writ, nor no man ever lov'd.

## PROSE PARAPHRASE

I will never admit that anything can hinder the union of two people truly in love. Love that is affected by circumstances or that fades because of distance is not true love. No, love is completely stable, unshaken by trauma. It is like a lighthouse or the North Star, which guides ships safely to harbor, and therefore is priceless. Time cannot change love, although time can change the physical appearance of the beloved. Love does not change over hours and weeks, but endures even until Judgment Day. If this belief in love is proved to be in error, then I have never written anything and no one has ever loved.

## THE PLACE OF THE SONNET IN THE CYCLE

Sonnet 116 is closely connected to the sonnets immediately before and after; all are concerned with the definition or proof of true love. Sonnet 115 argues that true love increases over time. Sonnet 116, of course, argues the exact opposite—that true love does not change or "alter when it alteration finds" (l. 3). Sonnet 117 then picks up on the language and themes of Sonnet 116 to argue that true love survives tests of (apparent) forgetfulness and unfaithfulness. The three sonnets together thus take on the challenge of understanding true love, but without coming to any conclusion, and the fact that Sonnet 116 comes in the middle, rather than at the end, of the extended consideration suggests that Shakespeare did not see it as the ultimate argument, even though most readers feel otherwise.

Sonnet 116 is also closely connected to sonnets 105 and 124 in theme, as they also attempt to describe or define idealized true love. However, neither of these sonnets uses the metaphors of 116, except for 124's "fools of Time" (l. 13), which echoes in the positive Sonnet 116's negative version: "Love's not Time's fool" (l. 9). Sonnet 124, like Sonnet 116, contrasts true love with affection that is subject to time, chance, and mutability. Through their folly, "fools of Time" bear witness to the nature of false love. Sonnet 105 is a meditation on constancy. The lines "Kind is my love today, to-morrow kind, / Still constant in a wondrous excellence" (105.5–6) share the attitude of Sonnet 116, but the focus in the earlier sonnet is clearly on a specific person, the poet's beloved, rather than on an impersonal definition of love in general.

Sonnet 116 rests within the large group of sonnets (1–126) concerned with the relationship between the poet and his friend, a handsome youth. It shares with all those sonnets a concern not only with the truth of what love is, but also a concern about the ravages of Time and how love or beauty might escape Time's destruction. The idea of doomsday shows up in Sonnet 55: "That wear this world out to the ending doom" (l. 12). Here, doomsday destroys the entire world, whereas in Sonnet 116 love survives even this cataclysmic event.

Personified Time with his sickle or, more usually, his scythe, shows up repeatedly, in sonnets 12.13, 60.12, 74.11, 100.14, 123.14, and 126.2. Most often when attempting to combat Time's ravages, the poet presents his poetry (or in the so-called Marriage group of sonnets 1–17 procreation) as a defense against time, but in Sonnet 116 poetry has only a walk-on in line 13, and it is not connected to the destruction caused by Time. Instead, love itself is presented as outlasting time and therefore needing no poetic defense against it.

## DEVICES AND TECHNIQUES

Sonnet 116 is composed with particular attention to structure. Each quatrain consists of a single sentence, with the couplet also a single sentence. The first quatrain has four enjambed lines, presenting a single, fluid thought describing the core of true love and the core of the poem. The fluidity of the poetic movement matches the positive nature of the idea, as well as the claim of the poet that there should be no impediments, not even those of punctuation. The second and third quatrains, in contrast, describe the possible impediments that love must and will overcome, and therefore the majority of lines are appropriately end-stopped, with only line 9's "rosy lips and cheeks" moving unencumbered into line 10, to be gathered up by the sickle of Time.

The sonnet begins with a command by the poet, but not to the reader; instead the poet addresses himself: "Let me not to the marriage of true minds / Admit impediments." Thus, although the poem is expansive in its theme, it is very narrowly focused in scope. The command to himself would seem to make this one of the most introspective of Shakespeare's sonnets, but the impersonal and general nature of the claims keep the poem from relating to the poet specifically. The self-command is followed by a series of statements, without any suggestion of uncertainty or doubt, until the final couplet. And even that final couplet only allows the possibility of doubt ("If this be error," 116.13) to indicate the extreme intensity of the speaker's belief through the impossibilities expressed in the second line of the couplet: "I never writ, nor no man ever loved" (116.14).

As Stephen Booth points out, Sonnet 116 has a clarity unusual in the sonnets; it is single-minded in its focus and tone (*Shakespeare's Sonnets*, p. 389). Aside from the structure, this clarity and focus are achieved by combining thoughts so general and so generally accepted as to be almost clichés, with detailed descriptions that "thus invest abstract statements with the urgency, vividness, and apprehensibility of concrete particulars" (Booth, p. 387). Thus the "ever-fixed mark" (5) is love itself, but also, by the next line, a person or personified thing that can "look" and not be "shaken." This shift in perspective could be confusing but is not because the sonnet is so tightly constructed around its single theme. The impersonality of the sonnet enhances the clarity, because it is almost immediately clear that the poet is concerned with a general definition of love, and there is no background or emotional layers that need to be understood before the meaning can be grasped.

## THEMES AND MEANINGS

As mentioned above, Sonnet 116 has a single-minded focus—the definition of true love as constant in the face of any and every obstacle. This focus is unfolded through, first, a definition that encompasses the first quatrain; and, second, through two metaphorical descriptions of the main obstacles love might face. Unlike so many sonnets, the couplet does not provide a twist or unexpected ending; instead it strengthens the main argument by presenting impossibilities as true if the rest of the poem is proved false.

Shakespeare begins with the famous phrase, "Let me not to the marriage of true minds / Admit impediments" (116.1–2). By focusing on "marriage" he appears at first to be shifting his focus from the handsome young man of previous sonnets. However, this is a spiritual marriage, one of minds rather than bodies. In type as well as in purpose, this "marriage" contrasts with the procreative and therefore clearly heterosexual marriage urged on the young man in the early sonnets. This idea of a spiritual union looks forward to Donne's metaphysical love poetry such as "The Ecstasy" and "A Valediction: Forbidding Mourning."

The metaphor of life as a sea voyage is a traditional one, used by Shakespeare and many other poets. In this example, the sea is appropriately stormy, and love is the stable force. Love is first presented as a man-made "mark" or beacon, the kind of guide that sailors can use only when they are close to land and, presumably, safe harbor. The power and stability of love is expanded in lines 7–8, when it is figured as the North Star, a natural or heavenly fixture rather than a man-made one. Shakespeare describes it as the guide to "every wand'ring bark" (l. 7). This universality continues the sonnet's focus on the general; the poem is not just about the poet's particular relationship. "Wand'ring" describes literally the movement of ships across the sea, but the word also has the suggestion of "error" and thus subtly implies falsity in the midst of truth. Since love is the star that remains fixed, Shakespeare is suggesting that love is something separate from the people engaged in a loving relationship; even though they might wander or stray, true love remains unchanging. This point is further emphasized by the astronomical language of the line, "Whose worth's unknown, although his highth be taken" (116.8). Just as the altitude of the North Star can be measured, but neither its value nor its true nature understood, a loving relationship can be described and itemized, but love itself will still not be adequately grasped.

In the third quatrain, Shakespeare returns to a theme he has used many times before, the idea of Time's destructiveness. However, here his focus is on what Time cannot do rather than on what Time can. The poet allows that "rosy lips and cheeks"—signs of both youth and life generally—are swept away by Time, but he claims that even doomsday itself cannot alter love. The use of the phrase "Love alters not" in line 11 returns to the beginning of the poem—"Love is not love / Which alters" (ll. 2–3)—and emphasizes the focus on constancy.

The couplet's use of the word "error" refers back to "wand'ring" (l. 7), but since the idea is now applied to love rather than lovers, the possibility of "error" is rejected with oxymoronic certainty. The speaker also re-enters the poem; he began with a command to himself, "Let me not," and ends by taking responsibility for the truth of what he has said. "If this be error and upon me proved / I never writ" (ll. 13–14). Thus, although the sonnet consists almost completely of generalities that can be applied to anyone, the poet maintains control of the argument and the poem by establishing his personal claims. In some sense, the poet has acted as a guide to or professor of love, lecturing the reader and therefore appearing as an expert in the subject, but without revealing any personal involvement or experience.

Helen Vendler, alone of all critics, sees Sonnet 116 not as a positive description of true love, but as a dramatic refutation of that claim. She points to the large number of negatives, such as "not" "never" and "no," which begin with the very first line ("Let me not") and appear in lines 2, 5, 6, 9, 10, and 14, along with "unknown" (8) and "but" (12). She also argues that the quatrains differ radically from each other, indicating not a continuous unfolding of a single line of inquiry, but reconsideration and change on the poet's part. "Without the differential model of refutation, reinscription, and authorial rethinking, the poem is imperfectly seen" (Vendler, p. 491). Vendler's argument is well presented within her critical framework, and opens the door for reconsideration of this best known and loved of Shakespeare's sonnets.

## THE RELATIONSHIP OF THE SONNET TO SHAKESPEARE'S OTHER WORKS

Sonnet 116 will for most readers be linked immediately and strongly to *Romeo and Juliet*, since it is that play that most fully deals with a marriage of true minds that refuse to bend to any obstacle. The metaphor of the lover as a ship in a tempest is twice used by Romeo, although his first use, "But He that hath the steerage of my course / Direct my sail!" (1.4.112–113), is connected to love only because Romeo himself is the prototypical lover. In his death scene, Romeo again uses the metaphor, but here to describe the failure of his voyage now that love no longer guides him. "Thou desperate pilot; now at once run on / The dashing rocks thy seasick weary bark!" (5.3.117–118). Romeo, as he views the supposedly dead Juliet, also makes reference to her crimson lips and cheeks, which echoes Sonnet 116's "rosy lips and cheeks" (l. 9); and the sonnet's claim that "Love's not Time's fool" (l. 9) finds an echo in Romeo's "O, I am fortune's fool!" (3.1.136). The sonnet's lines 11–12, "Love alters not with his brief hours and weeks / But bears it out even to the edge of doom," might be considered an adequate one-sentence summary for the entire play.

The idea of a tempest as a metaphorical obstacle to love is literalized in *Othello*, when Othello and Desdemona are separated by a storm at sea before they are separated by internal tempests, and Titania describes how her lover's quarrel with Oberon results in unseasonable storms which "Hath every pelting river made so proud / That they have overborne their continents" (*A Midsummer Night's Dream*, 2.1.91–92). Shakespeare also uses storms in both *The Tempest* and *King Lear* to signal dramatic changes in circumstances and psychological upheavals.

The North Star is used to describe constancy and firmness in *Julius Caesar* when Caesar describes himself as "constant as the northern star, / Of whose true-fix'd and resting quality / There is no fellow in the firmament" (3.1.60–62). Coriolanus makes a similar point when he expresses his hopes for his son while echoing the other nautical metaphor of 116: "that thou mayst prove / To shame invulnerable, and stick i' th' wars / Like a great sea-mark, standing every flaw, / And saving those that eye thee!" (*Coriolanus* 5.3.72–75).

The use of "compass" to relate to the end of a life is used in *Julius Caesar* (5.3.25), but is more generally used to mean encompass or circumscribe, as in *The Rape of Lucrece* (l. 346), *Richard III* 1.3.283, and *Titus Andronicus* 5.1.126. It is also used generally to describe a man holding a woman in his arms or attempting to win her favor, as in *The Two Gentlemen of Verona* 2.4.212. These other meanings of "compass" thus resonate with the word's significance in Sonnet 116 ("range") to indicate that though Time may win the beloved's physical attributes, true love will endure.

### Annotated Bibliography

Booth, Stephen. *An Essay on Shakespeare's Sonnets.* New Haven: Yale UP, 1969. This book-length essay is an intelligent and detailed consideration of the problem of the sonnets as a coherent sequence since, as Booth points out, there are varying and conflicting patterns rather than an overarching, consistent narrative. Booth also considers individual sonnets, some in great depth.

———, ed. *Shakespeare's Sonnets.* New Haven: Yale UP, 1977. Here, Booth presents an en-face edition of the 1609 quarto and a modernized version. In addition, Booth provides scholarly commentary that ranges from specific word and line explication to discussions of connections among sonnets and to various other Shakespearean and other sixteenth- and seventeenth-century texts. Invaluable.

Fineman, Joel. *Shakespeare's Perjured Eye: The Invention of Poetic Subjectivity in the Sonnets.* Berkeley: U of California P, 1986. Fineman argues that in the sonnets Shakespeare invents a new poetic subjectivity that disrupts the previously normalized relationship between the poetic persona and the poet himself, especially in the lyric praise poem.

Vendler, Helen. *The Art of Shakespeare's Sonnets.* Cambridge, MA: Harvard UP, 1997. Vendler presents in-depth, intelligent, and occasionally startling readings of each sonnet. By rejecting the lure of a narrative pattern, Vendler is able to provide more sensitive readings than many past critics, who were forced to emphasize those elements that fit into their particular pattern.

Weiser, David K. *Mind in Character: Shakespeare's Speaker in the Sonnets.* Columbia: U of Missouri P, 1987. Weiser focuses on the poet-speaker and distinguishes between "soliloquies" and "dialogues" to suggest that readers identify with the speaker as a character and that there is a pattern of growth in the sonnets as arranged in the 1609 quarto.

# Sonnet 126

## Steven Doloff

O thou, my lovely boy, who in thy power
Dost hold Time's fickle glass, his sickle hour;
Who hast by waning grown, and therein show'st
Thy lovers withering as thy sweet self grow'st;
If Nature, sovereign mistress over wrack,
As thou goest onwards, still will pluck thee back,
She keeps thee to this purpose, that her skill
May time disgrace and wretched minutes kill.
Yet fear her, O thou minion of her pleasure!
She may detain, but not still keep, her treasure:
  Her audit, though delay'd, answer'd must be,
  And her quietus is to render thee.

## PROSE PARAPHRASE

The speaker, addressing his "lovely boy," warns him that despite the youth's physical beauty, the perfection of which seems to defy the ravages of personified Time, his condition is still temporary. Nature, personified as a doting mistress to her creation, the boy, is portrayed as having only limited power to sustain his beauty, which she does as a gesture to deny and shame Time. The speaker explains that Nature must eventually submit to the authority of Time and pay for her gesture by handing the boy over to Time's "withering" ministrations which he, the speaker, has already begun to experience (126.4).

## THE PLACE OF THE SONNET IN THE CYCLE

Sonnet 126 has often been cited as part of an argument for a thematic division within Shakespeare's sonnet sequence. Since, starting with Sonnet 127, the remainder of the sequence, when gender specific, addresses or concerns a woman, Sonnet

126 would appear to be the envoi of the preceding 125 that, when gender specific, involve a young man, something of an oddity in Elizabethan sonnet cycles.

It is possible that a numerological significance may be found in the sonnet as well. As number 126, it constitutes the sonnet sequence's second "grand climacteric." The *Oxford English Dictionary* notes that in Shakespeare's day, individuals' ages that expressed multiples of 7's and multiples of 9's were traditionally regarded as "climacteric" ages, or particularly subject to changes in health or fortune. The age of 63 (the "grand climacteric"), a multiple of both 7 and 9, was believed especially critical. This may explain why Sonnet 63 (the sequence's first "grand climacteric") emphasizes the speaker's own physical decline at Time's hand, and graphically anticipates the same for his beloved boy. As the second "grand climacteric," Sonnet 126 revisits this same theme of the speaker and youth's common mortality.

## DEVICES AND TECHNIQUES

Formally, Sonnet 126 joins sonnets 99 and 145 in deviating from the uniform pentameter, fourteen line English rhyme scheme (*abab cdcd efef gg*) of all the other sonnets in the sequence. Sonnet 99 has a fifteenth line and Sonnet 145 is written in tetrameters.

Sonnet 126 is constructed of six iambic pentameter couplets followed in the 1609 edition by two pairs of italicized parentheses. While the inclusion of "twelve liners" (under the looser definition of sonnet as simply a short lyric) in Elizabethan sonnet sequences, and even of those consisting of couplets, is not unheard of, it is rare. For this reason, scholars have speculated as to whether the terminal parentheses are of editorial or authorial origin. Editorialists suggest that the printer of the 1609 quarto may have bracketed what he perceived to be the missing thirteenth and fourteenth lines of a standard sonnet (Evans, p. 241). (Authorialists' interpretations appear below.)

The sonnet does adhere to Shakespeare's common rhetorical mode of posing an assertion or complaint in the first eight lines and then turning with the ninth line to some modified point of view. The former here is the speaker's marking of Nature's physical gifts to the boy, the latter, his warning of her inevitable abandonment of the youth to Time's ruin. Also in keeping with the norms of the cycle, the poem is organized grammatically into what would constitute three quatrains in a regular sonnet.

The accounting metaphors in which death is couched at the end of Sonnet 126 mark the culmination of the financial imagery developed through earlier sonnets. In sonnets 2 and 4 the speaker urges the boy to propagate heirs to whom he may bequeath as his "legacy" (4.2) the "treasure" (2.6) of his beauty, and in Sonnet 6 he protests that the multiplication of that "treasure" (6.4) in progeny is not an illegal form of "usury" (6.5). In Sonnet 30, "th' expense" (30.8) of personal sorrows causes the speaker to "pay" (30.12) in tears. Sonnet 49 imagines an "audit," or reckoning (49.4), by the boy of his feelings for the speaker. Sonnet 67 describes a "bankrout" (bankrupt) Nature relying upon her "exchequer" (treasury), the lovely boy, for the "wealth" (beauty) he alone possesses (67.9, 11, 13), and in Sonnet 125 the speaker seeks "mutual render" (equal exchange) of commitment between the boy and himself (125.12).

None of the uses to which Shakespeare puts these earlier financial tropes, however, would seem to anticipate the final sepulchral "audit" (examination of accounts) in 126.11 to which Nature is to be called by Time, or the "quietus" (discharge of debt to clear accounts) for which she must "render" (hand over in payment) (l. 12) her "treasure" (l. 10), the boy. Death presides over this "quietus" in the form of its alternative Elizabethan meaning, to discharge or release from life, made famous by Shakespeare's only other use of the term, in Hamlet's reflection upon how one might "his quietus make / With a bare bodkin [mere dagger]" (3.1.74–75). An additional implication in "quietus" here may be the settling of accounts or putting to rest, with Sonnet 126, of the speaker's self-obligated debt of praise to the beloved boy (Evans, p. 242–243).

The accounting metaphor evokes, as well, the commonplace cited by Shakespeare in *1 Henry IV* that life is a debt to God, as Prince Hal tells Falstaff: "Why, thou owest God a death" (5.1.126). Alternative Elizabethan uses of "rend" and "render," appropriately, include to tear apart and to melt down.

In Sonnet 126 Shakespeare shapes even his poetics to his argument. Just as we are told that Nature holds back the boy as long as she can from Time's dominion, the speaker holds back until the last two words of the poem to announce the boy's fate ("render thee"). Moreover, the signal words of doom in the last line, "quietus" and "render," would seem at least phonically anticipated by the poem in preceding groups of thematically linked words. The "k" sound in "quietus" is heard earlier in "sickle," "wrack" and "kill"; and the "r" in "render," in "withering," "wrack" and "wretched" (Vendler, pp. 534–535).

## THEMES AND MEANINGS

As the last in the beloved boy series of sonnets, Sonnet 126 reprises several recurring themes, along with their associated images and metaphors. The dominant theme in this poem is that of Nature's war with time, "that her skill / May Time disgrace and wretched minutes kill" (126.7–8). However, the beauty of Nature's creations, exemplified in the boy, can only briefly escape Time's ruinous power. This theme appears prominently in sonnets 1–19, and repeatedly through to Sonnet 126. The "glass," or mirror, in Sonnet 126 (l. 2), used also in sonnets 3, 22, 62, 77, and 103, attests to either the temporary abeyance of Time's visible damage to the boy, or its evident toll upon the speaker. Similarly, the "sickle" (l. 2), as a metaphor for Time's disfiguring function, appears first in Sonnet 116 and, synonymously as "scythe," is used for its fatal function in sonnets 12, 60, 100, and 123.

The theme of the speaker's love for the boy in Sonnet 126 merits some note specifically for its subdominant role. Given the sonnet's valedictory position in the series, the primary motif of which is arguably the speaker's devotion to the youth, and given that the preceding three sonnets reaffirm that devotion, there would seem placed upon Sonnet 126 expectations of a similar emphasis. Yet the speaker's love for the boy is noted in the sonnet merely in passing, as we assume the speaker to be among the boy's aging "lovers" (l. 4). Indeed, in a somewhat antipetrarchan conclusion to the series, the speaker's much protested admiration for the boy leads to no final transformation or transcendence. The speaker ends both the sonnet and the series, rather, by directing the boy's and the reader's attention admonitorily into the grave.

If the theme of love in Sonnet 126 is notable for its understatement when viewed in context with the preceding series, within that same context the theme of death is remarkable for its ascendancy. Highlighted at the end of Sonnet 126, predictions of death weave also through many of the earlier 125 sonnets. Direct reference to the fair youth's death appears in sonnets 1, 3–4, 6–7, 11–14, 64, and 104; and to that of the speaker's in sonnets 32, 71, and 73–74. Sonnet 81 (perhaps significant because of its climacteric numbers, $81 = 9 \times 9$) specifically links the deaths of both. In many of these earlier sonnets the speaker offers various defenses against death (or Time), such as the youth's power to propagate in sonnets 1, 3–4, 6, 9, 11–14, 16–17; the speaker's power to preserve the boy's graces through poetry, for example, Sonnet 63 (the sequence's first "grand climacteric") as well as in sonnets 15, 17–19, 60, 65, 100, 107; and even the speaker's own irrevocable love for the boy in sonnets 116 and 123–125. None of these defenses, however, return in Sonnet 126 to mitigate the grim finality of the "quietus" (l. 12) to come.

Critical attention to Sonnet 126, by itself, has focused upon several aspects, such as the possible double meaning to be found in the term "glass" in line two. Some critics have resisted the more common usage here of the word as "mirror" because, while it may literally reflect time's power, it is not an object conventionally carried by Father Time. Taken, alternatively, to mean "hourglass," a shortening used only one other time by Shakespeare, in *The Winter's Tale* (4.1.16), the image joins "sickle" as Father Time's two traditional possessions. Such a reading, however, would then appear to make "hour," the third element in the line as printed in the 1609 quarto, "Doest hould times fickle glasse, his sickle, hower," redundant as a reference to the passage of time. Thus some sonnet editors have dropped the comma between "sickle" and "hower" to create the single idea of "sickle hower," meaning variously the specific moment of life's reaping (death), the period of diminished time (like the sickle-shaped phase of the moon), or the destructive time unit itself (the sickle-like, rending hour), all of which offer approximate appositives to "fickle [hour]glass" (Booth, p. 431).

Another aspect of critical attention in the sonnet is the paradoxical expression in line 3, that the youth "hast by waning grown." It has been suggested that this may be an allusion to the activity of an hourglass (possibly figured in the preceding line) that wanes on top as it grows below. As such, it may describe the boy's increasing beauty even as he simultaneously diminishes his total allotment of time (Evans, p. 241).

A third critical question involves the inconsistent distribution of authority among the boy, Nature, and Time. In the first line, the lovely boy is personally ascribed the "power" to forestall the ravages of Time upon himself. In line five, however, Nature is portrayed as "sovereign mistress over wrack," making her the ruler over the forces of ruin, to which the boy is now subject. And by poem's end, Nature herself is made accountable to a more formidable, unnamed authority (arguably Time) to whom she is ultimately obliged to cede dominion over the youth (see Joseph Pequigney's *Such Is My Love: A Study of Shakespeare's Sonnets* [Chicago: U of Chicago P, 1985], 204).

The empty parentheses of lines 13 and 14 in the 1609 quarto (which modern editors usually choose to omit) have elicited much scholarly speculation. If we assume they appear because Shakespeare and not the printer put them there, then they would seem to constitute some kind of pictographic coda to the sonnet, if not to the entire young man sequence. Understandably, the range of interpretations is fairly wide. A commonly held opinion is that the two sets of parentheses are meant to imitate specific imagery already found or alluded to in the sonnet. Thus, to different scholars they have suggested an empty hourglass (see Rene Graziani's "The Numbering of Shakespeare's Sonnets 12, 60 and 126," *Shakespeare Quarterly* 35 [1984]: 79–82), "waning" lunar crescents (see John Lennard's *"But I Digress": The Exploitation of Parentheses in English Printed Verse* [New York: Oxford UP, 1991], 41–43), marks in an accounting book (Duncan Jones, p. 366), or the blades of sickles. The excising of two lines might also be seen as representing or recapitulating Nature's "plucking back" or "rendering" (as in "tearing off") of the boy. It has been proposed that the bracketed empty lines imply two empty graves, one for the youth and one for the speaker (as the results of the two "grand climacterics"), thus indicating, perhaps, their ultimate union, even if only in death (Duncan Jones, pp. 100, 364). Another opinion is that the missing couplet reflects the boy's barren legacy, should he continue to refuse to "couple" (have children) as the speaker has urged him (Duncan Jones, p. 366). A numerological interpretation has it that the seventh couplet is missing because, while the number six was traditionally associated with human perfection (as attributed to the boy), seven was identified with divine perfection, beyond mortal reach (Duncan Jones, p. 364).

Finally, the "quietus" suggestive of death in line twelve has reminded some scholars of Prince Hamlet's departing declaration, "The rest is silence" (5.2.358), prompting the idea that the "silent" couplet at the end of Sonnet 126 expresses that death-like stillness (Duncan Jones, p. 366).

## THE RELATIONSHIP OF THE SONNET TO SHAKESPEARE'S OTHER WORKS

The theme of time's ruinous authority that develops through the initial lovely boy sequence to govern Sonnet 126 may be found in several of Shakespeare's plays, but in minor or very circumscribed roles. For example, it appears in Macbeth's despairing speech:

> To-morrow, and to-morrow, and to-morrow,
> Creeps in this petty pace from day to day,
> To the last syllable of recorded time;
> And all our yesterdays have lighted fools
> The way to dusty death. (5.5.19–23)

This vision of a meaningless, "dusty death" to which Macbeth believes time's "petty pace" leads him is not, however, a controlling theme in the play, but rather a symptom of the moral dissolution to which Macbeth has reduced only himself.

We can also find a similarly despondent view of time expressed in passing by the dying Hotspur in *1 Henry IV*. More despairing over his loss of "proud titles" to Prince Hal than his "brittle life," he bitterly observes life to be "time's fool" (5.4.79, 78, 81). And in *As You Like It*, Jaques' well known "seven ages" of man speech presents what is (within the context of that comedy) solely the melancholic's perspective on time's compelled decrepitude and "mere oblivion / Sans teeth, sans eyes, sans taste, sans every thing" (2.7.165–166). Earlier in that scene Jaques reports how in his conversation with Touchstone, the fool "very wisely" does "moral [moralize] on the time" (2.7.29):

> And so from hour to hour, we ripe, and ripe,
> And then from hour to hour we rot and rot;
> And thereby hangs a tale. (2.7.26–28)

While it may seem we have found another expression of Sonnet 126's rueful contradiction "by waning grown" (l. 3), its thematic weight is negligible. For the fool's pronouncement on time's paradoxical operations is most appropriately understood as a parody rather than an affirmation of Jaques' truly morose attitudinizing on mortality.

**Annotated Bibliography**

Booth, Stephen, ed. *Shakespeare's Sonnets*. New Haven: Yale UP, 1977. A useful edition with helpful commentary on each sonnet. Also reprints the 1609 (first) edition of these poems.

Duncan-Jones, Katherine, ed. *Shakespeare's Sonnets*. The Arden Shakespeare. London: Thomas Nelson and Sons, 1997. A standard edition that offers up-to-date textual and critical commentary for each of the poems.

Evans, G. Blakemore, ed. *The Sonnets*. The New Cambridge Shakespeare. Cambridge: Cambridge UP, 1996. Another useful edition. The notes will prove informative to students at any level.

Vendler, Helen, ed. *The Art of Shakespeare's Sonnets*. Cambridge, MA: Harvard UP, 1997. Offers a thorough study of the individual sonnets' complex prosodic and rhetorical patterns and devices. Excellent analysis of Shakespeare's use of language.

# Sonnet 128

## Gayle Gaskill

How oft, when thou, my music, music play'st,
Upon that blessed wood whose motion sounds
With thy sweet fingers, when thou gently sway'st
The wiry concord that mine ear confounds,
Do I envy those jacks that nimble leap
To kiss the tender inward of thy hand,
Whilst my poor lips, which should that harvest reap,
At the wood's boldness by thee blushing stand!
To be so tickl'd, they would change their state
And situation with those dancing chips,
O'er whom thy fingers walk with gentle gait,
Making dead wood more bless'd than living lips.
   Since saucy jacks so happy are in this,
   Give them thy fingers, me thy lips to kiss.

## PROSE PARAPHRASE

To me you are melody and harmony, so whenever your gracious hands touch the lucky virginal to command a wordless song from its well-tuned wires, you so confuse me with delight that I grow jealous of the little keys that hop up to caress your dear fingertips. Standing beside you, I grow hot with envy and desire to see that pushy instrument gather all the pleasures that my lips deserve. Those lips now dote so pitifully that they would gladly trade places with the lifeless wooden instrument in order to feel your fingertips tenderly tripping over them. If you must satisfy those cheeky rascals, the virginal's keys, then thrill them with your fingers but kiss me with your lips.

## THE PLACE OF THE SONNET IN THE CYCLE

This second of the Dark Lady sonnets playfully combines two notions from the sonnets to the fair young man, music and jealousy, and with heightened sexual emphasis redirects them to the lady. It identifies the love object with beautiful music, a rare conceit in Shakespeare's sonnets. Only Sonnet 8 ("Music to hear, why hear'st thou music sadly?") joins Sonnet 128 in employing the word "music" to name the beloved. That earlier sonnet addresses a mellifluous speaker or perhaps a singer who is "music to hear" (l. 1). In this quality the youth exceeds the lady, for according to Sonnet 130, compared to her speech, "music hath a far more pleasing sound" (l. 10). Though the poet admits he loves "to hear her speak" (l. 9), nevertheless in Sonnet 128 he portrays her only as an instrumentalist, calling her "my music [who] music play'st" (l. 1). She commands the tune solely with her hands.

The other musical resemblance between sonnets 8 and 128 is their juxtaposition of the same pair of like-sounding opposites, terms for harmony and confusion. In Sonnet 8, the poet uses the noun "concord" (l. 5), meaning "agreement or harmony between things" (*Oxford English Dictionary sb.* 4), as he tells the stubborn young bachelor that musical concord should by analogy persuade him of his duty to marry and to father an heir. Then with emphatic alliteration he introduces the verb "confound" (l. 7), that is, "to defeat utterly, discomfit, bring to ruin" (*OED v. trans.* 1.a.), in order to rebuke the youth's self-destructive resistance to his patriarchal duty.

In Sonnet 8 the rhetorical confrontation between "concord" and "confound" amiably chides the young man for lost opportunity, but in Sonnet 128 the same musical rhetoric chides the speaker himself by portraying him as a lover completely bemused by the musician who "gently sway'st / the wiry concord that mine ear confounds" (ll. 3–4). The lady creates musical concord from what Kerrigan calls "the sinewy twanging which characterizes the virginals" (355) and thereby confounds the speaker's reason as she rouses his sexual desire.

Sonnet 128 comically portrays a second concept of the young man sonnets in the speaker's jealous accommodation of his rivals. In envying "those jacks that nimble leap / To kiss the tender inward of thy hand" (ll. 5–6), the poet confesses what Vendler describes as an adolescent phase of "abject . . . doting—longing to blush, to be tickled, to dance, to kiss, to worship every motion of the beloved, even at the price of sharing her with others" (547). The speaker first hints he is willing to share his mistress with an amorous rival in sonnets 40–42, where he detects the young man's interest in the woman and unhesitatingly offers her to him, dubiously insisting that his consuming affection for the youth exceeds his interest in the woman. Coyly, he phrases the offer in conundrums. In Sonnet 40 he twice addresses the young man as "my love" (ll. 1, 3), reiterating his claim upon his friend with the possessive pronoun, and he twice repeats the same phrase to name the female love object he freely surrenders, thereby reinscribing his claim to her as well. With a combination of noble generosity and pathetic capitulation, he insists, "All mine was thine, before thou hadst this more" (l. 4). The teasingly self-contradictory offer invites diverse interpretations. In its words "mine" and "thine," Colin Burrow finds an echo of the Anglican marriage vow, "With all my worldly goods I thee endow" (*The Complete Sonnets and Poems* [New York: Oxford UP, 2002], 460). Meanwhile, Duncan-Jones suggests its concluding word, "more," may be "an anticipation of the sonnet [144] alluding to 'a woman colored ill'" (190). Sonnets 40–42, with affected word games, anticipate the intense sexual jealousy that recurs in the Dark Lady sonnets. Sonnet 42 ends the discussion with a wanly self-deluding sophistry: "my friend and I are one; / Sweet flattery! then she loves but me alone" (ll. 13–14). Only with deft wordplay can the speaker balance self-esteem with self-abasing devotion to his rival. Like the more lightly self-mocking Sonnet 128, sonnets 40–42 gingerly approach the topic of a shared sexual relationship, dodge the dilemma with verbal dexterity, and promptly change the subject.

In its context near the start of the Dark Lady subsequence, Sonnet 128 delicately introduces the bitter jealousy and self-contempt that recur more vividly throughout the speaker's dramatization of his relationship. Notably, in Sonnet 137 the speaker fears his eyes of desire are "anchor'd in the bay where all men ride" (l. 5), that is, as Duncan-Jones puts it with emphatic italics, "where *all men* find sexual release" (388). Sonnet 144 doubles the jealousy by imagining the woman tempting the beloved young man, and the poet elaborates his anguished self-portrait as a jealous lover by confessing his lack of proof, for he admits that "suspect I may, yet not directly tell" (l. 10). In a devastating fulfillment of the quizzically self-abnegating offers he made in sonnets 40–42, he casts the youth and the mistress, as G. Blackmore Evans (*The Sonnets* [Cambridge: Cambridge UP, 1996], 262) and others have observed, as Virtue and Vice in a morality play or in Marlowe's *Dr. Faustus*:

> To win me soon to hell, my female evil
> Tempteth my better angel from my side,
> And would corrupt my saint to be a devil,
> Wooing his purity with her foul pride. (ll. 5–8)

Joking nervously in sonnet 128, the lover excitedly declares his only rivals for his lady's touch are the "jacks" of her instrument, and he puns lightly as he personifies the "saucy jacks" (l. 13), who "nimble leap / To kiss the tender inward of thy hand" (ll. 5–6) in terms that define a *jack* as "a low-bred or ill-mannered fellow, a 'knave' *Obs.*" (*OED sb.* 2a.). Instantly in the next sonnet the speaker transmogrifies that flirtatious confidence into a curse on the humiliation of sexual desire as he denounces "the heaven that leads men to this hell" (l. 14). In comparison to that grim sequel and those that follow, Sonnet 128 seems a frail piece of rhetoric. In his introduction to Stephen Orgel's Pelican edition of the sonnets (New York: Penguin, 2001), John Hollander finds it "trivial" (xxxv), and Booth calls it "a mere labor at cleverness" (439), but Vendler regards the poem as "a triumphant *jeu d'esprit* on the dangerous subject of sexual infidelity" (544). For a moment of amusing sprezzatura, Sonnet 128 controls vicious sexual anxieties with graceful wit.

## DEVICES AND TECHNIQUES

The syntax of Sonnet 128 strains against the traditional confining iambic pentameter structure of three rhymed quatrains and a couplet. Enjambment hurries the movement of lines 1, 2, 3, 5, and 9, and the first two quatrains form a single sentence with no punctuation stronger than commas. Thus the poem imitates the sight of "frantic action one sees when one looks inside a keyboard instrument while it is being played" (Booth, p. 438), the sound of rapid polyphonic music performed on plucked instruments, and the kinesthesia of its own controlling dance metaphor.

Like dancers of an Elizabethan volte or jig, the instrument's "dancing chips" (l. 10) "nimble leap" (l. 5), while the lady's more temperate fingers "walk with gentle gait" (l. 11) as she "gently sway'st / The wiry concord" of her instrument (ll. 3–4) and simultaneously stirs desire in one who does not dance but stands with his poor blushing lips. Rhythmically, the sonnet's concluding phrase is as remarkable for abrupt closure as the octave is for breathless enjambment. Having relinquished his lady's fingers to the virginal's "saucy jacks" (l. 13) with mock generosity, the speaker in his last five syllables suddenly commands her to give "me thy lips to kiss" (l. 14). He will not stop her music, so he stops her mouth.

The metaphor of dance requires personification, so Sonnet 128 animates two rival troupes of wooers for the lady. At first, the troupe belonging to the musical instrument is victorious. This includes first the virginal itself, the "wood," which is initially "blessed" (l. 2), then "bold" (l. 8), and finally "dead" (l. 12); next, the strings, "the wiry concord that mine ear confounds" (l. 4), and last the keys, the enviable "dancing chips" (l. 10), also known as "saucy jacks" (ll. 13, 5), that, when "tickled" (l. 9), "nimble leap / To kiss the tender inward of thy hand" (ll. 5–6). To oppose this formidable ensemble, the poet personifies "mine ear," which promptly surrenders to "the wiry concord" (l. 4), and "my poor lips" (l. 7), which "blushing stand . . . at the wood's boldness" (l. 8). Synecdoche reduces the lover to ear and lips and the lady to "fingers" (ll. 2, 11) and "hand" (l. 6). With dramatic efficiency the speaker delays the lips' victory over the jacks until the last words, which note that the lady herself has "lips to kiss." As Vendler reveals, he foreshadows his miniature triumph with a "homonymic phrase" (546): where the jacks "leap / To kiss" (ll. 5–6), the poet demands "lips to kiss" (l. 14).

The first line of this highly elaborate sonnet employs the technique of antistasis, as Booth points out, the "repetition of a word in a different sense" (439). The first "music," "thou, my music," is vocative; the second, "music play'st" is the object of the verb. Shakespeare reverses the same "self-conscious rhetorical gimcrack" (Booth, p. 439) in the first line of Sonnet 40: "Take all my loves, my love, yea, take them all." Here the direct object precedes the vocative, but the antistasis nonetheless links the poems as convoluted circumlocutions that dance daringly around a disturbing topic.

## THEMES AND MEANINGS

With a tone of giddy affection, Sonnet 128 intertwines two familiar themes of love poetry: the power of music and the lover's erotic jealousy of his lady's touch. According to Pythagoras, harmonious music issued from movements of the planets as they circled the stationary earth. In Sir John Davies's 1596 poem "Orchestra, or A Poem of Dancing," a suitor tells his lady that Love creates the universe out of chaos by setting the four elements dancing in harmonious motion. Nature, human affairs, and even her own hands dance:

> And when your ivory fingers touch the strings
> Of any silver-sounding instrument
> Love makes them dance to those sweet murmurings
> With busy skill and cunning excellent. (ll. 330–333)

Davies's lady thus participates in the divine creative act as she imitates Shakespeare's lady at the virginal.

Shakespeare's poetic figure of erotic identification with an object the mistress touches is also familiar. In Sir Philip Sidney's 1591 sonnet sequence *Astrophil and Stella*, the speaker watches "with envy" as his lady's pet sparrow touches her neck and lips. Anticipating Shakespeare's "saucy jacks" (l. 13), he asks the bird, "Is sauciness reward of courtesy?" (83.5, 10). The conceit is best known in Romeo's exclamation: "O that I were a glove upon that hand, / That I might touch that cheek!" (2.2.23–24). The practical absurdity of the lover's wish does not negate its enthusiasm. Though the sparrow is a trivial pet, Juliet wears no glove, and the jacks are merely "dead wood" (l. 12), each speaker manufactures jealousy for amatory purposes.

Juxtaposed, the metaphors of solemn divine harmony and jealous erotic empathy invite a satirical reading, as Ben Jonson proves in his 1599 comedy *Every Man out of His Humor*. Jonson's courtly object of ridicule, Fastidious Brisk, watches his mistress play the viola da gamba, and between doses of tobacco he remarks, "You see the subject of her sweet fingers, there? . . . Oh, she tickles it so, that . . . I have wished myself to be that instrument" (3.9.101–106). In Sonnet 128 the allusion warns a reader against empathizing with the lover by introducing him as the fool of both his affections and his affectations.

He is a little less crude than Jonson's Fastidious, dwelling on an instrument that lies beneath his lady's fingers rather than between her legs, but he is equally focused on the musician rather than the music. He even misnames the virginal's parts, mistaking the key for the jack, "an upright piece of wood fixed to the back of the keylever, and fitted with a quill which plucked the string as the jack rose on the key's being pressed down," according to the *OED* (*sb.* 14), one of several glosses to note Shakespeare's gaffe. In 1928, E. W. Naylor ingeniously announced the lady must be tuning the virginal, not playing it (Rollins 1:326), and in 1977 the misnomer made Booth declare "the poem comes to grief" (438), though he delineates the puns that denote "jack" as "a term of abuse for . . . impudent upstarts" (439). Whatever Shakespeare understood of the virginal's mechanism, his anxious, amorous fictive speaker twice substitutes the jarring metonymic jacks for the harmonious literal keys. The little joke betrays serious fears.

## THE RELATIONSHIP OF THE SONNET TO SHAKESPEARE'S OTHER WORKS

In the plays Shakespeare repeats the concepts of music and erotic jealousy of a lady's hands, but he never unites them in a player at the virginal. Had he done so, he might have given that role to Juliet. Before Romeo longs to be a glove on Juliet's hand, he enacts the sonnet speaker's part: he offers his lady lips that stand and blush, he fails to kiss her hand, and finally he kisses her lips (1.5.93–106). The pleading dialogue creates a perfect English sonnet in a scene of music and dancing; however, Romeo's instant success denies him the sonnet speaker's frustrated jealousy.

In *Titus Andronicus*, the recollection of a desirable woman's hands touching musical strings grows bitterly grotesque. After assailants rape Lavinia and amputate her hands, her uncle moans,

> O had the monster seen those lily hands
> Tremble like aspen leaves upon a lute,
> And make the silken strings delight to kiss them,
> He would not then have touch'd them for his life! (2.4.44–47)

In this bizarre context, the speaker's choice of a traditionally erotic image emphasizes the lady's vulnerability and his own frustrating failure to protect her from brutality.

The comedies show that music shapes and conveys human feeling. In *The Merchant of Venice*, Lorenzo expounds on the power of music to change the nature of both animals and people "with concord of sweet sounds" (5.1.84), and Portia orders music to accompany Bassanio's fateful choice of the casket containing her picture. "If he lose," she explains, "he makes a swan-like end, / Fading in music," and if he wins, music is the "dulcet sounds in break of day / That creep into the dreaming bridegroom's ear, / And summon him to marriage" (3.2.44–45; 51–53). Whereas in the play music itself asserts power and conveys sweetness to the ear, in the sonnet it is the musician's hands that are empowered with sweetness under her lover's anxious eye.

In *Twelfth Night* a shared response to music signals harmony of affection. Calling for an old song, the Duke turns to the loving but disguised Viola, asking, "How dost thou like this tune?" When she replies, "It gives a very echo to the seat / Where Love is thron'd," he commends her and for the first time invites her to speak intimately (2.4.20–22). Before he meets Viola, the same lovesick duke introduces the play with an association between music and love, but he crudely distorts the metaphor into an image of gluttony:

> If music be the food of love, play on,
> Give me excess of it; that surfeiting,
> The appetite may sicken, and so die. (1.1.1–3)

The intuition of love that Viola rouses in the duke expresses itself in his heightened sensitivity to music well before his reason recognizes her as a fit love object. Initially, he is like the sonnet speaker, too distracted by his own frustrations to hear music feelingly.

When a man gazes at a woman's hands with erotic jealousy, he makes her the object of rising tension. The sonnet diffuses that tension with its concluding comedy, but the same gaze in the plays puts the woman in danger. In *Othello*, Iago conceives his plan to implicate Desdemona with Cassio as the latter "takes her by the palm" (2.1.167). Using their mere touch to indicate that "Desdemona is directly in love with [Cassio]," he asks the lady's rejected suitor, Roderigo, "Didst thou not see her paddle with the palm of his hand?" When Roderigo maintains "that was but courtesy," Iago confuses him with conceits: "Lechery, by this hand; an index and obscure prologue to the history of lust and foul thoughts" (2.1.167, 219, 254–258). Unconscious of Iago's scrutiny of her innocent handclasp, Desdemona is vulnerable to his gaze. The sonnet lady, however, is fully apprised of her fingers' erotic effects.

Like Desdemona, Hermione in *The Winter's Tale* falls victim to the jealous male gaze upon her hands. Watching his wife give her hand to his old friend Polixenes,

Leontes abruptly stammers, "Too hot, too hot! / ... to be paddling palms and pinching fingers." His jealous thought leaps wildly to cuckoldry and back to her hands, this time through the keyboard image from the sonnet: "Still virginalling / Upon his palm?" (1.2.108, 115, 125–126). The comic tension of Sonnet 128, which draws upon an adolescent obsession with the lady's touch, has dark parallels in female vulnerability and male jealousy as portrayed in the plays.

**Annotated Bibliography**

Booth, Stephen, ed. *Shakespeare's Sonnets*. New Haven: Yale UP, 1977. Offers comprehensive annotations for every poem.

Duncan-Jones, Katherine, ed. *Shakespeare's Sonnets*. The Arden Shakespeare. London: Thomas Nelson and Sons, 1997. A thorough and helpful annotated edition that includes an introduction that historically contextualizes the sonnets and persuasively nominates William Herbert, the future third Earl of Pembroke, as the fair young man.

Kerrigan, John, ed. *"The Sonnets" and "A Lover's Complaint."* Rev. ed. New York: Penguin, 1995. Thorough contextual analysis that includes *A Lover's Complaint* within the sonnet sequence.

Rollins, Hyder Edward, ed. *The Sonnets*. New Variorum Edition. 2 vols. Philadelphia: J. B. Lippincott, 1944. The most comprehensive critical survey of commentary on each sonnet from 1609 until 1944.

Vendler, Helen. *The Art of Shakespeare's Sonnets*. Cambridge, MA: Harvard UP, 1997. Original close readings of the sonnets that focus on a schematic of key words and couplet links.

# Sonnet 129

### Annalisa Castaldo

The expense of spirit in a waste of shame
Is lust in action; and till action, lust
Is perjur'd, murderous, bloody, full of blame,
Savage, extreme, rude, cruel, not to trust,
Enjoy'd no sooner but despised straight,
Past reason hunted, and no sooner had
Past reason hated, as a swallow'd bait
On purpose laid to make the taker mad:
Mad in pursuit and in possession so;
Had, having, and in quest to have, extreme;
A bliss in proof—and proved, a very woe;
Before, a joy propos'd; behind, a dream.
   All this the world well knows; yet none knows well
   To shun the heaven that leads men to this hell.

## PROSE PARAPHRASE

Sexual intercourse (the acting out of lust) is a shameful waste of vitality or life-force. Before it is satisfied, lust is deceitful, deadly, bloody, savage, extreme, cruel and untrustworthy. Once lust is satisfied, it is hated. Sex is desired beyond reason, but once sex is over, it is hated beyond reason, as the fish hates the bait, once it discovers the hidden hook. Lust drives people mad, both in pursuit of their goal and in possession of that goal. At all points—seeking, having, and having had—lust is excessive. Sex provides bliss at the moment of achievement, but immediately after provides only sorrow. Before it has been experienced, it is a joy looked forward to, but afterwards, it is only an unreal, unhappy memory. All of this is known to everyone, yet no one knows enough to avoid the temporary pleasures that lead to such misery.

## THE PLACE OF THE SONNET IN THE CYCLE

Sonnet 129 is part of the Dark Lady sequence, which begins with Sonnet 127. Sonnet 129 does not explicitly deal with the attractions of the Dark Lady, as sonnets 127 and 130 do, but the theme of satisfied lust causing disgust separates it from the sonnets that deal with the love of the young man and sets this poem in the realm of heterosexual attraction. In fact, apart from the vast difference in tone, Sonnet 129 pairs neatly with Sonnet 128, since the latter sonnet has the poet watching the lady playing the virginals and wishing that he were the instrument. Sonnet 128, therefore, presents the situation that Sonnet 129 will come to regret. However, Sonnet 129 stands out from those immediately surrounding it in two ways. First, it is the only one that does not directly mention a woman at all, let alone a specific, dark-haired woman. Second, and more important, the tone is quite different, one of savage disillusionment rather than lighthearted flirting. It is difficult to turn from the idea that lust leads men into hell to the playful poetic satire of "My mistress' eyes are nothing like the sun" (130.1). However, Sonnet 130 does deal with the same theme—that love (or lust) causes the poet to ignore the evidence of his eyes and consider his mistress beautiful.

The tone of Sonnet 129, as well as the theme of disgust and shame, is more closely connected to sonnets 137–138 and 147–152, especially 147. The idea expressed in the couplet, that lust leads to an inability to recognize physical and moral virtue, is explored in detail in Sonnet 147, which ends with a similar juxtaposition of hell and goodness (in 147, the lady's physical blackness or fairness, rather than heaven and hell specifically). Sonnets 137 and 148 also turn on the realization that lust has misled the poet about his Dark Lady's beauty, both physical and spiritual. Line 10 invests "had" with sexual overtones, a use that is found in sonnets 52.14 (Being had, to triumph, being lack'd, to hope") and 87.13 (Thus have I had thee as a dream doth flatter"), although both these sonnets are part of the handsome youth cycle. The image of sex as hell appears in Sonnet 144.12, where the poet imagines that "one angel," the fair youth, is "in another's hell," that is, having sex with the Dark Lady.

## DEVICES AND TECHNIQUES

Sonnet 129 is written in an impersonal voice, without use of either the first or third person pronoun. The speaker thereby gives the sonnet a philosophical or homiletic tone, although the bitterness that builds up through the piling on of negative adjectives contradicts the seemingly objective approach. Lines 2 and 3 begin symmetrically with the verb "is," and throughout the sonnet the meaning hangs on these nonspecific verbs, since the three quatrains make up a single sentence. Lust is thus constantly the subject, but more and more elided. This elision complicates the meaning of the poem, as the question of who is acting and who is to be held responsible for the actions becomes distanced and ambiguous.

The syntax of Sonnet 129 is tortuous, especially in the first line, when the formal pause at the end of the line comes before the verb has appeared, and the entire structure of the sentence is reversed, since the subject turns out to be "Lust in action" in line 2, not "Th' expense of spirit" that begins the poem. Although the specific grammatical structure can often be hard to follow, the fact that the first 12 lines are a single sentence gives the poem a great deal of momentum, keeping the reader's eyes and thoughts moving forward until the conclusion provided by the couplet. The single sentence also conveys the sense of lust's insistence as the poem drives the reader onward without respite.

Stephen Booth points out that Sonnet 129 also gains a great deal of its power from its "succession of *s* sounds frustrated by stopped consonants: the lines spit" (*Essay*, 149). Words such as "expense," "spirit," "shame" and "lust" (129.1, 2) give way to more complicated patterns such as "Is perjured" and "murd'rous, bloody" (129.3). This start-stop action is continued by the broken parallelism of lines 6–7, where the first elements of each line are exactly parallel ("Past reason hunted" and "Past reason hated"), but the second elements are not. Line 7 does not even end grammatically at the line break, ensuring that the lack of parallelism is obvious. This pattern is repeated in a smaller form in line 12; a parallel structure would call for a modifier of some kind for "dream" to match "joy proposed," but dream is unmodified and so breaks the balance of the line. The poem also imitates the heavy breathing of the lustful person: "Had, having, and in quest to have" (l. 10).

The question of the techniques used in Sonnet 129 deserves special attention because of several editorial decisions, which are discussed at length by Robert Graves and Laura Riding in their essay, "A Study in Original Punctuation and Spelling Sonnet 129" and by Stephen Booth in his commentary on both the sonnet and the Graves and Riding essay. For example, the 1609 quarto gives line 9 as "Made In pursut and in possession so;" but modern editors have emended the first word to "Mad." Sixteenth-century spelling recognized "made" as an alternative to "mad," and Shakespeare's original readers would have had available to them both options. In much the same way, line 11 in the quarto reads, "A blisse in proofe and proud and very wo." The late-eighteenth-century editor Edmond Malone, and editors following, emended the line to "proved, a very woe." As with mad/made, "proud" was a recognized spelling of both "proved" and "proud," since the "u" was often used in printed texts for "v." This orthographic ambiguity provided a visual pun now lost to us. In both instances, the original word continues to make grammatical sense, although certainly requiring more work by the reader. Graves and Riding (and some other editors) argue for the complexity of the text as presented in the 1609 quarto, while Booth and most other editors point out that since these are well known alternative spellings, it is just as likely that the more straightforward meaning was the primary one and that interpretation should be presented to modern readers. No matter what choice an editor makes, the linguistic ambiguity and richness is forever banished to footnotes by the arrival of regularized spellings.

## THEMES AND MEANINGS

Sonnet 129 describes the poet's disgust at lust in general, and specifically sexual lust that is either unsatisfied or has just been satiated. Lust is here personified as both the cause of all manner of evil—until lust is satisfied it (and the person suffering from it) is "Savage, extreme, rude, cruel" (l. 4) even "murd'rous" (l. 3)—and physically and emotionally appalling in its own right—"no sooner had, / Past reason hated" (ll. 6–7). Although there is a physicality to the sonnet in the violence of the language and the vividness of the word choice, the impersonal tone and the lack of specific sexual detail and metaphors that directly relate to the body suggest that the theme is the emotion of lust rather than just the act of sexual intercourse. Even while the lust is unfulfilled, the sonnet suggests that the control it exhibits over man is dangerous and dehumanizing. In fact, the sonnet personifies lust in the first two lines, so that men who are consumed by lust actually become lust incarnate.

The sonnet gives equal weight to the evils of lust unsatisfied and lust satisfied. The former is the cause of many, if not all, crimes and sins, from lying to murder. A man (and "men" in line 14 seems to be gender-specific) motivated by lust will do anything to attain his goal, but once he has achieved it, he immediately discovers that it is not at all what he thought and wanted. It is this second theme that makes the sonnet especially despairing and bitter. The poet argues that a man who lusts will destroy anything and anyone in his way, but that once the lust is satisfied, the same man finds he himself has been destroyed from within, driven mad by the awareness that his long-sought object is poisoned bait.

The last two lines before the couplet seem to pull back slightly from this view of complete disgust; lust unsatisfied is described as "a bliss in proof" and "a joy proposed," while the final description of satisfied lust is "a dream." These more positive or at least moderate terms prepare the reader for the argument of the couplet, which is that even though "the world well knows" that lust leads to despair, sin, and madness, it still presents itself as "heaven." In the end, therefore, the poet pulls back from his absolute condemnation, at least to the point of admitting that before the moment of agonized awakening, the dream that lust creates is an attractive one. This slight shift in tone does not make the sonnet less powerful; instead the sonnet is more realistic because it more closely matches the experience of most readers.

The final couplet of Sonnet 129 is not as straightforward as it as first appears, although the general meaning is easily grasped. The last phrase "yet none knows well / To shun the heaven that leads men to this hell" (ll. 13–14) is ambiguous. What exactly is "this hell"? Is it lust in general, or only lust satisfied? Is it the vagina, as in Sonnet 144? If it is lust in general, then what is "the heaven" that leads to lust? It could be the moment of orgasm and sexual satisfaction, but that places it in the middle (between unsatisfied and satisfied lust), rather than the end (as the logic of the line suggests). The poet could also be suggesting that romantic love is the heaven that leads inevitably to feelings of lust, and this reading would make the poem especially bitter since it would argue against any feelings of love between men and women. Either way, the heaven the poet refers to is clearly not truly divine, but only the baited hook described earlier.

## THE RELATIONSHIP OF THE SONNET TO SHAKESPEARE'S OTHER WORKS

The disgust at sexuality that is exhibited so savagely in Sonnet 129 shows up repeatedly in later Shakespearean plays, from *Hamlet* to *The Winter's Tale*. In *Troilus and Cressida*, Cressida expresses fear that her surrender to Troilus will evoke just such a reaction: "Women are angels, wooing: / Things won are done, joy's soul lies in the doing" (1.2.286–287). Although it is the war rather than disgust that separates Troilus and Cressida, when he sees her with a new lover, he rejects the very notion that this woman is Cressida; her sexuality, separate from Troilus's love, literally unmakes her in Troilus's eyes. Like Cressida, Diana in *All's Well That Ends Well* recognizes that men, "when you have our roses, / You barely leave our thorns to prick ourselves, / And mock us with our bareness" (4.2.18–20).

Many of the later comedies and romances—*Measure for Measure* and *The Winter's Tale* especially—are linked to Sonnet 129 because they demonstrate the violent emotions and actions that can occur when feelings of lust are involved. *The Winter's Tale* opens with Leontes' sudden and unmotivated certainty that his wife has been unfaithful with his best friend; Hermione's advanced pregnancy provides conclusive evidence that she has been sexually active with a man, and that realization is enough to lead Leontes to the disgust that makes up Sonnet 129. There is an echo of the couplet's comparison of the heaven of lust that leads to hell in the conversation between Polixenes and Hermione (1.2.67–75), when he claims that before women, he and Leontes were innocent even of original sin. In *Measure for Measure*, Angelo is suddenly sexually attracted to the novice Isabella as she pleads for her brother's life, and after she has gone, asks himself, "Dost thou desire her foully for those things / That make her good?" (2.2.173–174). Throughout the play, sexuality and desire are seen as deadly and perverted, and even lawful matches such as Claudio and Juliet's are cause for punishment.

*Antony and Cleopatra* is the play most concerned with the danger sexuality presents to a man, as Antony is torn between Cleopatra and Egypt's sensuality on the one hand and his duty to Rome and his wife Octavia on the other. Each time he sways towards Rome, he recoils from Cleopatra's overt sexuality and his own response to it. Enobarbus describes the essential paradox of Sonnet 129, although from a positive standpoint, when he says of Cleopatra, "Other women cloy / The appetites they feed, but she makes hungry / Where most she satisfies" (2.2.235–237).

Hamlet's diatribes about lust replicate the language of Sonnet 129 as well as the themes. He ends the nunnery speech to Ophelia by declaring that feminine wiles have made him mad (3.1.147), as Sonnet 129 describes lust as driving "the taker mad: / Mad in pursuit and in possession so" (ll. 8–9). Othello, of course, is driven mad by Iago's continual descriptions of Desdemona's lust for other men.

### Annotated Bibliography

Booth, Stephen. *An Essay on Shakespeare's Sonnets.* New Haven: Yale UP, 1969. An intelligent and detailed consideration of the problem of the sonnets as a coherent sequence since, as Booth points out, there are varying and conflicting patterns rather than an overarching, consistent narrative. Booth also considers individual sonnets, some in great depth.

———, ed. *Shakespeare's Sonnets.* New Haven: Yale UP, 1977. Presents an en-face edition of the 1609 quarto and a modernized version. In addition, Booth presents scholarly commentary that ranges from specific word and line explication to wide ranging discussion of connections among sonnets and to various other Shakespearean texts and sixteenth- and seventeenth-century writers. Invaluable.

Graves, Robert, and Laura Riding. "A Study in Original Punctuation and Spelling Sonnet 129." In *Discussions of Shakespeare's Sonnets.* Ed. Barbara Herrnstein. Boston: D. C. Heath and Co., 1964. 116–123. Although Stephen Booth (in *Shakespeare's Sonnets, Edited with Analytic Commentary*, 447–452) convincingly argues that Graves and Riding are incorrect in their claims, this remains a seminal argument in early textual analysis as an interpretive tool. The authors argue that modernizing spelling and punctuation changes the meaning of the poem.

Vendler, Helen. *The Art of Shakespeare's Sonnets.* Cambridge, MA: Harvard UP, 1997. Vendler presents in-depth and intelligent readings of each sonnet. By rejecting the lure of a narrative pattern, Vendler is able to provide much more sensitive readings than many past critics, who were forced to emphasize those elements that fit into their particular pattern.

Weiser, David K. *Mind in Character: Shakespeare's Speaker in the Sonnets*. Columbia: U of Missouri P, 1987. Weiser focuses on the poet-speaker, and distinguishes between "soliloquies" and "dialogues" to suggest that readers identify with the speaker as a character and that there is a pattern of growth in the sonnets as arranged in the 1609 quarto.

# Sonnet 130

## Gina Macdonald with Andrew Macdonald

My mistress' eyes are nothing like the sun
Coral is far more red than her lips' red:
If snow be white, why then her breasts are dun;
If hairs be wires, black wires grow on her head.
I have seen roses damask'd, red and white,
But no such roses see I in her cheeks;
And in some perfumes is there more delight
Than in the breath that from my mistress reeks.
I love to hear her speak, yet well I know
That music hath a far more pleasing sound:
I grant I never saw a goddess go,—
My mistress, when she walks, treads on the ground:
   And yet, by heaven, I think my love as rare
   As any she belied with false compare.

### PROSE PARAPHRASE

The speaker in the poem, presumably the young Shakespeare, spends the first twelve lines contrasting the qualities of his "mistress" or loved one with the traditional qualities normally attributed by poets like himself to lovely young women they seek to praise. The word "mistress" at this time simply meant "young woman," without the connotations of a sexual liaison carried by the modern word. The poet says that this young woman's eyes are in no way like the sun in brightness or power. Her lips are not as brilliantly red as is coral, nor are her breasts as pale and white as snow; instead they are a grayish mouse brown. Traditionally, a young woman's hair, despite reality, was praised as "golden," like spun gold or fine, gleaming golden wires, perhaps reflective of the traditional Renaissance gold wire net used to hold the hair in place. Here the speaker likens the woman's hair to low-cost black wire. That is, her hair is black and unkempt and ordinary.

The poetic tradition had been to describe the facial coloring of the poet's beloved in terms of red and white roses, that is, pale skin and rosy cheeks and red lips. The word "damask'd" in line 5 suggests damasked cloth, a type of cloth in which the colors are mingled or woven together in mixed sets of colors, as well as damask (that is, Damascus) roses. The idea is a mix of reds and whites, the colors commingled to create beauty. In modern terms we might call this a strawberries and cream complexion. The narrator admits that he has seen such lovely flowers, soft of petal and colorful of hue, but fails to find these colors in his mistress' face—no roses in her cheeks. In the social system of the time, pale skin, protected from the sun, was associated with the aristocracy, whereas darker hues signaled the peasantry, working outdoors in the fields. Likewise her breath is not fragrant like the perfumes that please with their lovely aromas; instead, her breath smells, and, in fact, the word "reeks" (l. 8) makes it sound particularly repulsive to a modern audience, though the term was not as negative in Shakespeare's day, when it was associated with steamy, smoky aromas.

Where other poets compare the voices of the woman they praise to sweet music, Shakespeare admits that the sound of music is lovelier than the voice of his beloved; however, despite that fact, he enjoys hearing her speak. Where other poets compare their "angelic" loves to "goddesses" who walk on air, Shakespeare finds his beloved more human. He says he has never seen a goddess walk (the Greek and Roman classical writers described the gait of a goddess like Venus or Athena as distinctive), so he cannot tell how light one's steps might be, but he knows that the woman of his poem takes solid steps and is firmly planted on the earthly ground, not the distant heavenly realms.

Throughout these first twelve lines, the pattern is one of contrast between the traditional, exaggerated praise other poets extend to the objects of their affections, and the frank realism of this description, which rejects artifice and instead plainly, bluntly admits the truth about the woman: her black hair, her brown skin, her bad breath, her heavy gait. However, in the last two lines, the conclusion of the sonnet and the final couplet, the speaker swears that, despite the fact that his beloved fails to meet the conventional standards of beauty of his day, in reality she is as beautiful as any other woman ("any she") who is lied to or about ("belied") by a poet using exaggerated, deceptive, or false comparisons ("false compare").

Shakespeare's Dark Lady's beauty lies in the fact that she is "rare" (l. 13), a term meaning "superior" or "of a high quality," and here suggesting that her beauty is uniquely hers rather than being conventional or orthodox. That is, other poets lie to (or about) their beloveds, but this narrator pays his beloved the compliment of telling her the truth. Furthermore, he loves her for herself, not for some artificial image of what beauty should be. His flattery involves trusting that she is strong enough and self-confident enough to appreciate a man who knows her true worth rather than one who creates unrealistic fantasies about some ideal beauty who never truly existed.

## THE PLACE OF THE SONNET IN THE CYCLE

This poem belongs to the sonnet set numbered from 127 to 152 that deals with the Dark Lady, an anonymous, promiscuous, dark-haired woman who is sometimes the audience and sometimes the subject of these verses. The Dark Lady poems explore passion, guilt, sexual desire, faithlessness, and the bitterness and misery of love. They are sometimes witty and playful, and at other times direct and accusatory. Together they create a fuller picture than the limited glimpse of the relationship provided by Sonnet 130 alone. For example, Sonnet 127 mentions the Dark Lady's "raven black" eyes (l. 9), mournful yet uniquely beautiful, while Sonnet 128 praises her musical skills at the spinet or virginal. Sonnet 129 calls her a "heaven" that leads to "hell" (l. 14), while Sonnet 131 calls her "tyrannous" (l. 1) yet a "precious jewel" (l. 4), but her deeds are "black" (l. 13). In Sonnet 133 the poet's heart has been imprisoned by her, in 134 he is "mortgag'd" to her will (l. 2), and in 137 "blind" Love has misled him to her (l. 1). Love for her is "a fever" and a "sickly appetite" in Sonnet 147 (ll. 1, 4). Nonetheless, in Sonnet 143 he hopes for a kiss.

These Dark Lady poems appear in their present order because they were so placed in the original printer's manuscript. It is thought that Shakespeare wrote two or three at a time to send on single sheets. Thus there is no overwhelmingly convincing external evidence as to sequence. However, there is some internal evidence as to the ups and downs of the alliance. Early poems often seem to reflect a good relationship with the lady addressed. Then, there is a more troubled period when the poet is trying to renew the connection (even reminding her of his name in sonnets 135 and 136, as if she had put him totally out of her mind). Still other poems discuss the relationship with an unidentified third party, a young man whose life is also touched by the Dark Lady.

## DEVICES AND TECHNIQUES

Sonnet 130 follows the traditional pattern of a Shakespearean sonnet, structured with three quatrains and a concluding couplet, all in iambic pentameter. The first two sets of four lines, rhyming *abab cdcd*, comprise a single sentence, with elements connected by semicolons. This section builds on contrasts between the parts of his beloved's face and upper torso and the traditional conventions for describing them. The movement is downward from eyes to lips to breasts, then back up to hair and an overview of her face—particularly skin tones and breath. The two basic methods of development are metaphorical images of beauty and contrasting realities to produce an overview that seems negative: this woman fails to live up to the ideal. Technically, the series begins with the simile "like the sun" and then shifts to a series of metaphors: coral red, snow white, rosy cheeked, golden haired, and so on. In line 8, the final line of the sequence, the choice of the verb "reeks" is particularly harsh and intended to jar. The last word in the sentence, the word on which a reader will inevitably pause, it seems inappropriate in a love poem, and is intentionally so. In the third quatrain (*efef*) and second sentence, the content focuses on the sound of the Dark Lady's voice and the heaviness of her walk. Again "treads" (l. 12), like "reeks," is jarring in a love poem, out of keeping with the traditional image of the woman. "Treads" sounds robust, tough, and masculine, not dainty and feminine, and the break in the iambic meter reinforces this break in convention. The negativity is softened somewhat by the initial positive clause, "I love to hear her speak," but this, too, leads to the concession that music sounds better.

As in all Shakespearean sonnets, the heart of the matter appears in the final couplet (*gg*). Therein, the transition "And yet" followed by the intensifier "by heaven" marks the shift in idea and the conclusion of the description: the poet's affirmation

of his beloved's uniqueness and his transformation of what has seemed like negatives into a resounding positive: "I think my love as rare / As any she." The end
rhyme with "rare" necessitates "compare," a word in Shakespeare's day that was an
acceptable abbreviated form for "comparison." Because Shakespeare is mocking the
once-popular Petrarchan poetic tradition, he imposes the two-part Italian structure
to his content, with the first eight lines, the Petrarchan sonnet's octave, setting up
the major contrasts that make the argument a rejection of Petrarchan conceits and
with the last six lines (the sestet) exploring the main topic a little further and concluding about it. In other words, form and content merge, as Shakespeare transforms the Petrarchan sonnet form of octave and sestet into his own unique
Shakespearean form, just as he rejects the Petrarchan conceits and replaces them
with his own reversals of the tradition. Thus, his structure makes clear that Shakespeare is playing a witty game in which all is not as it at first seems, neither form
nor content.

Part of the game depends on his double audience. Shakespeare addresses his
poem directly to young men like himself and indirectly to his beloved, with distinct
messages for each. His series of statements about his "mistress" putatively addresses
his contemporaries, young men like himself who, no matter their role or occupa-
tion, communicated their feelings of love through the popular Petrarchan conventions of the Italian sonnet. Petrarch, for example, praised his beloved Laura's walk
as resembling that of angels and her voice as heavenly, the music of the spheres. The
exaggerated praise so common in the Petrarchan tradition that preceded Shakespeare and that shaped his contemporaries' poetry employed conventions or conceits that were repeated in poem after poem. These conventions praised the beloved
as having eyes like stars, diamonds, or suns; lips red as roses, sugarplums, or ripe
cherries; snow-white, pearl-white, lily-white, or ivory skin set off by rosy cheeks or
peaches-and-cream/strawberries-and-cream complexions; and golden hair as fine
as spun gold. These better-than-life young women had perfumed breath and voices
like music or angels. So light and delicate were they that they floated on air, or at
the very least had a feather-light step. In the early 1580s Sir Philip Sidney popularized such Petrarchan conventions in his sonnet cycle, *Astrophil and Stella*. In Sonnet 9 of that collection, for example, Sidney describes Stella's face as being "of
alabaster pure" (l. 3) and topped with golden hair. Her lips are "Red porphyr," her
teeth pearls (l. 6), and her cheeks are "mixed red and white" (l. 8). As with modern-
day greeting cards, these conceits and conventions quickly became clichéd and trite,
a one-size-fits-all ready-made rhetoric suitable for the most tongue-tied lover. Even
much later, in the early seventeenth century, poets at a loss for what to say were
still employing these old-fashioned and well-worn conventions, as did Thomas
Campion in "There is a Garden in her Face" (1617). One can imagine a Renaissance
male audience used to engaging in the game of love and courtship with such images as tools in their repertoire laughing raucously at what they might anticipate
will be the outraged reaction of Shakespeare's "mistress." However, Shakespeare is
setting them up so that the twist of his ending will win their appreciation for the
skill of a man who can seem to criticize so harshly and who then can gamely turn
his criticism on its head and transform it into high praise. In the game of male competition, he will have overcome by proving himself the better poet and the better
man. Shakespeare's evocation of this conventional language of love in the negative—"my mistress' eyes are nothing like"—is thus mockery of the linguistic-poetic

orthodoxy of this time, as well as a put-down of his poetic competition: Shakespeare's art, like his mistress, is above the conventional.

The second audience is the black-eyed, black-haired mistress herself, who might expect extravagant praise, but who initially receives only what seems to be a series of insults. What woman wants to be told that her coloring is not perfect, her eyes are not dazzling, and her breath leaves much to be desired, as do her voice and her walk? Like Shakespeare's male Renaissance audience, his modern audience might well expect an angry response from the object of the poet's desires and wonder whether his final strategy will truly work on her, for the real praise does not come until the "pirouette," or turn, of the last two lines. This final couplet changes the negatives into a graceful and realistic compliment: this mistress is "rare," a unique person who need not be lied to/about ("belied") with false comparisons. If we can imagine the mistress as "overhearing" Shakespeare the poet describing her to his male contemporaries, we can again see the game he is playing: involving her emotionally in his poem, even though the emotions may be shock and anger, then hoping to create an emotional shift as she realizes that she is indeed being praised. Though his praise is that she is superior to the women who accept mindless flattery as sincere, Shakespeare himself comes off as honest and truthful, refusing to resort to the insincerities that plague the language of love.

In other words, the dominating techniques of metaphorical imagery and contrast depend for effect not only on the paradoxical twist of the last two lines, but also on the perspective of a dual audience, one male, one female, both aware in different ways of the use of exaggerated praise as a viable or not-so-viable strategy in the game of love.

## THEMES AND MEANINGS

Commentators have sometimes found that the prevailing theme of Sonnet 130 is the rarity and even uniqueness of Shakespeare's mistress, a woman who creates her own standards of beauty in defiance of convention and whose down-to-earth reality Shakespeare values more than he does the fake golden-haired goddesses of poetic tradition. He loves her voice and thinks her "rare"; she is a real woman, not a poetic construct or young man's fantasy. This interpretation of theme is in keeping with Shakespeare's argument in other of the Dark Lady sonnets. For instance, in Sonnet 127 he concludes that, even though her beauty is of the type ordinarily "not counted fair" (l. 1) it nonetheless has "nature's power," and is "suited" to her (ll. 5, 10); Shakespeare therefore concludes about her that though "not born fair, no beauty lack[s]" (l. 11), so much so "That every tongue says beauty should look so" (l. 14). Shakespeare challenges conventional ideas of female beauty and rejects insincere flattery.

The central theme, however, is another that recurs in his work: Shakespeare's power and superiority as both an artist and as an appreciative lover. His message to his contemporaries, that is, to his competing poets, is that he can outwrite them. He can use all their clichés to show their emptiness and lack of imagination. Thus, he rejects images that recur in the poetry of Michael Drayton, Ben Jonson, Sir Philip Sidney, Edmund Spenser, John Wooton, and Sir Thomas Wyatt. Furthermore, he has the special gift of rhetorical skill that enables him to transform seeming insults into high praise. He can make statements that would mortify most women and turn those statements into compliments to soothe the Dark Lady he addresses. The lady herself cannot help but be flattered by being appreciated for herself rather than as a stimulus for a threadbare poetic tradition and by winning the love of a poetic talent capable of truly praising her beauty. Her rarity deserves more than the artifice of poetasters, although, of course, Shakespeare's praise is itself a form of witty artifice, a construct of clever manipulative rhetoric. In point of fact, his praise is that the lady is no better (and no worse) than the ladies whom other poets describe with lies. So wherein lies the truth? If they are no better than she, does that make her superior to them? Or are such comparative measures irrelevant, with only the personal relationship mattering? Shakespeare loves to hear her speak and understands her weaknesses and accepts them; his focus is on communication, not beauty, but ultimately what he communicates is how very devious he can be with language, and therein lies both his charm and his weakness.

## THE RELATIONSHIP OF THE SONNET TO SHAKESPEARE'S OTHER WORKS

Sonnet 130 is very much in keeping with the concerns and themes of Shakespeare's canon. Shakespeare frequently plays off shallow, conventional praise against realistic, mature appreciation. Young men, such as Romeo in *Romeo and Juliet*, Lysander and Demetrius of *A Midsummer Night's Dream*, and Orsino in *Twelfth Night*, frequently resort to Petrarchan excesses to woo their beloved ladies; in turn, the young women answer with tart, deflating responses, calling into question a love expressed in generic language. Any poetic tradition can become quickly conventionalized and thus insincere; true appreciation lies in responding to the particular individual, not in using a common social currency artfully. A sign of Romeo's youth and insincerity is the ease with which he changes from exaggerated praise of Rosaline to exaggerated praise of Juliet, just as the Petrarchan conceits of the immature and insincere Lysander and Demetrius in *A Midsummer Night's Dream* are as easily transferred to a new love object as their affections and their verbal expressions of them during the madness of love of the midsummer night. This is the indulgence of emotion for its own sake, not true love. Being in love with being in love is a common satiric touchstone summed up in Shakespeare's Duke Orsino in *Twelfth Night*, a romantic who indulges feelings of love far beyond their supposed stimulus.

Another common Shakespearean theme is the power of art, and especially of poetry, to capture truths no other form of inquiry can manage, and to make transient flesh and blood live on as long as readers read, as in Sonnet 65, where Shakespeare describes the artist's ability to stop time as a "miracle . . . / That in black ink my love may still shine bright" (ll. 13–14), or in Sonnet 63, which praises black ink that makes beauty live on and keeps life fresh and green in spite of time.

Finally, this poem stands in contrast to another in the Dark Lady series, Sonnet 138, a cynical poem based on the premise that love thrives best on lies, only this time the lie of the man is his pretence that he does not recognize that the woman is lying and the lie of the woman is the flattery and false-speaking normally associated with male courtship. The two poems call for realism in love, though at the same time both recognize artifice as basic to the survival of the relationship in question.

**Annotated Bibliography**

Stapleton, M. L. "'My False Eyes': The Dark Lady and Self-Knowledge." *Studies in Philology* 90 (Spring 1993): 213–231. An analysis of the ambiguous and inconsistent nature of "Will" and his Dark Lady in the sonnets, with a balance between revelation and pose.

Thomas, Paul R. "Shakespeare's Sonnet 130 and the History of Two Ideas: The Effictio and the Topos of the World Upsidedown." *Encyclia: The Journal of the Utah Academy of Sciences, Arts, and Letters* 66 (1989): 70–78. Thomas explores medieval patterns that Shakespeare draws on. The idea of a world reversed from what it should be is a common motif, but in love, if the beloved is the lover's world, then the negative images reflect a lover's world turned upside down.

Woolway, Joanne. "An Overview of 'Sonnet 130.'" In *Poetry for Students: Presenting Analysis, Context, and Criticism on Commonly Studied Poetry.* Ed. Marie Rose Napierkowski and Mary K. Ruby. Detroit: Gale P, 1998. 1: 252–255. Woolway examines Shakespeare's success in turning the poetic convention of the blazon, or detailed summary, around and particularly examines the way Shakespeare uses stressed and unstressed syllable's to support the poem's meaning.

# Sonnets 135 and 136

## Elizabeth Moore Willingham

### Sonnet 135

Whoever hath her wish, thou hast thy *Will*
And *Will* to boot, and *Will* in over-plus;
More than enough am I that vex thee still,
To thy sweet will making addition thus.
Wilt thou, whose will is large and spacious,
Not once vouchsafe to hide my will in thine?
Shall will in others seem right gracious,
And in my will no fair acceptance shine?
The sea all water, yet receives rain still,
And in abundance addeth to his store;
So thou, being rich in *Will* add to thy *Will*
One will of mine, to make thy large *Will* more.
   Let no unkind 'No' fair beseechers kill;
   Think all but one, and me in that one *Will*.

## PROSE PARAPHRASE

While other women may make a wish, you have your "Will" (your vagina, the speaker's penis, the sexual desire of each, and one or more men named Will). Moreover, you have enough "Will" and even "Will" in excess. I am so much a pest that I tire and annoy you after you are satisfied; thus I augment your delicious desire (and your vagina). Won't you, whose desire is great and whose vagina is spacious, just this once (or at once) agree to keep me, my desire, and my penis safely hidden away within yourself? While you look favorably on the sexual desires (or parts) of others, are you going to frown upon mine? As the sea with all its waters still receives the rain and does not mind adding more water to its abundance, so you, already rich in desire and sexual parts, add to yours my own as one more, to make your abundance of these even greater. Do not allow your cruel "no" to destroy these pretty petitioners (me, my desire, my penis); think of all of them (us) as one entity, of me as composing or making part of it.

### ▩  Sonnet 136

If thy soul check thee that I come so near
Swear to thy blind soul that I was thy *Will*,
And will, thy soul knows, is admitted there;
Thus far for love my love-suit, sweet, fulfil.
*Will* will fulfil the treasure of thy love,
Ay, fill it full with wills, and my will one.
In things of great receipt with ease we prove
Among a number one is reckon'd none:
Then in the number let me pass untold,
Though in thy stores' account I one must be;
For nothing hold me, so it please thee hold
That nothing me, a something sweet to thee:
    Make but my name thy love, and love that still,
    And then thou lovest me,—for my name is *Will*.

## PROSE PARAPHRASE

If your instinct alerts you because I get too close, remind yourself that without a doubt I was once your Will ("will" in all senses noted above). And your soul knows that "Will" is welcome to enter. In a metaphysical sense, the will is necessary to direct the soul and so is welcome. In a physical sense, the speaker is asking for sex. Go this far in granting my request for the sake of love, sweetheart. My penis and desire will fill your vagina. Fill yourself with desires and phalluses and let mine be one of these.

When we get large gifts, one small thing is entirely overlooked. So let me enter you unnoticed, though in the counting of your possessions I can be one item. Regard me as nothing, as long as you hold on to me, a nothing that is precious to you. Make only my name your beloved and love my name forever afterward. By loving my name, then you will love me as well, for I am "Will." That is, by loving desire, sexual parts, and myself, you will turn to me for the act of love.

## THE PLACE OF THE SONNETS IN THE CYCLE

These sonnets appear early in the second sequence of the collection known as the "Dark Lady" sonnets (127–152) and share elements with those that precede and follow them. The speaker begins his addresses to the Dark Lady in 127 by seeking to justify placing his affections on this "black" mistress and next (128) offers a charming praise of the lady and a pretty plea that she give her smaller favors to others and reserve her greater ones to him. He turns against his desire in 129, lamenting and cursing it and its effects. Companion sonnets 133 and 134 use language related to criminal and civil law and banking to introduce the mistress's infidelity with the speaker's "friend" and employ "will" with its multiple intentions.

Sonnets 135 and 136 mark a difference in tone from that of the previous sonnets, since they do not treat the lover's shifting perceptions of and feelings for the lady, but the importunate tone and specific language ("vex thee still," 135.3; "I was thy Will," 136.2) confirm a rupture between the former lovers that is introduced in 133–134. With only a few comparatively tender interludes following 135–136, the speaker becomes progressively more condemnatory of his passion for the dark mistress. Sonnets 135–136 are the most playfully and importunately sexual of the series, and Fineman (1984) would surely include these among "the voluptuary sonnets" which he makes personal to Shakespeare by referring, tongue-in-cheek, to "what Shakespeare calls his 'will'" (76). On the other hand, Feinberg (1987) describes the Dark Lady sonnet environment, using terms that are clearly associated with this pair of sonnets, as frequently "a wilderness of sexual contempt and self-deception, inhabited solely by an unstable Will" (100). It seems that in 135–136 the ambience is more a playground than a "wilderness" for Shakespeare's "will"—though "Will" is clearly aware that he may get hurt at the competitive level of play implied there. Whereas in sonnets 133–134 Shakespeare wishes that either his male friend or he himself were free of the Dark lady's enchantment, in sonnets 135–136 the speaker is willing to share her, to be one "in the number" of lovers (136.9).

## DEVICES AND TECHNIQUES

The chief device in each of these sonnets is the crowded significance attached to "will" and "Will." The word makes thirteen appearances in 135 (and also "Wilt"), seven in 136 (once as a verb). Some examples are capitalized and italicized in both 135 and 136 in the 1609 quarto, but the fonts do not appear to change or limit meaning. Evans describes the word play of these two sonnets as "frankly bawdy and frenetically witty exercises" (253).

McGuire (1987) finds that the poem's "willful" punning is mirrored in and "augmented by" the "willfulness of the sonnet's idiosyncratic rhyming and form" (311). He writes that no Shakespearean sonnet "has a rhyme scheme more extravagantly atypical" than that of 135 (311) in which lines 1, 3, 9, 11, 13, and 14 end in -ill (Will / still; still / will; kill / Will. The line-end words form an interesting declarative sentence that suggests a negative response to the speaker's plea. McGuire also proposes that the final syllables of lines 2 (-plus), 4 (thus), 5 (spacious), and 7 (gracious) are all a part of the b-rhyme ("over-plus" and "thus"). In McGuire's scheme, only four elements set into three quatrains and a couplet compose the rhyme scheme: *abab bcbc adad aa*. Sonnet 136 will offer reader an off-rhyme in the first quatrain with "near / there" and in the second with "love / prove." However, these rhymes probably were exact for an early-seventeenth-century reader.

Also notable in the lover's desperate rhetoric is his alternating use of first and third person references to himself and his possessions. The lover speaks of himself, his desire, his penis, his person, and his name in both persons. In Sonnet 135 he refers to himself in the third person three times in the first two lines. In 136, he refers to himself as "I" in lines 1 and 2 and in the third person in line 3 with the transition of "thy Will" at the end of line 2. In line 5, he refers to himself in the third person ("Will will fulfill") and in lines 9, 10, and 11 he uses the first person with "me" and "I." In line 12, he refers to himself, alternately, in both terms as "that nothing, me, a something."

## THEMES AND MEANINGS

The meaning of these poems lies mainly in their somewhat subversive sexual language and images. Feinberg asserts that the Dark Lady's voice is suppressed by the speaker throughout the sequence. Both Sonnet 135 and Sonnet 136 address their discourse to the Dark Lady, and each is a plea for her sexual attentions. Perhaps we hear her voice paraphrased in the opening speech of each sonnet and in her saying "no" in Sonnet 135 on three occasions: in the speaker's two questions of lines 5–6 and 7–8; these lines seem to come as responses to her rejection, and perhaps she refuses him again to spur the refutation of the couplet, where he refers directly to her "unkind no"—though it may not have been yet spoken (13–14). Sonnet 135 seems more playful, and perhaps more self-assured, than its successor, despite any implied rejection. Here the Dark Lady has had her "Will" in all its senses, whereas in Sonnet 136 she seems to begin by recoiling from that "Will."

A particular phrase in Sonnet 136—the central mention of the "blind soul" along with "soul" twice—recalls the "poore soul" of Sonnet 146.1, but the latter is contained in an environment that is nothing like that of 136, and it is useless to force a seventeenth-century Christian interpretation on the "soul" references of 136. Booth notes that the "reference is to the seat of intuition" but that the sonnet's "immediate context does nothing to activate the philosophical and religious connotations of *soul*" (469), and later that sexual meaning is "evoked" by the conflict. Evans writes, similarly, that the word is "used as the seat of intelligence and its resulting emotions, without any necessary suggestion of 'spiritual' qualities" (254). Booth goes on to suggest that there may be a "sexual meaning" to "blind soul" (470). The "blind" quality of the "soul" is like that of the woman's sexual organs, the visible opening of which is in the almond shape of an eye. The frankly sexual topic and language of the sonnet suggest that the "soul" may be a paradoxical reference to the sexual parts of a woman whose "soul" is perceived pejoratively as governed or contained there. When we find that it is the "soul" that will admit "Will," the significance assigned to "soul" becomes more clearly sexual. If the first instance of "soul"—recalling Booth's identification of "soul" as "the seat of intuition"—is not entirely sexual, it may be read as the conscience—perhaps now blinded by love for another; something like the conscience provides the impulse (the "check," 136.1) to pull away from the former lover ("I was thy Will," in the past tense). In the same sense, the "soul" may be some blindly instinctive component of the woman addressed, who is somehow viscerally repelled by the lover's final approach. His "com[ing] so near" (136.1) may refer to physical proximity or, more likely, with the use of the sexual verb "come"—to the approach of the speaker's sexual parts to hers. The latter is supported in the adverbial "thus far" as a measure of her "fulfill[ing] his "love-suit" or gratifying his desire (136.4) and his assurance of reciprocal sexual performance: "*Will* will" fill the "treasure of thy love" (thinly veiled code for vagina) "full with wills" (136.5, 6).

The speaker of Sonnet 136 constructs three persuasive strategies to win over his mistress: he is first reassuring: she knows him because he was hers (1–3); the second appeal is an extravagant but concise promise of sexual favors (5–6); the third

(7–12) is a paradox of the second, implying that his "one" Will (taken, perhaps, from the abundance that he has just described in 5–6) will be hardly noticeable to her, insignificant as he is, but all the more (precious) to the mistress. The couplet reduces the mercantile-imaged "Will" to a name merely, and asks that she love only the name, and by doing so—and going to no further trouble—will thus give her love to him. The mercantile and legalistic language of Sonnet 136 (7–12) suggests an accounting document, perhaps a bill of lading, or an enumeration of items in the papers ("will") of an estate, where small items would not be officially documented, but where one particular small item might be held as "sweet," presumably for sentiment's sake (12); the speaker suggests such an attachment with the sentimentally implied ownership of "thy Will" in line 2. The lover appeals to the mistress's sense of pity, as well as to the notion that, being a "nothing," he would not be costly or troublesome; he bargains in the commercial sense, discarding the expansive offers made in lines 5–6. The sexual references persist among the mercantile ones: "things of great receipt" (l. 7) and "store" (l.10) continue the idea suggested by "treasure" (that is, treasury) as the mistress's body of line 5, or more specifically, her vagina. The anxious and importunate lover further deprecates his use and value in the last four lines and places himself at the feet of the Dark Lady.

## THE RELATIONSHIP OF THE SONNETS TO SHAKESPEARE'S OTHER WORKS

Interpretation and debate about the sexual word play is responsible for much of the interest these sonnets, and they remain, in the minds of many readers, "the bawdy 'Will' Sonnets" (Rowse, p. xxi). Sexual play on "will," coming in battalions in these sonnets, comes single spies in the plays, rather as in *King Lear* ("O indistinguish'd space of woman's will," 4.6.271), *Troilus and Cressida* (2.2.53ff), and *All's Well That Ends Well* (4.3.16–17). In this last, the second lord says that Bertram "this night fleshes his will in the spoil of [a gentlewoman's] honor." As in these sonnets, erotic word play lightens or expands a bit of dialogue in the plays. Such references appear in the interludes of comic relief in the tragedies, such as *Macbeth*'s porter's speech on the effects of drink, the frequent sexual puns of Mercutio and the Nurse in *Romeo and Juliet*, and the puns and broad metaphors of *Othello*. As expected, considerable sexual punning appears in the comedies, which are often directly concerned with sexual desire.

Yet the sonnets express a laxness about sex that the plays shy away from. Even premarital sex is shunned in the plays, and adultery is rejected. Goneril and Regan in *King Lear* both want Edmund, and Goneril writes a letter urging Edmund to kill her husband (4.6.262–268). All three would-be adulterers are evil, and all three end up dead. The sonnets in general, and these two in particular, take a freer approach. The only bar to their adulterous affair is the Dark Lady's possible rejection of the speaker. While the Dark Lady sonnets are probably not in chronological order, in Sonnet 138 the feared rejection is not evident, since the speaker says, "I lie with her, and she with me" (l. 13).

### Annotated Bibliography

Booth, Stephen, ed. *Shakespeare's Sonnets*. New Haven: Yale UP, 1977. One of the most valuable collections/editions for its introduction and discussions of each sonnet with attention to literary and mechanical technique as well as to language, and for its reproduction of the 1609 quarto text in facsimile on facing pages with the edited versions.

De Grazia, Margreta. "The Scandal of Shakespeare's Sonnets." In *Shakespeare's Poems*. Ed. Stephen Orgel and Sean Kellen. New York: Garland, 1999. 89–112. De Grazia suggests a reading for the Dark Lady sequence, rather than the Fair Youth sequence, as "abnormal and unnatural" or as "perverse and menacing" in that the former delineates a love of desperation that threatens "social peril" via indiscriminate sexual activity and miscegenation (that is, the Anglo Will with the "Black" lady).

Duncan-Jones, Katherine, ed. *Shakespeare's Sonnets*. The Arden Shakespeare. London: Thomas Nelson and Sons, 1997. Annotated sonnets with facing-page notes to language and phrases; thorough introduction includes textual background, a comparative review of historical criticism, and the editor's fresh critical view.

Evans, G. Blakemore. *The Sonnets*. Cambridge: Cambridge UP, 1996. Commentary section organized by phrases as they appear in the sonnet and are sometimes helpfully detailed beyond recording entries from the *Oxford English Dictionary*.

Feinberg, Nona. "Erasing the Dark Lady: Sonnet 138 in the Sequence." *Assays* (1987): 97–108. Feinberg shows how the Lady is effaced and her voice stifled by the lover whose voice suppresses hers and is, thereby, diminished himself.

Fineman, Joel. "Shakespeare's 'Perjur'd Eye.'" *Representations* 7 (1984): 59–86. Earlier exposition and comparison of the two divisions of the sonnets. Before de Grazia, he juxtaposed the restrained and idealistic relationship of the Fair Youth poems with the "misogynistic" language and sexual excesses of the Dark Lady sonnets. His view exposits "an idealist homogeneity disrupted by a supplementary heterogeneity" (78).

Ingram, W. G., and Theodore Redpath, eds. *Shakespeare's Sonnets*. London: Hodder, 1978. An edition of the sonnets of interest principally in the facing page notes and rather detailed and documented summaries of critical thought.

McGuire, Philip C. "Shakespeare's Non-Shakespearean Sonnets." *Shakespeare Quarterly* 38.3 (1987): 304–319. McGuire shows connections between structure and theme ("formal identities and meaning") in the sonnets he points to as having "deviant" or "atypical" rhyme schemes. McGuire treats sonnets 29, 46, 55, 88, 125, and 135, among others. He cites 76, 105, and 108, in which the speaker comments on variation in poetic form, as bolstering the "fiction" of a unified Shakespearean rhyme scheme.

Orgel, Stephen, and Sean Kellen, eds. *Shakespeare's Poems*. New York: Garland, 1999. A collection of essays on a wide range of topics related to the sonnets. Includes work by Edward A. Snow, Jonathan Bate, Katherine Duncan-Jones, Joel Fineman, and others.

# Sonnet 138

## Elizabeth Moore Willingham

When my love swears that she is made of truth
I do believe her, though I know she lies,
That she might think me some untutor'd youth,
Unlearned in the world's false subtleties.
Thus vainly thinking that she thinks me young,
Although she knows my days are past the best,
Simply I credit her false speaking tongue:
On both sides thus is simple truth suppress'd.
But wherefore says she not she is unjust?
And wherefore say not I that I am old?
O, love's best habit is in seeming trust,
And age in love loves not to have years told:
    Therefore I lie with her and she with me,
    And in our faults by lies we flatter'd be.

**PROSE PARAPHRASE**

When my lover swears that she is faithful, I believe her "though I know she lies" (l. 2), that is, she tells me falsehoods and also lies with other lovers. I pretend as I do so that she will think me a novice in love. So "vainly" (l. 5), that is, both uselessly and out of vanity of wanting to be thought young and innocent, I pretend that she sees me as youthful, even though I know that she knows that I am old. In turn, I claim to believe her when she deceives me. With her lies and my pretense of belief, we hide truths that are easy to see. But why does she not admit that she is false? And why not admit that I am old? We act as we do because trust, or at least the appearance of trust, is essential for love, and an old man in love does not want to be reminded of his age. For these reasons, we lie together—as lovers and speakers—and our lovemaking and our falsehoods hide our mutual failings and please us both.

## THE PLACE OF THE SONNET IN THE CYCLE

Sonnet 138 is one of the "Dark Lady" sonnets, in which the speaker's stance is often self-reflective and condemnatory, both of self and of the lady. One finds resonance in the speaker's voice in Sonnet 138 from Sonnet 126 (a sort of epilogue to the Fair Youth sequence), where the poet laments the transience of youth just prior to his turning to the Dark Lady. In tone, 138 is one of the kinder of the misogynistic sonnets (see also sonnets 137, 144, 147, 148), in which the Dark Lady appears to serve as a mirror for the speaker's misgivings and self-loathing, for his doubts about his age, for his compromises with ideals of love, and for his shortfalls as a lover. Edward Snow points to Sonnet 138 as setting its world view against those of sonnets 116 and 129, using a quality of acceptance in which the "apocalyptic metaphors" (and absolutes) of the latter are "entirely inappropriate" (479–480). The speaker's compromise here, however, perhaps lays the groundwork for resentment revealed in the self-reproaches of sonnets like 148, 150, and 152.

If the order of the sonnets is authentic, one may plausibly observe that the speaker continues to dwell in Sonnet 138 on the language of Sonnet 137, considering the paradoxes of true versus false and lovers' blindness versus the testimony of seeing clearly. In Sonnet 138, though, the speaker approaches the paradoxes and laments of the previous poem in a mood of reconciliation. As in Sonnet 137, he continues here to play with words having sexual as well as mundane meaning ("lie," "made," "truth") and creates interplay between other contrasts: youth and age; experience and inexperience; easy and difficult; unknowing and sophisticated. Following Sonnet 138, Sonnet 139 speaks again to the issue of the mistress's faithfulness and the speaker's wish not to be confronted with her dalliances, matters which were central in 133 and 134. In a holistic view of the sonnets, Barbara Herrnstein Smith groups 138 with the "finest" and "most characteristic" of the sequences, in spite of her perception of its "figurative language" as "austere" and far from "sensuously evocative" (40). The speaker's concern about his age echoes similar expressions in his poems addressed to the Fair Youth (for example, Sonnet 73). In those sonnets the speaker also repeatedly pardons offenses that may be sexual betrayals (for example, sonnets 35, 40).

## DEVICES AND TECHNIQUES

In addition to the absence of "imagery" that Smith notes (above) as an unusual element of this sonnet, the Lady's implied utterance in the first line also sets the sonnet apart. Her statement serves two pivotal functions: it creates the narrative tension of the sonnet, and the abrupt overture sets the reader in the middle of a conversation.

Sonnet 138 takes the typical English form of three internally rhymed quatrains followed by a couplet, all in pentameter. However, Shakespeare treats the first two quatrains as if they were an octave (an eight-line stanza in the Italian sonnet style) to present the first part of the poetic argument: the tacit agreement of supposed trust between the speaker and his mistress. The first quatrain opens with a promise attributed to the Dark Lady (that she is "made of truth") and immediately shows the lover (speaker) complicit with his mistress in believing her falsehood. The second quatrain (ll. 5–8) justifies the lover's acceptance of his mistress's lies by explaining what he barters in exchange, and the final line (8) concludes that each "suppress[es]" truth.

Like the Italian sestet (the last six lines of an Italian sonnet, which in the English are the third quatrain and the couplet), lines 9–14 here mark a shift in the speaker's tone as he poses—or redirects—two questions to the listener (ll. 9–10) and justifies his solution (ll. 11–12). The speaker responds to the questions in a direct and matter-of-fact sentence, whose two imbedded rationales are coordinated with an under-stated "And." The final lines (13–14) follow the couplet function and rhyme of the English sonnet and provide the resolution of the poetic tension by showing that in-deed the "seeming trust" (l. 11) works well for this couple.

## THEMES AND MEANINGS

The theme of mutability, described aptly in tone and substance by Prince as "Shakespeare's laments on time and transience" (25), informs the Dark Lady son-nets, as well as those addressed to the Fair Youth (sonnets 1–126), but in sonnets 127–152 the preoccupation with time and age grows more somber. In the second se-quence, the remedy for the deterioration of physical beauty and power under the passage of time is not—as it was in the Fair Youth sonnets—marriage and the beget-ting of children (see Sonnet 3, for example), or even the poetic transcendence of time (Sonnet 55, for example), but a practical, personal mediation of an inexorable fact. In the medieval or renaissance view, one might say that the lovers opt for seiz-ing the day over retiring to a convent or a hermitage with their ideals of love intact.

This matter of recognition, compromise, and resignation creates for Cruttwell (1960) "the most terrible, and also the nakedest" of the Dark Lady sonnets, as the speaker reveals "things that are not easily confessed" and puns in "grim serious-ness" on "lie" (ll. 13–14). Barber (1967), citing the reciprocal advantage to the two lovers, calls the poem "jaunty as well as devastating" (317, quoted by Feinberg n. 7). Booth (1977) marks its tone as "downright smug" (477). Noting these assessments, Feinberg (1987) writes that the male lover "displaces his own existential fears onto her [his mistress's] behavior" when he accuses her of faithlessness and "articulates his disappointment that she too [sic] is a changing, aging creature . . . a fallen mor-tal like him" (107).

Discussion of the paradoxical language of Sonnet 138 centers on issues of truth-telling and belief. Margreta de Grazia (1999) points out that, at the replacement of the Fair Youth with the Dark Lady, a variety of distinctions "collapse," among them, in Sonnet 138, the difference between truth and a lie (104). The lover references his mistress's assurance of her fidelity with "[w]hen" (l. 1), an iterative adverb of time used with the present tense; thus, he implies that the mistress is regularly prompted to make this oath, and he, to pretend to believe it. In addition, "swears" (l. 1) im-plies, according to Booth's reading, that some event indicating contrary evidence has led to the swearing (478). Booth notes that when "lie" signifies "falsehood," the lover's assertion of belief is impossible and that "though" does not "effectively me-diate" the paradox (478); Fineman writes that the statement stands as "proof of its own paradoxicality" (77).

The opening sentence of Sonnet 138 likely communicates a second paradox: that the mistress is—or was—a true maid ("made of truth") where the lover is con-cerned. As an experienced lover, the speaker cannot believe his mistress's patently false protestations, yet he declares his willful belief in her "lie" (2)—only logical in the sense that he knows that she "lies" with others, which overturns "made of truth." His sleight-of-hand allows him to avoid—what is, for him—a more worrisome "truth" and a more distressing betrayal: aging (ll. 3–6). This concern shows in circumlocution and softened phrases: the speaker associates "vainly thinking" (that is, both a useless act and a self-congratulatory one) with "young," rather than make a direct statement about his age (l. 5). He next buffers the language with which his mistress regards his age—we have only his word for this—as "past the best" (l. 6). While the speaker describes his acceptance of her falsehoods with "[s]imply" (l. 7), his action is not so simple—neither in the sense of simple-minded nor of easily done. In the first place, he is perceptive enough to know that she "lies" with others and also lies to him about her perception of his age; in the second, he is crafty enough to disguise his awareness of the truth out of self-interest.

The speaker is well acquainted with love's games, but pretends to be ignorant—"simple"—feigning no suspicion that his mistress deceives him. (One may well conclude that she shows no sign of knowing that he deceives her, either.) The speaker toys with "simple" and presents the notion that he is sufficiently experienced to know how to appear to be inexperienced, and his mistress is as well. This speaker is no longer the youthful lover, "untutored" and "unlearned" (ll. 3–4), but an aging man whose view of love is practical, cynical, and a bit desperate (ll. 7–8). Booth points out a gender reversal of this argument from the real Elizabethan world: "passing off commercially experienced women as virgins" (that is, as "true maids") to inexperienced youths (477).

The last line of the second quatrain (8) provides the speaker's synthesis: we are both guilty of obvious falsehoods, and we each accept the lies of the other. Although the romantic stand-by of the blindness of lovers is a part of other sonnets in this sequence, here the lovers are not blind, but mutually and customarily turn a blind eye to infidelity and age, remaining reciprocally aware of what the other is feigning not to see. It seems that their mutual experience—in love and with life—has taught these two something about love's practical realities that makes their bargain palatable and, paradoxically, more honest than one based on the impossible idealism of youth.

The next two lines (9–10) ask why the lovers do not simply confess the truth. These questions, like the mistress's oath, are rephrased at second hand, here from the mouth of the implied audience. After all, this sonnet is not an address to the mistress like sonnets 135, 136, 137, 139, 140, and 141 or internally to the speaker, like sonnets 144, 146, 153, 154. It is more in the style of a late-night confessional for the barman or friend. The questions prompt the speaker to validate the lovers' choices. The transitional "O" (138.11) may be read as a weary vocalization, a monosyllabic elegy on the ideals of love and youth from the age-worn, love-worn speaker. On the other hand, it may be reasonably read in the spirit of a second wind, a vowel of bravado prefacing an upward transition. The lover affirms that he indeed creates for his mistress the appearance of trust ("seeming trust"), and she validates him because he does not like to be reminded of his age. Thus as they support one another's lies and lie together in lovemaking, the lovers mutually flatter one another, perhaps in the sense of delude (but here with an awareness that makes delusion impossible) and more appropriately in the sense of pleasing or satisfying one another.

## THE RELATIONSHIP OF THE SONNET TO SHAKESPEARE'S OTHER WORKS

Smith notes that Shakespeare, in common with some of his own tragic heroes—Macbeth, Lear, Hamlet, and Othello—betrays an "absolutist" viewpoint, and that in the sonnets, a compromise of his values and resultant expectations meant "corruption or betrayal" (21). Although Smith's comment is directly attached to the Fair Youth sonnets, it is particularly telling in the frank compromise of Sonnet 138. Both Hamlet and Othello reject the love of "true maids" who are also "made of truth," while the speaker of Sonnet 138 accepts the love of one who is neither. Hamlet does so with deliberated pretense and innuendoes of sexual promiscuity that only confuse and dismay Ophelia. Othello manages not to believe the truth by accepting Iago's claims about Desdemona's alleged lying (again in both senses of the word). Even in the comedies any hint of unchastity leads to rejection, as in *Much Ado about Nothing*. The difference in outlook in Sonnet 138 is clear.

Probably the history of *Antony and Cleopatra*, as a sort of tale of "love among the ruins," provides the greatest number of parallels with Sonnet 138. Snow (1980) compares the "brittle idealism" and "insecurities" of Othello's worldview (467) with Cleopatra's conscious embrace of "passionately embodied fictions" over the "Roman-minded difference between truth and falsity" (466), a distinction that Othello and Lear, for example, fail to understand at every opportunity until it is too late. The lovers of Sonnet 138, embracing the compromise and each other, preempt the separation of the lovers at the final curtain or—in Shakespearean terms—the dignified removal of the corpses from the stage.

### Annotated Bibliography

Booth, Stephen, ed. *Shakespeare's Sonnets*. New Haven: Yale UP, 1977. Of particular value for the facsimiles of each sonnet from the 1609 quarto facing his edited versions and for Booth's general preface, which provides a sound overview of the whole to accompany his extensive notes on each sonnet.

Cruttwell, Patrick. *The Shakespearean Moment*. New York: Random House, 1960. An older work that eschews a "subjective" reading of the sonnets, and that remains useful for contextual criticism; the lead essay, "Shakespeare's Sonnets and the 1590s," is the only extended treatment of the sonnets in this book, but the detailed article provides terse and telling critical opinion, insight, and interpretation.

De Grazia, Margreta. "The Scandal of Shakespeare's Sonnets." In *Shakespeare's Poems*. Ed. Stephen Orgel and Sean Kellen. New York: Garland, 1999. 89–112. De Grazia suggests a reading for the Dark Lady sequence, rather than the Fair Youth sequence, as "abnormal and unnatural" or as "perverse and menacing" in that the former delineates a love of desperation that threatens "social peril" via indiscriminate sexual activity and miscegenation (that is, the Anglo Will with the "Black" lady).

Duncan-Jones, Katherine, ed. *Shakespeare's Sonnets*. The Arden Shakespeare. London: Thomas Nelson and Sons, 1997. Annotated sonnets with facing-page notes to language and phrases; introduction includes textual background, a comparative review of historical criticism, and a fresh critical view.

Feinberg, Nona. "Erasing the Dark Lady: Sonnet 138 in the Sequence." *Assays* (1987): 97–108. Comparing Sonnet 138 with material from *Othello* to Petrarch, Feinberg shows how the Lady as "other" is effaced and her voice stifled by the lover whose voice suppresses hers, and is, thereby, diminished himself.

Fineman, Joel. "Shakespeare's 'Perjur'd Eye.'" *Representations* 7 (1984): 59–86. Before de Grazia, Fineman juxtaposed the restrained and idealistic relationship of the Fair Youth poems with the "misogynistic" language and sexual excesses of the Dark Lady sonnets. His view exposits "an idealist homogeneity disrupted by a supplementary heterogeneity" (78).

Prince, F. T. "The Sonnet from Wyatt to Shakespeare." In *Elizabethan Poetry*. Ed. John Russell Brown and Bernard Harris. Stratford-upon-Avon Studies. London: Arnold, 1960. 10–29. Comparison of Italian and French forms and the English (principally Wyatt, Sidney, Spenser, and Shakespeare).

Smith, Barbara Herrnstein. *William Shakespeare: Sonnets*. New York: New York UP, 1969. An edition with criticism and a solid introduction to the sonnet form and features that is both readable and scholarly.

Snow, Edward. "Loves of Comfort and Despair: A Reading of Shakespeare's Sonnet 138." *ELH* 47.3 (1980): 462–483. A careful analysis of language between the two versions of the sonnet (in *The Passionate Pilgrim*, 1599, and *Sonnets*, 1609) and its echoes in Shakespearean drama. Emphasizes the transforming quality that the lover's view in this sonnet brings to the more general preoccupations with transience, faithfulness, and despair of the two sequences.

# Sonnet 144

## Andrew James Hartley

Two loves I have of comfort and despair,
Which like two spirits do suggest me still:
The better angel is a man right fair,
The worser spirit a woman colour'd ill.
To win me soon to hell, my female evil
Tempteth my better angel from my side,
And would corrupt my saint to be a devil,
Wooing his purity with her foul pride.
And whether that my angel be turn'd fiend
Suspect I may, but not directly tell;
But being both from me, both to each friend,
I guess one angel in another's hell:
    Yet this shall I ne'er know, but live in doubt,
    Till my bad angel fire my good one out.

### PROSE PARAPHRASE

The speaker of Sonnet 144 says that he is in love with two different people, one male, and one female. Both tempt ("suggest") him (l. 2), but in different ways. The young man is beautiful and apparently virtuous, the woman dark in appearance (and therefore, according to the fashion of the day, unattractive) and sexually promiscuous. The former urges him to virtue, the latter to vice. To make matters worse, the woman seems to be trying to seduce the young man, so that the speaker feels torn not just by the sense that his own affections are divided, but by the jealous fear that his "two loves" (l. 1) will actually go off together. The speaker cannot be sure that the young man has given in to the woman's excessive sexual enticements, but he feels the extent to which they have both drawn away from him and into each other. Since he sees the man as angelic and the woman as demonic, he sees their possible union as the triumph of hell. At the end of the poem, the speaker confesses that he cannot know the truth of what has actually happened, and will not know, until the man (the "better angel," line 3) is shown to have been obviously corrupted by the woman (the "bad angel," line 14), a corruption possibly manifested by some venereal disease (as suggested by the phrase "fire . . . out," line 14), and is smoked out, like an animal from its den.

## THE PLACE OF THE SONNET IN THE CYCLE

This is the last sonnet in which the young man appears explicitly. If we are to trust the sequence of the sonnets as printed (and there is no hard evidence to assume the order of the sonnets was not dictated by the author), then we may make the assumption that the young man who dominates the first 126 sonnets (at least in so far as gender can be determined from pronouns) is the same as the "better angel" of Sonnet 144. This young man is the subject of the sequence's first seventeen sonnets, which urge him to marry, and then the succeeding sonnets sing their love of him in various ways before switching attention to the "woman color'd ill" (l. 4), usually referred to as the Dark Lady, who appears first in Sonnet 127 and who, beginning in Sonnet 133, seems to have attracted the love of the young man as well as the speaker. In the sonnets between 133 and 144, the woman is thus characterized as faithless, manipulative, and deceptive, even as she continues to be the object of the speaker's increasingly conflicted obsession.

The writer had earlier feared or suspected betrayal by the fair youth, whether because the youth switched allegiance to a rival poet (sonnets 78–86) or found another lover (92–95), perhaps the writer's mistress, a fear also suggested by Sonnet 35, where the images of the rose thorn (l. 2) and rose worm ("canker") boring within the "sweetest bud" (l. 4) have sexual connotations. In Sonnet 92 the writer comments, "Thou mayst be false, and yet I know it not" (l. 14). Whereas in these earlier sonnets, however, the poet feared the loss of the youth's love, in Sonnet 144 he seems at least as troubled by the Dark Lady's deception/defection as by the young man's behavior. And while in Sonnet 35 the writer makes excuses for the youth, in Sonnet 144 he is angry with the Dark Lady.

If the sonnet sequence can be said to contain a narrative, then the story comes to a head between sonnets 133 and 144 as the idealized young man and the more problematic Dark Lady, both of whom the speaker has been infatuated with albeit in different ways, seem to get involved with each other. The resultant love triangle creates extreme anxiety and depression on the part of the speaker, who feels increasingly left out. Sonnet 144 thus falls at the sequence's emotional low point, a moment in which the speaker's love for his mistress seems least rational, least rewarding, and least in his control.

While the poem was published with the rest of Shakespeare's sonnets in the 1609 quarto (which also contained *A Lover's Complaint*), an alternative version of Sonnet 144 was published in the 1599 collection *The Passionate Pilgrim*, which was reissued in 1599–1600. This collection contains poems by several authors (including Shakespeare), and the version of Sonnet 144 that appears there, though demonstrating that it was written significantly before the publication of the entire sonnet sequence in 1609, looks unrevised. Other than some small differences in pronouns that are altered for the better in the later publication, the 1599 version contains no significant variations from the 1609 version.

## DEVICES AND TECHNIQUES

Sonnet 144 uses the standard Shakespearean sonnet form of three quatrains and a couplet (rhymed *abab cdcd efef gg*) and in this poem each of those units is a sentence. The poem has no clear "turn," in which the direction of the poem is radically altered, though line 9 begins a sestet in which doubt and foreboding take over from the octet's playful angel/devil extended metaphor, showing not so much a taking back of what has been said as a second thought that reshapes and modifies the sentiment of the poem.

The dominant poetic device within the sonnet is the oppositional relationship that juxtaposes the heavenly attributes of the young man against the hellish associations of the Dark Lady. The two "spirits" (a generic term for supernatural beings) are defined through a whimsical use of conventional Christian tradition that sets angels against devils in a constant battle for the soul of earthly humankind. Here, the contested ground is the speaker of the poem himself, his soul being torn in contrary directions by the appeal of both the angel and the devil. This central metaphor feeds the entire poem, moving toward the final image of the angel being plunged into hell, and it gives rise to the image of infernal heat that ends the poem.

The idea of the human being thus led and misled by heavenly and demonic agents is a common one, particularly in medieval religious drama such as morality plays, in which a central Everyman figure picks his passage through the moral minefield of life, trying to separate the good and bad advice given to him by various metaphorical characters bent on either his salvation or his damnation. The poem ironically twists this conventional psychomachia (a kind of internal struggle) by making the Everyman figure (the speaker) a bystander, the angelic force being the one that is tempted by the devil. While the psychomachia of the Mystery plays emphasized the individual's control of his soul's afterlife, grounding his destiny in what choices he made during life, the poem's speaker finds himself powerless to determine his own earthly future. He can only watch as the devil turns all her powers on luring the angel away from him and into sin. The consequence of the angel's giving in to her temptation takes the idea of damnation further, since the process would actually turn the angel into a devil ("fiend," 144.9): the fallen angel would be damned because of his unlawful sexual contact with the demonic dark angel, but would also become a fiend to the speaker in that such an act would show that the speaker had been completely replaced in the angel's affections by the devil. The last line of the poem renders both lovers angels, implying the extent to which their probable alliance has muddied the moral waters, undercutting the original good/evil binary with a word that emphasizes their ultimate similarity as seen from the perspective of the speaker, whose love for both of them has been, apparently, rejected.

The effect of creating a moral binary and then undermining it by conflating the good and evil figures by intertwining them is central to Fineman's argument about how the poet's two loves ironize each other and cause a problematic devaluing of both that, in turn, produces a sense of crisis in the narrator. This crisis disrupts the speaker's sense of self in ways that, according to Fineman, revolutionized poetic subjectivity (Fineman, 57).

On a verbal level, the poem exploits the closeness in sound and appearance of words that should be virtual opposites like *fiend* and *friend*, the rhyming of *angel* with *hell* and the fact that *evil* and *live* are visually linked through anagram. The result is a sense of paradox and conflict that is perfectly in keeping with the uneasy binaries and moral/psychological ambiguities at the heart of the poem. The weight given to these words is especially notable because of the way they frequently fall at the end of the line. Similarly, the poem's final anxiety is present in the endings of the last couplet, where *doubt* and *out* suggest both pain and finality in sound (the open vowel sound and the closed final consonants) as well as sense.

## THEMES AND MEANINGS

It is, of course, common to some Christian traditions that the influence of the devil is seen in the part of the tempting woman, who echoes Eve in leading men towards damnation. It was a common point of Christian misogyny to conflate the Bible's first human woman with the satanic power that tempted her and, as was seen in the writings of church fathers such as St. Augustine, it was similarly common to see the evidence of the woman's devilish nature in her sexually alluring appearance and actions. In versions of both the older Catholic and newer more Puritanical traditions, that which made women desirable physically is what made them dangerous, taking prisoner the male will and capacity to reason, leading them towards sin and damnation. It is therefore appropriate that the poem's final sexual overtones (in which the angel is tempted to enter the female devil's hell in ways suggesting actual sexual intercourse) imply—albeit playfully—the hellish nature of the woman's sexual organs. Once tempted into this expressly sexual "hell," the poem easily plays on the idea that the figurative hell is made literal in the resultant venereal disease (which confirms the sense of demonic "looseness" frequently linked to any manifestation of female desire).

The word "despair," which appears in the poem's first line, is used commonly today, but in the Renaissance it had greater weight, partly because of its theological associations. In the New Testament, Jesus refers to one sin, the sin against the Holy Spirit, being unforgivable (Matthew 12:31–32). This unforgivable sin was sometimes considered to be despair: the idea that the extent of one's sin makes forgiveness and salvation impossible. Since this attitude denies God the capacity to redeem the sinner regardless of his or her fault, it was considered a kind of blasphemous arrogance. The poet's use of the term here suggests, therefore, not merely depression, as it might do today, but a morbid self-involvement that puts one's self (or soul) in jeopardy. While one love offers comfort (as it is appropriate for an angel to do, promising that all is not lost), the demonic love provides only the certainty of self-destruction. A similar dynamic is present in Christopher Marlowe's play *Doctor Faustus* (probably written a few years before this poem, though the dates of both the poem and the play are uncertain) in which the good angel continues to tell the hero that he might yet be saved, while the evil angel insists that he is damned already.

Under the playful image of the angel/devil binary, the speaker explores a deep-seated sense of rejection and a feeling of increasing irrelevance as he is forced to recognize that despite the depth of his love, he cannot force either of his angels to love him as he loves them. The idea of being ignored by one's beloved is, of course, a common one in life and art, but it is made doubly painful and darkly funny when one considers that here the poet has two beloveds, and that he has been forgotten because they have fallen for each other!

Most painfully, of course, the poem leaves the speaker in a state of uncertainty, not knowing the extent to which he has been driven out of the affections of both his angel and devil. The poet is paralyzed by doubt and suspicion, unsure of just how bad his predicament is and unwilling to find out for sure and push the situation into crisis. In some ways, not knowing is worse than having the truth, however bad that truth might be, because it prevents him from moving on. As things are, he can only speculate and wait, terrified of doing something that will lose one or both of his angels forever. This paralysis is a kind of emasculation that, as with the unusual problem of having both a male and a female lover, seems to make him uncertain of his own manhood, manhood being customarily associated with sexual aggressiveness and being active instead of passive as he is here. As is often the case with unrequited love, then, the speaker finds that his situation does not stay conveniently in one area of his life but detrimentally affects his entire world and sense of self.

## THE RELATIONSHIP OF THE SONNET TO SHAKESPEARE'S OTHER WORKS

The unease about female sexuality is a familiar preoccupation in the English Renaissance, and it surfaces frequently in Shakespeare's plays. One of the most famous examples is King Lear's crazed statement that women are human only above the waist. From the waist down they are "Centaurs." Above the girdle they are divine, but "Beneath is all the fiends' " (4.6.124, 127), an image suggesting a bestial monstrosity located specifically in their genitalia and sexual desires. One of the most extreme instances of this misogyny comes from Posthumus in *Cymbeline*, who denounces his wife and all women as driven by lust and thus contaminating all the children they produce. As is usually the case in Shakespeare, however, Posthumus's misogyny is, like Othello's or like Leontes' in *The Winter's Tale*, grounded in his own mistaken jealousy about his wife's fidelity. His wife, like Othello's, is innocent of the adultery Posthumus suspects, and this innocence undermines the idea that the audience is supposed to accept what he says at face value. Part of the problem is that virgin/whore binary alluded to earlier. The man who idolizes his beloved in ways denying her any sexual desire sees the evidence of such desire in her as utterly corrupting, so she turns in his mind from virginal goddess to prostitute. While the men in Shakespeare are always wrong about their beloved's infidelity, the importance they place on chastity suggests a persistent and neurotic preoccupation with the dangerousness of female sexuality. When Hamlet's mother weds his uncle after his father's death, Hamlet assumes that this remarriage manifests a basic truth about all women: they are inconstant and driven by sexual appetites. "Frailty," he says, "thy name is woman!" (1.2.146). While this jealous preoccupation with female chastity is usually the subject of tragedy in Shakespeare (or in tragedy narrowly averted in a comedy like *Much Ado about Nothing*), it takes center stage in the satirical comedy *The Merry Wives of Windsor*, in which a jealous husband is taught to allow his faithful wife more liberty.

Shakespeare is fond of exploring triangles of desire, in which three people are involved in love relationships that somehow leave one of them out in the cold. Sometimes, as in *Othello* or *The Winter's Tale*, one of these relationships is the product only of jealous imaginings and doesn't really exist, but in a play like *Twelfth Night*, the triangles of desire are very real. In this play, Viola, disguised as a boy, is in love with her master, Orsino, who is, in turn, in love with Olivia. Olivia, believing Viola to be a boy, falls in love with her. Antonio loves Sebastian (Viola's brother), who falls for Olivia, and similar triangles can be observed in the supporting cast of Feste, Maria, Sir Andrew, Sir Toby and Malvolio. Throughout the play the audience is presented with these three-person love affairs, revolving them so that the grief and loneliness of one of the characters is always just visible. As in the sonnet, Shakespeare seems to reveal the idea that much of what makes love interesting as a literary subject has less to do with beauty and happiness than it does with the melancholy, isolation, and pain one feels when one is ignored by one's beloved, particularly when he or she is romantically fascinated by someone else.

The overall theme of the sonnet—the dividing and destructive effects of the love triangle on the speaker—might be linked to Iago's gleeful warning to Othello to beware of jealousy, "the green-ey'd monster which doth mock / The meat it feeds on" (3.3.166–167).

## Annotated Bibliography

Duncan-Jones, Katherine, ed. *Shakespeare's Sonnets*. The Arden Shakespeare. London: Thomas Nelson and Sons, 1997. An excellent, modern-spelling edition, with thorough, facing-page notes, and a valuable introduction that covers much previous scholarship and contextualizes the sonnets historically. The edition also makes a cautious but compelling attempt at locating the poems and the people in them in terms of Shakespeare's own biography.

Evans, G. Blakemore, ed. *The Sonnets*. The New Cambridge Shakespeare. Cambridge: Cambridge UP, 1996. A useful edition of the poems that includes a separate and detailed commentary devoted largely to unpacking difficult or suggestive phrases, simultaneously pointing to textual variants and historically relevant notes.

Fineman, Joel. *Shakespeare's Purjured Eye: The Invention of Poetic Subjectivity in the Sonnets*. Berkeley: U of California P, 1986. A compelling and provocative study. The author claims that Shakespeare's shift from the idealizing and visual poetry of praise toward something "corruptingly linguistic" disrupts the usually unified and unifying eye/voice of the sonnets creating a new kind of poetic subjectivity. In part this change comes from a consciousness of the beloved other's less-than-ideal status that focuses attention on the poet's problematic desire, revealing fissures and paradox within the narrative voice and, effectively, a different and more complex sense of self. "This is why the poet has 'two loves of comfort and despair' (144) because desire *in* itself is equal to 'one angel in another's hell' (144)" (22).

Kerrigan, John, ed. *Shakespeare: "The Sonnets" and "A Lover's Complaint."* Harmonsworth, Eng.: Penguin, 1986. An edition of the poems with a separate commentary and an introduction that takes a strong historicist approach to the sonnets, emphasizing their placement within the larger sequence and insisting on the importance of *A Lover's Complaint* as an end note to that sequence.

Vendler, Helen. *The Art of Shakespeare's Sonnets*. Cambridge, MA: Harvard UP, 1997. A thoughtful and accessible series of close readings of each sonnet in turn, focusing primarily on its aesthetic features, but also addressing the poem's ideas and psychological mood.

# Sonnet 146

### Yashdip S. Bains

Poor soul, the centre of my sinful earth
Fool'd by these rebel powers that thee array;
Why dost thou pine within and suffer dearth,
Painting thy outward walls so costly gay?
Why so large cost, having so short a lease,
Dost thou upon thy fading mansion spend?
Shall worms, inheritors of this excess,
Eat up thy charge? Is this thy body's end?
Then soul, live thou upon thy servant's loss,
And let that pine to aggravate thy store;
Buy terms divine in selling hours of dross;
Within be fed, without be rich no more:
   So shalt thou feed on Death, that feeds on men,
   And Death once dead, there's no more dying then.

## PROSE PARAPHRASE

Following the traditional Christian distinction between the eternal soul as the animating principle and the body as mortal and perishable, the speaker is admonishing his soul for its failure in controlling the body's sensual inclinations and catering to its desires by spending too much on them. In a formal address to his "Poor soul" (146.1), which has become a virtual prisoner of his body, the speaker is trying to make it realize its perilous state. He says that you, the soul, have let yourself be surrounded by the rebel powers or senses of my body. Why are you letting yourself starve and waste away and suffer hardship? You are spending a lot of money on adorning the body. Since you have only a short-term lease on the building, why are you spending so much on a structure that is not going to last long? Will you let the worms become inheritors of this extravagance and devour your expenses or outlay? Is this the final destiny of your body in death? Is this the purpose of the life of your body? Answering this question, the speaker urges the soul to make itself the master of its servant, the body, and have it serve the soul.

Let your body expend itself and go to waste, the speaker counsels his soul, so that you can increase your own stock of divine possessions. You should get rid of your drudgery and hours of wasteful labor and purchase heavenly and durable terms of life. Feed yourself and satisfy your inner needs and abandon the worldly ambitions of gaudy or outward appearances of wealth. By compelling the body to enhance your future, you will feed on death that kills human beings; once you have overcome death, there is no more dying then. The body, your servant, should work for your eternal life.

## THE PLACE OF THE SONNET IN THE CYCLE

This sonnet belongs to a group that focuses on the poet's anxiety and unease about living in luxury and letting his soul cater to the body's needs. If only the soul would exercise its spiritual authority and keep the rebellious flesh and blood under control, the poet would have no fear about the future. Duncan-Jones has proposed, "The problem of ageing is here approached in an individualistic way, posing the question of why an ageing body should be expensively dressed or generously fed" (408).

In Sonnet 63, Shakespeare had lamented the rot that overcomes beauty and mentioned "confounding age's cruel knife" (l. 10). In Sonnet 71, he had characterized his death as fleeing "From this vile world with vildest worms to dwell" (l. 4). In Sonnet 73, he had spoken of the decline of his youth and had advised contentment after death in Sonnet 74 (ll. 1–2). In Sonnet 81, Shakespeare imagines the day "when I in earth am rotten" (l. 2). Shakespeare had written about immortality through breeding or his own poetry and thus had gone beyond the contrasting futures of the immortal soul and the mortal body. While dealing with the body's end, Sonnet 146 stands apart from the rest in its concern for the spiritual destiny of the soul and the final end and purpose of the body. But Shakespeare does not explicitly acknowledge a narrow belief in Christ and Resurrection. Thus, he is allowing the possibility of appealing to the general readers who have fears about aging and death and have some kind of belief in the immortality of the soul. Hence it is Shakespeare's sole sonnet that deals unambiguously with a spiritual crisis resulting from the subordination of the soul to the body's needs.

The unreasonableness of sensuality surfaces repeatedly in the sonnets. In Sonnet 129 Shakespeare devotes twelve lines to showing the evils of lust, but the couplet concludes that no one can avoid "this hell" (129.14). In Sonnet 147 he recognizes that his love of the Dark Lady is a fever, a disease, but he cannot cure that ailment. The two "Bath" sonnets (153–154) acknowledge that the speaker cannot escape his love, much as he wishes he could. So here the speaker recognizes the supremacy of soul over body. The poem does not indicate whether the good advice will be followed. However, the other sonnets suggest that it will not be. In the context of the Dark Lady sonnets that surround it, this poem may be yet another protest against a love that the speaker recognizes to be at once destructive and irresistible.

## DEVICES AND TECHNIQUES

Shakespeare has composed Sonnet 146 in his usual Petrarchan or Italian arrangement of an octave and a sestet in terms of argument, though in form he divides it into three quatrains and a couplet (rhymed *abab cdcd efef gg*). He uses punctuation and "Then" in line 9 to mark the division between the octave and sestet. Line 2, however, presents the reader with a major difficulty with a repetition of "My sinful earth:"

> Poor soul, the centre of my sinful earth,
> My sinful earth these rebel powers that thee array[.]

The repetition of "My sinful earth" in the 1609 edition is attributed to a printer's error, and most modern editors omit the repetition of line two. Some, however, emend the line in various ways, since, as Stephano remarks in *The Tempest*, "Thought is free" (3.2.123). Among the proposals are: "Thrall to," "Hemm'd with," "Fool'd by," "Feeding," "Spoiled by." Vendler opts "for *feeding* as the missing word, chiefly because it 'explains' the presence of the word *fading* used of the mansion" (611).

The first two lines, in the vocative case, constitute the speaker's formal address to his soul. In lines 3–8, in the interrogative mode, the speaker raises three serious questions about the soul serving the body. These questions are couched in the imagery of spending or economic exchange. In line 8, the speaker poses another short question that indicates a break in the rhythm and in the logical forward motion. "Is this thy body's end?" The speaker faces a real problem about the end or purpose of his body. Adopting the imperative case in lines 9–12, he employs images of feeding in addition to the economic or commercial ones of buying and selling. In lines 13–14, the speaker follows the affirmative mode.

There is an immense urgency with which "why" in lines 3 and 5 forces the reader to pay attention to the homily to the soul. Vendler points out a structural feature of the sonnet: "[I]t is that lines 1–2 generate line 9; lines 3–4 generate line 10; lines 5–6 generate line 11; and lines 7–8 generate line 12" (615). The "soul" in line 1 leads to "soul" in 9; "pine" from line 3 re-appears in line 10; "spend" in line 6 parallels "buy" in line 11, and "eat" (l. 7) matches "fed" (l. 12). These repetitions and reversals establish links between the octave and the sestet separated by a question about the body's end.

Pointed phrases in Sonnet 146 like "pine within" (l. 3), "large cost" (l. 5), and "excess" (l. 7) dramatize the addressee's situation. Images of extravagance underline the folly of painting the body or outward walls "so costly gay" (l. 4). The soul has leased a fading mansion, on the decoration of which it is spending enormous sums of money. The worms in lines 7–8 capture vividly the terrible fate of every human being. "Then" in line 9 strikes the note of change, and the speaker becomes assertive and authoritative in providing guidelines to the soul. The situation of a master living off his servant carries a spiritual message, but it also suggests the secular sense of keeping the lower ranks under control. Forcing one's servant to waste away and increase one's own stock refers back to the commercial scene. The images of a conscientious master and a smart merchant bring to mind economic relations of the marketplace. Shakespeare's elaboration of spiritual concerns in terms of concrete imagery of economic relationships makes the situation real for the reader.

The soul's selling "hours of dross" (l. 11) or worthless hours of living or giving up the material and short-lived life and buying long periods of devotion to higher goals sounds immediately persuasive to the reader, but it also reminds him or her of the drudgery of labor. Since a majority of people spend their lives in laborious jobs to earn a living, the divine alternative sounds especially attractive. The soul should control the body in return for eternal life. "Within" and "without" (l. 12) represent the soul and the body. By starving away the body or not catering to its carnal needs, the soul would defeat death. Death can kill the body, not the soul. Death can feed on people because they have corporeal forms. If there is no body, there is no death, so "there's no more dying then" (l. 14). The buying of divine terms is contingent upon the selling and control of the body. Shakespeare's strategy of specifying the spiritual in terms of the material activities like buying and selling and feeding makes the reader believe how easy and simple a task it would be to kill death and gain eternal life.

As Vendler points out, Shakespeare proceeds by using antitheses and repetitions (612). Alliteration and repetitions are striking: earth, dearth, death, dead, dying; [feeding], fading, fed, feed, feeds; pine, painting, pine; dost thou, dost thou; why, why, buy; costly, cost. Shakespeare elaborates "sinful earth" or body in terms of gaudily dressed or arrayed people and outward walls of fading mansions, suggesting that a body is a mansion in which a soul dwells. The body is also its servant. Normally, death feeds on bodies; Shakespeare reverses the traditional image so that a soul will feed on death. The soul can feed on death only after killing it; hence there will be no more dying. The concrete act of feeding invokes the corporeality of death, thus equating body and death.

Instead of adopting the medieval technique of dialogues between body and soul, Shakespeare personalizes the argument by using a speaker's direct address to his soul. The speaker transforms his own apprehensions about his fashionable and decadent life into a homily to his soul, thus distancing himself from the personal crisis and objectifying it. By constantly playing on the literal and metaphorical, he brings the reader back to the speaker and his soul surrounded by "my" sinful earth (l. 1) and his earthly mansion and the excessive costs of maintaining it; similarly, the expense is unjustifiable because worms will inherit the body. Buying and selling, decorating, and augmenting or increasing one's stock are commercial activities. The key question is, "Is this thy body's end?" (l. 8). To answer is to confront one's own struggle with aging, decay, disintegration, and death.

In the language of Sonnet 146, the speaker displays considerable awareness of the Bible while explaining his spiritual condition. "Fading mansions" is reminiscent of 2 Corinthians 5.1: "For we know that if the earthly tent we live in is destroyed, we have a building from God, a house not made with hands, eternal in the heavens." The "hours of dross" brings to mind the lines from Matthew 6.20: "But store up for yourselves treasures in heaven, where neither moth nor rust consumes and where thieves do not break in and steal." Line 13 reminds the reader of Psalm 49.6 which condemns "those who trust in their wealth and boast of the abundance of their riches." In the last couplet, Shakespeare may allude to Isaiah 25.8: "He will swallow up death forever. Then the Lord God will wipe away the tears from all faces." Relevant here is 1 Corinthians 15.26: "The last enemy to be destroyed is death." And 1 Corinthians 15.54 declares: "Death has been swallowed up in victory." But in spite of these biblical echoes and allusions, as Helen Vendler has stressed, "The gloominess of this sonnet has little of the radiance of Christian hope" (614).

## THEMES AND MEANINGS

What is the body's purpose or destiny? Will it just die and rot, or does it have another purpose or goal? Sonnet 146 deals with anxieties about the relationship between soul and body and the perils of catering excessively to the demands of the flesh. If a person lets the body or flesh and blood dominate over the soul, the future promises nothing but rotting in a grave and becoming a feast for worms. Since the soul is the animating principle of the body and the cosmos, a person should ensure his or her immortal future by letting the material body waste away and die. The speaker knows this but cannot quite implement it in his own life.

The vanity of spending money on oneself, living in luxury, buying clothes and jewelry, and building mansions is part of the common human experience. Aging, death, mortality, and immortality are constantly disturbing and destroying the human scene. This theme runs through Shakespeare's poetry and plays. Shakespeare also focuses on the difficulty of dealing with human desire for material possessions and worldly glory. The soul may pay no heed to the speaker's advice; death, however, is claiming its victims while the soul is wasting away and suffering. The immediate reality for Shakespeare is the excesses of the body and the "worms, inheritors of this excess." The physical desires should not take precedence over the future of the soul. Yet one has to be cautious in asserting that Sonnet 146 is Christian and that Shakespeare is presenting an orthodox view.

This sonnet's theme is both one's consciousness of the ultimate goal of life and the difficulty of achieving it. While reminding his soul of its wrong direction in favor of the body, he is dodging his own responsibility. He cannot stand back and address his soul without evading the problem of his own complicity and regret. Hence the sonnet has an immediacy and poignancy missing in medieval dialogues between body and soul. It is a dilemma for a human being, not an error, if one cannot follow a narrow path for eternal salvation. Hence Michael West and others are not justified in stressing a relationship between this poem and medieval body-and-soul dialogues ("The Internal Dialogue of Shakespeare's Sonnet 146," *Shakespeare Quarterly* 25 [1974]: 109–122). Stephen Booth also obscures the imaginative and spiritual reach of the sonnet when he asserts that its first line "suggests the beginning of human history, implies its course, and implies its end, which is also the focus of the poem's end, the Last Judgment, doomsday—when the bodies and souls of the righteous shall be reunited in eternal life and death shall have 'no more dominion' over them (Romans 6:9)" (*Shakespeare's Sonnets*, p. 503). Shakespeare finds a way to keep the sonnet free of dogmatic certainties. B. C. Southam makes this point:

> There are in the Sonnet a number of Biblical echoes which superficially run the poem along a conventional course, and the values of the poem seem to be those of the prosperous Elizabethan world. But it is Shakespeare the humanist speaking, pleading for the life of the body as against the rigorous asceticism which glorifies the life of the spirit at the expense of the vitality and richness of sensuous experience. Neither spir-

itual nor bodily life can be fulfilled at the other's cost, for the whole man, body and spirit indivisible, will suffer thereby. We can see how very much higher is the charity which motivates this sonnet than the type of Christianity which moves on the surface of the poem, and at which the irony is directed. (71)

While acknowledging the central position of the soul, Shakespeare finally concludes that the body is the only concrete human reality. Hence, as Melchiori has stressed, "The end, the purpose of the Body is indeed this: to be the only constant, and therefore *true*, thing in an arbitrary universe dominated at all levels, physical, and metaphysical, by greed and hypocrisy, the deception of 'appearance'" (194).

## THE RELATIONSHIP OF THE SONNET TO SHAKESPEARE'S OTHER WORKS

"Is this the body's end?" This question appears frequently in Shakespeare's poems and plays. Should human beings accept their mortality without protest and not raise questions about their sense of disappointment and disbelief about their future? Confronted with horror, tragedy, and death, everyone asks questions and wonders instead of just falling and ceasing. When Lear has been shut out of his palace in a storm, he says, "No, I will weep no more. In such a night / To shut me out? Pour on, I will endure" (3.4.17–18). He sees Edgar posing as a mad beggar and perceives the truth about human life: "Thou art the thing itself: unaccommodated man is no more but such a poor, bare, fork'd animal as thou art. Off, off, you lendings!" (3.4.106–108), and Lear tears off his clothes. In the last scene, Lear enters with dead Cordelia in his arms and howls (5.3.258). Kent, Edgar and Albany are observing the scene and stunned by it:

> *Kent*: Is this the promis'd end?
>
> *Edgar*: Or image of that horror?
>
> *Albany*: Fall, and cease! (5.3.263–265)

Hamlet's last dying words are, "the rest is silence" (5.2.358). Humanistic queries about aging, dying, and decay bore on Shakespeare's mind throughout his life. Skeptical as he was of any answers, he kept laboring the question.

**Annotated Bibliography**

Booth, Stephen, ed. *Shakespeare's Sonnets*. New Haven: Yale UP, 1977. In his conservatively modernized text of the 1609 edition, Booth seeks to provide what "a Renaissance reader would have thought as he moved from line to line and sonnet to sonnet" (ix). Full commentary on the richness of language and shades of meaning.

Dubrow, Heather. "'Conceit Deceitful': The Sonnets." In *Captive Victors: Shakespeare's Narrative Poems and Sonnets*. Ithaca: Cornell UP, 1987. 169–275. Shows how Shakespeare's sonnets are more subtle in their use of narrative and dramatic techniques than those of other Renaissance poets.

Duncan-Jones, Katherine, ed. *Shakespeare's Sonnets*. The Arden Shakespeare. London: Thomas Nelson and Sons, 1997. A modernized text of the sonnets, with detailed notes and commentary; a full introduction to historical, intellectual and cultural contexts of the sonnets, with a review of critical approaches.

Melchiori, Giorgio. "Sonnet 146 and the Ethics of Religion." In *Shakespeare's Dramatic Meditations: An Experiment in Criticism*. Oxford: Clarendon P, 1976. 161–196. Analyses the sonnet in its socio-historical and linguistic contexts. Cautions against dogmatic tendencies of critical methods.

Southam, B. C. "Shakespeare's Christian Sonnet? Number 146." *Shakespeare Quarterly* 11 (1960): 67–71. Shakespeare the humanist is "pleading for the life of the body as against the rigorous asceticism which glorifies the life of the spirit at the expense of the vitality and richness of sensuous experience" (71).

Vendler, Helen. *The Art of Shakespeare's Sonnets*. Cambridge, MA: Harvard UP, 1997. In her detailed analysis of each sonnet as a work of art and in her commentary, Vendler focuses on the language: words choices, and sound patterns. Vendler does not explore any narrative theme in the sequence but rather provides close readings of the individual poems.

# Sonnet 147

## Robert Appelbaum

My love is as a fever, longing still
For that which longer nurseth the disease;
Feeding on that which doth preserve the ill,
The uncertain sickly appetite to please.
My reason, the physician to my love,
Angry that his prescriptions are not kept,
Hath left me, and I desperate now approve
Desire is death, which physic did except.
Past cure I am, now reason is past care,
And frantic-mad with evermore unrest;
My thoughts and my discourse as madmen's are,
At random from the truth vainly express'd;
   For I have sworn thee fair and thought thee bright,
   Who art as black as hell, as dark as night.

## PROSE PARAPHRASE

My love is like a fever: it keeps longing for the thing that stokes it and only makes it worse; it feeds on what makes it sick in order to gratify a volatile, pathological appetite. My rational mind, which would act as a physician and cure me of this morbid love, is angry because its prescriptions have not been followed, and so it has abandoned me. In a desperate condition, I now find by experience that desire, which rejected medicine (or which medicine proscribed), is death. I am past being cured; my rational mind that should cure me is past caring for me. I am frantically mad, ever unable to sleep. My thoughts and words are like a madman's, at odds with the truth and poorly articulated. For I have sworn that you are fair, and have regarded you as beautiful physically and morally, although you are "as black as hell, as dark as night" (147.14).

## THE PLACE OF THE SONNET IN THE CYCLE

This poem recalls sonnets 118 and 119. In the earlier poems, the speaker writes about having spent time with someone other than the young man—probably a woman, and very likely the Dark Lady of sonnets 127 through 152. He has likened his desire for both individuals to the operation of an appetite, and has claimed that he attempted to "frame his feeding" (118.6) on the other person as if on bitter sauces, the better to appreciate the sweetness of the young man. But the bitter sauces made him sick. He has even, in his error, "drunk of Siren tears" made from a distillery as "foul as hell within" (119.1–2).

Sonnet 147 occurs toward the end of the Dark Lady sequence, however, when thoughts of the young man have largely been put aside. The poet's relationship with the Dark Lady is, to say the least, vexed. But what is most vexed about the relationship is the behavior that being with her has forced upon him. Whether the Dark Lady is dark without but fair within, or whether her dark features are in fact "fair" since they are beautiful, though she is in some way "foul" or "black" within, his love for her entices him into a condition that seems at once true and false, at once bright and grim, at once a foretaste of heaven and a sentence in hell. "In faith," he says in Sonnet 141, "I do not love thee with mine eyes, / For they in thee a thousand errors note" (ll. 1–2). Yet the poet loves her anyway, making him "Thy proud heart's slave and vassal wretch to be" (l. 12). "O, from what pow'r hast thou this pow'rful might," he asks in Sonnet 150, "[w]ith insufficiency my heart to sway, / To make me give the lie to my true sight, / And swear that brightness doth not grace the day?" (150.1–4). "Who taught thee how to make me love thee more, / The more I hear and see just cause of hate?" (150.9–10). In the context of his affair with the dark lady, the poet speaks of sexual relations as a "heaven that leads men to . . . hell" (129.14). Given the words he and the lady have exchanged, and the thoughts he had kept to himself, he complains "I am forsworn" (152.1), "I am perjur'd" (152.6), "And all my honest faith in thee is lost" (152.8). In words that echo the conclusion of Sonnet 147, Sonnet 152 ends with the complaint that "I have sworn thee fair"—meaning "fair" in her behavior and values as well as her looks—and thus he has only perjured himself the more, "To swear against the truth so foul a lie!" (152.13–14).

## DEVICES AND TECHNIQUES

In the context of the poet's ongoing battle with his feelings for the lady, Sonnet 147 arrives as an exercise in what Joel Fineman calls "the paradox of praise," or "the mock encomium" (29). Not that poems like Sonnet 147 are themselves paradoxical or comic, Fineman adds; but they are "written as though by a poet who had already essayed the paradox of praise, who has tried it out in misplaced earnest, and who now draws from this appropriate and consequent conclusions" (29). The conclusions in this case reflect both upon the lady and the poet. Building to them by way of an elaborate conceit of illness and madness, which seems to lay the fault upon the poet only, but to lay it upon him in a way that makes the reader sympathize and perhaps even approve of his plight, the sonnet's conclusions may come as something of a surprise. Certainly they are powerful, even though they depend on proverbial expressions ("black as hell, . . . dark as night") that may otherwise seem a bit tired. They accuse the woman of congenital treachery, and they accuse the poet himself of the kind of perjury and self-delusion that other Dark Lady sonnets also discuss. The accusations are both powerfully convincing and unexpected; indeed they are powerfully convincing precisely because they are unexpected.

The language of the concluding couplet sounds rather different than the language of the first twelve lines and states a rather different position, too. The meditative, somewhat convoluted and soft-sounding language of lines 1–12 gives way to overt pronouncement in heavily accented, clearly structured, and emphatic expressions (with especially hard stresses on "sworn," "thought," "black," and "dark"). Meanwhile the arguments in lines 1–12, all about the poet and his forgivable weakness (forgivable because it is the weakness of love), give way in the concluding couplet to a denunciation, posed objectively about an objective state of affairs. The disparity is worth emphasizing. What the denunciation says about the poet does not quite fit the conceit of illness and madness that has been so painstakingly developed, and what it says about the lady has nothing at all to do with illness and madness. It comes as a clear and direct revelation of an emphatic, even proverbial truth that gives the lie to all the paradoxical funny business that the poet's relationship with the Dark Lady has entailed. After the histrionics of love, the exchanges of insincere or impossible oaths, and the paradoxes of praise, these simple truths are expressed as if they have been at the heart of the matter all along.

Entirely subjective in outlook, the conceit of the first twelve lines is developed with a rigor that may suggest the metaphysical poems of John Donne. It reveals an ingenious analogy. And in doing so it dramatizes a condition of the inner life, at once physical and mental, through which an individual has failed to prevent himself from falling into the extreme, unhealthy madness of love. Each of the three quatrains makes a related statement that moves the conceit along while also dramatizing the process of mad love and leading toward a need for a conclusion such as is supplied by the final couplet. The statements, each of which dominates the quatrain in which it appears, are as follows: (a) my love is like a fever. (b) My reason has left me. (c) I am past cure. To explicate: (a) As it is like a fever, this is a love that burns. But more important, it operates as pre-modern medicine believed that fevers operated, not by way of an infectious pathogen, but by way of something eaten, and something that the feverous subject continues to desire, even though to consume more of this product is only to feed or stoke or "nurse" the disease even farther. (b) As my reason has left me, I cannot keep myself from continuing to feed on the cause of my illness—and the idea of death approaches. And finally, (c) as I am past cure, and nothing can restore my reason to me, I am frantic, restless, full of crazy thoughts and empty words.

So the first twelve lines of Sonnet 147, divided into three quatrains as is typical of the English (or Shakespearean) sonnet, develop the idea of a man who, having contracted a pathological condition, has spun out of control, in the course of which a truth that is not truth at all (perhaps!) begins to form in his mind: "Desire is death" (l. 8). From the subjective meditation of the first twelve lines—whose logical elegance, by the way, gives a lie to the idea that the speaker is "frantic mad" (l. 10) and whose thoughts are "vainly express'd (l. 12)—the objectively posed statements of the concluding couplet emerge. The tone changes. The conceit is dropped, and the cautious and difficult inward language of the meditation gives way to the easy and incautious language of denunciation.

## THEMES AND MEANINGS

One of the more interesting aspects of this poem is the insight it affords into the psychology of inward experience that Shakespeare's age took for granted. The conceit of the first twelve lines expresses several related ways in which an individual may experience what today might be termed a divided self. In the first instance, the poet is divided from his own passion, which obeys a logic (or illogic) of its own. This is a division of the self where love and desire are experienced like an illness, and the illness itself experienced like a gluttonous fever. Such a phenomenon is not recognized today, but in keeping with humoral psychology and Galenic medicine of Shakespeare's day (named after the second-century Roman physician Galen), a fever could be triggered by eating something too "cold," though not necessarily something cold in a literal sense: it may be a question of something "cold" in a medical, analogical sense. The body would heat up (literally) in order to compensate for this "coldness." But as the body was heated up, the individual might then crave to eat more of the "cold" substance to cool himself, though the effect would only be to trigger more heat. So a depraved or "sickly appetite" would be avaricious for a substance that would seem to make the individual better but could only make the individual worse. And this, the speaker of the poem asserts, is what love is like! One desires more and more of the thing (that is, the person) that makes one sick with love, and "feeding" on this love-object ends up making one both sicker and (as this is the paradox of desire) more and more in love.

In this circumstance, as one gets sicker with passion for a thing that can only cause harm, one may still understand and disapprove of what one is doing; one's "reason" may tell one to stop, just as one's reason may tell one to put down that second slice of cake. Thus, in the second instance, the divided self can be experienced as a division between one's rational mind and one's passionate behavior. The mind may prescribe a treatment for the passion (stop eating!), but the passion goes on. The poet imagines then that one's reason can actually (and unreasonably: but this is how "rational" authorities often work) get angry and abandon the self, making the self "desperate" (l. 7), without hope, but still conscious enough to recognize the most stunning idea of the poem: "Desire is death." Readers often intimate a foreshadowing of Freud's idea of the conflict between Eros and Thanatos in this line; and indeed the conscious but unreasonable self fixated on a dangerous passion is a lot like the Ego in Freud when it has surrendered its interests to the Id, and forsaken the wisdom of the Superego.

Once the self has been abandoned by its own rational faculties, the self being "past cure" and the rational faculty being "past care" (l. 9), the self can in the third instance find itself divided from any principle of coherence. "[F]rantic mad," the individual is "At randon [that is, at random] from the truth" (ll. 10, 12). In this case we might say that the passion has led the individual from a fixation to a dissipation, from a troubled emotional life to insanity, from a neurotic obsession to a psychotic break. Whatever we may think of this progression to madness from a modern medical point of view, it correlates with early modern thinking about how a "perturbation" of the self could lead to a "raving" madness. The mechanisms of this psychology are amply revealed in Timothy Bright's *A Treatise of Melancholy* (London, 1586), which Shakespeare probably knew, and Robert Burton's *An Anatomy of Melancholy* (Oxford, 1621), which, though published after Shakespeare's death, codified the Renaissance psychology of Shakespeare's period. But the poet, of course, pretends at the end that this idea of a divided self, deteriorated to a condition of raving madness, is an explanation for something much simpler: the fact that the poet has been in love with someone who does not deserve his affection.

## THE RELATIONSHIP OF THE SONNET TO SHAKESPEARE'S OTHER WORKS

Because of the reflection on the psychology of love and desire featured in the poem, Sonnet 147 may be thought of as a key to the psychological drama of Shakespeare's plays—comedies, tragedies, histories, and romances alike. Whether Shakespeare is consistent in his understanding of divided or passionate selves is a subject the student may investigate for herself, but the relevance of the sonnet to Shakespearean drama is unmistakable. Sonnet 147 finds especial resonance in plays that talk about or dramatize the relationship between "appetite," "desire," and "love." *Twelfth Night* is one of those plays, beginning as it does with the line "If music be the food of love, play on," and going on in many ways to think about the body and its passions, including its passions both for food and love. *Othello* is another one of those plays. The student may wish to investigate what Iago says about love and its similarities to the appetite for food (especially with regard to Desdemona, for example, 1.3.347–352; 2.1.231–235), and even to think about the divided self that Othello becomes in acts 4 and 5. In *A Midsummer Night's Dream* Demetrius concludes that when he spurned Helena he was like a sick man who rejects wholesome food, "But, as in health, come to my natural taste, / Now I do wish it, love it, long for it, / And will evermore be true to it" (4.1.174–176).

In the plays, and indeed elsewhere in the sonnets, Shakespeare distinguishes between love as appetite and love as something more spiritual. Iago regards love as no more than lust, but Desdemona's love for Othello belies that position. Proteus's lust for Silvia contrasts with Valentine's love in *The Two Gentlemen of Verona*. In the sonnets addressed to the Dark Lady the poet seems unable to sort out his feelings. Sometimes, as in this sonnet or Sonnet 129, the poet is attracted to the Dark Lady only physically, and even as he is attracted to her he is repulsed by that attraction. Yet elsewhere, as in Sonnet 130, the Dark Lady's appearance is irrelevant to his feelings, which seem to be more love than lust. Even in the punning sonnets 135–136, which are rife with sexual innuendo, the relationship seems to be more than just physical. Renaissance sonnet cycles traditionally vacillate in their emotions as the lover hopes, despairs, renounces his lady, and then pursues her again. Sonnet 147 thus shows a moment in an ongoing relationship, one that changes again by Sonnet 149.

### Annotated Bibliography

Booth, Stephen. *An Essay on Shakespeare's Sonnets*. New Haven: Yale UP, 1969. The book that changed the way we read the sonnets, emphasizing complexities and unresolvable tensions and contradictions in the experience of reading the poems.

———, ed. *Shakespeare's Sonnets*. New Haven: Yale UP, 1977. An indispensable edition that includes a reproduction of the 1609 quarto, amply and ingeniously annotated.

Felperin, Howard. "The Dark Lady Identified; Or, What Deconstruction Can Do for Shakespeare's Sonnets." In *Shakespeare and Deconstruction*. Ed. G. Douglas Atkins and David M. Bergeron. New York: Peter Lang, 1988. 69–94. Challenges intuitive notions of character and identity as they apply to the lyricism of the sonnets.

Fineman, Joel. *Shakespeare's Perjured Eye: The Invention of Poetic Subjectivity in the Sonnets*. Berkeley: U of California P, 1986. The most influential book on the sonnets since Booth's *Essay*.

Often difficult to read, it studies the sonnets by way of the theme of Shakespeare's poet-ics of praise, adopting the language and critical tools of poststructuralism and Lacanian psychoanalysis. Sonnet 147 plays a major role in Fineman's analysis of the "paradox of praise."

Hoeniger, F. David. *Medicine and Shakespeare in the English Renaissance.* Newark: U of Delaware P, 1992. The most comprehensive account of its subject.

Hunt, Marvin. "Be Dark but Not Too Dark: Shakespeare's Dark Lady as a Sign of Color." In *Shakespeare's Sonnets: Critical Essays.* Ed. James Schiffer. New York: Garland, 1999. 369–389. An essay that begins to question the many implications of darkness and black-ness as they apply to the Dark Lady, including racial implications.

Kerrigan, John, ed. *Shakespeare: "The Sonnets" and "A Lover's Complaint."* Harmondsworth, Eng.: Penguin, 1986. A fine and useful edition, with helpful annotations.

# Sonnets 153 and 154

### Yashdip S. Bains

 Sonnet 153

Cupid laid by his brand and fell asleep:
A maid of Dian's this advantage found,
And his love-kindling fire did quickly steep
In a cold valley-fountain of that ground;
Which borrow'd from this holy fire of Love
A dateless lively heat, still to endure,
And grew a seething bath, which yet men prove
Against strange maladies a sovereign cure.
But at my mistress' eye Love's brand new-fired,
The boy for trial needs would touch my breast;
I, sick withal, the help of bath desired,
And thither hied, a sad distemper'd guest,
   But found no cure: the bath for my help lies
   Where Cupid got new fire, my mistress' eyes.

## PROSE PARAPHRASE

In the first eight lines, or octave, the speaker tells the instructive and amusing story of Diana's votary's futile attempt to put out Cupid's torch. Cupid put aside his love-inducing brand—a torch was a more ancient implement of Cupid than a bow and arrow—and went to sleep. One of the virgin nymphs, who had vowed to lead an uncorrupted and chaste life, seized this opportunity and quickly got hold of his torch that kindled the fire of love and steeped or immersed it in a nearby cool valley-fountain or spring associated with Diana. Before the flame was extinguished, the hallowed or sacred fire of love set the water of this fountain ablaze with an ever-burning heat and changed it into one of boiling hot water. People soak themselves in this water for "a sovereign," that is, efficacious, "cure" (l. 8). Hot baths were used for the treatment of venereal and other diseases.

In the following six lines, or sestet, the speaker shifts the focus from Cupid to his own experience. Cupid re-ignited his love's torch by the heat of the speaker's mistress's eyes. To test whether his flame was still potent, that is, able to induce love, Cupid touched the speaker's breast. Feeling sick because of this contact with Cupid's brand, the speaker went immediately looking for the warm and healing water but did not find any cure. The therapy he was seeking would be found where Cupid got fresh fire for his torch; that is, the eyes of the speaker's mistress.

## ❁ Sonnet 154

The little Love-god lying once asleep
Laid by his side his heart-inflaming brand,
Whilst many nymphs that vow'd chaste life to keep
Came tripping by; but in her maiden hand
The fairest votary took up that fire
Which many legions of true hearts had warm'd;
And so the general of hot desire
Was sleeping by a virgin hand disarm'd.
This brand she quenched in a cool well by,
Which from Love's fire took heat perpetual,
Growing a bath and healthful remedy
For men diseased; but I, my mistress' thrall,
    Came there for cure, and this by that I prove,
    Love's fire heats water, water cools not love.

### PROSE PARAPHRASE

This sonnet tells the same story as Sonnet 153, but with slight variations. Here Cupid falls asleep first and then lets go of his "heart-inflaming brand" (l. 2). In this version many nymphs, not just one, who have taken a vow of chastity pass by, and the most beautiful takes the torch, thus disarming the god of love.

As in the previous sonnet, she puts out the torch, though this time she uses a well (154.9) rather than a "cold valley-fountain" (153.4). The effect, however, is the same: Cupid's torch heats the water and creates a healing bath. The speaker here, as in Sonnet 153, goes to this bath seeking a cure for love and fails to find that cure. Here he learns that love can heat water (inflame even the least passionate), but water cannot quench love.

### THE PLACE OF THE SONNETS IN THE CYCLE

Sonnets 153 and 154 have a significant connection with the rest of the sequence and serve as a bridge between the preceding 152 poems and *A Lover's Complaint*, published together with the sonnets in the 1609 first edition of these works. These concluding sonnets stand apart in their use of mythology; they are the only ones in which Cupid appears. However, thematically they are consistent with the preceding poems. These two sonnets demonstrate that however hard Diana's votaries may try, they cannot extinguish human desire. Shakespeare's sonnet sequence begins with a stress in Sonnet 1 on "increase": "From fairest creatures we desire increase,

/ That thereby beauty's rose might never die" (ll. 1–2). The sequence closes with a reminder in Sonnet 154 of the persistence of that desire: "Love's fire heats water, water cools not love" (l. 14). Warnings about the dangers of passion and the urgings of the chaste votaries of Diana will not dampen the sexual impulse, a point also made by Sonnet 129.

These two "Bath" sonnets—the Roman baths in that town are the subject of Shakespeare's mythmaking here—follow logically from the sonnets addressed to the Dark Lady (127–152). She is the speaker's mistress here. In the Dark Lady sonnets the speaker sometimes seeks in vain for a cure for his love, which he regards as a disease. In Sonnet 137 he likens that love to the plague (l. 14). In Sonnet 147 he compares it to a fever. His physician, reason, has given up hope for the patient's recovery. As in sonnets 153–154, the speaker is "[p]ast cure" (147.9).

While the speaker in sonnets 153–154 may have gone to Bath to seek a remedy for an emotional ailment, he may suffer from physical illness as well. The baths were considered a cure for venereal disease, and in Sonnet 144 the speaker alludes to the Dark Lady's infecting the Fair Youth of sonnets 1–126 with syphilis (144.14). Love's fever in sonnets 153–154 may thus refer to a sexually transmitted disease. The speaker finds that the baths are ineffectual in removing either his desire for his mistress or the consequences of that desire.

## DEVICES AND TECHNIQUES

In sonnets 153 and 154, Shakespeare draws on a conceit from a six-line epigram by a sixth-century Byzantine poet, Marianus Scholasticus, which reads in a literal translation (Duncan-Jones, p. 422):

> Here beneath these plane trees, exhausted Love was sleeping softly. He had entrusted his torch to the Nymphs. But the Nymphs said to one another, 'Come on, why are we waiting? Let's put out the torch and with it quench the fire in human hearts.' But the torch set light even to the waters, and the Nymphs of Love have filled the bath with hot water ever since.

Shakespeare may have come upon this epigram in a version by Ben Jonson; if Duncan-Jones is right in her conjecture, "the two sonnets cannot have been written before 1603" (422). Shakespeare transforms this epigram into a thesis about love and women's eyes.

Shakespeare wrote Sonnet 153 in the standard form of three quatrains and a couplet (rhymed *abab cdcd efef gg*). While the rhyme scheme is thus typical of the English or Shakespearean sonnet, its structure follows the Petrarchan or Italian arrangement of octave and sestet in the presentation of the argument. In the octave, Shakespeare narrates the epigram in words that stress Cupid's supreme function of stimulating erotic desire among human beings. Cupid's torch is characterized as a "love-kindling fire" (l. 3) and the "holy fire of love" (l. 5) that is full of "dateless lively heat" (l. 6). The sestet develops further the human dimension of the epigram by noting that even Cupid derives the potency of his flame from a woman's eyes. Shakespeare uses words like "fire," "torch," "cure," "bath," and "eyes" to enrich the sonnet with bawdy suggestions. Hot baths were associated with sexual rendezvous where men contracted syphilis and with cures for sexually transmitted diseases. The "cold valley-fountain" (l. 4) implies "one of the cool springs associated with the goddess Diana, and the female genitals in which the hot male member seeks to be cooled or quenched" (Duncan-Jones, p. 422). Similarly, "strange maladies" (l. 8) alludes to "diseases possibly contracted through contact with *strange*, or foreign, women" (Duncan-Jones, p. 423).

Sonnet 154 employs the same standard English sonnet rhyme scheme as the preceding poem, but here the structure is also English rather than Italian. The first eleven and a half lines develop the myth of creation of the hot waters at Bath. In the middle of line twelve the speaker introduces his own experience, which disproves the water's ability to cure him. The conclusion or turn is therefore limited nearly to a couplet rather than a sestet.

Both poems are filled with bawdy allusions that make them fables about human sexuality. The chaste nymph who picks up Cupid's hot brand may be yielding to the temptation of sex. The "cold valley fountain" or "cool well" in which she quenches the torch could be a reference to female genetalia. The sickness (l. 11) or disease (l. 12) that prompts a trip to Bath could be venereal in nature. Moreover, since Roman times spas and baths have been associated with lasciviousness (Booth, p. 533). In going to Bath for a cure, the speaker may be seeking gratification of his desire, not a way to end it. Certainly, he discovers that relief is to be found only by being with his mistress, not by fleeing her.

## THEMES AND MEANINGS

The universality of love and the persistence of desire form a prominent theme in all of Shakespeare's sonnets. Desire cannot be suppressed. People may seek chastity, but they are always on the brink of losing it. Cupid tempts Diana's votaries by inducing them to come close to his torch. Their decision to pick up the torch exposes them immediately to the excitement of desire. Even if they succeed in putting out the flame, Cupid can relight it with fire from a woman's eyes. The votaries can preserve their chastity only by staying away from Cupid and his torch. But they cannot keep their distance, so they lose their will and submit to love and desire. Shakespeare may condemn lust, but he does not uphold chastity as a worthy goal for human beings.

Shakespeare stresses a woman's eye as the stimulant for love and desire. He thus echoes the Renaissance view that the male derives exhilaration and pleasure by exchanging glances with the female and seeks her company for love. Without a male's erotic response to the female, beauty's rose would perish. Even Cupid has to rely on the female eye as the source of fire.

The physical union of the male and female is a necessary condition for the fulfillment of desire, but it also can give rise to numerous ailments. In a humorous manner Shakespeare treats venereal disease as an inevitable part of sexual desire without underestimating the seriousness of the ailment. A healthy or sound person can get infected. Yet even then the real help "lies / Where Cupid got new fire: my mistress' eyes" (ll. 13–14). Superstition claimed that a virgin's "cool well" could cure sexually transmitted diseases. The perpetual heat of love's fire turns the cool well or cold fountain into a hot source for treating love's disease. In the same place a man may find both sexual satisfaction and the cure for the illness he caught there. In a metaphorical sense, sexual gratification cures desire, but it also drives one to seek additional such experiences. As Shakespeare describes lust in Sonnet 129, "Had, having, and in quest to have" (129.10).

## THE RELATIONSHIP OF THE SONNETS TO SHAKESPEARE'S OTHER WORKS

Shakespeare's poems and plays constantly demonstrate the supremacy of passion and sex over chastity. The poet transcends the limitations of Christian doctrine and examines the subject in the larger human setting. As Costard states in *Love's Labor's Lost*, "Such is the simplicity of man to hearken after the flesh" (1.1.217–218). Touchstone expresses the same idea in *As You Like It*: "As the ox hath his bow, sir, the horse his curb, and the falcon her bells, so man hath his desires; and as pigeons bill, so wedlock would be nibbling" (3.3.79–82). When Escalus contends in *Measure for Measure* that law will not allow brothels in Vienna, Pompey responds in all seriousness: "Does your worship mean to geld and splay all the youth of the city?" (2.1.230–231). So in sonnets 153–154 Diana's votaries may steal Cupid's brand, but they discover that they cannot extinguish it when they immerse it in water.

One of the results of copulation is venereal disease, and Shakespeare's work is full of its devastating impact on society. The word "sound" in the sense of free of disease occurs frequently in his poetry and plays. The impact of the disease on the sex trade naturally worries Mistress Overdone, a bawd, in *Measure for Measure*: "Thus, what with the war, what with the sweat [diseases causing fevers], what with the gallows, and what with poverty, I am custom-shrunk" (1.2.82–84). The plays contain many jokes and puns about ailments of the flesh and cures like sweating in hot tubs. Love and disease are interlinked so closely that one cannot be analyzed without the other. Eros cannot be suppressed in the name of finding a cure for the disease.

Shakespeare uses Cupid in a variety of serious and humorous ways in his plays. In *Love's Labor's Lost*, Armado, a fantastical Spaniard, thinks "I should outswear Cupid" (1.2.64). As Berowne testifies in the same play, Cupid can impose a plague upon him for neglecting the god's "almighty dreadful little might" (3.1.201–203). Oberon, the king of fairies, recalls in *A Midsummer Night's Dream* that he saw "Flying between the cold moon and the earth, / Cupid all arm'd" and talks about a flower called love-in-idleness and its juice (2.1.155–174). In *Much Ado about Nothing*, Beatrice ridicules Benedick by saying: "He set up his bills here in Messina, and challeng'd Cupid at the flight, and my uncle's fool, reading the challenge, subscrib'd for Cupid, and challeng'd him at the burbolt" (1.1.39–42). Benedick states that if anyone can prove that he has ever been in love, he can "hang me up at the door of a brothel-house for the sign of blind Cupid" (1.1.250–254). Cupid in his numerous manifestations can be found inserting love in people's lives, thereby making them happy or miserable.

Shakespeare constantly dramatizes the significance of women's eyes as the original source of love. Berowne, one of the lords attending on King Ferdinand of Navarre, expounds the doctrine he has derived from women's eyes: "They are the ground, the books, the academes, / From whence doth spring the true Promethean fire" (*Love's Labor's Lost*, 4.3.299–300). Prometheus had stolen fire from heaven and given it to human beings; Shakespeare's Prometheus seems to have found it in a woman's eye. Even Cupid cannot perform his role without help from a woman's eye. There would be no love without the senses, especially sight. By using classical mythology in these sonnets and in his other works, Shakespeare is shifting the context for love and sex from Christianity to a universal human desire that transcends any system of belief.

## Annotated Bibliography

Booth, Stephen. *An Essay on Shakespeare's Sonnets*. New Haven: Yale UP, 1969. A reading of the entire sequence and of individual sonnets, with stress on the "multitude of different co-existent and conflicting patterns—formal, logical, ideological, syntactic, rhythmic, and phonetic" (ix).

———, ed. *Shakespeare's Sonnets*. New Haven: Yale UP, 1977. In his conservatively modernized text of the 1609 edition, Booth seeks to provide what "a Renaissance reader would have thought as he moved from line to line and sonnet to sonnet" (ix). Full commentary on the richness of language and shades of meaning.

Burrow, Colin, ed. *The Complete Sonnets and Poems*. The Oxford Shakespeare. Oxford: Oxford UP, 2002. Discusses date of composition, order of the sonnets, and structural influences. Argues that the sonnets have various themes and thoughts rather than a systematic sequence about specific relationships.

Dubrow, Heather. "'Conceit Deceitful': The Sonnets." In *Captive Victors: Shakespeare's Narrative Poems and Sonnets*. Ithaca: Cornell UP, 1987. 169–275. Maintains that Shakespeare's Sonnets are more subtle in their use of narrative and dramatic techniques than those of other Renaissance poets.

Duncan-Jones, Katherine, ed. *Shakespeare's Sonnets*. The Arden Shakespeare. London: Thomas Nelson and Sons, 1997. A modernized text of the sonnets, with detailed notes and commentary; a full introduction to historical, intellectual, and cultural contexts of the sonnets, with a review of critical approaches.

Hutton, James. "Analogues of Shakespeare's Sonnets 153–154: Contributions to the History of a Theme." *Modern Philology* 38.4 (May 1941): 385–403. Hutton tries to solve the puzzle of how Shakespeare came upon the epigram by Marianus Scholasticus in the *Greek Anthology* and examines the sonnets from the perspective of a literary tradition.

Rollins, Hyder Edward, ed. *The Sonnets*. New Variorum Edition. 2 vols. Philadelphia: J. B. Lippincott, 1944. A thoroughly assembled record of writings about the sonnets from 1609 to the early 1940s.

Schalkwyk, David. *Speech and Performance in Shakespeare's Sonnets and Plays*. Cambridge: Cambridge UP, 2002. Schalkwyk seeks to interpret the sonnets as he imagines a Renaissance reader would have understood them. That is, he maintains that the poems serve to establish relationships between the speaker and his subjects. Schalkwyk looks at the nature of these relationships and how the language of the poetry tries to determine them.

Vendler, Helen. *The Art of Shakespeare's Sonnets*. Cambridge, MA: Harvard UP, 1997. In her detailed analysis of each sonnet as a work of art and in her commentary, Vendler focuses on the language of the poems. She is not concerned with the narrative structure of the sequence but rather with how the individual sonnets make meaning.

# THE LONG POEMS

# A Lover's Complaint

## Ilona Bell

### PROSE PARAPHRASE

*A Lover's Complaint* begins when an unidentified narrator, out for a walking tour in the countryside, hears a "double voice" (l. 1) resounding through the hills from the valley below. He sees a pale young woman and, unbeknownst to her, observes her from afar. She is weeping uncontrollably, wiping her eyes with a napkin or handkerchief bearing a coded message. Her eyes jump distractedly from the distant sky to the ground below, unable to find a point of stability or rest. She wears a straw hat typical of a simple county girl; her hair and clothes are disordered, suggesting that her life is in shambles and that she is too upset to keep up appearances. As the narrator watches, she begins removing keepsakes from a basket: letters written in blood and rings inscribed with secret posies or poems—the signs of a clandestine love affair. Kissing them and sobbing, she cries out against her lover's perfidy and lies. She still desperately loves him; she reads his messages over and over. Since only privileged early modern women could read, we can infer that the female complainant is not a simple country lass as we may have assumed but a well-educated gentlewoman who has been dishonored and ostracized as the result of an illicit love affair gone awry.

At this point, "a reverend man" (l. 57) who has been grazing his cattle on the riverbank and who is presumably living a secluded pastoral life in the countryside nearby approaches the female complainant and compassionately urges her to tell him her story. He sits down by her side, implying that he is quite literally prepared to take her side. Even before she begins to speak, he acknowledges that she has a valid "grievance" (l. 67) and urges her to share with him the "grounds and motives of her woe" (l. 63). The "reverend man" has been compared to a father confessor figure, but he is described as a distinctly secular man who once lived amidst the bustle and internecine strife of court and city. It is this personal experience from his own more active past that prompts him to sympathize with the female complainant and to offer "in the charity of age" (l. 70) to do whatever he can to help her recover her reputation and ease her misery.

Calmed by his compassion and trust, she proceeds to tell her story. She explains that she allowed herself to fall in love with a beautiful, androgynous young man who inspired love and admiration in everyone with whom he came in contact. He was "maiden-tongu'd" (l. 100), that is, his voice had barely begun to deepen or he spoke mildly and meekly as a maid (that is, a virgin). He was a masterful horseman and an enchanting conversationalist. He charmed young and old, men and women alike. The more women he conquered, the more his allure grew.

The female complainant moved in his social circles. She had heard the gossip about the women with whom he had slept and the children he had fathered out of wedlock. Yet like so many others, the female complainant found the androgynous young man irresistibly attractive, but for some time she guarded her virginity—"held my city" (l. 176)—knowing that her well-being depended on preserving her honor, until one fateful day when the male lover gave a long, persuasive speech that dissolved her resistance. The speech, which she quotes verbatim, began by offering her "holy vows" of love (l. 179), claiming that although he had had many lovers, she was the first he ever loved. His rhetoric is seductive but specious, especially the claim that the "shame" that befell his previous lovers was theirs alone since he had merely succumbed to their desires (ll. 187–188). His persuasion concludes with a "strong-bonded oath / That shall prefer and undertake my troth" (ll. 279–280). The carefully chosen words that begin and end the speech ("holy vows," "oath," and "troth") all seem to promise a clandestine lover's contract, a troth-plight or betrothal leading to marriage.

When the male lover's speech ends, the female complainant resumes her narrative. She describes the tears that fell upon his cheeks, tears that convinced her, despite her better judgment, that he loved her and intended to marry her. Moved by the intensity of the moment, she "shook off [her] sober guards and civil fears; / Appear to him as he to me appears, / All melting" (ll. 298–300). They slept together, after which he quickly lost interest.

As her complaint draws to a close, the female complainant admits with remarkable frankness that she is still so attracted to the male lover, for all his flaws, that she might do it all over again, should the opportunity arise. But of course, it will not. The poem ends with her plaintive, despairing words.

## COMPOSITION AND PUBLICATION HISTORY

After acquiring an extraordinary popularity in sixteenth-century England, sonnets and lovers' complaints had gone out of fashion by 1609 when Shakespeare's *Sonnets*, including the long poem *A Lover's Complaint*, was first published by William Thorpe. *A Lover's Complaint* is not mentioned on the title page of the volume but is instead introduced by its own title, "A Lovers Complaint by William Shake-speare." Sales were apparently disappointing, for the volume was not reprinted again until 1640.

The authorship of *A Lover's Complaint* was called into question in 1912 by J. W. Mackail, who argued that the poem was too artificial, pedantic, clumsy, and imperfectly constructed to be by Shakespeare. Put off by the difficulty and artificiality of the language and puzzled by the oddity of the frame, scholars disregarded the poem for much of the twentieth century, at the very moment in history when Shakespeare's other works were receiving unparalleled scholarly and critical attention. Finally, in the 1970s a number of independent studies of the poem's language and substantive grammar revealed compelling connections between *A Lover's Complaint* and the plays Shakespeare wrote after the turn of the century, convincing most Shakespeareans that the poem (rather like the female complainant herself) had been belied.

In 1986 William Kerrigan published a carefully edited and extensively annotated edition of *The Sonnets and A Lover's Complaint*. In his introduction and notes Kerrigan demonstrated that *A Lover's Complaint* was integrally connected to the sonnets and that the volume would have been seen as a unit by Shakespeare's audience, accustomed to reading sonnet sequences followed by and connected to narrative poems. Although a few critics continued to doubt Shakespeare's authorship, Kerrigan's edition was a turning point: *A Lover's Complaint* has been widely accepted as a canonical Shakespearean text ever since. There are still only a handful of essays devoted to *A Lover's Complaint*, and criticisms of its structure and language continue. Yet in the past few years interest in Shakespeare's nondramatic poetry has grown. Thanks to new scholarly editions, reader's companions, and a forthcoming collection of essays, *A Lover's Complaint* is becoming more comprehensible and enjoyable than ever before.

## LITERARY ANTECEDENTS AND SOURCES

*Shakespeare's Sonnets* and *A Lover's Complaint* belong to a well-established English Renaissance literary tradition—the sonnet sequence conjoined to and printed with a narrative poem, the two parts often linked, as in Shakespeare, by brief Anacreontic poems describing Cupid's escapades (sonnets 153–154). Shakespeare's most notable precursors in this tradition are Samuel Daniel's *Delia and A Complaint of Rosamond* (1592); Thomas Lodge's *Philis and The Tragical Complaint of Elstred* (1593); Richard Barnfield's *Cynthia. With Certain Sonnets and the Legend of Cassandra*; Spenser's *Amoretti and Epithalamion* (1596).

*A Lover's Complaint* itself belongs to the literary genre of the female complaint. These complaints, spoken by a female persona, are to be distinguished from Petrarchan complaints spoken by a dejected and rejected male lover, works which were also extremely popular during the Renaissance. The genre or literary tradition of female complaint traces its roots back to the *Heroides*, which were written by the Latin poet Ovid around the time of Christ. Rather like the dramatic monologue, the Ovidean complaint invites sympathy for its female speaker, even as it exposes her to the ironic judgment of the male writer and reader. The *Heroides* were widely read in England from the Middle Ages on. Medieval and Renaissance lyrics, ballads, and popular love songs include many a woeful, abandoned young woman complaining of her fate and bemoaning her lover's betrayal.

Next to Ovid, probably the most influential male-authored female complaint was *Shore's Wife*, a didactic poem written by Thomas Churchyard, first published in the *Mirror for Magistrates* in 1563, revised and republished in 1593, approximately ten years before Shakespeare wrote *A Lover's Complaint*. Shore's Wife, the female speaker, bemoans her fall from fortune following the death of her lover, King Edward IV. *Shore's Wife* and many of the complaints that it inspired were didactic tales designed to titillate male readers with tales of female sexual transgression while warning readers that man's well-being is subject to fortune's constantly turning wheel. *Shore's Wife* and many of the subsequent poems spoken by a grieving woman, or the ghost of a fallen woman, allowed the female persona to present her point of view vigorously and movingly; at the same time, they were didactic poems designed to teach women to guard their chastity and good name lest they suffer an equally forlorn fate.

Shakespeare's poem seems closer in spirit and purpose to exculpatory complaints that became increasingly popular during the reign of Elizabeth I (1558–1603). Written by both men and women (Samuel Daniel, Isabella Whitney, Sir Henry Lee, Anne Vavasour, and George Gascoigne among others), exculpatory complaints often doubled as veiled poems of courtship. While Churchyard and other authors of *de casibus* (fall from fortune) complaints presented the female complainant as a sinful, fallen woman who had been justly punished for her sexual liberty and moral failing, exculpatory complaints invited sympathy and support for the female speaker who had been, or was in danger of being, seduced and betrayed by a man whose callousness and dishonesty the poem exposes.

Sir Henry Lee's "Sittinge alone upon my thought" provides a literary model for a male-authored female complaint that defends a woman's honor even after she has lost her virginity and affirms her sexual desire even without the sacrament of marriage. Lee represents his female complainant as a lovable, soft-hearted woman who naturally deserves mercy not because she is repentant but because she is so sad and so vulnerable. Following the poet's introductory description, which has interesting similarities to Shakespeare's opening narration, Lee's complaint consists of a series of questions posed by the female complainant and followed by an echo that repeats her final words, answers her questions, and explains that she has been abandoned and betrayed by a male lover whose youthful pride and arrogant self-absorption make him incapable of "ruthe," meaning both compassion and remorse for breaking the vows he made to her.

Isabella Whitney's *The Copy of a Letter . . . With an Admonition to al yong Gentilwomen and to al other Mayds in general* (1567), the first original poem known to be written and published by an Englishwoman, provides an example of a female-authored female complaint, written to an inconstant male lover upon her discovering that he had secretly betrothed himself to another woman. Whitney wrote the letter to remind her lover that their prior clandestine marriage contract made him honor-bound to marry her. Hoping to convince him that she deserves his love, Whitney in her letter, written in meter and packed with classical allusions, displays her learning, magnanimity, and devotion. Whitney maintains her dignity, saying that if he does not respect her mind, she will free him from his vows. Apparently, she did not receive the answer she sought, for Whitney decided to publish the letter in order to inform the world that the shame and dishonor were his, not hers. It was a radical act. Like Shakespeare's female complainant, Whitney rebels against the double standard that condoned sexual dalliance for men while expecting women to be chaste, silent, obedient, and long-suffering.

The title, *The Copy of a Letter*, announces that this is a private poem of courtship, written to Whitney's male lover, and subsequently printed, perhaps after having been rewritten, along with *With an Admonition to al yong Gentilwomen and to al other Mayds in general*, which defends female desire and freedom of choice. The admonition specifically addressed women like Shakespeare's female complainant who had already been passionately aroused by a particular suitor and who "good advice do lack." Whitney refrains from giving the kind of moralizing warnings that Shake-speare's female complainant deems so useless in lines 155–161, but she also warns her female readers to beware the deceptiveness of male rhetoric and the risks of clandestine marriage contracts. She hopes to help her readers distinguish between desirable suitors who are "constant, true, and just" and undesirable suitors like Shakespeare's male lover who use deceitful rhetoric and false vows to seduce and betray innocent young women. Whitney advises her female readers to "trye him well before," both *before* exchanging vows of love and *before* consummating those vows. The climax of Whitney's admonition, like the climax of Shakespeare's female complaint, occurs when the false lover crowns his lover's persuasion with a seem-ingly heartfelt but calculatedly false display of tears.

Isabella Whitney could have taken her inconstant lover to court because a prior marriage contract was legally binding, but like Shakespeare's female complainant she was not interested in forcing him to marry her. Instead, she wrote her letter to try to convince him to marry her if, and only if, he still desired her as much as he once seemed to love and respect her. Elizabethan lovers' complaints such as Lee's and Whitney's provide a precedent for interrogating the sexual double standard and conventional gender roles that Shakespeare's female complainant contests at the end of the poem.

An even closer analogue to Shakespeare's paired poems can be found in Samuel Daniel's sonnets and complaint. A shorter, unauthorized version of Daniel's son-nets, containing "the priuate passions of my youth" and now largely unread, was published along with the pirated edition of Sidney's *Astrophil and Stella*. Distressed to find his "secrets bewraide [betrayed] to the world, uncorrected" and feeling "forced to publish that which [he] never meant" (9), Daniel transformed his pri-vate poetry of courtship and seduction, addressed to an unnamed lady, into pub-lic poetry of praise, addressed to a conventional sonnet lady he called Delia, an anagram for *ideal*. Daniel removed the most erotic and derogatory poems, inter-spersed a large number of new poems designed to commemorate and idealize his love, and completely reordered the sequence, thereby concealing the courtship the poems originally enacted. To complete the volume, Daniel added *The Complaint of Rosamond*, in which Rosamond speaks to Delia through Daniel so that Daniel can speak through Rosamond to Delia, urging her not to sacrifice youthful passion for money and power as Rosamond did when she allowed herself to be persuaded to become mistress to the aging Henry II.

It is the longer, expurgated, authorized sonnet sequence, published along with *The Complaint of Rosamond* in 1592, that modern scholars have related to Shake-speare's sonnets and complaint, but Shakespeare himself almost surely knew the whole story. Like Daniel, Shakespeare concealed his private lover's dialogue by omitting names and biographical details that might have identified the young man, the Dark Lady, and the female complainant, leading to centuries of scholarly spec-ulation and controversy. Like Daniel, Shakespeare may also have omitted some son-nets that were biographically revealing, potentially scandalous, or overtly critical of the young man.

The unauthorized publication of Sidney's and Daniel's poems was a watershed moment in English literary history, for it proved that private manuscripts were no longer safe from public exposure. English love poetry from the 1590s and early 1600s is still primarily manuscript poetry, written not for publication but for a private lyric audience known to the poet. Yet the best love poetry from this period—including Shakespeare's *Sonnets* and *A Lover's Complaint* as well as Spenser's *Amoretti* and Donne's *Songs and Sonnets*—is also conscious of and at least partially addressed to a potential, wider lyric audience that was eager to learn the "secrets" of the poet's "private passions." Shakespeare, Spenser, and Donne did not conceal the courtships their poems enact; instead, they veiled allusions to persons or events outside the poem in ambiguity or obscurity.

## DEVICES AND TECHNIQUES

*A Lover's Complaint* is written in the rhyme royal stanza used in Shakespeare's *Rape of Lucrece*: seven lines of iambic pentameter verse in the rhyme scheme abab-bcc, where each new letter stands for a new rhyme. The stanza has close connections to the English sonnet form (*ababcdcdefefgg*) pioneered by Henry Howard, Earl of Surrey and perfected by Shakespeare. Like the Shakespearean sonnet, *A Lover's Complaint* begins with a quatrain in alternating rhymes (*abab*). The repetition of the "*b*" rhyme begins to dissolve the quatrain to make a couplet which in the sonnets typically sums up or overturns the poem's argument. In *A Lover's Complaint*, the *bb* couplet is followed by another couplet that leads to the next quatrain; the couplets, therefore, provide only a temporary or even a false sense of closure. Of course, that is also true of a sonnet sequence, where a concluding couplet leads to a new opening quatrain. As the complaint continues stanza after stanza, the conclusions or explanations reached in one couplet are complicated and often undermined by subsequent stanzas. For example, the female complainant's resolve to maintain her chastity gives way to the male lover's persuasion. Thus the stanza form looks back and sums up in order to move on to another reworking of the same imprisoning pattern, much as the female complainant looks back at her lover's earlier affairs, sees the "patterns of his foul beguiling" (l. 170), sums it all up, only to begin the cycle of attraction and repugnance all over again—a cycle already familiar to readers of the sonnets.

*A Lover's Complaint* is full of neologisms (or coinages), archaisms, and archaic sounding neologisms reminiscent of Spenser's poetry. With an unknown word appearing every twenty lines or so and an unusually condensed and contorted sentence structure, the poem can be difficult to understand, even for readers familiar with Shakespeare's language. The abstruse language, convoluted syntax, mysterious imagery, and puzzling or problematic conclusion suggest that the poem, like the sonnets, contains a subtext of private meanings that Shakespeare was not ready to explain to the wider reading public.

*A Lover's Complaint* is a study in the uses and effects of rhetorical persuasion. Rhetoric, which refers to language, both spoken and written, whose express purpose was persuasion, was a primary subject in the Elizabethan curriculum, widely taught to Elizabethan men but not to Elizabethan women. Shakespeare's male lover, whose speech the female complainant quotes in full, uses a number of familiar rhetorical strategies to convince her to sleep with him. His basic argument is as follows: first, he claims that, although he has had many lovers in the past, he never loved or wooed anyone before; second, he pretends to propose marriage and to betroth himself to her; third, he describes a holy nun who fell so deeply in love with him that she was willing to renounce her vows, thereby endowing his love for the female complainant with a patina of spiritual truth; and fourth, he gives her the lover's tokens he received from his previous lovers, thereby imparting concrete substance to his protestations that his previous affairs meant nothing to him because he never loved any other woman as he now loves her. He concludes his speech by reiterating in even more forceful terms his desire to betroth himself to her. Finally, he gives his words a dramatic physical embodiment by bursting into tears. This performative enactment of his oral persuasion was recommended by Ovid in *The Art of Love* and denounced by Isabella Whitney's *Admonition* as a specious rhetorical device commonly used to deceive innocent young women: "Some use the teares of Crocodiles, / contrary to their hart: / And yf they cannot alwayes weep: / they wet their cheekes by Art."

The opening description by the male narrator is a framing device, used by Lee, Daniel, and Spenser, and typical of male-authored female complaints. Shakespeare departs from convention, however, in two important ways. First, he introduces the reverend man who becomes the female complainant's private lyric audience, leaving the male narrator to eavesdrop on a conversation that he cannot influence and does not judge. Shakespeare's second and even more visible departure from convention is to leave the frame open by not bringing either the narrator or the reverend man back to speak at the end of the poem. Critics have censured the poem for this omission, and some have concluded on that basis that the poem is a draft that Shakespeare left unfinished. These critics have failed to understand the conclusion of the poem, which, in fact, has a perfectly balanced formal structure: seven stanzas of introductory description spoken by the male narrator; fifteen stanzas of narration spoken by the female complainant; fifteen stanzas of rhetorical persuasion spoken by the male lover; seven stanzas of summary judgment spoken by the female complainant whose two-part narrative frames the male lover's speech.

## THEMES AND MEANINGS

Shakespeare warns us from the very outset that we are entering a symbolic universe full of veiled allusions and double meanings: "From off a hill whose concave womb reworded / A plaintful story from a sist'ring vale, / My spirits t'attend this double voice accorded" (ll. 1–3). "[T]his double voice" not only describes the redoubling formal structure of *A Lover's Complaint*—the male narrator quoting the female complainant, who in turn quotes her male lover—but it leaves us to make our own way through the dualities and duplicities the poem presents. Because the poem ends without the conventional didactic exegesis, we must decide for ourselves how to interpret and judge the male narrator, the reverend man, the female complainant, and her male lover.

Since we only hear the male lover's persuasion through the female complainant's recollected quotation, we might reasonably ask whether she belied him in order to exonerate herself. Does the poem give us any reason to think that she is the one who is manipulative and deceitful (or self-deceived) as critics have suggested? The female complainant is certainly "fickle" in the sense of changeable (l. 5), as her distracted appearance in stanza 4 attests; after hearing her tale, however, there is little reason to think she is also "fickle" in the by-then archaic sense of deceitful or unreliable. She not only provides a remarkably frank account of her thoughts and feelings but also accepts full responsibility for her actions: "Ay, me, I fell, and yet do

question make / What I should do again for such a sake" (ll. 321–322). Some critics have been skeptical or even critical of the female complainant because she neither expresses remorse nor renounces her former passion, but she is believable
precisely because she tells the reverend man (and us) what she feels rather than what
an early modern woman was told she ought to feel.

The conventional male-authored female complaint subjects the female complainant's vanity and weakness to the male narrator's irony and judgment. Typically, the introductory narrative frame introduces the female complainant, while
the concluding narrative frame summarizes the lessons to be drawn from her mea
culpa. By contrast, Shakespeare's male narrator sets the scene only to subside into
silence. In the conventional didactic complaint, the male narrative frames and
judges the female complainant; in *A Lover's Complaint* the female complainant
frames and judges the male lover's speech. This structural innovation confirms what
the narrative itself reveals: the unreliable narrator whose sins are revealed by the
poem is not the female complainant but the male lover.

Shakespeare's unusually multilayered narrative structure invites us to reexamine
the moral assumptions perpetuated by conventional male-authored female complaints and encourages us, if we so choose, to accept the reverend man's invitation
to side with the female complainant. If we trust the poem's formal structure, the
female complainant's narrative exposes the hypocrisy of the social, ethical, and literary codes that allowed an aristocratic male lover to seduce, betray, and calumni-
ate any number of women, enhancing his own reputation by his innumerable
conquests while destroying their honor—and, at that time in history, their lives.

## THE RELATIONSHIP OF THE POEM TO
## SHAKESPEARE'S OTHER WORKS

Published with Shakespeare's *Sonnets* and following a literary tradition of narrative poems linked to sonnet sequences, *A Lover's Complaint* is most closely connected to the sonnets themselves. Indeed, the more one immerses oneself in the
language of the sonnets and the complaint, the more one is flooded by echoes, allusions, and intricate interconnections so complex, numerous, and perplexing that
one can only get a glimpse of them here.

Probably the most evident similarity is the description of the androgynous male
lover whose "Small show of man was yet upon his chin, / His phoenix down began
but to appear / Like unshorn velvet on that termless skin" (ll. 92–94) and who "had
the dialect and different skill, / Catching all passions in his craft of will, / That he
did in the general bosom reign / Of young, of old, and sexes both enchanted" (ll.
125–128). The beautiful young man of the sonnets whose "woman's face with Nature's own hand painted" also "steals men's eyes and women's souls amazeth" (20.1,
8). The female complainant says that the male lover's admirers "dialogu'd for him
what he would say, / Ask'd their own wills and made their wills obey" (ll. 132–133).
This punning reference to Will Shakespeare's own "craft of will" hints that the poetic fiction of the complaint is somehow linked to the biographical truths concealed
in the sonnets (and Shakespeare puns shamelessly on his own name in sonnets 135
and 136), where Shakespeare "dialogued for" the young man, anticipating his response, blurring the identities of poet/lover and reader/beloved.

The parallels between the sonnet speaker and the female complainant, the young
man and the male lover, come together when the male lover woos the female com-

plainant as he himself has been wooed, with poems of courtship: "th annexions of fair gems enrich'd, / And deep-brain'd sonnets that did amplify / Each stone's dear nature, worth, and quality" (ll. 208–210). Shakespeare's sonnets also woo the young man with poems of courtship that are valuable tokens of love, "stones of worth . . . / Or captain jewels" (52.7–8) precisely because they reflect the young man's glimmering beauty. The poetic connections between the young man and the male lover, the female complainant and the sonnet speaker, reach a climax when the male lover completes his persuasion and promptly bursts into tears: "For lo his passion, but an art of craft, / Even there resolv'd my reason into tears, / There my white stole of chastity I daff'd" (ll. 295–297). Her resistance dissolves, just as Shakespeare's does when confronted by the young man's tears in Sonnet 34.

Shakespeare's *Sonnets* help to explain the intricate structure and obscure language of *A Lover's Complaint*. Even more important, *A Lover's Complaint* helps to explain the gaps and contradictions that make the sonnets such a riddle. When read together, Shakespeare's *Sonnets* and *A Lover's Complaint* provide further evidence that the 1609 text is a brilliantly imagined and intricately interconnected volume of poems. The pervasive and insistent links between the ways in which the young man beguiles the sonnet speaker and the ways in which the male lover beguiles the female complainant indicate that Shakespeare conceived *A Lover's Complaint* as the conclusion to and commentary upon *Sonnets* (1609).

Statistical analyses of Shakespeare's language link *A Lover's Complaint* to plays written after 1600, and even more closely between 1603 and 1609. These conclusions are confirmed by critical interpretation: the bleak, complicated view of love and human nature, the searing effects of deception and betrayal, the shift from youthful, playful courtship to its dangerous and ominous aftermath connect *A Lover's Complaint* to Shakespeare's later plays, especially *All's Well That Ends Well*, *Measure for Measure*, and *Cymbeline*.

## Annotated Bibliography

Bell, Ilona. " 'That which thou hast done': Shakespeare's *Sonnets* and 'A Lover's Complaint.' " In *Shakespeare's Sonnets: Critical Essays*. Ed. James Schiffer. New York: Garland, 1999. 455–474. One of the first critical interpretations of *A Lover's Complaint*, this essay links the ways the young man beguiles the sonnet speaker to the ways the male lover beguiles the female complainant and argues that Shakespeare conceived *A Lover's Complaint* as the conclusion to and commentary upon *Sonnets* (1609).

Burrow, Colin, ed. *The Complete Sonnets and Poems*. The Oxford Shakespeare. Oxford: Oxford UP, 2002. This edition, with extensive annotations and introduction, argues that the complexity of the language in *A Lover's Complaint* creates an "effect of excluded intimacy" that "plunges the reader into a world where interpretation is all" (142, 141).

Duncan-Jones, Katherine, ed. *Shakespeare's Sonnets*. The Arden Shakespeare. London: Thomas Nelson and Sons, 1997. The introduction and notes present a strong argument that Shakespeare was himself responsible for publishing the 1609 edition, for ordering the sonnets, and juxtaposing sonnets and complaint.

Hyland, Peter. *An Introduction to Shakespeare's Poems*. London: Palgrave Macmillan, 2003. This fine introduction to Shakespeare's nondramatic poetry includes general discussions of Shakespeare as poet and Shakespeare and the literary marketplace, as well as individual analyses of the poems. Treats *A Lover's Complaint* as a coda to the sonnets.

Kerrigan, John, ed. *Motives of Woe: Shakespeare and "Female Complaint": A Critical Anthology*. Oxford: Clarendon P, 1991. Here Kerrigan surveys the literary tradition of the male-authored female complaint before and after Shakespeare, and reprints important examples, edited and annotated, from medieval lyrics to Pope.

———. *Shakespeare: "The Sonnets" and "A Lover's Complaint."* Harmondsworth, Eng.: Penguin, 1986. This ground-breaking edition includes an introduction describing the complaint genre and the tradition of sonnets published with narrative poems. Insightful annotations clarify the poem's abstruse language and connect *A Lover's Complaint* to the sonnets and the plays.

Sharon-Zisser, Shirley. *Suffering Ecstasy: Essays on Shakespeare's "A Lover's Complaint."* Burlington, VT: Ashgate, forthcoming. This is the first collection of essays devoted entirely to *A Lover's Complaint*. The wide range of critical approaches situates the poem in its generic, cultural, and historical contexts.

# Venus and Adonis

### Yashdip S. Bains

## PROSE PARAPHRASE

Adonis rises at dawn and prepares to go hunting, but lovesick Venus stops him. Boldly asking for a kiss, she removes Adonis from his horse. She ties the horse to a tree, pushes Adonis to the ground, and, when he protests, stops his mouth with kisses. Finally, she promises to let him go if he will give her just one kiss in return. Adonis agrees, but then leaves her frustrated by not kissing her. In lengthy and rhetorically embellished speeches, Venus lists reasons why he should love her. Comparing him with Narcissus, she urges him to leave heirs to posterity. Unaffected by her pleadings, Adonis says that the sun is burning his skin, so he must leave.

Venus replies that her sighs will cool Adonis, her hairs give him shade, and her tears will quench them if they catch on fire. She will cover him with her body. Adonis responds with scorn to all her pleas. He moves away toward his horse, but having caught the scent of a lusty mare appearing from the nearby grove, Adonis's horse breaks his reins and pursues her. The two horses escape into the wood, leaving Adonis sitting there angry. Venus returns to him, holds his hand, and implores him to learn to love by his horse's example. Still untouched by her wooing, Adonis says he is not ripe for love.

Undiscouraged by his reluctance, Venus persists in her courtship. Afraid that Adonis may reject her again, she faints. Adonis seeks to revive her by various means. He slaps her cheeks, "wrings her nose, . . . bends her fingers" (ll. 475–476), and finally tries to awaken her with his kisses. This last method succeeds; Venus opens her eyes and speaks ecstatically of her pleasure at being kissed by Adonis.

Adonis reminds her that he is not mature enough for her. Night is approaching, and Adonis kisses her farewell. Enraptured, Venus begins to kiss again. They fall to the ground, where Venus kisses and fondles him, "takes all she can, not all she listeth" (l. 564). Still, Adonis shows no desire. Venus at last lets him go but asks to meet him the next day. He replies that he intends to "hunt the boar, with certain of his friends" (l. 588).

THE ROMANCES AND POETRY

Fearing for his safety, she clings to him, sinks to the ground, and pulls him down on top of her. She alerts him to the hazards of hunting ferocious boars and advises him to opt for only hares, foxes, or deer. She speaks of her love again, once more urges him to have sex with her so that he can leave an image of himself to posterity, but Adonis admonishes her for prettifying her lust with the rhetoric of love and leaves her.

Feeling lonely, Venus roams aimlessly in the dark. She listens to the echoing of her moans and broods over the pangs and agonies of love. After sunrise, she rushes quickly to a myrtle grove and catches the sounds of Adonis's hunt. She discovers that his dogs are afraid of the blood-stained boar. Having come upon a number of wounded dogs, Venus is worried that Adonis may have perished and exclaims against death. She weeps, but when she notices the huntsmen again, she believes that Adonis is alive and censures her own trepidations. She retracts her criticism of death.

Then Venus realizes that the boar has killed Adonis by pushing his tusk into his groin. She imagines that the beast only wanted to kiss him. She composes an elegy for her beloved. Stricken with grief, she falls on his body and catches a glimpse of his dead eyes. She prophesies that, because Adonis has died, love will always be accompanied by the pain and sorrow of inequality and unrequited desire. Adonis's body melts away from her sight and in its place "A purple flow'r . . . check'red with white" springs (l. 1168). Venus plucks it and pledges to hold it dearly in her breast. Thus weary of the world, she goes back to Paphos in Cyprus in her dove-drawn chariot to mourn his death in private.

## COMPOSITION AND PUBLICATION HISTORY

Although it is difficult to assign a precise date of composition for *Venus and Adonis*, editors believe that Shakespeare wrote it toward the end of 1592 when the theaters were closed because of the plague. There is no reason to eliminate the probability that he had worked on it before.

*Venus and Adonis* was entered in the Stationers' Register on April 18, 1593, and was available in bookstalls by June of the same year. Bearing Shakespeare's name on the title page, it was his first published work. Dedicated to Henry Wriothesely, third Earl of Southampton, it was printed in quarto format by Richard Field, who was born in Stratford and may have gone to the King's New School with Shakespeare. Only a single copy of the first quarto has survived and is in the Bodleian Library at Oxford. Because it is so carefully printed, editors postulate that Shakespeare may have given the printer his own manuscript and supervised its proofreading. It is one of the most reliable of his printed texts. *Venus and Adonis* became popular immediately, appearing in ten editions before the poet's death in 1616 and in another six by 1636. In his dedication Shakespeare modestly offered it as the "first heir of my invention" and vowed "to take advantage of all idle hours, till I have honored you with some graver labor."

## LITERARY ANTECEDENTS AND SOURCES

Venus, in Roman religion, was originally a goddess of gardens, but this notion was later modified under the influence of ideas from Sicily and Greece. She became identified with Aphrodite and emerged as the deity of love. In Greek mythology Aphrodite was the daughter of Zeus and Dione. Hesiod records that she sprang from the foam of the sea that had stuck to the severed member of Uranus, who had been mutilated by his son Cronos. She was married to Hephaestus but did not stay faithful to him. After learning of Aphrodite's affair with Ares, Hephaestus caught the two in a net and submitted them to ridicule in an assembly of gods. The Romans honored her because, as the mother of Aeneas, she was their ancestor.

Mythological figures can personify human passions, and Shakespeare uses their supernatural status in different ways to create a tension between myth and human reality in the domain of love and desire. Venus and Adonis both resemble and differ from human beings. Venus, the goddess of love, physical desire, and procreation, is not one fixed personality, nor is she merely the Eternal Feminine. She embodies the Neoplatonic idea of Love's pursuit of Beauty, but she also behaves aggressively and relentlessly in satisfying her sexual passion. Shakespeare emphasizes her complexity by playing on her various attributes as a mother (of Cupid and Aeneas), a conqueror of Mars (in the bedroom), a deceiver, a prophet, and an expert in love's verbal artifices and techniques of enticement. She can be comic, sensual, and violent.

Venus frequently takes on physical attributes of mortals. She pleads with Adonis to appreciate her beauty. After advising him about the need for procreation (ll. 157–174), the "love-sick queen [begins] to sweat" (l. 175). She kisses passionately and "she weeps" (l. 221). When Adonis "struggles to be gone, / She locks her lily fingers one in one" (ll. 227–228). When Adonis looks at her with disdain, she faints. Venus, expert in verbal devices, uses various rhetorical strategies to lure Adonis to have sex with her. She promises to reveal to him the secrets and mystery of love. She invites him to "be my deer" in her "park" (l. 231).

In Greek mythology, Adonis, a beautiful youth, was born as a result of the incestuous love Myrhha (or Smyrna) had for her father, Cinyras, King of Cyprus. Angry that Myrrha had refused to worship her, Venus had induced her to develop an erotic passion for her father, just as she cursed Hippolytus for not worshiping her by causing his stepmother, Phaedra, to fall in love with him. When Cinyras discovered the horrible reality, he tried to kill his daughter, but she was transformed into a myrtle, from which Adonis was born. Venus fell in love with Adonis, who was killed by a boar during a hunt. Upon his death, she caused a rose or an anemone to spring from his blood. Venus and Persephone (goddess of the underworld) laid claim to him, but Zeus determined that he should stay part of the year with each. In the course of their worship of Adonis, devotees surrounded his images with beds of rapidly withering plants, "Gardens of Adonis." Shakespeare refers to the garden in *1 Henry VI* (1.6.6–7), as do Edmund Spenser in *The Faerie Queene* (book III, canto vi) and John Milton in *Paradise Lost* (book IX). Shakespeare has Venus characterize him in two metaphors that suggest such ephemeral floral arrangements:

> The field's chief flower, sweet above compare,
> Stain to all nymphs, more lovely than a man. (ll. 8–9)

Nature has created him as a physically perfect specimen of a male, and when he dies the world will perish with him:

Nature, that made thee with herself at strife,
Saith that the world hath ending with thy life. (ll. 11–12)

Being vigorously wooed by Venus, Adonis rejects her for several reasons. He prefers chasing the boar to chasing a woman (ll. 409–410). Love is contradictory, "a life in death, / That laughs and weeps and all but with a breath" (ll. 413–414). He insists repeatedly that he is too young and immature to respond to Venus's pleas. He thinks of himself as "a garment shapeless and unfinish'd" (l. 415), a "bud before one leaf put forth" (l. 416), and a "springing" thing (l. 417). Adonis stresses his youth when Venus does not want to let him go (ll. 524–525). Clinging to a perfect, untarnished boyishness, he voices the fatal reluctance to enter manhood and all the grief and strife sexual maturity will bring. Adonis also rejects Venus because she argues falsely (l. 787). Venus justifies love "for increase" (l. 791), but Adonis dismisses her reason as "the bawd to lust's abuse" (l. 792). He proceeds to suggest that lust has usurped love's name on earth (ll. 793–796). Adonis draws a contrast between the two: "Love is all truth, Lust full of forged lies" (l. 804).

Ovid's book X of the *Metamorphoses* provided the main source for Shakespeare, who could have read it in the original Latin and in Arthur Golding's English translation of 1565–1567. Shakespeare expanded Ovid's brief story of less than 100 lines to his own 1,194 lines. In addition to rhetorically elaborate imagery and descriptions, Shakespeare included a number of digressions like Adonis's horse running away with a mare and the hunting of Wat the hare. In Ovid, however, Adonis reciprocates Venus's love for him; the two hunt together. Venus returns after Adonis has suffered from a mortal wound and changes him into an anemone. Shakespeare significantly alters the story by making Adonis reject Venus and devoting himself exclusively to hunting. His Adonis is beautiful and chaste and abhors love; he goes hunting the boar to avoid Venus's attentions. In the struggle between the principles of eros and chastity, Shakespeare's Venus may have failed, but she succeeds in the sense that Adonis's tragic experience forces the universal recognition that the alternative to erotic fulfillment is violent death. Shakespeare also may have been influenced by Ovid's narrations of Salmacis and Hermaphroditus and Echo and Narcissus.

In the 1590s, the erotic narrative poem, also called a minor epic or epyllion, had become extremely popular. A typical epyllion was an elaboration of a single tale from Ovid's *Metamorphoses*. Each poet tried to excel his predecessors by developing the form further and by turning marginal points into central events. The first narrative had appeared in 1560 under the title *The Fable of Ovid Treating of Narcissus*. In 1565 Thomas Peend published his *Pleasant Fable of Salmacis and Hermaphroditus*. Ovid's "erotic epyllion" had become fashionable with the publication of Thomas Lodge's *Scilla's Metamorphosis, Interlaced with the Unfortunate Love of Glaucus* in 1589. Christopher Marlowe may have composed his *Hero and Leander* about the same year, but it was not published until 1598. These erotic treatments of passionate and sensual topics had a comic and narrative voice. Marlowe's poem and Thomas Heywood's *Oenone and Paris* made the minor epic still more popular. Shakespeare entered the market for erotic narratives to establish his reputation as a new poet and to display his ability to alter and amplify an Ovidian tale. With *Venus and Adonis*, as Colin Burrow has stressed, Shakespeare emerged "as someone who could outdo his predecessors in the arts of miniaturization and orna-mentation" (18).

In 1593, Shakespeare enlivened the literary scene with this minor epic, in which he took pride in his craft by citing an epigraph from Ovid's *Amores* (1.15.35–36) that reads in Marlowe's translation: "Let base-conceited wits admire vile things, / Fair Phoebus lead me to the Muses' springs" ("*Vilia miretur vulgus: mihi flavus Apollo / Pocula Castalia plena ministret aqua*").

## DEVICES AND TECHNIQUES

In the early nineteenth century Samuel Taylor Coleridge championed Shake-speare's nondramatic poems and initiated a discussion of imagery in *Venus and Adonis*. He selected the following stanza as a suitable example of powerful imagery:

> With this he breaketh from the sweet embrace
> Of those fair arms which bound him to her breast,
> And homeward through the dark laund [glade] runs apace,
> Leaves Love upon her back, deeply distress'd.
>> Look how a bright star shooteth from the sky,
>> So glides he in the night from Venus' eye[.] (ll. 811–816)

Coleridge elucidates the effectiveness of the image of the shooting star: "How many images and feelings are here brought together without effort and without discord—the beauty of Adonis; the rapidity of his flight; the yearning, yet hopelessness of the enamoured gazer; and a shadowy ideal character is thrown over the whole" (*Coleridge's Criticism of Shakespeare*, ed. R. A. Foakes [Detroit: Wayne State UP, 1989], 22). The narrator describes sympathetically Venus's shock at seeing Adonis's dead body; her eyes withdraw like the stars that despise daylight: "Which seen, her eyes as murder'd with the view, / Like stars asham'd of day, themselves withdrew" (ll. 1031–1032). Like a snail shrinking into its shell, "her eyes are fled / Into the deep-dark cabins of her head" (ll. 1037–1038). Shakespeare draws much of his imagery from the world of nature, an apt source given that Venus and Adonis are both fig-ures of fertility. Shakespeare invokes the patterns of natural growth and death.

Narrating an erotic encounter between mythological and legendary figures, Shakespeare opens with a typically classical but hackneyed image of dawn, but he also introduces realistic diction like "[s]ick-thoughted" and "bold-fac'd" in his por-trayal of Venus (ll. 5, 6). Shakespeare creates a luxuriant setting for Venus's amorous hunting of Adonis (her version of venery, a word that derives from the name of Venus and refers to both hunting and love-making), but he constantly brings the reader back to earth by describing Venus in human terms and Adonis as an indig-nant and impatient adolescent. The narrator, however, constantly speaks about the goddess as well as a woman. Lying in the sun she sweats; but, also, she is so light that even flowers can support her. When Adonis does not warm up to her wooing, she loses patience and scolds him for his fake appearance as a man (ll. 211–214). Adonis lacks the instinctive or innate desire for sex, and she puts herself into such a rage that she even wishes she were a man and Adonis a woman so that he could experience the degree of her frustration.

Clark Hulse underlines the significance of the poem's use of red and white: "The style of *Venus and Adonis* might best be epitomized in the metaphors of red and white: a constant shifting of the significance of the images and the syntactic structure linking them, which are held together as a series simply by the repetition of the image itself" (174). Venus considers Adonis "more white and red than doves or roses are" (l. 10). She wants to make his lips "red, and pale, with fresh variety" (l. 21). Holding the tender boy under her arm, she is "red and hot as coals of glowing fire, / He red for shame, but frosty in desire" (ll. 35–36). She revels in the changes of color in Adonis's face: "Being red, she loves him best, and being white, / Her best is better'd with a more delight" (ll. 77–78).

Red, for Venus, stands for her sensuality and desire. She concedes that her lips may not be as fair as Adonis's, "yet they are red" (l. 116). In her cheeks, "white and red each other did destroy" (l. 346) when she sneaks up on Adonis and alternately blushes and turns pale. When Venus faints, Adonis "Claps her pale cheek, till clapping makes it red" (l. 468). Grieving over Adonis's death, her heart has turned to lead, but her leaden heart will "melt at mine eyes' red fire, / So shall I die by drops of hot desire" (ll. 1073–1074). Hence, it is fitting that at the end of the poem Adonis turns into a flower that is purple checked with white.

The narrator captures the intensity and ferociousness of the goddess's actions by comparing them to a hungry eagle's devouring its prey, but he also modifies it significantly by mentioning Venus's feeding on Adonis's breath. Devouring flesh and bone and kissing are quite different. The narrator proceeds with the comparison:

> Even as an empty eagle, sharp by fast,
> Tires with her beak on feathers, flesh, and bone,
> Shaking her wings, devouring all in haste,
> Till either gorge be stuff'd, or prey be gone;
>    Even so she kiss'd his brow, his cheek, his chin,
>    And where she ends, she doth anew begin. (ll. 55–60)

"Even as" is a prelude to "Even so she kissed his brow, his cheek, his chin." Venus the bird of prey is devouring Adonis. But the narrator modifies his view by altering the situation in the next stanza:

> Forc'd to content [submit], but never to obey,
> Panting he lies, and breatheth in her face.
> She feedeth on the steam, as on a prey,
> And calls it heavenly moisture, air of grace,
>    Wishing her cheeks were gardens full of flowers,
>    So they were dew'd with such distilling showers. (ll. 61–66)

The movement from Venus as an eagle to Venus as a garden registers the development of the images; the same can be seen in Adonis as a victim and as a gentle shower. Venus feeds on his hot breath, "as on a prey," and "calls it" heavenly moisture given by divine grace. She would have liked to irrigate her gardens, that is her cheeks, with his dew or water. She has not torn apart Adonis's flesh and bones. Yet her appetite is so enormous that she cannot stop kissing.

Recalling the story of Venus and Mars caught by Vulcan in a net, Shakespeare draws attention to Adonis lying "tangled" in the net of her arms (ll. 67–68). Venus may catch Adonis, but she cannot satisfy her desire. She pleads with Adonis for a kiss, and he promises it. He raises his chin; when her lips are ready, he "turns his lips another way" (l. 90). Venus's tears cannot put out Venus's fire. Here lies the comedy and pathos of her situation. As Shakespeare describes her plight, "She's Love, she loves, and yet she is not lov'd" (l. 610).

Venus's attempts at wooing are not entirely soft and tender; even the gesture of holding Adonis's hand is seen as harsh: "A lily prison'd in a jail of snow, / Or ivory in an alabaster band (ll. 362–363). Her desire is so overwhelming that it becomes aggressive and destructive. Shakespeare's imagery shows the inherent pain and brutality of the moment.

Shakespeare's imagery also accentuates the impact of gestures or silences or words alluded to but not recorded. Venus acts annoyed that Adonis stays silent or hardly reacts to her ardent kisses. Sometimes he speaks; the narrator compares his red lips or "the ruby-color'd portal" (l. 451) to "a red morn" (l. 453) that signifies a stormy day. His "meaning" works like the wind or a wolf or a berry or a bullet of a gun, and almost kills her (ll. 457–462). She faints. She lies on the grass "as she were slain, / Till his breath breatheth life in her again" (ll. 473–474).

Adonis attempts several times to stop the wooing and leave, but Venus uses various devices to prolong the scene and to keep Adonis engaged there. One of the devices for slowing down the passage of time is digressions. Two of the digressions focus on Adonis's horse, which has bolted to be with "A breeding jennet, lusty, young, and proud" (l. 260), and Venus's story of the hunting of Wat the hare. The horse provides an example that, according to Venus, Adonis should learn from (ll. 403–405). Later, when she has pulled Adonis down on top of her, to make sure that he stays where he is, she tells the story of the hare and urges him to mark carefully what the hare does to evade his hunters (ll. 679–708). Venus, however, has spoken in vain: "Your treatise makes me like you worse and worse," Adonis says (l. 774). Colin Burrow explains how the hare tale "is placed at this climactic moment of sexual non-fulfillment in order to give readers from the 1590s the combined pleasure of hearing at length about a hunt, and of imagining, also at length, a woman attempting to rape a man" (30). According to Burrow, these digressions "also work to defuse the eroticism of the poem for a censorious reader" (30).

## THEMES AND MEANINGS

In this story of Venus's futile attempts at introducing Adonis to the pleasures of sex, Shakespeare is exploring different aspects of love. He is aware of but does not limit the scope of his poem to the idealistic notions of Neoplatonic philosophy. His erotic narrative focuses on sexual desire and the possibilities of its fulfillment or absence in human experience. The principle of love operates as an impersonal force in the cosmos, as does procreative desire; however, in the human sphere it is experienced as entirely personal and subjective. It is also the site of struggle for power and control among men and women. It can lead to harassment, violence, and death. Ovid's stories in the *Metamorphoses* illustrate the twisted path and the variable results of erotic craving. Mutual love is so mysterious that it baffles and confounds even Venus, who carries an astonishing arsenal of rhetorical and other techniques of persuasion and still cannot penetrate the defenses Adonis has built.

Since Venus is the goddess of love, it is inevitable that she should initiate the wooing of Adonis. Her duty is to uphold passionate love and procreative sex. In patriarchal cultures, this role falls to men who woo women. Through Venus's amorous addresses to Adonis, Shakespeare is questioning the effectiveness of clichés, stale imagery, and worn-out arguments in the Petrarchan discourse of love, which had permeated the vocabulary of erotic narratives. Venus's exuberant and flowery diction and imagery glorify erotic impulses and the subordination of reason to passion. Adonis's rejection of sexuality destroys him in his adolescence. She makes known the vagaries and anguish of love through her prophecies after Adonis's death. Love may have a "sweet beginning," but it will lead to an "unsavory end" (l. 1138) when its beloved has died. "It shall be fickle, false, and full of fraud" (l. 1141), she says, if one of the sexes does not respond to the other. This is how Shakespeare accounts for the origin of pain and suffering in human love.

Shakespeare conducts a significant debate about love and lust in the discourse between Adonis and Venus. Adonis contends that love has become something ugly because of its physicality and believes that it should be pure and unearthly. He disapproves of the physical link between the sexes, without which love cannot exist. As caterpillars destroy the tender leaves, love stains and ruins beauty; it makes beauty shameful and corrupt. He maintains that "Love is all truth, Lust full of forged lies" (804). If there were no bodily contact, Adonis would opt for love. He finds Venus's wanton talk offensive to his ears. But Venus without Adonis does not make sense to Shakespeare; there can be no love if there is no physical desire and no other as the object of desire. By turning against Venus, Adonis will be metamorphosed into what Venus says he is when he was still alive but cold to her entreaties, a "liveless picture, cold and senseless stone, / Well-painted idol, image dull and dead" (ll. 211–212). In fact, by becoming a flower, he is more alive after death than he is earlier when he rejects passion.

Shakespeare never forgets that love is affected by the passing of time. The goddess of love will live forever, but human beings do not. Adonis uses his youth and immaturity as reasons to repel the advances of his wooer. But Shakespeare's narrative underlines the elegiac note of decline and decay of passion. Venus's "beauty as the spring doth yearly grow" (l. 141), but mortal women grow ugly and wrinkled and lose their spirit. Hence Venus's advice rings true to Shakespeare's readers:

> Make use of time, let not advantage slip,
> Beauty within itself should not be wasted.
>> Fair flowers that are not gath'red in their prime
>> Rot, and consume themselves in little time. (ll. 129–132)

Nobody can transcend the domain of time; love cannot escape the destructive limits of mortality.

## THE RELATIONSHIP OF THE POEM TO SHAKESPEARE'S OTHER WORKS

Shakespeare's primary concerns in this poem about sexual desire, the inequalities and effects of passion on individuals, the changeable nature of relationships, and love as arena for power and control appear prominently in his comedies and tragedies. Venus can be treated as a prototype for Shakespeare's delineations of a number of powerful and desiring women: Titania in *A Midsummer Night's Dream*, Portia in *The Merchant of Venice*, Rosalind in *As You Like It*, Goneril and Regan in *King Lear*, Lady Macbeth in *Macbeth*, Volumnia in *Coriolanus*, Cleopatra in *Antony and Cleopatra*, and Paulina in *The Winter's Tale*. Some of them are charming and virtuous heroines, while others are nasty and destructive. The subject of a supernatural being madly in love with a mortal can be seen in *A Midsummer Night's Dream*, in the wooing of Bottom by Titania. Rosalind's pursuit of Orlando in *As You Like It* and Helena's search for Bertram in *All's Well That Ends Well* indicate Shakespeare's fascination with the subject: the woman's primary role, instead of the male's, in the pursuit of love.

Shakespeare grapples in his poem with the problem of the nature of love in the fallen world. Venus's prophecy about difficulties in the pursuit of desire represents the themes of plays like *Romeo and Juliet* and *Othello*. Unresolved conflicts culminate in tragedies. However noble and sincere one's attempts in love and marriage may be, one cannot predict the outcome. In *Venus and Adonis* Shakespeare stresses the gulf between desires and ideals and the disasters that result from it.

In all his works Shakespeare deals constantly with the impact of time on everyone's life and the human attempts to cope with the process of decay and disintegration. In sonnets 1–17 he pleads with his young friend to overcome the ravages of time by having children, just as Venus urges Adonis to do. Sonnet 129 decries lust, just as Adonis does. The humorous aspects of love in *Venus and Adonis* pervade Shakespeare's comedies, just as the tragic consequences of Adonis's rejection of love underlie his tragedies. Thus, in *Venus and Adonis*, Shakespeare announced some of the themes and concerns that would preoccupy him throughout his life.

## Annotated Bibliography

Burrow, Colin, ed. *The Complete Sonnets and Poems*. The Oxford Shakespeare. Oxford: Oxford UP, 2002. A modern-spelling text that provides detailed introductions and biographical and literary background to the poems and the dating and textual problems.

Dubrow, Heather. "'Upon Misprision Growing': *Venus and Adonis*." In *Captive Victors: Shakespeare's Narrative Poems and Sonnets*. Ithaca: Cornell UP, 1987. 21–79. Regards *Venus and Adonis* as "a subtle exploration of human emotion, a coherent analysis of human character" (18). Venus is an advocate of "an amoral delight in sexuality," and Adonis rejects her "in the name of higher philosophical verities" (48). Analyzes the effects of the poem's language and the conventions of the epyllion on the reader.

Duncan-Jones, Katherine. "Much Ado about Red and White: The Earliest Readers of Shakespeare's *Venus and Adonis* (1593)." *Review of English Studies* 44 (1993): 479–501. An account of the poem's popularity during Shakespeare's time as an erotic courtship poem and its changing fortunes from the eighteenth to the twentieth century.

Hamilton, A.C. "*Venus and Adonis*." *Studies in English Literature, 1500–1900* 1 (1961): 1–15; reprinted in Kolin, 141–156. Shakespeare presents Venus's pursuit of Adonis according to the Platonic tradition of Love as the desire for Beauty. When Adonis "dies, Beauty dies, Love leaves the world with her place usurped by 'lust,' Nature lies ruined, creation reverts to original chaos, and there is the 'mutuall ouerthrow of mortall kind'" (8).

Hulse, Clark. *Metamorphic Verse: The Elizabethan Minor Epic*. Princeton: Princeton UP, 1981. Discusses the relationship between *Venus and Adonis* and mythography. Shakespeare relies on symbols or emblems that represent specific attributes of character or events. Adonis's symbol is a flower whose beauty fades. Venus is compared to a jennet, a milch doe, and the boar.

Kahn, Coppélia. "Self and Eros in *Venus and Adonis*." *Centennial Review* 20.4 (1976): 351–371; reprinted in Kolin, 181–202. Reads the poem in psychological terms "as a dramatization of narcissism—self-love in the form of withdrawal from others into the self" (352). Adonis must choose between sex with Venus, which signifies his entry into manhood, and the isolation of narcissism, which leads to his death.

Kolin, Philip C., ed. *"Venus and Adonis": Critical Essays*. New York: Garland, 1997. The first section is a review: "Venus and/or Adonis among Critics." The second part is a selection of criticism from Coleridge to Catherine Belsey. "*Venus and Adonis* in Production" forms the third part, and the fourth is "New Essays on *"Venus and Adonis."* Finally, Kolin provides a chronological bibliography of scholarship, including editions and reviews.

Mortimer, Anthony. *Variable Passions: A Reading of Shakespeare's "Venus and Adonis."* New York: AMS P, 2000. The erotic conflict will go on because "Venus sees no difference between lust and love; Adonis refuses to recognize the continuities between them" (32). They are both absolutes; in their rigid domains, sexuality and chastity belong in opposite camps that will not come together.

Roe, John, ed. *The Poems*. New Cambridge Shakespeare. Cambridge: Cambridge UP, 1992. Provides an introduction and a discussion of problems of dating and text.

Rollins, Hyder Edward, ed. *The Poems: A New Variorum Edition of Shakespeare*. Philadelphia: Lippincott, 1938. An edition that includes an exhaustive record of commentaries on the poems until the 1930s in addition to discussions of composition date, text, and sources of *Venus and Adonis*.

# The Rape of Lucrece

### Bruce E. Brandt

## PROSE PARAPHRASE

**Lines 1–126: Tarquin comes to Collatium to rape Lucrece.** Tarquin gallops in haste from the Roman siege of Ardea to Collatium, where he intends to rape Lucrece. The night before, in Tarquin's tent at the Roman camp, Lucrece's husband, Collatine, had been boasting about his wife and thereby foolishly calling attention to her chastity and beauty. Perhaps, the narrator suggests, Lucrece's reputation for chastity makes Tarquin desire her; or perhaps Tarquin, the son of a king, is envious that one less nobly born should be married to such a peerless woman. Or perhaps some other wrongful thought has spurred him on. When he reaches Collatium, Tarquin is welcomed by Lucrece, whose virtue and beauty are evident in the blushes that color her white cheeks, and Tarquin finds her even more attractive than her husband had claimed. Tarquin's behavior seems appropriate, and the innocent Lucrece cannot read his intentions in his eyes. To Lucrece's delight, he praises Collatine's military prowess and makes excuses for coming to Collatium. After supper and a long conversation with Lucrece, Tarquin is shown to a bedroom. However, his troubled mind does not allow him to sleep.

**Lines 127–161: A meditation on the consequences of desire.** Tarquin lies in bed thinking about the dangers of going through with the rape, and although the faint hope that he might successfully woo Lucrece argues against the use of force, he remains resolved. The narrator comments that the fear of not obtaining what one wants may drive one on, that great rewards cause one to ignore the risk of death, and that covetousness may cost one more than one gains. Everyone desires honor, wealth, and ease of life in old age, but these goals may conflict, as when we risk life for honor on the battlefield, or sacrifice honor for wealth, or find that pursuing wealth leads to death. In doing evil we abandon what we are for the things we expect to obtain, and through always wanting more we foolishly neglect and lose what we already have. This is the risk that Tarquin now takes, sacrificing his honor to satisfy his lust. How can he expect truth from others if he is not true to himself?

How can he expect a stranger to live justly when he betrays himself and lays himself open to slander and unhappiness?

**Lines 162–302: Tarquin hesitates, but resolves to proceed.** The dead of night comes, when the benevolent stars shed no light, and the only sounds are the death-threatening cries of owls and wolves hunting the defenseless lambs. Pure thoughts are asleep, but lust and murder are awake. Tarquin leaps from his bed and throws his cloak over his arm. He is torn between desire and fear, but desire wins out. Creating sparks by striking his sword against a flint, Tarquin lights a torch and says that he will force Lucrece to his desire just as he forced fire from the flint. Pale with fear, he then thinks about the dangerous consequences of his intended rape and rebukes himself for his unjust thoughts. He asks the torch to extinguish itself and not contribute to the darkening of Lucrece's light, and he tells his unholy thoughts to die before they lead to blotting Lucrece's purity. He considers that humanity abhors such a deed and that it will dishonor his knighthood and his family. He argues that a valiant man should not be a slave to love, that the shame will outlive his own life, and that winning such a fleeting prize is not worth the cost in the long run. He thinks about what Collatine would do if he were aware of the danger to his wife and asks himself what excuse he could possibly offer. Collatine has never wronged him and is his kinsman and friend. He could beg Lucrece for her love, but he knows she is not free to respond as he wants. However, his desire remains stronger than his reason, and thinking of Lucrece's beauty, he dismisses his fears and seeks Lucrece's bed.

**Lines 302–365: Tarquin goes to Lucrece's bedroom.** As Tarquin forces open the locks on the doors that stand between him and Lucrece's bedroom, they creak in rebuke. The household weasels (kept to catch rats) shriek at him, the wind tries to extinguish his torch, and a pin in one of Lucrece's gloves pricks his finger, but these events do not deter him. He interprets them as tests of his resolve rather than as bad omens. When he reaches Lucrece's door, his impiety has so changed him that he actually begins to pray for the success of his rape before he abruptly recalls that the heavens abhor such acts. He then claims Love and Fortune for his gods and denies that there will be lasting consequences for his sin.

**Lines 365–743: Tarquin rapes Lucrece.** Tarquin enters Lucrece's bedroom, draws back the bed curtains, and is dazzled by her beauty. His gaze lingers on her hands, her lips, her closed eyes, her hair, and her breasts. He touches her breast, and she fearfully awakes. He tells her that he is going to rape her because of her beauty, that he knows the consequences of his action, and that he will not be deterred. Holding up his sword, he says that if she denies him, he will kill her and one of her slaves and claim that he found them in bed together, thus destroying her family's reputation. However, if she acquiesces, he says that no one will ever know. Lucrece pleads with him, urging that he consider her hospitality, his friendship with her husband, his own princely name, the love of his subjects, and the authority that God has given him. He tells her to stop, but she continues pleading. He then puts out his torch and rapes her. Immediately afterward, Tarquin is overcome by guilt and departs.

**Lines 743–1022: Lucrece rails against Night, Opportunity, and Time.** The distraught Lucrece prays for day never to come since she can not dissemble her feelings and her disgrace will be revealed. She attacks Night as a time of tragedies, sins, and death and asks it to obscure the coming day with its mists since it is guilty of the crime against her. She says that if Tarquin were Night rather than Night's child, he would defile the moon and stars, giving her copartners in her grief. However, she feels alone in her sorrow and fears that she will become the subject of talk and gossip once the coming day makes evident the breach of her chastity. Moreover, she reflects that if her reputation is doubted, then Collatine's reputation will also be questioned. If Collatine's honor lay in her, it has been stolen, and she feels guilty for having welcomed Tarquin, even though she did it for Collatine's sake. Thinking about how evil can hide within an apparent good, Lucrece then complains against Opportunity for providing the occasion for sin and suffering. She next attacks Time for allowing Opportunity to rob her of the hours that Time had allotted her. She prays, though, that Time will punish Tarquin, causing him to live in sorrow and poverty, to see his friends become his foes, and to run mad and seek to kill himself. Tarquin's baseness is even greater, she argues, because he is the son of a king.

**Lines 1023–1358: Lucrece resolves to kill herself, but sends for her husband first.** Ending her tirade as fruitless, Lucrece concludes that the only way to preserve her honor is to kill herself. When Tarquin threatened her, she had wanted to live, but now all that she had wanted to live for has been taken from her. Her death will prevent slander and protect Collatine from the ignomy of a bastard child and the mockery of Tarquin. Dawn has now come, but Lucrece wishes it were still dark. Everything she sees aggravates her grief, and the mirth of the morning birdsongs disturbs her. She desires instead the song of the nightingale, thus identifying herself with Philomela, who was transformed into the nightingale after her rape by Tereus.

Then, like a frightened deer that does not know which way to flee, Lucrece debates her decision to commit suicide. Would killing herself add to her soul's pollution? Both body and soul had been dear to heaven and to Collatine. However, her soul will now wither like a pine tree whose bark has been pulled away, so freeing it from its sacked and corrupted bodily dwelling place would not be sinful. But before she dies, Lucrece will reveal the reason for her death to Collatine so that he can vow revenge on Tarquin. In language reminiscent of a last will and testament, she says that she will bequeath her stained blood to Tarquin, her honor to her knife (for in dying her honor will be reborn out of the ashes of her shame), and her resolution to Collatine, so that from the example of her death he will learn to kill Tarquin. Her blood will thus wash away the slander of her rape. Lucrece then calls for her maid, who does not dare to ask why she is crying, but begins to weep in sympathy for her. The narrator comments that women often weep in response to another's grief because their minds are more impressionable than men's and their natures are more open.

After they have wept together for a considerable time, Lucrece tells the maid that her tears cannot help her. She ascertains that Tarquin has departed but refuses to tell her maid what has happened. She writes a letter to her husband asking him to come from Ardea immediately. When the servant who will deliver the letter blushes from humility and his sense of duty, Lucrece misreads his blush and feels certain that her shame is known.

**Lines 1359–1582: Lucrece contemplates a picture of the siege of Troy.** During her tedious wait, Lucrece calls to mind a detailed painting of the siege of Troy. It shows the eyes of dying soldiers and grieving wives, Greek soldiers digging trenches, and Trojans peering out at the Greeks. One can see brave commanders and pale cowards. The face of Ajax reveals his rage, while Ulysses shows his wisdom and self-control. One can see Nestor encouraging a crowded throng of Greeks to fight. Many things are imaginatively suggested by details. For example, the image of Achilles is evoked solely by his hand and spear. Hopeful and fearful, Trojan mothers stand on the wall and watch the bloody battle taking place between the Dardanian shore and the banks of the Simois (a battle imitated by the waves). Lucrece has come to this picture to find the distressed and grieving face of Hecuba, to whom she compares her own woes. Feeling that the artist has wronged Hecuba by depicting her face but giving her no tongue, Lucrece says that she will speak for her, railing against Pyrrhus and scratching out the faces of her Grecian enemies with her knife. She offers to mar the beauty of Helen, the strumpet who caused the war, and asks why the lust of Paris should have led to the destruction of so many. Lucrece then finds the image of Sinon, the betrayer of Troy. His honest appearance gives no sign of his inner treachery, and Lucrece at first objects that such guile could not lurk in a man with such a face. But thinking of Tarquin, she decides that the painting is right. Priam was beguiled just as she was. Enraged, she tears the image of Sinon, but then collects herself. Lucrece's emotions thus ebb and flow as she loses her own sorrow in thinking of the sorrow of others.

**Lines 1583–1729: Lucrece's suicide.** When the messenger returns with Collatine and other Roman nobles, they find Lucrece wearing black mourning garments, and her tear-stained eyes threaten more weeping. Collatine is at first struck speechless but finally takes her hand and asks her to share her grief so that they can help her. Sighing sorrowfully, Lucrece tells her husband she has been violated in their own bed. She describes the rapist's threat to kill her along with a slave and claim that the two had been taken in adultery, thus destroying her reputation. The rapist had commanded her silence and told her that her own beauty was to blame. However, Lucrece emphasizes that her mind has remained pure even though her body has been defiled. Collatine is struck silent as grief and anger war within him. Seeing his turmoil, Lucrece says that his sorrow adds to hers, and that what she wants from him is not tears, but revenge. Before she will name the rapist, Lucrece demands that the other Romans also swear to avenge her, which they do. Continuing, she asks how such a stain can be wiped away, and the men all respond that her pure mind is what counts. But she insists that no future woman will be able to refer to Lucrece to excuse unchaste deeds. Then, with some difficulty, Lucrece finally speaks the name of Tarquin. Saying that he is responsible for her death, she plunges a knife into her breast, and her soul is released from her body.

**Lines 1730–1855: Lucrece is revenged.** The Roman nobles stand amazed until Lucrece's father Lucretius throws himself on her body and Brutus pulls the knife from her breast. The blood bubbling forth divides into two streams, one red and pure and one black and stained. Her father cries out that children ought not to die before their parents, and Collatine then falls upon the body, almost appearing to die himself until his manly shame bids him live to pursue revenge. He cannot speak coherently because of his emotion. Weeping vigorously, Lucretius and Collatine begin to outdo each other in their clamorous grieving. This sight prompts Brutus to put aside his disguise of foolishness, and he assumes a new dignity. He tells Collatine that weeping is no revenge, and asks him to kneel with him and invoke the gods. Swearing by the Capitol, Lucrece's chaste blood, heaven's sun, their rights as Romans, and Lucrece's soul, he kisses the knife that killed her and vows revenge.

He urges the others to join him, and they drop to their knees and repeat the vow. They then carry Lucrece's bleeding body through Rome to show what Tarquin has done, and the Romans consent to his banishment.

## COMPOSITION AND PUBLICATION HISTORY

*The Rape of Lucrece* clearly appears to be the "graver labor" that Shakespeare had promised to write for the Earl of Southampton in the dedication to *Venus and Adonis* in 1593, which means that *Lucrece* was written between then and 1594, when it was first published. Shakespeare's focus on narrative poetry during this time may be related to the closing of the theaters from June 1592 to May 1594 because of plague. The 1594 edition was carefully printed, most likely directly from Shakespeare's manuscript, by Richard Field, who also printed *Venus and Adonis*. Since printers at that time made corrections while printing was in progress, there are some minor variations among the eleven surviving copies (some imperfect) of this edition. Though not as popular as *Venus and Adonis*, *Lucrece* was quite successful, being reprinted five times in Shakespeare's lifetime and three more times by 1655. None of the changes in any later edition derive from Shakespeare. Interestingly, the original title page read simply *Lucrece*, but the use of *The Rape of Lucrece* in the heading at the beginning of the text and as the running title printed at the top of each page suggests that the longer title may be what appeared in Shakespeare's manuscript. The sixth edition changed the title page to *The Rape of Lucrece*.

## LITERARY ANTECEDENTS AND SOURCES

The ancient story of Lucretia's (Lucrece's) rape and its consequences is an etiological myth explaining the origins of the Roman Republic in the same way that the story of Aeneas or Romulus and Remus may be said to explain the foundation of Rome. The surviving classical versions of the story vary in their details, and all were written centuries after the actual founding of the Republic. Literary polishing and the incorporation of folkloric elements into the legend had already long obscured whatever factual basis it may have had, if indeed, there ever was any. For Romans such as Ovid and Livy, the myth embodied important truths about kingship, wifely duty, and political liberty; Lucretia's suicide was considered heroic. However, as Ian Donaldson has shown, the myth has been transformed greatly over the centuries by changing ideas about suicide, heroism, and government. The resulting literature, art, and intellectual concepts are far too numerous to explore here, but a major turning point in the way Lucrece was understood is found in St. Augustine's *The City of God*, written in the fifth century. Opposed to suicide, Augustine argues that if Lucrece were truly chaste she should not have killed herself and then suggests that she might have killed herself from guilt because she had adulterously consented to Tarquin.

Shakespeare's *Lucrece* primarily follows Ovid's *Fasti* (2.721–852), which he very likely knew from the edition of Paulus Marsus, whose commentary includes the relevant portions of Livy's *History of Rome* and of the Greek historian Dionysus Halicarnassus. He may, of course, also have read Livy's *History of Rome* (1.57–59) in some other edition, and he may have known the translation in Painter's *The Palace of Pleasure*. Additionally, he appears to have known Chaucer's depiction of Lucrece in

*The Legend of Good Women*, and Gower's translation of Ovid's *Fasti* has been suggested as a source. Details in the painting of the Trojan War derive from the first two books of *The Aeneid* and book 13 of Ovid's *Metamorphoses*.

## DEVICES AND TECHNIQUES

Shakespeare's Lucrece has far more to say, and says it far more eloquently, than in any previous version of the myth. The poem belongs to the literary genre known as the complaint, which had become particularly popular in the 1590s. Indeed, six other complaint poems appeared in the two years immediately prior to the publication of *The Rape of Lucrece*. One of these, Samuel Daniel's *The Complaint of Rosamund* (1592), has been shown by verbal parallels to have been an influence on Shakespeare. Both poems use rhyme royal, a seven-line iambic pentameter stanza rhyming ababbcc. This was the stanza Chaucer used in *Troilus and Criseyde*, and in Shakespeare's time it was seen as an appropriate choice for serious and tragic topics.

## THEMES AND MEANINGS

Interpretation of *The Rape of Lucrece* is complicated by questions concerning the relationship of the Argument to the poem. An Argument usually abstracts or summarizes the actual contents of the poem that it introduces, but *Lucrece*'s Argument briefly describes the overall story of the Tarquins' seizure of power in Rome and their loss of this power as a consequence of Sextus Tarquinius's rape of Lucrece. It thus provides the necessary background for understanding Shakespeare's poem, but it mentions events that Shakespeare does not include in the poem itself, or to which he only very briefly alludes, and it says nothing about matters that occupy a large part of the poem. Moreover, in some details the Argument follows Livy's account of events while the poem reflects Ovid's version of those details. Various explanations have been suggested, ranging from the possibility that someone other than Shakespeare added the prose Argument when the poem was being printed to the possibility that Shakespeare deliberately wanted his readers to grapple with differing versions of the story. The fundamental point is that the decisions one makes about the relationship between the poem and its larger, traditional context as embodied in the Argument affect one's understanding of how to read the poem, as is evident in the two main areas of discussion in current criticism.

One major area of debate over the meaning of *The Rape of Lucrece* has been the degree to which it embodies or responds to ideas about republican government. Livy, whose position is largely summarized in the Argument, strongly endorses the republican form of government that resulted from the expulsion of the Tarquins. However, the details of the Tarquins' seizure of power are omitted from the poem, and the end of the poem refers only to the banishment of Tarquin himself, and not to the subsequent establishment of the Republic. Some critics have felt that Shakespeare has thus chosen to exclude the political dimension of the myth, while others are certain that he is highly interested in the political issues that it raises.

The gender politics of the poem have been an even more prolific area of discussion in recent criticism. Nancy Vickers's influential study of Lucrece also invokes the Argument-poem dichotomy. She argues that the poem's omission of the first visit to Rome (which is included in the Argument) significantly alters the story, making Tarquin's initial incitement to rape depend on what he has heard about Lucrece rather than on his visual impression of her beauty. Thus, the poem emphasizes the power of language. Other studies focusing on gender explore Lucrece's assumption that she is the embodiment of her husband's and family's honor, the sixteenth-century understanding of rape and consent, and female subjectivity. For Vickers and many others, Lucrece is a passive victim of patriarchal values, and has no voice of her own. However, for Philippa Berry, Lucrece consciously and deliberately takes control of her fate by setting into motion the revenge that will lead to the establishment of the Republic.

## THE RELATIONSHIP OF THE POEM TO SHAKESPEARE'S OTHER WORKS

Written within a year of each other, *Venus and Adonis* and *The Rape of Lucrece* clearly invite comparison. Despite their differences in tone and subject matter, both poems place great emphasis on the display of eloquence and rhetorical ornamentation, both explore questions of gender and power, and both are creative expansions of material taken from Ovid.

Shakespeare's use of Ovid in the narrative poems is not surprising, for Ovid animates the entirety of Shakespeare's canon. Not only do an overwhelming majority of Shakespeare's mythological allusions come from Ovid, but as Jonathan Bate has demonstrated, Shakespeare's use of Ovid remains profoundly creative from the early comedies through the Romances at the end of his career.

Shakespeare explores issues of gender and power from a number of perspectives, including the farcical violence of *The Taming of the Shrew* and the cross-dressing heroines of the festive comedies. Violence against women can be seen in Othello's murder of Desdemona and in the sexual demands made by Angelo in *Measure for Measure*. Rape is threatened but averted in *The Two Gentlemen of Verona*. The only rape outside of *Lucrece* occurs in *Titus Andronicus*, where the Philomela and Hecuba imagery invoked by Lucrece is used to describe Lavinia. However, Iachimo's violation of the sleeping Imogen's privacy in *Cymbeline* constitutes a kind of psychological rape, and Iachimo's intrusion into her bedchamber (where she had been reading the tale of Tereus) and his careful noting of the mole on her breast are reminiscent of Tarquin's entrance into Lucrece's bedchamber.

The Roman setting of *Lucrece* also continued to interest Shakespeare, who went on to write three plays based closely on Roman history: *Julius Caesar, Antony and Cleopatra*, and *Coriolanus*. More generally, critics have often felt that Lucrece and Tarquin are precursors of Shakespeare's later tragic characters. The most sweeping claim for *The Rape of Lucrece*'s importance as a turning point in Shakespeare's development as a dramatic artist is Harold R. Walley's argument that in the process of writing the poem Shakespeare systematically worked out a dramatic methodology that affected his entire subsequent treatment of tragedy. A similar but more specific argument is Mary Jo Kietzman's suggestion that Shakespeare's self-conscious use of the complaint to display a character's mental life in *Lucrece* parallels his use of the soliloquy to depict Hamlet's inner life. Many critics have also seen a parallel between Tarquin and Macbeth in their deliberate choice of evil.

**Annotated Bibliography**

Bate, Jonathan. *Shakespeare and Ovid.* Oxford: Oxford UP, 1993. Bate provides a comprehensive overview of the sophisticated and innovative ways in which Shakespeare used and transformed the works of Ovid, his favorite poet. Chapter 2 focuses on *Venus and Adonis* and *The Rape of Lucrece.*

Berry, Philippa. "Woman, Language, and History in *The Rape of Lucrece.*" *Shakespeare Survey* 44 (1991): 33–39. In contrast to Vickers, Berry argues that Lucrece is not a passive victim, but that through language she becomes a shaper of history.

Bromley, Laura G. "Lucrece's Re-Creation." *Shakespeare Quarterly* 34 (1983): 200–211. Bromley notes that although modern readers find it difficult to accept Lucrece's suicide as a response to rape, Lucrece and her society would have believed that the effects of rape were permanently corrupting. She then shows that Lucrece is not a passive woman whose death is imposed upon her by patriarchal attitudes, but a powerful and independent person who resists evil through an act that will lead to the overthrow of tyranny.

Bullough, Geoffrey. *Narrative and Dramatic Sources of Shakespeare.* Vol. 1. London: Routledge and Kegan Paul, 1964. Bullough conveniently reprints the texts of Shakespeare's major sources. Volume 1 contains the sources for *Lucrece.*

Burrow, Colin, ed. *The Complete Sonnets and Poems.* The Oxford Shakespeare. Oxford: Oxford UP, 2002. Burrow's introduction to *Lucrece* includes insightful discussions of Shakespeare's engagement with his sources, the contemporary political implications of Shakespeare's poem, its explorations of the difficulties of reading texts and people, and the legal understanding of rape and consent in Elizabethan England.

Donaldson, Ian. *The Rapes of Lucretia: A Myth and Its Transformations.* Oxford: Oxford UP, 1982. Donaldson explores the evolution of the story of Lucretia from Roman times to our own, looking particularly at how changes in the way the story is depicted in art, literature, and the history of ideas reflect changing ideas about suicide, republicanism, and heroism. Chapter 3 focuses on Shakespeare's *Lucrece.*

Kietzman, Mary Jo. "'What Is Hecuba to Him or [S]he to Hecuba?': Lucrece's Complaint and Shakespearean Poetic Agency." *Modern Philology* 97 (1999): 21–45. Kietzman discusses the relationship between *The Rape of Lucrece* and *Hamlet,* focusing on Shakespeare's use of the complaint mode to dramatize "the sheer complexity and the agonizing difficulty of choosing who to be and how to act" (22).

Stimpson, Catharine R. "Shakespeare and the Soil of Rape." In *The Woman's Part: Feminist Criticism of Shakespeare.* Ed. Carolyn Ruth Swift Lenz, Gayle Greene, and Carol Thomas Neely. Urbana: U of Illinois P, 1983. 56–64. Stimpson argues that "Shakespeare's sympathy toward women helps to create an attitude that is more generous and less foolish than that of many of our contemporaries" (56). He looks shrewdly at the psychological reasons that lead some men to rape and is acutely sensitive to the agony felt by women who have been raped.

Vickers, Nancy. "'The blazon of sweet beauty's best': Shakespeare's *Lucrece.*" In *Shakespeare and the Question of Theory.* Ed. Patricia Parker and Geoffrey Hartman. New York: Methuen, 1985. 95–115. Vickers finds that Shakespeare's omission of the previous visit mentioned in the sources is significant since it means that Tarquin's initial decision to rape Lucrece is based solely on what he has heard and not on a visual impression of her beauty. Lucrece's rape, and indeed the entirety of her role as a woman in this patriarchal system, is determined by contending male rhetoric.

Walley, Harold R. "*The Rape of Lucrece* and Shakespearean Tragedy." *PMLA* 76 (1961): 480–487. Walley argues that in the process of writing *Lucrece* Shakespeare systematically worked out his characteristic dramatic method and his entire subsequent treatment of tragedy.

# The Phoenix and Turtle

## Nicholas Birns

### PROSE PARAPHRASE

Let the bird who sings the loudest, the one who sits on the lone tree in Arabia, sing. Let him sing the sad but decorous song that serenely rallies all the other birds to come to the funeral. But the screech owl, a bird that exhibits devilish hostility and is a kind of figure of death, shall not approach this celebration. Nor shall all the birds who like to dominate other birds be allowed, except the eagle, whose kingly station merits admission. The swan will be the priest, because his white feathers are like the white robes of a priest. The swan has the right to officiate at the funeral and to preside over the funeral music that is played there. The black crow, which lives three times as long as the other birds, and like the phoenix can reproduce itself though its breath (that can both bestow life and wipe it out), also has a right to be there because of these unusual properties.

Let the funeral song begin! The mutual devotion exemplified by the two birds, the phoenix and turtle-dove, is gone because they are gone. Their love was so intense, bestowed such concord, that their individuality was erased. Love made them one compound thing. Even when they were far apart in geographical space, their love provided such a connection that it seemed that there was no distance between them. For each other, the phoenix and turtle-dove were not separate beings. When they looked into each other's eyes, they saw themselves. Our customary ideas of personhood, of one being as a distinct entity, are breached. Neither one being nor two, through the closeness of their union the phoenix and turtle-dove presented a challenge to rational thought. If either the phoenix or turtle were to be alone, each would lose its identity. The more complicated state was, for them, the preferable one. Their relationship shows the superiority of love over mere reason. Because reason was so impressed by love, it composed this dirge for the dead lovers: All singular and extraordinary beauty is here in ashes. All they once had, and all they once were, is now simply part of death. They left no children, not because they were physically unable, but because their marriage was about constancy of heart and not mere sexuality. Without the phoenix and turtle-dove living among us, we can have neither genuine truth nor genuine beauty. There may still seem to be truth and beauty in our world, but these are imposters. If you seek truth or beauty, you must go to the urn where the mingled ashes of the two birds lie. Pray for these birds and remember the faithfulness of their love.

## COMPOSITION AND PUBLICATION HISTORY

Shakespeare's poem was originally included in an anthology, *Love's Martyr, or Rosalin's Complaint*, compiled by Robert Chester in 1601. The anthology was dedicated to John Salusbury (spelled Salisbury in many historical records, but Salusbury in the text itself). Salusbury was an aristocratic landowner whose seat was at Lleweny (Lleweni) in Denbighshire in North Wales. Through his mother, Katharine Tudor, Salusbury was distantly related to the ruling Tudor dynasty. He was active in the politics of the day and at one point was a member of Parliament. Robert Chester, not judged by scholars to be someone of great literary talent, wrote most of the anthology. Importantly, it was not really a "vanity" piece since the collection was designed to honor John Salusbury, not Chester himself. Chester compiled the anthology presumably to celebrate Salusbury's love for his wife, Ursula Stanley, an illegitimate daughter of the Earl of Derby. (Shakespeare had some interaction with the Stanley family earlier in his career. He is thought to have written verses on the Stanley tomb at Tong, prompting speculation that this was one of the reasons he was asked to contribute.) Presumably, the poem was commissioned by Chester for this anthology, in which it appears on pages Z3v–4v. The anthology is large and contains many lengthy, allegorical and complex works, dwarfing Shakespeare's grave, soft-spoken lament in size, though not coming near it in majesty. Chester attempted to get the most prominent and successful of his contemporaries to contribute: George Chapman, Ben Jonson, and John Marston. The first of these was famed as a poet and translator of Homer as well as dramatist. Jonson was a lyric poet as well as a comic and, with less success, tragic, dramatist. Marston, who concentrated his energies mainly in drama, is known for his dark comedies and tragedies of London life. All of the poems in the anthology were more or less produced on demand. So there are dangers in attributing any direct personal or biographical emotions felt by their creators to these pieces. Indeed, *The Phoenix and Turtle* is one of the great "anonymous" poems of the English language. It is one of those poems, like Keats's late odes, where the poet seems to have completely transcended the biases and vagaries of personality.

## LITERARY ANTECEDENTS AND SOURCES

The theme of the phoenix and turtle, which serves as the motif of the anthology compiled by Robert Chester in 1601, has a long, if not particularly clear, ancestry. Considering that the story of the phoenix is one of the most famous of legends from ancient times, it is surprising how obscure its genealogy is. Herodotus (fifth century B.C.) is the first Greek author to mention the phoenix. In book 2 of his *Histories* he tells the story of a bird that lives for 500 years and then dies. This bird is replaced by a new phoenix, which preserves the body of the old phoenix in fragrant spices, takes it to its burial site in Arabia, and then returns to Egypt to live for another 500 years. Here we already have the idea of the phoenix's unusual relationship to time, its compound identity, and its Arabian provenance. This last element supplied to the West, and even to Egypt, a sense of exoticism. It also signified associations with fertility springing forth, spontaneously, from otherwise barren desert. This paradoxical fertility underlies the stress on the uniqueness of the tree. It as if the phoenix, of which there is only one at a time, came from the only tree in Arabia.

Herodotus was followed by many other classical authors, including the fourth-century Christian Latin author Lactantius, a writer well-known in the Middle Ages and Renaissance. But the idea of the phoenix that seems to sustain Shakespeare's poem (though never explicitly articulated, and indeed tacitly denied, in it), the vision of the bird dying and then being reborn from its own ashes, does not occur in the very early writings. It is available to us only from as late a writer as the early fifth-century Roman poet Claudian. This image was taken up by the fourteenth-century English writer Sir John Mandeville in his *Travels*, where it either reached Shakespeare directly or through contemporary sources. (It was also used earlier in English poetry in a poem sometimes ascribed to the ninth-century Anglo-Saxon poet Cynewulf, but there is no way for Shakespeare to have known of his work. The Anglo-Saxon poem, like Lactantius's, reworks the phoenix legend into a heavily Christian allegory.)

In contrast to the idea of the phoenix, the turtle-dove imagery, despite its attestation in classical sources, seems to stem largely from the Bible. In the Hebrew Bible, the turtle-dove was one of two birds (the other not being the phoenix, unmentioned in the Bible, but the pigeon) able to be offered in sacrifice. The famous line about the "voice of the turtle" heralding the return of spring in the *Song of Songs* (2.12) associates the turtle with renewal and fertility. The turtle-dove represents renewal in the biological sense much as the phoenix is associated with renewal in a metaphysical sense. (This is another way of saying that the turtle-dove actually exists whereas the phoenix, as far as we know, does not.) Also, during Mary's purification in the New Testament (Luke 2.2) two turtle-doves are sacrificed. This is the source of the line about "two turtle-doves" in the popular English Christmas carol *The Twelve Days of Christmas*. Given that the turtle-dove is largely associated with fertility, and the phoenix is a kind of signal of recovery or temporal change, it is striking to realize that in Shakespeare's poem the phoenix is the female, the turtle-dove the male. This seems, from all evidence, to have been a conceit particularly suggested by Robert Chester. It is also fascinating that the mating of the two birds involves the union of previously very separate biblical and classical traditions of aviary symbolism.

The entire notion of an assemblage of birds mimicking a human collective was a time-hallowed one. It was made famous in English poetry in the fourteenth century by Geoffrey Chaucer's *Parlement of Fowles* and, though this may not have been a direct influence on either Chaucer or Shakespeare, by the medieval Persian poet Farid ud-din Attar's *The Conference of the Birds* (*Mantiqu't-Tair*).

Certainly, the symbolic use of birds as a motif had many precedents in medieval allegories and emblem-books. A Renaissance example of the latter possibly familiar to Shakespeare is Andrea Alciati's *Emblematum liber*. The idea of the individual surrendering his or her identity to a greater whole, even though Shakespeare, in this poem, casts that whole as the perfection of love, also has other embodiments. As A. Kent Hieatt pointed out in writing of the relation of Shakespeare's sonnets to

Edmund Spenser's *Ruines of Rome* (*PMLA* 98 [Ocotober 1983]: 800–814), the immortality promised by the lover to his beloved through poetry is also the kind of immortality that Joachim du Bellay and Spenser deliberately promote as superior to the temporal immortality of the Roman Empire. The merely political version of timelessness is mutable and doomed to crumble and fade, even though memories and ghosts of its power linger.

## DEVICES AND TECHNIQUES

For such a short poem, *The Phoenix and Turtle* is exceedingly complex. Unlike Shakespeare's sonnets, or for that matter his narrative poems, this work is not written in a long-established form. Despite its lyric intensity, there is a dramatic quality to the poem. This is unsurprising. A funeral is a dramatic occasion, with entries, speeches, exits, and with the remains of the deceased being, somewhat incongruously, a prop. So the poem is a kind of lyric three-act drama. There is a proem, where the officiant and audience come in; the actual anthem, a eulogy of the love of the phoenix and turtle-dove; and the lament—*threnos*—to this love. The threnos also operates as an exit or outward procession from the funeral. The players sing it as they leave the stage.

Despite its brevity, the poem has a stately and unhurried tone. It is gravid with emotion, but not bursting with it. But this ceremonial quality does not make it monotonous. The sudden exclamation, "[T]hou shrinking harbinger" (l. 5) is unexpected. The force of the revulsion that is resonant in this injunction against the owl is like a tremor rolling through the poem. We see a show of emotion from within the formal obsequy, and we never forget that this quality is, thus, in reserve for the rest of the poem. If there is deliberate overstatement here, in other words, if the villainy of the owl is being overplayed as in the case of, for instance, a monster in a pageant for children, we see a genial, kindly humor along the baseline of the denunciation. That is to say, the poet in this scenario would be using the owl image not so much to ward off evil as to accentuate the gentle and kindly regard in which he wants readers to hold the entire tableau, to have their sensibilities prepared for the understanding of the unique love of the phoenix and turtle-dove. On the other hand, the owl may not just represent itself but night and, by extension, death, so the force of the execration may be fully justified. There is almost an onomatopoetic aspect to the language here, as the sudden harshness of the language comes near to mimicking the disruptive nature of the owl's hoot.

The rhyme scheme of the quatrains in the proem and anthem—the main part of the poem—bears close scrutiny. It is officially *abba*. But sometimes the two rhyme-sounds are so close to each other that every line-ending has a discernable phonic relation to every other one in the stanza. This can be seen as early as the parallel "lay" / "obey" "tree" / "be" pairings (ll. 1–4). In the eighth stanza, the "n" sound carries over in the "asunder" / "wonder" and "queen" / "seen" rhymes (ll. 29–32). In the following one, the long "i" is held in common by all four rhymewords, "shine," "right," "sight," and "mine" (ll. 33–36). The "n" pattern returns in the penultimate stanza of the anthem with the "twain" / "remain," "one" / "none" rhymes (ll. 45–48).

Some of the primary rhymes, though, might not seem immediately obvious to today's reader. Differences in modern pronunciation mask the rhymes "can" /

"swan" and "together"/ "neither" (ll. 14–15, 42–43). Some of what might be called the "ambient rhymes," the lines that are wrapped around the stanza at beginning and end (the first and fourth lines of the quatrain) verge on doggerel. This is true of "confounded" / "compounded" in lines 41/44 or even "twain" / "remain" in lines 45/48. But the internal couplets that separate these rhymes help shelter them from any sense of silliness. This quality of teasing the limits of rhyme while remaining within proper and accustomed language, if not literally imitating the jagged rhyme scheme of the early sixteenth-century poet John Skelton, does evoke his off-kilter rhythmic sensibility. In the threnos, all three lines of each stanza rhyme with each other. Modern pronunciation affects only a few of these rhymes, such as "rarity" / "simplicity" / "lie" in the first stanza of the threnos (ll. 53–55). The repetition of the rhyme intensifies the dirge-like, compressed quality of the verse. This is so whether the rhyme words are short, as in most stanzas, or multi-syllabic, as in the third with "posterity" / "infirmity" / "chastity" (ll. 59–61). This stanza again testifies to the poem's intermixing of philosophical terms with everyday ones, without making this juxtaposition outlandish or unwieldy. The final two stanzas of the threnos, like the first of the poem as a whole, rely almost entirely on basic monosyllabic words: "urn," "true," "fair," "dead," "birds," "prayer" (ll. 65–67). From the simplest of elements, the poet has assembled a poem the complexity of which has remained a captivatingly impenetrable mystery to readers.

The meter of the poem is seven syllables, thereby technically "catalectic trimeter." This seven-syllable line is a favorite of Shakespeare's for use in songs attributed to characters within plays. For instance, the meter is used in the song "Who Is Silvia" in *The Two Gentlemen of Verona* (4.2.39–53), Ariel's "Full Fathom Five" song in *The Tempest* (1.2.400–409), some of the witches' speeches in *Macbeth*, and some of the speeches of Puck in *A Midsummer Night's Dream*. This meter is at once playful and slightly eerie, less earnest than normal discourse but also possessing a suspended state of relation to reality that enables a more incantatory, even ecstatic resonance. Enhancing this effect is the way that some of the words are sounded out differently than they would be in modern English: for instance, "Arabian" is three syllables, not the four it would be today (l. 2). Similarly, "requiem" has to be two syllables here, not three (l. 16). It is staggering to see how much meaning the poem gets into seven syllables. For instance, "To themselves yet either neither" (l. 43) poses within severe limits the essential dilemma of the possibility of compound identity. When one compares the meter of this poem to the iambic pentameter famous from the plays and sonnets (or to the significantly longer lines used, for instance, by George Chapman in his contribution to the Chester collection), there is a natural feeling of compression. But because, perhaps, these are uncharacteristic forms for Shakespeare, one feels also a fresh quality that is quite different from that of the sonnets, where the argument is advanced through sustained repetition of both theme and form. This poem is a one-time occasion. It is a component of no greater union. Its message is delivered with a power that emanates from its knowledge of its own exclusivity (that is to say, from the author's viewpoint—in the anthology of which it is a part it is merely one reiteration of the theme among many).

Nonetheless, there is a sense of regularity to the rhythm of the poem. We are reassured by this regularity, as funeral chants generate a rhythm whose basic integrity lends a reassurance amid the pain of loss. This regularity heightens the "concordant" (l. 46) quality evinced both in the love of the two birds and the verbal harmony of the poem. The diction is more unusual, even given differences between Shakespeare's language and our own. Most striking is the Englishing of "threnos," the technical term used for the final elegy of the dead pair, in "threne" (l. 49). This word is not found even in most glossaries at the back of collected editions of Shakespeare. But it demonstrates the poet's ingenuity, manifest not only in making the rare word "threne" an integral part of the rhyme-scheme but also in the poet's seamlessly, and in rhyme, making a statement of intent. Shakespeare is one of the first to introduce this technical term, threnody, into English, and he immediately assimilates it as much into that language's spoken register as he can. He is making organic a technical term external to the matter, as opposed to the form, of the poem. At the same time, the poet is announcing to the reader that he is about to write a threnos! This strategy is paralleled in line 21, "Here the anthem doth commence." This line, which ordinarily would be a gloss, like the poetic equivalent of a stage direction, is wound integrally into the poem. In this poem, there are no externals; even the indicators and dividing-markers are firmly part of its rigorous and intricate architecture.

There is also "defunctive" in the fourth stanza. This means funeral music, stately, sad music that is sanctioned by the presence of the swan-priest. But to modern ears it sounds almost comic, due to the greater popularity of the word "defunct" to mean simply expired or no longer operative. Even in Shakespeare's day "defunctive" was a formal way of describing this sort of mournful music. "Harbinger" in the second stanza (l. 5) is also striking. The word is not an uncommon one. But, because the diction in the first stanza is so sparse and severe, it stands out.

As is typical in Shakespeare's poetry, though, the most philosophically complex parts of the poem use simple language to clothe these difficulties. "[T]he self was not the same; / Single nature's double name / Neither two nor one was called" (ll. 38–40). There are multiple meanings in these lines. "Either was the other's mine" (l. 36) can mean that for, say, the phoenix, the turtle was as much "herself" as her own soul and body were. Love has made her other herself. Love has wiped out all boundaries between inside and outside, herself and her husband. It can also mean, by extension, that either one was the consummate possession of the other, the thing about which they each most yearned to say, "This is mine." As A. Alvarez puts it, "mine" can function both as "a concrete metaphor and a grammatical tool" (Alvarez, p. 5). There can even be another meaning: either was the other's "mine" as in a source of minerals, a gold mine, a trove of resources. The lovers found their ultimate resources in each other.

The poem is brief, but its theme, the life and death of love, has endless implications. The poet has put considerable emotion into the poem. This emotion is heightened and made stronger by the way the poem's tightly constructed syntax nonetheless allows all sorts of excursions into eddies of language and meaning. There is a surprising amplitude to the discussion of the metaphysical paradox of two-in-one. The poet seems genuinely delighted, or bemused, by paradox. As Cleanth Brooks puts it, "If the poet is to be true to his poetry, he must call it neither two nor one; the paradox is his only solution." (See Cleanth Brooks, "The Language of Paradox: *The Canonization,*" in *John Donne, A Collection of Critical Essays,* ed. Helen Gardner [Englewood Cliffs, NJ: Prentice-Hall, 1962], 108.) Partially because of this elaboration, the anthem does not quite have the almost measureless emotional reservoir of the proem and threnos. But its intellectual concentration is powerful. This is also true of its word-play. "Property" (l. 38) almost hints at the alternative: impropriety. "Appalled" usually has a negative connotation (ibid.). We have the slight sense that the phoenix and turtle, in the intensity and mutuality of their love, do not only outshine the world, but embarrass it. At the very least, it is a counter-cultural love, waged against normal expectations. The subject is elegiac. But the tone is euphoric and celebratory. The poet is filled with fervor in describing how diminished we are without the love of the phoenix and turtle. The sadness is so formal that the constituent elements in the poem are immersed in it but not overwhelmed. A rhythm of celebration underlies the language and tone of severe tragedy. An inspirational joy parallels the sadness of the poem. Joy is engendered by the poem's sonorous evocation of unadorned mortality. The words "trumpet" and "herald" in line 3 are more commonly associated with announcements of triumph, not lamentation. In many ways, the poem seems a wedding song in a funeral song's body.

## THEMES AND MEANINGS

Many commentators have emphasized the importance of the poem's being called *The Phoenix and Turtle* and not "*The Phoenix and the Turtle*," although today professors and students commonly refer to it as such. (In any event, the title was not applied to the poem until 1807. The 1601 text calls it "The Turtle and Phoenix," and the 2002 Oxford edition of the poem just calls it by its opening lines, "Let the bird of loudest lay," thus evading the issue of the title entirely.) *The Phoenix and Turtle* title emphasizes the unitary nature of the two birds' compound love: the poem is not about two protagonists, but a couple as protagonist, two made into one. The phoenix and turtle become their own new being, given a kind of immanent logic by their love. The very title, it is argued, is integral to the poem's dominant conceit. Excessively scrupulous critics may over-argue this point. But it operates as a salutary reminder of how important the confounding of usual notions of self is to the poem's philosophical essence.

In a poem replete with paradoxes, perhaps the deepest one of all is unarticulated. The loss of the phoenix and turtle-dove is presented as devastating. Yet the tone and import of the poem is nonetheless affirmative. Love and suffering, gain and loss, are, of course, in any human experience, closely intertwined. Weddings and funerals bear a particular resemblance to each other. Both define significant stages of life. Both are large pageants with a massive cast of characters who dress and act with particular ceremony. Both are public acknowledgments of the most primal emotions, those of cherishing another person's presence, or mourning his or her absence.

The line "bird of loudest lay" (l. 1) at the beginning of the proem has excited comment. It seems to refer to the phoenix, especially in the reference to the sole Arabian tree, given the longtime association of the phoenix legend with Arabia (alluded to many times within Chester's collection). But an attentive reading of the poem will yield the question: How can the phoenix serve as herald to her own funeral? How can she survive her own death? Or is this a new phoenix, a regenerated phoenix, as would be true if Shakespeare is following the legend? Does Shakespeare assume the legend and thus not have to explain it to the reader? But if a new phoenix begins the poem, does this not puncture the note of finality in the threnos? And if the chaste wings obey the bird of loudest lay, and that bird is the phoenix, then do not the chaste wings belong to the turtle? But is not the turtle already dead? These are issues of perpetual fascination, and vexation, for critics.

Of all the paradoxes in the poem, "married chastity" has spurred the most debate. There is a potential meaning here. Chastity usually means restraint from sexual activity. In that the phoenix and the turtle leave no offspring, this definition of chastity could be applicable to the marriage of the two birds. But marriage, in this society and in ours, is the one relationship where sexual activity is not only permitted, but encouraged. Given that sexual activity in marriage is sanctioned, is indeed a premise of marriage, the married chastity to which the poem refers could well have been a consummated marital relationship. Even in the most conventional rendition of the phoenix legend the phoenix does not reproduce normally. Hence, the absence of offspring is not the indicator it would be if this legend were not involved.

Still, this poem, unlike the classical phoenix legend, provides no new phoenix to replace the dead one. Why does Shakespeare offer no immortality? The common simile "like a phoenix from the ashes" is a cliché in our culture. Yet Shakespeare, in the most famous literary use of the phoenix image, emphatically does not have the phoenix rise from the ashes. (The image of rising from the ashes does occur when the phoenix is mentioned in the second stanza of "The Canonization," a poem by John Donne, Shakespeare's slightly younger contemporary, with strikingly similar themes, though Donne's poem is not a contribution to the anthology compiled by Chester.) Indeed, there is a curious silence concerning the afterlife in Shakespeare's poem. As with the *Song of Songs* in the Bible, the poem presents erotic passion within a theological context, though the latter is far weaker here. The swan is said to be a priest and wears the appropriate vestments. But nothing that is said in the poem indicates a trust in an afterlife or in a presiding higher power. This omission does not mean that the poem takes a position against these ideas, simply that it does not take a position either way. The swan/priest reference is certainly not sarcastic. It highly values the swan's whiteness and its resemblance to the white vestments of a priest that stand for purity and sanctity. (The fact that the swan's song is usually associated with his own death, and not that of others, seems to be elided by the poem.) The exhortation to prayer at the end of the poem certainly indicates a belief in the efficacy of that prayer. John Marston, in his contribution to the anthology, seems to follow up from Shakespeare by pursuing a transcendental dimension that Shakespeare has not allowed. George Chapman, in contrast, treats the entire conception as comic and preposterous. Shakespeare uses diction that skirts the havoc of nonsense. He manifests an idealism that registers an awareness of ultimate spiritual realities. But Shakespeare disciplines his poem in a way that avoids the obvious psychological allegiance of both alternatives offered by his fellow poetic contributors.

Many commentators have noticed the similarity between the argument of *The Phoenix and Turtle* and that of so-called "metaphysical" love poems by John Donne (1572–1631). In poems like "The Canonization" and "The Extasie" Donne speaks of pairs of lovers who, through love, become one entity. In "The Extasie," for instance, the language of the lovers is described as one in which "both meant, both spake the same." Whether Shakespeare meant to emulate the younger poet's style, whether this idea was just in the air of poetic practice at the time, or whether the resemblance is happenstance is open to continued speculation. But both poets are certainly interested in how love complicates any simple concept of personal identity. Donne seems more interested in the married couple as constituting a kind of syzygy, a yoked being, animated by life and by a shared spirit of love. Shakespeare seems more fascinated by how the very concept of a person, an individual, is annihilated by truly fulfilled love. Shakespeare was a playwright accustomed to juggling the idea of individual character against the backdrop of a preconceived dramatic tableau. So perhaps this side of the question had particular meaning for him. Like Donne, Shakespeare understands the close kinship of love and mortality. The "mutual flame" (l. 24) that overtakes the two lovers, a line made famous by the critic G. Wilson Knight's use of it as the title for his book on visionary and transcendental love in Shakespeare, is a shared death, not a shared love.

One of the most radical positions taken by the poem is its stance on the effect on the world of the death of the couple. It is not just a case of the phoenix and turtle's having died, and the community's mourning their passing. If this were the situation, the occasion would be a tragic loss of two individuals (or, as the case is here, one compound individual). But, as in the aftermath of so many of Shakespeare's tragedies, life would go on afterward. One has only to think of *Romeo and Juliet* and the way the death of Romeo and Juliet, the young married couple, reunites their city and heals its wounds. We might expect a similar kind of healing pathos for the community of birds here. But there is none. The phoenix and turtle serve as ideals of transcendental truth and beauty. But these ideals are no longer instanced in the incarnate world. In fact, truth and beauty, we are told, do not even exist in the strict sense after the death of the couple. Truth and beauty may seem to exist. But they are really not there. They died with the birds. Genuine truth, authentic beauty, are forever gone. The fair (beautiful) and true must go to the urn to derive their fairness or truth, like, to use a modern comparison, an electrical fixture that has to be plugged into an outlet in order to work. This is a radically pessimistic assertion to make in a funeral dirge, which, traditionally, has the twin tasks of lamentation for the death of the dead and reaffirmation of life for the living. Given the brevity of Shakespeare's poem and its situation in an anthology containing poems of far greater optimism, one does not necessarily have to take the poem's pessimism at face value. Even without the context, the poet, through the vigor of his language, expresses a discernible jubilation even in lamenting how bereft we are after the birds' expiration. This tone leavens the pain prescribed by a strict reading of the words. But we cannot escape the fact that the literal level of the poem as we most often read it conveys an irremediable sadness. The "prayer" at the very end, and also the word "repair" do brighten matters a bit (ll. 65, 67). Even though here "repair" literally means just the action of going to the urn for sustenance, it also carries associations of reconstruction and renovation. This second meaning helps tinge the sadness with a positive overtone. But speculations like this are only the result of determined inference on the part of the reader.

The poem eloquently speaks of the absolute sovereignty of love. Love surpasses everything else. It even abolishes the individual personalities of the lovers. Once they have loved each other, neither the phoenix nor the turtle-dove is of any interest individually. But the idea of human identity not being singular but conglomerate also has other implications. For instance, the medieval idea of "the King's two bodies," articulated for the twentieth century in a famous 1957 book of that name by Ernst Kantorowicz, says that the Christian ruler has a body in two senses: his own literal body, which will die and is capable of sin, and his spiritual body, which, as God's anointed and vice-regent, can transcend death and be passed on, intact, to the king's corporeal successor. It is the latter, spiritual body of the King through which God's authority is truly manifest. Sir Frank Kermode has applied this idea to *The Phoenix and Turtle* through the idea of the *aevum*, the intermediate time of the angels that lies between the eternity of God and the mere immediate time of humanity. The phoenix and his love, the turtle-dove, persist on a level of time equivalent to the time of the angels.

A more immediate political interpretation sees the phoenix and turtle-dove as representing Queen Elizabeth I and Robert Devereux, Earl of Essex. Essex as a favorite of the Queen was considered a possible candidate not to succeed the Queen herself, since he was not of the blood royal, but to be regent for whoever would follow her as monarch. Essex was put to death for treason in 1601. Given the inevitable involvement of Salusbury, Chester, and many of the contributing writers with the issues of the day, and given the close temporal contiguity between the foiling of the Essex conspiracy and the compilation of *Love's Martyr*, it is possible to trace various associations of significant or weighted imagery in the poem with the activities of those involved with the anthology. Though these have provided much fodder for scholarly articles, no wholly persuasive connection has been ascertained.

In the *Times Literary Supplement* for April 18, 2003, John Finnis and Patrick Martin propose another contemporary reference, linking the poem to the execution of the Catholic Anne Line together with two priests. Finnis and Martin argue that Anne is the phoenix, her husband, Roger, who lived in exile in France, the turtle-dove. Physically separated, the two remained united in the celebration of the Mass, a conceit echoed in *Cymbeline* 1.3.31–33. On the way to their execution, the two priests, Fathers Mark Brakworth and Roger Fieldcock, sang a motet by William Byrd, punningly alluded to in the poem's first line.

## THE RELATIONSHIP OF THE POEM TO SHAKESPEARE'S OTHER WORKS

The most obvious connection of *The Phoenix and Turtle* to Shakespeare's plays is with *Romeo and Juliet*. In that play we have two lovers becoming one, tragically dying, and serving as an example for the rest. Not only, though, do the different genres and lengths of lyric and drama impose different articulations of love, but the character of the lovers is different. Romeo and Juliet, though their love is genuine and admirable, are too young to know what they are doing. Whether or not attributable to Shakespeare's greater maturity at the time of the writing of *The Phoenix and Turtle*, the view of love here is more complex, even though the tragic outcome is similar. The greater wisdom of *The Phoenix and Turtle* is not due to love's being any more lost; it derives from a greater awareness of just what has been lost.

The *Sonnets* offer a kind of contrast to the poem. Though many of the themes are the same, the idea of mutual, married love is not present in the *Sonnets*, as it is in Spenser's earlier sonnet-sequence, *Amoretti*, because in the sonnets the person whom the speaker loves, in the most spiritual sense, is a man; and when the speaker focuses on a woman he is filled with such profound skepticism about her character as to make marriage impossible. Also, both the Dark Lady and the speaker are apparently married to other people (Sonnet 152). Hence, in the Dark Lady sonnets there is no marriage and not much chastity. But the general ideals of the *Sonnets*, such as love as a paragon of what transcends death, are a common denominator between the sonnet-sequence and Shakespeare's other great lyric poem.

The sonnets are about a persona very close to Shakespeare himself. The narrative poems, *The Rape of Lucrece* and *Venus and Adonis*, are as detached from the individual sensibility of the author as any of the plays. The remaining miscellaneous poems ascribed to Shakespeare often assume conventional poetic stances. Only in *The Phoenix and Turtle* do we see Shakespeare writing on a subject that, presumably, he could have made personal but electing not to do so. This may be the reason that, from the nineteenth century onward, critics have at once seen the poem as an example of pure poetry and fervently sought to situate it in an allegorical or historical context. There is a liberating lack of personality to the poem. Shakespeare has taken what many would have found a burden, executing a poem on a theme completely set by an outside commission, yet finds within that commission potential for an influx of great poetic energy. We sense that the poet is making the material as distant as possible from his own emotions and letting a kind of deep, collective emotion instead occupy the work. The poet, at the end, in effect asks the entire cosmos to mourn for the dead bird-lovers and to pray for their souls. By this time, there has been so much weight put behind what the poem says that the reader unflinchingly finds this plea apt.

Sir Frank Kermode has argued that the two-in-one rhetoric of the poem led to a greater interest in dyads and multiple identities on the part of the writer, yielding the greater richness of language in *Hamlet, Othello, King Lear,* and the late romances. A more tangible common denominator between the poem and much of the later works is a greater interest in ceremony and the emotional catharsis afforded by formalized ritual. We see this sense of the possibilities of ceremony in the conclusion of *The Winter's Tale* and in act 5 of *Henry VIII.* In this latter the praise of the young Princess Elizabeth, later to become Queen, contains, in Archbishop Cranmer's prophecy of what will happen after her death, an image of discontinuous transmission for which the phoenix story once again becomes a fit example:

> Nor shall this peace sleep with her; but as when
> The bird of wonder dies, the maiden phoenix,
> Her ashes new create another heir
> As great in admiration as herself,
> So shall she leave her blessedness to one
> (When heaven shall call her from this cloud of darkness,)
> Who from the sacred ashes of her honor
> Shall star-like rise as great in fame as she was,
> And so stand fix'd. Peace, plenty, love, truth, terror,
> That were the servants to this chosen infant,
> Shall then be his, and like a vine grow to him. (5.4.39–49)

James VI of Scotland (James I of England) was not Elizabeth's son. He was a rather distant relative. He established a new (Stuart) dynasty, not continuing the old (Tudor) one. Given Elizabeth's virginity and lack of an heir of her body and blood, conventional metaphors of succession—such as the idea of a new branch growing from an old tree used in *Cymbeline*—are not suitable in these moving lines. So the new phoenix, which is not the same as the old one, and which cannot exist at the same time as its predecessor (as King James did not live in England as long as the old Queen was alive, but came south to occupy her throne), yet is its true, sole, and legitimate heir, is an apt image. The two-in-one rhetoric might have to do with James's promising to become king of both England and Scotland. Or, given the Welsh associations of the Salusbury family, it might refer to the English crown extending over Wales. This political background might fortify the general understanding that the sense of urgency the poem possesses may have something to do with the succession crisis—or that Shakespeare might have remembered his old poem when writing the later play and seen the applicability of it. But the issue of succession should not necessarily lead to a determinate political reading of the phoenix image, especially since there is no mention of a new phoenix in the poem unless one reads "the bird of loudest lay" at the beginning of the poem (l. 1) as such a reference. Shakespeare may have found the phoenix image of particular pertinence to his late romances (of which *Henry VIII*, despite its historical basis, is one in spirit). The phoenix conveys a sense of miraculous regeneration. It encapsulates how magic can work within ordinary structures to revive seemingly obliterated life. But, on the immediate level, there is no resurrection for Shakespeare's lover in his poem of 1601.

As Kermode notes, the poem was composed close to the time in which *Hamlet* was written. The funeral rites for Ophelia—her being honored with "the bringing home / Of bell and burial" (5.1.233–234) and the catalogue of flowers strewn upon her grave—have some of the incalculable mourning of the obsequies recorded in this poem. The burial song of the supposedly dead Fidele (Imogen) in *Cymbeline* (4.2.258–281) is also a dirge, and written closer in terms of meter (one extra beat per line, making it full tetrameter) to the Phoenix poem, but the mood seems far different.

Some critics have made much of the mention of the phoenix in *The Tempest*, when Sebastian, dismissing Prospero's magic, says, mockingly, that "Now I will believe / That there are unicorns; that in Arabia / There is one tree, the phoenix' throne, one phoenix / At this hour reigning there" (3.3.21–24). The traditional legend of the phoenix, articulated more explicitly (in the idea of there being only one phoenix at any given time) than in *The Phoenix and Turtle*, is dismissed as incredible. Some have concluded that this rejection in *The Tempest* means that Shakespeare, when writing the poem, had fervently believed in the phoenix. Ten years later, when writing the play, he had become skeptical of the phoenix and been convinced of its imaginary status.

This conclusion neglects several factors. First, the line in *The Tempest* is spoken by a character and is not attributable to the dramatist, even if it can be argued that Sebastian's assumption of what is and is not real reflects a consensus. Second, Prospero's magic certainly conjures real effects that work with real consequences on people. So if Sebastain dismisses Prospero's magic (so explicitly likened to Shakespeare's own stagecraft) as unreal, his view of the imaginariness of the phoenix must similarly be qualified. Third, as each work of Shakespeare's is in many ways its own world, Sebastian's opinion may not represent a personal view of Shakespeare's on the phoenix, any more than Brutus's opinion of monarchy in *Julius Caesar* is Shakespeare's own. Finally, no reader of *The Phoenix and Turtle* should conclude that it does not regard the story it is using as a profoundly felt conceit rather than an observed reality. The depth of feeling the poem summons on behalf of the phoenix and turtle is not a consequence of the poet's supposing they actually exist. He is not feeling sorrow on behalf of the birds as empirical entities. He is talking about the death of love as a principle. In order for love to exist as a principle, there must exist beings who love each other. This sense of the principle of love being illustrated symbolically by the birds persists even if the reader chooses to reject the various explicitly allegorical interpretations of the poem. To suppose that Shakespeare believes in the phoenix the way a young child may believe in ghosts or fairies is profoundly to misunderstand the way he uses images in his poetry and plays.

## Annotated Bibliography

Alvarez, A. "Shakespeare's 'The Phoenix and the Turtle.'" In *Interpretations: Essays on Twelve English Poems*. Ed. John Wain. London: Routledge, 1955. 1–16. A close reading that emphasizes the love theme over the spiritual one; a useful corrective to the Wilson Knight book cited below. Praises the poem's "logically and passionately attained sense of proportion."

Broek, R. van Den. *The Myth of the Phoenix, According to Classical and Early Christian Traditions*. Leiden, the Netherlands: E. J. Brill, 1972. Technical and academic discussion of the Phoenix tale. Astonishingly, this book is the only full scholarly discussion of this very well known strand of classical/Christian legend.

Davies, H. Neville. "*The Phoenix and Turtle*: Requiem and Rite." *Review of English Studies: A Quarterly Journal of English Literature and the English Language* 46 (November 1995): 525–530. Analyzes the poem in light of existing funeral liturgies and poems concerning burial rites; aptly notes its ceremonial qualities and the strength of the language that Shakespeare generates from those associations.

Empson, Sir William. "The Phoenix and Turtle." *Essays in Criticism* 16 (1966): 147–153. In a few pages, this most resourceful of twentieth-century literary critics gives basic historical and contextual background, a close reading of the poem, focusing on its rhetorical and metaphysical aspects, and a glimpse of the poem's relations to later ideas of pure poetry and nonsense verse.

Hume, Anthea. "*Love's Martyr*, 'The Phoenix and the Turtle,' and the Aftermath of the Essex Rebellion." *Review of English Studies: A Quarterly Journal of English Literature and the English Language* 40 (February 1989): 48–71. One of the best argued of those studies that presume a link between the poem and the political turmoil and intrigue of the last few years of the Elizabethan era.

Kermode, Sir Frank. *Shakespeare's Language*. New York: Farrar, Straus, and Giroux, 2000. Argues that *The Phoenix and Turtle* heralds a new inwardness made possible by its two-in-one imagery, which is the prerequisite for the linguistic achievement of the later tragedies and romances.

Klause, John. "'The Phoenix and Turtle' in Its Time." In *In the Company of Shakespeare: Essays on English Renaissance Literature in Honor of G. Blakemore Evans*. Ed. Thomas Moisan. Madison, NJ: Fairleigh Dickinson UP, 2002. Less narrowly political than many of the contextual analyses; looks at how the imagery, tone, and field of symbolic reference are all embedded in the poem's late-Elizabethan milieu of production. Klause, who teaches at Hofstra University, is one of the few Americans to write well on the poem. Perhaps the poem's concern with ceremony and symbolism have rendered it more susceptible of interpretation by British sensibilities.

Knight, G. Wilson. *The Mutual Flame: On Shakespeare's Sonnets and "The Phoenix and the Turtle."* London: Methuen, 1955. Fervid, allegorical interpretation of the poem as expressive of a Platonic Christianity. Goes too far in a good direction, but Knight's idiosyncrasy is a valuable quantity when applied to the poem. Knight's use of the title *The Phoenix and the Turtle* has aroused a sizable amount of ire among the more pedantic of Shakespeare scholars.

Matchett, William. *"The Phoenix and Turtle": Shakespeare's Poem and Chester's "Louues Martyr."* The Hague: Mouton, 1965. This book is devoted exclusively to *The Phoenix and Turtle*. Offers an intense close reading of the poem, followed by a consideration of the *Love's Martyr* volume and the contemporary political situations. Matchett concludes, somewhat controversially, that Shakespeare wrote the poem as a supporter of the Essex rebellion with a Roman Catholic agenda.

# The Passionate Pilgrim

## Peter Kanelos

### CONTENTS OF THE ANTHOLOGY

*The Passionate Pilgrim* is part puzzle, part mystery. First appearing in 1599, five to six years after the release of Shakespeare's long narrative poems *Venus and Adonis* (1593) and *The Rape of Lucrece* (1594) and a decade before the publication of his *Sonnets*, this slim volume, bearing Shakespeare's name on its title page, was most certainly not authored in its entirety by Shakespeare. Only five of the twenty poems contained in the first edition can be attributed with confidence to Shakespeare; four of the remaining pieces are without doubt the work of his contemporaries; eleven are of uncertain authorship. Several factors, discussed in further detail below, combined to bring *The Passionate Pilgrim* to the world: an ambitious, and perhaps unscrupulous, publisher, a vogue for sonnet sequences, the popularity of Shakespeare's name, and the loose publication practices of the period. The debate over what to do with this hybrid and elusive work has remained lively for centuries and continues to this day.

Given that Shakespeare did not write the bulk of *The Passionate Pilgrim* and did not endorse its publication, its place in the canon is equivocal. Some editors include it in its entirety in anthologies (the Riverside edition); others publish it partially (the Oxford and Norton editions group the five poems by Shakespeare apart from the eleven of unknown origin, leaving out those that are assuredly by other poets); some choose not to print it at all (the Bevington edition). Yet for those curious about Shakespeare, *The Passionate Pilgrim* does hold value. Three of the poems are also found in *Love's Labor's Lost*, published in quarto form in 1598. Because the verses in *The Passionate Pilgrim* differ in several critical aspects from the "same" poems found in Shakespeare's play, questions emerge about the ways in which Shakespeare incorporated poetry into his dramatic works. Two other pieces in *The Passionate Pilgrim* surface in print later, with significant alterations, as sonnets 138 and 144; the points at which the versions diverge offer insight into Shakespeare's process of writing and revising his poetry and give proof that he had been working on his sonnets for at least a decade. And the sequence as a whole is apparently meant to complement Shakespeare's earlier long poem, *Venus and Adonis*, thus presenting a means to reflect upon that work as well.

The poems by Shakespeare in *The Passionate Pilgrim* appear as numbers 1, 2, 3, 5, and 16. Four sonnets on the theme of Venus and Adonis (numbers 4, 6, 9, and 11) are in all probability from another poet's pen; the likely candidate is Bartholomew Griffin, who is almost certainly the author of number 11. Numbers 8 and 20 were written by Richard Barnfield, appearing in his *Poems: In diuers humors* (1598). Christopher Marlowe is responsible for the first sixteen lines of number 19; it is possible that Sir Walter Raleigh is the author of "Love's Answer," the brief response that concludes this poem; the verses are attributed to him in Izaak Walton's *Complete Angler* (1655). As is evident from this tangle, *The Passionate Pilgrim* is one of the most unorthodox works that we associate with Shakespeare.

## COMPOSITION AND PUBLICATION HISTORY

*The Passionate Pilgrim* was first published in 1599, by William Jaggard. Two copies of the second edition (also published in 1599) are known to exist: one in the Library of Trinity College, Cambridge, the other in the Huntington Library in San Marino, California. The title page of this edition reads: *The Passionate Pilgrim. By W. Shakespeare. At London Printed for W. Iaggard, and are to be sold by W. Leake, at the Greyhound in Paules Churchyard. 1599.* The Victorian poet and critic Algernon Charles Swinburne, holding that Jaggard had committed an act of literary larceny, branded the publisher an "infamous pirate, liar and thief" (*Studies in Prose and Poetry* [London: Chatto & Windus, 1894], 90). Given the irregular publication practices of the Elizabethan era, this allegation may be a bit extreme. It was not uncommon for publishers during the period to gather together assorted poems from various authors and to issue them under a single title. Richard Tottel initiated this practice in 1557 when he brought forth a collection called *Tottel's Miscellany*. The immense popularity of this work spawned many imitators for decades to come. Yet Jaggard took certain liberties with his project that may have pushed the boundaries of propriety.

By 1599, Shakespeare's star had risen. A contemporary critic, Francis Meres, praised him as one of the leading playwrights of the age and confirmed that Shakespeare was also well-regarded as a poet: "the sweet and witty soul of Ovid lives in mellifluous & honey-tongued *Shakespeare*, witness his *Venus and Adonis*, his *Lucrece*, his sugared *Sonnets*" (*Palladis Tamia*, 1598). Jaggard clearly sought to profit from Shakespeare's renown. By claiming that *The Passionate Pilgrim* was the work of Shakespeare and by locating near the front of the collection sonnets that were genuinely his, Jaggard suggested to the book-buying public that his volume contained those "sugared sonnets," which were believed to be circulating in closed circles amongst Shakespeare's intimate friends.

There are at least two credible theories as to the "composition" of *The Passionate Pilgrim*. Poetry in Elizabethan England was regularly a private affair. Poems in manuscript were passed liberally between friends and associates or between poet and patron, with no intention of publication on the part of the author. As these traveled from person to person, they were frequently copied down by an appreciative hand, reduplicating the poems and extending their availability. Collectors would often gather together a number of these loose pieces in commonplace books. The original authors held no definable right over their work, and publishers would frequently print these poems without any acknowledgment given to the poets. It is quite possible that such a commonplace book landed in the hands of Jaggard, and that he, recognizing that some of the poems contained therein were the work of Shakespeare, decided to publish the entire volume under Shakespeare's name. The other possibility is that Jaggard, a struggling young publisher at this time, gathered together this work himself, using the five poems by Shakespeare to lend credibility to a larger design, the crafting of a sequence loosely based on the amorous pursuit of Adonis by the goddess Venus. Although we are uncertain as to the manner in which Jaggard assembled what he would title *The Passionate Pilgrim*, we have no direct record of Shakespeare's complaining about its appearance in print, or of his even acknowledging its existence.

By affixing the Venus and Adonis theme to his collection, Jaggard was manifestly capitalizing on the earlier success of Shakespeare; he attempted to create the impression that these poems were developing further the subject matter of Shakespeare's popular narrative poem. His marketing strategy was made most explicit in 1612, when he brought out a third edition of *The Passionate Pilgrim*. To ensure that the public was aware of what was being offered, the publisher added a supplementary title: *Certaine Amorous Sonnets, betweene Venus and Adonis, newly corrected and augmented. By W. Shakespeare.* Jaggard evidently believed that his readers still retained their appetite for this tale and that Shakespeare's name was still a draw.

Perhaps feeling, however, that *The Passionate Pilgrim* was too slight to justify a new printing, and aware that he could no longer insinuate that these were Shakespeare's "sugared sonnets" (the *Sonnets* having been published in 1609), Jaggard added material to the 1612 edition, almost doubling the volume in length. Among the new poems, several were brazenly lifted from a work that Jaggard had himself published in 1609, *Troia Britannica*, by the popular writer Thomas Heywood. This time, Jaggard's appropriation did not pass without response. Heywood and Jaggard had already been at loggerheads over what Heywood perceived as the shoddy editing and printing of his *Troia Britannica*. The filching of his poems, and their attribution to Shakespeare, was too much for Heywood to endure quietly, and he launched a rebuke. In his *Apology for Actors*, he declared,

> Here likewise, I must necessarily insert a manifest injury done me in that worke, by taking the two Epistles of *Paris* to *Helen*, and *Helen* to *Paris*, and printing them in a lesse volume, under the name of another, which may put the world in opinion I might steale them from him; and hee to doe himselfe right, hath since published them in his owne name: but as I must acknowledge my lines not worth his patronage, under whom he hath publisht them, so the Author I know much offended with M. *Jaggard* (that altogether unknowne to him) presumed to make so bold with his name. (*Apology for Actors*, 1612, in Samuel Schoenbaum, *William Shakespeare: A Documentary Life* [New York: Oxford UP, 1975], 219.)

We have no way to judge whether or not Heywood is reporting Shakespeare's displeasure accurately, but we do know that Jaggard removed the title page from unsold copies of *The Passionate Pilgrim* in 1612 and inserted a new one, from which Shakespeare's name had been stricken. However shady Jaggard's poetic venture may have been, and however much Shakespeare may or may not have been distressed by it, Jaggard's reputation among those who cared about the Bard's work was not permanently blighted. In 1622, at the peak of his career, Jaggard was invited to participate in the publication of the First Folio edition of Shakespeare's plays.

## LITERARY ANTECEDENTS AND SOURCES

Two literary trends merge together in *The Passionate Pilgrim*: a fashion for Ovidian poetry and a lingering demand for sonnets. Publius Ovidius Naso (Ovid) had been one of the leading poets of Augustan Rome. His mythological narratives, focusing on moments of physical, emotional, and spiritual transformation, established him as one of the most glittering literary figures of an already gilded age. His work—witty, sensual, sophisticated—resonated with writers of the Elizabethan period as well. Many of Shakespeare's contemporaries drew upon the tales of Ovid and imitated his open-ended narrative style. In 1589, Thomas Lodge's *Scilla's Metamorphosis* initiated a particular vogue for this form, which would last into the early Jacobean period. The most celebrated example of the Elizabethan epyllion (or "minor epic," as these poems are sometimes categorized) was Christopher Marlowe's *Hero and Leander*, detailing an episode found in Ovid's *Heroides*. Digressing from the original tale, Marlowe's narrative concludes before the drowning of Leander, who is left swimming across the Hellespont to reach his beloved, Hero. By bringing the story to a premature close, Marlowe leaves the reader with a sense of frustration mirroring that of the protagonist and shows that the Elizabethan epyllion could be handled with flexibility and ingenuity.

Shakespeare's immediate source for his *Venus and Adonis* was Arthur Golding's immensely influential translation of Ovid's *Metamorphoses*, first published in 1567, as well as Ovid's *Metamorphoses* in the original Latin. Shakespeare took from Golding's account the basic outline for his story: Venus, struck by her son Cupid's arrows, falls irrevocably in love with the handsome youth, Adonis; she grows concerned over his fondness for hunting, warning him against some of the more savage beasts of the woods; he ignores her admonitions, is slain by a boar, and is subsequently turned by the goddess into a flower, bearing the whiteness of his purity and the purple of his shed blood. Yet Shakespeare drew from at least two other tales in the *Metamorphoses* to add complexity to his story. From Ovid's account of "Echo and Narcissus" he seized upon the notion of a beautiful, self-absorbed young man resisting the advances of an infatuated, persistent goddess. From Ovid's tale of "Hermaphroditus and Salmacis" Shakespeare drew a lusty woman wrestling down the unruly object of her desire, portraying this episode with particular eroticism in his *Venus and Adonis*.

If William Jaggard had his way, the Elizabethan book-buyer, browsing casually over this volume, glancing at the title page and then flipping through the first few poems, would have laid down his or her money for what he or she thought was a sequence of sonnets, authored by Shakespeare, on the racy theme of the goddess of love seducing a mortal boy. Reading the work through, the purchaser would have discovered some rather surprising twists. By recasting the relationship of Venus and Adonis, and specifically Shakespeare's modified version of this relationship, in the shape of a poetic sequence, heavily colored by sonnets and thus by the expectations accompanying this form, *The Passionate Pilgrim* plays with and against the established conventions of the sonnet form: the idealization of a beloved object elides into obsessive desire; the line between pursuer and pursued blurs; a clear demarcation between male and female is lost. Yet *The Passionate Pilgrim* was first and foremost a commercial venture. If it appears to the reader in the guise of a sonnet sequence it is only because the publisher calculated that a sonnet sequence, attached to the name of William Shakespeare, was what the market called for. It does seem serendipitous, however, that many of the conventions challenged, perhaps accidentally, by this collection would be tested again a decade later when Shakespeare's *Sonnets* were finally printed for the public.

## DEVICES AND TECHNIQUES

Given the cobbled nature of *The Passionate Pilgrim*, it is not surprising that the poems exhibit inconsistencies in meter, form, and style. Only nine of the pieces conform to the traditional sonnet structure (1, 2, 3, 4, 5, 6, 8, 9, and 11). Five use the six-line stanza found in Shakespeare's *Venus and Adonis* (7, 10, 13, 14, and 18). Two of the poems are in rhymed couplets with lines of seven-syllables (16 and 20). Three are in varied meters, most likely intended for musical accompaniment (12, 15, and 17). Number 19 is in stanzas of four lines, consisting of two couplets apiece. Because so many hands are at work in this collection, and because the guiding force in assembling these poems was editorial, not artistic, the only consistency in the work appears to be an implied consistency of theme.

## THEMES AND MEANINGS

Although the poems collected in this volume are culled from a variety of sources, they are arranged in a manner that suggests a coherent subject. Numbers 4, 6, 9, and 11 are all explicitly on the theme of Venus and Adonis: Venus courts Adonis unsuccessfully with lascivious embraces and seductive words (4 and 11); the goddess cautions Adonis, who is hunting with his hounds, about a dangerous boar nearby, using her concern as a pretext to reveal her "wounds" to him suggestively (9.13); Venus spies on Adonis as he bathes, lamenting, "why was not I a flood?" (6.14). Scholars have conjectured that the author of these four sonnets is Bartholomew Griffin, based on the grounds that a poem very much like number 11 appears in his work *Fidessa* (1596). The pieces by Shakespeare (1, 2, 3, 5, and 16), and those by other poets not explicitly on this theme, placed in proximity to these poems, read as if they are further reflections upon this mythological tale.

Some assimilate the Venus and Adonis story more easily than others. Number 10 is a lament on the death of a beautiful young friend, compared to a flower "untimely pluck'd" (10.1). Number 18 looks sardonically at the course of seduction. The poems by Shakespeare, however, seem to fit awkwardly into the pattern. Number 1, for example, a near duplicate of Sonnet 138, details the deception and self-deception that sustains a love relationship. A male speaker, whose "years are past the best" (1.6) believes the flattering falsehoods told him by his female lover, even though he is aware that she is lying; this is hardly the voice of a youthful, recalcitrant Adonis. Number 2 (Sonnet 144) echoes the conceit in *Venus and Adonis* that the woman is a temptress and the man the "better angel" (2.3). Yet the speaker is situated precariously between these two figures in a way that seems inconsistent with the youth in the narrative poem, grappling with temptation in a very un-Adonis-like manner. In number 3, the speaker explains that he is eager to break vows abjuring the company of the opposite sex (this is Longueville's sonnet from *Love's Labor's Lost*, 4.3.58–71), but argues that he should be forgiven because he had forsworn women, while his beloved is a "goddess" (3.6); of course, he means this only figuratively. The "divine" status of his lover forms a tenuous link to the next poem, number 4, in which "Sweet Cytherea" (4.1) watches Adonis in the brook. Number 5 returns to the theme of forswearing (another speech from *Love's Labor's Lost*, 4.2.105–118) and to the beloved cast in heavenly terms; it concludes with the couplet, "Celestial as thou art, O, do not love that wrong: / To sing heaven's praise with such an earthly tongue" (5.13–14). In each of the poems by Shakespeare included in *The Passionate Pilgrim*, a link with the story of *Venus and Adonis* can be teased out, but the association is always strained.

The fifth poem by Shakespeare (number 16, from *Love's Labor's Lost*, 4.3.99–118) is printed in the latter part of the collection, and points to another odd feature of *The Passionate Pilgrim*. Following number 14, a page with a supplementary title is found: *Sonnets to sundry notes of Musicke*. The appearance of this page is surprising and enigmatic, suggesting that the remainder of the work is of a distinct character. Number 17 was certainly set to music; it was originally printed in Thomas Weelkes' *Madrigals to 3.4.5 and 6 voyces* (1597). Yet number 12, not included in this section, was also first published as a ballad, appearing in a musical anthology printed in the 1590s. Musical references do abound in the late pieces: "For now my song is ended" (15.16); "All my merry jigs are quite forgot" (17.5); "I fear— / Lest my mistress hear my song" (18.49–50); "Melodious birds sing madrigals" (19.8); "[the nightingale] there sung the dolefull'st ditty" (20.11). The compiler suggests that the final six poems in *The Passionate Pilgrim* are all lyrics to songs. While Shakespeare's poem does not refer explicitly to music, "On a day (alack the day)" can be said to be song-like in its meter. It is tempting to consider that it may have at some point been set to music, perhaps even before it was utilized as Dumaine's sonnet in *Love's Labor's Lost*; tantalizingly, it appears in another miscellany, *England's Helicon* (1600), under the title, "The Passionate Sheepheards Song." Of the five Shakespearean pieces in *The Passionate Pilgrim*, number 16 adheres most closely to the Venus and Adonis theme: Love is personified, the male lover is youthful, and there is reference to an immortal pining for a mortal's love. Yet, as in the other poems, the connections to the mythological story are delicate and can only be inferred.

## THE RELATIONSHIP OF THE POEMS TO SHAKESPEARE'S OTHER WORKS

Situated between the publication of his narrative poems and the release of his *Sonnets* fifteen years later, *The Passionate Pilgrim* helps shed a bit of light on this gray period in Shakespeare's career as a poet. Apparently Shakespeare's reputation as a poet was sufficiently robust during this intermediate time, even though he had not brought out new poems for years, to tempt a publisher to profit from it. Moreover, on the evidence that versions of at least two of his sonnets were then circulating, it also appears that Shakespeare may have not entirely retreated into the world of the theater; we cannot be certain as to how actively he participated in the vibrant exchange of private poetry during this period, but his poems, it seems, did travel. The three poems lifted from *Love's Labor's Lost* also indicate that however much Shakespeare was revered as a dramatist, some appreciative readers turned to the printed texts of his plays then available for the poetry contained therein. Although *The Passionate Pilgrim* is a "Shakespearean" text only in a peripheral and anomalous sense, attending to its intersection with his other works does allow us a broader understanding of Shakespeare and his artistry.

Since the versions of sonnets 138 and 144 printed here differ somewhat from the texts in the 1609 edition, *The Passionate Pilgrim* may offer some insight into Shakespeare's compositional process, though there is no guarantee that the 1599 poems record Shakespeare's words. Still, line 11 in Sonnet 138 reads, "O, love's best habit is in seeming trust." In *The Passionate Pilgrim* this is printed as "O, love's best habit's in a soothing tongue." Similarly, in the 1609 *Sonnets* the poem ends, "Therefore I lie with her, and she with me, / And in our faults by lies we flattered be." The earlier version ends: "Therefore I'll lie with love, and love with me, / Since that our faults in love thus smother'd be."

Sonnet 2 of *The Passionate Pilgrim* is closer to Sonnet 144 (1609), but even here the two texts show minor differences. The 1599 version refers to the Dark Lady's "fair pride," which in 1609 is printed as "foul pride" (l. 8). Line 11 in 1599 reads, "For being both to me, both to each friend," meaning that the fair youth and Dark Lady are friends of the speaker and each other. In 1609 the line appears as "But being both from me, both to each friend," referring to the pair's being physically away from the speaker but not repeating the information already given in line 1 that both are the speaker's "loves." *The Passionate Pilgrim* may be showing us versions of the sonnets that were circulating among Shakespeare's friends in the 1590s and may suggest that these friends were also exchanging and copying not only poems that would be printed in 1609 but also others from the plays. William Jaggard's probable piracy may thus let us join those whom Francis Meres called Shakespeare's "private friends" as they read the latest verses fresh from his quill.

### Annotated Bibliography

Hyland, Peter. *An Introduction to Shakespeare's Poems.* New York: Palgrave Macmillan, 2003. Hyland's discussion of *The Passionate Pilgrim* locates the work in relation to Shakespeare's career as a poet. His chapters on Ovidian poetry and the Elizabethan sonnet tradition are useful.

Lee, Sidney, ed. *The Passionate Pilgrim.* Facsimile of First Edition (1599). Oxford: Clarendon P, 1905. Lee provides an extremely detailed account of the publication history of *The Passionate Pilgrim*, following the complex route a work of this period would have taken on its way toward reaching the public. The facsimile is actually of the second edition; the true first edition was not identified until 1920.

Prince, F. T., ed. *The Arden Shakespeare: The Poems.* Walton-on-Thames, Surrey: Thomas Nelson and Sons, 1998. This edition has impressive notes on each poem, making accessible much of the scholarship on *The Passionate Pilgrim*. There is also a valuable discussion of the physical text and its composition.

Roe, John, ed. *The New Cambridge Shakespeare: The Poems.* Cambridge: Cambridge UP, 1992. Roe argues interestingly that *The Passionate Pilgrim* was not only an attempt to capitalize on the popularity of Shakespeare's *Venus and Adonis*, but that it was also a conscious response to issues raised in that earlier work.

*Shakespeare's Poems: "Venus and Adonis," "Lucrece," "The Passionate Pilgrim," "The Phoenix and the Turtle," "The Sonnets," "A Lover's Complaint."* Published for the Elizabethan Club. New Haven: Yale UP, 1964. This edition reproduces, *inter alia*, the Huntington copy of the 1599 second edition of *The Passionate Pilgrim*. It provides a general introduction to the print history of the poem, portraying William Jaggard in a pointedly negative light.

# Appendix: Shakespeare Resources on the Web

## General Sites

British Broadcasting Company (BBC). *In Search of Shakespeare*. http://www.bbc.co.uk/history/programmes/shakespeare/. Accessed September 2004. Part of BBC's History Web site, giving links to articles on Shakespeare's life, Elizabethan England, and related topics.

Davis, Terry. *Mr. William Shakespeare and the Internet*. http://shakespeare.palomar.edu/. Accessed September 2004. An award-winning, comprehensive and annotated site (and a metasite to other Shakespeare sites on the Web), it provides information on Shakespeare's works, life and times, theater, criticsm, the Renaissance in general, educational resources, links to what Davis believes are the best sites, and more. From the site's introduction: "This is the fourth edition of these pages. . . . My motive in publishing these pages remains to help and stimulate others in Shakespeare studies, and especially those who might contribute their work to the Internet. . . . From the beginning these pages have been an annotated guide to the scholarly Shakespeare resources on the Internet."

*Folger Shakespeare Library*. http://www.folger.edu/Home_02B.html. Accessed September 2004. The Folger Shakespeare Library, established in 1932, is an independent research library located on Capitol Hill in Washington, D.C. According to the site, "The Folger is home to the world's largest collection of Shakespeare's printed works, as well as magnificent collections of other rare Renaissance books and manuscripts on all disciplines—history and politics, theology and exploration, law and the arts. Included in the collections are over 310,000 books and manuscripts; 250,000 playbills; 27,000 paintings, drawings, engravings, and prints; and musical instruments, costumes, and films." In addition, the Folger serves as a museum on Shakespeare and his life and times.

*Internet Movie Database*. http://www.imdb.com. Accessed September 2004. More than 400,000 movie and video titles are catalogued in this well-known Web site, now owned by Amazon.com. It is perhaps the most comprehensive site to search for movies and TV productions based on Shakespeare's work. Plot synopses and full cast and credit information are usually provided as well as links to criticism and other resources.

Liu, Alan, and the English Department at the University of California at Santa Barbara. *The Voice of the Shuttle*. http://vos.ucsb.edu/. Accessed September 2004. An extensive, well-respected metasite of links to humanities resources on the Internet. According to the site, it "models the way the humanities are organized for research and teaching as well as the way they are adapting to social, cultural, and technological changes." By searching under "Shakespeare," users are linked to a large number of sources related to literature, culture, current festivals, college courses, and more.

Massachusetts Institute of Technology (MIT). *The Complete Works of William Shakespeare.* http://the-tech.mit.edu/Shakespeare/. Accessed September 2004. According to the site's description this is the Web's first edition of the Complete Works of William Shakespeare. "This site has offered Shakespeare's plays and poetry to the Internet community since 1993."

Oxquarry Books. *The Amazing Web Site of Shakespeare's Sonnets.* May 31, 2004. http://www.shakespeares-sonnets.com/. Accessed September 2004. This site provides text for all of the sonnets, with descriptive commentary for each. Also included are sonnets by other Elizabethan poets, Spenser, Sidney, Drayton, and a few others; the poems of Sir Thomas Wyatt are also offered.

*Perseus Digital Library Project.* Ed. Gregory R. Crane. September 9, 2004. Tufts University. http://www.perseus.tufts.edu. Accessed September 2004. *Perseus Garner Collection.* Ed. Clifford E. Wulfman. September 9, 2004. Tufts University. http://www.perseus.tufts.edu/cgi-bin/ptext?doc=Perseus%3Atext%3A1999.03.0024. Accessed September 2004. Perseus is an evolving digital library for the study of the humanities. The Perseus Garner Collection is a part of this library, containing primary materials from the English Renaissance and some secondary materials from the nineteenth and early twentieth centuries. Among the Garner materials are the complete works of Shakespeare and some Shakespeare glossaries (by Alexander Dyce and C. T. Onions); the site is in the process of adding Alexander Schmidt's *Shakespeare's Lexicon and Quotation Dictionary*, as well as Hakluyt's navigation texts and the Holinshed *Chronicles*, which are the source of many of Shakespeare plays.

Pressley, J. M. *Shakespeare Resource Center.* http://www.bardweb.net/. Accessed September 2004. Aims to provide useful links to Shakespeare resources on the Web. Includes numerous links and features information on Shakespeare, his works, his will, Elizabethan England, theater companies, and so forth.

Royal Shakespeare Company. http://www.rsc.org.uk/home/index.asp. Accessed September 2004. At the official Web site of the Royal Shakespeare Company (RSC), which performs year-round in Stratford-upon-Avon, London, and throughout the United Kingdom, users can book tickets for RSC productions, tour its archives, and find out more about Shakespeare's life and work. From the site: "Our mission at the RSC is to keep audiences in touch with Shakespeare—understanding his work through today's artists, actors and writers."

Rusche, Harry. Emory University. *Shakespeare Illustrated.* http://www.emory.edu/ENGLISH/classes/Shakespeare_Illustrated/Shakespeare.html. Accessed September 2004. *Shakespeare Illustrated* "explores nineteenth-century paintings, criticism and productions of Shakespeare's plays and their influences on one another" (from the Web site). According to the site, "pictures from Shakespeare accounted for about one fifth—some 2,300—of the total number of literary paintings recorded between 1760 and 1900."

*The Shakespeare Birthplace Trust.* http://www.shakespeare.org.uk/homepage. Accessed September 2004. The Shakespeare Birthplace Trust was started after the purchase of Shakespeare's Birthplace in 1847 in order to preserve it as a national monument. The Trust's main objectives are to promote appreciation of Shakespeare's works; to provide an education department that offers educational activities at all levels; and to promote exhibitions, concerts, and an annual poetry festival as well as special events. It also maintains the five houses, including Shakespeare's birthplace and Anne Hathaway's cottage, owned by Shakespeare family members; a library; and museum.

*Shakespeare's Globe.* http://www.shakespeares-globe.org/. Accessed September 2004. The official Web site of Shakespeare's Globe Theatre, which was torn down in 1644 and not rebuilt until 1996, provides links and resources. The theater is now a playhouse and educational center, "whose goal is to be a unique international resource dedicated to the exploration of Shakespeare's work" (from the Web site).

Ulen, Amy. *Shakespeare High.* http://shakespearehigh.com/. Accessed December 2004. Ulen, a teacher, maintains *Shakespeare High*—a Shakespeare classroom resource center—which provides ideas for teachers and students, including student guides, photos, chat rooms, and more. The site is arranged as a "school," with sections called "Faculty" (resources for teachers), "Students" (study guides and more), "Library" (reference resources), and so forth.

University of Virginia. *Electronic Text Center*. http://etext.lib.virginia.edu/shakespeare/. Accessed September 2004. From the site: "The Electronic Text Center's holdings include a variety of Shakespeare resources that range from early Quartos, the complete 1623 First Folio, and early playhouse promptbooks, to more modern editions and to many bibliographical articles that discuss Shakespeare's works."

Victoria University of the University of Toronto. The Centre for Reformation and Renaissance Studies. *Romeo and Juliet Prompt-Books Databases*. http://www.crrs.ca/publications/electronic/romeo.htm. Accessed September 2004. This site includes two searchable databases containing information from approximately 170 promptbooks for productions of *Romeo and Juliet*, from the seventeenth century to the 1980s. These databases were "assembled by Jill Levenson during the preparation of her Oxford Shakespeare edition of the play" (from the site).

# Selected Bibliography

Students should also consult the bibliographies at the end of the individual discussions.

**Bibliographies**

Champion, Larry. *The Essential Shakespeare: An Annotated Bibliography of Major Modern Studies*. New York: G. K. Hall, 1993.
*Garland Shakespeare Bibliographies*. New York: Garland, 1980–.
Harner, James L., ed. *World Shakespeare Bibliography*. Published annually in *Shakespeare Quarterly*. Baltimore: Johns Hopkins UP, 1950–.
Modern Language Association of America. *MLA International Bibliography*. 1921– (print). 1963– (database).
Rosenblum, Joseph. *Shakespeare: An Annotated Bibliography*. Pasadena, CA: Salem P, 1992.
Wells, Stanley, ed. *Shakespeare: A Bibliographical Guide*. New ed. New York: Oxford UP, 1990.

**Age of Shakespeare**

Bindoff, S. T. *Tudor England*. Harmondsworth, Eng.: Penguin, 1965.
Briggs, Julia. *This Stage-Play World: English Literature and Its Background, 1580–1625*. New York: Oxford UP, 1997.
Byrne, Muriel St. Clare. *Elizabethan Life in Town and Country*. London: Methuen, 1961.
Frye, R. M. *Shakespeare's Life and Times: A Pictorial Record*. Princeton: Princeton UP, 1967.
Halliday, F. E. *Shakespeare in His Age*. New York: T. Yoseloff, 1956.
Harrison, G. B. *England in Shakespeare's Day*. 2nd ed. London: Methuen, 1949.
Kermode, Frank. *The Age of Shakespeare*. New York: Modern Library, 2003.
Knights, L. C. *Drama and Society in the Age of Jonson*. London: Chatto and Windus, 1937.
Lee, Sidney, and C. T. Onions. *Shakespeare's England*. 2 vols. Oxford: Clarendon P, 1916.
Picard, Liza. *Elizabethan London: Everyday Life in Elizabethan London*. London: Weidenfeld and Nicolson, 2003.
Rowse, A. L. *The England of Elizabeth: The Structure of Society*. New York: Macmillan, 1950.
Singman, Jeffrey L. *Daily Life in Elizabethan England*. Westport, CT: Greenwood P, 1995.
Tillyard, E.M.W. *The Elizabethan World Picture*. New York: Macmillan, 1944.
Wright, Louis B. *Middle-Class Culture in Elizabethan England*. Ithaca: Cornell UP, 1935.

**Biographies**

Bradbrook, Muriel C. *Shakespeare: The Poet in His World*. New York: Columbia UP, 1978.
Burgess, Anthony. *Shakespeare*. New York: Alfred A. Knopf, 1970.

Chambers, E. K. *William Shakespeare: A Study of Facts and Problems*. 2 vols. Oxford: Clarendon P, 1930.

Greenblatt, Stephen. *Will in the World*. New York: W. W. Norton, 2004.

Halliday, F. E. *The Life of Shakespeare*. Rev. ed. London: Duckworth, 1964.

Holden, Anthony. *William Shakespeare: The Man Behind the Genius: A Biography*. Boston: Little, Brown, 1999.

Honan, Park. *Shakespeare: A Life*. New York: Oxford UP, 1998.

Quennell, Peter. *Shakespeare: A Biography*. Cleveland: World, 1963.

Rowse, A. L. *William Shakespeare*. New York: Macmillan, 1963.

Schoenbaum, Samuel. *Shakespeare's Lives*. New ed. New York: Oxford UP, 1991.

———. *William Shakespeare: A Documentary Life*. New York: Oxford UP in association with Scolar P, 1975.

Wood, Michael. *In Search of Shakespeare*. London: BBC, 2003.

## Textual Studies

Black, M. W., and M. A. Shaaber. *Shakespeare's Seventeenth-Century Editors, 1632–1685*. New York: Modern Language Association of America, 1937.

Bowers, Fredson T. *On Editing Shakespeare and the Elizabethan Dramatists*. Philadelphia: Published for the Philip H. and A.S.W. Rosenbach Foundation by the U of Pennsylvania Library, 1955.

Greg, W. W. *The Editorial Problem in Shakespeare: A Survey of the Foundations of the Text*. Oxford: Clarendon P, 1951.

———. *The Shakespeare First Folio: Its Bibliographical and Textual History*. Oxford: Clarendon P, 1955.

Hart, Alfred. *Stolne and Surreptitious Copies: A Comparative Study of Shakespeare's Bad Quartos*. Melbourne, Australia: Melbourne UP, 1942.

Hinman, Charlton. *The Printing and Proof-Reading of the First Folio of Shakespeare*. 2 vols. Oxford: Clarendon P, 1963.

Maguire, Laurie E. *Shakespearean Suspect Texts: The Bad Quartos and Their Contexts*. Cambridge: Cambridge UP, 1996.

Pollard, Alfred W. *Shakespeare's Fight with the Pirates and the Problems of the Transmission of His Texts*. Rev. ed. Cambridge: Cambridge UP, 1937.

———. *Shakespeare's Folios and Quartos: A Study in the Bibliography of Shakespeare's Plays, 1594–1685*. London: Methuen, 1909.

Taylor, Gary, and John Jowett. *Shakespeare Reshaped, 1606–1623*. Oxford: Clarendon P, 1993.

Vickers, Brian. *Shakespeare, Co-Author*. Oxford: Oxford UP, 2002.

Walker, Alice. *Textual Problems of the First Folio*. Cambridge: Cambridge UP, 1953.

Walton, James Kirkwood. *The Quarto Copy for the First Folio of Shakespeare*. Dublin, Ireland: Dublin UP, 1971.

Williams, George Walton. *The Craft of Printing and the Publication of Shakespeare's Works*. Washington, DC: Folger Shakespeare Library, 1985.

Willoughby, Edwin Elliot. *The Printing of the First Folio*. Oxford: Oxford UP, 1932.

## Shakespeare's Language

Berry, Ralph. *The Shakespearean Metaphor: Studies in Language and Form*. Totowa, NJ: Rowman and Littlefield, 1978.

Blake, N. F. *Shakespeare's Language: An Introduction*. New York: St. Martin's P, 1983.

Crane, Milton. *Shakespeare's Prose*. Chicago: U of Chicago P, 1951.

Doran, Madeleine. *Shakespeare's Dramatic Language*. Madison: U of Wisconsin P, 1976.

Evans, Benjamin I. *The Language of Shakespeare's Plays*. London: Methuen, 1952.

Halliday, F. E. *The Poetry of Shakespeare's Plays*. London: Gerald Duckworth, 1954.

Hulme, Hilda M. *Explorations in Shakespeare's Language: Some Problems of Lexical Meaning in the Dramatic Text*. London: Longmans, Green, 1962.

Hussey, S. S. *The Literary Language of Shakespeare*. London: Longman Group, 1982.

Joseph, Sister Miriam. *Shakespeare's Use of the Arts of Language*. New York: Columbia UP, 1947.

Kermode, Frank. *Shakespeare's Language*. New York: Farrar, Straus, and Giroux, 2000.

Mahood, M. M. *Shakespeare's Wordplay*. London: Methuen, 1957.

Partridge, Eric. *Shakespeare's Bawdy: A Literary & Psychological Essay and a Comprehensive Glossary*. New York: E. P. Dutton, 1948.

Sipe, Dorothy L. *Shakespeare's Metrics*. New Haven: Yale UP, 1968.

Spurgeon, Caroline F. E. *Shakespeare's Imagery and What It Tells Us*. Cambridge: Cambridge UP, 1935.

Vickers, Brian. *The Artistry of Shakespeare's Prose*. London: Methuen, 1968.

Willbern, David. *Poetic Will: Shakespeare and the Play of Language*. Philadelphia: U of Pennsylvania P, 1997.

Wright, George T. *Shakespeare's Metrical Art*. Berkeley: U of California P, 1988.

## Shakespeare's Theater

Bentley, G. E. *The Jacobean and Caroline Stage*. 7 vols. Oxford: Clarendon P, 1941–1968.

———. *The Profession of Dramatist in Shakespeare's Time, 1590–1642*. Princeton: Princeton UP, 1971.

———. *The Profession of Player in Shakespeare's Time, 1590–1642*. Princeton: Princeton UP, 1984.

———. *Shakespeare and His Theatre*. Lincoln: U of Nebraska P, 1964.

Berry, Herbert. *Shakespeare's Playhouses*. New York: AMS P, 1987.

Bradbrook, Muriel C. *The Rise of the Common Player: A Study of Actor and Society in Shakespeare's England*. Cambridge: Cambridge UP, 1979.

Chambers, E. K. *The Elizabethan Stage*. 4 vols. Oxford: Clarendon P, 1923.

Cook, Ann J. *The Privileged Playgoers of Shakespeare's London, 1576–1642*. Princeton: Princeton UP, 1981.

Foakes, R. A. *Illustrations of the English Stage, 1580–1642*. Stanford: Stanford UP, 1985.

Greg, W. W., ed. *Dramatic Documents from the Elizabethan Playhouses*. 2 vols. Oxford: Clarendon P, 1931.

Gurr, Andrew. *Playgoing in Shakespeare's London*. 2nd ed. Cambridge: Cambridge UP, 1996.

———. *The Shakespearean Stage, 1574–1642*. 3rd ed. Cambridge: Cambridge UP, 1992.

———. *The Shakespearian Playing Companies*. Oxford: Clarendon P, 1996.

Gurr, Andrew, with John Orrell. *Rebuilding Shakespeare's Globe*. London: Weidenfeld and Nicolson, 1989.

Harbage, Alfred. *Shakespeare's Audience*. New York: Columbia UP, 1941.

———. *Theatre for Shakespeare*. Toronto: U of Toronto P, 1955.

Hodges, C. Walter, Samuel Schoenbaum, and Leonard Leone, eds. *The Third Globe: Symposium for the Reconstruction of the Globe Playhouse, Wayne State University, 1979*. Detroit: Wayne State UP, 1981.

Hotson, Leslie. *Shakespeare's Wooden O*. London: Rupert Hart-Davies, 1959.

Knutson, Roslyn L. *Playing Companies and Commerce in Shakespeare's Time*. Cambridge: Cambridge UP, 2001.

Lawrence, W. J. *The Physical Conditions of the Elizabethan Public Playhouse*. Cambridge, MA: Harvard UP, 1927.

Nagler, Alois M. *Shakespeare's Stage*. Trans. Ralph Mannheim. Enlarged ed. New Haven: Yale UP, 1981.

Shapiro, Michael. *Children of the Revels: The Boy Companies of Shakespeare's Time and Their Plays*. New York: Columbia UP, 1977.

Smith, Irwin. *Shakespeare's Blackfriars Playhouse: Its History and Design*. New York: New York UP, 1964.

———. *Shakespeare's Globe Playhouse: A Modern Reconstruction*. New York: Charles Scribner's Sons, 1956.

Thompson, Peter. *Shakespeare's Theatre*. London: Routledge & Kegan Paul, 1983.

## Comedies

Barber, C. L. *Shakespeare's Festive Comedy: A Study of Dramatic Form in Relation to Social Custom*. Princeton: Princeton UP, 1959.

Berry, Edward. *Shakespeare's Comic Rites*. Cambridge: Cambridge UP, 1984.

Berry, Ralph. *Shakespeare's Comedies: Explorations in Form*. Princeton: Princeton UP, 1972.

Bradbury, Malcolm, and David Palmer, eds. *Shakespearian Comedy*. Stratford-upon-Avon Studies 14. New York: Crane, Russak, 1972.

Brown, John Russell. *Shakespeare and His Comedies*. 2nd ed. London: Methuen, 1962.

Champion, Larry S. *The Evolution of Shakespeare's Comedy: A Study in Dramatic Perspective*. Cambridge, MA: Harvard UP, 1970.

Charlton, H. B. *Shakespearian Comedy*. London: Methuen, 1938.

Charney, Maurice, ed. *Shakespearean Comedy*. New York: New York Literary Forum, 1980.

Evans, Bertrand. *Shakespeare's Comedies*. Oxford: Clarendon P, 1960.

Friedman, Michael D. *"The World Must Be Peopled": Shakespeare's Comedies of Forgiveness*. Madison, NJ: Fairleigh Dickinson UP, 2002.

Frye, Northrop. *A Natural Perspective: The Development of Shakespearean Comedy and Romance*. New York: Columbia UP, 1965.

Hunter, Robert G. *Shakespeare and the Comedy of Forgiveness*. New York: Columbia UP, 1965.

Leggatt, Alexander. *Shakespeare's Comedy of Love*. London: Methuen, 1974.

Levin, Richard A. *Love and Society in Shakespearean Comedy: A Study of Dramatic Form and Content*. Newark: U of Delaware P, 1985.

Macdonald, Ronald R. *William Shakespeare: The Comedies*. New York: Twayne, 1992.

Mangan, Michael. *A Preface to Shakespeare's Comedies*. New York: Longman, 1996.

McFarland, Thomas. *Shakespeare's Pastoral Comedy*. Chapel Hill: U of North Carolina P, 1972.

Nevo, Ruth. *Comic Transformations in Shakespeare*. London: Methuen, 1980.

Ornstein, Robert. *Shakespeare's Comedies: From Roman Farce to Romantic Mystery*. Newark: U of Delaware P, 1986.

Phialas, Peter G. *Shakespeare's Romantic Comedies*. Chapel Hill: U of North Carolina P, 1966.

Richmond, Hugh M. *Shakespeare's Sexual Comedy: A Mirror for Lovers*. Indianapolis: Bobbs-Merrill, 1971.

Sen Gupta, S. C. *Shakesperian Comedy*. London: Oxford UP, 1950.

Swinden, Patrick. *An Introduction to Shakespeare's Comedies*. London: Macmillan, 1973.

Vaughn, J. A. *Shakespeare's Comedies*. New York: Frederick Ungar, 1980.

Wilson, J. Dover. *Shakespeare's Happy Comedies*. Evanston, IL: Northwestern UP, 1962.

## Tragedies

Battenhouse, Roy W. *Shakespearean Tragedy: Its Art and Its Christian Premises*. Bloomington: Indiana UP, 1969.

Bayley, John. *Shakespeare and Tragedy*. London: Routledge & Kegan Paul, 1981.

Bradley, A. C. *Shakespearean Tragedy: Lectures on "Hamlet," "Othello," "King Lear," "Macbeth."* London: Macmillan, 1904.

Bulman, James C. *The Heroic Idiom of Shakespearean Tragedy*. Newark: U of Delaware P, 1985.

Campbell, Lily B. *Shakespeare's Tragic Heroes: Slaves of Passion*. Cambridge: Cambridge UP, 1930.

Champion, Larry S. *Shakespeare's Tragic Perspective*. Athens: U of Georgia P, 1976.

Charlton, H. B. *Shakespearian Tragedy*. Cambridge: Cambridge UP, 1948.

Dickey, Franklin M. *Not Wisely But Too Well: Shakespeare's Love Tragedies*. San Marino, CA: Huntington Library, 1957.

Evans, Bertrand. *Shakespeare's Tragic Practice*. Oxford: Clarendon P, 1979.

Frye, Northrop. *Fools of Time: Studies in Shakespearean Tragedy*. Toronto: U of Toronto P, 1967.

Goldman, Michael. *Acting and Action in Shakespearean Tragedy*. Princeton: Princeton UP, 1985.

Grene, Nicholas. *Shakespeare's Tragic Imagination*. New York: St. Martin's P, 1992.

Harbage, Alfred, ed. *Shakespeare: The Tragedies, a Collection of Critical Essays*. Englewood Cliffs, NJ: Prentice-Hall, 1964.

Harrison, G. B. *Shakespeare's Tragedies*. London: Routledge & Kegan Paul, 1951.

Heilman, Robert B., ed. *Shakespeare: The Tragedies, New Perspectives*. Englewood Cliffs, NJ: Prentice-Hall, 1984.

Held, George F. *The Good That Lives After Them: A Pattern in Shakespeare's Tragedies*. Heidelberg: C. Winter, 1995.

Holloway, John. *The Story of the Night: Studies in Shakespeare's Major Tragedies*. London: Routledge & Kegan Paul, 1961.

Jorgensen, Paul A. *William Shakespeare: The Tragedies*. Boston: Twayne, 1985.

Kirsch, Arthur. *The Passions of Shakespeare's Tragic Heroes*. Charlottesville: UP of Virginia, 1990.

Knight, G. Wilson. *The Imperial Theme*. 3rd ed. London: Methuen, 1951.

———. *The Wheel of Fire*. Rev. ed. London: Methuen, 1949.

Lawlor, John. *The Tragic Sense in Shakespeare*. New York: Harcourt Brace, 1960.

Lerner, Lawrence, ed. *Shakespeare's Tragedies: A Selection of Modern Criticism*. Harmondsworth, Eng.: Penguin, 1963.

Long, Michael. *The Unnatural Scene: A Study of Shakespeare's Tragedies*. London: Methuen, 1976.

Mangan, Michael. *A Preface to Shakespeare's Tragedies*. London: Longman, 1991.

Margolies, David. *Monsters of the Deep: Social Dissolution in Shakespeare's Tragedies*. Manchester, Eng.: Manchester UP, 1992.

McAlindon, Thomas. *Shakespeare's Tragic Cosmos*. Cambridge: Cambridge UP, 1991.

McElroy, Bernard. *Shakespeare's Mature Tragedies*. Princeton: Princeton UP, 1973.

Mehl, Dieter. *Shakespeare's Tragedies: An Introduction*. Cambridge: Cambridge UP, 1987.

Muir, Kenneth. *Shakespeare's Tragic Sequence*. London: Hutchinson U Library, 1972.

———. *William Shakespeare: The Great Tragedies: "Hamlet," "Othello," "King Lear," "Macbeth."* London: Published for the British Council by Longman's, Green, 1961.

Nevo, Ruth. *Tragic Form in Shakespeare*. Princeton: Princeton UP, 1972.

Rackin, Phyllis. *Shakespeare's Tragedies*. New York: Frederick Ungar, 1978.

Reid, Robert Lanier. *Shakespeare's Tragic Form: Spirit in the Wheel*. Newark: U of Delaware P, 2000.

Ribner, Irving. *Patterns in Shakespearean Tragedy*. New York: Barnes & Noble, 1960.

Rosen, William. *Shakespeare and the Craft of Tragedy*. Cambridge, MA: Harvard UP, 1960.

Spivack, Bernard. *Shakespeare and the Allegory of Evil: The History of a Metaphor in Relation to His Major Villains*. New York: Columbia UP, 1958.

Stirling, Brents. *Unity in Shakespearian Tragedy: The Interplay of Theme and Character*. New York: Columbia UP, 1956.

Whitaker, V. K. *The Mirror up to Nature: The Technique of Shakespeare's Tragedies*. San Marino, CA: Huntington Library, 1965.

Wilson, H. S. *On the Design of Shakespearian Tragedy*. Toronto: U of Toronto P, 1957.

Young, David. *The Action to the Word: Structure and Style in Shakespearean Tragedy*. New Haven: Yale UP, 1990.

## Histories

Armstrong, William A. *Shakespeare's Histories: An Anthology of Modern Criticism*. Harmondsworth, Eng.: Penguin, 1972.

Becker, G. J. *Shakespeare's Histories*. New York: Frederick Ungar, 1977.

Blanpied, John W. *Time and the Artist in Shakespeare's English Histories*. Newark: U of Delaware P, 1983.

Campbell, Lily. *Shakespeare's "Histories": Mirrors of Elizabethan Policy*. San Marino, CA: Huntington Library, 1947.

Champion, Larry S. *"The Noise of Threatening Drum": Dramatic Strategy and Political Ideology in Shakespeare and the English Chronicle Plays*. Newark: U of Delaware P, 1990.

———. *Perspectives in Shakespeare's English Histories*. Athens: U of Georgia P, 1980.

Hart, Jonathan. *Theater and World: The Problematics of Shakespeare's History*. Boston: Northeastern UP, 1992.

Hodgson, Barbara. *The End Crowns All: Closure and Contradiction in Shakespeare's Histories*. Princeton: Princeton UP, 1991.

Holderness, Graham. *Shakespeare Recycled: The Making of Historical Drama*. Hempstead, Eng.: Harvester Wheatsheaf, 1992.

———. *Shakespeare's History*. New York: St. Martin's P, 1985.

Howard, Jean E., and Phyllis Rackin. *Engendering a Nation: A Feminist Account of Shakespeare's English Histories*. London: Routledge, 1997.

Kelly, Henry A. *Divine Providence in the England of Shakespeare's Histories*. Cambridge, MA: Harvard UP, 1970.

Knights, L. C. *William Shakespeare: The Histories*. London: Longmans, Green, 1962.

Leggatt, Alexander. *Shakespeare's Political Drama: The History Plays and the Roman Plays*. London: Routledge, 1988.

Norwich, John Julius. *Shakespeare's Kings: The Great Plays and the History of England in the Middle Ages, 1337–1485*. New York: Scribner, 1999.

Ornstein, Robert. *A Kingdom for a Stage: The Achievement of Shakespeare's History Plays*. Cambridge, MA: Harvard UP, 1972.

Paris, Bernard J. *Character as a Subversive Force in Shakespeare: The History and Roman Plays*. Rutherford, NJ: Fairleigh Dickinson UP, 1991.

Pearlman, E. *Shakespeare: The History Plays*. New York: Twayne, 1992.

Pierce, Robert B. *Shakespeare's History Plays: The Family and the State*. Columbus: Ohio State UP, 1971.

Prior, Moody E. *The Drama of Power: Studies in Shakespeare's History Plays*. Evanston, IL: Northwestern UP, 1973.

Pugliatti, Paola. *Shakespeare the Historian*. New York: St. Martin's P, 1996.

Rackin, Phyllis. *Stages of History: Shakespeare's English Chronicles*. Ithaca: Cornell UP, 1990.

Reese, M. M. *The Cease of Majesty: A Study of Shakespeare's History Plays*. New York: St. Martin's P, 1961.

Ribner, Irving. *The English History Play in the Age of Shakespeare*. Rev. ed. New York: Barnes & Noble, 1965.

Saccio, Peter. *Shakespeare's English Kings: History, Chronicle, and Drama*. London: Oxford UP, 1977.

Sen Gupta, S. C. *Shakespeare's Historical Plays*. London: Oxford UP, 1964.

Siegel, P. N. *Shakespeare's English and Roman History Plays: A Marxist Approach*. Rutherford, NJ: Fairleigh Dickinson UP, 1986.

Smidt, Kristian. *Unconformities in Shakespeare's History Plays*. Atlantic Heights, NJ: Humanities P, 1982.

Sprague, Arthur Colby. *Shakespeare's Histories: Plays for the Stage*. London: Society for Theatre Research, 1964.

Tillyard, E.M.W. *Shakespeare's History Plays*. London: Macmillan, 1944.

Vetz, John W., ed. *Shakespeare's English Histories: A Quest for Form and Genre*. Binghamton: Medieval & Renaissance Texts and Studies, 1996.

Wilders, John. *The Lost Garden: A View of Shakespeare's English and Roman History Plays*. New York: Macmillan, 1978.

Winny, James. *The Player King: A Theme of Shakespeare's Histories*. New York: Barnes & Noble, 1968.

## Romances

Bieman, Elizabeth. *William Shakespeare: The Romances*. Boston: Twayne, 1990.

Bishop, T. G. *Shakespeare and the Theatre of Wonder*. Cambridge: Cambridge UP, 1996.

Cutts, John P. *Rich and Strange: A Study of Shakespeare's Last Plays*. Pullman: Washington State UP, 1968.

Fawkner, H. W. *Shakespeare's Miracle Plays: "Pericles," "Cymbeline," and "The Winter's Tale."* Rutherford, NJ: Farleigh Dickinson UP, 1992.

Felperin, Howard. *Shakespearean Romance*. Princeton: Princeton UP, 1972.

Foakes, R. A. *Shakespeare: From the Dark Comedies to the Last Plays: From Satire to Celebration*. Charlottesville: UP of Virginia, 1971.

Frye, Northrop. *A Natural Perspective: The Development of Shakespearean Comedy and Romance*. New York: Columbia UP, 1965.

———. *The Secular Scripture: A Study of the Structure of Romance*. Cambridge, MA: Harvard UP, 1976.

Hartwig, Joan. *Shakespeare's Tragicomic Vision*. Baton Rouge: Louisiana State UP, 1972.

Hunter, R. G. *Shakespeare and the Comedy of Forgiveness*. New York: Columbia UP, 1965.

Kermode, Frank. *William Shakespeare: The Final Plays*. London: Longmans, Green, 1963.

Knight, G. W. *The Crown of Life: Essays in Interpretation of Shakespeare's Final Plays*. Oxford: Oxford UP, 1947.

Mincoff, Marco. *Things Supernatural and Causeless: Shakespearean Romance*. Newark: U of Delaware P, 1992.

Mowat, Barbara A. *The Dramaturgy of Shakespeare's Romances*. Athens: U of Georgia P, 1976.

Nelson, Thomas A. *Shakespeare's Comic Theory: A Study of Art and Artifice in the Last Plays*. The Hague: Mouton, 1973.

Palfrey, Simon. *Late Shakespeare: A New World of Words*. Oxford: Clarendon P, 1997.

Peterson, D. L. *Time, Tide and Tempest: A Study of Shakespeare's Romances*. San Marino, CA: Huntington Library, 1973.

Richards, Jennifer, and James Knowles, eds. *Shakespeare's Late Plays: New Readings*. Edinburgh: Edinburgh UP, 1999.

Ryan, Kiernan, ed. *Shakespeare: The Last Plays*. New York: Longman, 1999.

*Shakespeare Survey* 11 (1958); 29 (1976).

Smith, Hallett. *Shakespeare's Romances: A Study of Some Ways of the Imagination*. San Marino, CA: Huntington Library, 1972.

Tillyard, E.M.W. *Shakespeare's Last Plays*. London: Chatto and Windus, 1938.

Traversi, Derek. *Shakespeare: The Last Phase*. New York: Harcourt, Brace, 1954.

Uphaus, Robert. *Beyond Tragedy: Structure and Experience in Shakespeare's Romances*. Lexington: U of Kentucky P, 1981.

Velie, Alan R. *Shakespeare's Repentance Plays: The Search for an Adequate Form*. Rutherford, NJ: Farleigh Dickinson UP, 1972.

Yates, Frances. *Shakespeare's Last Plays: A New Approach*. London: Routledge & Kegan Paul, 1975.

## Poems

Beauregard, David N. "*Venus and Adonis*: Shakespeare's Representation of the Passions." *Shakespeare Studies* 8 (1975): 83–98.

Belsey, Catherine. "Tarquin Dispossessed: Expropriation and Consent in *The Rape of Lucrece*." *Shakespeare Quarterly* 52 (2001): 315–335.

Booth, Stephen. *An Essay on Shakespeare's Sonnets*. New Haven: Yale UP, 1969.

——, ed. *Shakespeare's Sonnets*. New Haven: Yale UP, 1977.

Calvert, Hugh. *Shakespeare's Sonnets and Problems of Autobiography*. Braughton, Eng.: Devon Books, 1987.

Campbell, S. C. *Only Begotten Sonnets*. London: Bell & Hyman, 1978.

Cousins, A. D. *Shakespeare's Sonnets and Narrative Poems*. New York: Longman, 2000.

Donaldson, Ian. *The Rapes of Lucretia: A Myth and Its Transformations*. Oxford: Clarendon P, 1982.

Dubrow, Heather. *Captive Victors: Shakespeare's Narrative Poems and Sonnets*. Ithaca: Cornell UP, 1987.

Ellrodt, Robert. "An Anatomy of *The Phoenix and the Turtle*." *Shakespeare Survey* 15 (1962): 99–110.

Empson, William. "*The Phoenix and the Turtle*." *Essays in Criticism* 16 (1966): 147–153.

Fineman, Joel. *Shakespeare's Perjured Eye: The Invention of Poetic Subjectivity in the Sonnets*. Berkeley: U of California P, 1986.

Garber, Marjorie. "Two Birds with One Stone: Lapidary Re-inscription in *The Phoenix and Turtle*." *The Upstart Crow* 5 (1984): 5–19.

Giroux, Robert. *The Book Known as Q: A Consideration of Shakespeare's Sonnets*. New York: Atheneum, 1982.

Hamilton, A. C. "*Venus and Adonis*." *Studies in English Literature* 1.1 (1961): 1–15.

Hernstein, Barbara, ed. *Discussions of Shakespeare's Sonnets*. Boston: Heath, 1964.

Hubler, Edward. *The Sense of Shakespeare's Sonnets*. Princeton: Princeton UP, 1952.

Hubler, Edward, Northrop Frye, Leslie A. Fiedler, Stephen Spender, and R. P. Blackmur. *The Riddle of Shakespeare's Sonnets*. New York: Basic Books, 1962.

Hulse, Clark. *Metamorphic Verse: The Elizabethan Minor Epic*. Princeton: Princeton UP, 1981.

Innes, Paul. *Shakespeare and the English Renaissance Sonnet: Verses of Feigning Love*. New York: St. Martin's P, 1997.

Kahn, Coppélia. "The Rape in Shakespeare's *Lucrece*." *Shakespeare Studies* 9 (1976): 45–72.

Keach, William. *"Venus and Adonis": Elizabethan Erotic Narratives: Irony and Pathos in the Ovidian Poetry of Shakespeare, Marlowe, and Their Contemporaries.* New Brunswick, NJ: Rutgers UP, 1977.

Knight, G. Wilson. *The Mutual Flame: On Shakespeare's Sonnets and "The Phoenix and the Turtle."* London: Methuen, 1955.

Krieger, Murray. *A Window to Criticism: Shakespeare's Sonnets and Modern Poetics.* Princeton: Princeton UP, 1964.

Landry, Hilton. *Interpretations in Shakespeare's Sonnets.* Berkeley: U of California P, 1963.

———, ed. *New Essays on Shakespeare's Sonnets.* New York: AMS P, 1976.

Leishman, J. B. *Themes and Variations in Shakespeare's Sonnets.* London: Hutchinson University Library, 1961.

Martin, Philip. *Shakespeare's Sonnets: Self, Love, and Art.* Cambridge: Cambridge UP, 1972.

Matchett, W. H. *"The Phoenix and the Turtle": Shakespeare's Poem and Chester's "Loues Martyr."* The Hague: Mouton, 1965.

Mortimer, Anthony. *Variable Passions: A Reading of Shakespeare's "Venus and Adonis."* New York: AMS P, 2000.

Muir, Kenneth. *Shakespeare's Sonnets.* London: George Allen & Unwin, 1979.

Newman, Jane O. "'And Let Mild Women to Him Lose Their Mildness': Philomela, Female Violence, and Shakespeare's *The Rape of Lucrece.*" *Shakespeare Quarterly* 45 (1994): 304–326.

Pequigney, Joseph. *Such Is My Love: A Study of Shakespeare's Sonnets.* Chicago: U of Chicago P, 1985.

Ramsay, Paul. *The Fickle Glass: A Study of Shakespeare's Sonnets.* New York: AMS P, 1979.

Schiffer, James, ed. *Shakespeare's Sonnets: Critical Essays.* New York: Garland, 1999.

*Shakespeare Survey* 15 (1962).

Smith, Hallett. *The Tension of the Lyre: Poetry in Shakespeare's Sonnets.* San Marino, CA: Huntington Library, 1981.

Vendler, Helen. *The Art of Shakespeare's Sonnets.* Cambridge, MA: Harvard UP, 1997.

Wait, R.J.C. *The Background to Shakespeare's Sonnets.* New York: Schocken Books, 1972.

Weiser, David K. *Mind in Character: Shakespeare's Speaker in the Sonnets.* Columbia: U of Missouri P, 1987.

Williams, Carolyn D. "'Silence, like a Lucrece knife': Shakespeare and the Meaning of Rape." *Yearbook of English Studies* 23 (1993): 93–110.

Wilson, J. Dover. *An Introduction to the Sonnets of Shakespeare for the Use of Historians and Others.* Cambridge: Cambridge UP, 1963.

Wilson, Katherine M. *Shakespeare's Sugared Sonnets.* London: George Allen & Unwin, 1974.

Wilson, R. Rawdon. "Shakespeare's Narrative: *The Rape of Lucrece* Reconsidered." *Studies in English Literature* 28 (1988): 39–59.

Winny, James. *The Master-Mistress: A Study of Shakespeare's Sonnets.* London: Chatto & Windus, 1968.

Witt, Robert W. *Of Comfort and Despair: Shakespeare's Sonnet Sequence.* Salzburg, Austria: Institut für Anglistik und Amerikanistic, Universität Salzburg, 1979.

# Subject Index

# Key Passages Index

# About the Editor and Contributors

**JOSEPH ROSENBLUM** received his Ph.D. in English from Duke University. He has taught courses in Shakespeare and is a drama critic for the High Point (North Carolina) *Enterprise*. His books include *Shakespeare: An Annotated Bibliography* (1992) and *Prince of Forgers* (1998).

**BARRY B. ADAMS** is Emeritus Professor of English at Cornell University, where he taught courses on Shakespeare, early English drama, and the history of the English language. He also served as Vice Provost for undergraduate education at Cornell. His current research project is a study of the language of thought in Shakespeare.

**ROBERT APPELBAUM**, Lecturer in Renaissance Studies at Lancaster University (England), is the author of *Literature and Utopian Politics in Seventeenth-Century England* (2002) and co-editor, with John Wood Sweet, of *Envisioning an English Empire: Jamestown and the Making of the North Atlantic World* (forthcoming). His essays on Shakespeare and early modern culture have appeared in *Shakespeare Quarterly*, *Textual Practice*, and other journals.

**YASHDIP S. BAINS** teaches English and Comparative Literature at the University of Cincinnati. He has published two books on making sense of Shakespeare's "bad" quartos, an annotated bibliography of *Antony and Cleopatra*, a critical edition of *1 Henry IV*, and a history of English Canadian theater, 1765–1826. He is managing editor of the journal *American Drama*.

**ILONA BELL** is Professor of English at Williams College. The author of *Elizabethan Women and the Poetry of Courtship* (1998), she has written widely on Renaissance poetry, early modern women, and Elizabeth I. Her first essay on *A Lover's Complaint* ("'That which thou hast done': Shakespeare's *Sonnets* and 'A Lover's Complaint'") was published in *Shakespeare's Sonnets: Critical Essays*, edited by James Schiffer (1999). Another, "Shakespeare's Exculpatory Complaint," will appear in *Suffering Ecstasy: Essays on Shakespeare's "A Lover's Complaint,"* ed. Shirley Sharon-Zisser (forthcoming). Bell is currently preparing an edition of John Donne's poems and completing a critical study, "We Adventured Equally: John Donne and Anne More."

**NICHOLAS BIRNS** teaches in the Humanities Department of New School University in New York City. He is editor of *Antipodes: A North American Journal of Australian Literature.* He has published articles in *Arizona Quarterly, Exemplaria,* and *The Hollins Critic,* and he is the author of *Understanding Anthony Powell* (2004).

**ROBERT G. BLAKE** received his A.B. from Harvard College and his M.A. and Ph.D. degrees from Duke University, where he specialized in Victorian literature. Since 1968 he has been the William S. Long Professor of English at Elon University, where he served as chair of the English department until 1977. He has published on a wide range of topics, from literary magazines to Shakespeare.

**OWEN E. BRADY** received his Ph.D. in dramatic literature from the University of Notre Dame. Currently Associate Professor of Humanities at Clarkson University (Potsdam, New York), he has published books and journal articles on a number of twentieth-century dramatists, including W. H. Auden, Amiri Baraka, David Rabe, Theodore Ward, Thornton Wilder, and Tennessee Williams.

**HAROLD BRANAM,** a retired college English professor, specialized in the English Renaissance. As a Marshall Scholar in Britain, he studied Shakespeare with the renowned critic G. Wilson Knight. He has published hundreds of articles, was an assistant editor for the *International Encyclopedia of Communications* (1989), and has been the featured poet on National Public Radio's "Writer's Almanac."

**BRUCE E. BRANDT** is Professor of English at South Dakota State University. His publications include *Christopher Marlowe and the Metaphysical Problem Play* (1985), *Christopher Marlowe in the Eighties: An Annotated Bibliography of Marlowe Criticism from 1978 through 1989* (1992), and numerous articles, notes, and reviews. He has long been active in the Marlowe Society of America and is currently serving as its president.

**REGINA M. BUCCOLA** is Assistant Professor of English at Roosevelt University (Chicago). Her primary research and teaching areas are early modern British drama and twentieth-century British and American feminist drama. Her publications include "Shakespeare's Fairy Dance with Catholicism," in *Shakespeare and the Culture of Christianity in Early Modern England* (2003), and " 'The top of woman! All her sex in abstract!': Ben Jonson Directs the Boy Actor in *The Devil Is an Ass*" (*Early Theatre Journal,* forthcoming).

**ANNALISA CASTALDO** is Assistant Professor of British Literature at Widener University (Chester, Pennsylvania). She has published articles on teaching Shakespearean film and on Neil Gaiman's use of Shakespeare in *The Sandman.* She is currently one of the editors of the CORD (Compendium of Renaissance Drama) CD-ROM project.

**SHERYL A. CLOUSE** is a Ph.D. candidate at the University of North Carolina at Greensboro. Her dissertation focuses on Shakespeare's use of the female body as spectacle in the romances and histories.

**DAVID W. COLE** is Professor Emeritus of English in the University of Wisconsin Colleges. He has published on a wide range of topics, including Shakespeare's *The Taming of the Shrew* and John Webster's *The Duchess of Malfi.*

**JOHN D. COX** is the DuMez Professor of English at Hope College (Holland, Michigan). He has published many articles and books on early drama, most recently *The Devil and the Sacred in English Drama, 1350–1642* (2000) and the third Arden edition of Shakespeare's *3 Henry VI* (2001), co-edited with Eric Rasmussen.

**NICHOLAS CRAWFORD** is Assistant Professor of English at the University of Montevallo. He has published articles in *Renaissance Papers, South Atlantic Review, The Comparatist,* and *English Literary Renaissance.* In 2003 he was a winner of both the Shakespeare Association of America's Open Competition and the *South Atlantic Review* Essay Prize. He is currently at work on a monograph that treats the relationship between subjectivity and the discourse of legitimacy in English Renaissance drama.

**STEVEN DOLOFF** is Professor of English and Humanities at Pratt Institute in New York City. His writing on Shakespeare has appeared in *Shakespeare Quarterly, Shakespeare Yearbook, Review of English Studies, The Huntington Library Quarterly, Shakespeare Bulletin,* and *The Shakespeare Newsletter.*

**MICHAEL EGAN** is Scholar in Residence at Brigham Young University–Hawaii. He earned his Ph.D. at Cambridge University and is the author of more than eighty professional articles and ten books. These include *Henrik Ibsen: The Critical Heritage* (1972), *Henry James: The Ibsen Years* (1972), *"Huckleberry Finn": Race, Class and Society* (1977), and *Extreme Situations: Literature and Crisis from the Great War to the Atomic Bomb* (1979; co-authored with David Craig). He is currently preparing the variorum edition of *The First Part of the Tragedy of King Richard the Second,* a previously unidentified play by Shakespeare, with an introduction, notes, and critical commentary (forthcoming).

**MICHELLE EPHRAIM** is an Assistant Professor of English at Worcester Polytechnic Institute. Her articles include "Jewish Matriarchs and the Staging of Elizabeth I in *The History of Jacob and Esau,*" published in the Spring 2003 issue of *Studies in English Literature,* and "Jephthah's Kin: The Sacrificing Father in *The Merchant of Venice,*" which will appear in a forthcoming issue of *The Journal of Early Modern Cultural Studies.* Her current book project examines the representation of Jewish women on the Elizabethan stage.

**CHARLES R. FORKER** is Professor of English Emeritus at Indiana University, Bloomington. In addition to many contributions to scholarly journals, his publications include critical editions of James Shirley's *The Cardinal* (1964), Christopher Marlowe's *Edward II* (1994), and Shakespeare's *Richard II* (2002). He is the author of a major study of the works of John Webster, *Skull Beneath the Skin: The Achievement of John Webster* (1986). His *Fancy's Images: Contexts, Settings, and Perspectives in Shakespeare and his Contemporaries* was published in 1990, and his survey of critical writings on *Richard II* appeared in 1998 as part of the series *Shakespeare: The Critical Tradition.* He is currently at work (with Joseph Candido) on the Variorum edition of Shakespeare's *King John.*

**GAYLE GASKILL** is Professor of English at the College of St. Catherine (St. Paul, Minnesota). She has published several articles on Shakespeare's plays and sonnets. Her recent publications include "Making *The Merchant of Venice* Palatable for U.S. Audiences," in *"The Merchant of Venice": New Critical Essays,* ed. John W. Mahon and Ellen Macleod Mahon (2002).

**PRISCILLA GLANVILLE** is a full-time English instructor at the University of South Florida.

**JAMES B. GUTSELL** is Professor Emeritus of English Literature at Guilford College (Greensboro, North Carolina), where he taught for thirty-six years and served as department chair. With a dissertation on George Chapman and a Ph.D. from the University of Connecticut, he specialized in Shakespeare but also taught African and Asian literature, Chaucer, and the Victorians. Turning a hobby into a profession, he is now a full-time potter, pottery teacher, and gallery owner.

**JAY L. HALIO,** Emeritus Professor of English, University of Delaware, has edited a number of Shakespeare plays and has written on Shakespeare's plays in performance.

**ANDREW JAMES HARTLEY** is Associate Professor of English at the University of West Georgia, Resident Dramaturg for the Georgia Shakespeare Festival, and the editor of *Shakespeare Bulletin,* a journal of performance criticism and scholarship.

**ROZE HENTSCHELL** is an Assistant Professor of English at Colorado State University, where she teaches British literature and culture of the sixteenth and seventeenth centuries, including Shakespeare and Milton. Her research interests include the study of material culture and popular literature in early modern England. She is especially interested in cultural representations of the textile industry in the early modern period and is at work on *The Materialities of Myth: The Culture of Cloth in Early Modern England.*

**PETER KANELOS** is an Assistant Professor of English at the University of San Diego. He has published on Shakespeare, Montaigne, and Giorgio Vasari, and he is presently one of the editors of the New Variorum edition of *Twelfth Night.*

**JEREMY LOPEZ** is Assistant Professor of English Literature at the College of William and Mary (Williamsburg, Virginia). He is the theater-review editor of *Shakespeare Bulletin* and the author of *Theatrical Conventions and Audience Response in Early Modern Drama* (2003).

**ANDREW MACDONALD** holds a Ph.D. in English (Renaissance Studies) from the University of Texas in Austin and is a Professor at Loyola University (New Orleans). Author of *Howard Fast* (Greenwood, 1996), he is also co-author of *Mastering Writing Essentials* (1996), *Shapeshifting: The Native American in Recent Fiction* (Greenwood, 2000), *Shaman or Sherlock? The Native American Detective* (Greenwood, 2001), *Jane Austen on Screen* (2003), and *Scott Turow* (Greenwood, forthcoming). He has published numerous articles for books, journals, and encyclopedias on a wide range of topics, including popular fiction, cross-cultural concerns, English as a Second Language, and cultural literacy.

**GINA MACDONALD** holds a Ph.D. in English (Renaissance Studies) from the University of Texas in Austin and is an Associate Professor at Nicholls State University (Thibodaux, Louisiana). Author of *James Clavell* (Greenwood, 1996) and *Robert Ludlum* (Greenwood, 1997), editor of *British Mystery and Thriller Writers since 1940, Dictionary of Literary Biography,* vol. 246 (2003), she is also co-author of *Mastering Writing Essentials* (1996), *Shapeshifting: The Native American in Recent Fiction* (Greenwood, 2000), *Shaman or Sherlock? The Native American Detective* (Greenwood, 2001), *Jane Austen on Screen* (2003), and *Scott Turow* (Greenwood, forthcoming). She has published numerous articles and encyclopedia entries about popular fiction, Shakespeare, English as a Second Language, and Spanish, Polish, and Russian authors.

**REBECCA FLETCHER McNEER**, Associate Professor of English and Faculty Coordinator at the Southern campus of Ohio University (Ironton, Ohio), has been teaching at the university level for more than thirty years. She received her undergraduate and Master's degrees at Marshall University (Huntington, West Virginia) and her doctorate in English Language and Literature at Ohio University (Athens, Ohio), with a specialization in twentieth-century British and American literature. In addition to Shakespeare, Dr. McNeer's research interests include women's fiction and Australian literature. She has published in the *Virginia Woolf Miscellany* and *Antipodes*, the journal of the American Association of Australian Literary Studies. At the Southern Campus, Dr. McNeer teaches advanced composition and a variety of literature courses, including a Shakespeare course every fall.

**KIRK BAZLER MELNIKOFF** is an Assistant Professor of English specializing in Shakespeare and performance at the University of North Carolina at Charlotte. He is currently co-editing a collection of essays on Robert Greene and is responsible for the *Shakespeare Film Newsletter*, which is published as part of the newly reformatted *Shakespeare Bulletin*. He has published in *Mosaic* and *Analytical and Enumerative Bibliography*. He has essays forthcoming in *Studies in Philology* and *Medieval and Renaissance Drama in England*.

**PATRICK PERKINS** received his Ph.D. from the University of Alabama in 2000. He teaches English Renaissance literature at Nicholls State University (Thibodaux, Louisiana).

**MICHELLE M. SAUER**, Assistant Professor of English and Coordinator of Gender Studies at Minot State University (Minot, South Dakota) and Managing Editor of *Medieval Feminist Forum*, holds degrees from Purdue University, Loyola University (Chicago), and Washington State University. Her edition of the *Wooing Group & a Discussion of the Love of God* is forthcoming. She has published on the anchoritic life, mysticism, asceticism, Church history, Christopher Marlowe, John Lyly, and queer theory.

**CHARLES R. TRAINOR** received his Ph.D. from Yale University and is Professor of English at Siena College (Loudonville, New York), where he specializes in courses on drama and Shakespeare. His publications include several articles on prenineteenth-century British literature and the book *The Drama and Fielding's Novels* (1988).

**GARY WALLER** is Professor of Literature and Cultural Studies at SUNY-Purchase. He is the author of many books, including *Shakespeare's Comedies* (1991), *The Sidney Family Romance* (1993), and *"All's Well That Ends Well": Critical Views* (forthcoming).

**ELIZABETH MOORE WILLINGHAM** is Associate Professor of Spanish at Baylor University and is a Fellow of the National Endowment of the Humanities (2004–2005). She is editor of a forthcoming series of editions of the Lancelot Prose based on the Manuscript Yale 229. Her recent articles include "Revisiting the *Baladro del sabio Merlin*: Perspectives Introduced by Editors of the Recent Facsimile Edition," in the Spring 2004 issue of *La corónica*.

**DEBORAH WILLIS** is Associate Professor of English at the University of California, Riverside, where she teaches Shakespeare, Renaissance drama, and Cultural Studies. She is the author of *Malevolent Nurture: Witch-Hunting amd Material Power in Early Modern England* (1995) and articles on Shakespeare, Marlowe, and Renaissance culture, including "'The gnawing vulture': Revenge, Trauma Theory, and *Titus Andronicus*," which appeared in volume 53 of *Shakespeare Quarterly* (2002). She is currently working on a project about witch families in early modern England.

**ROBERT F. WILLSON JR.** is Emeritus Professor of English at the University of Missouri–Kansas City. He has published numerous books and articles about Shakespeare, concentrating mainly on filmed versions of the plays. His most recent study is *Shakespeare in Hollywood: 1929–1956* (2000). He is also editor of the *Studies in Shakespeare* series for Peter Lang Publishing.

**JESSICA WINSTON** is an Assistant Professor of English at Idaho State University. She is currently writing a book on the poetry and drama of the early Elizabethan Inns of Court. Her recent articles on this topic have appeared in *Studies in Philology* and *Early Theatre*.

**MATTHEW WOODCOCK** is Lecturer in Medieval and Renaissance Literature at the University of East Anglia (Norwich, England). He is the author of *Fairy in "The Faerie Queene": Renaissance Elf-Fashioning and Elizabethan Myth-Making* (2004) and editor of a collection of essays on Fulke Greville, published as *The Sidney Journal* 19.1–2 (2001). He is currently producing a critical edition for the John Nichols project of entertainment narratives from Elizabeth I's 1578 progress to East Anglia.